INSIDE JOB

Stephen Pizzo, Mary Fricker
and Paul Muolo

INSIDE JOB

The Looting of America's Savings and Loans

McGraw-Hill Publishing Company

New York   St. Louis   San Francisco
Hamburg   Mexico   Toronto

6 7 8 9 DOC DOC   9 2 1 0

ISBN 0-07-050230-7

Library of Congress Cataloging-in-Publication Data

Pizzo, Stephen.
    Inside job : the looting of America's savings and loans / Stephen Pizzo, Mary Fricker, and Paul Muolo.
        p.   cm.
    Bibliography: p.
    Includes index.
    ISBN 0-07-050230-7
    1. Building and loan associations—United States.   2. Building and loan associations—United States—Deregulation.   I. Fricker, Mary. II. Muolo, Paul.   III. Title.
HG2151.P59   1989   89-12519
332.3'2'0973—dc20   CIP

Book design by Sheree Goodman

Contents

Acknowledgments

This book was three years in the making, and more people deserve our gratitude and thanks than space here allows. First among them are our families: Steve Pizzo's wife, Susan Pizzo, and sons, Nicholas and Christopher Pizzo; Mary Fricker's mother, Sibyl Dameron, and sons, Glenn and Scott Fricker; Paul Muolo's wife, Ann Leger. High also on our list are our agent, Denise Marcil, and our editors, Tom Miller and Anne Sweeney, who saw the importance of this book long before the thrift crisis became standard fare on the evening news. We are certain that had they not embraced this project early on, this book might never have seen print. In addition, we'd like to extend our thanks to Debra Kass Orenstein for her insightful and intelligent legal commentary, and to John Carter, copy editor par excellence. Thanks also to *National Thrift News* editor (and thrift guru) Stan Strachan, who patiently endured as two of his reporters were distracted by this project. Special thanks to all those we could not name in this book: the U.S. attorneys, FBI agents, federal regulators, and attorneys who, at risk to their careers, spoke to us and sent us critical documentation because they believed the public had a right to know what happened. They all know who they are, and we thank them sincerely. Finally, we want to acknowledge the fine reporting being done around the country by dozens of good journalists. Without access to their investigative work, we could not have written this book.

DRAMATIS PERSONAE

Descriptions include only information that is relevant to the stories in this book.

John B. Anderson: California farmer who bought the Dunes Hotel and Casino in Las Vegas from Morris Shenker in 1984 and put it into bankruptcy in 1985; borrowed from many S&Ls.

Ottavio A. Angotti: Chairman, Consolidated Savings Bank, Irvine, California.

Frank Annunzio: Democratic congressman from Illinois.

Jack Atkinson: Vernon Savings borrower.

George Aubin: A consultant to Mercury Savings, Witchita Falls, Texas; and Ben Milan Savings, Cameron, Texas; associate of Herman K. Beebe.

Farhad Azima: Director, Indian Spring State Bank, Kansas City, owner Global International Airways.

James Baker: White House chief of staff, 1981–1985; treasury secretary, 1985–1989.

Tyrell Barker: Owner, State Savings in Lubbock, Texas, Brownsfield Savings in Brownsfield, Texas, and Key Savings, Englewood, Colorado.

Doug Barnard: Democratic congressman from Georgia; chairman of the Commerce, Consumer and Monetary Affairs sub-committee of the House Committee on Government Operations.

Ben Barnes: Lieutenant governor of Texas 1968–1972; associate of Herman K. Beebe and John Connally.

Charles Bazarian: Oklahoma loan broker; owner CB Financial.

Gilbert Beall: Borrower from Acadia Savings, Crowley, Louisiana; purchased Poconos property from Jilly Rizzo and Anthony Delvecchio.

Herman K. Beebe: Louisiana businessman; owner AMI Inc. and Bossier Bank &

Trust; subject of 1985 comptroller of the currency report which listed 109 financial institutions related to Beebe.

Richard Binder: Borrower from Centennial Savings, Guerneville, California; associate of David Gorwitz.

William Black: Director of litigation in the FHLBB Office of General Counsel 1984–1986; deputy director, FSLIC, 1986–1987; general counsel, FHLB San Francisco, beginning in 1987.

Spencer Blain: chairman, Empire Savings, Mesquite, Texas.

Ellis Blount: FBI special agent on the Herman K. Beebe case.

Jack Bona: borrower with Frank Domingues at San Marino Savings, San Marino, California; purchased Atlantic City Dunes Hotel in 1983.

Douglas Bosco: Democratic congressman from California; borrower from Centennial Savings, Guerneville, California.

L. Linton Bowman: Texas savings and loan commissioner, resigned in 1987.

Joseph Boyer: FBI special agent on the State Savings of Corvallis, Oregon, case.

Eric Bronk: attorney and consultant for Robert Ferrante's Consolidated Savings Bank, Irvine, California.

Mitchell Brown: owner with E. Morton Hopkins of First National Bank of Marin; borrower at State Savings of Corvallis, Oregon.

Neil Bush: former director, Silverado Savings, Denver.

Christopher Byrne: senior trial attorney, FDIC.

Joseph Cage: U.S. attorney, Shreveport, Louisiana, on the Herman Beebe and Acadia Savings cases.

Lance Caldwell: U.S. attorney, Portland, Oregon, on the State Savings/Corvallis case.

Carl Cardascia: President, Flushing Federal Savings, New York.

Duayne Christensen: chairman, North American Savings, Santa Ana, California.

James Cirona: president, FHLB San Francisco.

Nick Civella: reputed boss of the Kansas City Mafia family.

Tony Coelho: Democratic congressman from California; chairman House Democratic Campaign Committee; became House majority whip in 1987.

John Connally: Secretary of the Navy 1961–1962; governor of Texas 1963–1968; Secretary of the Treasury 1971–1972; candidate for Republican presidential nomination in 1980; partner with Ben Barnes in the 1980s.

Patrick Connolly: California deputy savings and loan commissioner and, later, executive vice president of Centennial Savings.

Ernie Cooper: FBI special agent on the Centennial Savings case.

Alan Cranston: Democratic senator from California, met with regulators on behalf of Lincoln Savings, Irvine, California.

William Crawford: California savings and loan commissioner, 1985–present.

Durwood Curlee: Director, Texas Savings and Loan League; later, Texas thrift lobbyist.

Sam Daily: Associate of Mario Renda in his linked financing scams; Hawaii real estate broker.

Morris "Moe" Dalitz: Reputed mob associate; owner Desert Inn Hotel and Casino and Sundance Hotel in Las Vegas; general partner La Costa resort.

Dennis DeConcini: Democratic senator from Arizona; met with regulators on behalf of Lincoln Savings, Irvine, California.

Anthony Delvecchio: Borrower at Flushing Federal Savings, New York; associate of Michael Rapp.

Daniel W. Dierdorff: President, Sun Savings, San Diego, California.

John Dioguardi: reputed to be a member of the Lucchese mob family; associate of Michael Hellerman.

Don Dixon: Controlled Vernon Savings, Vernon, Texas.

Frank J. Domingues: borrower with Jack Bona at San Marino Savings; owner South Bay Savings, Newport Beach, California.

Edwin Edwards: Louisiana governor 1972–1980, 1984–1988.

Frank Fahrenkopf: chairman Republican National Committee, 1982–1988.

Robert Ferrante: Owner, Consolidated Savings Bank, Irvine, California.

Ed Forde: chairman, San Marino Savings, San Marino, California.

Lorenzo Formato: president, World Wide Ventures; associate of Michael Rapp.

Jack Franks: southern California loan broker.

Jake Garn: Republican senator from Utah; chairman, Senate Banking Committee; co-author, Garn-St Germain Act.

Thomas Gaubert: Former head and major shareholder, Independent American Savings, Irving, Texas; treasurer 1986 Democratic Congressional Campaign Committee.

John Glenn: Democratic senator from Ohio; met with regulators on behalf of Lincoln Savings, Irvine, California.

Henry Gonzalez: Democratic congressman from Texas; chairman House Banking Committee after St Germain was defeated for re-election in 1988.

David Gorwitz: reputed mob associate; friend of Richard Binder who was a borrower at Centennial Savings.

Camille Gravel: Louisiana attorney; represented Herman Beebe; close friend of Judge Edmund Reggie.

Edwin J. Gray: Chairman, FHLBB, 1983–1987.

Roy Green: president FHLB Dallas, resigned 1987.

Alan Greenspan: thrift consultant; chairman, Federal Reserve Board.

Mary Grigsby: member FHLBB, 1984–1986.

Beverly Haines: Executive vice président, Centennial Savings, Guerneville, California.

Craig Hall: Dallas real estate syndicator.

Erwin Hansen: President, Centennial Savings, Guerneville, California.

J.B. Haralson: Owner, Ben Milam Savings, Cameron, Texas, and Mercury Savings, Witchita Falls, Texas; associate of George Aubin.

Richmond Harper: member of the 1970s Rent-a-Bank scandal in Texas and a Ben Barnes associate.

Michael Hellerman (aka Michael Rapp): Mob's stock broker; borrower, Flushing Federal Savings, New York; purchased Florida Center Bank with rubber check from Charles Bazarian.

Lee Henkel: Brief member, FHLBB; associate of John Connally and Charles Keating.

E. Morton Hopkins: owner, Commodore Savings in Dallas, partner with Mitchell Brown in First National Bank of Marin in San Rafael, California.

Donald Hovde: member FHLBB, 1983–1986.

Lawrence S. Iorizzo: reputed mob associate and associate of Mario Renda.

William Isaac: Chairman, FDIC, 1981–1985.

Norman B. Jenson: Las Vegas attorney; casino owner; borrower, Alliance Federal, Kenner, Louisiana; alleged member international drug smuggling ring.

Charles Keating: Chairman, American Continental Corporation in Phoenix, parent company of Lincoln Savings, Irvine, California.

John Keilly: Las Vegas loan broker; associate of Norman B. Jenson, Wayne Newton, Frank Fahrenkopf; did 27 months in prison in 1970s in connection with a union bribery case.

Carroll Kelly: owner with David Wylie, Continental Savings, Houston; associate of Herman K. Beebe.

Murray Kessler: reputed mob associate; involved with a figure in the Texas Rent-a-Bank scandal in the 1970s.

Adnan Khashoggi: Saudi Arabian middleman, associate of Mario Renda; borrower from Mainland Savings, Houston, Texas.

Kenneth Kidwell: President, Eureka Federal Savings, San Carlos, California.

Charles Knapp: Former head of Financial Corporation of America, parent company of American Savings, Stockton, California; the "Red Baron."

Sig Kohnen: a senior officer of Charles Bazarian's CB Financial.

John Lapaglia: loan broker; head of Falcon Financial, San Antonio, Texas.

William Lemaster: President, Indian Springs State Bank, Kansas City.

Woody Lemons: CEO, Vernon Savings.

Donald E. Luna: associate of Herman K. Beebe and Carl Cardascia.

Bruce Maffeo: Assistant U.S. attorney, Organized Crime Strike Force, Brooklyn, New York, on the First United Fund case.

George Mallick: Fort Worth developer and friend of Speaker of the House Jim Wright.

Michael Manning: Attorney; fee counsel, FDIC and FSLIC, on the First United Fund case.

Ed McBirney: Chairman, Sunbelt Savings, Dallas.

John McCain: Republican senator from Arizona; met with regulators on behalf of Lincoln Savings, Irvine, California.

Ed Meese: U.S. Attorney General, 1985–1988.

John Mmahat: CEO Gulf Federal Savings, Metarie, Louisiana.

Donald P. Mangano: owner, Ramona Savings, Ramona, California.

Scott Mann: chairman CreditBanc Savings, Austin, Texas.

Carlos Marcello: reputed New Orleans Mafia boss.

Ronald J. Martorelli: vice president, Flushing Federal Savings, Flushing, Queens, New York.

Frederick Mascolo: borrower at Acadia Savings, Crowley, Louisiana; purchased Poconos property from Rizzo and Delvecchio.

Harvey McLean: director, Paris Savings, Paris, Texas; owner, Palmer National Bank, Washington, D.C.

Walter Mitchell, Jr.: Redondo Beach, California, city councilman and associate of Robert Ferrante.

Ed Mittlestet: president, Charles Bazarian's CB Financial.

John L. Molinaro: owner, Ramona Savings, Ramona, California.

Patrick Murphy: FBI special agent on the Centennial Savings case.

John Napoli, Jr.: convicted of bank fraud in connection with his dealings at Aurora Bank in Denver; an associate of Michael Rapp.

Tom Nevis: borrowed over $100 million from savings and loans; convicted of bank fraud at State Savings of Corvallis, Oregon in 1989.

William O'Connell: President, U.S. League of Savings Institutions.

Guy Olano: Chairman, Alliance Federal Savings, Kenner, Louisiana.

J. William Oldenburg: San Francisco loan broker; owner, State Savings, Salt Lake City.

Michael Patriarca: Director of Agency Group, FHLB San Francisco.

Leonard Pelullo: chairman, Royale Group Ltd; purchased Atlantic City Dunes in 1988.

Gene Phillips: chairman, Southmark Corp.

Salvatore Piga: reputed mob associate and friend of Mario Renda.

Robert Posen: thrift attorney, associate of loan broker John Lapaglia.

Richard Pratt: FHLBB chairman, 1981–1983.

Albert Prevot: French businessman from Houston whose testimony led to the indictment of Herman K. Beebe.

G. Wayne Reeder: Southern California developer with connections to Southmark, Herman Beebe, San Marino Savings, others.

Donald Regan: CEO and chairman of the board, Merrill Lynch, 1973–1981; treasury secretary 1981–1985; White House chief of staff 1985–1987.

Edmund Reggie: Louisiana judge; founder and director, Acadia Savings, Crowley, Louisiana; associate of Herman Beebe.

Lionel Reifler: Associate of Michael Rapp; borrower at Acadia Savings in Crowley, Louisiana.

Mario Renda: Deposit broker; owner First United Fund, Garden City, New York.

John Riddle: Vernon Savings borrower.

Don Riegle: Democratic senator from Michigan; met with regulators on behalf of Lincoln Savings, Irvine, California; later returned contributions from Lincoln.

Jilly Rizzo: Borrower, Flushing Federal Savings; associate of Michael Rapp, and close friend and bodyguard to Frank Sinatra.

Peter Robinson: Assistant U.S. attorney, Santa Rosa, California, on the Centennial Savings case.

Stuart Root: head, FSLIC.

Heinrich Rupp: Borrower, Aurora Bank, Denver; claimed to be CIA contract pilot; associate of Michael Rapp.

Anthony Russo: Vice president, Indian Springs State Bank, Kansas City.

Richard Sanchez: supervisor, FHLB San Francisco.

Nicholaas Sandmann: Dutch investor; borrower and stockholder, Centennial Savings, Guerneville, California.

Philip B. Schwab: Owner, Cuyahoga Wrecking Company, Great Neck, New York; owner, Players Casino, Reno.

Martin Schwimmer: Financial advisor, First United Fund, Garden City, New York.

Joe Selby: Chief supervisory agent, FHLB Dallas.

Siddharth Shah: Executive vice president, Centennial Savings, Guerneville, California.

Morris Shenker: Owner, Dunes Hotel and Casino, Las Vegas, until 1984; former attorney for Teamster boss Jimmy Hoffa.

William Smith: associate of Michael Rapp; claimed to be former CIA agent.

Leif and Jay Soderling: owners, Golden Pacific Savings, Windsor, California.

Rosemary Stewart: head, enforcement division, FHLBB.

Fernand St Germain: Democratic congressman from Rhode Island; chairman, House Banking Committee; co-author, Garn-St Germain Act.

David Stockman: director, Office of Management and Budget, 1981–1985.

Larry Taggart: California S&L commissioner 1983–1985.

R.B. Tanner: founder, Vernon Savings, Vernon, Texas.

Laurence B. Vineyard, Jr.: attorney for Brownfield Savings, Brownfield, Texas; owner with Tyrell Barker of Key Savings, Englewood, Colorado.

Paul Volcker: chairman, Federal Reserve Board, 1979–1987.

M. Danny Wall: Sen. Jake Garn's aide until 1985; became FHLBB chairman in 1987.

Bruce West: Vernon Savings borrower.

Chuck Wilson: owner, Sandia Savings, Albuquerque, New Mexico.

Franklin Winkler: Associate with Marlo Renda in linked financing scams; Hawaii real estate developer.

V. Leslie Winkler: International con man and associate of Mario Renda.

Jarrett Woods: owner, Western Savings, Dallas.

Jim Wright: Democratic congressman from Texas; became Speaker of the House January 1987.

David Wylie: owner with Carroll Kelly, Continental Savings, Houston; associate of Herman K. Beebe.

Al Yarbrow: Beverly Hills loan broker.

Original Sin

President Ronald Reagan stepped through the tall French doors of the White House Oval Office into the bright sunlight of a lovely fall morning. Whispers and nudges rippled through the crowd, and a hush fell over the Rose Garden. A squad of Secret Service agents melted into the audience as Reagan, smiling broadly, strode across the lawn to the podium.

The president stood at ease for a moment and looked out over the assembled guests, beaming with pride and satisfaction. He had promised the American people that he would get government off their backs, that he would deregulate the private sector. This day, October 15, 1982, less than two years into his presidency, he had invited 200 people to witness the signing of one of his administration's major pieces of deregulation legislation.

Reagan told the audience of savings and loan executives, bankers, congressmen, and journalists that they were there to take a major step toward the deregulation of America's financial institutions. He was about to sign, he said, the Garn-St Germain Act of 1982, which would cut savings and loans loose from the tight girdle of old-fashioned, restrictive federal regulations. For 50 years American families had relied on savings and loans to finance their homes, but outmoded regulations left over from the era of the Great Depression, Reagan believed, were preventing thrifts from competing in the complex, sophisticated financial marketplace of the 1980s. The Garn-St Germain bill would fix all that, he promised.

At the conclusion of his remarks, and following enthusiastic applause, Reagan took his seat at a table surrounded by the bill's proud political parents. He flashed a broad smile for the cameras and launched into the signing process. With each sweep of a souvenir pen, thrift regulations crumbled. It was an exhilarating moment for Ronald Reagan. The bill was "the most important

1

legislation for financial institutions in 50 years," he said. It would mean more housing, more jobs and growth for the economy.

"All in all"—he beamed—"I think we've hit the jackpot."

Less than four years later, at the lavish Dunes Hotel and Casino in Las Vegas, Ronald Reagan's words could well have served as the chorus to Ed McBirney's company song.

Ed McBirney was the fun-loving 33-year-old chairman of Sunbelt Savings and Loan, one of Dallas's largest S&Ls with nearly $3 billion in assets. He was playing host at one of his periodic parties in his plush penthouse suite at the Las Vegas Dunes. One of the guests later described the party: McBirney smiled slyly as he surveyed his guests. Slouched on the floor against a couch, he puffed on a large cigar as Sunbelt executives and customers, whom he had flown from Dallas to Las Vegas on a private 727 jet, mingled and chatted, enjoying predinner cocktails and hors d'oeuvres on Sunbelt's tab. McBirney seemed to enjoy living up to his reputation as an outrageous swinger who conducted business deals between, and during, parties, and entertainment had been secretly arranged tonight that promised to be . . . interesting.

He glanced toward the door as it opened. Four attractive, well-dressed women entered the room full of men. The buzz of conversation paused as McBirney's guests noticed the new arrivals. They watched expectantly, curiously, as the women smiled seductively and drifted quietly to prominent positions in the room. Suddenly, without explanation, they began to undress.

The savings and loan guests, well aware of McBirney's reputation, were only momentarily surprised. Then they settled back to enjoy the show. They did assume, however, that once the women were naked, the entertainment would end. They were wrong. When the women finished undressing they moved toward the center of the room and engaged in an enthusiastic lesbian romp. The all-male audience did some embarrassed shuffling, but for the most part they went along for the ride. After the lesbian routine the girls separated and moved among the guests, many of whom were still frozen in amazement. Targeting the older members of the audience, the women began performing oral sex on them while McBirney, sitting on the floor, grinned widely and puffed on his cigar.

McBirney was skillfully riding a cresting wave of power, and he certainly must have felt like he had hit the jackpot, though it was not quite the one President Reagan had had in mind that morning in the Rose Garden. But just four months after the March 1986 party in Las Vegas, McBirney would be forced to resign from Sunbelt, and he would leave the institution hopelessly insolvent. When the dust finally settled regulators would say Sunbelt's cash drawer was $500 million short. Worse yet, the cost of playing out the thrift's losing hand would be $1.7 billion. Quite a jackpot.

McBirney, and dozens like him, were a new breed of savings and loan executive that had sprung like weeds out of the rich soil of the October 1982 Rose

Garden ceremony. At first no one quite knew what to make of these flamboyant new "entrepreneurs." They were very different from the old traditional thrift officers, but wasn't that precisely the point of deregulating the thrift industry—to attract the best and brightest from America's private sector and give them free rein to work capitalism's magic on an industry clogged with dead wood? Wall Street's wunderkind, arbitrager/financier Ivan F. Boesky, acquired a small upstate New York thrift. Then-Vice President George Bush's son Neil became director of Silverado Savings in Denver. New York Governor Mario Cuomo's son Andrew tried to purchase Financial Security Savings in Delray Beach, Florida. Former Governor of Illinois Dan Walker acquired First American Savings in Oak Brook, Illinois. Surely, people thought, if men of such stature wanted to own savings and loans, the industry must be headed in the right direction.[1]

But only 18 months after the Rose Garden signing, Edwin Gray, chairman of the Federal Home Loan Bank Board (FHLBB),[2] discovered something had gone very wrong. On March 14, 1984, he received in the morning dispatch a classified report and videotape from the Dallas Federal Home Loan Bank. Gray summoned fellow Bank Board members Mary Grigsby and Donald I. Hovde to a darkened meeting room on the sixth floor of the Bank Board building, just down the block from the White House, to view the tape. Gray, in his late forties, a solid but tired-looking man with graying hair, sat at the head of the conference table. Microphones recorded the moment for history. In the dimly lit room, a videotape began to roll.

Gray, Grigsby, and Hovde watched in rapt horror. The narrator, a Dallas appraiser, appeared to be in the passenger seat of a car driving along Interstate 30 on the distant outskirts of east Dallas. The camera panned slowly from side to side, catching in sickening detail the carrion of dead savings and loan deals: thousands of condominium units financed by Empire Savings and Loan of Mesquite, Texas. The condominiums stretched as far as the camera could see, in two- and three-floor clusters, maybe 15 units per building. They were separated by stretches of arid, flat land. Many were only half-finished shells. Most were abandoned, left to the ravages of the hot Texas sun. Like a documentary film, the camera zoomed in on building materials stacked rotting in the desert dust. Loose wiring and shreds of insulation swayed in the warm, dead, quiet air. Siding had warped, concrete cracked, windows broken. In many cases only the concrete slab foundations remained—"Martian landing pads," a U.S. attorney would later call them.

"I sat in that board meeting," Gray said later, "and I was so shocked and stunned at what I was seeing that it had a profound effect on me. It was like watching a Triple X movie. I was sick after watching it. I could not believe that anything so bad could have happened."

Empire Savings and Loan had rocketed gleefully into the newly deregulated thrift universe in apparent disregard of the ethical and legal implications of its wild ways, growing seventeen-fold in two years. Later the Federal Savings and Loan Insurance Corporation (FSLIC) would charge that Empire's officers had "sold" land back and forth with associates, to make it look like the land was increasing in value, in order to justify huge loans from Empire Savings for the condominium projects along the I-30 corridor. They seemed to have completely ignored cautions normally taken by prudent thrifts to ensure the safety and security of money entrusted to them by their depositors. And now the savings and loan was not only broke but deeply in the red.

The Bank Board closed Empire Savings that very day and about a year later the federal government would file both civil and criminal charges against over 100 companies and individuals involved in Empire's collapse.[3] In the end the Empire case alone would cost the FSLIC[4] about $300 million. But Empire, costly as it was, represented just the first small hint of the financial holocaust to come. Deregulation of savings and loans sparked a period of waste and corruption, excess and debauchery the likes of which the nation had not seen since the roaring twenties. The ink wasn't dry on the Garn-St Germain legislation, deregulating the thrift industry, before high-stakes investors, swindlers, and mobsters lined up to loot S&Ls. They immediately seized the opportunity created by careless deregulation of thrifts and gambled, stole, and embezzled away billions in an orgy of greed and excess.

The result was the biggest financial disaster since the Great Depression and the biggest heist in history. Tens of billions of dollars were siphoned out of federally insured institutions. Following Empire Savings thrift after thrift collapsed, the victims of incompetent management, poor or nonexistent supervision, insider abuse, and, most important, outright fraud.[5] By the time the problem was discovered, there was little left for the FSLIC to do but pay back the depositors whose money the thrifts had squandered. In just two short years the FSLIC insurance fund paid out the equivalent of all its income for the past 52 years.

In early 1987 thrift regulators said it would cost the FSLIC $15 billion to close all insolvent thrifts. (Out of about 3,200 thrifts, at least 500 were insolvent and another 500 were nearly insolvent.) By the end of the year that estimate had jumped to $22.7 billion. In mid-1988 regulators said the cost could go to $35 billion. In October they upped the figure to $50 billion. But at the same time the General Accounting Office[6] was saying the shortfall was more like $60 billion. In late 1988 experts[7] said costs were increasing by as much as $35 *million* a day and floated total loss figures of $100 billion or more. When President George Bush announced his S&L bailout plan in February 1989, analysts put the cost at $157 billion to $205 billion for the first ten years and a total of $360 billion over three decades. They were conceding that the cost of bailing out the S&Ls would be more than the entire federal deficit. As everyone in Washington and the thrift industry (except President Reagan, who went eight years without mentioning the problem) haggled over just how many billions might be missing, the late Senator Everett Dirkson's favorite Washington joke came to mind: "A billion dollars here and a billion there and pretty soon we're talking real money." The halls of Congress began to hear the first quiet whispers of a taxpayer bailout.

The meltdown of the savings and loan industry was a national scandal, a scandal that left virtually no player untouched or unsullied. It was above all a story of failure—failure of politicians, failure of regulators, failure of the Justice Department and failure of the federal courts. But even as the crisis was being unraveled and the alarm sounded, thrift executives and their customers continued to revel in life in the fast lane, surrounded by their women and their mansions, their Lear jets and their Rolls-Royces. And billions of dollars drifted off into the ozone never to be seen again. Of the missing money, as much as half had been stolen outright. Yet few of the hit-and-run artists who infiltrated the thrift industry went to jail and little of the money was recovered. In short, these inside jobs not only paid but paid very well indeed. And the savings and loan industry as Americans had known it for 50 years teetered on the edge of collapse.

Coauthors Steve Pizzo and Mary Fricker were jarred to attention by thrift deregulation's fallout when tiny, conservative Centennial Savings and Loan in their rural Northern California hometown of Guerneville began acting strangely in December 1982 (two months after the signing of the Garn-St Germain Act) and announced it was going to pay $13 million cash for a construction company. Pizzo was editor of the Guerneville weekly, the *Russian River News*, and Fricker was news editor. Pizzo wrote a news analysis highly critical of Centennial's plan to spend seven times its net worth[8] on a construction company, and he began aggressive coverage of a succession of strange happenings at Centennial Savings and Loan.

Centennial officers suddenly were awash with money. Their names popped up in complex real estate transactions documented at the county recorder's office. Out-of-town visitors from places like Holland, Las Vegas, and Boston mysteriously came and went, taking money with them. Still the thrift's financial statements recorded phenomenal growth. And the small-town rumor mill geared up to churn out dozens of explanations for this bizarre behavior. In the *Russian River News*, Pizzo began asking some fairly obvious questions of the Centennial officers: "Where is all this money coming from?" "Who are you lending it to, and why?" "How can you justify these extravagant salaries, benefits, perks, planes, luxury cars, boats, and trips?" Was this, Pizzo asked, the proper role for a savings and loan, heretofore the most conservative, predictable, and reliable of all American financial institutions?

Pizzo's journalistic probings infuriated Erv Hansen, the president of Centennial Savings, and he exploded. He dispatched his assistant to complain to the paper's publisher. Periodically he threatened that tellers at Centennial would monitor withdrawals, and if they were substantial, he would sue the *News* for causing a run on the thrift. Drunk in a local bar one night, Hansen told Pizzo's business partner, Scott Kersnar, "You tell your partner he better stop sticking his nose where it doesn't belong or I'll do to him what I did to that San Diego reporter on that stock manipulation deal." Pizzo had no idea what had happened to the San Diego reporter, but he took the warning seriously because he had already discovered that some of those customers buzzing around Centennial's loan window had organized crime backgrounds.

For four years Pizzo pursued the Centennial Savings and Loan story, and gradually his *Russian River News* articles about Centennial Savings found their way outside tiny Guerneville. They circulated quietly at the Federal Home Loan Bank in San Francisco and Washington and at the Justice Department. In late 1985 Centennial collapsed—$165 million was missing.

A few months later Pizzo ran a full-page story entitled "Bust-Out," which explained the decades-old mob scam of gaining control of legitimate businesses and then looting, gutting, and abandoning them. Pointing to characters he had discovered in association with Hansen at Centennial, Pizzo raised the possibility that Centennial might have been a victim of such an operation. After the article appeared FBI agents quietly working on the Centennial case took Pizzo aside and behind closed doors told him they personally believed his premise was correct.

Three thousand miles away, in New York City, Stan Strachan, editor of a trade publication called the *National Thrift News*,[9] described by *USA Today* as "the Bible of the thrift industry," heard of Pizzo's pursuit of Centennial. He called associate editor Paul Muolo into his office and told him to go to California to find out if there was a story in all that alleged skullduggery. Two days later Muolo sat in Pizzo's small, cluttered Guerneville office and wondered if Pizzo was actually onto a story or was just a nut—his bust-out theory left little room for neutral ground. Was it even remotely possible that deregulation had allowed organized crime and their legions a foothold in the thrift industry? Muolo had to admit that thrift failures suddenly were multiplying exponentially around the country. The *National Thrift News* was reporting on the collapses every week. Something frightening, and not at all understood, was going on, and Pizzo's profile of Centennial's collapse was practically a template that could be laid over several others Muolo was writing about for the *National Thrift News*. Pizzo complained that he had tried to alert regulators about Centennial in one way or another for months, but they had ignored him. The implications of Pizzo's suspicions were enormous. Muolo went back to New York to sort out what he had heard.

A week later Mary Fricker called Pizzo. She had left the *News* and now worked for a daily newspaper nearby, but she had followed Pizzo's Centennial stories and had for a year been working on a related investigation of her own. She wanted to sit down and go through his files. Pizzo's Centennial "file" was a big, disorderly cardboard box stuffed with documents and notes. For a day she dug through the box and weighed the evidence that more had been going on at Centennial than met the eye.

In December 1986 the three of us agreed that whatever was going on at thrifts was too big a story for any one writer to get his or her arms around alone. We decided to cooperate in a thorough investigation of savings and loan failures. We were still running on hunches at that point, but we had enough information to sense that we were on the threshold of what could be the story of a lifetime. And so we began sorting through Humpty Dumpty's eggshells scattered coast to coast. While industry professionals told us time and again that the growing number of thrift failures were simply the result of natural selection following deregulation, we steadily amassed evidence that suggested otherwise—Humpty Dumpty had been pushed.

By the end of 1988, Centennial Savings and 581 other thrift institutions were dead and another 800 were in regulatory intensive care and might not survive. Some of the people who had run those institutions were also dead— garroted, shot, or victims of suspicious accidents. And still the looting continued. In fact, it threatened to get worse as, incredibly, Congress made plans to deregulate banks. The multibillion-dollar problem created by the insolvency of over 500 of the 3,200 federally insured S&Ls, and the near insolvency of over 500 more, mind-boggling as it was, would be peanuts compared to an equivalent problem among the 14,000 federally insured banks.

We were driven in our investigation by evidence that much of the looting in progress at many of the savings and loans around the nation was in fact not the work of isolated individuals but instead was the result of some kind of network that was sucking millions of dollars from thrifts through a purposeful and co-ordinated system of fraud. We saw evidence that classic "bust-outs" were in progress at thrifts everywhere we looked. At each step of our investigation our suspicions grew because, of the dozens of savings and loans we investigated, *we never once examined a thrift—no matter how random the choice—without finding someone there whom we already knew from another failed S&L.* Yet there was no coordinated national investigation into the causes of the savings and loan crisis. Individual reporters and individual FBI agents around the country were pecking away at their own local thrift failures, but no one seemed to be pursuing the common links between geographically disparate thrift failures. Pizzo's sus-picions since 1984 that there was a connection behind much of the looting had met with scoffs of disbelief at the highest levels of the Justice Department and the Federal Home Loan Bank Board in Washington. If some group or groups had successfully orchestrated the theft of tens of billions of dollars from financial institutions, in broad daylight, without firing a shot, and had gotten away with it without raising the Justice Department's suspicions, the implications for the country were grim.

We believed we were in a race to identify the players in this massive looting operation. In the process we uncovered mobsters, arms dealers, drug money launderers, and the most amazing and unlikely cast of wheeler-dealers that ever prowled the halls of financial institutions. The damage they did to this country's thrift industry will be with us well into the next century. It will significantly add to our national debt and will cost every taxpayer in the country another $2,000 in taxes over the next ten years. The 150-year-old thrift industry itself may not survive.

CHAPTER ONE

A Short History Lesson

The deregulation of savings and loans in the early 1980s was prompted by a series of new problems that suddenly beset an industry that had been a stable member of the American financial community for 150 years. The first savings and loan in the United States—then called a "building and loan" and tailored after building and loan societies in England—was the Oxford Provident Building Association, formed in 1831 in Frankford, Pennsylvania (now part of Philadelphia). Savings and loans filled a vacuum created by banks, which were primarily interested in making consumer and commercial loans, not home loans.

There were 12,000 savings and loans in operation by the 1920s but they were not part of an integrated industry. Each state regulated—or failed to regulate—its own S&Ls, and regulations differed widely from state to state. At the same time competition between thrifts and banks was creating friction between the two kinds of financial institutions. Congress had created the Federal Reserve System for banks in 1913, thereby giving banks an aura of federal control and safety that S&Ls did not enjoy.[1]

In this environment a movement began to initiate federal regulation of thrifts, but before Congress could take concrete action the stock market crashed in 1929 and the Great Depression followed.[2] Over 1,700 thrifts failed and depositors lost $200 million in savings. Thrifts were desperate for help, and their lobby, the U.S. League of Local Building and Loan Associations (later to become the U.S. League of Savings Associations, the nation's largest and most powerful thrift trade association), urged the federal government to come to the industry's aid.

By then thrifts had become a critical element in the national economic machinery and their troubles could not be easily ignored. President Herbert Hoover responded to industry pressure and signed the Federal Home Loan Bank Act in 1932, creating a federal S&L pyramid with the Federal Home Loan Bank

9

Board (FHLBB) in Washington at the top, 12 semi-independent regional federal home loan banks (FHLBs) beneath it, and individual savings and loans at the base of the pyramid.[3] Thrifts were given the option of being state or federally chartered, but those who chose a federal charter had to operate under strict federal regulations and examiners were sent to make sure they did.

Many Americans had lost their life savings during the "bank holidays" of the Depression and they were slow to put their money back into banks and thrifts. To encourage them to fund their neighborhood savings and loans with their meager savings, Congress decided the industry needed to insure its depositors' money against loss. In 1934 Congress established the Federal Savings and Loan Insurance Corporation (FSLIC),[4] which insured deposits up to $5,000— big money in those days. The FSLIC (pronounced Fizz-Lick by industry insiders) insurance system was funded not by the government but by assessments made on its member thrifts.[5]

In this new and improved federal thrift system, local insured deposits were loaned out to local home buyers, who then became solid members of the community, and new depositors—a business cycle that worked beautifully for 50 years. Savings and loans occupied a special place in America, making home ownership affordable for the emerging middle class primarily through 30-year, fixed-rate mortgages. Thrifts provided the fuel for the home-building engine that for almost half a century acted as the fountainhead of America's dynamic domestic economy. Headlines reading "Housing Starts Decline" always predated recessions, and "Spurt in Housing Starts" always announced the recovery. The American life-style centered around the single-family home funded largely by the little neighborhood savings and loan, a system immortalized in the classic Frank Capra film *It's a Wonderful Life*. In the film, Jimmy Stewart played George Bailey, the head of a sleepy little hometown thrift that lent money to residents of the mythical Bedford Falls. Insiders called those days the 3-6-3 days, when savings and loan executives borrowed (from depositors) at 3 percent, loaned (to home buyers) at 6 percent, and were in a golf cart by 3 p.m.

The first real trouble for this comfortable savings and loan world appeared during a mildly inflationary period in the 1960s when Congress worried over the increasing cost of homes. Since the Second World War affordable housing had become an American birthright. Congress' solution to rising home prices was to put a cap on the interest rate that thrifts could pay on deposits placed with them. Congress' reasoning was that if S&Ls didn't have to pay too much for deposits, they wouldn't have to charge too much to the homeowners who borrowed from them.

It was here that Congress' tinkering with the thrift system began going terribly wrong. The interest rate cap, designed to help the housing sector, became a serious handicap for thrifts in the 1970s. The wildfire of inflation that then swept the economy put savings and loans in a bind[6] because by 1979 inflation was running at 13.3 percent but thrifts were limited to paying only 5.5 percent on deposits, and depositors were not willing to invest their money at such low rates.[7] To compound the thrifts' problems, in the 1970s wily entrepreneurs introduced an entirely new product, the money market fund, which paid higher interest rates.[8] Other companies—like Sears, American Express, and Merrill Lynch—saw the possibilities and also developed investments to attract savers' deposits. This increased competition was aided by new technologies. A twenty-first-century rail of satellite dishes and fiber optics enabled depositors to place their savings nationwide, even worldwide. They were no longer confined to their community bank or thrift in their search for a better return on their savings.[9] Thrifts hemorrhaged from a steady outflow of deposits. By 1982, for example, there was over $200 billion in money market funds.

The outflow from thrifts quickly reached crisis proportions. In 1972 the nation's savings and loans had a combined worth of $16.7 billion. By 1980 that figure had plummeted to a *negative* net worth of $17.5 billion, and 85 percent of savings and loans were losing money. Regulators began to warn that if nothing were done, all thrifts would collapse by the end of 1986.

Throughout the years, when savings and loans experienced financial difficulties, federal regulators had traditionally added more layers of regulation. But they could not regulate away the effects of inflation, so in the mid-1970s they decided the opposite approach might work—deregulation.[10] In 1980 Congress finally passed its first thrift deregulation bill, the Depository Institutions Deregulation and Monetary Control Act, designed to phase out interest rate controls on deposits placed with banks and S&Ls. At the same time Congress increased the FSLIC insurance coverage on deposits from $40,000 per account to $100,000.[11] Regulators later said this may have been the most costly mistake made in deregulating the thrift industry. Suddenly thrifts could attract $100,000 blocks of (insured) money with which they could wheel and deal at no risk to the depositor or to the thrift officers. Ironically, this increase in FSLIC coverage was made with little debate and no congressional hearings. While legislators were hammering out the details of the Depository Institutions Deregulation and Monetary Control Act in a late-night session on Capitol Hill, Glen Troop, chief Washington lobbyist for the powerful U.S. League of Savings Institutions, and an associate convinced congressmen to make the increase.[12]

"It was almost an afterthought," a House staffer later told a reporter.[13]

Deregulation of interest rates by the Depository Institutions Deregulation and Monetary Control Act was a mixed blessing for thrifts. It did increase their deposits but it created a deadly profit squeeze in the process. As the cost of deposits increased, the spread between the price thrifts paid for the short-term deposits and the rate thrifts had charged for the long-term loans they held (some of which they might have made 30 years earlier) increased. Thrifts were paying significantly more interest on deposits than they were receiving on old loans. In the first half of 1982 S&Ls lost a record $3.3 billion. Thrifts from around the country found their balance sheets bleeding a sea of red ink, and lobbyists from the U.S. League of Savings Institutions and other trade organizations begged Congress to throw them another life preserver. The result this time was the most significant thrift legislation in 50 years, the Garn-St. Germain Depository Institutions Act of 1982, which Ronald Reagan signed in the Rose Garden ceremony in October 1982. Garn-St Germain went beyond simple tinkering. It was a complex piece of legislation that changed the face of an entire industry with a pen stroke. Two key elements were:

S&Ls would be allowed to offer money market funds,[14] free from withdrawal penalties or interest rate regulation.

Thrifts could invest up to 40 percent[15] of their assets in nonresidential real estate lending. Commercial lending was much riskier than home lending, but the potential returns were higher. This provision made thrifts vulnerable to enormous losses.[16]

Also in 1982, in a move designed to reassure worried depositors who heard about the thrift industry's problems, Congress passed a Joint Current Resolution that placed the full faith and credit of the U.S. government behind the FSLIC.[17] Thrift regulators also got the deregulation fever:

To combat the dying off of S&Ls, a regulation requiring a thrift to have 400 stockholders with no one owning more than 25 percent of the stock was changed in April 1982 to allow a single shareholder to own a thrift. This did result in the start-up of many new savings and loans, but it completely changed the character of the industry. Approval for a new thrift charter had traditionally been based on a clear community need and widespread local support for the thrift. Now the thrust was to attract innovative, visionary entrepreneurs to be the saviors of the thrift industry. What the industry got was a rush of brash, new owners with no other stockholders to buffer the S&L's well-being from the controlling owner's ambition, bad judgment, or greed.[18]

To make it even easier for an entrepreneur to purchase a thrift, regulators allowed buyers to start (capitalize) their thrift with land or other "noncash" assets rather than money. (This provision was a boon to land developers who had extra land lying around that they had not been able to develop.)

To encourage more loan business for savings and loans, regulators said thrifts could stop requiring traditional down payments from borrowers. Instead, thrifts could provide 100 percent financing, with the borrower not having a dime of his own money in the deal.[19]

Thrifts were permitted to make real estate loans anywhere.[20] They had until now been required to loan on property located in their own market area, with an emphasis on community home building and ownership. But with this new regulation (which was intended to encourage a freer flow of funds from cash-rich to cash-poor areas and to increase loan opportunities for thrifts), thrifts were allowed to loan on property too far from home to monitor properly.

On top of these revolutionary changes, owners of troubled thrifts began stretching already liberal accounting rules—with regulators' blessings—in order to squeeze their balance sheets into compliance. (Traditional accountants termed the liberalized thrift accounting methods "voodoo accounting.") For example, "goodwill"—defined as customer loyalty, market share, and other intangible "warm fuzzies"—accounted for over 40 percent of the thrift industry's net worth by 1986.

In all these ways—Congress passing legislation and regulators easing regulations and accounting standards—the federal thrift industry was systematically deregulated between 1980 and 1983. And for a while it *looked* like deregulation was working. In 1983 and 1984 the thrift industry *appeared* to grow by $300 billion. Empire Savings, for example, had assets of only $20.7 million in 1982, but by 1984 it recorded assets of $320 million. George Bailey's little sleepy building and loan became a powerful money lending/development conglomerate that could make loans on, or even own, hotels, shopping malls, mushroom and windmill farms, tanning beds, Arabian horses, Wendy restaurants, and hot-tub spas—or invest in junk bonds and the futures markets. The sky was the limit and it could all be done with federally insured deposits.[21]

Unfortunately, many of the "entrepreneurs" attracted by these changes were actually con men intent upon draining as much money from the system as they could and then moving on. Simply put, Congress and Bank Board officials failed to add into the deregulation equation almost everything mankind has learned about human nature since the dawn of recorded history. Greed, avarice, ambition, and ego dictate that some things in the social order just can't be left on the honor system, and at the top of that list is the care and feeding of other people's money.

One former swindler, speaking to us from Fort Leavenworth federal penitentiary, where he was serving time for loan fraud, said his compatriots knew immediately what deregulation could mean to them. Imagine how they felt, he recalled, when "they realized they could have access to all the money they ever wanted."

It's not hard to understand why savings and loans in the 1980s became known as "money machines." As one regulator remarked years later, "They didn't deregulate the industry, they *unregulated* it."

Perhaps conditions could still have been kept under control, in spite of deregulation, if the examiners responsible for watching over savings and loans had done their job. So where was that diligent cadre of solemn bank examiners who had once traveled the country making certain that bankers stayed honest? Well, first of all, there were a lot fewer of them. The philosophy of the Reagan administration was that deregulation meant *fewer* regulators and examiners, so their number was cut. States, too, cut their supervision staffs. Turnover by 1984 was running at 16 percent. Those examiners who were left were simply outgunned, overworked, undertrained, underpaid,[22] and ill-equipped to face down the new breed of banker attracted by deregulation. Each FSLIC employee was responsible for watching $18.7 million in assets, about four times the $4.7 million in assets watched by each employee of the FDIC, which insured banks. As the industry deregulated, inspectors accustomed to examining nearly identical sets of books at each thrift, books based on simple 30-year home mortgages, suddenly were expected to be able to follow the intricate machinations of highly speculative finance. Examining a $20,000 loan on a home was a far cry from trying to judge the quality or prudence of a $20 million loan on a shopping center or a multitiered master limited partnership.

It wasn't long before thrift failures rippled across the nation like one of those elaborate displays of dominoes that are erected and then destroyed for the *Guinness Book of World Records*. But the destruction didn't all happen in a day or a week or a month. It was four years in the making, and as we followed it we often asked ourselves the same question that Charles Bazarian, one of the borrowers convicted of fraud, demanded of us:

This all didn't happen just yesterday. This happened over a long period of time. So where were the regulators, huh? They like to run around now, acting like they just discovered all this. Where were they when it was going on? Where were the goddamn regulators then?

Where, indeed, were the regulators[23] while thrifts were being looted? During our investigation we got very little in the way of answers to that question. Spokesmen at the FHLBB either flatly refused to discuss thrift failures or they lied about them. In 1983 they told us there was no problem. Then later, when the trouble burst into the open, they lied to us about the size of the problem. Then they lied to us about the causes of the problem. There was no fraud, no organized crime involvement—it was the economy's fault, they said. Then they threw a blanket of secrecy over the solutions they said they had in mind.

In the thrift industry itself, trade groups like the powerful U.S. League of Savings Institutions worked overtime during the years following deregulation to make sure the industry's dirty little secret never got out. They feared that if the public learned that some people were using deregulation to loot thrifts, they would demand re-regulation.

It was only after we were well along in our investigation, and had cultivated solid sources within the Justice Department and the law firms working for the FSLIC, that we began to learn just why everyone was so afraid to talk. If what we saw at crooked thrifts had concerned us, nothing had prepared us for the abuses of power we found in Washington. But we also found courage, and we found the story of a lonely and painful passage for a most unlikely man—Edwin Gray. U.S. League members had talked Gray into becoming chairman of the FHLBB. When he took office, in May of 1983, he assumed control of a regulatory apparatus completely unequipped to handle the coming thrift explosion.

CHAPTER TWO

Shades of Gray

On a Monday in November 1982, stocky, congenial Edwin Gray was in New Orleans to attend the annual convention of the U.S. League of Savings Institutions. Gray represented Great American First Savings Bank of San Diego, California; he was their PR man. His old friend from California, Ronald Reagan, was to be the keynote speaker at the convention. Gray and Reagan went way back together—Gray had been Reagan's press secretary during his years as governor of California. Gray, 47, was a mainstream Reaganite. He believed in Reagan and his free market philosophy. When Ronald Reagan was elected president, Gray had briefly taken a job with the administration as assistant to the president and director of the White House office of policy and development. But Gray's wife, Monique, had disliked Washington and its humid climate and wanted to return to their home in sunny San Diego, so Gray left the administration and went back to his post at Great American First Savings Bank.

President Ronald Reagan was coming to New Orleans to tell members of the U.S. League of Savings Institutions that their industry was well on its way back to its halcyon days. With the signing of the Garn-St Germain bill less than a month earlier, Reagan believed he had personally unfettered a mighty industry which could now rise to towering heights. Gray believed the same, and in fact he had spent a good deal of time in Washington lobbying for the bill before its passage. Once, when he submitted a $2,000 expense voucher, his superiors at Great American Savings quipped, "Since you're spending so much time working for the U.S. League, lobbying for Garn-St Germain, maybe they can pick up part of this." One of the items on the tab was $600 for a dinner Gray had hosted for another old California friend, Ed Meese.

Ed Gray was enjoying being a gadfly at the New Orleans convention when suddenly Leonard Shane, the 1983 chairman of the U.S. League, pulled him aside. The position of chairman of the Federal Home Loan Bank Board (the

Washington, D.C., agency that regulated the nation's federally chartered savings and loans) was coming up for grabs, Shane told Gray. Its current chairman, Richard Pratt, a Mormon and a burly former educator from Utah, was returning to private business.[1] Traditionally the U.S. League had a major say in picking the FHLBB chairman.

"Ed, we want you to be the next chairman," Shane told Gray.

Gray was flattered. Bill O'Connell, president of the U.S. League, also asked him if he'd consider being chairman. Gray told them only that he'd think about it, but the word had already gone out among the membership that Gray had been given the League's benediction. Delegate after delegate came up to him and asked him to take the job. It became a little embarrassing, but the refrain was like music to Gray's ears. A thrift executive becoming chairman of the Federal Home Loan Bank Board was like a priest being elected Pope. How could he say no? Ed Gray's chimney soon issued forth the white smoke of acceptance.

On May 1, 1983, Ed Gray was sworn in as the seventeenth chairman of the Federal Home Loan Bank Board (FHLBB or the Bank Board), a three-member board that consisted of the chairman and two directors who were referred to as "members." Under law, one board member had to be a Republican and the other a Democrat.[2]

With his wife at his side, Gray raised his right hand and took the oath of office, administered by his friend attorney general Ed Meese. Then Gray took off his horn-rimmed glasses and smiled. Those who were there that day remembered that he already looked tired. But being chairman of the FHLBB wasn't a hard job, and he'd promised Monique he'd stay only two years. Gray would have to make a lot of upbeat speeches about how well the industry was doing, and he was expected to support legislation the industry wanted—or that's what the job had been like for his predecessors. Had Gray known what really lay ahead, and that his term would turn out to be one of the longest and most tumultuous in FHLBB history, he might have put his right hand back in his coat pocket and taken Monique home to San Diego.

In the coming four years, until the end of his term in June 1987, Gray would be investigated by the FBI and the Government Ethics Committee and badgered by congressmen and senators, including the powerful speaker of the House, on behalf of their constituents. His own administration, and his longtime friend Ronald Reagan, would turn their backs on him, turning him down when he asked for more money and more regulators to help deal with the massive abuses and insolvencies besetting the S&L industry. And that very same thrift industry that had begged him to take the job would vilify him for his efforts to save it. Ed Gray would become a pariah.

Gray didn't know it then, but he had just been sworn in as the central character in an epic drama. And how unlikely a protagonist he was. Ed Gray was in no way prepared for the task that was about to be handed him. Some would say he wasn't qualified for it either. He was a public relations flack by trade. He gave warm smiles, firm handshakes and great back slaps, and he told a good story. He was an old-fashioned gentleman with thinning, graying hair who called his women acquaintances "dear." A nice guy, an honest guy . . . but he did not have the national stature of a Paul Volcker.[3]

But then Gray had not been selected on the basis of his qualifications. He was supposed to be a cheerleader for the thrift industry and a tool of the administration. That point was driven home his first day on the job when he received a phone call from Treasury Secretary Don Regan.

"You're going to be a team player, I take it?" Regan asked him.

"Sure," Gray said, leaning back in his swivel chair. "Sure."

Regan hung up with Gray still holding the receiver. What was that all about? Gray wondered.

He threw himself into the job of chairman. He loved the idea of being a public official, and he took the responsibility to heart. He was a *Mr. Smith Goes to Washington* kind of guy. Ed was no monetary genius, but what he lacked in experience he tried to make up for by putting in long hours. He wanted to know what was going on in the industry and, conversely, he felt it would be helpful for thrift executives to know what was on his mind. So Gray had his staff mail copies of all his speeches to the directors and chief executives of the nation's major thrifts. "The Thoughts of Ed Gray" became a regular part of industry mail call. Stodgy industry leaders viewed all this with amusement, and the joke started to circulate that if you suddenly realized you'd been dropped from Ed's mailing list, it probably meant the Bank Board was getting ready to close your thrift.

Gray was a very different kind of regulator than his predecessors. Like the president, who had appointed him, he held strong, sometimes simplistic views of what he considered to be right and wrong. And when he had to make decisions on technical matters, he let those instincts mold his course.

Gray's first few months in office passed in relative quiet. The only problem on his plate at the time was untangling the mess left by the collapse of Manning Savings and Loan in Chicago. The Bank Board had closed Manning Savings just before Gray was made chairman. The $117 million thrift had failed after growing rapidly, not by attracting local deposits but by using deposits from deposit brokers to invest in questionable real estate ventures.

Deposit brokers handled[4] billions of dollars for institutional investors like pension funds, insurance companies, even Arab nations looking for a profitable place to park their oil revenues. They scoured the nation each morning for the highest interest rates being paid that day on certificates of deposit (CDs), and then purchased $100,000 insured CDs with their investors' money. Such brokered funds became known to regulators as "hot money" because they were temporary. When the certificates matured[5] the money would again flow to whomever was paying the best rate that day. The fickleness of these deposits forced thrifts to offer higher and higher interest rates to attract them.

Brokered deposits, in small doses, could help a thrift stabilize its deposit base and give it a quick, though expensive, source of funds when the thrift was a little short. But Manning Savings had overdosed on brokered deposits. An old adage came to Gray's mind: The only thing that separated a medicine from a poison was the quantity in which it was used. Gray remembered another time, back in the 1960s, when thrifts had turned to brokered deposits in a big way. The result was a wave of cut-throat thrift competition for deposits that drove up the interest rate the S&Ls had to pay to attract those deposits. Thrifts willing to pay the highest price then grew too fast. The FHLBB in Washington had ended the practice in July 1963 by limiting the amount of brokered deposits a thrift could hold to 5 percent of its total deposits.

But that was old-fashioned regulation. In 1980, when thrifts were having a hard time attracting deposits, regulators had repealed the 5 percent limit, and brokered deposits once again became all the rage. But unlimited brokered deposits combined with Garn-St Germain, which deregulated what thrifts could do with those deposits, created a volatile chemistry. Thrifts could get their hands on all the money they wanted and could invest that money in almost any scheme they thought might turn a profit.[6]

Gray saw immediately the risk inherent in the combination of ambitious entrepreneurial thrift owners, with their quest for high-yield investments, and the easily available brokered deposits to fund those investments. He knew that the Federal Deposit Insurance Corporation (FDIC)[7] under chairman William M. Isaac[8] was struggling with a similar problem, following the 1982 collapse of Penn Square Bank, a small shopping-center bank in Oklahoma City. Brokered deposits had fueled Penn Square Bank's wild speculation in oil industry investments and had contributed to an unhealthy atmosphere of management fraud. (In 1988 a bank official would plead guilty to criminal charges in a scheme that regulators said involved risky loans and kickbacks.) But few people in Washington other than Isaac, and almost no one out in the 50 states, shared Gray's assessment.

Since the creation of the federal S&L industry in 1932, state and federal savings and loans had coexisted peacefully. State thrifts could receive FSLIC insurance if they chose to pay the premiums,[9] but they were regulated by state agencies and state regulations instead of the FHLBB and federal regulations (except that they did have to adhere to FSLIC standards). On the whole the differences between state and federal regulations were slight (though state regulations tended to be more liberal than federal regulations) until federal deregulation in the early 1980s changed the rules of the game. Then, many say, *real* deregulation happened on the state level. Notable among the states with more liberal thrift regulations were Arizona, Florida, Illinois, Louisiana, Michigan, Mississippi, Missouri, New York, North Carolina, Ohio, Virginia, and Washington. But Texas and California outdid them all, grabbing the lead in deregulation one-upmanship (Texas won first place, but California ran a close second).

Actually, deregulation was not new to Texans. They had significantly liberalized regulations for state-chartered thrifts in 1972 and again in 1981. In addition, banking had for years been done differently in Texas. Typical features of the state thrift business included risk-taking, wheeling and dealing, and domination by a good-old-boy network that had close ties to the most powerful Texas politicians. When oil prices went from $7.64 per barrel in 1975 to $34.50 per barrel in 1981, the Texas economy boomed, building permits quadrupled, and Texans thought they were invincible. All the thrift industry needed then to rocket into the stratosphere was for the feds to approve brokered deposits and for the FSLIC to decide to insure S&L deposits up to $100,000 each, all of which happened in 1980. In the early 1980s Texas thrifts attracted huge deposits by promising to pay a higher interest rate than anyone else in the country, and they invested those deposits in commercial real estate ventures. Texas thrifts grew at roughly three times the national average. So many new owners were attracted to thrift ownership in Texas—because Texas thrifts seemed to be able to get their hands on endless supplies of money and the Texas real estate market was booming—that by 1987, when Texas thrifts finally were failing in large numbers,[10] 50 percent were run by managers who had entered the business after 1979 (over 80 percent were former real estate developers).

Typical of the new thrift owner in Texas was Harvey D. McLean, a Dallas developer and chairman of Paris Savings and Loan. Reports in *BusinessWeek* that he had attended a costume party wearing punk regalia and blue hair and joked that he was dressed that way to visit his banker surprised no one in the out-of-control Texas thrift environment. Durward Curlee, a Texas thrift lobbyist who had been executive director of the powerful Texas Savings and Loan League, was referring to Texas thrift owners' penchant for fleets of airplanes when he remarked to a *BusinessWeek* reporter, "That's not criminal. That's Texas."[11]

Out in California state-chartered savings and loans had been struggling to survive since 1975 under a state administration[12] that employed hard-nosed regulators. When the federal government eased up on regulations between 1980 and 1982, over half of the state's S&Ls, including most large California thrifts, switched to federal charters.[13] The result was a precipitous drop in S&L contributions to state politicians and also in income (from fees charged to member thrifts) for the California Department of Savings and Loan, which regulated state S&Ls. The department lost more than half its income and had to lay off more than 60 state examiners. Under those dire circumstances Governor Edmund Brown, Jr. decided to treat S&Ls more kindly.

Former State Assembly Minority Whip Paul Priolo told us later that the

California League of Savings Associations (the Cal League), the thrift industry's statewide lobbying group, lobbied the state legislature every year with the same theme: "They told us every year that we had to pass legislation to match any federal legislation that might cause thrifts to switch to federal charters. The buzzword was 'parity.' They constantly lobbied for parity, or better, with federal legislation. And they almost always got what they asked for." Priolo said legislators knew little about the thrift industry and relied on the Cal League for guidance in drafting new state regulations. A former federal regulator said state politicians were also concerned they would lose contributions if state-chartered thrifts switched to federal charters.

In response to the political and financial pressure, Republican state assemblyman Pat Nolan, who was an associate of a number of S&L executives,[14] sponsored the Nolan Bill, which became law January 1, 1983. Under the terms of the new California law, virtually anyone could own an S&L, attract as many deposits as he could pay for, and invest all those deposits in anything. And it could all be insured by the FSLIC and backed by the full faith and credit of the U.S. government. California's deregulation made Garn-St Germain look conservative by comparison, and in retrospect it was a terrible mistake. But only one lawmaker voted against it, and traditionalists in the thrift industry who worried about it kept their concerns to themselves. (Five years later, however, they would claim that the thrift industry's problems were not their fault.)

Later Ed Gray would remark, "Can you imagine? Any business, any entrepreneur [in California] could get a charter and could run whatever operation he wanted on the credit of the U.S. government? Imagine that! It didn't matter. You could choose any business you wanted to be in. . . . Just incredible."

Ed Forde, who owned San Marino Savings and Loan in Southern California (which failed in 1984 soon after Empire Savings collapsed), told us years later how he felt when he learned of the new California regulations at a seminar sponsored by state regulators. " 'My god,' I said to myself, 'this is what I've been waiting for all my life!' " Clever consultants and law firms began canvassing the state offering seminars on owning one's own savings and loan. Jeffer, Mangels and Butler, for example, was a Los Angeles law firm that gave seminars called "Why Does It Seem Everyone Is Buying or Starting a California S&L?"[15]

The strategy failed to attract back most of the thrifts that had recently switched to federal charter, but it did attract hundreds of entrepreneurs interested in starting new S&Ls. What politicians and regulators later claimed they could not foresee (the loopholes and opportunities created by deregulation) were instantly recognized by those who wasted no time flooding the state with applications—235 between April 1982 and the fall of 1984. Unfortunately, the rush of applications far exceeded the state savings and loan commissioner's ability to investigate the applicants.

When the job of state commissioner became available in March of 1983 (with the new Republican administration of George Deukmejian), Ed Gray recommended his friend Lawrence W. Taggart for the post.[16] But Taggart, it turned out, had a very different regulatory philosophy from Gray. Gray was deeply troubled by the brokered deposits that by 1983 were fueling fearful growth in California, but Taggart saw no problems. When many of the new California thrifts ballooned their assets from the minimum start-up capital of $2 million to tens and then hundreds of millions of dollars, using brokered deposits, and when growth rates at some California thrifts exceeded 1,000 percent a year, Taggart wasn't worried. On the contrary, he took a real shine to the new breed of thrift owners, accommodated them in every possible way, and approved their thrift applications as soon as the paperwork could be completed (he approved 60 charters in his first six months in office).

And look who showed up as California savings and loan owners:

Dr. Duayne Christensen, a Southern California dentist-turned-real-estate-speculator, got tired of begging for loans from straitlaced thrift officers and in January 1983 he opened North American Savings and Loan in Santa Ana, California. A married man with teenage children, Christensen had undergone a midlife crisis of some sort and had taken up with a flashy real estate lady from Oak Grove, California, Janet F. McKenzie. Both apparently shared a burning desire to be rich.

In short order, according to an FSLIC lawsuit, the two began to wheel and deal with North American's deposits, investing them in grossly overappraised real estate projects in which they held a secret interest. One project alone (a 20-unit condominium project in Lake Tahoe, Nevada), which they acquired for less than $4 million, they sold back and forth to artificially increase its value to $40 million, regulators said. Reno mortgage broker John Masegian helped put together loans for the condominium deal. The next month, February 1983, while he was attending a savings and loan convention in Miami, he was garroted in the stairwell of the Fountainebleau Hilton. The murderers had tried to stuff his body down the trash disposal chute but it wouldn't fit.[17] No one was charged with his murder. A security guard claimed that a few months later Christensen tried to hire him to kill a business partner who lived in Arkansas, but later Christensen changed his mind.

North American collapsed in June 1988 and cost the FSLIC $209 million. The day before North American was seized by federal regulators, Christensen was killed in a mysterious single-car accident when his Jaguar slammed head-on into a freeway abutment at six o'clock in the morning, leaving a $10 million life insurance policy that named McKenzie as sole beneficiary and a will Christensen had signed three days earlier that named McKenzie as his sole heir. The coroner ruled out foul play in Christensen's death and the $40 million that regulators said Christensen and his associates spirited out of North American

Savings remained missing. In April 1989 McKenzie and four others were indicted and charged with racketeering. The case was pending as of this writing.

A few miles away, in Ramona, California, former rug salesman John L. Molinaro and his partner Donald P. Mangano, who owned a construction company, were granted a charter and opened Ramona Savings and Loan in April 1984. In short order the thrift made loans to condominium construction projects being built by Mangano & Sons Construction Company, condominiums whose floors were later covered by carpets from Molinaro's carpet store. Regulators and the Justice Department later charged that the two men became more and more bold in devising ways to part Ramona Savings from its deposit money as time passed. Two years after opening its doors Ramona Savings collapsed into insolvency. FSLIC officials said Ramona Savings would cost them $70 million.

Ten months after Ramona Savings' collapse, a San Francisco passport clerk caught Molinaro trying to get to the Cayman Islands[18] on a dead man's passport. When the FBI arrested him and searched his Mercedes, they found false IDs and materials on how to establish a false identity and launder money. They also found, and filed in court, his list of things to remember, which included . . . "consider storing gold in Cayman deposit box . . . write out a plan for depositing Cayman cash and bringing some back thru (sic) Canada" . . . etc. When FBI agents checked inside the Cayman safe-deposit boxes, they found what the FSLIC believed was some of Ramona's money. Molinaro told FBI agents he had deposited $3 million at First Cayman Bank, and in safe-deposit boxes he had stashed $278,000 in cash and $100,000 in gold and diamonds . . . all accessible by secret code.

The list of colorful characters who showed up at thrifts in California following deregulation was a long one, and they arrived at a time when the state regulatory commission was crippled by the recent loss of 60 examiners (caused by the budget crunch when state thrifts defected to federal charter from 1980 through 1982). Not until Taggart was succeeded by William Crawford as state savings and loan commissioner in 1985 would the examining staff begin to be rebuilt.

During those undersupervised years high fliers and swindlers looted the thrift industry of billions of dollars, right under the overworked examiners' noses. They even developed shoptalk to describe their crooked deals: "dead cows for dead horses," "cash for trash," "kissing the paper," "land flips," "daisy chains," and "white knights." Each was a sleight of hand that rogue thrifts employed around the country to confuse regulators and hide the frauds that underlay their operations.

The profligacy of thrifts around the country, especially in Texas and California[19] (and secondly Florida and Arizona), didn't begin to catch Ed Gray's eye in Washington until the Empire Savings failure in 1984. By that time the horse was definitely out of the barn. Most of the problems were developing at state-chartered thrifts rather than federally chartered institutions (because the states adopted regulations even more lenient than were enacted on the federal level), but Gray was affected in a very important way by what happened on the state level because the FSLIC, which he and his fellow board members at the FHLBB administered, insured most of those state thrifts and would have to bail them out should they fail.[20] Ironically, it was precisely the FSLIC coverage that made the looting of thrifts so lucrative and relatively risk free—for everyone except the FSLIC and, ultimately, the taxpayer. Thanks to the FSLIC insurance, depositors didn't have to worry about their money, and the people who were spending it certainly didn't.

CHAPTER THREE

Centennial Gears Up for Deregulation

Before deregulation most thrifts were small. One did not go into the savings and loan business to get rich. In fact, starting a small community-based savings and loan bordered on performing community service—local people pooling their resources to assure there would be a safe place for their savings and a source for home loans. These small-town thrifts were just barely eking out a living when deregulation passed Congress and they became the prime targets for the wolves that deregulation unleashed. They were easy targets for the fast-talking high rollers who showed up to wow the mostly unsophisticated managers and boards of directors with promising projects or to offer top dollar to local shareholders for their stock. Hundreds of small thrifts across the nation fell into the wrong hands in the weeks and months following deregulation, and one of those was Centennial Savings and Loan, a state-chartered thrift in Northern California. From its plain vanilla beginnings, Centennial rocketed to unimaginable heights within just a few months after deregulation. But few people became concerned about the metamorphosis until Centennial's officers threw a spectacular Christmas party at the end of 1983.

It was the most lavish Christmas party anyone could recall. "Elegant Renaissance Faire" was the theme. Couples gasped as jesters proclaimed their entry into the hall, now transformed into an Elizabethan forest of 300 living trees sparkling with 75,000 tiny white lights. Candlelight shimmered through piped-in fog that simulated the moors and woods of Nottingham. Oriental rugs covered the floor.

Once seated among the trees, the 500 invited guests were entertained by a hundred roving Robin Hoods, fiddlers, jugglers, jesters, and pantomimes. Waiters and waitresses, one for every two guests, wore Elizabethan costumes—swagger plumed hats, ruffled laced bodices, yards of velvet. They rolled the ten-course, three-hour meal into the hall on flaming carts, meats crackling on open spits, each course heralded by twelve trumpeters.

Men and women visiting the rest room were attended by shoeshine boys for the men and maids-in-waiting with an array of makeup and perfumes for the women. Dancing continued until three o'clock in the morning, and to this day many say it was the most romantic evening of their lives.

It was Christmas 1983 in Santa Rosa, California, and Centennial Savings and Loan officers spent $148,000 to show their friends, stockholders, and area politicians that the S&L had arrived. For the little thrift it was as much a coming-out party as a Christmas fete. But for those of us who had been paying close attention, it was another reason for concern. This was a very different Centennial from the small thrift that had opened in 1977 in Guerneville (population 1,700), 20 miles west of Santa Rosa.

Guerneville was on the banks of the Russian River 60 miles north of San Francisco. It had been a popular summer resort among the redwoods in the 1940s and 1950s, but it had faded considerably as tourists passed it by for more exotic destinations in the sixties and seventies. Property values slid as the only takers for the old summer cabins were realtors and speculators betting Guerneville would soon become a bedroom community of its fast-growing neighbor, Santa Rosa (population 70,000). A handful of local investors drawn from Guerneville's hard-hit business community joined resources to raise the $2 million regulators required of a new savings and loan, and they opened Centennial in the hope that the realtors and speculators were right. Their plan was to make home loans to those who would live in Guerneville and work in Santa Rosa.

But the vision was slow in materializing and the little thrift spent its first three years going through a succession of lackluster presidents, none of whom left a memorable mark on the town or the institution's bottom line. However, as 1980 approached so did the dawning of the deregulation of the savings and loan industry. Centennial's directors wanted someone at the helm who could sail their little thrift out of becalmed seas and into the uncharted potential promised by this newly deregulated industry.

One of Centennial's directors recalled his acquaintance with a man who had plenty of experience in the thrift industry. Erwin "Erv" Hansen, age 48, had been bouncing around the industry a long time. He had worked as a senior executive for Imperial Savings and Loan in Southern California, as a deputy commissioner and the number two person in the California savings and loan commissioner's office, as CEO for Far West Financial in Newport Beach, California, and as chief accountant for the Federal Home Loan Bank Board in Washington, D.C. He was well known in the industry and was regarded as a conservative banker.[1] As frosting on the cake, Erv was married to a local gal, Gayle, who told friends she looked forward to returning home someday.

Early in December 1980, Erv Hansen drove into town in an aging car packed with family and belongings and on December 16 Centennial's board of directors voted to make Erwin Hansen the thrift's fourth (and last) president.

Everyone just called him Erv. He shunned traditional banker's garb. Instead he would have looked right at home on the street in Dallas, with his Western sports coat and slacks, open-collar shirt, shiny bucking-bronco belt buckle, and pointed-toe cowboy boots. A tall man, he wore the outfit well.

Erv cut a very different figure than Centennial's former presidents and he quickly won the friendship of Guerneville's redneck cowboy community with his love of drink and good company. His office away from the office was the Appaloosa Room at Buck's bar and restaurant, where he routinely held court after work and late into the evening. He'd buy drinks all around and regale those present with well-told stories, mostly about himself and his past exploits in the bigger world outside Guerneville. But Erv's favorite tales soon switched to a new theme: what he was going to do, what deregulation meant to him and Centennial, how the sky was the limit.

"The beauty is that there's going to be enough money in this for everyone," he liked to boast.

Erv swept the townsfolk off their feet. Even those put off by his sometimes arrogant ways found it hard to criticize him. He seemed a cross between John DeLorean and J. R. Ewing. But there were two dangerous unknowns: no one understood just what deregulation of thrifts meant in practical terms, and no one really knew Erv Hansen.

It took time for Hansen to spur the lazy little thrift to a gallop. With its net worth of just $1.87 million, there wasn't much he could do, and shallow-pocketed locals were clearly not going to be the source for the kind of money he needed. But he had a plan. He knew where he could get plenty of capital, practically overnight—hundreds of millions of dollars in brokered deposits, just for the asking. But Centennial's directors, officers, and shareholders weren't ready just yet for the kind of moves Erv had in mind. So he decided to bide his time for a while and build alliances at Centennial with those who shared his vision.

Beverly Haines began as a teller at Centennial when it opened its doors in 1977. Haines, 44, had been married to a well-to-do San Francisco contractor, but an unpleasant divorce in the early 1970s left her at times living at the pleasure of friends and relatives. She eventually moved into the family's summer cabin in Guerneville with her teenage son, who had recently been paralyzed in an auto accident. His injuries left him in a wheelchair and in need of 24-hour care. Haines was totally dedicated to her son, caring for him at night while working at Centennial during the day.

She was bright and articulate, a short, well-dressed blonde with a cultured way of speaking and moving that attracted fawning admirers. She moved from teller to receptionist and held that position when Erv Hansen arrived on the scene in 1980. Haines was clearly a woman used to better circumstances, and Hansen felt he and Haines had something to offer each other. The two became fast confidants, often meeting behind closed doors. Beverly was clearly on her way up. Hansen soon appointed her executive vice president of Centennial and put her in charge of the thrift's money desk, the entry point for large deposits from pension and trust funds and deposit brokers. It was a key position that later would become the fulcrum of the wheeling and dealing that Hansen had in mind.

At this time Siddharth "Sid" Shah was in Santa Rosa trying his hand as a developer and not having much luck. Shah, 47, an East Indian, had come to the United States in 1963. He had majored in engineering at Stanford University near San Francisco and had gone to work for nearby Piombo Corporation, a heavy-construction company.[2] Shah worked for Piombo for 13 years, during which time he managed the company's projects in Saudi Arabia and, later, around Santa Rosa.

Shah oozed a confidence that some found repulsive and others found captivating. He was quiet, shrewd, and inscrutable. Associates described him with amazement as someone who "got things done," "knew how to work all the angles," "was always working on some kind of deal . . . a genius with paper" who could wring every penny out of a construction job.

During his stay with Piombo, Shah acquired 8 percent of the company stock. In early 1982 Shah and Piombo had a parting of the ways and Shah announced he was leaving Piombo to strike out on his own. Piombo had a long-standing policy of purchasing any stock that a departing employee had accumulated during his stay with the company, but in this case Shah and Piombo's owners were not even close to a mutually agreeable price. Shah wanted $1 million for his shares. Piombo said the stock was worth only $200,000. Shah said he felt his price was fair because he believed the company could be sold for $13 million. Piombo's shareholders, eager to give Shah the opportunity to prove it, gave him an option to purchase Piombo for $13 million—but only if he could close the deal within a year.

Meanwhile, Shah's Lakewood Enterprises—a development company in Santa Rosa—was going nowhere, and in the spring of 1982 Shah turned to Erv

Hansen and Centennial. Both men had big plans. Both told associates they wanted to make big things happen. And both saw a deregulated thrift industry as the opportunity of a lifetime.

Shah introduced Hansen to Dutch investor Nicholaas Sandmann, 36, who had sailed mysteriously into town with plans to develop the old 1,000-acre George Ranch east of Santa Rosa. Handsome and charming, with a lovely young wife, "Neik" quickly captured the imagination of the San Francisco area jet set. Herb Caen, columnist for the San Francisco *Chronicle*, described Sandmann as the "high-flying newcomer from Holland." Other press reports said he was "a reclusive Dutch businessman who lives in a multimillion-dollar mansion in Amsterdam."

He fit perfectly into the genteel Sonoma County horse-and-winery set of which Santa Rosa was the center. There the gentry played polo and croquet and sipped chardonnay and cabernet—made in their own cellars—on their magnolia-shaded verandas overlooking vineyards soothed by Pacific Ocean mists. Sandmann knew how to play that game. Shah and Hansen were eager to learn.

In July of 1982, regulators said, loan money began to flow among the three men. Centennial loaned Sandmann $5.4 million on his George Ranch development and paid Shah's company, Lakewood Enterprises, a $150,000 finder's fee for introducing Sandmann to Centennial. Later the George Ranch deal would collapse in a flurry of defaults and allegations of fraud, inside deals, and kickbacks, but in 1982 it looked brilliant and significantly improved Centennial's financial statement.

Such large loans improved a thrift's financial picture because thrifts were allowed to book a lot of income immediately upon making a loan. For example, they collected points—usually 1 percent to 6 percent of the loan. On a $1 million loan with 5 points, a thrift could immediately book $50,000 in income. Fees, such as "loan origination fees," were also added to the borrower's bill. These, too, went right on the thrift's books as income as soon as the loan was made. Simply put, loans generated instant income for thrifts, and the bigger the loan, the bigger the income. Often thrift executives used inflated appraisals to justify even larger loans, so they could book even larger profits, which in turn justified large bonuses for the executives.

Unfortunately, all this profit was only on paper because thrifts routinely added the points, fees, and even the interest to the amount of the loan.[3] For example, if a borrower wanted a $1 million loan, the S&L might loan him $1.2 million and put the extra $200,000 in a reserve account to cover the first two years' worth of interest. In effect, the S&L was paying itself until the reserve account ran out. The reserve accounts made a loan appear current for a long time regardless of the true state of the project (or the whereabouts of the borrower).[4] And if the loan came due and the project then turned out to be phony, the loan could be rolled over (renewed) on the theory, California Savings and Loan Commissioner William Crawford later quipped, that a rolling loan carried no loss.

With such tricks up his sleeve, Hansen had no worries about the generosity of Centennial's loan on the George Ranch. He was on a roll. Sensing the momentum he was building, he struck quickly. One bold move would follow another, starting with the boldest of all: In August of 1982 Hansen convinced Centennial's board of directors, which now included one-time receptionist Beverly Haines, to purchase Shah's option on Piombo Corporation for $100,000 and to pay Shah $1 million for his Piombo stock—five times more than Piombo itself was willing to pay. Centennial would then exercise the option and purchase the giant construction company for $13 million cash, proving Shah to be a man of vision by validating his boast to skeptical Piombo shareholders that their company was worth $13 million. Shah would become head of Piombo and an executive at Centennial the day the deal closed.

Centennial would benefit, Hansen argued, because deregulation was making it possible for thrifts to invest in commercial real estate and become development companies, and Centennial needed to position itself to take advantage of the new opportunities for fun and profit. California's Nolan Bill, which allowed state S&Ls to invest 100 percent of their assets in speculative ventures, was set to go into effect January 1, 1983. Hansen was pushing Centennial up onto the cutting edge of California's thrift deregulation movement.

Centennial's board of directors approved the plan but kept it secret, and in September, four months before the deal was set to close, Shah, still technically only a customer and therefore exempt from banking regulations that forbade large loans to thrift officers, received a last-minute flurry of loans from Centennial. In a nine-day period, FSLIC documents indicate, Shah and Lakewood Enterprises received four loans, totaling $1,450,000, secured by various properties that the FSLIC would later claim were worth far less than the amounts of the loans. In 1981 Shah's company had reported to the IRS only $100,815 in assets and a loss of $16,576. Needless to say, most bankers would not consider that sufficient security for a $1.45 million loan. (All four loans would ultimately end up in default.)

In late November, Hansen made the Piombo deal public. Centennial was purchasing Piombo Corporation, he announced, for $14,100,000 ($13 million in cash to Piombo, $1,100,000 to Shah). Steve Pizzo had just taken over as editor of the *Russian River News* and immediately began to hear complaints from friends who were Centennial shareholders. They were confused, angry over being frozen out of the decision, and concerned about the way the deal appeared to have been ramrodded through Centennial's board of directors.[5] Pizzo, a former real estate broker and investor himself, also found the deal perplexing. It was a highly speculative move on Centennial's part and he couldn't figure out where Centennial was getting the $13 million in cash to purchase Piombo Corporation.

After a couple of days of stalling, Hansen finally agreed to an interview for the local paper. It was Pizzo's first encounter with Hansen, who greeted him dressed in brown Western slacks, cowboy boots, and Western shirt with open collar. Hansen's six-foot-plus frame filled the small four-by-eight office. A gold Rolex watch glittered on his wrist, a gold chain and pendant hung around his neck, and a large gold-and-silver cowboy buckle cinched his belt.

Deregulation was going to be a real boon to Centennial Savings and Loan, Hansen told Pizzo. It was going to pull the little thrift out of the doldrums and into the financial fast lane. And part of the steam for this engine, he said expansively, would be generated by the construction company, with its ability to develop large real estate projects.

Hansen and Pizzo did not hit it off. There were big holes in Hansen's analysis and Pizzo wrote a commentary that raised questions about the wisdom of the deal itself and about the potential conflicts of interest inherent in a lender owning its own development company. What would prevent the lender from making risky loans to that subsidiary, especially during recessions, when development companies invariably fell on hard times? Pizzo's editorial hit the street a few days later and provoked a roar of outrage from Hansen. He threatened to sue the *Russian River News* if the piece resulted in any substantial withdrawals by depositors, simply the first salvo in what would turn out to be a three-year diatribe to silence opposition.

When Pizzo asked Erv where Centennial was getting the $13 million in cash to buy Piombo, Hansen waved his hand in the air and brushed the question off by stating that the money was "brokered deposits from the East Coast and from the Bureau of Indian Affairs." Hansen had strapped Centennial onto the roller coaster of brokered deposits, the "hundreds of millions of dollars just for the asking" that he had all along intended to tap as soon as he built alliances and had Centennial's board of directors under his control. He had acquired these deposits simply by placing ads in *The Wall Street Journal* guaranteeing to pay interest rates on insured certificates of deposit (CDs) that were slightly higher than the going market rate (in 1982 the going market rate was averaging 10.4 percent and in 1983, 9.22 percent).

Once a thrift began to depend on brokered deposits, it was in for a wild ride. Like using cocaine, the lure of easy brokered deposits often began innocently but soon became a compulsion and finally a physical necessity. Brokered deposits were a way for a thrift to grow larger than the resources of its local depositors would normally allow. Centennial's total assets at the beginning of 1983 stood at $49 million. By the time regulators seized the thrift in August 1985, its assets had ballooned to a grotesque $404.6 million, thanks in large part to brokered deposits.

. . .

When Hansen told Pizzo he was using "brokered deposits from the East Coast" to purchase Piombo Corporation, Pizzo understood. But Hansen's "Bureau of Indian Affairs" comment, which Hansen wouldn't clarify, left Pizzo baffled for five years. Finally, one day in 1988, after we were well along in our investigation of savings and loans elsewhere, we received a thick, unmarked package from an attorney on the East Coast. The contents of the package had nothing to do with Centennial (they related, instead, to Mario Renda, an East Coast deposit broker who was placing deposits at Centennial. See First United Fund chapters), but they provided the clue that enabled us to piece together the Bureau of Indian Affairs (BIA) puzzle.

Among the dozens of enclosures in the package was a handwritten letter to the East Coast attorney from an inmate at Fort Leavenworth federal penitentiary. He said he was serving a five-year prison sentence for wire fraud that involved a credit union, brokered funds, and linked financing. He told the attorney that the Bureau of Indian Affairs was involved in many of the failures of financial institutions, and he said he knew the names of companies and people in those companies whose job it was to take gifts to BIA officials.

Ringing in Pizzo's ears as though it had been the day before and not five years earlier was Hansen's comment that he was getting money from the BIA. We called the attorney on the East Coast, but she had no idea what the BIA reference meant and, in fact, had paid no attention to it because it didn't make sense to her. So we contacted the prisoner at Fort Leavenworth who had written the letter and he gave us the leads we were after.

We discovered that the BIA controlled one of a number of large government trust funds that deposit brokers tapped into for deposits—brokers got deposit money from pension funds, credit unions, and oil sheiks, and they also got deposit money from government trust funds. The BIA at that time managed $1.7 billion for American Indians. The Bureau was required by law to invest the money with government-insured institutions (by purchasing short-term CDs), and as often as several times a week they notified brokers that they had money to invest. Brokers served as middlemen, searching the nation for institutions offering the highest interest rate on short-term CDs on the day the BIA money became available for investment.

Brokers placing funds for the BIA were paid a commission from the institution that received the BIA deposits. There was fierce competition among brokers for the BIA money, and in depositions taken in the Fort Leavenworth prisoner's case in 1985, a deposit broker told the court it was his understanding that bribes to BIA officials in exchange for deposits were a routine business expense for deposit brokers.[6]

Since the S&Ls paying the highest interest rate on deposits were the S&Ls that were so desperate for money that they were willing to pay whatever it took to get it, this process put government in the position of rewarding, i.e., pouring money into, the nation's weakest financial institutions. For this reason regulators in Washington vehemently opposed the use of deposit brokers by managers of government trust funds. Their opposition centered on the BIA fund because it was the largest government trust fund, but when they tried to halt the investment practice they ran up against the political opposition of a tough lobby, the Indian lobby, which naturally enough wanted to get the highest possible return on its investments. FHLBB Chairman Ed Gray complained bitterly during this time that the BIA was channeling much of its deposit business to the country's weakest thrifts. He said that the BIA had funds in practically every thrift that had recently failed.

We now knew where Centennial got the fuel to power its enormous growth—from deposit broker Mario Renda and the money changers handling deposits for the BIA trust fund. There was enough money out there to feed hundreds of Centennials.

Centennial's purchase of Piombo, funded by brokered deposits, closed on January 6, 1983. In a staggering increase of assets, Centennial went almost immediately from a neighborhood savings and loan with a net worth of $1.87 million to a development conglomerate with thrift, construction, and development subsidiaries. The deal made Shah and Hansen wealthy and powerful, virtually overnight. Using the $1 million Centennial paid him for his Piombo stock, Shah bought up Centennial shares from disaffected Centennial shareholders until he became the thrift's largest single stockholder. He became executive vice president of Centennial, chief executive officer of Sonoma Financial Corporation (Centennial's new development subsidiary), and chief executive officer of Piombo, at a salary of $120,000 a year for five years, plus a yearly bonus (like Hansen's) of 10 percent of Centennial's profits. In a short six months Sid Shah had gone from construction engineer and failing developer to Northern California mover and shaker.

Hansen and Shah came to rely on brokered deposits to fund much of their activity at Centennial. But brokered deposits, with their combination of high interest rates and commissions to deposit brokers, were an expensive way to get money, so Hansen and Shah had to come up with a profitable use for it. And Erv, though he began short on funds, was never short on ideas. He planned to turn Centennial the sow's ear into Centennial the silk purse through real estate speculation. By early 1983 the critical pieces of the plan were in place, with one exception: Hansen wasn't satisfied with just his fat salary. He needed access to even more money.

A regulation prohibited thrifts from making more than $100,000 in unsecured commercial loans to their employees, officers, directors, or major shareholders unless the Federal Home Loan Bank approved. Clearly that was an inconvenient rule for thrift officers with expensive tastes. How could Hansen and his cohorts participate personally in the real estate developments and reap the massive financial rewards they envisioned? A mechanism had to be triggered to circumvent this regulation. To that end Hansen formed close alliances with officers at other savings and loans. Immediately money began to flow like artesian spring water among the main players.

Hansen had an old friend who had become the head of his own thrifts— Columbus Savings and Loan in San Francisco and Marin Savings and Loan in nearby San Rafael, later combined to become Columbus-Marin Savings and Loan. Regulators would later charge that the two men conspired to make loans to one another in order to circumvent the loans-to-affiliated-persons regulations. Before it was over Hansen received three loans totaling $174,000 from Columbus-Marin, loans on which regulators said he was routinely delinquent. Court documents showed that Hansen's friend received $550,000 in loans from Centennial, and he then approved a $250,000 line of credit for Hansen at Columbus-Marin. The FSLIC later charged that Columbus-Marin also loaned $50,000 to Shah and made at least 14 loans to other Centennial executives, including a $505,000 loan for Dutch investor and Hansen/Shah business partner Nicholaas Sandmann.

Another reason to have like-minded thrifts "on the program" was to have a way to get rid of bad loans, and this was the role Hansen envisioned for Atlas Savings and Loan in San Francisco. Thrifts routinely sold parts or all of their loan portfolios to other thrifts. These transactions, called "participations," were a perfectly legitimate way for the selling S&L to raise cash and the purchasing S&L to fatten its loan portfolio. But Hansen needed someone to sell his *bad* loans to—someone who might miss the fact that the loans had been made to shaky borrowers on property that was grossly overappraised. In short, Hansen needed a sucker, and that's precisely what he had in mind for Atlas Savings. Atlas soon found itself the proud owner of $6.5 million in loan participations purchased from Centennial, and Centennial had some of Atlas's hard-earned cash. A year later these participations would turn out to be a package of rotting, "nonperforming" loans, according to an FSLIC lawsuit. These, plus other loans Atlas bought from Centennial, ultimately led to Atlas's collapse in 1985.

We would discover as our investigation matured that participations like the ones Hansen sold Atlas were the AIDS virus of the thrift industry. Innocent thrifts exchanging loans with a thrift infected by fraud would find months later that they had picked up some terminally ill loans. Through the use of participations in the 1980s, the thrift industry spread its problems much more widely than otherwise would have been possible.

In another case Erv fathered an ally when he had Centennial help two young Sonoma County brothers, Leif and Jay Soderling, break into the thrift industry by loaning them $1 million of the $2 million they needed to start Golden Pacific Savings and Loan in Windsor, near Santa Rosa. Centennial promptly packed Golden Pacific's management team with people from its own ranks, ensuring that a close relationship would ensue. And it did.

"Erv just picked up the phone one day and called Jay Soderling," Beverly Haines said. "He told Jay he needed $250,000 right away. Jay cut a cashier's check out of Golden Pacific and drove right over with it." Haines tapped Golden Pacific for $125,000 (which she said she gave to Erv), and regulators claimed Shah got at least $1 million.[7] All these loans later went into default.

Meanwhile, back at the George Ranch, things were not going well on the Sandmann loan. Less than a year after getting the $5.4 million from Centennial, Sandmann was already in default, FSLIC attorneys later claimed. Legally, Centennial could have foreclosed on the project, taking it over for what Sandmann still owed. But Hansen and Shah interceded on behalf of their friend (and business partner). Rather than foreclose on the property, Centennial bought it from Sandmann's company, Damstraat (named for a street in Amsterdam), for *$8.1 million*, the FSLIC charged, allowing Sandmann to pocket a quick $3.7 million profit. Centennial then hired Sandmann as a project manager for six months and paid him yet another $300,000.

In 1983 Centennial moved its corporate offices from Guerneville to Santa Rosa, an appropriate move for a company quickly becoming a financial power in Northern California. The thrift bought and remodeled a large office building downtown on Fourth Street, and the total cost was pegged at somewhere near $7 million—30 times the value of its former Guerneville home. Everything at the new office was first-class: oak, brass, etched glass, box-beamed ceilings, mirrored walls, plush carpets. There was a board room big enough to jog in with a conference table long enough to skate on. Western oil paintings graced the walls and cowboy sculptures stood on cabinets and desks. A five-foot-high solid crystal horse head dominated the conference room. Finally, Centennial Savings and Loan executives had the setting and accoutrements that reflected their ambitions.

But as plush as Centennial's new home was, Hansen and Shah wanted more, and Shah had just the ticket. Back in 1980 he had purchased an old stone building on the outskirts of Santa Rosa, county records showed, for about $150,000. Built in 1909 as a hotel, the building had fallen on hard times and had last been home to a topless bar. Hansen immediately saw the big-ticket opportunity in that old stone building. He, Shah, and Sandmann transferred the property into a partnership they formed called Stonehouse Partners and later sold it to Centennial for $1 million, "as is." Erv told Centennial's board of directors that the old building would make a wonderful headquarters for Centennial Corporation, the new holding company of Centennial Savings and Loan. Regulators said he did *not* tell the directors or the regulators (because it would have been a conflict of interest for him to benefit from the purchase) that he was one of the Stonehouse Partners.

Then the buying spree really began. Hansen, a renowned ladies' man, had made the acquaintance of a stunning young woman who fancied herself an interior decorator. He took an immediate liking to her, and the two began a relationship that ultimately would cost Centennial hundreds of thousands of dollars. When Hansen needed a decorator for the Stonehouse, according to Haines, he hired his young friend. Over the next few months the two of them flew often to Los Angeles and Las Vegas, on Centennial's twin-engine Cessna, on "buying trips." And buy they did. Hansen never required that she submit invoices for the furniture and art she bought, Haines told us, but simply had Centennial pay whatever she submitted in the way of bills. There were antique desks: Hansen's cost $48,000 and he paid extra to have American eagles carved on the front; Beverly Haines's, an old French Provincial, cost $12,000 and she complained that the drawer was too heavy to open. Then there was the $35,000 French Provincial gold-and-silver chess table with an inlaid marble top and matching gold-and-silver chessmen. Hansen wanted to use it as an end table, but a couch has two ends, after all, so a second table, a reproduction, was ordered for an additional $35,000.

In addition, Centennial spent over $1 million renovating the Stonehouse offices. A full gourmet kitchen was installed so the European chef, hired at $48,000 a year, could prepare meals for Centennial's business guests. Hansen spent $90,000 decorating his own office, which featured a full wet bar. The conference room was appointed with the finest in antique tables, chairs, settees, and Persian rugs. The building was simply magnificent. Santa Rosa had never seen anything like it. For those who had known Hansen just a few short months earlier, it was a disorienting sight.

Hansen moved the corporate office into the Stonehouse as soon as the work was completed. But four months later he moved everyone back to the Fourth Street building. The Stonehouse proved to be cold and uncomfortable.

"It reminded me of a mortuary," Haines told us later. It was placed on the market, but there were no takers for the $2 million white elephant.[8]

Hansen and Shah then decided Centennial needed a place in San Francisco where they could entertain out-of-town dignitaries. So they purchased a penthouse ("a pied-à-terrific," gushed San Francisco columnist Herb Caen) on Lombard Street in San Francisco for $773,487. Again Hansen's interior decorator friend was employed to redecorate the place, for an additional $150,000.

Hansen wanted Centennial to have a way to chauffeur dignitaries from one place to the next, so Haines said that Sandmann, by then a Centennial vice president, arranged the purchase of a 1971 stretch Mercedes limousine for a mere $30,000. Unfortunately, the car was in Holland. By the time it was re-trofitted in the U.S. to meet American smog and safety standards, Haines said, the car cost Centennial $77,000. Paying the bill, though, didn't mean Centennial owned the car, which FSLIC investigators later discovered was registered in Hansen's name.

Cars were an obsession with Hansen, and one afternoon he decided to go out during lunch and kick some tires. Before the afternoon was out he had purchased five cars for himself and his family: three station wagons, a four-wheel-drive pickup for his son-in-law, and a snappy Datsun 280Z for himself. The FBI reported the cars were paid for with an $89,792.42 Centennial Savings and Loan cashier's check. Hansen called Haines and told her to bring the check down right away. He told her he would reimburse the thrift later, but the FBI said he never did.

On special occasions, like weddings and civic events, Hansen made a point of being seen around town behind the wheel of his 1930s-vintage Rolls-Royce, for which he paid $137,000. And to ensure they did not feel left out, Hansen arranged for the heads of each of Centennial's several subsidiaries to receive brand-new Mercedes-Benzes, except Haines, who requested, and got, a BMW.

"I didn't want a big car," Haines told us.

It wasn't long before these spending sprees caught the attention of the public. Few knew quite what to make of them, but most people accepted the ostentatious life-styles of Centennial's top officers as one more piece of proof that the area was becoming a playground for the rich and famous. Almost everyone felt that Santa Rosa and the surrounding areas were destined for explosive growth. Looking at all the Centennial glitter, some saw it as the first positive proof that the boom times had arrived. And if that were so, then perhaps Shah and Hansen were the vanguards and visionaries who would blaze the shining path to success and riches for the rest. By throwing money around, Hansen and Haines rose to positions of considerable prestige in Northern California.

CHAPTER FOUR

$10,000 In a Boot

Erv Hansen was building Centennial into a center of financial power in Northern California. But not everyone shared his vision. A small but growing number of people began to openly express concern about Centennial's rapid growth and feverish activities. Something was fishy, people whispered. Savings and loans, "thrifts," were supposed to be thrifty, not splashy, deregulation or not. S&L executives were supposed to be staid, dour, predictable, thoroughly dependable fellows. What was Centennial up to?

The *Russian River News* continued to nip at Centennial's heels, and in May of 1983 Hansen gave $50,000 to a small competing tabloid in Guerneville called *The Paper*, which was having money troubles. *The Paper*'s manager, Tom Richman, was soliciting financial support from the community to keep his publication in business. He dropped by Centennial, and Hansen was more than happy to help out. He paid the first installment—which sources said was $10,000—right on the spot.

"Hansen just reached down into his cowboy boot and pulled out a wad of cash and handed it to him," an FSLIC attorney told us. Hansen later said he hoped the extra money would tip the competitive balance between the two publications and put the *Russian River News* out of business. Fifty thousand dollars went a long way in a town of 1,700. Richman later described the $50,000 as a gift. Documents filed in a FSLIC suit showed Centennial even considered becoming *The Paper*'s partner.

But Hansen was interested in buying more than good press. Success and money always attract politicians, and Centennial attracted its share. Congressman Douglas Bosco, a Democrat, came from a small town near Guerneville where he had been a Haines family friend. A born politician, he was an attorney and former member of the California state legislature (where he was a member of the Assembly Finance, Insurance and Commerce Committee). Centennial was quick to lavish attention on Bosco. Bosco's mother was given a job working for Haines at Centennial, and Shah hired a friend of Bosco's to manage Shah's company, Lakewood Enterprises.

Hansen, Shah, Haines and various family members were listed as contributors to Bosco on his 1983 and 1984 disclosure statements. In addition, Bosco borrowed $124,000 from Centennial and $65,000 from Golden Pacific between 1982 and 1984.[1] His payments were often late and a thrift executive told us S&L officers had to call Bosco in Washington to discuss bringing his payments current. Bosco said the tardiness was caused by frequent moves. In 1984 Bosco used Centennial's private plane to attend the funeral of a constituent and failed to report it on his federal financial disclosure form. He said the failure was an oversight. In 1986 he was questioned by the FBI about Centennial Savings but he was not accused of any wrongdoing. (An FBI agent told us that if the FBI investigated Bosco for his relationship with Centennial, they'd have to investigate all congressmen because they all did the same thing.) Bosco said his relationship with Centennial was completely above board, that he never asked them for any personal favors, nor did they ever do him any. But with powerful friends Centennial Savings' influence in the community prospered nicely.

One of the more remarkable political relationships that developed at Centennial was between Sonoma County's chief law-enforcement officer, Sheriff Roger McDermott, and Hansen. The sheriff was a guest on several flights of Centennial's corporate plane and accompanied Hansen and others on trips to Canada and Las Vegas. McDermott also became a partner in a construction company that was working almost exclusively on Centennial projects, including a multimillion-dollar condo development in Bullhead City, Arizona, on the Colorado River about 60 miles south of Las Vegas.

Centennial's sweet scent went out beyond Sonoma County, and like bees to honey, individuals with criminal backgrounds and organized crime connections found their way to the savings and loan. For them, we would learn, deregulation of the thrift industry was the best thing that had happened since Prohibition poured millions of dollars into their ever-waiting hands.

The first person to raise Pizzo's suspicions was Norman B. Jenson. A slight, silver-haired man, he was a Las Vegas attorney, but he had various other interests. He told us later that he had had, for example, significant business dealings with Sid Shah and Piombo Corporation before Shah teamed up with Centennial. Jenson had met Shah some years earlier when Piombo was bidding for work at Murrieta Hot Springs, a project near Palm Springs being developed by Morris Shenker, owner of the Dunes Hotel and Casino in Las Vegas. (Shenker had been Teamster President Jimmy Hoffa's attorney and was described by the President's Commission on Organized Crime as an associate of Kansas City organized crime boss Nick Civella.) Jenson was a potential investor in Shenker's Murrieta Hot Springs development, and he said he had met Shah when Piombo was positioning itself to get a construction contract on the project. Jenson also had real estate investments near Santa Rosa, and he and Piombo had joined in several joint-venture partnerships.

Soon after Shah became a central figure at Centennial, Pizzo went to the county recorder's office to research Shah's land holdings and real estate transactions, and he discovered documentation of several local deals between Piombo and Jenson. Pizzo found Jenson to be a shadowy character who left a confusing paper trail. He drifted in and out of complex deals in ways that left Pizzo wondering what was in the deals for Jenson. In many of Jenson's joint-venture partnerships with Piombo, Jenson eventually, mysteriously, deeded without remuneration his portion of the joint ventures to Piombo. Property didn't seem to get bought and sold, it just appeared and then got transferred. Jenson was maddening to trace, always hidden behind several layers of paper corporations and powers of attorney. To Pizzo he seemed to be acting like a man with a lot to hide.

Pizzo checked further into Jenson's past and more questions surfaced. Jenson had been a principal in the Holiday Casino in Las Vegas, and he and a partner had held a $1.7 million mortgage on the Shenandoah Hotel and Casino. Evidently he carried some weight in Las Vegas casino circles. A computer search on Jenson's name coughed up a 1981 United Press International story about the indictment of two men from New Jersey charged with extortion. According to the article, Thomas Principe, 49, described by the FBI as "one of the most prolific hit men on the East Coast," and Dominick D'Agostino, 64, who had interests in the trucking business, were charged with extorting $300,000 from two Philadelphia developers. The money, according to federal investigators, had been extracted under threat of violence to their persons, property, and families to finance a Las Vegas casino project. The $300,000 was allegedly delivered to Thomas DiBiasi, an attorney, who then made out a check in that amount to Norman B. Jenson and his partner, owners of the proposed casino site. (Jenson later told us he became a government witness in the case.)

As the months went by Pizzo periodically checked filings at the county recorder's office, but nothing new appeared in Jenson's name, and there was no evidence to connect him directly to Centennial Savings. His relationship seemed to be with Shah and Piombo, not Centennial. Not until three years later would Pizzo get the tip that unraveled the Norm Jenson mystery:

One afternoon in August 1986 Pizzo was sitting in the *Russian River News* office reading a recently delivered copy of the *National Thrift News*. He spotted a story about the collapse of three thrifts, one in Washington state, one in Texas, and another in Louisiana, and he glanced through the article, wondering how such widely separated thrifts might have been related. A name buried on the third page, near the end of the story, jumped out of the gray text—*Norman B. Jenson*. The FSLIC was claiming in a lawsuit that the three thrifts had conspired to make Jenson a $4 million loan on a Las Vegas casino, the DeVille Casino, for which they said Jenson had paid a $50,000 kickback to the president of the Louisiana thrift, Guy Olano. The loan later went into default.

The fact that Jenson had been dealing with thrifts in Louisiana, Washington, and Texas had staggering implications for Pizzo. He had developed a nagging suspicion that what he was seeing at Centennial might be happening at other thrifts as well. His suspicion was based on nothing more than the belief that if a looting were in progress at Centennial, perhaps other thrifts were also being victimized. He had mentioned his suspicions to state regulators, but they treated him more like someone reporting a flying-saucer sighting than someone sounding an alarm. He continued to worry nonetheless. The deals were just too smooth and too slick, and too much money was disappearing, for this to be no more than a pack of amateurs fleecing a bank.

The *National Thrift News* story lent unexpected support to these concerns. If Jenson was out there working over other thrifts—in a deal that had involved thrifts in three states—then maybe he wasn't alone. Were there others? Who were they? Was this a nationwide conspiracy? How bad was it? Could the Mafia or other organized crime figures be involved? Were they networking? How? How many thrifts were threatened? Pizzo made some phone calls to defense attorneys and learned that Jenson's loan had been arranged for him by a loan brokerage firm in San Antonio, Falcon Financial, owned by loan broker John Lapaglia, who was in federal prison serving a 14-month sentence for failing to report $169,000 in income on his 1979 federal tax return. In John Lapaglia we had our first clue as to how events at several savings and loans might be connected.

Loan brokers put borrowers together with lenders for a commission—and sometimes a piece of the action. If the borrower were on the up and up, the broker's service was a service to all. But if the borrower were a crook, the loan broker knowingly or unknowingly could become a kind of traveling host to that dangerous virus, introducing it to thrifts from coast to coast. We learned that a handful of roving loan brokers traveled this country like nomads, putting deals together. They were the synapse across which both legitimate and illegitimate business jumped in the thrift industry. When deregulation of the thrift industry greatly expanded thrifts' ability to invest in multimillion-dollar real estate projects, it created a gold mine for loan brokers (whose commission was based on a percent of the loan). Deposit brokers pumped money into thrifts and loan brokers pumped it out.

Jenson's involvement in the complex DeVille Casino deal put him in a new light, and Pizzo decided to investigate him more intensely. During a search for documents relating to Jenson, Pizzo turned up a deed for a Santa Rosa home that he learned had been the subject of an arson probe by county investigators after a predawn fire on December 2, 1982. He contacted a county fire chief who had become an important source for him on fire-related news stories, and the fire chief outlined the facts surrounding the arson. Then Pizzo gradually pieced together the rest of the story.

Residents in a prestigious hillside neighborhood above Santa Rosa had been jolted from their sleep by the dreaded sound of fire sirens one night in December 1982. From their bedroom windows they had peered through oak trees at the glow of a fire that lit up the night sky as it destroyed a three-bedroom redwood home on Lower Ridge Road. When firemen arrived they had to pry open a locked security gate to get inside, and by that time the expensive home on the five-acre estate was engulfed in flames. Firemen found no sign that anyone was at home. Later, when questioned, neighbors told strange stories of a young couple named Miller who kept mostly to themselves, of limousines with darkened windows that came and went at all hours of the night, of Doberman pinschers that roamed the grounds.

Arson investigators determined that someone had set the fire by dumping gasoline down the hall and stairs. They also discovered that before the fire someone had thoroughly ransacked the house. Walls had been torn open, floor-boards ripped up. Fire officials began a records search for the property's owner and they came up with Jenson and a company in Las Vegas, D.J. Investments. Calls to Las Vegas turned up no D.J. Investments, so they phoned Jenson. When first asked if he were the owner of a home on Lower Ridge Road, he told arson investigators he was, but after being told the circumstances that led to the call, he quickly backed away from his earlier statement, saying that he had been mistaken, that he didn't have anything to do with the house.

County arson investigators continued to sift through the charred ruins until, on the third day, federal agents suddenly appeared on the scene.

"There were eight of us investigating the fire," recalled fire investigator Kevin O'Shea. "These feds called us together and told us our investigation was over. They told us to forget everything we had seen there, that as far as we were concerned, it never happened. They even told us to destroy any notes we might have taken. 'This never happened,' they said." At that point federal agents took over the investigation.

Jenson continued to refuse comment and no fire insurance claim was filed. But an investigator told us they discovered a tantalizing clue in the rubble: a smoke-stained business card that simply read "Morrison Energy International, Dean Chandler, sales." On the back someone had penciled instructions on how to work the security gate. Investigators called the Santa Rosa phone number printed on the card and a secretary answered, "Lakewood Enterprises." Lakewood was Sid Shah's real estate company. Questioned by arson investigators, Shah disclaimed any intimate knowledge of Dean Chandler or Morrison Energy International, saying only that he let Chandler use his phone number for messages. However, Pizzo discovered on a 1982 financial statement prepared by Shah that he owned 5,804 shares of Morrison Energy International stock, which he valued at $60 a share. Why was Shah trying to hide from investigators his involvement with Morrison Energy?

Questions surrounding the 1982 fire at the Lower Ridge Road home grew as time passed but no answers were forthcoming. The house sat charred and empty. No one made a move to clean it or fix it. Occasionally federal agents would arrive at the scene and sift through the ashes. The home's former occupants, the "Millers," had vanished. Neighbors in the tony neighborhood began to complain that the place was an eyesore. Their complaints finally forced Norman Jenson to come forward and assure them the property would be cleaned up. Who would be doing the work? "Piombo Construction Company," they said he told them.

Going back again and again to his federal sources knowledgeable about Jenson, Pizzo learned that the burned house, the "Millers," Norm Jenson, and Sid Shah had become the center of a massive Organized Crime/Drug Enforcement Task Force investigation that had set up shop in the Federal Building in Santa Rosa. For five years a 12-agency team would investigate a $300 million international drug ring. Then the U.S. attorney would hand down an indictment alleging that the ring laundered its money through Sid Shah's and Norman B. Jenson's complex real estate deals.

Jenson was the first red flag that went up for Pizzo. Then a second warning flag was raised when Pizzo learned that reputed Mafia associate Richard Binder had shown up at Centennial's loan window and had borrowed over $1 million. With Binder had been Dave Gorwitz, a fellow with a long criminal record and established Mafia ties. Gorwitz was also old friends with Paul Axelrod, according to mobster Jimmy "the Weasel" Fratianno, who described Axelrod as Morris Shenker's "banking expert."

Binder's friend Gorwitz had pulled swindles on the West Coast before. In 1975 Gorwitz had made San Francisco headlines when he was caught up in the high-profile prosecution of California State Senator Richard Dolwig. Dolwig had lent his name and influence to an advance-fee loan scam run by Gorwitz and David Kaplan, another minor hood.[2] Kaplan turned state's evidence and in open court described Gorwitz as a muscleman for the mob. Other court testimony stated that Gorwitz was a financial advisor to Salvatore M. Caruana (described by federal officials as a highly placed organized crime figure with links to the

Patriarca family).[3] Gorwitz, "Uncle Dave" to his friends, was convicted and
served four years in prison, his second prison term. He had served time earlier
on a counterfeiting conviction.

After serving his sentence in the Dolwig case, Gorwitz headed for Massachusetts, where he became involved with Richard (Dick) Binder in a mysterious
precious metals venture, the Bay State Gold Exchange, which later was the
subject of a Boston *Globe* investigative piece.

The *Globe* reported that Binder had started Bay State Gold Exchange in
Plymouth, Massachusetts, outside Boston, with an $800,000 grubstake allegedly
provided by mobster Salvatore Caruana. Along with the money, Caruana apparently sent trusted aide Dave Gorwitz to keep an eye on Caruana's new investment and on Binder. Bay State Gold Exchange was supposed to be dealing
in reclaimed gold and silver, but authorities said they believed Caruana used it
as a vehicle to launder money from his drug operations.

Three times a week, the *Globe* reported, Binder withdrew cash from a nearby
bank, mostly in $20 bills. He visited the branch over 100 times and withdrew
$8.1 million from Bay State's checking account in just 11 months. He stuffed
it into a brown suitcase and left. Caruana would show up regularly to make six-
figure withdrawals from Bay State's "petty cash" drawer, according to former
Bay State employees. When precious metal prices crashed in 1981 so did Bay
State, not long after a Bay State associate was found shot to death and stuffed
in the trunk of a car. Federal investigators were interested in Binder's activities
at Bay State by that time, but a fire at Binder's home destroyed all of Bay State's
records.

"Bay State emerged from the foam of the sea and dipped back beneath the
waves," one investigator told the *Globe*.

Binder and Gorwitz left Boston in a hurry after their little "enterprise" ended
in the probing story in the Boston *Globe*. When Binder and Gorwitz emerged
from the sea of foam to start a new life in Santa Rosa, they were immediately
put under FBI surveillance. Nevertheless, Binder zeroed in right away on Centennial. Hansen became a customer at Binder's newly opened Santa Rosa jewelry
store, and in November 1982 Binder borrowed $5,800 from him, which bank-
ruptcy records say he never repaid. Between 1984 and 1986 Binder also borrowed,
and then defaulted on, over $3 million from Centennial and two other Northern
California lenders. (Between 1984 and 1986 bankruptcy court documents showed
Binder borrowed $385,000 from Bank of America, $1,151,000 from Central
Bank of Walnut Creek, and $1,450,000 from Centennial.)[4]

Centennial might have lost even more to Binder and Gorwitz if a certain
$6 million land deal had gone through. The pair had their eyes on five acres
of land on the outskirts of Santa Rosa. Binder brought Gorwitz in as a "consultant," for which Uncle Dave was to get 25 percent of the action, according
to later court testimony. A lawyer began a draft agreement but Gorwitz insisted

his name not appear on any of the documents, that instead his interest be hidden in an offshore corporation. Suddenly the owners of the land backed out of the sale. Shortly thereafter federal regulators swooped down on Centennial and closed the thrift (in August 1985), and Binder declared bankruptcy and returned to the East Coast, his four-year stay in Santa Rosa abruptly terminated.

The Gorwitz connection left little doubt in Pizzo's mind that organized crime figures, or people with ties to organized crime, were sucking money out of Centennial.

While Erv Hansen was welcoming borrowers with questionable credit records, he was proving there was no end to the ways he could pull money out of little Centennial. In early 1984, soon after the fabulous Christmas party that had all of Northern California talking, the board of directors of Centennial announced that Shah and Hansen would receive kingly bonuses of $818,000 each. The combined amount, $1.636 million, represented nearly two-thirds of the $2.6 million net profit Centennial claimed for 1983.

Federal regulators would later learn that in reality the $2.6 million "profit" was an engineered illusion. Hansen had created $4 million in "profits" by "selling" to Atlas Savings and Columbus-Marin Savings Centennial's interest in some partnerships it held with Atlas and Columbus-Marin. The sales were reversed almost immediately in 1984, with Centennial buying the same interests back from the two thrifts and paying them a profit for their trouble. In other words, whatever profit Centennial made on the sale in 1983 was wiped out in the buy-back a few months later. The deal fattened Centennial's bottom line at the end of 1983. This was the stuff bonuses were made of.

But there was nothing phony about the $1.6 million bonus Shah and Hansen got. With bonuses and salary together, the two had each earned well over $1 million after the first year together as a team at Centennial.[5] Understaffed regulators had let Centennial go its own way for nearly two years, but the huge bonuses finally caught their attention and they dubbed them "excessive," stating that Hansen's compensation was five times that of any other thrift president in the FHLB's eleventh district.[6]

But even under the hot breath of angry regulators Hansen found a way to compound his larceny. In response to regulators' criticism of his bonus, Hansen called Centennial's board of directors together and told them that if his management contract—which allowed him a salary of $100,000 a year plus a chunk of the profits (real or imagined)—was going to cause Centennial problems with the regulators, he was willing to renegotiate his contract. But first the board would have to buy out his old contract, and he wanted $350,000 for that. Hansen also demanded his salary be increased to $250,000 a year if he had to give up profit sharing. Like everything else Hansen proposed, his offer was accepted by his board of directors. (A former chairman of Centennial's board explained the board's acquiescence by telling us that whenever the board opposed Hansen, he became furious and threatened to replace them with people who would do what he wanted, when he wanted.)

Hansen's new contract, and the $350,000 he extracted from Centennial to set aside his old one, just added insult to injury and regulators hit the roof. Of course in 1984 "hitting the roof" meant regulators wrote Centennial a letter and demanded that the board do everything possible to get Hansen and Shah to return some of their "excessive compensation." The board agreed but regulators later charged that the board made little or no effort to get the money back, and regulators soon had other matters to occupy their attentions.

Hansen reveled in his new role as empire builder, even if those empires were built in the clouds. He formed a Centennial "hunting club" and purchased $500 shotguns for himself and his covey of rural groupies. He hosted a gala fishing expedition to Canada, bringing along his drinking buddies and Sheriff McDermott. After admiring a Western belt buckle he had seen on another high flier, Hansen had one made for himself. Built into the gold-and-silver buckle was a small pistol that snapped out and could actually fire a .22-caliber bullet.

No deal was too big or too small. During a slow afternoon one day, Beverly Haines, Hansen, and a business associate purchased a small, run-down rural house for $40,000. Documents on file at the county recorder's office told us the rest of the story. The same day the group bought the property they deeded it back and forth among themselves several times, each time raising the recorded value. (This maneuver is called a "land flip," and it is illegal if it is being used to defraud a lender.) The final deed recorded was a trust deed securing an $80,000 loan from Atlas Savings and Loan on the property. This little impromptu partnership had spent a couple of hours signing documents and turned a $40,000 purchase into a $40,000 profit. Kind of a "nooner," financially speaking. Naturally the loan went into default.

On another occasion Hansen, Shah, and Dutch investor Neik Sandmann paid $50,000 for a two-thirds share of an old stone warehouse near the railroad tracks where bums jumped freights. County records showed they "flipped" the property among themselves and their partnership several times, raising the value each time, and capped off the transactions with a $487,000 loan, again from Atlas Savings. Eventually they defaulted on the loan and regulators said Atlas had to sell the property at a considerable loss.

Shah took an interest in mushrooms and he purchased a small mushroom farm near Santa Rosa, making Hansen and Haines partners in the operation. Hansen then had Centennial put $1.5 million into a large, bankrupt mushroom company in Washington state. Regulators claimed Shah's plan was to merge all the mushroom operations into one and corner 80 percent of the West Coast market, but in 1984 he left Centennial holding the bag for $4 million in nonperforming loans to the project and Shah ultimately placed his mushroom empire, Mushroom King, into bankruptcy.

And just where were thrift examiners while all this frolicking in the vault was going on? Centennial should have been under scrutiny by both state and federal examiners because it was a state-chartered thrift and a member of the FSLIC. But the state examination staff had been decimated by the defection of thrifts to federal charters, and the numbers of examiners on the federal level had also been cut. In 1980, prior to deregulation, there had been over 700 federal examiners to cover the country's 4,002 thrifts. But deregulation was interpreted by Washington to mean there would be less need for regulation, and examiners had been cut to 679, even though the number of institutions in trouble had begun a sharp rise.

"Haven't you heard of deregulation?" a frustrated regulator told Pizzo one day when he called to ask them why they weren't all over Centennial. "We don't supervise these institutions like we used to."

Since frequent on-site examinations were impossible, regulators often relied on supervision by mail. Examiners would study records supplied by Centennial and fire back complaints. "We got dozens of these warning letters," Beverly Haines later told us. "They'd send us a warning letter on a deal or transaction they felt was unsound or a violation, and tell us not to do that anymore. Then they'd say that since it was already done, that at the very least we should go back and get the board of directors' formal approval for it." For well over three years that was the extent of the "punishment" handed out to Hansen et al. The demoralized employees who remained at the California Savings and Loan Department and Federal Home Loan Bank, after staffs were cut, were paralyzed. Higher up, in the policy-making levels of the regulatory apparatus, the reluctance of the system to admit it had a self-induced cancer was enormous.

Hansen had his own way of appeasing regulators. He'd hire them. Pat Connolly, former state deputy savings and loan commissioner, became a Centennial director, executive vice president, and managing officer in 1984. His job, in Hansen's mind, was to keep the staff at the state commissioner's office off Centennial's back, Haines told us. And he was paid handsomely for his services.

"One minute Connolly was working for the state of California earning $40,000 a year," explained Haines. "Hansen hires the guy and suddenly he's pulling down $80,000 a year. In December of 1984, just two months after being hired, he gets another $40,000 bonus. All he had to do was calm the regulators down." (Connolly did not reply to our requests for an interview.)

Banks and savings and loans were required to have periodic audits of their activities. The audits had to be done by recognized, qualified accounting firms. Centennial used, first, Alexander Grant[7] and, later, Peat, Marwick, Mitchell & Co. But even though the FHLBB required an independent audit of thrifts, the tab for the auditor's services was paid by the thrift being examined. Furthermore, the law did not require the auditor to report irregularities to the FHLBB or law enforcement but only to thrift management. It was then up to the thrift officers to take corrective action or, presumably, to turn themselves in if they had broken the law. This policy resembled requiring a fire marshal to report to Nero that Rome was ablaze. (During our investigation we heard of several occasions when thrift officers would offer auditors kickbacks, gifts, or a high-paying job with the S&L in exchange for a clean audit. If the auditors refused to cooperate, the thrift would change firms.)

"At Centennial an auditor for the independent auditing firm actually sat in on board meetings and helped them structure the Piombo deal [purchase]," said Haines. Later the auditor became a Centennial officer. Investigators told us Centennial eventually hired seven of its former auditors in a revolving-door pattern investigators said they found troubling.[8]

With the money flowing at full force, Centennial generated an almost irresistable momentum about it. All who came within its orbit felt that force and many bent to it. Was Centennial the promise of deregulation realized? Or was it a hijacked thrift careening out of control? No one seemed to want to try to sort out the answer to that question during 1983 and 1984. Centennial appeared successful and powerful, a trend setter, and most people were content to climb on board and enjoy the exhilarating ride.

CHAPTER FIVE

The Downhill Slide

Everything went Erv Hansen's way at Centennial for nearly two years. When anyone on Centennial's staff or board of directors dared challenge him, he flew into a fury of self-righteous indignation. He bragged, cajoled, and bullied his way through the months. With Beverly Haines running the money desk, brokered deposits and jumbo CDs poured into Centennial's coffers—and out the other end. Regulators alleged that Hansen, Shah, Sandmann, and others pumped that money off into projects of their own. For a time the examiners and auditors, who were supposed to ensure that precisely this kind of looting never occurred, seemed not to care. And their former colleagues, who were by that time working for Centennial, assured them all was well.

But hiring former examiners and auditors wasn't going to keep Hansen's house of cards together forever, and by mid-1984 he came under increasing pressure from regulators who began to make the kinds of noises that Hansen, a former regulator himself, knew preceded real action. Someone had to take the fall. Behind the scenes it was somehow agreed to lay the blame for Centennial's excesses on Shah. Hansen informed the feds that Shah was the problem and that Shah would resign. Stories were even floated in the local press that Hansen and Shah had had a falling-out. Shah told reporters he had private interests to pursue (mushrooms among them). He said he was not the corporate type and no longer fit in at Centennial. The truth, it was later revealed, was that regulators had required Centennial's management to sign a supervisory agreement in which they agreed to cease any dealings with Shah.[1]

Shah's contract was terminated, but, like Hansen before him, Shah exacted a price for voiding his contract and, regulators said, took one more dip in Centennial's pool of liquid assets. Shah received $450,000 for his stock and $300,000 to buy out his employment contract with Centennial. FSLIC attorneys later charged Hansen arranged the stock purchase by inducing Centennial's directors, whom the FSLIC would refer to later as "a rubber-stamp board," to buy Shah's shares. Under the scheme the directors would pay $60 a share for Shah's shares, $25 in cash and $35 in promissory notes.

Hansen made Centennial lines of credit available to the directors in excess of the cash amount they needed to purchase Shah's shares. Regulators said the excess funds were intended as an incentive to the directors to participate in the scheme. The result was that Shah received $450,000 directly out of Centennial's coffers for his shares. Later the promissory notes signed by the directors/straw purchasers were "forgiven" by Shah, regulators charged, thereby relieving them of that obligation. The FSLIC claimed Shah's departure cost Centennial another $750,000.[2]

Despite Shah's sacrifice on the regulatory altar, Hansen's life continued to get more complicated, even dangerous. In May 1985 Hansen, Haines, and Shah learned through Hansen's friend Sheriff Roger McDermott that two disgruntled former associates may have hired a hit man to deal with the trio. Haines said that on a spring evening in May, after dinner and drinks, McDermott took Hansen back to the courthouse and swore him in as a special Sonoma County deputy. He gave him a badge and Hansen began carrying two pistols for protection. Deputy Erv was born. Hansen had a photo taken of his swearing-in, which he proudly hung on the wall behind his desk. As for the hit man, no one ever came forward. (After Centennial's collapse and the ensuing FBI investigation, it was discovered that sheriff's office files referencing Erv's special deputy status and gun permit were missing. Sources within the department said that only a three-by-five, cross-reference card remained to show that a master file had ever existed. McDermott was not reelected as Sonoma County sheriff, quietly left office, and maintained his silence on these events.)

For a while Hansen was successful in promoting the myth that all of Centennial's problems had been caused by the uncontrollable Sid Shah. Now, with him gone, Hansen said he was "trying to hold this thing together." But by late spring of 1985 Hansen was telling friends that he expected regulators to remove him from office—though not before he made one more valiant effort to hold off Centennial's day of reckoning. Regulators had told Hansen that, to avoid being declared insolvent, Centennial needed an infusion of $7 million. Undeterred, Hansen had another rabbit up his sleeve.

Centennial's wild ride had begun with its purchase of Piombo and, ironically, would end with its "sale." Hansen announced that he had found a buyer for Piombo, a buyer who would pay a whopping $25 million for the construction company, $12 million more than Centennial had paid for it two and a half years earlier, even though Piombo had been gutted of most of its valuable real estate holdings during its short stay at Centennial. This "profit" would produce the cash that regulators were demanding Centennial raise in order to stay in business. Here for the first time we ran into a tactic that nearly every thrift bandit we met would employ as a last desperate effort to ward off an FSLIC takeover—the White Knight.

Piombo's purported buyer was Sierra Diversified Investments (SDI), head-quartered in Shingle Springs, California. But when we tried to find SDI we discovered it had no phone listing or utility company accounts there. Equally mysterious were SDI's two principals, Dave Bella and Edward Blair. Sources inside Centennial complained to us that they knew little of the pair except that "we hear they are in the tire recapping business, or something like that."

Not only did the mysterious company and its owners raise regulators' eyebrows, but the transaction's terms turned out to be a regulator's nightmare: SDI would pay only $100,000 in cash. The rest of the $5.75 million down payment was to be in the form of promissory notes and deeds. SDI agreed to make other cash installments of $2.6 million in four months and $1.5 million in eight months. Nineteen million of the $25 million was to be carried by Centennial as a 30-year loan.

Regulators sent no weak-kneed warning letters this time. Finally, enough was enough. They gave Hansen a clear, unmistakable order: Do not consummate the Piombo sale. But Hansen rushed the sale to completion anyway, quickly transferring Piombo to SDI. At the closing SDI put up $100,000 and in return got the keys to Piombo. They also got Piombo's bank accounts, which contained over $800,000, *and* Hansen extended $1 million in operating loans from Centennial to Piombo's new owners. (Several weeks after Centennial was seized, FSLIC negotiators wrestled control of Piombo back from SDI, but not without additional cost. Since possession is still nine-tenths of the law, and since Hansen had given SDI possession of Piombo, the FSLIC had to pay SDI to let go. According to a source close to the negotiations, the tab was $300,000.)

The Piombo sale was the final outrage. At 5 p.m. on August 20, 1985, a small army of FSLIC examiners, auditors, and private security guards stormed Centennial's branches. A representative of the Federal Home Loan Bank Board[3] walked up to Hansen, handed him a letter from Washington, and said, "Mr. Hansen, we are declaring Centennial insolvent. You are hereby removed as chairman of the board and president. Please give us your keys and do not touch anything on or in your desk."

If there was ever a moment to call in one's IOUs, that was it, and that night Centennial's favorite congressman, Doug Bosco, announced from his home in Washington, D.C., that he was outraged by the Bank Board's action. He said that he was concerned for Centennial's shareholders and that he knew Hansen and considered him to be a kind, generous, and humanitarian man. He said he was going to personally investigate the Bank Board's seizure of Centennial.

Bosco was just one of the first in a long line of congressmen and senators who would interfere with the regulatory process in the name of constituent service. Bosco was later forced to make an embarrassing public retraction when a group of conservative bankers threatened to withdraw their financial support for Bosco if he did not distance himself from the likes of Erv Hansen. A spokesman explained their reasoning: "My feeling is that a legislator should have all the facts before criticizing federal regulators. Centennial was a high-flying organization that was headed for trouble for a long time."

The headline in *The Paper* that week (the tabloid Hansen had given $50,000 to, as a "gift") read, "Centennial is dead. Long live Centennial." The paper ran an editorial that was a eulogy to Centennial written by the publisher.

The day after the takeover Pizzo ran into Hansen in a bar that Beverly Haines owned in Guerneville, and they spent a couple of hours talking things over. Hansen showed none of the animosity he had earlier displayed toward Pizzo. Now he wanted sympathy. Over a beer he sang the blues.

"They came in and fired me," Hansen said. "One little punk looked me in the eye and said, 'Hansen, we're going to put a number on your back.' No, they won't, because I didn't do anything wrong."

When the boom fell Centennial had swollen to $404 million in assets, a 1,000 percent increase in just 32 months. Eighty percent of Centennial's $435 million in deposits were high-cost brokered funds in certificates of deposit.[4] The days following the takeover found regulators gasping in horror and disbelief, we were told, as they picked through Centennial's rubble. Thirty-six percent—$140 million—of all of Centennial's outstanding loans were tied up in high-risk development ventures owned by Centennial's own subsidiary companies or cronies.

The feds immediately fired Haines and 14 of the thrift's officers. Centennial was dissolved as a privately held, state-chartered stock thrift and was converted to a federal mutual, an institution that is theoretically owned by its depositors and borrowers. At that instant $7 million in stock, owned by 300 stockholders, some of them Centennial's founders, became worthless. The day after the takeover Pizzo walked into Centennial's small Guerneville branch and found an elderly Centennial employee in tears.

"I should have known," he said. "I invested every penny I'd saved for retirement—$50,000—in Centennial stock, and now it's all gone. I'm too old to start over. I should have known. It's my own fault. I should have known when Hansen walked by me every day, never even shook my hand or said hello."

Centennial became known among federal regulators in San Francisco as the Eleventh District's "dirtiest thrift"—a reference to what they said they saw as a sordid and wide-ranging labyrinth of fraud and self-dealing. With every day that passed the magnitude of the mess mounted. Centennial was $36 million in the red, then $60 million, $90 million, $112 million, and on it went. The further examiners looked, the more rot they found. There were loan files, for multi-million-dollar loans, that contained no appraisals or other required documentation. The FSLIC "SWAT" team found the $48,000-a-year European chef on the payroll, the company plane that was costing $35,000 a month in tie-down fees and maintenance, and the San Francisco penthouse. They seized over 25 company cars that ranged from Mercedes sedans to a stretch limo. And the $2 million Stonehouse, filled with European antiques, still sat vacant on the outskirts of town.

Hansen retired to his $500,000 home in Santa Rosa while officials began sorting through the wreckage to determine if any federal laws had been broken. In a last-ditch effort to salvage his dream, Hansen filed suit against the FHLBB, charging that their seizure was precipitous and premature. The case was soon dismissed and Hansen went back home to spend the next two years brooding in his Santa Rosa mansion.

On the heels of the takeover an FBI investigative team, specialists in white-collar crime, arrived in Santa Rosa to investigate violations of banking regulations. Special Agent Pat Murphy, an accounting specialist, and his partner, Special Agent Ernie Cooper, an attorney, got the thankless task of unraveling thousands of pages of old loan documents, title reports, deeds, and loan applications. There were a lot of unanswered questions, and, at that time, no one was talking.

For ten months the investigation limped along with little progress. The deals were mind-bogglingly complex, and the chance of nailing someone for clear criminal activity began to seem remote. Then chance dropped a veritable Rosetta Stone right in the FBI's lap, and at 8 a.m. on September 3, 1986, Pat Murphy, accompanied by a woman FBI agent, knocked on the door of Beverly Haines's magnificent home in Guerneville. A sleepy Haines, still in her bathrobe, answered.

"Beverly Haines," said Murphy, "I have a federal warrant for your arrest for embezzling $1.6 million from Centennial Savings and Loan."

Haines and an accomplice, who worked as the manager of the headquarters branch of Centennial in Santa Rosa (he had not been among those fired after the federal takeover), were taken into federal custody the same day. What was remarkable about the charges was that the money they embezzled was taken both before *and after* the federal seizure of Centennial, while the place was thick with federal auditors and FBI agents. Haines had become accustomed to having unrestricted access to Centennial's petty cash drawer, and after she was tossed out by regulators it hadn't taken her long to figure out a way to keep the money flowing.

Haines, who had been the young branch manager's boss at Centennial, had convinced him to aid her in a complex check-kiting scheme.[5] Over $5.8 million

was missing, though investigators said they could specifically tie only $1.6 million to Haines. She had facilitated the complicated fraud by opening over thirty checking accounts at Centennial and Bank of America.[6] Haines wrote checks for large sums of money—$145,000, $90,000, $125,000—on her Centennial accounts and deposited them at Bank of America. She then had Bank of America issue her cashier's checks for like amounts, which she converted to cash. When Haines's checks came back to Centennial for collection, her accomplice admitted, he sent the money to Bank of America but hid the checks in his desk or briefcase so there would be no record that Haines's accounts at Centennial were grossly overdrawn.

Federal investigators could not say what Haines did with all the money, and though Haines provided detailed testimony on alleged wrongdoing by others,[7] she remained vague about where her money was.

"They just don't understand," she told us. "It was all just kited checks, there really wasn't all the money they say there was." But she put those checks to very real uses. A workout specialist hired by the FSLIC to collect on bad Centennial loans said Haines even tried to pay off a $50,000 Centennial loan with a kited check.

"She readily agreed to repay the loan when we confronted her with the demand," he said. "She was really gracious about it and wrote us a check in full. What we didn't know then was that she was kiting checks out of Centennial and so what she did was repay us with our own money."

Another place a goodly chunk of Haines's money went was into her home in Guerneville. From practically the day things began to roll at Centennial in early 1983 until well after the federal takeover in 1985, workmen and craftsmen worked day in and day out on the Haines home. They transformed a once modest summer cabin into a luxurious two-story, 3,000-square-foot home suitable for the pages of *Architectural Digest*. It had over a dozen handmade stained-glass windows, three fountains, an elevator, a tile workout room complete with sauna, electrically operated skylights throughout, a sunken hot tub in the master suite, Italian-marble showers with gold-plated fixtures, suede carpets, and hand-carved doors. There was even a vault to store furs.

Haines began cooperating with the investigation almost immediately in a desperate effort to stay out of prison. Perhaps to inspire just such behavior, the assistant U.S. attorney in charge of the case, Peter Robinson, had Haines, following her arrest, held over the weekend in the Oakland County jail. Jail was definitely not Beverly's cup of tea, and when she was let out on bail, the feds' only problem was keeping up with the furious pace with which she began turning evidence against her former compatriots. She even agreed to give speeches to banking executives about bank fraud.

Haines's arrest and decision to turn state's evidence was a severe blow to Hansen. Acquaintances said his normally cocky, self-assured demeanor gave way to an increasingly sullen mood. A heavy drinker, he now indulged even more.[8] Finally, one night in early 1987, he showed up at Community Hospital's emergency room with what was reported to be a self-induced drug overdose. With Haines talking to the feds, and his attorney advising him not to be seen talking with Sid Shah, Hansen felt isolated and sent tentative feelers out to the federal authorities to see if he, too, could cut a deal. The question was met with stony, ice-cold silence, investigators told us. The U.S. attorney wanted to sweat him out while the FBI debriefed Haines. Four months after the first suicide attempt, Hansen was rushed to the emergency room a second time. Friends had found him unconscious in his car, in the garage, with the engine running.

After being stabilized Hansen was transferred to Oak Crest mental hospital on a mandatory 72-hour hold. This time federal investigators decided they had better talk to their prime suspect since he seemed to be going to extraordinary lengths to get their attention. Assistant U.S. Attorney Peter Robinson, an FBI agent, and a psychologist met with Hansen at Oak Crest. It was then that Hansen was given a description of the kinds of charges that would be brought against him. Some 26 in all were contemplated, including charges that he had embezzled at least $872,000 from Centennial between 1982 and 1985. The investigation had revealed that Hansen had routinely used his institution's funds to fuel his own extravagant life-style, taking $20,000 here, $25,000 there, $55,000 for antiques, $137,500 for jewelry, $80,000 for his taxes, $85,000 for cars, $25,000 for art, $45,000 for a vacation . . . and on and on (according to documents we obtained through the Freedom of Information Act). He had arrogantly used Centennial's treasury as his own personal petty cash drawer.

Hansen was released from Oak Crest and went home to resume waiting for the FBI to contact him. In the months that followed federal agents continued to debrief Haines and went right back to giving Hansen the official cold shoulder. They also handed down 17 indictments of mostly minor figures in the Centennial daisy chain.

What was left of Centennial was now in the hands of a crack management team from Great Western Savings and Loan, appointed by the FSLIC. In one final irony, on January 26, 1987, 18 months after regulators took over Centennial, the FHLB of San Francisco issued a confidential memorandum addressed "To the Board of Directors, Centennial Savings and Loan." The memorandum warned sternly, ". . . you may have found evidence of fraud and criminal collusion by and between former officers, directors, and outsiders, including professionals such as appraisers, and lawyers. You as directors have an obligation to review such acts for possible referral to a local prosecutor, or the United States Department of Justice." By that time, of course, the Justice Department probe was well under way and the crooks were long gone. So, for any practical purposes, was Centennial.

• • •

Golden Pacific Savings and Loan was seized a month after Centennial, in September 1985.[9] Leif Soderling, the older of the two Soderling brothers, had resigned as president in February, saying, "I don't want to be in the savings and loan business. It's got a lot of regulations and I don't want to learn them." His resignation didn't help him avoid trouble, however. In March 1987 he and his brother, Jay, were charged with loan fraud in connection with a complex series of land transactions that had netted them $10 million from their own thrift. The brothers pleaded guilty and were sentenced to one year in prison and ordered to pay restitution. (Critics of the lack of consistency in sentencing pointed to a front-page newspaper story about the Soderlings' sentence. On that same front page was news of another sentence, that of a man who had held a friend's parrot for ransom and received seven years in prison for the extortion attempt. The juxtaposition of the two stories led one disillusioned FBI agent to quip bitterly, "Use a parrot, go to jail.")

Contributing to the Soderlings' light sentence was an eloquent presentation by the prosecutor, Assistant U.S. Attorney Robinson, who described the brothers as two young men who "did not intend to establish the savings and loan for the purpose of ripping it off" but simply took the wrong fork in the road. During the hearing an attorney for the FSLIC repeatedly implored the judge to take a stronger stance with the two brothers, saying that evidence indicated that the pair had secreted some assets away and transferred others to third parties in order to hide them from investigators. The judge asked the U.S. attorney if this were so. Robinson replied that his agents had not conducted any search for secreted assets. (In March 1989, just months after the two brothers got out of prison, another U.S. attorney would accuse them of secretly receiving payment on a $800,000 note and spending most of the money on thoroughbred horses, a home computer, and car phones, in violation of probation, which required that any money they acquired be used for restitution. The brothers denied the accusation and the matter was pending as of this writing. The court had restricted the brothers to a living allowance of $2,500 a month for themselves and their families.)

In February 1988 the FSLIC filed a $10 million civil suit against the brothers. The FSLIC claimed they had manipulated substantial assets in order to defraud the FSLIC. Evidently the FSLIC didn't buy the Soderlings' tale of woe that Jay had a minus net worth of $1.5 million and Leif a negative net worth of $1 million. The FSLIC also filed a $100 million civil suit against Centennial's former directors and a number of former executives. And to round out the group the FSLIC filed a similar $50 million suit against several former Columbus-Marin Savings and Loan executives.[10]

From information provided by Haines, investigators were finally able to develop a solid case against Hansen. Investigators said they hoped that, once faced with the sobering reality of a multicount grand jury indictment and years in prison, Hansen would give them the evidence against Shah.

Nice idea, and it might have worked. Except that time ran out for the FBI when, on July 30, 1987—two years after the feds took over Centennial and just one day before Hansen was to enter into negotiations with the Justice Department—Hansen, 55, was found stone dead in bed. Nearly everyone suspected suicide or foul play, so the coroner gave the case special attention. The official report: Hansen had died of a cerebral aneurysm. A blood vessel on the right side of his brain had burst while he slept.

A pall fell over the sordid Centennial story after Hansen's death. Shah was the only major player left unscathed. He had boasted in the newspapers, through his high-powered lawyer, that he was guilty of nothing more than taking advantage of good business opportunities. Sure, he'd made a lot of money. What was wrong with that?

But quietly, behind the scenes, the multiagency investigation into the December 1982 fire on Lower Ridge Road had continued. Then suddenly, on October 5, 1987, special agents Pat Murphy and Ernie Cooper met Sid Shah as he was leaving his Sonoma, California, home—the opulent Spreckles mansion, of sugar fame—and hauled him off to appear before a federal magistrate in San Francisco. The grand jury had indicted Shah, accusing him of being part of an elaborate $300 million international drug-smuggling and money-laundering operation that imported marijuana, hashish, and cocaine from Mexico, Morocco, Colombia, and Thailand and that had done the bulk of its business between 1979 and 1985. Shah denied the charges. The ring was headed, the indictment said, by Ronald Stevenson, alias Ronald Miller, who had lived in the expensive Lower Ridge Road house with his wife and child at the time it was torched. Investigators speculated he had since been murdered in Mexico.

"Sid Shah Indicted" roared the headlines. Santa Rosa buzzed with the news. The indictment, drafted by the federal Organized Crime Drug Enforcement Task Force, charged that Shah, Las Vegas attorney Norman Jenson and others had laundered the drug proceeds through a complex web of real estate projects, including some connected to Centennial Savings and Loan and Piombo Corporation. At Shah's bail hearing a prosecutor cited Shah's recent trips to Amsterdam to meet with Sandmann as reason to fear that Shah might flee if released from jail before the trial. Nevertheless the judge ordered Shah released on $500,000 bail.[11] (The case was pending as of this writing.)

Unbeknownst to Shah, during the lengthy inquiry federal investigators had secretly recorded a meeting and phone calls between Shah, Norm Jenson, and Ronald Stevenson's brother, Michael. Shah, Jenson, and Stevenson discussed ways to best deal with the grand jury, which had subpoenaed records of their complex real estate transactions. The transcript of the meeting showed Shah reassuring the others:

"You don't have to worry 'bout me saying anything. Where the money was coming from, don't worry about that part of it if anything could hurt you guys."

Members of the drug ring began to talk, and transcripts of the interrogations show they told investigators that Norman Jenson, the man who had done millions of dollars' worth of business with Piombo, was at the very center of the high-rolling, international drug operation. One informant, William Olof Henrickson, told the FBI that Jenson had "mob" affiliations. A confidential DEA source said Jenson owned his own freighter, which prowled the waters from South America to Oregon. The informant told investigators that Jenson complained that the freighter was stuck in South America because it was being watched by the feds and that Jenson was willing to pay $1 million to anyone who would pilot it back to the United States. Transcripts showed investigators were also told that Jenson held drug kingpin Ron Stevenson's properties in his name and in the names of various shell corporations, and that Jenson used his own Coos Bay, Oregon, marina as an importation point for millions of dollars' worth of pot and cocaine. An FBI agent said he was told Jenson had placed the drug ring's vast fortune in safe havens in Switzerland, the Bahamas, Panama, and Thailand, once with the help of a Swiss consul general and once with the help of a Thai embassy employee in Los Angeles.

One technique used by Jenson to launder all this high-temperature money, a source in prison told us, was to purchase expensive property with a cash down payment and take out as large a loan as possible on the property. Jenson could then make the monthly payments on the loan with drug proceeds. The interest he paid on the loan he simply considered to be the cost of cleaning the money—the laundry bill. Jenson associates, including Henrickson and Michael Stevenson, told investigators that 50 percent of the Lakewood Hills development had been financed by Stevenson's drug proceeds.

How much did the ring launder through Lakewood Hills? an investigator asked Henrickson.

"Half a billion [sic] at Lakewood Hills, I think," he replied. "That's what he [Ronald Stevenson] told me one time. Five hundred thousand dollars."

A county politician had eased the paperwork for the Lakewood Hills development through the county bureaucracy, he added:

"They had the politician in their pocket, one of 'em, you know. And they could get permits through him and shit like that."

Later Centennial bought Lakewood Hills, thereby cashing out the asset for Jenson and the others.

A raid on Jenson's offices in Las Vegas netted investigators a treasure trove of documentation on Jenson's far-flung enterprises. An inventory of items taken in that search included paperwork on various real estate transactions allegedly used to launder drug money (including files on Lakewood Hills and Jenson's deals with Piombo Corporation) and numerous plastic bags and bottles containing "green leafy substances, and white powders and white powder residues" (according to the FBI receipt for property received).

With such damning evidence in federal hands, Jenson agreed to cooperate with the government in its investigation of the drug ring, Sid Shah, and individuals at savings and loans in Texas, Washington, and Louisiana. In return Jenson sought and received partial immunity from prosecution. Then, just before the drug trial was scheduled to begin, informant Michael Stevenson disappeared. The drug case was pending as this book went to press.

At this point the wind went out of the Centennial criminal investigation. The feds' technique of sweating out Hansen had blown up in their faces, and now that he was dead, Assistant U.S. Attorney Peter Robinson announced he was going into private practice to become a defense attorney, and the FBI had to scale back its investigation.[12] After 12 years as a federal prosecutor, Robinson would now defend clients accused of some of the same kinds of crimes he had formerly prosecuted. In an article he wrote for a legal publication he said his new clientele gave him something he had not found as a prosecutor:

> . . . the feeling I have experienced as a defense lawyer getting a dismissal for a client is euphoric—and addicting . . . the gratitude for helping one real person is much greater than I received as a prosecutor helping the public . . . my days as a champion of the underdog have just begun. It is a daunting challenge. But I already feel at home.

In a final twist of irony, Robinson revealed that his new offices would be located in Centennial's former executive quarters, the Stonehouse.

With his departure the Centennial investigation lost its drive and dribbled to a close. Beverly Haines went off to Giger Correctional Facility in Spokane, Washington, to serve a five-year sentence for embezzling $1.6 million from Centennial, but in two months she was out, released by Judge Robert Peckham to a halfway house in San Francisco to perform community service and serve three years' probation. She was allowed to go home on weekends.

Centennial, born in 1977, finally passed completely from sight in April 1987 when its garments were divided between the FSLIC and Citizens Federal Savings and Loan of Miami, which paid only $8 million for what was left of Centennial's "goodwill" and for the right to operate an interstate network of thrifts that would have branches in Florida and California (interstate banking was forbidden except when it suited regulators' needs).[13] In less than five years, from December 1980 to August 1985, when federal regulators took over the thrift, over $165 million vanished, and no one ever served more than a year in prison for the theft.[14] In

1985 there were 5,995 bank robberies in the U.S. that involved a total loss of $46 million.[15] But at Centennial alone the heist netted $165 million.

By the time Citizens Federal bought the remnants of Centennial in April 1987 we were well into our investigation of failed thrifts coast to coast. We had decided in December 1986 that the evidence Pizzo had collected at Centennial was too compelling to ignore. We *knew* we were onto an important story. The strategy we adopted was to approach our investigation in the same way an epidemiologist would track a spreading virus. We took a random selection of failed thrifts across the country and examined each to see if we found common elements in their deaths. We had a theory to prove or disprove: that "bust-outs" and other forms of orchestrated fraud were underlying the sudden crisis in the thrift industry. Pizzo and Fricker would work out of an office in Guerneville; Muolo, out of the *National Thrift News* office in New York. We spent over two years on the investigation, years in which we collected bits of information every day that expanded our understanding of the puzzle we were piecing together. In the process we uncovered a cast of bank-fraud artists that were working every single savings and loan we examined. The interwoven relationships astonished even us, and by the time we completed our investigation, in June 1989, our original hypothesis had been eclipsed by the reality we discovered: deregulation had unleashed a holocaust of fraud upon the thrifts it had been designed to save.

CHAPTER SIX

Lazarus

When the California legislature deregulated state-chartered thrifts in order to stem the flow of state thrifts to federal charters after Garn-St Germain passed, it virtually threw the rule book out the door and made California thrifts irresistible. In one important provision the legislature decreed that a savings and loan could invest or loan 100 percent of its assets in real estate,[1] and it set no standards for the type of property or the qualifications of the borrower. Suddenly the state was so flooded with applications for thrift charters that almost anyone who could prove he had the $2 million required as start-up capital got the nod. By 1984 it was easier to get approval to own a California savings and loan than it was to get a casino license in neighboring Nevada. As a result some people who might not have qualified to run a casino in Nevada got thrifts in California instead and ran them like they *were* casinos.

Toward the end of our Centennial investigation a source close to the Soderling brothers slipped us a copy of a letter the pair had prepared as part of their plea bargain negotiations with the FBI. The letter outlined what the former thrift owners agreed to tell the feds in return for a soft sentence. Near the end of the letter was a cryptic reference to "Robert Ferrante and Consolidated Savings and Loan. . . ." We asked one of our FBI sources who Robert Ferrante was; we'd never run across the name and the Soderlings' letter did not explain further.[2]

"Ferrante . . . huh, there's one you should look at," our source told us. "He's a good example of the kind of business person California's new thrift laws let into this business. You won't believe it. Go on down to L.A. and look in the court records . . . that's all I can tell you." When we did research Ferrante we discovered all that the FBI agent had promised and more. There was no shortage of colorful information on Mr. Ferrante, in both public records and the local press. He had first made headlines in 1982.

It was late on a Monday night, April 12, 1982, when Robert Ferrante and his trusted aide Raymond Arthun decided to call it a day. They locked up their office in the Brookside Village condominium conversion project in Redondo Beach, California, on the outskirts of Los Angeles, and walked to their cars in the dimly lit office parking lot. Arthun stopped at his car and Ferrante continued down three spaces to his.

Suddenly Arthun heard a noise. Looking up he saw a man with a sock over his head leap from behind a bush in front of Ferrante's car. The man ran up to within a few feet of Ferrante and opened fire on him with a .22-caliber semiautomatic pistol equipped with a silencer. Ferrante screamed for help but the would-be assassin continued his work with polished precision, even coming closer to fire a few last shots into Ferrante as he crumbled to the pavement. Then the gunman walked briskly out into the parking lot, where he was picked up by a waiting tan Toyota hatchback.

But Robert Ferrante was not to be killed off that easily. Miraculously, of the nine rounds fired, only four hit their mark and only two caused any serious damage. One passed through Ferrante's left thigh and a second lodged in his chest. The police report showed he told police he knew who had shot him, but he refused to give them the identity of the attacker. Later, in a sworn declaration filed in connection with a partnership gone sour, Ferrante claimed he had been targeted by two former business partners with ties to the Israeli Mafia.[3]

Less than two years after he lay bleeding from a hit man's bullets, and while he was publicly involved in a tangled web of civil lawsuits as well as a criminal case involving bribery of a public official, Ferrante was granted a charter from the State of California, and approved by the Federal Savings and Loan Insurance Corporation (FSLIC), to open his very own savings and loan.

What a perfect example of how the once-conservative thrift industry had changed, we thought. Old-line thrift owners would have been horrified to have someone like Ferrante as a colleague, almost as horrified as Ferrante probably would have been to be stuck in such a boring occupation. But now would-be tycoons like Ferrante were welcome in the savings and loan industry . . . and S&Ls were no longer boring. Far from it.

Robert Ferrante, an attorney, liked to describe himself as a product of blue-collar working-class parents, a hard worker who grew up near Los Angeles and put himself through college and law school. His brother, Rocco, described him as "one hell of an entrepreneur." Detractors called him a "little arrogant Napoleon." He was short—about five feet seven—trim and handsome, and he exuded the polished corporate image.

In 1972 Ferrante, then 24, married the daughter of wealthy San Fernando real estate developer Chester Anderson. Anderson owned and operated Day Realty and Day Escrow Company, with 20 offices and 1,500 employees in the Los Angeles area. Ferrante immediately became a partner with his father-in-law and the two began investing in condominium conversion projects together. But the bloom later faded from the family rose and by 1979 Chester Anderson was suing son-in-law Ferrante and two Israeli businessmen who were partners of Ferrante in other projects. Anderson alleged in his suit that they had used his company as though it was their own. The judge agreed, ruling:

"It is clear that the defendants used large sums of Condor Development [the Anderson-Ferrante company] money, directly and indirectly. . . . They also used the credit of Condor Development by pledging proceeds from the sale" of its projects to guarantee a $1.3 million loan for projects of their own.

The judge also disclosed that Ferrante and his partners had even tried to handicap Anderson's attempt to recover the missing funds from them. "The defendants upon being served with the complaint herein decided to take $540,000 of corporate funds which they believed was owing [sic] to Chester Anderson, in order to prevent him from using that money to finance his lawsuit against them." The suit was an ugly family affair and got plenty of press in Southern California, but apparently state regulators missed the stories.

Ferrante's feud with his father-in-law didn't get in the way of his relationship with his two Israeli partners. The three men continued to do condo conversions together until they had a falling-out in 1981 and Ferrante went to court to have their partnership dissolved—on his terms. (The suit was later settled out of court.) Angry accusations flew back and forth. In April 1982 the masked assassin ambushed Ferrante, and a month later he went to court to demand a protective court order to keep his two former partners away from him.

Ferrante testified that he believed he was the target of an Israeli hit man to whom his two former partners had paid $25,000 to kill him. He told the court that he was repeatedly warned by the pair that they were going to kill him.

"I can recall over 30 threats in the 22-day period prior to the actual assassination attempt on my life," Ferrante told the court. Employees at Ferrante's office corroborated his contention that someone was out to get him. Robin Bohannon told the court that in November a man had stormed into the office looking for Ferrante.

"Where's Robert Ferrante? I'm going to break his head, and Ray Arthun's too." Bohannon said the man kept yelling that he had a gun and was going to use it on Ferrante and Arthun. (In 1987 Ferrante's then ex-wife would tell Los Angeles *Times* reporters, "It was and still is my husband's policy to take extreme risks with money, even to the point of nearly being murdered because of its use.")

Despite Ferrante's accusations against his former business partners, and ensuing police and private investigations, no one was charged with the attempt on Ferrante's life. And despite the wide publicity accorded the events surrounding the shooting, Ferrante's reputation was evidently not sufficiently damaged to make regulators later question his suitability as an S&L owner.

But there was still more, we found. Ferrante made headlines again in May

1983 when the United States attorney indicted former Redondo Beach, California, City Councilman Walter Mitchell, Jr., for allegedly taking bribes from Ferrante to gain city approval in 1979 for Ferrante's Brookside Village condo conversion project—where Ferrante was shot in 1982. Voters recalled Mitchell in 1980 after a public row and a series of newspaper articles on the controversial condominium conversion issue.

Mitchell, a slight man in his thirties, pleaded innocent. But during his three-day trial in 1983 witnesses told the jury that Mitchell himself had said he was being paid by Ferrante to get approval for the Brookside Village project. Under the alleged Brookside Village scheme, Mitchell, a painting contractor by trade, received lucrative painting contracts on Ferrante-owned construction projects in return for his help with the city council, the prosecutor charged.[4] The jury convicted Mitchell of mail and tax fraud and sentenced him to a year and a half in prison. (In 1988 Mitchell's mail-fraud convictions were overturned on appeal when the court ruled that officials could be convicted of mail fraud only if the fraud cost the government money or property. The tax-fraud conviction was upheld.)

To the end Mitchell denied he had accepted bribes from Ferrante, and the district attorney dropped that aspect of the investigation. Later, FSLIC investigators learned, Consolidated made $52,000 in loans to Mitchell's wife while her husband *quietly* served his sentence. And when Michell got out of jail, he went to work for Ferrante in Hawaii, according to exhibits filed in a FSLIC lawsuit in 1988.

Ferrante's problems did not occur in private. We found volumes written on his exploits, both in public records and in the press, but apparently none of this verbiage had filtered up to the green eyeshades of state and federal regulators when, in 1983, Ferrante applied for a state charter for his own savings and loan. Regulators may not have heard of him, but he had certainly heard about deregulation and he now wanted his own S&L. The processing of Ferrante's application for Consolidated Savings Bank proceeded without a hitch, thanks to California's new ultraliberal savings and loan regulations passed just that year.[5]

So at the very time that Ferrante's relationship with Redondo Beach City Councilman Walter Mitchell was being investigated and openly discussed in the press during the Mitchell trial in May 1983—prompting a public rehashing of the 1982 murder attempt on his life and the 1979 lawsuit filed against him by his father-in-law—Ferrante's application to run his own thrift sailed through the application process. Even Ferrante's application for FSLIC insurance coverage, a separate step requiring federal approval, progressed uneventfully. Federal Home Loan Bank Board spokeswoman Martha Gravlee later explained that FBI checks of prospective thrift or bank owners might turn up prior criminal *convictions* but would reveal nothing on current investigations, and Ferrante had never been convicted of anything.

Ferrante's application was a perfect example of one government hand not knowing what the other hand was doing. "The U.S. attorney had subpoenaed every document in my office with Ferrante's name on it," recalled one senior loan officer in Southern California. "That was at the same time the state and the Federal Home Loan Bank were considering his application for a savings and loan and FSLIC insurance. Somebody wasn't talking to somebody else."

Ferrante later said of the approval process, "I assumed they checked me out thoroughly." Not so.

The California Savings and Loan Commissioner's office approved Ferrante's application in May of 1983. At the dawning of 1984 Consolidated also received the blessing of the Federal Home Loan Bank Board when, after the FHLBB's "investigation," it approved Ferrante's new thrift for FSLIC insurance. The next day, February 28, 1984, Consolidated opened its doors for business. Ferrante now owned his own money machine. He would serve as chairman of the board until December 7, 1984, when he gave that position to banker Ottavio A. Angotti. Ferrante would remain the sole stockholder throughout the thrift's short life.

Consolidated Savings Bank's offices first were located in a shopping center in Brea, about 30 miles east of Los Angeles. "It was basically a post office drop, a storefront, not like a real bank at all," recalled a reporter who covered the opening. Eighteen months later Ferrante would move his bank to Irvine, in Orange County, 30 miles south of Los Angeles, into a fancy three-story building in Douglas Plaza, adjacent to Orange County's John Wayne Airport.

Firmly in the saddle, what Ferrante needed now was to fuel Consolidated with deposits as fast as he could. Like Erv Hansen at Centennial, Ferrante turned to deposit broker Mario Renda and First United Fund, even though Consolidated's application for a savings and loan charter had said Consolidated would be a hometown thrift filled with passbook savings accounts. But passbook savings were small and took time to build up, whereas brokered deposits came with a phone call and gave thrifts all the money they wanted when they wanted it. An FHLBB examination revealed that 16 months after Consolidated Savings opened for business, 70 percent of its savings deposits would consist of brokered and jumbo ($100,000) certificates of deposit, much of it from Mario Renda's First United Fund.

With the brokered deposits rolling in, Consolidated had all the money it needed. Regulators later complained that Ferrante bellied right up to his own loan trough to get some of those deposits for his own projects, the largest of which was a 157-acre landfill at the southern edge of Los Angeles called the Carson landfill. Years earlier the property had been a dump for the city, and the state considered it a toxic waste site. Nevertheless over the next few months, according to an FSLIC lawsuit, Ferrante would arrange to have Consolidated loan just over $15 million on the property through a confusing maze of companies he had formed and controlled. Many of the Carson loans were obscurely noted on Consolidated's books as simply "sundry debit items,"[6] federal examiners reported.

Ferrante's right-hand man at Consolidated was its president, Ottavio Angotti, who had been born and raised in Italy and who had come to the U.S. in 1957. He still spoke with an Italian accent and when angry sometimes slipped into Italian. It was Angotti who was left to do battle with suspicious examiners wanting to know where those several million dollars in "sundry debit items" were going and what interest Ferrante had in the Carson project. When we interviewed Angotti by phone two years later, he told us he hadn't been hiding anything from anybody.

"The examiners, both state and federal, were auditing the bank at the very time we were doing this," Angotti said, his Italian accent growing thicker with each angry word. "They saw all those debit items. How can they say we were trying to hide anything?"

The $15 million Carson loans only slightly exceeded regulators' $100,000 limit on unsecured commercial loans to affiliated persons and also immediately put Consolidated Savings in violation of the loans-to-one borrower regulation, regulators claimed. (The Carson loans, according to FSLIC reports, were three times Consolidated Savings' reported net worth and consumed a quarter of its deposits.) Despite the $15 million that was headed into the Carson project, Ferrante never developed the property,[7] maybe because of its continuing problem as a toxic waste dump.

Perhaps anticipating the wrath of regulators, Ferrante decided to "participate out" (sell) some of the Carson loans to other institutions.[8] Ferrante arranged these participation deals with United Federal Savings and Loan of Durant, Oklahoma, and Savings Investment Service Corporation (also known as SISCorp) of Oklahoma City, a loan brokerage firm.[9] The key figure in Consolidated Savings' deals with United Federal Savings and SISCorp was Charles Bazarian of Oklahoma City. Bazarian was described by one former savings and loan executive who knew him well as "an original piece of work."

In Charlie Bazarian we came face-to-face with one of the most active con artists working the thrift circuit coast to coast. As our investigation progressed we were stunned by the number of times we would be sifting through the ashes of a failed thrift and come across a Bazarian deal.

Bazarian was not an Oklahoma native. He was a Connecticut Yankee, the son of an Armenian immigrant produce salesman. Charlie was a living caricature of a tycoon, an obese, gregarious fellow, five feet nine inches tall, 245 pounds, who eventually had to have quadruple heart bypass surgery. He chewed expensive handmade cigars and had never bothered to clean up his malapropisms and bad grammar. He and his wife, Janice Lee Bazarian, were well-known figures in Oklahoma City society. Friends said Charlie had a need to associate with the great and near great. On one occasion the couple arranged for their friend Las Vegas entertainer Wayne Newton to perform free at a benefit for their favorite charity, a rehabilitation center for the mentally handicapped. On another occasion former heavyweight boxing champ Muhammad Ali, who was visiting for a few days at the Bazarians' home, stopped by the center and signed autographs for the patients.

Charlie and Janice were great party givers. Every year Bazarian, whom friends had nicknamed Fuzzy, threw an elaborate birthday party for his son, nicknamed Buzzy. Buzzy, born in 1982, was only a baby, but the guest list was a Who's Who of Oklahoma City. One year Fuzzy, in Buzzy's honor, had an entire circus set up on the vast lawn of his 19,000-square-foot, $2.4 million mansion. At one end of this lavish spread the Bazarians reportedly had an indoor swimming pool with a retractable dome ceiling and a waterfall. The Bazarians listed as assets artworks worth $100,000 (including one jade boat appraised at $65,000), $775 worth of exotic fish, and a $60,000 Rolls-Royce Camrogue. Bazarian had a Rolex watch (gold with diamonds) worth $15,000 and an economy duplicate worth $1,000. Janice had a gold-nugget-and-diamond pendant that cost $1,500 and Charlie countered with his $1,500 sapphire-and-diamond cuff links. But the *real* Charlie, we speculated, was the $1,700 gold-and-diamond oil-well belt buckle.

For someone living such an exalted life-style, Bazarian had a most unlikely history. He quit school after the eighth grade. In the 1960s, already the father of three children, he moved his family to Oklahoma and worked as a restaurant cook. Later he got into the insurance business and by 1977, when he was 37, he had his own insurance company.

"He couldn't do enough for his family," a brother-in-law told a reporter. "He would give you the shirt off his back."

Well, maybe. But his generosity didn't extend to his clients. In the 1970s he and associates set up an insurance company that agreed to pay up to $1 million in lifetime medical benefits to clients who paid the $30 membership fee and the monthly insurance premiums, but no one ever bothered to set aside any money to pay the medical claims. In 1978 he pleaded no contest to felony charges of mail fraud. Prosecutors charged that he and his cohorts bilked 700 farmers and ranchers out of more than $347,000 in fees and premiums. Bazarian was sentenced to four years in prison, which was reduced to four years' probation in exchange for his testimony against his partner, who was convicted and sent to prison.

Bazarian immediately filed for bankruptcy, claiming to owe $276,000, including $24,000 in unpaid Las Vegas hotel-casino bills. In June 1979 the bankruptcy trustee determined that Bazarian had no assets at all and he was forgiven his debts. Five years later he was chairman, CEO, and sole shareholder in CB Financial, a company purportedly worth $141 million.

"Charlie is a very entrepreneurial person," said Sig Kohnen, who started CB Financial with Bazarian in 1983. "He has picked himself up by the bootstraps." Unfortunately they were attached to someone else's boots.

CB Financial was Bazarian's baby. He told us the company borrowed money from thrifts and re-loaned it to investors in real estate partnerships, some of which were tax shelters. Bazarian formed some of these partnerships himself, and in those cases he was loaning to his own limited partners. He made part of his profit by charging his borrowers more for the money (in interest and fees) than the thrifts charged him for the money. But Bazarian got double duty out of his investors. He took the notes they signed when he made them loans and either sold the notes at a discount or pledged them as security for more loans from thrifts and banks.

Charlie had a veritable perpetual-motion money machine going. The more loans he made to his investors, the more investors' notes he held that he could sell or pledge for more loans, an arrangement that appeared to us to closely resemble a Ponzi scheme. At its height CB Financial had a total debt approaching $200 million. Bazarian used some of the money to buy stock in savings and loans as one way to win the hearts and minds of lenders, according to his associate Sig Kohnen. In 1985 Bazarian owned $15 million of stock in at least nine institutions. Among the lenders he did business with were United Federal Savings and Loan and SISCorp (the two companies Ferrante would soon sell loans to).

When, in August 1985, Ferrante wanted to dispose of some of the $15 million in Carson loans, Beverly Hills loan broker Al Yarbrow introduced Ferrante to Bazarian. Again we saw what a critical role loan brokers like John Lapaglia (who arranged loans for Norm Jenson) and Al Yarbrow played in the thrift crisis. They found willing lenders for needy borrowers, and for the introduction the broker received a commission based on a percent (usually 2 to 5 percent)[10] of the loan. The shakier the borrower or deal, the higher the commission. Some loan brokers, looking for crazy lenders, traveled the country with their briefcases stuffed with crazy deals.

Al Yarbrow was a particularly well-connected loan broker, having been in the business since the 1960s. He was a bright, articulate, distinguished-looking man in his fifties, over six feet tall. A conservative dresser, he projected the classic corporate U.S.A. image. Those who did business with him said he worked hard, was always well prepared, and gave the impression of being a real professional.

Be that as it may, in the late 1960s Yarbrow was charged with diverting over $300,000 from his Bradley Mortgage Company's impound accounts. The money had been paid to Bradley Mortgage by homeowners who had arranged their

FHA mortgages through Bradley, and it was supposed to be used to pay insurance and property taxes. Instead, Yarbrow had used the money to finance his other business ventures. Nearly 400 homeowners got a rude surprise when the tax man informed them that their property taxes were delinquent. We learned that Yarbrow repaid the money as part of an arrangement with the Los Angeles County prosecutor.

When Yarbrow introduced Ferrante to Bazarian in 1985, Charlie sent Ferrante over to United Federal Savings and SISCorp. United Federal Savings agreed to buy $3 million worth of Consolidated Savings' Carson loans and SISCorp agreed to purchase $5 million more. The ice thus broken, Ferrante and Bazarian found a number of ways to do business together. Along the way, regulators said, $3.5 million disappeared. As FSLIC attorneys later described the deal in court, Consolidated had agreed to buy a package of loans from SISCorp and had sent $3.5 million to Bazarian to forward to SISCorp. SISCorp said they never got the money. Consolidated didn't seem to care, regulators said, and did virtually nothing to recover the money.

Even while he was wheeling and dealing with Ferrante, Bazarian was building onto his house of cards. His CB Financial empire, fed on loans and enmeshed in complicated financial transactions, began to collapse when in 1986 federal tax changes sharply reduced the allure of the kind of tax shelters Bazarian was offering his investors. Bazarian was sued at least 16 times in Oklahoma courts in 1986 by people who claimed he owed them more than $77 million.[11] Bazarian claimed his problems were caused by federal thrift and bank regulators who sabotaged his growing empire. But in a moment of candor he also admitted to us, "I just borrowed tremendous amounts of money. . . . I just had an appetite that was absolutely incredible for, you know, money."

When regulators stopped thrifts from making loans to Bazarian's operation and began suing him for recovery of old loans, his wife literally broke into song. Janice Lee Bazarian fancied herself a singer, and in 1986 she recorded, with her group, "Janice and the Deadbeats," a song they called "FDIC" about the horrors of dealing with hard-hearted bank regulators. Sung to the tune of "YMCA," made popular by the Village People, the chorus went:

> F-D-I-C,
> It's time to pay to the F-D-I-C.
> They can have everything that you signed and agreed
> You can hang out in bankruptcy.
> F-D-I-C,
> It's time to pay to the F-D-I-C.
> You can get yourself clean, you can make an appeal
> Your bank is gone and these guys won't deal.
> (copyright 1987, used with permission of Janice Lee Bazarian)

By May 1987 more of Bazarian's schemes were catching up with him. Vernon Savings and Sunbelt Savings, two Dallas institutions, and Borg-Warner Acceptance Corporation, an industrial lender in Chicago, tried to force Bazarian into bankruptcy, asserting claims of over $16 million. When Bazarian and CB Financial finally agreed to the involuntary bankruptcy in October, a long list of thrifts and banks lined up to sue for recovery.[12] Among them was Consolidated Savings Bank (then in the hands of regulators), which said Bazarian had defrauded the thrift of $12.3 million.[13] CB Financial was about $90 million in debt. Bazarian estimated his personal debts totaled about $108 million, which included Las Vegas gambling debts of $469,000.

But Bazarian didn't let these problems affect his life-style. In the same year he and Janice Lee bought a new home in Oklahoma City. Bazarian didn't say what he paid for the house but two years earlier, in a hotter real estate market, it had been on the market for $2 million. From his new home Bazarian complained expansively to reporters that people were bringing him great deals but, because of all the charges swirling around him, he couldn't find a bank willing to lend him money. Friends said Bazarian was just misunderstood, that he was well-meaning but too trusting of others and too eager to make deals. Even an assistant U.S. attorney admitted that Bazarian had charm: "He's a very endearing, charming fellow. He has a way of becoming very likable."[14]

Try to tell that to the process server hired by the FSLIC to serve a subpoena on Bazarian in relation to his deals with Consolidated. According to testimony during court proceedings the process server made numerous trips out to the Bazarian mansion with no results. Then when someone finally did come to the door, they were two thugs brandishing guns. The process server ran to his car and sped off, only to look in his rearview mirror and see that the two men were following in their car. A half-hour, Hollywood-style car chase through the streets of Oklahoma City ensued. The process server was finally able to lose his pursuers, and he returned home to tell the FSLIC to find someone else to serve Bazarian. A FSLIC attorney told the story to a Los Angeles judge who quipped, "That's the way they do things in Oklahoma."

Consolidated Savings' Chairman Angotti claimed he had been misled about Bazarian and wished he'd never heard of him. "We had no information about his former criminal activities," Angotti claimed. "If we had, we wouldn't have done business with him." Angotti said he believed there was a darker side to the Bazarian affair. "I was fooled and defrauded by more than Bazarian. I was defrauded by the Federal Home Loan Bank itself. When I contacted them to get a reading on SISCorp and Mr. Bazarian, those sons-a-bitches just told me that he [Bazarian] was okay. They let me walk right into that thing because you see I was a pain in the ass as far as they were concerned. The Federal Home Loan Bank boards of Topeka and San Francisco, they framed me. They ruined the good name of Ottavio A. Angotti."[15]

(In 1988 a bankruptcy court trustee alleged that Bazarian had been secretly transferring assets to trusts for his children and concealing them from the trustee. Later Bazarian reached a settlement with the trustee in which he agreed to relinquish his Oklahoma City mansion and many other assets to satisfy creditors. The trustee did agree, however, to let the Bazarians keep the copyright to Janice's song, "FDIC.")

By mid-1985, a little over a year after opening for business, Ferrante had made a big dent in Consolidated's bottom line. Finally federal regulators were eyeing him nervously. They conducted an examination of the S&L's books, which they claimed showed major inconsistencies between Consolidated's records and the facts:

1. Consolidated *said* 84.8 percent of its loans were mortgage loans secured by real property; the *truth*, according to examiners, was that 52.7 percent of its loans were *unsecured* commercial loans, a majority of which were in excess of loans-to-one-borrower limitations.

2. Consolidated *said* it had no brokered deposits; the *truth* was that at the time 70 percent of its deposits were brokered and more were pouring in every day.

3. Most of Consolidated's loans were to 15 borrowers, most of whom regulators reported had suspiciously close ties to Ferrante.

4. The net worth Consolidated reported included substantial noncash assets of questionable value.

5. Loans lacked adequate documentation and Consolidated had no written formal loan policy and procedures.

Given the extent of Consolidated's alleged infractions, we wondered why regulators let the thrift continue to operate for a year after the examination. The answer, we learned, was that regulators had lengthy procedures to follow, and they had to proceed in an orderly manner.[16] The modus operandi in the banking world was not to panic. *Panic* was the "P" word of banking. Instead, there were careful, measured steps to be followed, calmly, quietly, and secretly, of course, so the public wouldn't *panic*.

Besides, Ferrante and Angotti weren't making it particularly easy, or comfortable, for regulators to examine Consolidated's books. Immediately following the critical June 1985 examiner's report, the regulatory apparatus tried to lurch into action, issuing a series of directives, restrictions, and cease-and-desist orders designed to jawbone Consolidated Savings into compliance. As a result Chairman Angotti, who was increasingly called upon to placate Consolidated's FHLB supervisory agent, particularly on the Carson deal, began harassing bank examiners. Eventually things got downright personal and came to a head when Angotti allegedly threatened federal examiners "with grave bodily harm including death."[17]

Depending on whose version you believe, the threat was either sinister or semi-sinister. According to one FHLB examiner, Angotti threatened to kill him. Regulators contended similar threats were made to another auditor as well. A public relations firm hired by Ferrante following the 1986 federal takeover of Consolidated Savings Bank told us it was all a big misunderstanding.

"Mr. Angotti is Italian," PR woman Sherry Twamley explained in a soft voice. "After weeks of struggling with federal regulators, Mr. Angotti just got angry one day and, instead of swearing at them in English, did so in Italian. If you translated what he said literally, it meant 'I'm going to cut your balls off.' But really," she added, "he's just a 'Mr. Harmless Professor.'"

Angotti agreed with Sherry Twamley's version of his threats, but he added that after his suffering at the hands of regulators he might have strengthened his threat. Angotti complained that they seemed obsessed with the "Mafia" and one federal examiner made constant allusions to Angotti's heritage and the mob. "He used to ask me all the time if I was taking my instructions from the Mafia," Angotti said incredulously, adding in his Italian accent that if he had known then what regulators had in store for Consolidated, he would have "eaten their blood."[18]

Angotti also speculated, "I think the state and feds had approved Robert for Consolidated but missed all the stuff about the bribery case and shooting and stuff. When they discovered it Consolidated had already been approved and I think they were just trying to force him out because their investigation of him didn't turn any of this stuff up."

Ferrante, in a counterclaim filed against the FSLIC, claimed that "Angotti, representing the new California-based S&Ls, arguing forcefully for the rights of an S&L to engage in all types of profitable commercial activities, including commercial lending," was anathema to FHLBB Chairman Ed Gray, who represented the interests of "the club," or the long-established large thrift institutions. Ferrante claimed that Ed Gray, in Washington, and regulators at the San Francisco FHLB conspired to "destroy Consolidated and Ferrante and Angotti, thereby removing them as political forces within the industry." He said the FSLIC colluded with newspapers and the media in a maniacal mission to destroy him.[19]

Whatever their reasons, Federal Home Loan Bank examiners from San Francisco continued to hound Angotti. They were cutting their way through the maze of partnerships, limited partnerships, trust assignments, and promissory notes Consolidated had erected around the Carson project. Ferrante later alleged in court documents that from November 1985 the thrift was hardly doing any banking at all. Instead, management and staff spent most of their time trying to satisfy regulators through two bank examinations, one agreement promising to correct any problems, eight meetings, and at least 41 long letters of instruction accompanied by hundreds of pages of documentation.

In what Ferrante characterized as a thoroughly unreasonable action, regulator Polly Cortez advised the FHLBB in February 1986 not to approve Ferrante's application to own another savings and loan. Then in March federal examiners began what would turn out to be the final inspection of Consolidated Savings' books. They later reported that Angotti, pushed for answers to embarrassing questions, again resorted to threats. He called examiner Darrell De Castro into an office to complain about the examination. The more Angotti talked, the more frightening his rhetoric became.

"If they want to fight, I can fight," Angotti vowed, according to De Castro. "And I don't lose. No one is going to close this bank. If they do, I will have to be dead. I mean that literally. And if they shoot me, I will have to shoot someone. And I hope it's not *you*." Unamused by Angotti's "Godfather" imitation, the FHLB asked for, and received from the court, a temporary restraining order barring Angotti or any other Consolidated official from interfering with examiners. Regulators returned with armed guards from the U.S. marshal's office, just for good measure. Left to do their job without distractions, regulators soon found the institution was insolvent.

On May 22, 1986, at 4 p.m., agents of the FSLIC pushed through the doors of Consolidated's new offices in Irvine and took control of the thrift. They were accompanied by FBI agents, some carrying automatic rifles, and local police. By now they were very familiar with the story of the Ferrante shooting incident, his claims of Israeli Mafia involvement, and Angotti's blunt threats to their examiners. FHLB attorney Bart Dzivi later testified they had also been warned by local law enforcement that there was an ongoing investigation into Ferrante's alleged links to organized crime.[20] Under those circumstances the green-eye-shaded regulators weren't about to walk in armed only with calculators.

Angotti was offended by his treatment that day. He said the FBI agents who accompanied the federal regulators held machine guns on him and the bank's tellers and also manhandled him personally.

"They came into my office and threw me up against the wall and frisked me," said Angotti. But Angotti had not been exactly caught off guard by the raid. Five hours earlier a reporter acting on a tip had called him.

"I hear they're going to shut you guys down today. Any comment?" the reporter had asked.

There was stunned silence on the line, and then Angotti blurted, *"Oh, shit!*

Thanks!" and hung up. (In 1986 and 1987 the reporter received a Christmas card from Angotti. In 1987 the card carried the simple message "Again, thank you, belated thanks. —Ottavio A. Angotti.")[21]

When the FSLIC team arrived at Consolidated's offices that afternoon, attorneys for regulators claim they found three large trash bags filled with shredded bank documents. Fifteen minutes after the takeover they found a bank official still frantically shredding. Regulators claimed later that other important documents were smuggled out the back door to Consolidated's corporate office even as the thrift was being seized.

While regulators secured Consolidated Savings' Irvine office, FBI agents and Bank Board officers simultaneously stormed the Newport Beach office that Ferrante shared with his attorney, Eric Bronk. A Mexican standoff ensued, with Bronk maintaining that neither Consolidated Savings nor Ferrante had any records at his office. While Bronk stalled, several people left the building carrying briefcases. Eventually Bronk went into a back office and after a long wait, regulators said, he returned with a single Consolidated-related file. After further altercation he repeated the process and produced another file. This stalling action continued for a couple of hours, during which time Bronk produced about half a dozen Consolidated files.

Finally examiners decided to call it a day and continue the next. It was late in the afternoon and everyone was tense and tired. Both sides were clearly standing their ground. But before they left the examiners had the locks changed on the doors, and they posted a Pinkerton guard outside for the evening. Then, just as everyone was filing out to their cars to leave, Ferrante suddenly appeared, walking out of a back office and, without saying a word, driving off. He had been there, apparently, the entire time, FSLIC's attorneys claimed.

Things didn't get any better the next day. Bronk/Ferrante associates scurried around clicking flash pictures of arriving FSLIC clerks and examiners. They also took photos of their license plates and leaped into the air to click pictures through the windows. Nervous FSLIC employees went to court and obtained another restraining order, in which they said they feared the photos were going to be used to track them down at their homes.

Bronk loudly, and occasionally physically, protested the search of his offices, and finally a restraining order had to obtained by the FSLIC against any further interference from Ferrante or Bronk. Bronk filed an $8 million lawsuit claiming "unlawful search and seizure." It was easy to understand why Bronk was upset. In the nine months prior to the takeover, court records show, Consolidated had paid him $1.2 million for legal and consulting fees and personnel, travel, entertainment, and office expenses.

When Superior Court Judge Richard Gadbois, Jr., listened in court to FSLIC complaints of photographing, threats, and interference, he warned the attorneys representing Ferrante, Angotti, and Bronk, "If I get downwind of any serious suggestion of anything like this, I'll be all over that thing like a cheap suit, and I really mean heavy." And in the event any FSLIC employees were actually harmed in any way, the judge warned, "You think you've seen FBI agents. . . . Judge Webster[22] and I had a little talk and I'm dead serious about that."

With the place to themselves, regulators quickly discovered just how bad things were at Consolidated. The total cost to the FSLIC would exceed $100 million, and regulators amassed enough evidence to file a civil suit against Ferrante, Angotti, Bazarian, and others for $52 million, the amount of money they estimated was missing.[23] Ferrante claimed he didn't have any of the contested millions and never had. The FSLIC spent hundreds of thousands of dollars on attorneys, seeking recovery from Ferrante and 19 other defendants. Some out-of-court settlements were reached, but such settlements fell within the Bank Board's veil of secrecy and were not made public. Sources told us pennies on the dollar were the norm. Meanwhile, Ferrante sued the FSLIC and the Bank Board, charging that they, not he, had ruined Consolidated.

"These guys remind me of the kid who killed his parents and then complained that the system should be kinder to orphans," said one federal prosecutor about Ferrante and other thrift officials who complained loudly when their thrifts were seized.

The FSLIC notified Ferrante that the U.S. attorney's office and the FBI had opened an investigation in the wake of Consolidated's failure, but as of the day this book went to press, no criminal charges had been filed and the money was still listed among the "disappeared." As for the regulators' efforts to rescue Consolidated, well, it's one thing to hold out hope you can catch a horse once it's out of the stable, but it's quite another to know what to do when the horse has already been rendered into glue. Consolidated Savings Bank had been bled white and could not be saved, and on August 29, 1986, regulators closed Consolidated Savings, claiming in their civil suit that Ferrante had used the thrift as "a slush fund for himself, members of his family, and various business associates." The stock, all held by Ferrante, was rendered worthless and Consolidated's wretched ruins were merged with a healthy thrift.

In a desperate attempt to stop state-chartered thrifts from switching to federal charters after passage of Garn-St Germain, California had thrown its arms open to all comers. "If you think that federal hussy is easy, come on up and see me sometime," the sign might as well have read on the door to the California savings and loan commission. Character, experience, and intentions of an applicant played little role in the commission's decision to grant an S&L charter. California officials were concerned primarily with starting the flow of contributions back to the politicians and assessments back into the state's regulatory apparatus. Larry Taggart, the state's new savings and loan commissioner, epitomized the laissez-faire mood of the time. He believed firmly in deregulation and apparently never met a thrift applicant he didn't like.

Asked in 1989, during his testimony before the House Banking Committee, how it could be that he approved 235 thrift applications in just 400 days in office, Taggart responded that he had no way of knowing how a person would do as a banker until they had tried. "How many of the thrifts you approved later failed?" Taggart was asked. "Take your pick, Congressman," Taggart responded.

As a result California, particularly Southern California, would lead the nation in aggregate losses at FSLIC-insured thrifts. To Consolidated Savings add Beverly Hills Savings, San Marino Savings, South Bay Savings, North American Savings, Ramona Savings, Westwood Savings, Butterfield Savings, Centennial Savings . . . 42 institutions failed in California between 1980 and 1987. (The closest competition for "most failed thrifts" came from Illinois with 33, Texas with 32, Louisiana with 29, Florida with 21, Ohio with 19, and New York with 18.) And more was yet to come. When thrifts began to collapse in large numbers in the mid-1980s, federal and state officials tried to blame the failures on a depressed oil economy. But in California oil played a very minor role in the state's robust business climate, yet thrifts nevertheless failed.[24] The oil excuse, we suspected, was a slippery way of avoiding the real issue—fraud.

CHAPTER SEVEN

Back in Washington

The important role played by deposit brokers in the epidemiology of the disease spreading through the thrift industry was becoming clear to us. Someone had to make huge deposits into thrifts so high rollers would have money to wheel and deal with. Local depositors were not a good source of money. Their accounts were often small and their balances fluctuated and were undependable. Deposit brokers, on the other hand, were totally dependable. If a thrift executive needed $2 million or $20 million deposited at his institution Monday morning, deposit brokers got it there. All the thrift had to do was guarantee to pay the highest interest rate offered that day. If someone were going to take the risks associated with defrauding a thrift, they would want to make sure the thrift had enough money to make it worth their while. Deposit brokers could make that guarantee.

By January 1984 Ed Gray, after eight months as chairman of the FHLBB in Washington, had become deeply worried about brokered deposits. He felt something needed to be done to limit them, and the solution he favored was to severely limit FSLIC insurance coverage of brokered deposits and thereby discourage their placement at thrifts. Gray called his friend Bill Isaac, then chairman of the FDIC, and asked him if he shared his concerns. Isaac told him the Penn Square Bank fiasco was all the proof anyone should need.[1] Together the two men mapped out a course of action that they knew would not be popular with either the industry or the Reagan administration. They planned to implement joint regulations that would strictly limit insurance coverage on deposits acquired through deposit brokerage firms.

As Gray saw it he was just doing his job—protecting the industry from a clear and present danger. After all, he reasoned, this wasn't the first time the FHLBB had limited brokered deposits. From 1963 to 1980 the Bank Board had forbidden a thrift to get more than 5 percent of its deposits from deposit brokers. The limit was enacted when thrifts on the West Coast used brokered deposits in the early 1960s to fuel rapid growth and to fund risky investments—the very characteristics that were worrying Gray now. The FHLBB had repealed the 5 percent limit in 1980 when thrifts were having a hard time attracting deposits.[2]

Gray and Isaac cemented their alliance against brokered deposits, however, and on January 15, 1984, the two men publicly proposed regulations that limited to $100,000 the amount of insured deposits any one money broker could place at a thrift or bank and still get federal deposit insurance coverage. Two months were set aside for public comment on the proposed rule and they soon had over 165 replies (about a fourth of the replies were form letters issued by major investment houses in opposition to the regulation). Responses were running two to one against the proposal, but many small S&Ls favored the rule. They feared brokered deposits were threatening the safety and soundness of the banking system. Many said they had no difficulty raising enough deposits without resorting to deposit brokers. Steven A. Grell, president of First Bank in Pipestone, Minnesota, said, "I have had many deposit brokers contact me concerning either buying or selling certificates. I find their business totally unjustified and hazardous to a federal insurance system." But most S&L officials objected to the regulation as penalizing all institutions for the abuses of the few.

Gray said he also faced stiff opposition from Treasury Secretary Donald Regan. Regan was the administration's most adamant champion of deregulation, and Gray's stand on deposits quickly earned Gray the tag of the great "re-regulator" among thrift industry lobbyists. Gray was not turning out to be Regan's idea of a team player. Regan was chairman of the Depository Institutions Deregulation Committee (established by the 1980 Depository Institutions Deregulation and Monetary Control Act to phase out all interest rate controls). Before coming to serve in the Reagan administration, Regan had headed the New York brokerage firm of Merrill Lynch, which later would become one of the nation's largest deposit brokers. Many came to refer to Regan as the father of brokered funds.[3] Now Regan's healthy stallion was about to be gelded by Gray's proposed regulation. Gray said later, "It seemed like almost every week the DIDC [Depository Institutions Deregulation Committee] is having a meeting and taking more of the wraps off. The money brokers began multiplying like crazy, and the growth was going like crazy, but there was no capital to sustain it."

According to Ed Gray, when Regan got wind of Gray's plan to rein in deposit brokers, he told Treasury Deputy Secretary R. T. McNamar that, Republican or not, old friend of the president's or not, "Gray has got to go." But Regan couldn't personally attack Gray. Regan's connections with Merrill Lynch were all too well known, as was the fact that brokered deposits were one of his favorite subjects. Instead, Regan put McNamar to work on the Gray problem.

McNamar was the complete antithesis of Gray. He was a slick, buttoned-down dresser who wore pin-striped suits and looked more like an investment banker than a government official. Gray, the son of a tractor salesman from Texas, occasionally wore loud sports jackets and looked uncomfortable even in loose-fitting suits.

McNamar picked up the phone and called Gray. They spent seven hours on the phone that day—during which Gray said McNamar tried every argument he could think up to convince Gray he should forget his brokered-deposit regulation. For seven hours McNamar talked, and talked, and talked. And for seven hours Ed Gray, like an old farm mule, didn't budge. Gray believed McNamar was lobbying more for Don Regan than reflecting the administration's position. Regan did not respond to our requests for an interview, but Gray said he heard later that Don Regan was furious with him. The difference between the two men was a fundamental one: Gray wanted the S&L industry to specialize more closely in what they knew best, home lending; Regan wanted to make thrifts just like banks. As a deregulator, Regan talked a lot about level playing fields, where all businesses were created equal and only the strongest survived. But evidently he didn't talk to Gray at all. Gray said Regan never once returned his calls during Gray's four years in Washington.

A few nights later, on January 30, 1984, less than eight months after taking office, Ed Gray stayed late into the night typing away at a speech he would give the next day to lawyers attending a conference of the National Council of Savings Institutions (NCSI). The lawyers represented both banks and savings and loans. Gray, who had started out as a reporter for a small radio station in Fresno, California, always wrote his own speeches. He chain-smoked as he tapped away on his typewriter. He was no doubt smoking a cigarette when he wrote that brokered money was "like a spreading cancer on the federal deposit insurance system."

The next day, with dark circles under his eyes from the night's work, Gray delivered his speech to the lawyers. Standing behind a podium at the Capital Hilton, he first took a deep breath. Then he prefaced his speech by saying, "I want to make it clear that as a champion of the free enterprise system myself, I am not against anybody making a fair profit." But by this time word had leaked that Gray had been unmoved by all attempts to change his mind on brokered deposits, and the audience knew the next word out of his mouth would be *but*. Before he even got to that point a couple of the lawyers sitting in the back of the room got up and left. Gray was "off the reservation," a term Don Regan used to describe anyone in the administration who did not toe the party line.

Gray was able to deliver his speech uninterrupted by any annoying applause. After all, most NCSI lawyers made a living representing thrift executives who took a free market approach to the S&L business. They didn't like being told by Gray that the brokered deposits fueling their enterprises—some of them from men like Mario Renda, who had brokered millions of deposits into Centennial and Consolidated—were bad medicine. (At the time over $34 billion in brokered deposits were at work at FSLIC-insured institutions.) And they didn't like Gray's opinion that the money was being used for risky investment schemes. Or that such easy money *might* encourage fraud.

Industry leaders were dumbfounded at Gray's remarks. They had thought he was their guy. "These people wanted me in the job because they thought I was going to be their patsy," Gray would tell us later. He was supposed to be on their side. Now he was embarrassing them. There could be only one explanation and the word spread quickly—*Ed Gray was a buffoon.* Even some old-timers on the Bank Board staff thought he was "off the reservation." They began to refer to him around the office as "Mr. Ed," a reference to television's talking horse. And what was he talking about? The terrible condition of the FSLIC. His own staff went out on damage control, telling Washington reporters, "Ed doesn't understand that brokered deposits are not the problem." Some staffers said even worse—that he didn't understand finance and was unqualified for the job. One told us, "It's an outrage he was ever appointed." But to Ed Gray this was not a complicated matter. And he did, too, understand brokered deposits —all too well.

But getting a handle on them would not be easy. There would have to be a fight, and the next salvo came directly from Merrill Lynch, which a week later released a report to the press that was critical of Gray's regulation. Edson Mitchell III, a young, fast-talking Merrill Lynch VP, told reporters he was going to follow Ed Gray around until the ban was overturned.

If all this uproar caused Gray to doubt for one moment the wisdom of his brokered-deposit regulation, those doubts didn't last. Within days of the Merrill Lynch news conference, Gray sat in the darkened board room at Bank Board headquarters, with Bank Board members Mary Grigsby and Don Hovde, and watched the videotape of the vacant, crumbling I-30 condos built with loans from Empire Savings and Loan near Dallas. Grigsby, in her early fifties, was a Texan who'd worked in the S&L business most of her adult life. She couldn't believe her eyes. A hundred million dollars of Empire's money, just rotting away in the Texas sun. Empire had been a tiny $20 million thrift that grew almost overnight to $330 million, using brokered deposits. The Board voted immediately to fire Empire's chairman, Spencer Blain, and close Empire, the first closing that regulators admitted was caused by fraud in the thrift industry's 50-year history.[4]

When the videotape was over Gray watched it again. Over and over he watched it. Empire Savings was the embodiment of everything he had feared might be wrong with the way thrifts used brokered deposits for risky, sometimes fraud-ridden, ventures. Gray showed the tape to his entire staff, including those doubting Thomases who had back-stabbed him to the press just days earlier. He told us he even called his friend Paul Volcker, head of the Federal Reserve Board, and Representative Fernand St Germain, House Banking Committee chairman, to his office for a screening. He must have shown the tape thirty times.

Now Gray was ready to take his message directly to the industry itself. He chose the upcoming U.S. League's annual convention to make a speech on the evils of brokered deposits. Less than two years earlier delegates at this convention had gushed for Gray to be their next FHLBB chairman. He knew only too well his reception this time would be far less pleasant, but so be it. Brokered deposits were destroying the industry, and the U.S. League and its members had to wake up before the damage was irreparable.

The night before Gray was to speak, Gray said U.S. League President William O'Connell begged him to water down his brokered-deposit regulation. O'Connell, in his early sixties, a slight man with a tuft of silver hair around his ears, was a seasoned lobbyist who employed a mildly persuasive manner. His consistent refrain to Gray was that the S&L industry needed to buy time and it was Gray's job to help. The League thought that maybe the ban was "a little too tough," O'Connell told Gray. Although the League's members weren't crazy about their growing dependence on short-term brokered funds and would officially support Gray's brokered-deposit regulation, O'Connell told Gray they did like the idea of being able to use long-term brokered funds (deposits of a year or more). Could Gray maybe amend the regulation to allow for long-term brokered deposits? But the next day Gray made his speech: brokered deposits were trouble, all of them, long and short. They were an accident waiting to happen. He announced that the ban was on and would continue unchanged. He hadn't budged.

His intransigence infuriated many in the industry, especially deposit brokers and the thrift executives who were using the brokered deposits. They were tired of Ed Gray. He was becoming a broken record on the subject of brokered deposits. To make matters worse, he had begun to rattle on in public, airing even more of the industry's dirty laundry, telling people that the FSLIC might run out of money if thrifts kept failing and that thrifts would have to pay higher FSLIC insurance premiums. O'Connell and other industry leaders also became uneasy. Gray was talking too much. Much too much. He was making people nervous.

Members of the Reagan administration started to wonder just how this loose cannon had gotten on deck. And the answer, some felt, was revealed a few weeks later during hearings to confirm Ed Meese as the nation's new attorney general. Testimony quickly focused on Meese's friends and favors, particularly sweetheart loans Meese had received from Ed Gray's old thrift, Great American First Savings Bank of San Diego. In the late 1970s Great American had loaned $120,000 on Meese's home in California. Then when Meese moved to Washington to be the White House counselor upon Ronald Reagan's assumption of the presidency in 1981, Meese bought a home in Virginia with the help of a $132,000 Great American loan on his California home. Combined payments on both homes (totaling $51,000 a year) were more than Meese could handle on his $69,800-a-year salary, and for 15 months he made no payments to Great American on the California home. Nevertheless, Great American did not foreclose. In fact, the thrift loaned Meese another $21,000 as a fourth trust deed on the house, for a total of $273,000 in loans on the California house. A Great American spokesman said the home had been appraised for $335,000. However, that appraisal was never borne out by the marketplace. The house finally sold in 1982 for $307,500.

Nearly everyone involved in the Meese home loans got a job with the administration. Gordon Luce, Great American Savings president, was appointed a delegate to the United Nations. In May 1983 Ed Gray landed the job of Federal Home Loan Bank Board chairman. Thomas Barrack, a wealthy Southern California developer, helped to locate a buyer for Meese's California house and was later appointed to a high post at the Interior Department. John McKean, who arranged two Meese loans totaling $60,000, was appointed to the U.S. Postal Service Board of Governors. Meese said none of these appointments had anything to do with the favors Great American Savings had done for him on his house.

However close Gray might have been to the top men in the Reagan White House, his role in the flap over brokered deposits had turned one of the most powerful men in the administration, Donald Regan, into an enemy. The Washington meat grinder went to work on Gray. Stories about Gray's lack of intelligence circulated from office to office like bad jokes.

The fact that Gray was an absentminded professor only added fuel to the rumor mill. White House Spokesman Larry Speakes had two favorite Ed Gray stories. In one he told about Gray's bad habit of losing cars. Gray would sign a car out of the motor pool, drive it to the airport, and then forget about it. When he returned from his trip he'd call a cab. Suddenly the motor pool noticed they had a half dozen cars missing, and a check of the airport parking lot turned them up right where Ed had left them.

In another case, so the story went, Gray was visiting the California legislature with a lot on his mind, as usual, and as he left he failed to notice a handwritten note on the elevator door: "Do Not Go to the Basement." Oblivious, Gray got on the elevator and pushed the button for the basement . . . which was flooded. Those waiting for the elevator above could hear Gray yelling for help as the elevator doors opened and the water rushed in on him.

And the tales went on and on. Gray heard about the stories, the Mr. Ed jokes, Don Regan's complaints to the president that Gray was not qualified for the job, and worse. But Gray was sure he was right. Everywhere he looked, it seemed, he saw brokered deposits fueling furious growth at once-modest little thrifts. The more deposits poured into an institution, the nuttier became the deals that the thrift's executives sanctioned. Champions of brokered deposits contended that Gray was simply watching the free market at work, efficiently transferring money to areas where it was needed. Brokered deposits weren't fueling fraud, they argued, they were fueling enterprise, innovation, growth. Now was not the time, they said, to get cold feet on the road to a deregulated America.

Gray was not convinced. "I believe in Reaganomics," he said, "but this isn't what I had in mind."

CHAPTER EIGHT

Tap-dancing to Riches

Deregulation of the interest rate that thrifts could pay to attract deposits in 1980, combined with the increase in insurance coverage to $100,000 per account and the removal by the Bank Board of any limits on brokered deposits, certainly revitalized the deposit brokerage business. Between June 1981 and June 1982 brokered deposits at savings and loans increased fivefold,[1] and in the next four months they went from $15.6 billion to $26 billion. Among the businessmen profoundly affected by the new deregulation was Mario Renda, who in 1980 became a deposit broker. Until that time he had been a man searching for a way to get rich. Through the years he was always where the money was, as, for example, in the mid-1970s during OPEC's[2] heyday, when Renda had made several trips to Saudi Arabia to insert himself into the orbit of the world's most notorious deal-maker, Adnan Khashoggi.

One day in 1977 Mario Renda, then 36, walked through the gates in a concrete wall on a narrow street in barren downtown Riyadh, Saudi Arabia. He crossed a small desert yard to a low stucco bungalow where a Sudanese servant silently motioned him to enter. He stepped into a living room that resembled a Holiday Inn converted into an oriental *suk* (bazaar). Dozens of men in Western business suits or flowing caftans and kaffiyehs milled around the smoky room or sat at the several tables littered with ashtrays and ashes. Obediently, Renda found a seat and settled in for a long wait.

A native New Yorker, Renda had arrived in Riyadh with a plan in his pocket to build precast concrete homes in Jidda, Saudi Arabia. He was a partner in IPAD (International Planners and Developers) Construction Consortium and wanted to build an empire on OPEC's purse strings. At that time Khashoggi was at the apex of his power.[3] The world's businessmen were rushing to his home in Riyadh, a jumble of added-on bungalows where Khashoggi held court 24 hours a day when he was in town[4] and made multimillion-dollar commitments the way a teller makes change. A nod from Khashoggi could set a man up for life.

Renda sat among that international gathering, described later that year in *Fortune* magazine, and waited his turn to make his pitch. Patiently he worked his way through the labyrinth and into Khashoggi's realm. When it came Renda's turn for an audience, he and Khashoggi reportedly closed a $5 million joint venture to build the concrete homes in Jidda. Renda went home a happy man, fancying himself an international financier.

The deal later fell apart, as did so many of Renda's highfalutin plans, but the collapse did not derail Renda's determined march toward a Khashoggi life-style. He didn't want to run a construction company. He wanted to be a mid-dleman, a broker like Khashoggi who claimed to have made $575 million in the past six years by simply doing deals. Renda coveted expensive possessions, ostentatious displays of wealth, and life on easy street.

"He wanted somewhere where he could park his Rolls-Royce, tell a few jokes, make a few phone calls, and go home and say he had a hard day at the office," Renda's IPAD partner Sy Miller said later. "He just came here to make phone calls." In the winter Renda reportedly kept a chauffeur-driven limousine running all day in front of the office to keep the car warm. He told Miller he wished he could put a big sign on one of his Rolls-Royces announcing the car cost $120,000 and then drive around New York City. "He said he wanted the world to know what it takes to own one of these and that he had it," said Miller.

In 1980 Renda would become the ultimate "middleman" when he created First United Fund and became a deposit broker. Being a deposit broker would be his ticket to that good life. It would also earn him the reputation as the Typhoid Mary of the savings and loan business.

Raised in the Queens section of New York, Renda had always had an entrepreneurial bent. He dropped out of Queens College, where he was majoring in music, to open his own tap-dance school on Long Island. By 1963 he owned and operated a music summer camp in the Berkshire Mountains in the northwest corner of Massachusetts. It seemed an idyllic life, but it was the slow lane as far as Renda was concerned. Bright, complex, charming, and lazy, Renda wanted more out of life. Suddenly, in 1975, he announced he was closing his camp and moving on to bigger and much better things. He told the owner of the camp next door that he had discovered a way to make real money. Within six months Renda went from tap-dance teacher to international financier. In 1976 he became partners with Sy Miller at International Planners and Developers (IPAD), a Panamanian-chartered company that Renda said provided "international financing on major private and governmental construction projects throughout the world."

"He was a sweetheart of a guy," Miller said. Renda would have the office staff "rolling on the floor laughing" at his stories. He seemed to be Mr. Wholesome, very straight, never told dirty jokes. He was a director on the executive committee of the Boy Scouts of America. But he wasn't much of a businessman.

In 1977 he closed the deal for IPAD with Khashoggi at Riyadh. Miller wasn't impressed. "Khashoggi was a big bullshit broker. He was a $3 bill." Later, Miller commented, "They ate a lot of rice and lamb, but Khashoggi, like Renda, sold blue skies." The deal never materialized, nor did any of the other big-shot deals Renda supposedly negotiated on his overseas trips for IPAD. Renda loved to hobnob with the rich and famous and that's apparently what he did on IPAD's expense account. Miller later said, "I would be a wealthy man today if we had nailed down some of the things we had going at the time." Instead, in July 1977, soon after Renda's trip to Riyadh, Renda left IPAD.

But IPAD had not been a total loss for Renda. He had made valuable contacts in the Arab world while traveling in Khashoggi's circles. Khashoggi also represented for Renda the kind of life he wanted for himself. He wanted to be a big shot, at the center of all the action, making deals with the wave of the hand, making or breaking the lives of others. Khashoggi, *Fortune* magazine reported in 1977, viewed himself as a J. P. Morgan or John D. Rockefeller. That probably sounded all right to Renda too.

After leaving IPAD, Renda spent a short time as a treasurer of an Arab bank (Arab International Bank), an offshore banking operation used to handle millions in Arab petro-dollars. At Arab International Bank he first learned the possibilities inherent in certificates of deposit (CDs)—information that would soon come in very handy.

Renda didn't stay long at Arab International Bank. In 1978, eager to strike out on his own, he formed Arabras, Inc., a one-man firm in New York City. The name of the new firm suggested Renda planned to continue to capitalize on his association with cash-rich Arab friends. The company's SEC filing said it would be doing business in the twin worlds of international finance and trade. But in 1980, when the U.S. Congress deregulated interest rates on savings deposits, Renda saw possibilities that transcended even the wealth of the Arabian oil sheiks. The new legislation was a boon to investors, who could then get a high return that was risk free (because the deposits were insured by the FSLIC). No doubt remembering what he had learned at Arab International Bank, where the bank's deposit brokers moved petro-dollar CDs around the world in search of the best daily interest rates, Renda grasped the full implications of interest rate deregulation. He quickly changed Arabras, Inc., to First United Fund and became a deposit broker. Before his arrest in 1987 he would broker $6 billion (buy $6 billion in CDs) for 6,500 investors into 3,500 financial institutions.

Renda started First United Fund in January 1980 with only $146,000 and two employees. (Forty-eight months later it would boast assets of $227 million, a brokerage business of $5 *billion*, an annual income of $5 million, and 100 employees.) To get First United Fund off the ground, he needed a steady flow of deposit money, lots of it. Renda's break came one day when he went to a local computer store to look for a computer for his new office. He later testified that while he waited for the salesman, another customer, Martin Schwimmer, struck up a conversation. Renda soon learned that Schwimmer managed pension funds for two New York unions, Local 810 of the International Brotherhood of Teamsters, Chauffeurs, Warehousemen and Helpers of America and Local 38 of the Sheetmetal Workers International Association. The two men retired to a nearby McDonald's for coffee, and that was the start of a beautiful friendship. Before Ronald McDonald could pour them a second cup, the deal was struck. Renda hired his *very new* friend, Schwimmer, to be financial advisor to his First United Fund, promising him $50,000 a year according to Schwimmer. (Later Schwimmer would report he made $400,000 in his first year with First United Fund and at least $1 million a year for the next three years.) Thereafter the advice Schwimmer gave to the union pension-fund bosses was to let First United Fund invest their money in certificates of deposit. In the following months Renda's network of banks and thrifts grew as he aggressively placed deposits for his new "clients."

Teamsters Local 810 had 7,000 members, who were employed as wireworkers and factory workers in Manhattan. Federal authorities later charged that its bosses agreed to throw their brokerage business Renda's way in return for kickbacks. The Sheetmetal Workers Local 38 had 650 members, employed as sheet-metal workers in New York and Connecticut. Their bosses didn't even know Schwimmer was putting the local's money at First United Fund. All they knew was that they had a financial advisor and he was investing their money somewhere. Between December 1981 and December 1984 the two locals invested about $100 million through First United Fund.

Renda had found a nice niche in the newly deregulated world of federally insured certificates of deposit. Using other people's money, he could get a percent of the action just by opening what amounted to savings accounts for them and collecting his commission from savings and loan officers, who were grateful for the deposits. Why would anyone work for a living when he could be a broker? But Renda and Schwimmer had an idea for a way to make an even larger profit from this arrangement. They told the 16 savings and loans and two banks that received this pension money to deposit their fees ($16 million over three years) in bank accounts that Renda and Schwimmer then kept secret from the IRS. (Though they didn't have to share with the IRS, Renda later admitted that he and Schwimmer did kick back a portion of their take to Teamster officials.)

With millions of dollars at his disposal, Renda began to act like a sheik.

Built like a fireplug, he had a platform installed in his office to elevate his desk so guests had to look up at him: "Power Desking." His office was described by one source as "a monument to bad taste," garish and ostentatious, with red velour wallpaper. He moved his family into a 30-room Garden City mansion surrounded by a couple of acres and a wall to guarantee privacy, and about this time he embraced yet another scheme for milking his brokerage business. His new idea involved a cast of "subcontractors" in Kansas City and Hawaii, and to understand the heist we first had to get to know them.

In Kansas City, back in 1980, little Indian Springs State Bank had been struggling to break out of its small shopping-center location, squeezed between Wig City and Athlete's Foot shoe store. The board of directors of Indian Springs was unhappy with the bank's lackluster performance, so they hired William Everett Lemaster, 56, away from a rural bank in Lexington, Missouri, because he had "impeccable credentials," a former chairman of Indian Springs bank told an *American Banker* reporter. One of Lemaster's first moves was to hire former local attorney Anthony Russo (whose credentials were anything but impeccable), who reportedly told Lemaster he could drum up all kinds of new business for the bank.

The two men were very different: Lemaster was tall, thin, and distinguished and reminded associates of an ambassador; Russo was ten years younger, short, fat, and talkative, and he wore an ostentatious display of jewelry. Russo was plugged into centers of power in Kansas City from his years as a prominent criminal attorney there, and Lemaster may have wanted to use those contacts to invigorate Indian Springs bank. The kind of contacts Russo had, however, were not necessarily the best medicine for a small financial institution. According to an official of the Kansas City Crime Commission, Russo had defended organized crime figures in Kansas City, in particular the Nick Civella crime family. Russo himself had served 16 months in Fort Leavenworth federal penitentiary in 1976–77 for bribery and interstate promotion of prostitution and had voluntarily relinquished his license to practice law rather than chance disbarment. Nevertheless, Lemaster hired him in 1981 to be vice president of Indian Springs bank.

Bank records showed that Lemaster's plan to make Russo a bank officer was met with dismay by bank regulators in Kansas City, who knew about Russo's reputation and his 16 months in prison. The Kansas City regulators passed the application along to Washington with a strong recommendation to deny approval. The warning was ignored by Washington and on August 19, 1981, the FDIC's board of review authorized Russo to be an Indian Springs officer but restricted his activities to "new business development." Russo's job at Indian Springs was to locate new depositors from among his wide-ranging business and personal contacts, and he had plenty to offer in that capacity. A former Indian Springs board member later told a reporter that Russo was well suited to his new job:

"He could walk up to someone and say that they were to move their account to Indian Springs State Bank, and people would do it with no questions asked."

At about the same time that he hired Russo, Lemaster also appointed Iranian-American businessman Farhad Azima, 39, to be a bank director. The three men had reportedly met when Lemaster was an "advisory director" and Russo was a "financial consultant" for a mysterious airline, Global International Airways, owned by Azima and headquartered in Kansas City. In 1978 Azima had founded Global International Airways to ship cattle to Iran, he told a Kansas City *Star* reporter, but when the Shah of Iran was ousted in 1979, Azima had to adjust his business plan. With money borrowed from an Arabian international bank, Global International quickly became one of the nation's largest charter airlines, with 900 employees worldwide and 20 planes, including seventeen 707s, two 727s, and one 747, the *Star* reported. But to this day it is not exactly clear what Global International really did, and Azima refused our requests for an interview.

Global International Airways first came to the public's attention in 1979 when it had an airplane stranded for three days on an airfield in Tunis, Algeria. The pilot had been paid $93,000 in advance to make the flight, but when his payment arrived in $100 bills in a suitcase, he became suspicious. And when cargo was loaded on his plane at the Tunisian airport, he demanded to see the relief supplies he was supposed to be flying from Lebanon to Nicaraguan refugees in Costa Rica.

Let me see the "lettuce," he insisted.

The "lettuce" turned out to be twin-barreled 57-millimeter guns with several dozen cases of ammunition labeled in Chinese. Later the Tunisian government said the Palestine Liberation Organization had been trying to send arms to the Sandinistas. A Global crewman later told the *Star* of a standing joke among the crew:

"They [airport personnel] would ask us what our cargo was and we'd tell them cabbages and cabbage launchers."

Apparently to discourage nosy airport personnel, former pilots said subsequent shipments stopped masquerading as cabbages. The munitions boxes "had Red Cross stickers all over the sides," one of Global's former pilots said.

Global International developed a reputation among insiders as one of the CIA's secret charter airlines. Former Air America pilots[5] showed up on its pilot roster. It flew arms shipments to Ecuador, Peru, Nairobi, Thailand, Haiti, and Pakistan. Azima later said the flights had been cleared by the U.S. State Department. Asked about the CIA, Azima told the *Star*, "No comment."[6]

When Lemaster appointed Russo and Azima to positions at Indian Springs bank in 1981, Global International Airways was at the height of its activities out of the Kansas City airport. Whether Azima got Indian Springs State Bank *directly* involved in covert activity, we could never determine. However, the following year Russo received a $25,000 check from Global Airlines, and later when he was questioned about the check in court (Russo was on trial for tax fraud. He was acquitted), he gave the following explanation:

> [Global International] was hired by the United States government to fly the president of Liberia, which was a new government, and its cabinet around the world on a goodwill tour. Liberia is a little country in Africa that I studied about, as a result, and learned a little bit about. After the War against [sic] the States, Lincoln, our president, sent some slaves to Liberia to live. And they lived on the, I believe, the west coast of Africa. Yes, the west coast of Africa. And formed this little country called Liberia.

> The United States has supported that country over the years. And about in 1981 they had a coup. Sergeant [Samuel] Doe, who was a sergeant in the Liberian Army, overthrew the government. The government was backed by the, our CIA and our government. And when the revolution or coup occurred, the United States then wanted to become friendly with the new government, wanted to continue to have ties between the United States and Liberia [not Libya, Liberia] and wanted us to continue our relationship with them. So they hired Farhad's airline, Global, to take Sergeant Doe, his entire cabinet, around the world on a goodwill tour.

> Farhad asked me if I would go as the "host" to the president and the cabinet, to escort them from country to country. It was at that time that, of course, I was an officer of the bank and I had to check with Mr. Lemaster, who was the president, and he covered for me and I took that trip around the world and we went all around the world with the president and his cabinet, and the president and I became friends and I would introduce them and kind of act like an ambassador. . . . The arrangement with Mr. Lemaster at the time was that any fee I would recover I would split with him because he covered for me at the bank.

Azima also testified during Russo's tax fraud trial, and the scheduling of his appearance had to be moved up one day because, he told the court, he had a luncheon meeting in Washington, D.C., the next day. A frustrated member of the prosecution team later told us that she believed Russo was acquitted of the tax fraud charges partly because of the aura of respectability the references to the CIA gave him.

Indian Springs State Bank treated Azima well. Examining bank records, we discovered his personal account at the bank was frequently overdrawn even as bank examiners demanded—on at least three occasions—that his loans be paid down. Each time examiners returned they found the loans still on the books and still in arrears. In 1983 Azima owed Indian Springs State Bank $800,000. At least $600,000 of the money went to Global International and a related company, even though Indian Springs State Bank's loans-to-one-borrower limit then was $348,881. Collateral for one of Azima's loans was his DeLorean.[7]

Azima also had other connections at Indian Springs State Bank. President Lemaster claimed in bank examination reports that Azima had sponsored the Dunes Hotel and Casino in Las Vegas for an unsecured loan of about $200,000 in 1982. The loan was guaranteed by Dunes owner Morris Shenker. Shenker was a millionaire St. Louis defense attorney who in the early 1980s was chairman and controlling stockholder of the Dunes Hotel and Casino in Las Vegas.[8] Shenker had been Teamster boss Jimmy Hoffa's attorney and confidant for over ten years, until Hoffa disappeared in 1975. Through him Shenker had access to the Teamster Union's $1.5 billion Central States, Southeast, and Southwest Areas pension fund.[9] Bank records revealed that a Shenker business associate from Las Vegas, Jay Fihn, also had a loan at Indian Springs. Russo testified he and Fihn teamed up to broker fuel to Azima's Global Airways, which, according to Russo, had a contract with some Las Vegas hotel-casinos to fly junkets (ferrying tourists to Las Vegas). Kansas bank regulators complained about the Dunes Casino loan, saying Shenker was not a creditworthy borrower and the casino was too far away from Kansas City. Regardless of demands by regulators that the loan be removed from the bank's books, it never was.[10]

Federal organized crime investigators said Shenker was an associate of the Nick Civella mob family in Kansas City.[11] Regulators found the Civella family at Indian Springs bank too. They were part of that "new business" they said Tony Russo brought to the bank. Members of the Civella family got $400,000 in loans from Indian Springs, bank records show, including one for an Italian restaurant. Their accounts were "habitually overdrawn," a bank examiner complained in one examination report. At the end of 1982 regulators alleged that bank officers kept a loan to a Civella current by rolling it over (renewing it) and increasing the amount of the loan at each renewal to cover the interest costs the loan had accrued since the last renewal.

At the same time that Indian Springs was making sweetheart loans to the Civella family, some of the Civellas were embroiled in a messy criminal prosecution in Kansas City. Federal organized crime prosecutors in 1981 had indicted brothers Nick and Carl Civella and others for skimming $280,000 off the gaming tables of the Tropicana Casino in Las Vegas. Nick Civella died of cancer before the trial ended in July 1983, but his brother Carl was convicted. Carl Caruso, convicted along with the Civellas, was also on the loan list at Indian Springs. Caruso operated junkets for the Las Vegas Dunes out of several Midwestern towns, including Kansas City. In court it was revealed that he was the bagman for the skimming operation, transporting the skim from the casino to Chicago and Kansas City for distribution to the mob families there.

• • •

In this setting Mario Renda was about to embark upon a new scam. He had recently met Franklin Winkler, the son of an old friend, and they had agreed to go into business together.

Franklin Winkler was an international wheeler-dealer. He and his dad, V. Leslie Winkler, were cosmopolitan con men. They were Hungarian Gypsies, smooth operators, and both spoke a number of languages. Franklin, who was in his forties, had been born in Istanbul and had lived all over the world, wherever his father Leslie's schemes took them. Franklin had most recently lived in Cuba, Italy, Australia, Kansas City, and Southern California and had lately settled temporarily in Hawaii. Leslie lived in Palm Springs. Franklin and his father were fat and affable. Franklin weighed over 300 pounds, but he was a charmer whom women found enchanting. Described by federal prosecutors as "a criminal financial genius," Franklin had reportedly already been convicted of felony frauds in both Italy and France but had never spent a day in jail. An attorney who had cross-examined him said he had a remarkable facility for slipping into a variety of nearly perfect foreign accents.

"He'd be talking to me about something during court recesses and all of a sudden he'd be speaking with a perfect French accent, or Italian, or Middle-European accent. He'd just throw it in for effect. The guy was really smooth."

Franklin Winkler had been losing money on real estate investments in Hawaii, and regulators said he agreed to cooperate with Renda in a scheme that would benefit them both. Renda would broker deposits into savings and loans or banks if the institutions agreed to make loans to Hawaiian real estate partnerships fronting for Winkler and Renda. "Linked financing," where deposits were promised to a bank or thrift in return for loans, was not always illegal but regulators didn't like the practice because they feared the promise of huge deposits would induce financial institutions to make risky loans that they would not otherwise have made. But the linked financing Renda had in mind *was* illegal because it was an end run around Indian Springs State Bank's loans-to-one-borrower limits, which at the time were between $250,000 to $350,000.¹²

The timing of this new friendship between Renda and Winkler was perfect because within weeks Anthony Russo went to Hawaii on vacation. Before he left he contacted an old friend who told Russo to look up a Franklin Winkler in Hawaii, which Russo did. The two men liked each other, and Winkler made Russo a business proposal. Authorities said Winkler suggested that under "the right circumstances" he and his friend Mario Renda could get Indian Springs bank all the deposits and all the loan business it could handle. Russo liked the sound of the offer.

A few months later, early in 1982, Russo traveled to Las Vegas, where he met again with Franklin Winkler. Accompanying Winkler this time was Sam

Daily, a retired Air Force colonel, then a Honolulu realtor. Daily was a Louisiana redneck, a short, fat man who looked like a TV huckster. He had black, greasy, plastered-down hair, a sailor's tongue, and a terrible temper.

Indian Springs State Bank Vice President Anthony Russo, con man and swindler Franklin Winkler, and Hawaii realtor Sam Daily met in a suite provided as a favor to Russo by Dunes owner Morris Shenker. Regulators charged that under the plan the men formulated at the Dunes, Renda would broker deposits into Indian Springs State Bank—"courtesy deposits" they were euphemistically termed. In return the bank would make loans to straw borrowers[13] who would be fronting for Renda, Winkler, and Daily.

The details of the plan would work like this: Renda would put the word out through First United Fund that he could place deposit money with banks and thrifts at rates a full percentage point or more above the going rate at the time.[14] Renda knew full well that the prospect of such a high interest rate would attract managers of credit unions and pension funds who were constantly on the prowl for the best rate for the money they managed. (Renda and his brokers mockingly referred to these credit managers as "rate junkies.")

All a bank or thrift had to do to get these deposits was agree to make a few loans to Renda's Hawaii "investors." Once the institution agreed to make the loans, Renda would send the deposits to the thrift or bank and, almost the same day, Winkler and Daily would send in their straw borrowers[15] to get the agreed-upon loans.[16] These individual borrowers (lined up by Winkler and Daily) would get a fee of between 2.5 percent and 6 percent of the loans obtained in their names.[17] When the loans were funded the borrowers would turn the money over to Winkler and Daily, who would tell the straw borrowers they could just forget about having to pay back the loan. Winkler and Daily would take care of that, they said. By sending in many straw borrowers, Winkler, Daily, and Renda disguised the fact that all the loan money was going to them. And when the loans went into default, the straw borrowers' names would be on the foreclosure papers and lawsuits, not their names.

The key to the whole arrangement was Renda's deposits. They were the bait that enticed bank officials to play along with the scheme. Without them little of the looting over the next five years would have been possible.

Russo later testified that he introduced Franklin Winkler to Indian Springs State Bank President Bill Lemaster. Winkler told Lemaster that First United Fund would broker into Indian Springs all the deposits he wanted in return for nothing more than some loans. To Lemaster this must have looked like a good way to pick up both deposits and loan business in one neat package, without having to pay the deposit broker a commission, and he agreed to the arrangement. In June 1982 Winkler, Daily, and Renda began shopping for straw borrowers.

By July 19, 1982, First United Fund had placed the first batch of brokered funds at Indian Springs State Bank, and the first crew of straw borrowers were in the starting gate. Winkler outlined the operation in one last letter to Renda that concluded:

"I suggest that we proceed with this first pilot transaction and then we should get together in order to formalize a proper modus procedendi for all future transactions of this type." In other words, if the scam worked at Indian Springs State Bank, they would expand their operation to other financial institutions.

Indian Springs State Bank made the loans to the straw borrowers as planned. The scheme worked perfectly. And on August 29 Franklin Winkler called a meeting with his dad, Leslie, and Renda at Southern California's luxurious La Costa resort to review the progress of their plan.[18] After the La Costa sit-down, Franklin's father, Leslie Winkler, sent Renda and Franklin a memo grandly entitled "Memorandum Premenoira." In the memo Leslie stated:

. . . Both Franklin and Mario have agreed to carry out a number of trial transactions under the contemplated terms and procedures. One transaction has already been concluded via K.C. Bank[19] and the intention is to repeat a few similar deposits which will demonstrate the feasibility of the operation of the program. (Leslie's interest in the project was not platonic. Because he had introduced Franklin and Renda, he was entitled to a "finder's" fee on each deal that went down.)

In the month following the meeting at La Costa, the three men formed at least eight companies and partnerships to conceal the paper trail left behind by their activities. Renda, Franklin Winkler, and Daily began visiting banks and savings and loans in areas they had targeted for high-growth potential—Kansas City, Southern California, Honolulu, Texas, Denver, Phoenix, Seattle, New York, and New Jersey—and pitched their linked financing schemes. The code name used for these transactions at First United was, appropriately, *special deals*.

Then Renda added a new wrinkle. He ran ads to let people know that for a fee he could supply deposits for anyone who needed a loan and wanted to get his own linked-financing deal going. Renda placed ads in major newspapers, including *The Wall Street Journal*, the Los Angeles *Times*, and the New York *Times*, which read:

MONEY FOR RENT
Borrowing obstacles neutralized
by having us deposit funds with
your local bank: New turnstyle
approach to financing. Write to:
FUND, Suite 311, 1001 Franklin Ave., Garden City, NY 11530

After these ads came out Renda was besieged by brokers or borrowers around the country who agreed to compensate Renda (in a variety of ways) if he would steer deposits to a thrift or bank that had already agreed to make them a loan upon receipt of the deposits. So, in addition to the "special deals" Renda had going with Franklin Winkler and others, he began supplying funds for other people's special deals as well. Later he would testify in court that he placed deposits for "hundreds" of special deals arranged by others.

These were perfect scams. Renda used other people's (federally insured) money to influence bank and thrift officials to make loans to the phony borrowers—the officials could even use the actual cash from Renda's deposits to make the loans. All Renda had to do was break the money into $100,000 chunks so it would be insured by the FSLIC. Even if Renda's scam eventually caused the bank to collapse (because the loans were not repaid), Renda had no worries—his deposits were insured and his straw borrowers already had the loans. Renda saw the possibility of arranging linked-financing scams at thrifts all across the nation. He could borrow hundreds of millions of dollars before anyone caught on, and then he could move the scheme on to the next institution. He knew over 3,000 thrifts and thousands more small banks that might take the bait. Even in Ed Gray's darkest nightmares over the potential evils of brokered deposits, he had never imagined abuses worse than the ones Mario Renda had in mind.

CHAPTER NINE

Buying Deposits

When regulators removed most restrictions on brokered deposits, beginning in 1980, officers at many financial institutions got in line to use the services of the new deposit brokers who set up shop around the country. Among the institutions whose officers saw the advantage of using brokered deposits was Penn Square Bank, a small shopping-center bank in Oklahoma City, and soon the officers on the bank's money desk knocked on Mario Renda's new door at First United Fund. The bank's officers used the brokered deposits from First United Fund (and from other deposit brokers) to finance risky lending in the oil business, which was booming.[1] In July 1982, Penn Square Bank collapsed, the sixth largest commercial bank failure in U.S. banking history.[2]

Thus it was that on September 30, 1982, at the very moment Winkler's and Renda's operation at Indian Springs State Bank was coming to life, Renda got some very unwelcome attention. Representative Fernand St Germain (D-R.I.), chairman of the House Banking Committee, conducted hearings into the Penn Square Bank failure and wanted to know, among other things, what role deposit brokers had played in the Penn Square disaster.[3] He summoned Renda and others to testify before the committee. The hearings put the spotlight on deposit brokers like First United Fund and threatened to result in a curtailment of their activities. By this time, however, the Reagan administration had put its full political muscle behind deregulation, and Treasury Secretary Donald Regan (a.k.a. "the father of brokered deposits") had the president's ear. Washington was marching in unison on a deregulation course that even the Penn Square catastrophe couldn't head off, and deposit brokers survived their congressional grilling unscathed.

Emboldened by this close encounter, Renda saw no need at all to stop his operation at Indian Springs bank. It went off like clockwork:

First United Fund proceeded to place $6 million in deposits at Indian Springs State Bank;

Daily's straw borrowers received $3.7 million in loans;

The straw borrowers were paid their fee and they turned the loan proceeds over to Daily, Winkler, and Renda.

Renda became bullish on the future. He moved First United Fund from its cramped offices on Old Country Road in Garden City, out in suburban Long Island, to elaborate suites on Franklin Avenue. He maintained a bull pen of brokers who spent their days on the phones placing deposits at institutions around the country. In late 1982 he employed 15 brokers (later to swell to 40) in First United's bull pen, and many of them were pulling down six-figure commissions.

But Renda's methods and those of a handful of other deposit brokers attracted still more unwelcome publicity. After a few large credit unions complained that their accounts had been "bilked" by such brokers, NBC-TV produced a news documentary on the problem and they interviewed Renda for the piece. Renda relished the exposure. After standing up to congressional scrutiny, he had become cocky. Following the airing of the NBC program he would end his morning peptalk to his staff by standing up and saying, "Okay, boys, get out there and bilk 'em."

A frequent visitor to Renda's new offices was Salvatore Piga, whom organized crime investigators identified to us as a Lucchese (Mafia) family associate. An assistant U.S. attorney described him as a "ruthless leg breaker," and his rap sheet showed a string of arrests for grand larceny, assault, robbery, burglary, extortion, and criminal possession of stolen property. Mario, on the other hand, called Piga a "teddy bear." Piga was in his early fifties, stocky, and in top physical shape, and he carried what the bull-pen brokers called a "cannon" under his coat. Sal, with his gun bulging, added more than just a touch of color around First United Fund.

As 1983 began the future was looking good at First United Fund. Mario and his brokers had placed $2.5 billion in 1982 and expected business to increase dramatically in 1983. Renda bragged widely that he could put $50 million into any institution on a day's notice. One day Winkler visited a banker and put forward the familiar linked-financing scheme. The banker was skeptical that Renda could actually produce the deposits. Winkler picked up the phone and called New York.

"Mario," he said, "deposit $1 million in this bank tomorrow morning." To the banker's amazement, it was done. What more needed to be said?

Franklin, Leslie, and Mario frequently visited each other in Hawaii and New York. Renda was becoming an important man in Hawaii, thanks to the straw borrowers' money, much of which was going into Hawaiian real estate. When we looked at Renda's Hawaiian activities, we found Consolidated Savings owner Robert Ferrante.[4] Renda and Ferrante were involved together in a company called Seaside Ventures, which was converting an old hotel into offices. Attorneys for the FSLIC said Consolidated Savings made Seaside Ventures a $2.2 million loan. Renda later testified that he wired the money straight to his personal Swiss bank account. Walter Mitchell, the Redondo Beach city councilman who went to prison after being accused of taking a bribe from Ferrante, got a job with Seaside Ventures in Hawaii after he got out of prison. (Part of his conviction was later overturned.)

When we found out that Renda and Ferrante were doing more than deposit business together, we looked deeper into their relationship. We discovered they had been associates for several years, and we obtained documents that showed they were also involved together in at least two other major projects, the Kailua Shopping Center in Hawaii and the Palace Hotel in Puerto Rico. (The casino deal was never completed and the project ended in bankruptcy.) An FSLIC attorney later told us that Renda and Ferrante vacationed together in the Caribbean in 1986, renting First United Fund's 100-foot yacht *Surrenda* for the occasion. Ferrante, invoices show, paid the boating tab with a $15,000 Consolidated check. Poking around these leads, we found out that the FBI in Los Angeles had a keen interest in the Ferrante-Renda relationship. Maybe that was why the folks at Consolidated were unusually concerned that Renda's association with Ferrante not become general knowledge. On at least one occasion, S&L records showed, Ottavio Angotti chastised a secretary who had written "copies to Mario Renda" on the bottom of a memo. Angotti X'ed out Renda's name and told her she was not to do that again.

Renda was building an empire in Hawaii, but his well-oiled machine suddenly developed a squeak in Kansas City. In February 1983, FDIC examiners, who had given the Indian Springs State Bank books a thorough going-over, said they weren't fooled by Winkler's and Daily's straw borrowers and declared that the numerous Hawaii loans, which totaled $3.7 million, were in reality one big loan. Examiners still weren't clear about what was going on there, but they were sure all these loans were part of one big venture of some sort. Since loans-to-one-borrower limits at Indian Springs State Bank were then about $350,000, examiners had identified what one former Indian Springs official termed "a monumental loan-limit violation." Regulators told Lemaster that these Hawaii borrowers had to repay the loans.

Lemaster gave Daily the bad news: Regulators had ordered that the Hawaii loans be repaid and no further loans made. The original plan to roll the loans over (renew them) through Indian Springs bank when they came due was now out of the question. But Winkler and Daily told Lemaster there was no way they could repay the loans. The money was long gone. It was then that Lemaster began to see he was caught in a trap. Renda had anesthetized his sound banking instincts with First United Fund's brokered deposits, which Lemaster had hoped to use to build Indian Springs State Bank into one of the leading banks in the state. But now his reputation for integrity, cultivated through years of hard work and dedication, was in real jeopardy. Acquaintances said it was at this point that Lemaster "began to go over to the dark side." Apparently he saw he had little to lose. The metamorphosis was startling to those who had known him for years. He lost his dignified ambassadorial air and replaced it with glitz, adopting Russo's more flashy image.

But Lemaster's problems in no way dampened Anthony Russo's enthusiasm for Renda's linked-financing scheme. Regulators learned that Russo had been holding seminars around town to teach other bank and thrift officials how they, too, could attract Renda's brokered deposits and then loan the money out to Winkler's and Daily's "qualified" investors as built-in customers. Renda paid Russo a finder's fee for bringing new institutions into the fold. Russo later admitted that, thanks to his efforts, just as Winkler and Renda were wondering how they were going to replace Indian Springs State Bank as a source of money a new convert showed up to fill the gap—Coronado Savings and Loan, a neighbor in the shopping center with Indian Springs State Bank. Renda promptly brokered $4.7 million into Coronado Savings, and Coronado in turn loaned Winkler, et al, $3.3 million. Renda discovered that savings and loans were even easier targets than banks because, on the whole, their management was less sophisticated.

"Renda used to tell his troops at First United Fund that as stupid and sheeplike as bankers were, savings and loan officials were on an even lower grade of intelligence," an investigator recalled later. "Consequently, Renda began focusing a great deal of energy on linked financing with savings and loans."

By May 1983 Lemaster was under severe pressure from regulators to resolve the Hawaii loan violation. In desperation, Lemaster bypassed Winkler and Daily and wrote directly to their straw borrowers, informing them that their loans were coming due and had to be repaid in full. Lemaster's letter came like a bolt of lightning out of a clear blue sky for the straw borrowers, who then converged on their keeper, Sam Daily. They'd been told by Daily not to worry about their loans, so why was Lemaster threatening them, they wanted to know. Daily turned to Winkler for help, demanding that he tell Renda to pump more money into the operation.

Despite all this regulatory attention being given to Indian Springs State Bank, bank examiners discovered, Anthony Russo regularly attended bank loan committee meetings in which bank directors discussed the bank's most important business—in clear disregard of earlier demands made by regulators that his activities at the bank be confined to drumming up new business. He exerted significant influence over daily operations at the bank. To make things even worse, examiners discovered that some of the Civella-related loans were in default. Those were no ordinary customers and the bank was having a hard time finding a law firm brave (or foolhardy) enough to try to collect on their loans.

"Law firms wanted no part of those particular cases," one former Indian Springs State Bank official told a reporter.[5]

This wasn't the kind of "new business" the board of directors had had in mind when they let Lemaster talk them into hiring Russo, and they told Lemaster to fire him. At first Lemaster resisted, but minutes of the June 1983 meeting showed that the board complained bitterly about Russo's alleged mob customers and about the Hawaii loans, which, after all, Russo had brought to the bank. At last Lemaster relented, agreeing to have Russo out by the end of the month.

With all this turmoil in Kansas City, no one was paying any attention to Sam Daily in Hawaii. Lemaster, Winkler, and Renda had their own problems as the scheme began to unwind, and they left Daily to twist in the wind. In desperation, Daily began penning a series of angry letters to Winkler, letters filled with accusations that Winkler and Renda had misled him, cut him out of his share, and left him to face the bank and the straw borrowers alone. Daily demanded that Renda use some of the loan proceeds he'd stockpiled to pay off the straw borrowers' loans at Indian Springs State Bank. The response Daily got from his first few letters was silence. He was furious.

On the evening of June 16, 1983, Franklin Winkler was relaxing in his Honolulu home when the phone rang. He got up from his easy chair and took the call. It was Sam Daily. Almost immediately a volley of shots rang through the house as an assassin, with a clear view of Winkler through the living-room window, opened fire. Franklin was hit three times, once in the arm, leg, and hand. No one was ever charged with the attempted murder. But nine days later Renda wrote in his desk diary that Winkler had called to say he suspected Daily:

> Sam (Daily) wrote ultimatum letter signed "or else." . . . Franklin didn't want to discuss particulars on phone . . . will meet in NYC Thursday.

Winkler returned to work in his Honolulu office a week later with a cast on his wrist but otherwise fit. His employees had hoped for a longer convalescence. His office manager, Chuck Downing, wrote in his desk diary on June 23:

> F.A.W. back in office for first time since shooting, wearing a cast on his wrist. My staff worried about going into his office and getting in the way of the next bullet.

By this time Daily was completely out of money. His wild letters had convinced Winkler and Renda that he was a real threat to them. He was talking too much. Daily wrote Winkler again, accusing him and Renda of all manner of underhanded double dealing, outlining his gripes in painful detail. On July 18 Winkler, trying to quiet the volatile Daily, shot off an equally detailed letter addressing Daily's complaints one by one.

Winkler reminded Daily that in 1982 both of them had been in dire financial straits, facing foreclosure on all sides, and that it was he, Winkler, who had come up with a scheme and let Daily in on it.

"Anyway the main point I am trying to make," Winkler wrote, "is that in some form or another we were able to obtain approximately $1,400,000 in cash to both of us in 1982 which amount allowed both you and I to stay in business."

At about the same time, thousands of miles away in Kansas City, William Lemaster's son, a Missouri doctor, began to receive strange phone calls. When he picked up the phone there was only long silence on the other end until the caller finally hung up. His father's white Lincoln Continental was vandalized several times over a two-week period.

"Someone was trying to rattle his cage," Lemaster's son said.

In the early morning hours of July 22, 1983, William Lemaster left a family party to drive home. Shortly thereafter a witness saw Lemaster's Lincoln cross a narrow bridge in Lexington, then suddenly make a wide U-turn at the end of the bridge and speed back across the bridge, heading in the direction from which it had come. When the car reached the end of the bridge it shot forward, as though someone had pushed the accelerator to the floor, leapt a curb, and slammed full speed into the concrete foundation of a roadside war memorial. The car burst into flames, burning the 59-year-old banker's body beyond recognition. What was left of the body, a handful of ashes and bone fragments, was swept up and officially cremated the next morning.

The incident could not have been an accident, according to investigators, but for several reasons it also didn't seem like suicide. When Lemaster had left the family gathering at 2 a.m., he had not given his family any hint that he intended to kill himself five minutes later. He had said no long good-byes, left no notes, made no final arrangements. The man who witnessed the accident said he could not identify Lemaster, or anyone else, as the driver of the Lincoln, so people began to wonder if Lemaster had really been in the car. Or if he had, had he been dead before the accident? they wondered. Maybe he had been drugged. Investigators determined that the fire had begun in the back seat, a place that contained no flammable liquid, a place where car fires seldom start. Further, the fire was a furious one that instantly consumed the entire passenger compartment. The fierce flames left no body to autopsy and made identification of the corpse impossible.

Could it have been murder? some asked. "It's a possibility," the young Lemaster said. "I would guess there were a few who had motives."[6]

While Lemaster's problems were over, his associates were left to deal with the fallout from his linked-financing arrangement with Renda. By midsummer 1983 most of the $6 million in Hawaii loans made by Indian Springs State Bank were in deep default and the bank was crawling with FDIC regulators. Over at Coronado Savings, FSLIC auditors had just found the new loans to the Hawaii partnerships, $3.7 million in all, that were also already in default.

In Hawaii, Daily was becoming increasingly frantic . . . and noisy. On August 8 Winkler called Renda, who jotted in his desk diary, "Franklin informed me that Sam Daily stole all the office furniture and equipment [from the partnership offices in Hawaii]." The following week some of the employees in Hawaii were told not to come to work because there was no money to pay them.

On September 6 Franklin Winkler penned a four-page letter to Daily (who was, after all, right there on the Hawaiian island of Oahu with him, merely a local phone call away. But maybe, after the shooting, Winkler didn't take phone calls any longer). Franklin's letter simply said:

> I learned that you are using me as a scapegoat to blame all of the wrongdoings on me so that you can exonorate [sic] yourself of any wrongdoings, & create an image of credibility for yourself. . . . Mario is aware of all these items and his only comment was that in the event you visit regularly a psychoanalyst, neither him nor I would have sufficient money to pay for such psychoanalyst to fully complete his cure on you.

On September 14 the FSLIC slapped a cease-and-desist order on Coronado Savings, stopping the thrift from making any future loans to the Hawaii partnerships or renewing the old ones. But regardless of these troubles, Renda and Winkler were reluctant to bid farewell to their beloved scheme, and a month after Coronado was lost to them, Renda's Hawaii office hosted lavish parties for bankers and savings and loan executives attending separate conventions there. It was an opportunity to find some new pigeons, and Renda spent $12,000 on the parties and sent several New York executives with their wives to assist in the grand event. He rented limousines to bring guests to the parties from their hotels. His employees were instructed to explain, if anyone asked, that the office furniture—which had been repossessed days earlier—had been moved out to make room for the party.

But keeping up appearances did nothing but infuriate Sam Daily, who was still trying to get Renda to pay off the Indian Springs loans so the straw borrowers would leave him alone. He did not appreciate having been left to juggle a crumbling empire of overencumbered properties with crushing negative cash flows and a small army of straw borrowers who were just now realizing that they had been had. On November 20, 1983, Daily penned another of his famous letters. This time he tried to get Franklin Winkler on his side by blaming Renda for all the troubles.

Franklin.

. . . I am sick and tired of protecting someone who has destroyed me. My firm intentions are that if Mario Renda refuses to do his part in helping us resolve these problems then I am going to hold a news conference with the Kansas City Business Journal and Kansas City Star, and I am going to tell them the whole sordid affair as it concerns First United Fund and Mario Renda. I want you to make Mario Renda well aware that I believe he deals with the Mafia and with known hit men. I had his one-eared friend checked out when he arrived in Honolulu, and he was rated as one of the top hit men in the United States. (An investigator told us he heard that Renda had sent Salvatore Piga—who was rumored to have lost a chunk of an ear when it was bitten off in a fight—to Hawaii to discover who shot Winkler. History has not recorded whether or not he was successful.)

In the event Mario Renda thinks that he would like to place a hit on me, I think you should tell him that that would probably not be too wise. I have sent another letter, in my best literate terms, outlining the whole series of events that have occurred as I know them concerning his business dealings and his association with the New York hit man. Should anything happen to me or my family I have three prominent attorneys who have a copy of that letter. Those three prominent attorneys are very good friends of mine. I can assure you that they will see Mario Renda behind bars if anything happens to me. I think he knows that I have the moral responsibility, the moral fortitude, and the pure guts that are necessary to see his company destroyed by revealing to the public the manner in which he carries on his business affairs and his involvement with Indian Springs State Bank.

First United Fund's high-water year was 1983, even though the Kansas City scams were falling apart. Renda's salary in 1982 had been $150,000. In 1983 he voted himself a bonus of $300,000 and in 1984 he would vote himself a bonus of $400,000.[7] First United Fund now had offices in Garden City, New York, in Woodland Hills, California, and in the Grosvenor Center in Honolulu.

But by late 1983 Renda's empire was seriously threatened, not by federal regulators, or by the FBI, or Sam Daily, but by Richard Ringer and Bart Fraust, two reporters working for the century-old newspaper the *American Banker*. Ringer first dented Renda's armor when he set out to cover the indictment of an East Indian who used Renda's linked deposits to swindle a number of small Midwest banks out of tens of millions of dollars. The *American Banker* story swept through the financial markets and First United Fund started losing customers right and left. Renda became obsessed with the story and he filled his desk diary for weeks with increasingly frantic scribblings:

Article in American Banker appeared very negative. Many clients called also negative after article. Prudential Bach will no longer do business or finance with First United. Very Damaging.

A.G. Becker cancelled us out. No more business because of American Banker Article. Contacted FBI for help.

Rumors on the street REALLY BAD. Street filled with rumors. No chance anyone will do business with us now.

Steve called to say Saudi's might not do business with us now.

On August 16, 1983, Renda filed a $90 million lawsuit against the *American Banker* for libel.[8] (Some time later Richard Ringer was jogging after work when a green Mercedes-Benz pulled alongside. Two well-dressed white men stepped from the car, walked up to him, and proceeded to administer a thorough beating. With their work done, they slipped back into the Mercedes and drove away. Neither man said anything to Ringer, but he certainly felt the beating could have been a message from Renda.)

In January 1984 the Kansas state bank commissioner determined Indian Springs State Bank was hopelessly insolvent and closed the bank down. (In December, Anthony Russo had suddenly quit, though he remained a director of the bank's holding company. No doubt he saw what was coming and figured the regulators who took over the bank wouldn't be developing his kind of "new business.") A team of examiners and attorneys moved in and began the tedious process of verifying bookkeeping entries line by line and examining each loan word by word to determine the true financial condition of the institution. The president of the bank, William Lemaster, who presumably would have had information crucial to the FDIC's understanding of what had happened at Indian Springs State Bank, was (reminiscent of Centennial's Erv Hansen) dead.[9] Unraveling Indian Springs State Bank was going to be a mess.

CHAPTER TEN

Renda Meets the Lawyer from Kansas

In Washington, Ed Gray had been working for months on his regulation that would deny FSLIC coverage to brokered deposits. He got the support of Bill Isaac, chairman of the FDIC,[1] and then he had to convince his fellow FHLBB members of the importance of the move. He had powerful statistics to make his point: use of brokered deposits was increasing at a frightening rate, from $3 billion industry-wide at the end of 1981 to an estimated $29 billion at the end of 1983.[2]

On March 26, 1984, the FHLBB approved the regulation, to go into effect October 1.[3] The period between approval of the regulation in March and its scheduled implementation date in October would prove to be a period of bitter regulatory war. Suddenly stories began to be leaked to the Washington press that Gray was abusing his expense accounts, that he might be under FBI investigation, and that he was a dullard who took hours to make even the simplest decisions. A story circulated that Gray had arranged a conference call with the district bank presidents and kept them all waiting on the line for an hour and a half while he agonized over artwork to be used in an in-house publication. Gray said the story was a complete fabrication.

In March 1984 Representative Doug Barnard (D-Ga.)[4] conducted new congressional hearings into the brokered-deposit issue, and the debate was heated. Once again Mario Renda was called to testify. When questioned specifically about his activities, he lied, denying any involvement in linked financing or in any other activities that would contribute to destabilization of financial institutions.

Barnard had submitted written questions to the FHLBB and the FDIC, and their written responses[5] were a tough, frank indictment of brokered deposits. The regulators complained about linked financing, and they used First United Fund as their key example.[6] They also complained that they were afraid the easy money would encourage risk-taking by thrifts looking for quick profits in high-risk investments. Gray said thrift failures could cost the FSLIC $2.2 billion (out of a $6 billion to $7 billion reserve) in 1984, more than double the $1 billion loss in 1983, and he was convinced that brokered deposits were an important part of the problem.[7]

The U.S. League, alarmed by Gray's doom-and-gloom message about the FSLIC fund, complained that Gray was nothing but a Johnny-One-Note. Such talk could only serve to scare the public away from thrifts, William O'Connell, League president, warned. If Gray didn't keep quiet, he would cause runs on thrifts across the country. In Congress legislation was introduced for the U.S. League that would have effectively gutted Gray's brokered-deposit regulation. Stumping for passage of the bill was the staff director from the Senate Banking and Urban Affairs Committee, Danny Wall. (Wall would replace Gray as FHLBB chairman in 1987.)

One of Gray's most vocal critics during this lengthy battle was his old friend California S&L Commissioner Larry Taggart, who in March 1984 took the fight into Gray's territory when he traveled to Washington to tell a banking law conference that brokered funds represented 80 percent of the new money pouring into S&Ls. Cutting off that supply, he warned, could do great damage to the institutions. Any abuses related to brokered deposits were not the fault of the brokers, he claimed, but were the fault of S&L managers who used the money improperly.

The deposit brokers weren't going to let Gray put them out of business without a fight. First Atlantic Investment Corporation Securities, Inc. (FAIC) of Miami and the Securities Industry Association sued in federal district court to have Gray's brokered deposit regulation overturned. On June 20, 1984, FAIC won a sweeping victory when federal judge Gerhard Gessell ruled that the broker ban was illegal and that action for such a ban had to come from Congress, not from the Bank Board. (Later FAIC would have the dubious distinction of having brokered the second highest [second to First United Fund] number of deposits into institutions that would later fail.) Gray then suggested Congress give the FHLBB and the FDIC the authority to impose such a ban, but Congress ignored his request. Danny Wall and members of the Senate and House banking committees breathed a collective sigh of relief. Their high-flying thrift constituents who'd opposed the ban were happy, and presumably their happiness would be reflected in their campaign contributions. Gray's many enemies could finally take pleasure in seeing him publicly humiliated.

Emboldened, the news leakers[8] picked up momentum. Word spread that Gray would not survive this defeat and was on the way out. In July a story broke in the Washington *Post* that Gray was under investigation by the FBI for underreporting expenses tied to the renovation of his office. Gray was also being investigated, the *Post* said, for abusing a $1,500 Bank Board expense account that was supposed to be used for entertaining Bank Board guests. Gray and his staff had supposedly used the money for staff lunches and cab fares. Gray denied any wrongdoing, pointing out that the lunches were tuna sandwiches he had brought in so he and his people could work late. The FBI cleared Gray of these charges, but the summer of 1984 was not a good one for Gray or for his fight to save the thrift industry from itself.

Mario Renda had had a tough summer as well. Soon after the Barnard hearings the *American Banker* sent a second salvo across Renda's bow (certainly a courageous move for a publication recently sued by Renda for $90 million). It was a lengthy piece headlined "Bank Board Document Lists Money Broker 'Horror Stories'; Abuses Include Questionable Loans in Exchange for Deposits," and it named First United Fund as one of the brokers involved. All hell broke loose. And a second wave of customer defections engulfed First United Fund. Once again Renda's desk diary was peppered with apocalyptic notes:

Account exec's reporting clients are uneasy about doing business with us.

A.G. Becker said no business, cash or otherwise because of the American Banker article. We're out of commercial paper business altogether now—gave us 90 days to clear out.

In May 1984 Franklin Winkler's Bank of Honolulu accounts were seized by the IRS. Apparently Winkler had failed to report something. Then more trouble when the FHLBB began an internal investigation of linked-financing deals involving deposit brokers and Ed Gray subpoenaed Renda's records. *The New York Times* ran a piece headlined "Money Broker's Books Subpoenaed," which disclosed that the FHLBB had subpoenaed First United Fund records to "determine the role it has played in about 20 banking institutions that have failed or are regarded as being in danger of failing."

Renda had responded in advance to the *Times* reporter's written questions with the following written responses: "We are not 'involved' in bank failures. We are the brokerage house that the greatest number of banks in the U.S. uses. We have quoted rates for over 1,000 banks. If 2 percent, or 20 of those banks, fail, naturally our name stands a good chance of being mentioned in each instance." Did First United engage in linked financing? "This is absolutely untrue. Neither First United nor any of its subsidiaries have ever borrowed any money whatsoever—nor have any of its officers borrowed any money whatsoever—from any banking institution for which we have quoted rates."

Bank records would later show that Renda was lying. In fact, at that very time he had just teamed up with a Houston-based swindler to pull a linked-financing swindle on Rexford State Bank in Rexford, Kansas. The Rexford State Bank scam was a classic bust-out in which they took out $2 million in loans in about three months and left the small 82-year-old bank insolvent. Why would Renda take the risk of continuing his "special deals" after Indian Springs State Bank was closed, when he must have known regulators were starting to scour Indian Spring's books trying to find out what went wrong?

"Renda felt he had nothing to worry about," said one source close to the FDIC. "He knew that, in those days before everyone wised up, the FDIC and FSLIC would send in two separate teams of auditors when they seized a bank like Indian Springs. One team would only look at the deposit side of the operation and the other the loan side. The two teams of auditors never ever compared notes. So he thought they'd never make a direct connection between First United Fund deposits and the Hawaii loans."

Renda was still brokering an enormous amount of deposits, and personal financial statements showed that by 1984 he was a very wealthy man. He surrounded himself and First United Fund with the trappings of success, including a $1.2 million BAC-111, an 80-seat jet that had been converted to a luxury corporate floor plan.[9] Renda already had purchased a $69,000 Rolls-Royce Silver Spirit and bought a second. To keep his wife, Antoinette, happy, he invested in a little jewelry, two rings worth $306,000 (a platinum ring with a 10.5-carat pear-shaped diamond and two baquettes, and an 18-carat gold ring with a 17.35-carat emerald-cut diamond and two triangular diamonds). For his desk nothing would do but a $1,100 silver inkwell and a $1,150 silver cigar box with two matching silver liquor canisters. For balance there was the $6,050 English silver tea and coffee service. Underfoot a $26,500 Kerman rug, a $7,000 Ant Bahktiari rug, and a $6,000 Tabriz rug. He finally had the Khashoggi life-style he had coveted.

As we unfolded the Renda story we began to wonder how many banks and thrifts Renda had infected and how many had succumbed.[10] We soon found out that no one had any idea. In October 1988, from a confidential source close to the Federal Reserve Bank, we did get a partial list of institutions known to have been used by Renda. There were 160 banks and thrifts on the list, scattered from coast to coast and even in Puerto Rico, and 104 had already failed. It became clear to us that the damage Mario Renda had done and was doing to thrifts and banks would be years in the unfolding.

In early 1984 the Indian Springs State Bank and Coronado Savings and Loan receiverships continued to try to figure out who owed what to whom at the two failed institutions. The FDIC and the FSLIC in Washington hired the Kansas City law firm of Morrison, Hecker, Curtis, Kuder & Parrish to handle some of the legal work, and one of the attorneys they assigned to settle some of the bank's problem loans was Michael Manning. Manning was a principled, hardworking Kansas lawyer in his mid-thirties. With no premonition that this would be anything but a routine bank case, Manning began as usual by dividing up the bank's problem loans with other attorneys in the firm. By pure chance he ended up with most of the Hawaii loans in his stack. When he looked over what he thought were about 30 simple collection cases, he was first puzzled that a small, landlocked bank in America's heartland would have loaned so much money on Hawaii real estate projects. A bank examiner shared Manning's puzzlement: "What in the world was a fly-shit bank in the basement of a shopping center in a suburb in Kansas City, Kansas, doing making these kinds of loans?" (The bank wasn't actually in the basement, but it was partially underground.)

One night Manning stayed late at his office and spread the loan files out on a table to study them together. He immediately spotted startling similarities. He noticed, for example, that many of the borrowers said they intended to use their loan to invest in the same limited partnerships. These were the same similarities that had driven bank examiners months earlier to determine that the many separate loans to the Hawaii partnerships were really part of one big loan. But the examiners had not pursued that insight beyond the point of demanding that Lemaster clean up the loans. If they had, they might have nipped Renda's scheme in the bud, thus saving dozens of financial institutions from Indian Springs' fate. Now Manning had picked up where the bank examiners had left off. He didn't know what the unifying factor was yet, but these were *not* unrelated loans. He decided to fly immediately to Hawaii to ask these borrowers some questions.

He took 30 depositions, in about that many days, from the Franklin Winkler-Sam Daily straw borrowers in Hawaii. Getting straight answers out of them was tough at first. They believed, the borrowers said over and over, that they were not responsible for repaying the loans. Winkler and Daily were, they said. The straw borrowers had broken federal law by allowing their names to be used on fraudulent loan statements, but they claimed they were as much victims as the FDIC and FSLIC.

From those depositions emerged a fuzzy picture of only the Hawaiian end of the operation. But Franklin Winkler and Sam Daily were clearly implicated in some larger scheme. Some of the borrowers mentioned someone in New York named Mario Renda. And the borrowers had bits and pieces of information concerning similar deals in other places like Texas and Los Angeles, but how those events tied together was still unclear. What Manning did know for certain was that he had stumbled upon an enterprise that reached far beyond his stack of 30 defaulted loans.

One Hawaii borrower realized immediately that Manning's questions were leading somewhere other than to a simple resolution of some overdue loans. He dug in his heels and took the fifth amendment 52 times during Manning's deposition. Ironically, the questions he refused to answer clued Manning in to the sensitive areas. Manning also deposed Franklin Winkler. Charming and friendly as usual, Winkler nevertheless took the fifth amendment to every question Manning asked him—even his name—for three days.

Manning went home to Kansas City more convinced than ever that he was onto something important. He began to keep a daily diary of clues, often isolated notes that made little sense but "seemed" important. The case was beginning to consume him. It was on his mind all the time. What had been going on at Indian Springs State Bank? It seemed to be bigger than Franklin Winkler and Sam Daily, somehow. Other states were involved, the borrowers had said. Were other banks in danger? he wondered. How widespread was this enterprise? Manning spent his days, nights, and weekends trying to piece together the answers to the puzzle.

Finally, after weeks of struggling with his conscience, the straw borrower who had taken the fifth 52 times phoned Manning and said he wanted to talk. He then exposed Mario Renda's key role in the scheme. There was a deposit broker in New York, he said, who had made "courtesy deposits" at Indian Springs State Bank. In turn, the bank loaned money to straw borrowers who gave the money to Franklin Winkler, Daily, and Renda and companies and limited partnerships they controlled. Manning realized now that he was dealing with a sophisticated form of linked financing, structured through a maze of interlocking partnerships and companies until it became almost impossible to detect. Who knew how many other banks and thrifts might have also been victims, he thought.

Though hired by the regulators[11] to pursue civil actions against those who owed money to Indian Springs State Bank and Coronado Savings, Manning felt he now had absolute evidence of criminal bank fraud (admissions from the straw borrowers) and he convinced Kansas City FBI Agent Ed Leon of his case. Leon, and later Manning, took this evidence to an assistant U.S. attorney in Kansas City, Kansas, expecting that she would immediately open an investigation. Instead they ran head-on into the frustrating realities of white-collar crime prosecution in America. She was not interested in his case, she told Manning. It would take too long to "turn." Her office's resources were limited. The Department of Justice demanded visible results, tangible statistics—indictments and convictions, and lots of them. Bank fraud cases took years to unravel. Thanks, but no thanks. Incredulous, Manning next carried his evidence to the Organized Crime Strike Force in Kansas City, where he got the same cold shoulder.

Manning reported his findings to Christopher "Kip" Byrne, senior trial attorney for the FDIC in Washington. Byrne had supervised Manning's pursuit of the Hawaii straw borrowers and shared his concerns about the strange nature of those loans. He had also heard of Mario Renda because of the periodic squabblings in Washington about the role of deposit brokers in bank failures since the collapse of Penn Square Bank in Oklahoma in 1982. Still, no one in the Justice Department would move on Manning's information.

Then, in September 1984, Manning got a break. Six of Renda's bull-pen brokers and Renda's personal secretary decided to break with Renda and start their own deposit brokerage firm. This resulted in a messy legal battle because, before hiring them, Renda had secured a pledge that they would not go into competition with him. So when they struck out on their own, Renda sued. The seven former employees later explained that they had read the *American Banker* articles about Renda, and one of them went to Washington to try to dig up some dirt on their old boss to further their side of the case. Byrne's name had appeared in the *American Banker* stories about Renda, so the former First United broker looked him up and offered to trade information. Was Byrne interested? Absolutely. It looked like Manning finally was going to get the inside scoop on First United Fund. But on the heels of the first meeting, just when Manning and Byrne were so close to Renda they could smell him, the seven former Renda employees settled with Renda and lost interest in their deal with Manning and Byrne.

The letdown was intense. To be so close and then to have Renda slip away, it was too much. Manning was beside himself. Questions plagued him: How big was Renda's operation? How many banks were at risk? The congressional hearings, the newspaper stories, all warned of the dangers of brokered deposits. Yet here was Manning, with tangible evidence of possible wrongdoing by one of the country's biggest deposit brokers, and he was being thwarted at every turn. It was crazy. So Manning took off the gloves and played a little hard ball. He went back to the six brokers and Renda's former secretary—"The Seven Dwarfs" he now called them. He threatened, he promised, he cajoled, he pleaded, and he threatened again. Finally it worked.

Their attorneys agreed to let Manning depose them, and he and Byrne rushed to New York before the Dwarfs could back out. Over four days, from dawn to late into the night, they took testimony. And when they were finished they had collected sworn testimony alleging labor racketeering, pension fraud, wire fraud, tax fraud, mail fraud, and bank fraud involving Renda, Winkler, Daily, and others. Never in Manning's wildest imaginings had he guessed he'd walked into a criminal enterprise of such breadth, such stunning magnitude. Not one of the rebel brokers had all the details of the operation, but when combined, their testimony was devastating—and the implications for the bank and thrift industries, terrifying.

On the third day of the interrogation Manning learned from a confidential source that Sal Piga had phoned Renda to say, "The Seven Dwarfs are talking to the FDIC." Manning told us later it was unnerving, to say the least, to have Piga use Manning's own nickname for the brokers. The nickname was an in-house joke at Manning's office in Kansas. How had Piga, in New York, learned of the term? Was one of the Dwarfs a plant? Were Manning's phones or offices bugged? What else did Piga know? Later, when two FBI agents went to the home of one of the Dwarfs to ask some questions, they found themselves staring down the barrel of a shotgun. The Dwarf had feared that the agents were Renda's men.

The sworn testimony Manning and Byrne had taken from the Seven Dwarfs was valuable and important, but by itself it could not carry the case. They needed documents, written proof from the files of First United Fund itself. But during the depositions the Dwarfs were adamant. No, they would not provide documents. That would be really pushing their luck. They were afraid. Manning and Byrne expected too much. Their lives were in danger. It was too much to ask. But just when Manning was about to give up, someone on the inside at First United Fund suddenly, and without explanation, produced the "smoking guns" Manning needed. [12]

Manning, on his way to catch a plane home to Kansas, pulled into a dark airport parking lot. He walked around to the back of the car and opened the trunk to take out his suitcase. There, in the trunk, was a fat stack of First United Fund documents. How they had gotten there Manning would never say. If he suspected anyone in particular, he knew it would be foolhardy and dangerous to speculate out loud. In ten days that silent stack of documents would collapse Renda's world.

Manning knew they had to move fast. Renda was no doubt prepared to take steps to protect himself if he learned they were getting close. Byrne took the evidence to Organized Crime Strike Force attorneys in Washington. They listened and sent Bryne and Manning and their evidence to the Brooklyn Organized Crime Strike Force, saying that Brooklyn Strike Force attorneys might have an interest in the case. They did. First United had come up in connection with an ongoing investigation the strike force was conducting into racketeering by the Lucchese crime family. Through the use of wire taps and bugs approved to investigate the suspected mob bribery of Teamster officials at Kennedy Airport, investigators had picked up an alleged mobster[13] talking about how Schwimmer, First United Fund's financial consultant, was helping him launder money through bearer bonds. [14]

The name First United Fund, therefore, got their immediate interest. "They were willing to spend the cerebral energy to understand the case," Manning told us later, and he spent the next ten days with them going over the details. Tough, straight-talking Assistant U.S. Attorney Bruce Maffeo (ironically pronounced like Mafia, with an "o": Mafio) picked up immediately on the importance of the case.

Now they needed to obtain a search warrant for a raid on First United Fund offices. Any documents still there had to be secured before Renda had a chance to remove or destroy them. But someone had to sign an affidavit setting forth the legal grounds on which they wanted to execute the search warrant. Manning was the obvious choice, since he was the one with the evidence against Renda, but Manning was working for the FDIC and had to have their approval for such a drastic action. The affidavit would contain slanderous allegations about the man who ran one of the largest brokerage firms in the United States. No, the execution of a search warrant by Manning, a representative of the FDIC, was out of the question, regulators said. At that point Kip Byrne, apparently outraged by the regulators' refusal, intervened. "Permit Manning to sign that search warrant or you can take my job and shove it," he said, in so many words. This was absolutely insane, he fumed. Was Mario Renda untouchable?

Voices don't often get raised at the FDIC and such an outburst by their own senior trial attorney shocked the stodgy regulators into reluctant action. They acceded to his demand . . . he just better be right. Ten days after Manning had found the First United Fund documents in the trunk of his car, Maffeo's troops, 30 FBI and IRS agents, assaulted the First United Fund offices at 1001 Franklin Avenue in Garden City, New York, with the search warrant in hand. Manning and Maffeo had been tipped that Renda was attending an all-day conference and would be out of the office—it seemed like a good day to go calling. For the next two days they filled box after box with First United Fund's books, records, files, and even personal notes. Six days later agents raided Franklin Winkler's company in Honolulu, hauling another 100 boxes of files off to Maffeo in New York.

For both Manning's civil case and Maffeo's criminal racketeering investigation, the haul was a windfall. Among the booty investigators found some revealing items—some deadly serious, some humorous. There were verses to a tongue-in-cheek song written for Renda by a First United employee. "The Twelve Days of Bilking," which was sung to the tune of "The Twelve Days of Christmas," outlined, stanza by stanza, how brokered deposits were used to con banks and thrifts. The last stanza referred to such things as "banks a-failing," "accountants auditing," "checks a-bouncing," "cops arresting," and "Steve Black hanging from a tree."[16]

Another song penned by Renda employees was entitled "Bilkers in the Night," sung to the tune of "Strangers in the Night."

The songs were amusing. A lot less amusing was evidence that Renda had used First United Fund as a giant Trojan horse that had been granted entry into dozens of banks and thrifts across the United States. A lot of the names of institutions where the Seven Dwarfs had said Renda had special deals going were found in the records seized at First United Fund:

Mission Bank, Mission, Kansas

Coronado Federal Savings and Loan, Kansas City, Kansas

The Metropolitan Bank, Kansas City, Missouri

Metro North Bank, Kansas City, Missouri

First Federal Savings and Loan, Beloit, Kansas

Farmers and Merchants Bank, Huntsville, Missouri

Rexford State Bank, Rexford, Kansas

Metropolitan Bank and Trust, Tampa, Florida

American City Bank, Los Angeles, California

Newport Harbour National Bank, Newport Beach, California

Sparta Sanders State Bank, Sparta, Kentucky

Community Bank, Hartford, South Dakota

Western National Bank of Lovell, Lovell, Wyoming

Emerald Empire Banking Company, Springfield, Oregon

Knickerbocker Federal Savings and Loan, New York, New York

State Savings and Loan, Clovis, New Mexico

Valley First Federal Savings and Loan, Van Nuys, California

Indian Springs State Bank, Kansas City, Kansas

First National Bank of Midland, Midland, Texas

The Teamster and Steelworker pension funds that Renda and his partner Schwimmer skimmed from were deposited at:

First Savings and Loan of Suffolk, Suffolk, Virginia

Westwood Savings and Loan, Los Angeles, California

North Mississippi Savings and Loan, Oxford, Mississippi

Old Court Savings and Loan Association, Baltimore, Maryland

First Progressive Savings and Loan, Westminster, Maryland

Sharon Savings and Loan, Baltimore, Maryland

First Border City Savings and Loan Association, Piqua, Ohio

Bank of San Diego, San Diego, California

Central Illinois Savings and Loan, Virden, Illinois

Montana Savings and Loan, Kalispell, Montana

Virginia Beach Federal Savings and Loan, Richmond, Virginia

Heritage Savings and Loan, Richmond, Virginia

Comstock Bank, Carson City, Nevada

Investors Savings and Loan, Richmond, Virginia

Standard Savings Association, Houston, Texas

Alliance Federal Savings and Loan, Kenner, Louisiana

Valley First Federal Savings and Loan, El Centro, California

Mainland Savings Association, Houston, Texas[16]

It was a long list and Manning couldn't even be sure it was complete. What investigators did notice was that more than just a few of the institutions listed also appeared on the FDIC and FSLIC's growing casualty lists. In fact, from January 1982 through June 30, 1985, First United Fund was number one in the nation in brokering deposits into banks that later failed, 28 in all, even though in 1985 it was only thirteenth in the nation in volume of deposits placed.[17] In comparison, Merrill Lynch, which brokered nearly 30 times the volume of deposits, brokered into only two institutions that closed.[18]

It appeared that Renda had supplied money to nearly all the go-go thrifts in the country.

By late in 1984 Sam Daily was all too aware that Renda and Winkler had left him to take the rap. Increasingly paranoid, he was certain they were trying to frame him. (He would eventually be convicted of conspiracy in the scam.) In an apparent attempt to short-circuit such a plot, Daily shot off two pages of his famous prose to the Honolulu police:

Dear Officer,

If you check your files you will find that some time about a year and a half ago, someone tried to put Mr. Winkler's lights out. Fortunately for Mr. Winkler they failed. . . .

After a rambling discourse outlining the troubles he'd seen, Daily finally got to the point:

> To that end, I am asking you to investigate this matter so that should one of Franklin Winkler's numerous enemy's [sic] eliminate his fat body from the face of our good earth, I will not be the suspect.

A month later Daily sent Winkler a letter that unquestionably outdid all his earlier literary efforts. This letter, which exposed Daily as an anti-Semite (the letter was referred to by investigators simply as "the fat, slimy hymie letter") also showed the stress Daily was under:

> Franklin:
>
> I just received your letter. It's really not worth commenting on, except to say that I had a friend and client, who is a criminal psychologist, review your letter.
>
> My friend is a Jew, and specializes in studying the behavior of the criminally insane and mentally ill Jew, under a grant funded by the Nation of Israel. The purpose of the grant is to identify Jewish individuals who degrade, by actions and deeds, the standards to which the true Jew adheres.
>
> He said the writer of the letter was obviously a psycho, and probably a fat, slimy, hymie and scared as hell.
>
> I said to my friend, "what is a hymie?" He replied: "Unfortunately, Sam, regardless of the high standards to which a group, such as us Jews subscribe, there is always that minority who degrade the rest of us. They are present in your Protestant Group, in the Catholic Religion, and in all other religious and ethnic groups as well. The most demented of the group, to which the author of the letter under discussion obviously belongs, is referred to by other Jews as a hymie. I believe the word first appeared in the 1920 dictionary of the underworld, published in New York."
>
> I congratulated him on his accuracy, and in our conversation he asked me, "Why is the fat, slimy, hymie so scared?" I replied; "my friend, if you had done all of the following in three short years, what would your emotional feelings be."
>
> . . . He may have framed [names deleted] and others into a murder for hire plot.
>
> . . . He was a major factor in Bill Lemaster, President of Indian Springs State Bank, committing suicide, or, "whatever,"
>
> . . . He stole some $800,000.00 from First United Partners Four, with some 10 Partners, all of whom are mad as hell,

. . . *He stole some $800,000.00 from Haiku Holdings and Haiku Partners, with some 27 Partners, all of whom are mad as hell,*

. . . *He and an associate made a phone offer to buy a bank to incite the bank into making loans which, in part, caused the failure of the bank, and an alleged loss of $5,000,000.00 to the shareholders of the bank,* [Indian Springs]

. . . *He is being investigated by the FBI on numerous accounts,*

. . . *He has over 130 lawsuits pending in Honolulu alone,*

and

. . . *He stole in excess of $500,000.00 from me.*

The criminal psychologist interrupted me. "Sam," he said, "I understand the SOB is a fat, slimy, hymie, crook who has taken some $3,000,000.00 from some 50 odd investors in three short years [a reference to Daily's straw borrowers], *and that he is probably going to prison, but that doesn't explain why he is so damned scared."*

I replied; "my friend, I spent my time in Korea, Vietnam, Thailand, Laos, and other parts of Southeast Asia. I have seen literally dozens of good men die. Some died bravely, most prayed, a few begged; all were scared. But in all of my experiences, I have never seen anyone so afraid of death as Franklin Winkler. I think the answer is simple. The men I have seen die had a cause that involved someone else; that is to say "Duty, Flag, Country, Family, or Friends." They had feeling for others; a sense of loyalty, honesty, truthfulness, and fairness to those with whom they dealt. Franklin Winkler has only himself and his Dad, who has one foot in the grave and one foot on a banana peel. He loves no one, and in turn, no one loves him. He has no God. He has only greed."

The criminal psychologist said, "Oh, now I understand. It is as plain as day. He is a fucking fat, slimy, hymie."

Franklin, if I were you, I'd be scared as hell, too. You've screwed over 50 families, ruined them. When you consider that probably 25% of our population, on a random basis, are nuts, there's probably at least 25% of 50 families out there who are capable of spilling your guts and your nuts on the paking [sic] *ramp floor, or in the alternative, putting a .38 slug thru your demented brain.*

Mind you, I have no interest in inflicting physical harm to your fat, slimy, hymie body. I'd rather hand you a bar of soap or a jar of vaseline as you walk into Leavenworth [prison], *and watch those big mean studs, there for violent crimes, line up to screw your fat, slimy, hymie ass.*

Have a good day Franklin,

Sam

Daily's literary thrashings came to naught. He was securely locked in the web woven by Franklin Winkler and Mario Renda, a web designed to leave them a safe arm's length away from the partnerships when the Hawaii loans went into default. On one side of Daily were the FDIC and FSLIC, who were looking for millions of dollars missing from their crippled institutions in Kansas, and on the other side were the nearly 50 straw borrowers who had been told to turn over their loan proceeds to Daily and "not to worry."

In early 1985 Manning sued Renda, Franklin and Leslie Winkler, Daily and others for $60 million on behalf of the FDIC and the FSLIC[19] for causing the collapse of Indian Springs State Bank and Coronado Savings. The suit accused them of racketeering and charged that the defendants had conducted and participated in an "ongoing criminal activity." The Manning lawsuit began the destruction of Mario Renda's empire.[20]

CHAPTER ELEVEN

The End of the Line

Manning filed the FDIC and FSLIC civil suit against Renda and his cohorts in U.S. District Court in Kansas in April 1985. In the lawsuit was a graphic description of Renda's "special deals" at Indian Springs State Bank, Coronado Savings and Loan, and Rexford State Bank. The Kansas City U.S. attorney's office, whom Manning had implored months earlier to take the case, was beginning to look more than a little silly. At last the Kansas City Organized Crime Strike Force took the matter to the grand jury. They contacted Maffeo and requested that he send them copies of the documents he and Manning had seized at Renda and Winkler's offices. Maffeo complied.

Nonetheless, Renda continued to do business out of First United Fund in New York, although things got pretty weird around the shop. First United Fund now was huge. It managed $5 billion in deposits. Most of its employees had nothing to do with Renda's wheeling and dealing but had come to suspect much. On the wall in the bull pen at First United was "the big board," which listed all the institutions dealing with First United Fund. Over the names of institutions that employees suspected were involved in one of Renda's "special deals" they would sometimes stick cutouts of army attack helicopters shooting missiles at the institution's name. On the side of the helicopters they'd write FDIC or FSLIC.

Word of the Kansas City grand jury probe sent a clear message to Franklin Winkler and his father, Leslie. As accomplished con artists, they knew when a gig was up, and if *even the Kansas City feds* were onto them, then this gig was most certainly up. In early 1987 both Franklin and his father skipped the country.[1]

Daily was obviously going to be named a defendant in any case brought by the Kansas City Strike Force, and as usual he was quick to take up pen in his own defense. This time he described his ideas for subverting Manning's inves-

119

tigation. In a report he called "Goals Achievable Through Use of Public Relations and Investigative Firms," Daily suggested to his cohorts that when Mike Manning came to Honolulu they "put a tail" on him. "The purpose would be to gather data on him, associate it with his billing, and try to pick up a little fraud upon the Federal Government by the Morrison, Hecker firm, as well as acquiring the capability to embarrass or discredit them, if need be." He also suggested they try to get a story on CBS's 60 Minutes that would portray Daily and his straw borrowers as victims rather than participants in the scheme.

But things were coming apart much too fast, and soon after Maffeo's search of the First United offices, Renda's own right-hand man and executive vice president, Joseph DeCarlo, Sr., began secretly negotiating with Maffeo and the Brooklyn Organized Crime Strike Force for immunity in exchange for testifying against his boss. When the talking was over DeCarlo agreed to plead guilty to a single count of conspiracy and another count of tax evasion in return for immunity on everything else. He also agreed to testify against Renda in return for a five-year cap on his sentence.

That was all Maffeo needed. Ten days later, in the early morning hours of June 16, 1987, a squad of FBI agents swooped down on Renda's New York mansion armed with a 145-count grand jury indictment. The federal agents read Renda his rights, and in front of his wife and children they handcuffed him and led him off to a waiting car. Renda was charged, along with codefendant Martin Schwimmer, with defrauding Sheetmetal Workers Local 83 and Teamster's Local 810 by skimming nearly $16 million off of the $100 million in pension funds brokered by First United Fund into thrifts and banks between December 1981 and December 1984. Renda and Schwimmer were charged with racketeering, mail and wire fraud, embezzlement and bribery. Prosecutors said the First United Fund case was the largest criminal union-pension fraud scheme ever prosecuted by the Justice Department.

The same day Renda was scooped up in New York—and three years after Manning had pleaded with the assistant U.S. attorney in Kansas City to prosecute Renda—a 31-count grand jury indictment was unsealed in Kansas City, charging Renda, Franklin Winkler, and Daily (and others) with embezzlement and with defrauding Indian Springs State Bank and Coronado Savings and Loan of $7 million. It was a bad day for Mario Renda. He now had a two-front war to fight. Maffeo was prosecuting him in Brooklyn for skimming from the pension funds, and the Kansas City Strike Force was prosecuting him for defrauding Indian Springs State Bank.

Renda and his attorney appeared before a federal judge in Brooklyn later that day. Renda's attorney objected to his client's rough handling earlier that morning by the FBI: "I understand there is little the court can do to help me, to raise my strenuous outrage at Mr. Renda's arrest this morning at seven o'clock in his home in Garden City in the presence of his children. . . . My client has asked me to apologize for the manner in which he appears before your honor. Having been taken out of his home this morning, he wasn't in a position to choose a tie or put on a suit."

To which a sober-faced judge replied, "Don't worry, I'm not fussy."

The Brooklyn indictment charged that Renda and Schwimmer had obtained union business the old-fashioned way, by bribing union officials. It charged that once the money was placed at thrifts, First United Fund was paid commissions that were shuttled to "off the books" bank accounts and not declared. With their profits in accounts not reflected on the books of First United Fund, the indictment claimed, Renda began lying on his taxes. In 1982 he claimed income of $2,251,478 for First United Fund when in fact First United Fund made $3,284,370 that year. In 1983 he told a whopper. He claimed First United Financial Corporation had made a profit of $137,206, when in fact income that year totaled $3,429,546. In all, Maffeo charged, Renda and Schwimmer had received over $16 million illegally from the two pension funds.

October 19, 1987 ("Black Monday" on Wall Street)—three years to the day after Maffeo's troops showed up with a search warrant at First United Fund's office in Garden City, New York—Renda was to go on trial along with Sam Daily in Kansas City. (Franklin Winkler was hiding out in Australia.) Jury selection had already begun when Renda and his attorney cut a separate deal with the head of the Kansas City Organized Crime Strike Force. Facing one count of conspiracy and 29 counts of federal wire fraud, Renda agreed to plead guilty to two counts of wire fraud for a two-year cap on his sentence.

Brooklyn Strike Force attorneys were furious with their Kansas City brethren because an attorney on the Kansas City Organized Crime Strike Force had earlier refused a much better offer from Renda: Before he was indicted Renda had offered to plead guilty to both the Brooklyn and Kansas City charges and take whatever sentence the judge gave him in Brooklyn in exchange for a maximum sentence of two years in the Kansas City case. He had also offered to repay the FDIC and FSLIC $20 *million in cash*. But the attorney on the Kansas City Strike Force refused the deal because he wanted to hold out for a prison sentence of five to seven years. By the time the trial rolled around, however, the head of the strike force had evidently gotten cold feet, and Stuart Steinberg, Renda's friend and attorney, cut a deal. But the offer to repay $20 million was off because Renda now claimed to be broke.[2] The FSLIC and the FDIC were left standing at the altar with that familiar empty feeling in the pits of their stomachs.

"Steinberg told me he couldn't believe how good a deal they were offered," an attorney close to the case told us. "He said they didn't even require Renda to testify against Daily or the others in the case."

The Kansas City acceptance of the Renda plea bargain particularly angered the Brooklyn Strike Force attorneys because they had gotten Renda's subordinate, Joe DeCarlo, to agree to testify against Renda in return for a *five-year*-sentence cap. How did it look when the main culprit made a better plea bargain than his lackey?[3]

The Kansas City Strike Force had let Mario Renda, one of the key figures in a nationwide scheme to defraud thrifts and banks, off with a two-year slap on the wrist. We had to wonder. Didn't the Justice Department know what kind of damage Renda had done at dozens of institutions? Weren't they aware by now of his associations with others who had swindled thrifts and banks across the country? (At least one member of the Kansas City prosecuting team certainly understood the significance of the case when he warned an investigator ominously after the trial, "This is much bigger than even you know. These are very nasty people.") Still, the Renda case had, from a prosecutor's standpoint, been "turned." For the record, the Kansas City Organized Crime Strike Force had its "conviction."

With Renda now out of the case and Franklin Winkler on the lam in Australia, that left just Daily and another minor player, Los Angeles investor and syndicator Fred Figge, to face 28 counts of wire fraud and one count of conspiracy.[4] The case droned on for two months. The loss of its star defendant, Renda, a key element in the original indictment, took all the focus out of the case. It bogged down badly as prosecutors tried to replace Renda with technical particulars. They threw over 670,000 pages of documents at the jury. The papers filled a dozen file cabinets and would have stood ten feet thick. When the trial ended in December 1987 the jury issued a muddled decision, finding Daily and Figge innocent of all the wire fraud charges but guilty of conspiracy.

The defense had contended that Daily and Figge were victimized by the Winklers, who then fled and left Daily and Figge holding the bag. After the trial some jurors said they agreed. But a defense attorney told a Kansas City *Times* reporter he wasn't sure the jury understood what they were doing, since they convicted the two men for conspiracy, which embraced the wire fraud counts, but did not convict them of the wire fraud.

"It's quite possible the jury was confused," he said. "I don't know whether they really knew what was going on or not."

Renda was not going to get off so easily in Brooklyn. Maffeo had all the evidence he needed tying Renda to the pension-fund embezzlement scam. And now, with DeCarlo telling all to federal prosecutors, Renda knew he was trapped. So he decided to follow DeCarlo's lead and turn against Schwimmer. Renda told Maffeo that he would testify against Schwimmer in return for consideration on his sentencing in the Brooklyn case and help with the judge on the Kansas City case, for which he had not yet been sentenced. Maffeo agreed. Renda pleaded guilty to racketeering and tax-evasion charges. In return Maffeo agreed to recommend to the Brooklyn judge that he limit Renda's jail sentence to 25 years and agreed to send notice to the Kansas City judge that Renda was now cooperating with federal prosecutors.[5]

After Maffeo settled matters with Renda, a source close to the case who knew we were investigating Renda sent us a package. Four years' worth of Mario's personal desk diaries arrived in a large UPS box one morning. Maybe in looking them over we'd see some familiar names, she said on a small yellow note attached to the first page of the foot-high stack.

The package included Renda's daily business diaries from January 2, 1981, through October 19, 1984 (when Maffeo's forces stormed First United Fund with a search warrant). Renda apparently kept the diaries on his desk and jotted down notes on important phone calls, reminders to himself, daily interest-rate quotes, and just plain trivia. The diaries were peppered with dozens of names we already knew.

Khashoggi was there. The Dunes Hotel and Casino. Winkler. Daily. Lemaster. Seaside. Teamsters. Ferrante and the Palace Hotel in Puerto Rico. Steelworkers. San Marino S&L. Bank of Irvine. Consolidated S&L., Bill Patterson of Penn Square Bank, First Atlantic Investment Corporation, Bureau of Indian Affairs, California Congressman Tony Coelho, all dutifully noted in Renda's own scrawl. Also, Morris Shenker was there: "Bill Wiss friend of Morris Shanker [sic]." "Morty Shanker deal." "B of A on Shanker deal." It took us days to pick through the diaries, trying to decipher Renda's careless handwriting and impossible spelling.

The scope of Renda's activities seemed to grow with every new piece of information. Given the allegations that Sal Piga was a Lucchese mob family associate and that the Brooklyn Strike Force had recorded an alleged Lucchese mob family member talking about how Schwimmer was helping him launder money through bearer bonds, we kept wondering if the mob was pulling Mario's strings. We asked several investigators if Renda was working with or for the mob, and one day we received a piece of unmarked mail. We opened the large envelope and found inside the sworn deposition of Lawrence S. Iorizzo. Attached was a handwritten note to us: "If you are focusing on mob bust-outs of savings and loans, then this is the definitive piece."

There were no shades of gray there, no subtleties to wade through. Larry Iorizzo was a bona fide hood. He was about five foot ten and weighed 300 pounds. He had been convicted of bootlegging gasoline on Long Island and he had fled to Panama, where he was silly enough to cross swords with Colombian drug lords. Rather than kill Iorizzo, the drug lords simply put him on a nonstop flight from Panama to Miami. As soon as the plane was airborne, they called the U.S. attorney in Miami and said, "Guess who's coming to dinner."

Iorizzo had decided at that point to save his skin by talking, and the feds placed him in the federal witness protection program. In return for protection he agreed to give evidence whenever he had information about a case. In a sworn deposition, September 30, 1987, Iorizzo told the feds what he knew about Renda. He said:

Back in 1981, when Renda and the Winklers were first formulating their linked-financing scheme, Iorizzo was the president and principal shareholder of a mob-front company called Vantage Petroleum Company in Bohemia, New York. He had been indicted in Suffolk County, New York, for obtaining contracts to distribute gasoline to turnpike and highway markets by collusive bidding. The case had been widely reported in the press and no one would loan either Vantage or Iorizzo any money.

This blacklisting was creating cash-flow problems for Iorizzo, and a friend steered him to Leslie Winkler. Leslie told Iorizzo that his friend Mario Renda was a New York "money man" who could help Iorizzo with his cash-flow problems. Leslie arranged a meeting between Renda and Iorizzo in late 1981. Iorizzo testified:

> During that meeting, held at Renda's home, I explained my financial dif-
> ficulties to Mario Renda. Renda told me that he was aware of the cash-flow
> problems and had been briefed on the situation by Winkler. Renda also
> indicated that he had read about my problems with law-enforcement au-
> thorities in the newspapers.

Renda explained to Iorizzo how his linked-financing scheme worked:

> I understood from our conversation that these brokered CDs could be used
> with banks that wanted to inflate their cash position, making the banks more
> liquid and in a more favorable position to extend loans. Renda told me that
> he could arrange for deposits to be put into a bank, if there was a bank that
> I knew well enough to talk to and explain that I could arrange for money
> to be deposited if the bank would give me a loan.

Leslie Winkler told Iorizzo that Renda was very close to Adnan Khashoggi and that Renda might be able to assist Iorizzo in getting a fat oil contract if Iorizzo used his powers of "persuasion" in New York to help Khashoggi. It seemed Khashoggi, who owned a home outside New York City, was having trouble getting the town fathers' approval for a helicopter landing pad at his home. Renda said that if Iorizzo could "remove these obstacles," Khashoggi would be most appreciative.

At that same meeting, Iorizzo later swore, he and Renda exchanged their Mafia bona fides, with Leslie Winkler telling Renda that Iorizzo was with the

Colombo crime family and Renda in turn bragging that he controlled "a lot of money being loaned for the benefit of the Paul Castellano family." Castellano was the New York City Mafia boss for the Gambino crime family.

According to Iorizzo, he and Renda came to an agreement under which Renda would place money at a bank of Iorizzo's choice, and he chose Central National Bank of New York (CNBY). The bank then made loans to a Panamanian shell corporation formed by Iorizzo. Renda got $35,000 under the table from Iorizzo as his share in the CNBY scheme and Leslie Winkler got a small percentage for making the introductions.

"I literally purchased the company's papers from a lawyer in Panama who maintained them, along with other such entities, on the shelf of a bookcase in his office in Panama," Iorizzo said. He had been introduced to the Panamanian lawyer by Leslie Winkler. Iorizzo told Renda he used the Panamanian shell corporation rather than Vantage Petroleum for this loan "because I had no intention of paying the loan off once it was made. Renda then suggested that I could use Panamanian shelf companies such as Houston Holding in order to borrow money from other banks in the United States and/or Europe, allow the loans to go into default, and then collapse these companies into bankruptcy, thereby discharging the nonperforming loans." What Iorizzo described was another classic bust-out.

Renda and Leslie Winkler also tried to enlist Iorizzo into their overall scheme to bust out banks and thrifts. "I understood from these discussions that the schemes involved getting banks to take in brokered deposits to make loans to limited partners who would turn the proceeds over to general partners in a partnership arrangement. . . . There was no intention of repaying anybody as the general partners had no obligation to pay the loans off . . . the loans would go into default and as the collateral was not worth as much as it was represented to be, the limited partners would be left with the responsibility of paying on the mortgage and/or promissory notes." Though interested in the scheme, Iorizzo had declined "due to other activities which required my presence in New York."

Renda's diaries and Iorizzo's deposition fleshed out for us Renda's role as a deposit broker. Taken together with the activities of his partner Schwimmer with the Lucchese crime family, they left little room for doubt that Renda's banking activities were intertwined with the mob's. Taken in a larger context, they were even more significant. Renda was a fellow who, in a matter of a few short years, went from tap-dance teacher to multibillion-dollar deposit broker and who was able to bilk dozens of thrifts and banks out of tens of millions of dollars. Ultimately, he put many of these institutions out of business—all of which he did with other people's money and newly promulgated government regulations that deregulated interest rates and thrift rules. The warnings issued by Ed Gray and a handful of others went unheeded as Congress listened instead to thrift lobbyists who insisted that brokered deposits were not a problem. When the court ruled that only Congress, not the FHLBB, could limit FSLIC insurance on brokered deposits, all hope of bringing the "hot money" under control vanished. The next step the FHLBB might have taken would have been to assign more examiners to watch institutions using large amounts of brokered deposits, but the FHLBB did not have enough examiners to do the job.

In the vacuum created by regulatory and congressional inaction, Mario Renda and others like him moved in and quickly subverted the role of deposit broker to that of extortionist and corruptor. Finding small thrifts struggling to make it against larger competitors, these brokers put a price on their millions —a cut. With the promise of huge deposits as the carrot, heretofore honest thrift officials agreed to accommodate the deposit brokers and their friends, who then spirited off their share of those deposits, never to be seen again. What did it matter? they reasoned. The deposits were insured—backed by the "full faith and credit of the U.S. Treasury."

The laws and regulations covering brokered deposits have not changed as of this writing. The potential for abuse by unethical deposit brokers like Mario Renda remains. We had hoped that the downfall of Mario Renda would have alerted regulators and examiners, but it was not so. In late 1988—three and a half years after the collapse of Indian Springs State Bank—when we interviewed *the* senior trial attorney at the FHLBB, we sat in shocked disbelief when we learned that he had no idea who Renda was or what Renda had done.

CHAPTER TWELVE

"Miguel"

The Mafia of the 1980s was a sophisticated $50 billion enterprise that employed financial consultants and attorneys and dealt on a daily basis with international currency fluctuations and the rise and fall of the Tokyo stock exchange.[1] Individual Mafia members had average annual incomes of over $200,000. The top 50 bosses made much more.[2] They traveled in the world of high finance, and even before thrifts were deregulated, upper-echelon Mafia financiers knew exactly how they would benefit from deregulation. They were ready to take advantage of the opportunity as soon as Congress passed the legislation. The lower echelons of the modern Mafia, a vast and assorted crew of "wise guys"[3] who were constantly sweeping the country for lucrative scams, also quickly got the word that savings and loans had changed. The Mafia on all levels struggled daily with a consuming need for cash and for a way to launder it. Thrift deregulation fulfilled both of those needs nicely, making it easier to launder money through multimillion-dollar development projects, using a thrift as a front, and making it easier to find thrift executives willing to make risky loans for a piece of the action. Not only had the rules been drastically eased, but the cops (thrift examiners) were no longer much of a threat, their ranks having been gutted after state and federal deregulation.

In our investigation we ran into the mob, or associates of the mob, at many of the thrifts we examined. Each of the "Big Five" New York families —Gambino, Genevese, Lucchese, Bonanno, and Colombo—turned up, along with the lesser families such as the Civellas from Kansas City, the Peter Milano gang in Los Angeles, Carlos Marcello in New Orleans, Santo Trafficante in Tampa, and others. Did the leadership of crime families have a sit-down[4] one day and decide to loot S&Ls? Clues that surfaced at dozens of savings and loans convinced us that some form of coordinated operation existed. The evidence was overwhelming that the Mafia was actively looting S&Ls—in

various, widely disparate locations, at the same time, in the same ways, often using the same people.

The mob was also using S&Ls to launder money. Thrifts' access to brokered deposits, as well as their new ability to make direct investments in real estate projects and partnerships, made deregulated thrifts a natural vehicle for laundering large sums of money. Among the most popular money laundering techniques were:[5]

> Buy an asset (a piece of property or a business, for example) with a loan from a thrift. Repay the loan over a period of time with dirty money. Once the loan was paid off, sell the asset and the money was laundered. (Or default on the loan and let the thrift repossess the property. Either way, you had an explanation for the origin of the money if anyone should ask.)

> A twist that would allow you to both launder money and steal some from the thrift at the same time was to borrow more on the asset than you paid for it (and more than it was worth) and then default on the loan, claiming you lost money on the project. The money in your possession would then clearly be the product of the defaulted loan and, therefore, laundered. Plus, you'd have the extra money you had made by overencumbering the asset (which the thrift would repossess and have to dispose of).

The permutations and possibilities were endless, especially when done in conjunction with a real estate transaction. The American way of handling real estate transactions was cluttered with 200-year-old ownership instruments like quit claim deeds, grant deeds, trust deeds, and deeds of reconveyance. Those arcane instruments might cross the sights of average people only once in their lives, when they bought their own homes. But to the white-collar swindler and money launderer, they were the tools of the trade. A routine heist or money-laundering operation involving real estate was a blizzard of such instruments, hiding true intentions behind a frenzy of deeds and note filings.[6]

Thrift deregulation came at a time (the early 1980s) when federal strike forces had targeted what they believed to be $100 billion[7] being laundered through U.S. financial institutions every year. The Bank Secrecy Act, passed in 1970, had several important provisions that fought against money laundering, including requiring banks and thrifts[8] to report all transactions over $10,000. But working against the Bank Secrecy Act was the 1978 Right to Financial Privacy Act (and many state laws), which severely limited what banks could tell law-enforcement officials.[9]

The role of savings and loans in money laundering made headlines in 1985 when results were made public of Operation Greenback, a federal money-laundering probe conducted in Puerto Rico from 1983 to 1985. Two senior FHLBB officials admitted they had altered bank examination reports that would have exposed possible currency reporting violations at a Puerto Rican thrift. The president of the Puerto Rican thrift was also vice chairman of the FHLB of New York. Senator William V. Roth (R-Del.), chairman of the Senate Committee on Governmental Affairs' subcommittee on investigations, said in hearings in July 1985:

> It is instructive to note that in 1983 the FHLBB examined 2,185 savings and loans nationwide, including Puerto Rico, and found two Bank Secrecy violations (primarily failure to report cash transactions over $10,000), whereas in the same year the FDIC found ten of the eleven Puerto Rican banks examined to be in some form of noncompliance with the Act. In 1984 the Bank Board found zero violations out of 1,906 examinations nationwide. In Puerto Rico alone the FDIC found six of the seven banks examined in noncompliance. Now this either means that the savings and loans are models of compliance with the Act, or that the Board just is not doing its job. There is little question in our minds that the latter is the case: The FHLBB has consistently dropped the ball regarding enforcement of the Bank Secrecy Act. In the entire history of the Act, since its passage in 1970, the Board has referred a grand total of two financial institutions to the Treasury Department for civil penalties, none for criminal penalties.

That complacent environment was nirvana for the mob, and they took every advantage of the opportunity. But the most prevalent mob activity we found at thrifts was individual mob members and associates getting and defaulting on loans—big loans and lots of them. The mob's survival depended on a constant flow of money. Before deregulation getting that money was a hit-or-miss proposition. Wise guys often had to shake down small businessmen. It was hard work. After deregulation thrifts bursting at the seams with brokered deposits were like the mother lode and the wise guys were the '49ers. If wise guys could get sufficient control of a thrift, they busted it out. If they failed to gain control, they took what loans they could get and moved on to the next thrift.

The frenetic pace with which they scoured the thrift industry looking for loans seemed also to be a function of the way the mob had changed since the 1960s. Twenty years ago the mob was still a fairly homogeneous entity made up of well-recognized "families" who controlled precisely described territories and took care of their own. Like Fortune 500 companies, mob families had their own now-familiar hierarchy, with each station bearing its own, sometimes paramilitary, title like capo, lieutenant, soldier, earner, wise guy. But the 1980s mob had undergone its own version of *perestroika*.[10] To survive a war on the mob that was being waged by law enforcement armed with high technology tools, wise guys were given far more independence of action. No longer were they required to get the Godfather's support for every little operation or scam.[11] Instead, mob operatives used their family associations (and one person might have several) as a reservoir of talent and influence when conducting an operation. Also, the young wise guys were far more independent-minded than in the old days when they virtually worshiped the Godfather. The conviction of 1,000 Mafia bosses and underlings since 1981 created a vacuum into which young, reckless, independent operators moved (to the dismay, apparently, of older Mafia members). They tended to organize their own jobs. "*Our* Thing has turned into *My* Thing," testified a former FBI agent.[12] When the job was done and the money in hand, the wise guys' only responsibility was "to do the right thing," meaning to be sure they passed enough of the booty up the line of command to satisfy the family.

In the past the Mafia had had little interest in a conservative thrift industry that only made home loans. But the deregulated thrift industry was an exciting new target for wise guys with busy minds always figuring out their next scam. Throughout our research, then, when we talked to regulators or FBI agents, we always asked them, "Are you coming across any mob-related people in your thrift investigations?" Coauthor Paul Muolo, headquartered in New York and living in New Jersey, got the tip that led us to the mob-related operation we later decided was most typical of such activity at a thrift. His New York source had told him:

"Well, check out Flushing Federal Savings and Loan over in Queens. Drop the name Rapp and see what happens. By the way, his real name's not Rapp, it's Hellerman. Michael Hellerman."

In late 1972, Michael Hellerman and his wife, Mary, a tall slender woman in her late twenties, had exited their car off the Cross Island Parkway and pulled into the driveway of their home in Bayside, Queens.[13] A stockbroker in his mid-thirties, Mike Hellerman had chosen to settle in this upper-middle-class enclave because of its relative proximity to New York City. Bayside was close enough that Hellerman could enjoy the city's nightlife while staying in touch with his clients, but far enough removed so he could escape the hustle and bustle. A suburb speckled with well-groomed single-family homes and small garden apartments, Bayside was a perfect place for Michael Hellerman to blend in with other professionals commuting daily to New York. It was also a perfect place for Hellerman to hide from his stock clients, who, perhaps, weren't prospering from some of Mike's recent trades.

Hellerman and his wife, returning from dinner, pulled their Cadillac into the driveway and climbed out. Four police officers came over to the couple as a crowd of curious neighbors watched.

"You Mike Hellerman?" a sergeant asked.

"Yeah."

The police led Hellerman and his wife to the house. "It looks like someone shot up your house, Mr. Hellerman," one officer told him. The Hellermans' home had been machine-gunned.

Only a few days earlier the couple had been held up at gunpoint in their home.

That night Hellerman's wife, Mary, became hysterical. The couple packed up their belongings and children and, using phony names, checked into the Diplomat Hotel across the river in midtown Manhattan. To neighbors and the police the event seemed out of place in the quiet neighborhood. But Mike Hellerman knew exactly what had happened and why. He also knew he needed help.

On October 19, 1972, two days after the shooting, he called a contact he had at the Federal Bureau of Investigation and baited his hook. He would be willing to tell the FBI everything he knew about the mob's activity on Wall Street, he said, if he could be guaranteed protection. He assured them he had plenty to tell and that members of the organized crime families he'd been dealing with wanted Mike Hellerman dead.

As his neighbors in Bayside would later learn, Mike Hellerman wasn't just any stockbroker. He was the mob's stockbroker. And he had enough information on mob stock scams to send key members of the Lucchese, Colombo, and Gambino crime families to prison for years. But it wouldn't be easy for Mike. One of Hellerman's best friends was John Dioguardi, better known as Johnny Dio, a big labor union racketeer who was reportedly a member of the Lucchese crime family. Dioguardi had once been instrumental in helping Jimmy Hoffa become president of the Teamsters Union. Dio and Hellerman were tight—so tight in fact that Dio was Hellerman's "protector" in the mob. From the late 1960s, up until he was sent to prison in October 1972 for bankruptcy fraud, Dio made sure that no harm came to Mike as Hellerman pulled stock swindle after stock swindle for the families.

Over the years Hellerman's stock scams had netted millions for Dio and mobsters like Vinnie Aloi, reputed to be the head of the Colombo crime family. There seemed no limit to the ways Mike Hellerman could turn a buck on a stock swindle. Hellerman bribed traders, artificially inflated the price of stocks by setting up phony buyers, and sold artificially inflated stocks at unheard-of profits. Other times Hellerman formed companies that had little or no assets, sold thousands of dollars' worth of stock in them, pocketed the profits, and left the buyers holding an empty bag when the bottom fell out of the stock price.

It seemed that no matter how many people he burned, Hellerman rarely got burned himself. Sometimes he sold stolen bonds. In other scams, using a phony company he'd created, he'd get a loan from a bank using stolen bonds as collateral. And in almost every scam the mob was there, riding a crest of stock scams engineered by their Wall Street wizard Michael Hellerman, who later referred to himself in his autobiography as a nice Jewish boy gone wrong.

From the mid-1960s up until late 1972, Hellerman had inhabited an underworld ruled by men like Dio and Vinnie. And he had no regrets. Along the way he had met a lot of people and seen a host of things that he would never have seen if he'd taken his father's advice and become an accountant.[14] Hellerman not only had helped the mob swindle millions but he had been involved in two major political scandals as well, including a brush with Watergate. He described the scandals in his 1977 biography, *Wall Street Swindler*.

In 1969 two aides to then House Speaker John W. McCormack had been convicted of attempting to peddle their influence with the SEC on behalf of a Hellerman company. And then in November 1971 Hellerman was implicated in a Watergate-related case, although he never was indicted. Robert Carson, an administrative aide to Hawaii Senator Hiram Fong (Carson had been president of the Honolulu Stock Exchange and also chairman of the Hawaiian Republican Party for eight years before he became Fong's aide), tried to quash the Justice Department indictment of Hellerman, Dio, and others in return for a $200,000 bribe. Richard G. Kleindienst, then deputy attorney general during the Nixon administration (Kleindienst later became attorney general), testified that Carson had offered to donate $100,000 of the money to the Committee to Re-Elect the President (CREEP) if Kleindienst killed the indictments against Hellerman and the other organized crime figures, including Vincent Aloi, Johnny Dioguardi, and Carmine Tramunti, reportedly head of the Lucchese family. Carson was eventually indicted and convicted.

Whatever else one might say about Hellerman's life, it had not been boring.

The son of a Polish immigrant, Hellerman grew up in Brooklyn and Long Island. When he finished college he headed straight for Wall Street. He was an imposing figure, over six feet tall and 200 pounds. He also was a quick study, with an uncanny ability with numbers, and he prospered almost from the start. His philosophy, he would later say in *Wall Street Swindler*, was simple.

"One of the first things I learned was that the investor, the buyer of stocks, is a sucker. He's just a turkey waiting to be plucked. He is totally at the mercy of his broker, who can manipulate him in such a way that the broker can wind up making more money than the customer and use the customer's money to do it."

By the time Hellerman was 22 the newspapers were referring to him as the

"Wizard of Wall Street." The more Hellerman made, the more he spent, and the money went quickly. Caught up in the glamour of Wall Street in the early 1960s, Hellerman always wanted more and his need for money became an addiction. Soon Hellerman was bribing stock clerks and taking his customers (and even his fellow brokers) for a ride. But some of Hellerman's honest customers complained and word got back to the Securities and Exchange Commission. At the age of 24 he was barred from engaging in the securities business in New York state.

By 1963 Hellerman, who'd developed a fierce gambling habit, was hanging out in Las Vegas, a down-and-out compulsive gambler. Cheating on Wall Street, Mike Hellerman was often a winner. But at the gaming tables, particularly the craps tables in Vegas, he was in way over his head. Following a drunken binge one night, Hellerman woke up thinking he'd won $15,000 only to discover that he'd dropped $240,000 at craps the night before.

In *Wall Street Swindler*, Hellerman said that in Vegas he fell in with the mob. He gravitated to Moe Dalitz, an old bootlegger and an alleged member of one of Cleveland's organized crime families. Dalitz wanted to hire Hellerman to work at his Vegas Desert Inn Hotel and Casino. Dalitz and Hellerman also cooked up a plan to open a hotel and casino in Reno. The deal flopped when Hellerman couldn't come up with a gambling license. It seemed that, like the SEC, the gaming control authorities in Las Vegas had certain standards that Mike didn't meet.

During his Las Vegas days in the mid-1960s Hellerman made friends with mobsters like Johnny Roselli, who was a one-time member of Al Capone's gang and the right-hand man of Sam Giancana, Chicago's Mafia boss. [15] But Hellerman's gambling problems—as well as his association with underworld crime figures—escalated, and it was only through the efforts of a special friend, Hellerman would later recall, that he was able to escape Vegas, at least for the time being, and return to New York, where Hellerman hoped to put his life, and scams, back together.

That special friend, Hellerman's savior, was Jilly Rizzo, who was almost 20 years older than Mike. Stocky Jilly Rizzo has often been described as Frank Sinatra's right-hand man, valet, personal body guard, and best friend. Rizzo and Hellerman became fast friends in spite of the fact that they appeared to have very little in common. Whereas Hellerman was a smooth talker, Rizzo was gruff and unrefined, which he made up for by being outgoing and gregarious. But Rizzo, despite his rough exterior, had a knack for making people, especially his restaurant customers, feel at home. He had slick, greased-back dark hair and he was starting to bald. As Hellerman said in his biography, "Jilly wasn't a handsome man." But Hellerman added, "If Jilly had a mission in life, it was to please Frank Sinatra."

Former mob enforcer turned informant Jimmy "the Weasel" Fratianno recalled, in *his* biography, a call he got from Rizzo that seemed to illustrate Rizzo's relationship with Sinatra. Fratianno said Rizzo told him:

> "Jimmy, Frank has asked me to speak to you about a jerk that used to work for him as a security guy. A real fucking animal. Hit a guy in the jaw and collarbone with one punch. . . . Frank fired him and the guy's had a hard-on for Frank ever since. He's been spouting off some bullshit to the scandal sheets. . . . we want this guy stopped once and for all. Know what I mean?"

> "You want the guy clipped? Just say the word and the motherfucker's good as buried."

> "No," Rizzo said. "Not right now. Just hurt this guy real bad. Break his legs, put the cocksucker in the hospital. Work him over real good and let's see if he gets the message."[16]

Hellerman had first met Rizzo when Rizzo was running Jilly's Restaurant, a popular New York nightspot that drew both entertainers and members of New York's well-known organized crime families. Jilly mingled with both—with equal success. Over the next 20 years Jilly and Mike would remain friends and Mike would make the bulky, tough-looking Rizzo an integral part of his life.

In 1963 Rizzo and Hellerman opened a restaurant together in New York called Mr. J's, named appropriately for Rizzo. The new Rizzo-Hellerman restaurant was a smashing success, at least at first, and Hellerman made even more contacts with men who made their living as part of the underworld. Hellerman later said he also met and became somewhat friendly with Rizzo's friend Frank Sinatra. And the Hellerman charm didn't fail him. Soon Sinatra was affectionately referring to Mike Hellerman as "Miguel." Mike, still in his early twenties, even proposed a joint-venture casino deal with "Old Blue Eyes." The deal never came off, but Sinatra reportedly liked the kid's pluck.

By 1968 Hellerman knew he wasn't going to get rich running a restaurant, and he decided to try to get back on Wall Street, where the money was. The SEC had barred him from the securities industry because of his earlier stock swindles, but that wasn't really a problem. To keep his name out of the deal, Hellerman set up a firm in the name of an old college chum who knew absolutely nothing about the brokerage business, and he hired a stable of brokers through whom he could move stocks.

During his earlier fling on Wall Street, Hellerman's mistake had been in trying to do his kind of business with the general public. They had taken umbrage and had turned him in to the SEC. Hellerman would have no such finicky customers this time around. Instead, he recruited customers like Johnny Dio and Vinnie Aloi. From 1968 to 1972 Hellerman pulled one stock swindle after another. On some of the deals he even swindled lower-level mobsters. Some complained to Aloi about the deals, but no harm ever came to Hellerman because Dio had become his "protector." For a piece of the action Dio would make sure no harm came Mike Hellerman's way. Besides, the two men had actually become very close friends.

Hellerman was raking in the money once again. And his old spending habits came back, too, just like it was yesterday. He was spending $10,000 a week in pocket change—jewelry, furs, expensive furniture and restaurants. Life was indeed blessed for Michael Hellerman. But again the good times were not to last. In October 1972 Dio was headed to prison for bankruptcy fraud. The night before Dio surrendered to U.S. marshals he and Hellerman got together at Dio's house in Bayside for a final farewell with friends. Hellerman was worried that with his protector in prison and with the SEC and FBI eyeballing his operation, his life was in danger.

"What's bothering you, Mike?" Dio asked Hellerman in private. "We knew this would happen sooner or later."

"I know," Hellerman replied. "But I'm scared. I'm going to move the hell out of New York as fast as I can. There are a lot of guys waiting for me now because you're going to be gone."

Hellerman was right. The mobsters he'd been swindling had a feeling that federal investigators from the SEC and the U.S. attorney's office in Manhattan were moving in for the kill. They were mad at Hellerman, not only for some of the unfavorable deals he'd cut for them, but also because, to save his own skin, Hellerman might be willing to sell out his old friends, including Dio, Aloi, and even Carmine Tramunti. There was plenty of sentiment within the families that they had better get to Hellerman before Hellerman got to them. They machine-gunned his house to warn him to keep quiet.

But the warning had the opposite effect. Hellerman quickly decided to cut a deal with New York Assistant U.S. Attorney Robert Morvillo, an old high school football buddy. Morvillo was now on the other side of the law, as head of the criminal division for the Southern District of New York.[17] The deal was this: Hellerman would get at least six years in prison for three large stock swindles that he masterminded, and he would testify against Tramunti, Aloi, and even his good friend Johnny Dio. Hellerman agreed. And in time all three would be sentenced to lengthy prison sentences because of Hellerman's testimony.

In the fall of 1973 Hellerman went from trial to trial as a protected government witness, testifying against Carmine Tramunti, Vinnie Aloi, and finally Johnny Dio. But by this time Michael Hellerman, a confessed and convicted felon himself, no longer existed. Under the wing of the federal witness protection program, Michael Hellerman had been transformed into Michael Rapp. As far as he and the U.S. government were concerned, Mike Hellerman was history, just a sealed file buried in the voluminous records of Foley Square in lower Manhattan. His new identity was created for him by the U.S. Marshal's Service.

With tongue in cheek, they gave him the name "Rapp." New Social Security cards were issued, a new birth certificate, driver's license, school records, personal history, everything short of a new bar mitzvah. (From this point forward we refer to Michael Hellerman as Michael Rapp.)

Mike Rapp also did a little time in prison, a situation he abhorred. When he was temporarily released in late 1973 to testify against Dio, he swore he'd "never commit another crime in my life." He begged Morvillo and the U.S. attorney's office not to send him back to prison. After the Dio trial Rapp went to a federal safe house in New England until he was scheduled to testify again in another trial involving Dio. To ingratiate himself with his captors, Rapp cooperated to the hilt. Rapp had no stomach for being a courageous prisoner of war. He sang like a canary. He was responsible for the indictment or conviction of more than 90 men.

What happened to Rapp after he finished testifying on the government's behalf is not clear. His life was in danger, and his best bet was to dissolve into his new identity. What is known is that he did very little prison time for the stock swindles he masterminded. Since he had testified against members of the mob, the U.S. attorney's office believed Rapp wouldn't dare step out of line.

By 1977 Rapp was living a quiet, simple life in Massachusetts, according to law-enforcement officials. Divorced from Mary, he remarried, opened a restaurant in Boston, and tried to settle down. With Thomas C. Renner, a reporter for the Long Island-based daily *Newsday*, he penned *Wall Street Swindler*, an autobiographical account of how a nice Jewish kid from Brooklyn got greedy, befriended mobsters, and pulled an untold number of stock scams on their behalf. (Ironically, some of Rapp's methods outlined in his book would later be used by convicted inside trader Ivan Boesky.) Nowhere in the book did Rapp disclose where he lived or what exactly he was up to. He wrote, "My future, whatever it may be, will depend on what I am willing to contribute. I have the tools, the education, and the mind to make a better life and I'm trying harder now than ever before in my life."

He also wrote, "I knew that no matter what the temptation, I would never commit another crime in my life. Those three short days, a flickering moment in my sentence, were enough to convince me that all the money, all the mink coats, jewels, fancy cars, and restaurants weren't worth one day in that prison again."

High-sounding promises aside, Rapp soon abandoned the straight and narrow path he had set for himself. After a run-in with Massachusetts revenue agents over the possibility that perhaps his Boston restaurant was underpaying its fair share of taxes, Rapp left in a huff and moved to Bar Harbor Island in Florida, just north of Miami, where in 1983 he resumed his relationship with Rizzo and made a host of new friends. He had to. He'd sent all his old friends up the river. No matter, his new friends were eager to do business with him. Soon, law-enforcement officials said, Rizzo introduced Rapp to Anthony Delvecchio,[18] a tall hulk of a man who weighed in at about 240 pounds and used to work as a bouncer in one of Rizzo's restaurants. Delvecchio, in his late forties, grew up on Delancy Street, a tough Italian neighborhood in New York's Little Italy. He later testified that Rizzo introduced him to Rapp in a Miami restaurant called Apples, which Rapp and reputed mobster Phil "Cigars" Moscotta had recently purchased.

Moscotta (who also went by the name Brother Moscotta), Rizzo, Delvecchio, and Rapp had dinner at Apples in May 1984 and one topic of conversation, Delvecchio later recalled, was Flushing Federal Savings and Loan in Flushing, Queens, New York. Rizzo and Delvecchio told Rapp that World Wide Ventures Corporation, in which Rizzo and Delvecchio said they held a stake, had just obtained an easy $500,000 loan from Flushing secured by some land in the Pennsylvania Poconos.[19] Delvecchio and Rizzo said World Wide had supplied Flushing Federal with an appraisal report that said the land, a hundred acres, was worth $2 million. The value was based on the fact that *some* day World Wide Ventures planned to build a hotel, timeshare and sports complex on the site. In fact, the land was worth only about $500,000 at the most, maybe less, thrift executives said later, yet the president of Flushing Federal had approved the $500,000 loan.[20] World Wide was a holding company in Orange, New Jersey, that invested in other business. It didn't matter that some of the businesses never got off the ground—like World Wide's self-chilling soda can.[21]

When Rapp was told the Flushing Federal story over dinner, he must have been intrigued. It sounded like his kind of bank. And it wasn't too far from Bayside, where he'd almost been murdered 12 years earlier. Rapp listened carefully. He also told Delvecchio he had access to European funds through a company called Swiss International, which was controlled by a man named Heinrich Rupp.

"If you need some money for the project in the Poconos, maybe I can help," Rapp said, according to Delvecchio. "I have a friend who's close with Rupp."

Rupp did become involved in another deal that they had on the table that night, a deal that involved the Aurora Bank in Denver and John Napoli, Jr., a man alleged to have close ties to New York's Lucchese crime family. Rupp and Napoli would both later be convicted of bank fraud for this scam. Court documents showed that Napoli had an opportunity to buy $9 million in stolen currency for $2 million from a contact named "Al." Napoli had arranged with Aurora Bank officers for the bank to loan millions of dollars to various people, and regulators later claimed that Delvecchio and Rizzo agreed to borrow $350,000 from Aurora.[22] (Later, when Rizzo was sued by the FDIC for his involvement in this deal at Aurora, he refused to answer questions and invoked the fifth amendment because he said he was the subject of a criminal investigation in another jurisdiction.)

Rupp claimed to be a longtime CIA contract pilot. His attorney told us that in the 1970s he flew for Global Air International out of Dallas. When Rupp was convicted of bank fraud in connection with the Aurora Bank case, a witness for the defense told the judge that the CIA commonly used financial institutions to launder drug money or scam loans before sending the money off to the Contras or to various other covert purposes.[23] Among the financial institutions the witness named as having been used in this way were Aurora Bank and Flushing Federal.[24]

Rapp apparently decided that taking out loans, or getting a share of loans that he arranged for others, might be a promising way to make ends meet. Clearly something new and exciting was happening in the once stodgy world of savings and loans, something that would welcome his kind of expertise. So Mike Rapp—former stockbroker to the mob, former jailbird, former informant— became Mike Rapp, loan broker and matchmaker. In short order a colorful cast of characters found their way to Mike's door. Delvecchio said a music publisher from Beverly Hills named Steve Metz arrived with big plans to buy his own bank. Texas investor Frank Negrelli, who was interested in oil and gas leases, also showed up, as did Owen Beveridge, a deposit broker from Long Island, and William Smith (he claimed to be a former CIA agent), who owned a travel agency that sponsored, among other things, gambling junkets to the Dominican Republic. And Rizzo and Delvecchio were around. Delvecchio said they all had business propositions for Mike Rapp—everything from investments in oil and gas leases to the purchases of banks, S&Ls, hotels, and casinos. For a finder's fee, or a piece of the action, Rapp's job was to put these men's ideas together with money to fund them. (Delvecchio has since sued Rapp over the collapse of their business arrangements.)

Another visitor to Rapp's home/office was Lionel Reifler, a man whose background was similar to Rapp's. In 1970 Reifler had pleaded guilty to stock fraud; in 1975 he pleaded guilty to selling unregistered securities and was sentenced to two years in prison. In 1973 Reifler had drawn the attention of investigative journalist and author Jonathan Kwitny, who gave him less than honorable mention in his book on white-collar crime in America entitled *Fountain Pen Conspiracy*. Reifler was now running a realty office in Fort Lauderdale, Florida.

These characters gravitated to Mike Rapp because he knew how to get money. Besides cutting his teeth on Wall Street, he had studied under master bank fraud artist Erwin Layne, a swindler who pulled scams for Vincent Gugliara, a soldier in New York's Colombo crime family. Layne's specialty involved a scam where he'd take possession of stolen bonds (usually obtained by the mob) and then move the bonds to banks and obtain loans against the bonds. During the days when he was still Michael Hellerman, Rapp had taken special note of the way

Layne operated. Hellerman even described Layne's system of scamming banks in *Wall Street Swindler*.

Speaking of Erwin Layne, Hellerman wrote, ". . . his next step was to borrow $10,000 or $15,000 from one of the wise guys, select a bank, and then open an account at that bank. He established himself at that bank as a construction executive and became friendly with a vice president of the bank. Once that friendship was established Layne began a carefully choreographed program of wining and dining the banker, providing a prostitute (whom the banker was led to believe was Layne's wife) and paying her to seduce the banker behind his back in a lavishly furnished apartment. . . . The setup for the scam might last six months, until Layne was convinced that he had the banker on the hook. . . ."

The banker thus compromised, the final step was to get large loans from the bank. The banker, torn between guilt and fear that Layne would find out he was sleeping with Layne's "wife," would bend over backward to accommodate Layne. Any resistance on the part of the banker was weakened by the "wife," who would beg the banker to make the loan so they could continue their affair. Once the loans were in hand, the only thing left for the swindler to do was to pull up stakes and leave town. It was a classic bank scam.

In the spring of 1984, Rapp had an idea that didn't stray too much from Layne's blueprint. Rapp, of course, would add some variations of his own, but the end result would be the same. His target would not be a bank, however. He was intrigued by thrift deregulation and the stories about Flushing Federal Savings, and he had decided to make friends with Carl Cardascia, the president of Flushing Federal.

CHAPTER THIRTEEN

Flushing Gets a Bum Rapp

Carl Cardascia, in his forties, had been president and chief executive officer of Flushing Federal Savings for about a year. Cardascia told friends he had never finished college and hated paperwork. Still, he had been a dedicated employee of the S&L since the late 1960s when he had begun working his way up the Flushing Federal ladder. He was no financial genius, but operating a savings and loan association did not exactly require an MBA. Cardascia picked close friend Ronald J. Martorelli as his right-hand man, making him a vice president and Flushing's chief lending officer. Prematurely balding, Martorelli was small-framed and wore glasses. He was a graduate of Hofstra University and, like Cardascia, had worked his way up the ranks at Flushing Federal, starting as a part-time teller in 1974 when he was just 17.

A federal judge would later describe Cardascia as a "careless," "incompetent" thrift president. He didn't like to waste his time studying financial statements and credit reports. Instead, he just made "an informal type of analysis within his own mind" about whether an applicant for a loan would be able to repay or not, Martorelli explained later. By mid-1984 Flushing Federal wasn't doing well. It was growing quickly (it had assets of about $578 million, thanks to brokered deposits) but was losing money. The Federal Home Loan Bank of New York slapped Cardascia with a supervisory agreement that forbade the S&L to make loans of more than $500,000 to out-of-state residents and more than $1 million to New York state residents. Flushing was also ordered to improve the documentation behind its loans.

But soon thereafter a realtor introduced Cardascia to World Wide Ventures. Cardascia apparently did some of his "informal analysis within his own mind" and decided World Wide Ventures looked like a pretty good risk. Court records showed Flushing Federal gave World Wide not only the $500,000 loan that Rizzo and Delvecchio later told Rapp about but also granted the company a $5 million line of credit. What Cardascia's informal analysis had not disclosed was that World Wide Ventures, according to regulators, was for the most part worthless. It had some rights to the bare land in the Poconos, but that was about it. On the surface World Wide looked like a company on the way up. But authorities would later claim that behind the scenes a friendly stockbroker was actually manipulating World Wide's stock and artificially inflating its price.

In June, World Wide President Lorenzo Formato brought a Florida businessman friend of his to Flushing Federal's corporate headquarters in New York and took him up to Cardascia's office on the second floor.

"Carlo," Formato said, "I'd like you to meet a friend of mine, Mike Rapp."

"Glad to meet you, Carlo," Rapp said, shaking Cardascia's hand. Michael Rapp told Cardascia that he was a businessman in search of financing for some projects he was considering, including the purchase of People's National Bank up in Rockland County. And there was a bank out in Oklahoma that he and a partner of his from Texas had their eyes on. Plus, he was looking at the purchase of oil and gas leases in Texas. Rapp mentioned that he could arrange for large deposits to be brokered into Flushing Federal. Cardascia, who evidently trusted Formato, listened to Rapp's rap. Over the next month or so, according to federal investigators, Rapp successfully applied the Erwin Layne formula to Flushing, with a couple of twists and flourishes of his own, of course.

Rapp began by wining and dining Cardascia and, according to one federal agent, even took the Flushing Federal president to Atlantic City on a little gambling trip. Although nothing was ever made of it, there were rumors that Rapp began buying presents for Cardascia and his wife—a set of golf clubs and a fur coat. Delvecchio said that along the way Rapp gave Cardascia an earful about his business plans. Then Rapp invited Cardascia and his wife to a benefit cocktail party in New York where Rapp's old friend Frank Sinatra was supposed to sing a song or two. Sinatra never showed, but his wife did, and since it didn't take much to impress Cardascia, that did the trick.

Rapp knew Cardascia's S&L was in trouble and needed money, and Mike knew where to get it. Delvecchio told authorities that Rapp, together with money brokers Owen Beveridge and others (Rapp would eventually tap into First United Fund too), made sure that Flushing received all the brokered money it needed in order to have enough cash to make loans to Rapp and his associates. Initially, a meeting was scheduled at Flushing Federal to talk about bringing money into the ailing S&L. Rapp, Reifler, and Delvecchio went into Cardascia's office, and Cardascia buzzed his young protégé, Martorelli, who then met Rapp and Reifler for the first time. Everyone shook hands. During the discussion Rapp told Cardascia he could bring at least $13 million in CDs into Flushing.

Martorelli and Delvecchio would later tell authorities how the deal worked: Rapp arranged to have the money deposited at Flushing free of any brokerage fees—all Flushing had to do was agree to loan to Rapp and his partners $250,000 of each million Rapp brought in. (Normally, the financial institution paid a 2 percent to 5 percent brokerage fee for brokered deposits it received. Rapp was taking a page out of Renda's book and offering to place the deposits at the institution without cost to the thrift.)

Rapp's friends started shaking the Flushing Federal money tree in June 1984 when according to the FSLIC, a World Wide associate was granted a $250,000 line of credit and Reifler's realty company got $250,000. Martorelli said no credit checks or applications were ever filled out by the two. All of the loans were unsecured. No sooner had Flushing shelled out $250,000 to the World Wide associate than the borrower's name appeared in the newspaper as the owner of a warehouse full of counterfeit highway tokens seized by FBI agents in Brooklyn. He was promptly arrested. Martorelli rushed into Cardascia's office waving the article about the arrest.[1] Cardascia looked it over. "I'll look into it, Ronnie. Don't you worry. I'll take care of it," he reportedly said.

Federal authorities claimed that even as the money flowed Rapp continued bringing new loan proposals to Flushing. The money from these loans, Delvecchio said, was supposed to go into high-yield oil and gas leases, and Rapp and his partners were buying a bank in Oklahoma. Also, Rapp, Rizzo, and Delvecchio were supposedly going to buy a hotel and casino in the Caribbean. All these investments would turn big profits and Flushing would get its money back, plus. By that time Rapp appeared to have gained Cardascia's total confidence. After all, how could Cardascia not trust a man who knew Frank Sinatra—personally? Rapp reassured Cardascia that he, Michael "Miguel" Rapp, would distribute loan proceeds to the borrowers he lined up. Martorelli said Rapp also promised Cardascia that he'd make sure the interest on the loans was paid in a timely manner.

With Flushing Federal under the watchful eye of federal regulators, Rapp couldn't take out too many loans under any one name without drawing suspicion so he set up a maze of phony corporations, prosecutors later proved. Through that paper corporate empire he and his friends could borrow money without putting their own names on paper. Rapp's scam at Flushing was just one big Ponzi scheme—regulators claimed he took out new loans to make payments on old loans and he and his friends pocketed any difference. Delvecchio told authorities that when Rapp set up a new company he'd show up at Flushing's headquarters, sometimes with Smith or Metz, other times with Rizzo and Delvecchio. They'd fill out a loan application for the new front company, Delvecchio said, and be out the door with a Flushing Federal check in hand the same day.

For example, Glen Grotto Inn, a Rapp company that was a mere shell with little or no assets, got a whopping $300,000 line of credit out of Flushing which later was increased to $700,000. By October 1984 Rapp was feeling so brazen that he even took out a $350,000 line-of-credit loan using his own name. He just walked into Flushing and filled out a loan application. Martorelli said Cardascia gave the nod and Martorelli cut the check. On that particular day Rapp brought his pal Jilly Rizzo with him, and regulators said Rizzo took the opportunity to pick up a quick $200,000 loan for himself while he was in the neighborhood.

Notwithstanding Martorelli's growing concern, Cardascia continued to turn on the loan spigot for Rapp and his friends. But Martorelli said that in late October, Cardascia (who later claimed he did not know at this time of Rapp's other life as Michael Hellerman) finally voiced concern to Rapp that regulators were due to inspect the S&L's books soon and if Rapp didn't come up with some collateral for all the loans he was arranging, there might be trouble.

"Carlo," Rapp reportedly said to Cardasica, "don't worry."

Rapp certainly wasted no time worrying. No oil leases ever materialized, nor did any of Rapp's other ventures that he spun elaborate stories about to Martorelli, who said he became increasingly skeptical. But Rapp feathered his own nest well. He lavishly furnished his Bar Harbor home and showered his new wife, Janet, with expensive diamond broaches, rings, and gold watches. Delvecchio said he saw Rapp refurnish his Florida ranch house with Flushing Federal loan proceeds and buy what he'd heard amounted to half a million dollars' worth of jewelry for his wife. In November, Rapp was having lunch with Delvecchio at the Waldorf-Astoria on Park Avenue in New York when a delivery boy arrived at Rapp's lunch table with two fur coats. Rapp told him to take the furs up to his wife's room. Janet Rapp soon returned the kind gift by throwing a party for her loving husband. The party cost around $100,000 but no matter, she just wrote a check, a Flushing check,[2] Delvecchio said.

By late October 1984 Cardascia was insisting that Rapp come up with collateral to cover the loans he'd received from Flushing. Most were still current, mainly because Rapp was using part of the newer loans to make payments on the others,[3] but Rapp probably figured he'd better cover the loans with something that at least *looked* like collateral before Cardascia had a nervous breakdown. Stock seemed like a good idea, so Rapp worked out a deal with a friend in Texas who needed a loan. The friend lent Rapp stock in a company he owned in return for a later loan. Rapp then put the stock up as collateral for most of the lines of credit he had previously arranged at Flushing. And while he was there he took the opportunity to get another $350,000, regulators later charged. (The stock later turned out to be worthless.)

But that was just a temporary fix and Rapp knew he would soon need a new source for loans. Flushing Federal was tapped out. Also the Flushing Federal loans were all coming due soon and he needed a way to deal with that too. Rapp began looking for a bank or savings and loan he could buy and control himself. He had been trying to set up a deal for Jilly Rizzo and Steve Metz to buy the People's National Bank in Rockland, County, Ramapo, New York. Rizzo and Metz were to be appointed to the bank's board of directors. Rapp said he had received assurances from his old friend Frank Sinatra that if Rizzo acquired the bank, Sinatra would serve as a director. Rapp was also telling interested parties that he had director commitments from singer Sammy Davis, Jr., and former President Gerald Ford. A lot of big talk . . . but no deal.[4]

Then a better opportunity to buy a bank came along at the end of 1984, and Rapp decided the least Flushing Federal could do for him, after all he had done for Flushing Federal, was to loan him the down payment. Martorelli said Rapp walked into Flushing accompanied by William Smith, the self-acclaimed ex-CIA agent. They clustered together in Cardascia's office. After a short time Cardascia buzzed Martorelli on the office intercom and asked him if he'd ever been to Texas. When Martorelli said he had not, Cardascia told him to pack his bags, he was leaving for Texas that day. Cardascia told Martorelli he would be representing Flushing Federal in a big deal.

It was Monday, December 4, and within an hour Flushing had cut Bill Smith a $700,000 check off a commercial line of credit. Rapp, Smith, and Rapp's attorney left to make the travel arrangements and said they'd return in an hour to pick up Martorelli. After they left Cardascia told Martorelli that the group was going to buy the First Bank & Trust Company in Duncan, Oklahoma, 140 miles north of Dallas. Once the bank deal was closed, Rapp would give Martorelli a check from the Duncan bank to pay off all the loans he and his friends had taken out of Flushing. Martorelli had two jobs on the trip: first, keep a close eye on the $700,000 check, and second, bring back the check paying off the Flushing loans.[5]

Within two hours Martorelli was on a plane to Dallas, carrying the $700,000 check Flushing had cut for Smith. That night they all stayed in a Dallas hotel and the next morning Rapp chartered two planes at a nearby airport and flew his entourage, including Martorelli, to Duncan, Oklahoma, "to check out the bank." A little tire kicking, as it were. Rapp told Martorelli, "We're going to meet the bank's president, the directors, and a couple of shareholders." Which Martorelli later said seemed reasonable enough to him. After all, he didn't expect Rapp to buy a pig in a poke. That afternoon Rapp and his entourage arrived at the Duncan bank. More meetings, dinner, and more meetings, but no deal. Martorelli waited outside while Rapp et al huddled with the bank officials. At one point during the negotiations Rapp came out of the meeting and asked Martorelli for the $700,000 check.

"They want to see it. It's the earnest money in the deal," Rapp told him. Ron handed over the check. Later that evening, after the meeting ended, Rapp gave the check back to Martorelli. Still no deal.

That night they flew back to Dallas, and Martorelli called Cardascia to inform him of the progress.

"Nothing so far," Martorelli said.

The next morning Rapp met Martorelli back at the Dallas hotel for breakfast. Martorelli asked him how the deal was going. "We're still trying to iron out some details. But it looks good though," Rapp said. "It should happen shortly." Rapp then asked Martorelli for the $700,000 check again. Martorelli handed the check over. It was Wednesday. Martorelli called Cardascia.

"Is the deal going to happen or not?" his boss asked.

"I don't know."

"Okay, if nothing happens by tonight, come back to New York."

"Okay."

The next morning Martorelli was on a plane back to New York. No deal and no check. The $700,000 was firmly in Rapp's hands.

Martorelli said Cardascia told him not to worry about the money. Cardascia said Rapp's purchase of the Duncan Bank was imminent and the deal was just awaiting approval of the Federal Reserve, the regulatory agency that had oversight responsibility for the First Bank & Trust Company of Duncan.[6] It seemed to Cardascia that the Duncan Bank acquisition was on the verge of being a done deal. But he informed Rapp that Flushing still needed more collateral on all the money it had lent to Rapp and his friends. The regulators were starting to sniff around the S&L's vault. Rapp told Cardascia not to worry, he'd take care of the situation. Rapp promised Cardascia that he would have enough deposits placed at Flushing to offset all the lines of credit that he'd arranged since May. Satisfied, Cardascia agreed to make more loans to Rapp and company. The FSLIC charged that Rapp got $350,000 for another dummy company that he had set up, Jilly's Enterprises got another $350,000 and a friend of Delvecchio's, acting as a straw borrower for Rapp, walked in and got a $575,000 line of credit. Authorities later alleged Rapp paid the straw borrower $5,000 and promised him a $50,000-a-year job with Jilltone, a new company Rapp was setting up with Jilly Rizzo and Delvecchio. (Delvecchio said Jilltone was trying to buy a hotel and casino in Santo Domingo.)[7]

Rapp told Cardascia to have Martorelli pick up the collateral for all the loans on December 17, 1984, at the Regency Hotel on Park Avenue in New York.[8] The last time Rapp had promised to produce collateral for the loans he was getting from Flushing, he had given Flushing worthless stock that he didn't own. This time the collateral was to be $8 million in certificates of deposit that Rapp supposedly had on deposit at Co-op Investment Bank, Ltd., an offshore bank based in St. Vincent in the West Indies. Dollar for dollar the face value of the CDs matched the lines of credit that Rapp and his friends had received at Flushing. Cardascia sent Martorelli to the Regency Hotel and as Martorelli walked into the room he looked at the familiar faces.

"You know everyone," Rapp said.

"Yes, I know everyone," Martorelli said.

Rapp read the pledge agreements that Martorelli had brought. He didn't like some of the language in the agreements and decided to change it.

Martorelli said Rapp snapped, "I don't like this clause." The clause he disliked would've allowed Flushing to claim the CDs as collateral *prior* to the maturity date of the CDs. Martorelli didn't argue with Rapp because the CDs were scheduled to mature before the loans came due anyway. Rapp took a pen from Martorelli and made the change. Now Flushing couldn't claim the CDs until they matured, which wasn't for several months. Rapp then handed the passbooks to Martorelli. The pledges and passbooks in hand, Martorelli headed back to Flushing, feeling that at last the bank had security for all the questionable loans Cardascia had approved for Rapp. Everyone breathed a sigh of relief. With the old loans now supposedly secured, Cardascia approved another round of loans totaling $1.2 million. Regulators claimed Rapp used part of the money to keep his earlier loans current. The CDs Rapp had given Martorelli were bogus, but it would be a while before Flushing found out. Rapp later admitted that he had paid a $1.5 million fee to Co-op Bank and the company's president to set up the phony CDs. Trying to cash them would be like grasping at a mirage.

By the early days of 1985 too many "interesting people" were hanging around Flushing Federal and too much money was heading out the door. Both regulators and the FBI were poking around asking questions. Matters got worse when a top executive of a company that had been selling home improvement loans to the S&L was found murdered in his car in Bayside, Queens—Mike Rapp's old neighborhood. New York's *Daily News* described the murder as a mob-style hit. The FBI declined to talk to us about the case, noting that its investigation was far from being a closed matter, but we did learn that Flushing had been losing millions of dollars on the loans it had been buying from the dead man's company.

The FBI zeroed in on the murder case, and while Agent Michael Shea was poring over Flushing's loan files he discovered a group of names that sounded terribly familiar, including Rapp's. By chance the FBI had found former protected witness Michael Hellerman. It took only a phone call to verify that Michael Rapp and Michael Hellerman were one and the same and that Hellerman had once been the mob's personal stockbroker. Another agent familiar with the case said that the lines of credit put together by Rapp "looked like a who's who of organized crime." The FBI also discovered the name of another convicted stock swindler: Lionel Reifler.

In early April 1985 Cardascia was forced out of his job by the New York FHLB. Later that month Flushing was taken over by the FSLIC. The S&L was in the hole by at least $50 million and would wind up costing the FSLIC close to $100 million. Starting in April, attorney Andrew Donnellan, with the New York law firm of Dewey, Ballantine, Bushby, Palmer & Wood, started investigating Flushing's failure for the FSLIC. Also on Rapp's trail were the FBI and the U.S. attorney's office in Brooklyn.

While the Flushing investigation was in its early stages, Rapp was allowed to continue to operate unimpeded, despite federal suspicions. We had seen this happen before: FBI agents in one city focusing only on what a suspect did in that jurisdiction and never checking to see if that person was operating (or had operated already) somewhere else. Rapp had similar scams in progress at thrifts and banks in California and Florida, so when Flushing collapsed he just shifted his attention to other fronts. But his relationship with his associates was becoming strained. He argued with Reifler and threw him out of his house. When the Texas businessman who had loaned Rapp the worthless stock was questioned by the FBI, he became furious with Rapp for getting him involved. Later he testified that Rapp threatened to have him killed if he didn't shut up.[9] Law-enforcement officials said Rizzo's deal to buy People's National Bank of Rockland fell through because the Federal Reserve wouldn't approve it, and Delvecchio said he and Rizzo, sensing trouble, started avoiding Rapp.

Later Delvecchio told investigators that Rapp essentially "robbed the bank," that he "finagled the bank out of money with other people involved." Delvecchio said he was mad at Rapp for the way he was wasting money when he was supposed to be investing it for the gang. Delvecchio brought his personal phone books to a deposition, apparently as a reference tool. Donnellan threatened to have Delvecchio's phone books entered as evidence in the case, and he grilled Delvecchio on whose names and numbers were in the book. Among them were all of the players involved with the Flushing lines of credit, including Rapp and Delvecchio's good friend Jilly Rizzo. Delvecchio had many different phone numbers for Rizzo, one of which was a New York phone number.

"Rizzo has a New York phone number?" Donnellan asked. Rizzo's residence had been listed as Rancho Mirage, California.

"Yes, he does," said Delvecchio. "Write that number down and call it up. Find out who answers."

"What is it?" asked Donnellan.

"Frank Sinatra's number," said Delvecchio. Donnellan let the matter drop. A couple of minutes later Donnellan took the book and found the name of John Wayne.

"You have John Wayne's number in here?" asked Donnellan.

"Yeah," said Delvecchio. "You want to talk to him? You'll have to get a shovel."

None of this slowed Rapp down. He was used to making and losing friends, and he was already building bridges to new ones. In 1985 a mutual friend, a banker in Houston, suggested to Rapp that he contact Charles Bazarian in Oklahoma City. Charlie had plenty of money, he said, and might be willing to loan to Rapp. Rapp liked the idea and in October he and William Smith flew to Oklahoma for a meeting with "Fuzzy." Mario Renda, who had gotten to know Bazarian at Consolidated Savings, had flown out from New York to attend one of Charlie's famous Halloween parties and was already at the Bazarian mansion when Rapp arrived.

The meeting between Bazarian, Renda, and Rapp came at a critical time for Renda and Rapp. Renda's indiscretions with Winkler at Indian Springs State Bank and Coronado Savings had led to the FBI raid on First United Fund headquarters a year earlier. Since then investigators had been all over him. He'd gotten bad press and cash flow was a real problem. Rapp was having similar troubles. His old friends didn't trust him anymore and he was having a hard time finding financial institutions that would take his bait. Bazarian, on the other hand, was still riding high. He was plugged right into a number of financial institutions, and his company, C.B. Financial, could still swing millions in loans anytime he wanted.

All the ingredients Rapp required to solve his current problems were present at that meeting. He had a scam in mind, but he couldn't pull it off alone. He needed help. Above all else he needed $10 million in seed money to prime the pump. Rapp laid out the deal for the other two men:

There was this bank in Florida, the Florida Center Bank in Orlando, he said. Its directors were anxious to sell out, if they could make a killing on their stock, and they were willing to work with him on a deal that could leave Rapp with the bank in his hands. To pull it off he needed just $10 million for two or three days. Five million would be used to buy a CD at Florida Center Bank, for which the bank agreed to pay him $3.1 million interest in advance (ten years' worth of interest in advance). In addition the bank would loan him $3.8 million (using the same $5 million CD as collateral). Then he'd combine the $3.1 million and the $3.8 million and buy a $6.9 million CD, on which the bank would pay him ten years of up-front interest and on which they'd grant him another, even larger loan. He would repeat the process three times, in about that many days, and it would generate enough money to repay Bazarian his $10 million plus $300,000 for his trouble.

The other $5 million that Bazarian loaned him, Rapp said, he'd use to buy controlling interest in the bank. And once Rapp controlled Florida Center Bank, he'd be in a position to make loans to Bazarian, especially if Renda funneled deposits into Florida Center Bank so it had plenty of cash. Rapp said he wanted to start a pay telephone business with loans from Florida Center Bank.

Charlie didn't have $10 million in cash right then, but he had a checkbook and an idea. He agreed to give Rapp two checks for $5 million each, but he didn't trust Rapp and asked his house guest and friend, Mario Renda, to accompany Rapp and the two $5 million checks to Florida. Bazarian offered to pay Renda $150,000, and Renda agreed to go.[10] Getting involved in the deal was a foolish move on Renda's part. He knew federal prosecutors were in possession of all his First United Fund records and those of his chief accomplice, Franklin Winkler. They would be watching his every move. But apparently he just couldn't refuse the $150,000—or the promise of a new scam.

With Bazarian's $10 million, Rapp finally had his best crack yet at getting his own bank. He flipped the CDs up to $10 million as planned, Bazarian's two $5 million rubber checks were covered before they could bounce, Renda started brokering deposits into Florida Center Bank, and Rapp started making sweetheart loans out the front door.

One successful deal under way, Rapp and Bazarian began looking for other business opportunities. Bazarian owned 9.9 percent of Local Federal Savings and Loan in Oklahoma, and he decided he wanted to sell his stock to Rapp and Rizzo. He set up a dinner meeting at Pier 66 in Tampa between Rapp, Rizzo, a stockbroker named Marc Perkins, his boss, and others. The purpose of the meeting, according to Perkins, was to discuss the sale of Bazarian's Local Federal stock. Perkins, referred by an acquaintance of Bazarian's, had never met any of the group. When he arrived at the restaurant Bazarian introduced him to the others. During cocktails Perkins listened as the men talked, then he excused himself. In the restaurant lobby he ran into his boss, who had earlier left the table, and he remarked to him, "You wouldn't believe the bullshit these guys are talking. I don't think these guys have enough money to pay for cocktails, much less an S&L."

The group settled in for dinner. The waiter brought the soup. Perkins made small talk with Rapp about their mutual interest, stocks. Suddenly, Perkins later told us, one of the men leaned across the table and nonchalantly asked Rizzo, "Hey, Jilly, you ain't packing a piece tonight, are you?"

Rizzo didn't respond and just looked the other way, as if to say "How indiscreet." Perkins almost choked on his soup. After composing himself, he left the table and phoned his wife.

"Honey, you have to call me back in a little while and have me paged. Say there's a family emergency or something. I have to get out of here. You wouldn't believe what's happening."

When he returned to the table the men were discussing Rapp's and Rizzo's proposed buyout of Bazarian's Local Federal stock. Rapp told Perkins about his prior conviction. Perkins told Rapp that a felony conviction precluded Rapp from participating in any such stock transfer and that he, Perkins, wanted no part of any of this business. Perkins liked his name and didn't want to have to change it.

"They were going to buy the Local Federal stock using Local's own money," Perkins said later. Just like the Florida Center Bank bust-out.

■ ■ ■

In June 1985 the FSLIC, on behalf of Flushing, sued Rapp, Cardascia, Formato, Rizzo, Delvecchio, Beveridge, Smith, the companies they controlled, and others. The FSLIC charged that Cardascia was "corrupted" by Rapp and his associates and that he aided and abetted in a scheme to defraud the S&L via 22 lines of credit, all of which went into default. The FSLIC charged that Cardascia didn't have the authority to grant the sizable lines of credit. (Several months later Cardascia was dropped from this RICO suit and named prominently as a defendant in a separate suit against just Flushing's former officers and directors, mainly Cardascia and Martorelli.)

A judge promptly imposed a $7,000-a-month spending limit on Rapp, but in February 1986 U.S. marshals in Miami arrested Rapp for exceeding those limits. According to court records, he had spent $44,000 in one month. The judge charged him with criminal contempt of court.

By the spring of 1986 the Justice Department had a better picture of Rapp's activities and knew he had to be shut down. One New York law-enforcement official familiar with the case put it this way:

"We knew what Rapp was up to but there was no program to nail him. He was running around bilking banks and thrifts and he had to be stopped. So we had a meeting down in Tampa. I said, 'This is what he's done and this is how he did it. I have an agent in Oklahoma who knows what he did there.' No one in the Tampa department could get up to speed on this. It was taking too long. So we cooperated—New York, Oklahoma, and Tampa—and we put a case together in six months."

A whistle-blower at Florida Center Bank helped bring Rapp's scam there to a screeching halt, but only after Rapp had withdrawn about $12 million to $15 million of a $30 million loan commitment the bank had made to him.[11] The three bustkateers, Renda, Rapp, and Bazarian, were indicted in September 1986 and charged with defrauding Florida Center Bank. Assistant U.S. Attorney Stephen Calvacca prosecuted the case and he said it was one of his most memorable trials.

He told us that he was about to present a key point to the jury when he suddenly noticed the jury's attention was focused out in the gallery. He turned to discover, to his amazement, that former heavyweight champion Muhammad Ali had strolled into the courtroom. Calvacca said Ali attended several sessions of the trial (as did former Gemini and Apollo astronaut Tom Stafford—the Tulsa *Tribune* reported that Stafford and Ali had both been involved in business deals with Bazarian) and always caused a stir. Calvacca knew the defendants had arranged this tactic, and he hit upon an idea to turn it around. When Calvacca began his closing remarks to the jury, he told them he knew they were wondering why Ali had been in the courtroom.

"I told them that Ali had long been an admirer of my courtroom style and often attended my trials."[12] Calvacca said the consternation at the defense table was extreme, but they had already had their last say in the case and they had no choice but to swallow hard and accept the fact that their little plan had backfired on them.[13]

Annoying the prosecution was something the three bad-boy defendants seemed to relish. Every day at noon the court broke for lunch, and defendants and prosecutors alike retired for their noon meal. But as prosecutors munched on their Wendy's hamburgers, Rapp, Renda, and Bazarian sat at a table covered with a white linen tablecloth while houseboys served them fresh gourmet delicatessen food flown in that morning from New York: pâté, luncheon meats, even fresh cheesecake from Leo Lindy's on Broadway.

"Hey, Calvacca, ya oughta try some of this cheesecake, it's really gooooood," Rapp would taunt.

In their closing remarks defense attorneys tried to convince the jury that their clients were simply misunderstood entrepreneurs, that stodgy regulators just didn't understand their revolutionary and innovative business deals. They even compared the three with the Wright brothers.

Calvacca retorted, "The Wright brothers? These were the Wrong brothers, the Blues brothers, the We-Take-the-Money-You-Lose brothers."

Rapp was found guilty of bank fraud in the case and sentenced to 32 years in federal prison and fined $1.75 million. Bazarian was found guilty of three counts of bank fraud and sentenced to two years in prison and fined $100,000. Renda was found guilty of one count of conspiracy and sentenced to two years in prison and fined $100,000.[14]

As the investigation into Rapp's role in the downfall of Flushing Federal and other financial institutions continued, Rapp's troubles mounted. Not only was he convicted and sentenced to 32 years in prison for the Florida Center Bank scam but he pled guilty to conspiracy and fraud charges in connection with the Flushing loans as well. He was sentenced to 10 years in prison for the Flushing bust-out, but his term was to run concurrently with the Florida Center Bank sentence.

When investigators began to learn the true extent of Rapp's activities, they opened investigations in New York, Los Angeles, Denver, Miami, and Orlando. Rapp had kited checks at Sun Bank of Miami (perhaps to the tune of $1 million in losses, some said) in 1984.[15] Similar troubles were also reported by the president of Western United National Bank in Los Angeles. When SSDF Federal Credit Union near Tampa collapsed in May 1986, regulators discovered it had made a large loan to a company allegedly controlled by Rapp because he promised to bring in millions of dollars in brokered deposits. Then, comparing notes with others, regulators learned that Rapp and his friends had tried unsuccessfully to buy several thrifts and banks in Oklahoma and Tennessee. The picture that emerged was one of Rapp and a band of associates clearly running a two-year looting operation while trying everything within their power to get control of a financial institution themselves.

Early in 1987 Lorenzo Formato, who served as president of World Wide Ventures, was sentenced to six years in prison for stock fraud in an unrelated case brought against him in New Jersey. However, while being sentenced in the New Jersey case, Formato cut a deal with the U.S. attorney's office in Brooklyn and pled guilty to mail fraud charges stemming from the use of World Wide stock as collateral to obtain loans from Flushing. Regulators claimed the World Wide stock was worthless. Formato agreed to cooperate in connection with the Flushing case.

Also indicted, and later convicted, were Harold Farrell and Robert Wolk, who'd been charged with defrauding Flushing out of $1 million.[16] The assistant U.S. attorney handling the Farrell-Wolk case would later recall how Farrell constantly begged him not to indict: "He came to my office telling me how he had heart problems and how prison would kill him," he said. Wolk and Farrell were both in their early sixties. "I didn't believe him," he said with a tinge of comic irony in his voice. "He'd been doing the same thing for years with other prosecutors. The other prosecutors listened. I didn't. I indicted him and he was convicted. A couple of months later he actually did die of a heart attack."

Regulators sued Rizzo in both the Flushing and Aurora Bank cases. Ken Merica, a private investigator in the Aurora case, recalled in 1988 that when Rizzo was subpoenaed he ran out the back door of his house in Rancho Mirage to avoid being served.

"You know where he went?" recalled Merica. "He ran over to Sinatra's house. He spent the afternoon over there. He thought we'd go away. Well, we waited. He came back four hours later and he didn't see us. We served him while he was walking up his driveway."

Cardascia was indicted in October 1988 for extortion and misapplication of funds in connection with a $240,500 loan he allegedly had Flushing Federal make to Donald Luna, a convicted swindler from Nashville, Tennessee. The case came to trial in early 1989, and after hearing all the evidence, the federal judge said Cardascia was clearly "a man of bad judgment" who probably should have been fired, but he found Cardascia not guilty of defrauding Flushing Federal in the Luna matter. Instead, the judge excoriated the Reagan administration, the FHLBB, and Congress for permitting the thrift's failure by their negligence. A disappointed prosecutor said the grand jury investigation of Flushing Federal would continue, and in 1989 Cardascia, Delvecchio, Martorelli, Rizzo, and others were indicted in connection with Flushing loans to World Wide Ventures Corporation, Rapp, and others. Cardascia was accused of receiving kickbacks, in the form of World Wide stock, in return for having Flushing make a $5 million loan commitment to World Wide. Delvecchio was charged with participating in the delivery of the stock to Cardascia, and Martorelli was accused of falsifying a document in relation to the World Wide loans. Cardascia was also charged with illegally making loans to Rapp and his associates in exchange for brokered deposits from Owen Beveridge and First United Fund. (At the time, regulators had forbidden Flushing to take any new brokered deposits.) Delvecchio and Rizzo were charged with using fraudulently overvalued security (the Co-op Investment Bank CDs and the Poconos property) as collateral for loans.

Rizzo's attorney said, "If it were not for his relationship with Mr. Sinatra, there would be no indictment. Mr. Rizzo is an honorable man."

In announcing the indictments the U.S. attorney said, "It would appear from the allegations in this indictment and earlier depositions of other borrowers that Flushing Federal was being run like a candy store."

Investigators were said to be looking into 80 questionable loan transactions at Flushing. An assistant U.S. attorney handling the case didn't want to talk about it, but she said she'd be using Rapp as a witness against his old buddies. Those sued civilly, but not charged criminally, denied wrongdoing in the case. Most of those charged criminally refused to talk. The case was pending as of this writing.

As for Mike Rapp, we never expected to hear from him. But in September 1988 Rapp called us collect from his jail cell in the North Dade Correctional Center in Miami in response to a letter we'd sent him asking about the Flushing Federal case. The first thing he wanted to know was how we found out where he was doing time.

"A law-enforcement official told us," Paul Muolo replied.

"No one's supposed to know where I am," he said. Rapp sounded concerned. "What's your book about?"

"The bust-out of S&Ls."

"Yeah, what's your angle?"

"Our angle is that the mob and others are busting out thrifts and banks. What do you think?"

"Yeah, that's partially true," he said, and then he paused. Rapp said he hoped we weren't going to sensationalize his role in financial failures. He rambled on about how "there was nothing illegal in my deal"—a reference to the Florida Center Bank case—and how he never told a lie on the witness stand. "Lending money to your friends shouldn't constitute fraud," he complained.

"Really?"

"I can't talk about any of this, not yet," he said. "I'm appealing my case. I may write another book of my own. I've had a couple of offers." Rapp said the real "story" behind the S&L debacle "is the regulators." He said they were, and are, "incompetent," but he declined to elaborate.

Paul told Rapp that we had a host of questions we wanted to ask and that we would send him a letter outlining our areas of interest.

We sent him a list of very frank questions about the Florida Center scam and waited. Two weeks passed and not a word from Rapp so Paul decided to call. Rapp was angry.

"Yeah, I got your letter and I don't like your questions. When are you going to start being a reporter and stop being a prosecutor? Don't bother me anymore. My lawyer is sending you a letter." Paul told him we'd add it to our growing collection. Rapp hung up. The lawyer letter never arrived.

Later, Tony Delvecchio told us that he did not participate in any of Rapp's swindles, but he did admit that "a lot of innocent people got hurt. Prominent people were swindled." He said Rapp and Napoli knew each other well in Florida and added, "One of these days I'll tell all about Rapp and World Wide Ventures. . . . Yeah, now the feds are talking to Napoli, trying to find out who all the top gears are." He said, "Rapp's money is in offshore banks. If he's smart enough to con all these people, he's smart enough to have offshore accounts."

Then Delvecchio hit the point that had been bothering us. "It's amazing. Rapp did all these scams 20 years ago and then he writes a book and does it all over again. He was good, Rapp was. He convinced a lot of people."

The beauty of the Rapp operation, from our point of view, was that it was so typical of a wise guy in action. Rapp loved to spend his days figuring out schemes. A brilliant man, he could have been successful as a legitimate businessman, but the excitement of swindles held too powerful an allure for him. From the day thrifts were deregulated, it was inevitable that Rapp would loot them. Opportunities of that magnitude could not possibly go unnoticed by swindlers like Rapp. But the unanswered question in the Rapp story (and in many of the other cases in this book) was—where did the money go? Delvecchio said in depositions that Rapp spent $500,000 on jewelry for a girlfriend and $500,000 in Las Vegas, which still left a large amount unaccounted for, since in a couple of years he got over $20 million from thrifts and banks.

One answer to that question finally came to us from a law-enforcement official who told us that two New York crime families, the Lucchese and Genovese families, were making demands on part of the take. When a dispute broke out over how the money was going to be divided up, the matter was finally settled, the official told us, when a friend of Rapp's, an officer in one of the families, organized a sit-down at which the families decided how the shell corporations would split up the loan proceeds. How much was divided up? Rapp's not saying.

Finding Rapp doing business with Renda and Bazarian was a real surprise. When Paul first got the tip to check out Flushing Federal, we did not know of any connection at all between the three men. But there they were, on Halloween 1985, at Bazarian's Oklahoma City mansion, planning a scam. It was a graphic illustration to us of the way the network of swindlers worked. They heard about each other by word of mouth. Some were Mafia members and associates; some weren't. But they all did business together, and the distinction between organized crime and mere white-collar crime blurred until it became almost meaningless. The looting of the savings and loan industry was carried out by a band of swindlers who operated, and cooperated, in their own best interests. We kept a list of the people we found looting each savings and loan we investigated. Bazarian would one day taunt us by bragging that he knew everyone on our list.

CHAPTER FOURTEEN

Casino Federal

In the movie *Quest for Fire* a band of Stone Age men, consumed with the need to acquire a cinder from which they could kindle their fires and reap the huge benefits fire could bring, scoured the countryside. To get a cinder they would steal and even kill. The quest became an obsession. When we investigated a close relationship that we discovered between savings and loans and gambling casinos, we learned that certain segments of the business community pursued casino ownership with the same passion that cave men searched for fire. They flocked to areas where it was rumored the public was about to approve gambling. They used every tool at their disposal, primarily political and financial, to ingratiate themselves with the local power brokers.

Because of the skimming and money-laundering opportunities inherent in a business that dealt in such a high volume of cash, no one was more dogged than the underworld in the pursuit of casinos. Owning a casino was a wise guy's most cherished dream. The propensity of organized crime to circle the casino flame had a dual result: Rumors of mob affiliation followed virtually everyone who applied for a casino license, and the gaming control boards that granted casino licenses developed a tough licensing procedure designed to weed out crooks. Nevada and New Jersey licensed casinos as a means of raising revenue and as a way of controlling casino ownership. Applicants underwent a rigorous investigation and interrogation during which Gaming Control Board investigators looked for any possible connection between the applicant and organized crime. If even a casual relationship could be established, the license was generally denied. In perhaps the ultimate irony, after thrift deregulation it was *much* easier to own a thrift than it was to own a casino.

To circumvent the licensing obstacle, men with organized crime connections often used "beards," individuals with clean records who could hold the casino license for them. In return a beard was generally rewarded with a piece of the action either at the casino or in some other business enterprise. The gaming control boards routinely uncovered beards and denied them licenses or, if they had already slipped by, threw them out. But other beards would replace them in short order, all part of the continuing quest for fire. Sitting on a gaming control board was like being a pest-control expert, some said. They sprayed regularly but the roaches always returned.

Conservative financial institutions shied away from making loans on an enterprise with such a colorful history. For this reason casinos were often financed by pension funds[1] or other large pools of money[2] that did not have to operate under the strict standards that regulators demanded of thrifts and banks. But then came the deregulation of the thrift industry and, with it, new owners and managers who were only too happy to make loans on casinos. The timing of thrift deregulation was serendipitous for those who aspired to own a casino because it came just as financing by the pension funds was being closed to them by fierce government antiracketeering prosecutions and seizures. Those who pursued casino ownership with a lifetime passion promptly saw the opportunities inherent in thrift deregulation. Time and time again, as we researched this book, we ran into the casino connection—thrift executives loaning on and investing in casinos.

We first encountered the casino connection when we met Norman B. Jenson at Centennial Savings. Jenson was a Las Vegas attorney with a 20-year history in Las Vegas gaming, including, at various times, connections with the Crystal Bay Club Cal-Neva in North Lake Tahoe and the Thunderbird Hotel, the International Hotel (now the Las Vegas Hilton), and the Royal Inn Hotel, all in Las Vegas. His "claim to fame," he told us, was the Las Vegas Holiday Casino, which he and partners developed, promoted, and operated. He and an associate held a $1.7 million mortgage on the Shenandoah Casino in Las Vegas,[3] and in the early 1980s Jenson was also trying to get control of two casinos in Nevada, the DeVille and the Crystal Palace.[4] We learned of Jenson's casino involvement when coauthor Steve Pizzo spotted Jenson's name in a *National Thrift News* article about a Seattle trial of executives of three thrifts that were located in Louisiana, Texas, and Washington. Jenson, the story said, was involved in a complex $4 million casino-financing agreement with the thrifts. We wondered how Jenson got involved with three such widely separated institutions, and he told us that a loan broker named John Lapaglia, whom he had known for 15 years, had made the introductions.

When we researched Lapaglia we found that he was a former Texas vice cop who had gone into the real estate business and at one time had maintained an office in Las Vegas, which was where Jenson had met him. In the mid-1970s Lapaglia owned East Texas State Bank in Beaumont, Texas, for a little over a year. In 1984 Lapaglia would apply to own his own savings and loan, Uvalde Savings Association, but federal regulators denied the application.

In the 1980s Lapaglia was the owner of Falcon Financial Corporation, a mortgage brokerage firm in San Antonio.[5] A smooth operator, he reminded people of an Arabian merchant. He traveled in a leased corporate plane, accompanied by his man Friday who doubled as a secretary. He said he did so because traveling with a woman secretary could raise questions. He was rumored to be a womanizer, ordering $100 bouquets for pretty receptionists he'd just met, but he told us the rumors weren't true. The brokerage business had been good to him—he claimed to have brokered $2 billion in loans, on which he earned his company hefty commissions of between $20 and $60 million over 20 years.[6] Perhaps that was why his wife had a dollar sign painted on the bottom of their swimming pool at his home outside San Antonio. Associates said he was a high flier, living the good life.

Through his trade as loan broker, Lapaglia had become well acquainted with the nation's savings and loans. He was a strong supporter of deregulation —as were most loan brokers, because it increased their income potential dramatically—and he had developed his stable of favorite institutions. He knew which thrift executives wanted to participate in the speculative opportunities (and risks) made possible by deregulation. In late 1983 Lapaglia[7] had sponsored a seminar in Acapulco, Mexico. About 25 thrifts, those on Lapaglia's most favored list, attended. The topic of the seminar was wheeling and dealing in a deregulated environment and those attending were the lenders of choice for Lapaglia's borrowers.

When Norm Jenson approached Lapaglia for help in getting loans for the Crystal Palace and DeVille casinos, Lapaglia knew just who to talk to—Guy Olano, chairman of Alliance Federal Savings and Loan in Louisiana.[8] Lapaglia had a close working relationship with Olano. Employees at Alliance said he often visited Olano in New Orleans, and one of Lapaglia's former employees worked for Olano. (Federal authorities told us Lapaglia brokered $40 million worth of loans to Alliance, including loans to himself, his family and his own projects, and the thrift lost several million dollars on the loans. Lapaglia denied the charge.) Alliance Federal was in Kenner, Louisiana, 40 miles up the Mississippi River from New Orleans in the bayou country of southern Louisiana. Guy Olano, a New Orleans attorney, was a founder of Alliance Federal and later became chairman. He was an arrogant young man in his early thirties, Italian, handsome, and stocky.

"He produced a physical revulsion in me," a fellow attorney told us. "He looked like a fat Moammar Gadhafi [sic], curly black hair, dark glasses, wafer-thin gold watch, Italian suits. He had a psycho-look in his eyes. He looked gangsteresque."

Once Olano got control of Alliance, it didn't take him long to get in trouble.

By August 1982, long before Lapaglia went to Olano on behalf of Norm Jenson, Olano had already earned his first cease-and-desist order from the Federal Home Loan Bank Board. Regulators' documents showed that Alliance Federal ignored the order for two years, and finally, on June 11, 1984, the FHLBB demanded (and got) court enforcement of the order—the first time in history that the FHLBB had resorted to court enforcement of one of its cease-and-desist orders. The Bank Board said it did not like Alliance's loose loan underwriting practices or the compensation Olano and some of his fellow directors and officers were paying themselves.

But Alliance Savings officers probably knew that short-handed regulators were paper tigers, and Olano went right on ignoring government saber rattling. In 1984 he tried to buy a Miami bank, and he was represented at that time by Miami attorney José Louis Castro. A New Orleans attorney described Castro as a "great dresser" who was "breathtakingly handsome." Castro was frequently in and out of Olano's office in New Orleans, an FSLIC attorney told us, and Olano visited him regularly in Miami. In addition, Alliance made several loans to Castro. Later, FBI agents testified in court that Castro had close ties with the Colombian Duque and Arosco organized crime families, which had been connected to money-laundering schemes at American financial institutions. They said Olano may have tried to set up bank accounts in the Netherlands West Antilles so he could use the account as a depository for money in the event he needed to flee the country. (Castro was later sentenced to ten years in prison for bank fraud in a case unrelated to Alliance.)

John Lapaglia told us that when he went to Alliance Federal to get a loan for Norm Jenson, he was only looking for interim financing (Home Savings in Seattle had agreed to assume the loan after one year), and Olano said he would be happy to arrange a one-year, $4 million loan.[9] The agreement was finalized during a meeting June 15, 1984, in a private suite at the Sands Hotel in Las Vegas. Among those at the meeting were John Lapaglia, Norm Jenson, and Guy Olano.

"We went up to Lapaglia's suite at the Sands," Jenson said. "We sat down and at the time they had loan forms with them, and I think somebody either had a secretary with them or someone from the hotel—I can't remember—but they had a typewriter they had gotten, and they actually executed final loan documents. . . ."[10]

The meeting at the Sands Hotel appeared to be a lucrative one for everyone involved. Initially Jenson received $500,000 as the first installment of the $4 million from Alliance. He promptly sent $50,000 to Olano for "legal fees." Regulators later called the $50,000 a kickback. (It was not illegal at that time for Jenson to pay a kickback, but it was illegal for Olano, an official of a federally insured thrift, to receive one. It later became illegal to receive or pay a bribe to a thrift or bank official.)

Within six months of the meeting at the Sands, Alliance Federal had released to Jenson $3.2 million of the promised $4 million for the DeVille Casino. The last installment the thrift paid, just before Alliance was seized by federal regulators, gave us a rare glimpse into just how loan money was often divided up among the players. Jenson signed for a $900,000 installment but claimed he saw only $22,000 of it. Apparently it was payday on this deal and others were in line ahead of Jenson. Jenson later testified that Lapaglia received $250,000 as his fee for referring Jenson to Alliance and took another $142,000 to pay off a loan he had at Alliance. In Jenson's words, the $142,000 was "scraped off the deal" by Lapaglia. Lapaglia told us the $250,000 and the $142,000 were his commissions for the DeVille and Crystal Palace deals. He said Olano took the $142,000 for Alliance out of Jenson's loan without Lapaglia's knowledge.

Asked by FSLIC attorneys why he would sign for $900,000 while getting only $22,000, Jenson responded, in essence, that you had to be there.

"You know, it's hard to put yourself in somebody's spot at the time," Jenson responded. "It's almost incomprehensible if you weren't there."

What did he think happened to the rest of the money?

"They just divvied up the fees and just cut it up. That's what they did." Jenson was referring to the principal players in the deal: the chairmen of the two lending institutions (Raymond Gray at Home Savings, Seattle, and Guy Olano at Alliance Federal, New Orleans) and the man who arranged the loan, loan broker John Lapaglia.

Alliance Federal didn't cough up the final $800,000 installment on the $4 million loan to Jenson because federal regulators stopped the deal. As soon as he saw he wasn't going to get the rest of the loan money, Jenson threw the DeVille project into bankruptcy. He never told how much of the $3.2 million that he did get was "divvied up" in his name. Alliance Federal Savings collapsed in 1985 with a negative net worth of over $150 million. Norm Jenson and Lapaglia testified against Olano in a bank fraud trial in Seattle in 1987 and eventually Olano got 15-year and 8-year sentences in federal prison, two of the few tough sentences we were to see during our investigation.[11] In June 1989 a federal judge awarded the FHLBB an $86 million judgment against Olano and four other associates of the thrift.

An attorney for one of the defendants in the Seattle trial described Lapaglia as "an unctuous witness who professed to be a born-again Christian." During his testimony Lapaglia lectured the jury on his deep personal code of ethics, but jurors weren't impressed. "The jurors didn't like him," one defense attorney recalled, adding that even the U.S. attorney who had called Lapaglia as a witness felt compelled to tell the jury they did not have to believe anything Lapaglia said unless it was corroborated by other testimony. In the Seattle trial five executives of Home Savings near Seattle, Irving Savings near Dallas, and Alliance Savings near New Orleans were convicted of bank fraud for creating a complex daisy chain in which officials of the three thrifts made illegal loans to each other. Loan brokers had made all the introductions. All three thrifts had, at one point or another, been involved with Norm Jenson's DeVille Casino loan.

One day in the fall of 1985 a mortgage trader walked into the New York office of the *National Thrift News* and told coauthor Paul Muolo that millions of dollars had disappeared from a company he worked for. That tip led us to investigate Philip Schwab, who owned Cuyahoga Wrecking Company, based in Great Neck, Long Island. In 1986 Cuyahoga was the largest demolition firm in the United States, with offices in 18 cities from Florida to New York to Michigan. Schwab also had a stake in about 40 other development, wrecking, and demolition companies and had business connections in every major city in the Midwest and on the East Coast. He and his wife, Mary, divided their time between a waterfront Mediterranean-style villa near West Palm Beach, Florida, and a sprawling home in posh Pelham, New York.

Schwab had been in trouble with authorities for years. In 1963 a Buffalo, New York, grand jury had indicted Schwab on three counts of perjury and two counts of grand larceny. Two of the trials ended in hung juries, and most of the charges were eventually dropped. (Schwab was acquitted ten years later of the remaining perjury charge when the witness could not testify—he was dead—and the key piece of evidence, a check, purportedly disappeared from the district attorney's files on the day of the trial.)

In 1965 the IRS filed tax liens totaling $128,000 against Schwab's company for failure to pay payroll taxes and seized the company's equipment and records. A few months later Schwab filed for bankruptcy. When his company didn't fulfill its contracts, the insurance company that had bonded Schwab took him to court. In court the insurance company demanded to see company records. Schwab refused to produce them. The judge cited Schwab for civil contempt and ordered him to spend 30 days in the Erie County Jail.

In 1966 Schwab's mother, who was home recovering from dental surgery, was tied up and gagged by a man dressed like a priest while thugs ransacked her modest Buffalo, New York, home. No money was taken, and police later speculated that the intruders were mob wise guys searching for files on Schwab's business.

Schwab's style was to keep his mouth shut when things began to go wrong. He consistently refused to talk to reporters and often refused to talk to authorities too. He was a tough, self-made man who had made his fortune armed with only a high school diploma. He looked like a cross between actors Gene Hackman and Ed Asner. A Catholic, he and his wife, Mary, were married in 1949 when she was 18 and had raised 14 children together.

Mary was his partner in all his businesses, and she filed for bankruptcy in

1969 when one of their businesses defaulted on $25 million in contracts after it was seized by the IRS. In her bankruptcy filing she listed assets of $3,500 and debts of $8.2 million. Although documents showed she was Philip's partner in the company, she claimed to know nothing about it. In court she testified that when she asked Philip for details about the family's business finances, "He sang to me a medley of songs."

"What did he sing?" U.S. Attorney Kenneth Schroeder, Jr., asked. " 'Impossible Dream'?"

"No," she replied. "He sang 'Raindrops Keep Falling on My Head,' 'I Can't Give You Anything but Love,' and 'You're My Everything,' and he told me to mind my own business." She added, "I don't know anything about any records. I only know that I sign papers." Schwab took the stand and confirmed he had sung to his wife but he declined to answer other questions. Consistent in his determination to keep his affairs private, he reportedly took the fifth amendment 156 times.

Despite his past financial (and legal) troubles, by the early 1980s Schwab had rebuilt his empire, and thrift and bank officials were falling all over themselves to make loans to him. Cuyahoga was by then touting a net worth of about $70 to $80 million. How could a banker say no?[12] Schwab's companies demanded such a healthy cash flow that he incessantly scoured financial institutions for cash, and finally he decided it would be useful to own a casino, the ultimate cash-flow machine. In 1984 he acquired the Mapes Money Tree in Reno for about $6.75 million. He renamed the casino Players Casino, and then he showed up at Eureka Federal Savings, near San Francisco, seeking financing to renovate his new gaming house.

How, we wondered, had a New Yorker made connections with a savings and loan near San Francisco? An attorney for Eureka Federal gave us the surprising answer—loan broker John Lapaglia, again. Schwab had hired Lapaglia to shop for a loan for him, and Lapaglia took him to Kenneth Kidwell, who was president of Eureka Federal Savings.[13] Kidwell was the son of Eureka Federal Savings' founder, and he had succeeded to power at the thrift just as deregulation changed all the rules that his dad had depended upon to build Eureka Federal Savings into a respected San Francisco Bay Area institution. Associates said Kidwell was cut from a very different cloth than his father. He was flamboyant and reckless, and he reveled in the Nevada casino scene. During the time Kidwell was head of Eureka Savings he was involved in a number of bizarre events that were widely publicized in California. One night police stopped his car after it was spotted weaving down the road. Officers suspected that Kidwell was drunk. When they searched him they found he was carrying two loaded pistols, a .38-caliber strapped to his leg and a .357 magnum. The guns were loaded with illegal, armor-piercing, Teflon-coated bullets. (The bullets had recently been outlawed because they could penetrate bulletproof vests worn by police.)

Kidwell lined up on the side of law and order when he provided the services of Eureka Federal to the FBI on at least two occasions. In 1981 he let the FBI and the DEA use Eureka Federal as a cover for a drug sting operation. He "hired" the agents and even let them rent a company car, a Mercedes 600. The FBI brought more than $3 million in cash into Eureka's vault as part of the sting, which did net a drug kingpin, Kidwell later told us. On another occasion, in 1982, Kidwell provided agents with covers as part of their sting operation to trap car manufacturer John DeLorean, whom they believed was dealing drugs (he was later tried and found not guilty). Kidwell let the feds wire and put video equipment in his 1,200-square-foot office, which adjoined a 3,000-square-foot suite in Eureka Federal Savings' main office building. The suite had a living room with two fireplaces, a bedroom with a huge round bed, a bar, and a wine cellar.

Kidwell got close to another FBI informant, Teamster union boss Jackie Presser, when Kidwell was contacted by a union official who said maybe "some lending activity" could take place through Teamster pension funds. Kidwell wrote to his lawyers in 1984 recalling the moment:

"I have been trying to do business with the Teamster pension fund for a lot of years. If I could obtain them as a client, surely every pension fund in the U.S. would want to do business with me." (One Teamster deal with Eureka Federal Savings, Kidwell said in his letter, would be brokered by Abe "the Trigger" Chapman, who has been widely alleged to be a former member of the infamous Chicago Murder Inc. gang.) When news accounts referred to Chapman's alleged mob connections, Kidwell dropped the deal. Eureka Federal employees told us Kidwell developed a social relationship with Presser.

Casino loans became a Kidwell specialty. Most lenders wouldn't go near them, but Eureka Federal made at least four major casino loans.[14] Regulators said Schwab received a $7.5 million loan from Eureka Federal and paid John Lapaglia a $30,000 finder's fee. Schwab also paid Lapaglia $630,000, which Schwab claimed was a commission for another loan but which looked to gaming board officials like part of the casino loan. If almost 10 percent of the Eureka Federal Savings loan ($660,000 out of a $7.5 million loan) went to Lapaglia for a finder's fee, gaming board officials later complained, it was an "inordinate amount."

But a little matter still needed to be cleared up before Schwab could pluck fruit from his new money tree—he was not yet licensed to operate a casino in Nevada. Schwab promptly filed an application with the Nevada Gaming Control Board. But if he thought that obtaining a casino license would be as easy as getting a loan out of Ken Kidwell, he was in for a rude surprise.[15]

While Schwab was awaiting word on his casino application, he took stock of thrift deregulation and decided he could also benefit by owning some savings and loans.[16] He had been a customer at Freedom Savings of Tampa since 1984 (Cuyahoga had offices in Tampa), and in December 1985 a Freedom Savings officer asked him to invest in Freedom stock. Freedom Savings, a $1.5 billion thrift that was well known among regulators for its use of high-cost brokered deposits to fund risky real estate development projects, was desperate for capital to meet a new regulation that increased the size of the reserves an S&L had to maintain. In January 1985, FHLBB Chairman Ed Gray had toughened the reserve requirements in an attempt to stop the fast growth and risky lending that he saw in progress all over the country.[17] The new regulation caught a lot of high-flying thrifts like Freedom Savings with their reserves down, and Freedom officers were looking for investors willing to pay cash into their reserves in exchange for stock.

When the Freedom Savings officer invited him to buy stock in the thrift, Schwab bluntly laid his cards on the table. "I informed him I would but that I am a businessman and if I were to invest in a losing bank to help it during a difficult time, I would expect a reasonable treatment when I applied for new loans. . . . It was agreed that I would pick up any shortfall that the other investors did not produce. In return I was able to borrow $3.2 million—without paying points—for each million worth of stock I purchased. . . ."[18] In other words, Schwab demanded the right to borrow from Freedom Savings three times the amount of his investment. It was strictly illegal for an S&L to make such a quid pro quo arrangement, but Freedom Savings agreed because it needed Schwab's investment.

Schwab paid about $7 million for a 5.9 percent stake in Freedom Savings, which promised him up to $24 million in loans, in disregard of regulations that forbade an S&L to make loans equaling more than 10 percent of its assets to any one borrower. Court records showed that, as it turned out, Freedom Savings actually loaned him $4.5 million on projects in Arizona and $7 million on a project in Philadelphia.[19] (All the loans eventually went into default. Freedom Savings failed in July 1987.)

When we checked further into Freedom Savings, we found our old familiar friend Charles Bazarian. Charlie was getting to be like a touchstone to our investigation—kind of a litmus test to see if a thrift was of the accommodating persuasion. Fuzzy had taken a shine to Freedom Savings, too, and he bought a 9.9 percent stake in the thrift. Sig Kohnen, a longtime friend of Bazarian who helped him start CB Financial in 1983,[20] told the Tulsa Tribune Bazarian bought stock in savings and loans as a way to meet lenders.[21] As co-shareholders in Freedom Savings, Bazarian and Schwab soon struck up a relationship, Bazarian told us, and before long CB Financial began arranging loans to Schwab ventures. (Those loans would later go into default, Bazarian said.)

At the same time that Schwab was buying into Freedom Savings in Tampa, he was taking control of Southern Floridabanc Savings Association in Boca Raton, Florida, by buying $3 million in preferred stock with a loan from First Federated Savings of West Palm Beach. Schwab was on a roll.

But if things were going well in Florida for Schwab, they were going poorly in Nevada. He had hired a consulting firm (that specialized in helping people get gaming licenses) to help him navigate the Nevada Gaming Control Board investigation. But after listening to Gaming Control Board concerns, the consultants handed Schwab a thick report so damning it became obvious that he would never pass muster. Schwab's gaming consultants reminded him, for example, that the main purpose for allowing casinos in the state was to generate tax revenues for Nevada, and the Gaming Control Board was not likely to look with favor on someone who had been successfully avoiding taxes for 20 years.[22] Schwab's consultants also zeroed in on his maze of companies and nonexistent records. In a written report they said Schwab admitted that he used money from his companies interchangeably, or funneled money from one through another, for whatever purpose he pleased. When asked why his companies didn't keep minutes of board meetings, he replied that he and his wife had a board of directors meeting every time they sat down together.

The consultants noted in their report that the Gaming Control Board might not be impressed when they learned that Schwab had been called to testify before the grand jury investigating the Abscam sting[23] and Morris Shenker (whom the consultants included on their "persons believed to be unsuitable by law-enforcement authorities" list). They were referring to an occasion when undercover FBI agents posing as Arabs met Schwab on a boat at Del Ray Beach, Florida, and asked him if he could guarantee them a gaming license in New Jersey. Their question was prompted, Schwab told the gaming consultants, by his association with Morris Shenker and the Dunes Hotel and Casino project in Atlantic City. Schwab said his answer to the "Arabs" was no.

Schwab's loan from Eureka Federal Savings, ostensibly to renovate the Players Casino, was also under scrutiny by the gaming board. He had put up property that had cost him only $1.4 million as security for the $7.5 million loan from Eureka Federal Savings. Schwab contended that, no matter what the property cost him, it was worth $16 million to $25 million, based on what it would be worth as a "going concern" someday. A bank appraisal obtained later said the property was worth $267,000, the gaming consultants noted in their report.

When the Gaming Control Board investigators interviewed Schwab, they asked him about "meetings at night with potential undesirables" and ten men with Italian surnames, prompting Schwab's gaming consultants to comment in their report to Schwab, "We have no specific records available to us regarding the backgrounds of these individuals. We can only presume at this point that the Gaming Control Board has information from law enforcement authorities associating these individuals with organized crime activities in the United States." Several of the men were connected to Schwab businesses. Schwab admitted knowing one of the men was a loan shark but he denied knowing the man was also a heroin dealer.

To top it all off, Schwab's own consultants said he failed to tell the truth, the whole truth, and nothing but the truth on his gaming licensing application: He told about the old perjury indictments but didn't mention the larceny charges because, he said, he thought they were the same thing. He also contended there were years when he was not employed. Schwab's consultants went on to say that he hadn't told about his gambling debts. Further, he hadn't told about all of his companies because, he said, "They never did anything" or were "owned by other members of the family."

It was hard, gaming board investigators concluded, to "get a handle on you [Schwab]." Schwab must have seen the handwriting on the wall. He dropped his application for a casino license, defaulted on the $7.5 million loan from Eureka Savings, and beat it back to the East Coast. (Regulators said Schwab used part of the Eureka Federal Savings loan for a project he had going in Philadelphia. Eureka Federal lost between $5 million and $7 million on the Schwab loan.)

What most intrigued us about the Schwab story was the ease with which he was able to become a major stockholder in two federally insured savings and loans (Freedom Federal Savings and Southern Floridabanc) at the very time that a Nevada gaming board was finding reasons to deny him a license to run a small gambling house.

After Schwab gave up on the Players Casino project, he overextended himself in real estate developments on Hilton Head Island off the coast of South Carolina. Within a year he claimed to be broke. In November 1986 Schwab and Mary filed personal bankruptcy in New York (chapter 7—liquidation). Soon Cuyahoga Wrecking filed chapter 11 (reorganization). The St. Petersburg *Times* reported that a bankruptcy command post was set up in a large room at the Columbia, South Carolina, courthouse right next to a similar one for the only other case that size, the bankruptcy of Jim and Tammy Bakker's PTL Club.

Schwab had been a very private man. Only in bankruptcy did the scope of his empire become public. Ultimately there would be 15 Schwab-related bankruptcies in New York, mostly the Cuyahoga companies, and eight in South Carolina. Investigators admitted Schwab's business affairs were so complex—and, as before, many important records had disappeared, according to Schwab's bankers—that they couldn't even tell how many companies Schwab owned. At first creditors filed claims totaling $135 million, but hundreds of millions were later added. Bankruptcy court records showed that as of July 1988 there were 103 creditors, including Bazarian's company, CB Financial. The overall debts of Philip Schwab, Cuyahoga Wrecking, and related companies were pushing the half-*billion*-dollar mark and growing. Schwab owed $200 million of that amount to thrifts and banks from Israel to California.

"This bankruptcy has already generated enough paperwork to kill half the national forests," said one attorney.

Representatives of several financial institutions got together to try to figure out how to best collect the money Schwab owed them. "It was like an Alcoholics Anonymous meeting, with all of the bankers standing up and confessing their involvement with Cuyahoga and Schwab," a Chicago lawyer present at one meeting told a reporter. Ultimately the bankers decided there was no hope. As they would later testify in court, they believed Schwab had bamboozled them, sometimes using the same collateral—by moving it secretly in the dead of night—to secure several loans at one time. He had operated a shell game, they said, that was nothing more than a fancy pyramid scheme, using oft-pledged assets (such as steel from demolition jobs) to get new loans that he used to pay off old ones. Thrifts banging on Schwab's door included: Crosslands Savings in New York, First American Bank and Trust in Lake Worth, Florida,[24] Freedom Savings of Orlando, South Chicago Savings in Chicago, American Pioneer Savings in Stuart, Florida, Harris Trust and Savings in Chicago, Community Savings in North Palm Beach, Eureka Federal Savings in San Carlos, California, Southern Floridabanc Savings in Boca Raton, Florida, First Federated Savings in West Palm Beach, and Concordia Federal Savings of Philadelphia.

In October 1988 Schwab was convicted of paying an Environmental Protection Agency inspector $25,000 in bribes between 1983 and 1987 to overlook violations Cuyahoga Wrecking Company committed while removing asbestos from building and construction sites. (Schwab had removed the asbestos from Carnegie Hall "so Frank Sinatra wouldn't get asbestos in his lungs" when he sang there, an employee said.) Schwab was sentenced to 42 months in prison. The national media reported that Schwab was also under investigation for violations regarding illegal handling of toxic wastes in Maryland and Delaware, for other environmental violations in Chicago, and for bank fraud in South Carolina. And in New York the U.S. attorney's office, headed at that time by headline-making Rudolph Giuliani, was digging into Schwab's deals with New York thrifts and banks.

Another one of Kenneth Kidwell's casino loans went to John B. Anderson. Anderson was a giant of a man, six feet three inches tall and barrel-chested, a farm boy, mostly a tomato grower, who had grown up in the agricultural communities near Yuba City, California. He put himself through the branch of the University of California in his hometown of Davis in the 1960s, majored in agriculture, and began work as a humble sharecropper. The fundamental values of hard work and living close to the land stayed with him while he became a millionaire many times over. An admirer told us that even after he made his fortune Anderson expected his children—to whom he was a good father, his neighbors said—to work for minimum wage.

But to the farmer's solid values Anderson added burning ambition. He told his hometown friends that his dream was to be the nation's single largest agricultural land owner. He knew he would have to accomplish that feat with borrowed money, of course, and borrow he did. Along the way he acquired vast holdings in Nevada, California, Arizona, and Louisiana. On paper Anderson was worth millions, but he was deeply in debt. When the agricultural recession hit in the early 1980s, his loans went sour. So, too, did his financial obligations elsewhere. By early 1985 newspapers would report that Anderson was being sued for $56 million by a host of creditors.

None of this misfortune dampened Ken Kidwell's willingness to extend Anderson credit. In 1984 Kidwell convinced Anderson to buy a controlling interest in the Dunes Hotel and Casino in Las Vegas.

When Kidwell first heard that the Dunes could be bought from reputed mob associate Morris Shenker, who had filed for bankruptcy in January 1984 (Shenker was neck-deep in trouble over about $197 million in debts, including loans from various union pension funds, banks and thrifts, and unpaid taxes of about $66 million), Kidwell first thought of his friend Wayne Newton as a potential buyer, he later told his Nevada attorney. But to his dismay he discovered that San Francisco loan broker J. William Oldenburg—whom Kidwell had introduced to Newton—had already convinced Newton to let Oldenburg broker the Dunes deal for him. Furious, Kidwell said he called Anderson, to whom Eureka Federal had already made several agricultural loans, and suggested that Anderson buy the Dunes. Anderson had first entered the gambling world with his 1981 purchase of the Maxim Hotel and Casino in Las Vegas and his 1982 purchase of the Station House hotel-casino in Tonopah, Nevada.

Anderson agreed. Eureka Federal was willing to put up the $25 million letter of credit (a guarantee to loan on demand) that would be required to swing the deal. In the meantime an option had to be acquired to ace out Oldenburg and Newton. Kidwell called San Antonio loan broker John Lapaglia for help with that end of the deal.

In the end the Kidwell/Anderson team beat out the Oldenburg/Newton team when those negotiating the Dunes sale said they preferred a letter of credit from a federally insured institution (Eureka Federal) to Oldenburg's financing package, which an associate said was mostly personal notes and guarantees. When Anderson applied for the Dunes gaming license, he sailed through the rigorous

Nevada State Gaming Control Board investigation. He assumed control of the Dunes from Shenker in 1984 but retained Shenker's son as a vice president and said Shenker himself would remain a board member.[25]

Some in Nevada's gaming industry wondered out loud if Anderson was "a beard" (fronting) for Shenker or for other interests that could not pass a Gaming Control Board muster. Such rumors had first surfaced a few months after Anderson had gotten control of the Maxim Hotel and Casino. The St. Louis *Post-Dispatch* broke a story that claimed organized crime figures from St. Louis, Kansas City, Chicago, and Denver had tried unsuccessfully to purchase the Maxim in 1982. The story said that sources in Las Vegas and Denver had told them, following that failure, that they had "put together another attempt to penetrate legal gambling in Nevada." The story identified the mobsters involved in the alleged plot as being Tony Giordano of St. Louis, Eugene Smaldone of Denver, Joe "Joey Doves" Aiuppa of Chicago, and Nick Civella of Kansas City. State Gaming Control Board member Dale Askew characterized the story as "street talk" and said that the related rumors that John Anderson was acting as a front for organized crime were "thoroughly checked out and discounted at the time Mr. Anderson was licensed. We did not find a thing."

Later the Las Vegas media reported that the Gaming Control Board was checking into Anderson's relationship with Eureka Federal Savings and Loan and Kenneth Kidwell. Following the Dunes deal, the Gaming Control Commission declared Eureka Federal an unacceptable source of funds for future casino acquisition. They gave no explanations for their action, but Kidwell complained in a letter to his attorney that the Dunes deal had caused him to become "trapped in Shenker's shadow."

Kidwell wrote that it had surprised him to read in the newspapers that he had ties to Morris Shenker and various mobsters. He complained that even some of his Eureka Federal customers thought he was working with the mob. He said that John Anderson called him one day and asked if it were true that he (Kidwell) was "washing money for one of the families."

Whatever problems there may have been at Eureka Federal Savings may never be known. Although the Nevada Gaming Control Commission was clearly concerned, the FHLBB was not. Even though some of the most prominent thrift looters we investigated were borrowers at Eureka Federal, even though one employee received phone threats just before she was to be deposed, even though a director told us he had been threatened by an officer, even though 170 loans were in default at Eureka Federal, regulators told us they had investigated Eureka Federal and found no evidence of fraud there. Mitchell Brown, a ubiquitous borrower who had also been co-owner of First National Bank of Marin in San Rafael, California, until he was forced out by regulators, felt differently.[26] Just before Brown was indicted for bank fraud in Oregon, according to investigators, he asked the U.S. attorney if he could cut a deal. He wanted blanket immunity, he said, for what he had done at Eureka Federal, but he would not tell regulators what he had done there (and they did not cut him a deal). His trial was pending as of this writing.

Six months after John Anderson's successful purchase of the Dunes, in May 1984, he submitted an application to the Gaming Control Board to purchase the Las Vegas Sundance Hotel, owned by M.B. "Moe" Dalitz, Mike Rapp's old Las Vegas buddy. The Gaming Control Board announced they were going to conduct another thorough review of Anderson's finances, including his association with persons doing business with San Marino Savings and Loan in Southern California. According to published reports, Anderson suddenly withdrew his licensing application without explanation. (In referring to San Marino officials may have had Jack Bona in mind. See next casino story.)

Like many other ambitious Anderson ventures, the Dunes turned out to be a giant money loser. Anderson put the Dunes into bankruptcy in September 1985 for protection from creditors, who were owed $117 million. Anderson would eventually leave Eureka Federal Savings stuck with nearly $32 million in his delinquent loans. A source close to the Eureka Federal Savings case said in late 1988 that Anderson was attempting to bring the loans current by making monthly payments of $500,000.

According to media accounts, Anderson also defaulted on $22 million in loans from Crocker Bank and $2.1 million borrowed from Aetna Life Insurance Company. He had $43 million in debts on his various real estate holdings and owed $68.6 million to Valley Bank of Nevada. After tapping out these sources Anderson headed north to Oregon, where authorities said loan broker Al Yarbrow helped him get $25 million in loans out of State Savings of Corvallis. Yarbrow also introduced Anderson to Charles Bazarian and Anderson later borrowed money through Bazarian's CB Financial. We would find Anderson's footprints at Vernon Savings in Dallas as well. (See Texas chapters.)

Jack Bona and his partner, Frank J. Domingues, got $200 million in loans from San Marino Savings and Loan in San Marino, California,[27] in ten months, even though tax records showed that three years earlier they had reported *combined incomes* of less than $30,000.[28] (Remember that the next time a banker tells you you don't earn enough to qualify for a $9,000 car loan.) The plan they submitted to San Marino was to convert apartment units to condos and sell them as tax-shelter rentals to investors in high income-tax brackets. When San Marino failed in December 1984[29] regulators charged that the properties on which San Marino lent Bona and Domingues $200 million were worth only about $100 million. Most of the loans were in deep default, and the properties turned out to be in such bad neighborhoods in Dallas and Los Angeles that even an internal memorandum at San Marino showed that the thrift's staff referred to them as "the Zulu projects." A California thrift director who went to Texas to look at the condos for himself sent back a memo with this discouraging word: "They are NOT convertible [into condos] except to a BLIND investor." Regulators claimed Bona and Domingues pocketed up to $50 million for themselves on these projects. Domingues told reporters that they made only about $10 million.

Remarkably, even as regulators were wringing their hands over what Bona and Domingues had done to San Marino Savings, the two new millionaires were buying their own savings and loan nearby, South Bay Savings. "Apparently the left hand didn't know what the right hand was doing," deputy California Savings and Loan Commissioner William Davis said later (he became deputy commissioner after the South Bay affair). The San Diego *Union* reported that Domingues said he would never allow *his* thrift, South Bay, to make the kinds of loans that San Marino had made to him and Bona. Be that as it may regulators later revealed that the day the two men bought South Bay, they had the thrift loan them $6 million.[30]

Shortly after opening South Bay, Jack Bona[31] split with Domingues. He sold out his share in South Bay to Domingues[32] and in 1983 purchased another kind of financial institution, Morris Shenker's troubled 664-room Atlantic City Dunes Hotel and Casino project. Shenker had begun the project just before defaulting on millions in loans from union pension funds. Now it was little more than a rusting abstract sculpture of I-beams in the middle of town. Shenker sold the project to Bona shortly before John B. Anderson bought Shenker out at the Las Vegas Dunes. Bona kept the Atlantic City Dunes for a couple of years, during which time he added a few more millions in loans to the project's crushing debt,[33] and then he defaulted and filed for bankruptcy in 1985.

The Dunes was put up for sale by the bankruptcy trustee and sold in 1988 to Royale Group Ltd., run since 1981 by Leonard Pelullo. We remembered Pelullo because his name had shown up without explanation in documents regulators had seized from Consolidated Savings. The handsome, swarthy Pelullo, who was 37 in 1988, worked out of an office in the Carlyle Hotel in Miami Beach's Art Deco district. *BusinessWeek* reported that he described himself as a "workout" specialist, a consultant who helped companies drowning in debt. The still-unbuilt Atlantic City Dunes project certainly qualified.

But Pelullo may have had a darker side. *BusinessWeek* also reported that he had recently worked under the alias Bob Paris because, Pelullo reportedly said, he wanted to avoid drawing attention to a New Jersey State Commission of Investigation report on boxing that described him as "a key organized crime associate from Philadelphia." Pelullo denied any ties to the mob.

In June 1989 a Cincinnati grand jury handed down an indictment against Pelullo and David A. Friedmann, a Houston businessman who from 1983 to 1985 was owner and CEO of Savings One, a thrift in Gahanna, Ohio (Mario

Renda and Martin Schwimmer attempted to purchase Savings One in 1983). The indictment charged the two men with conspiring to obtain loans from the thrift that were used for purposes other than stated on the loan application. The indictment also charged that Pelullo paid Friedmann $145,000 in kickbacks for arranging the loans. Pelullo said the money was pre-paid interest on a loan extension he expected to receive. The case was pending at this writing.

We had run into the casino connection at Consolidated as well. One of Consolidated Saving's problem loans, regulators claimed, was a $614,311 loan to Robert Shearer and Llewellyn Mowery for refurbishing the Treasury Hotel and Casino in Las Vegas. Shearer and Mowery refused to repay the loan, according to regulators, unless Consolidated loaned them $3 million more.

Consolidated Saving's owner, Robert Ferrante, got into the casino act personally, court records showed, when he and Mario Renda teamed up for a casino project in Puerto Rico that they called the Palace Hotel and Casino.[34] After Consolidated failed and Renda found himself enmeshed in all manner of criminal and civil difficulty, the Palace Casino was allowed to go into bankruptcy and Las Vegas newspapers reported that the project was purchased out of bankruptcy by the Pratt Hotel chain, a division of Southmark, Inc., a Dallas-based conglomerate that also owned San Jacinto Savings and Loan in Houston (see Chapter 21).

By far the most frequent casino connection we ran into at failed thrifts around the country was the Las Vegas-based Dunes Hotels and Casinos company and its chairman, Morris Shenker. Shenker, born in Russia in 1907, had been an attorney in St. Louis since 1932. He first came to national attention in the early 1950s during the congressional hearings of the Kefauver committee, which investigated the influence of organized crime in interstate commerce. Twenty years later *Life* magazine detailed his alleged mob ties in an exposé of a former St. Louis mayor (by then, ironically, Shenker had been appointed chairman of the St. Louis Commission on Crime and Law Enforcement, a position he held from 1969 to 1972). In 1975 *Penthouse* magazine said Shenker was under investigation by a federal strike force and grand jury in St. Louis and added, "His Byzantine financial maneuvering astounds investigators in and out of government."

The source of Shenker's power appeared to be his lengthy and well-publicized relationship as chief attorney and confidant of Teamster union president Jimmy Hoffa. Hoffa was Teamster boss from 1957 until he went to prison in 1967, and he continued to run the union from prison for several years. (He was released from prison in 1971 and disappeared in 1975 as he was attempting to regain control of the Teamsters. Authorities believe he was murdered.) The President's 1986 Commission on Organized Crime reported that the Teamsters, the nation's largest union, had been "firmly under the influence of organized crime since the 1950s." In 1989 the FBI released material collected for the FBI by Teamster president Jackie Presser during the nine years he was an FBI informant, until he died in 1988 of brain cancer. The documents showed a union dominated by organized crime and corruption.

As Teamster leader, Hoffa controlled the massive ($400 million in 1967, $1.6 billion in 1977) Teamsters' Central States Pension Fund. He directed that millions of the fund's dollars be loaned to associates and mobsters, and over the years the fund became, as author Steven Brill wrote in *The Teamsters*, "a special bank where loans depended almost always on the right kickbacks or the right organized crime connections." By 1974 Shenker had more than $100 million in loans from the fund, for the Las Vegas Dunes and other properties, according to Brill. The President's 1986 Commission on Organized Crime said that Shenker received the largest single loan ever made by the fund, a portion of which had never been repaid. With that access to millions came, apparently, tremendous power.

Hoffa pioneered the use of Teamster pension funds to finance casinos in 1960. The *Penthouse* piece said Michael Rapp's buddy Moe Dalitz helped persuade Hoffa to finance Nevada hotels and casinos.[35] In Las Vegas the Teamsters at one time backed Dalitz's Desert Inn, Circus Circus, the Fremont, the Lodestar, the Plaza Towers, the Stardust, the Landmark Hotel, the Four Queens, the Aladdin, and Caesar's Palace; in Lake Tahoe, the King's Castle, the Lake Tahoe, and the Sierra Tahoe; in Riverside, the Riverside; and in Overton, the Echo Bay, according to investigative reporters Jonathan Kwitny and Steven Brill. Presser told the FBI that profits from Las Vegas casinos were illegally skimmed and mob couriers took the cash away in suitcases.

Shenker got control of the Las Vegas Dunes with the promise of a $40 million advance from the Teamsters' Fund, and we came across him or the Dunes numerous times in our investigation. Erv Hansen at Centennial gambled at the Dunes regularly, reportedly sometimes dropping $10,000 at the roulette table in a single night. Norman B. Jenson had been a Shenker business associate. Shenker made the Dunes a hospitable place for thrift officials and even occasionally provided suites where deals could be cut, as when Winkler, Daily, and Russo met there to formalize their Indian Springs State Bank project. The Dunes Hotel and Casino and several of Shenker's associates received loans from Indian Springs State Bank. Jack Bona bought the Atlantic City Dunes from Shenker and John Anderson bought the Las Vegas Dunes, both using S&L credit, when Shenker was in deep financial trouble. Shenker was mentioned in Renda's 1981 desk diary. Nevada gaming documents revealed Philip Schwab was a Shenker associate, as was Eureka Federal Savings President Kenneth Kidwell, who also knew Jackie Presser well.

When Sun Savings in San Diego failed in July 1986, court documents showed that the president, Daniel W. Dierdorff, had loaned Shenker almost $2 million, which he never repaid. Shenker often entertained Dierdorff at the Dunes, regulators said, and Dierdorff used Shenker's jet for gambling trips to the Dunes and other personal trips. Shenker maintained a $25,000 line of credit in Dierdorff's name at the Dunes. Also around that time Dierdorff opened an account at another savings and loan under an assumed name and deposited more than $200,000 to that account in 1983. Dierdorff later pleaded guilty to two felony bank fraud charges, but the source of the money remained a mystery. He was sentenced to eight years in prison in 1989.

Why would Shenker, who appeared to have a direct pipeline to limitless Teamster pension-fund money, be so solicitous of his connections within the S&L industry? Because in 1983 the Labor Department finally wrestled control of the Teamster Central States Pension Fund away from the mob. With its immense appetite for money, Shenker's empire was in crisis. How serendipitous for Shenker, then, that at that very moment Congress was obligingly deregulating savings and loans. Without missing a beat Shenker swung into his savings and loan mode, and when he had to sell the Dunes in 1984 (a massive court judgment against him, on behalf of a pension fund he owed millions, forced him into bankruptcy), his hunt for fresh money intensified. Legitimate bankers wouldn't loan to him, so he needed insiders like Dierdorff, over whom he had some control. Better yet, suppose he could use a beard to front for him and take control of a thrift? That's apparently when he thought of Charles Bazarian, a heavy gambler at the Dunes (his 1987 bankruptcy filing revealed he owed the Dunes $174,000).

In early 1985 Bazarian was buying stock in savings and loans as a way to meet lenders. (Not until his indictment in September 1986 at Florida Center Bank with Rapp and Renda did his wheeling and dealing begin to catch up with him.) He bought 9.9 percent of Freedom Savings in Tampa (the maximum that could be acquired without regulatory approval), where he met Philip Schwab. A month later he bought 9.9 percent of Bloomfield Savings and Loan (for a reported $731,000) in a ritzy suburb of Detroit, and two weeks later, in early April 1985, he showed up there with his hand out for a loan. He didn't come alone, however. With him were Shenker and loan broker Al Yarbrow. Bazarian later said in court depositions and in conversations with acquaintances that the Bloomfield connection was Shenker's idea. He said Shenker had a friend with connections to the chairman of Bloomfield, and Shenker wanted Bazarian to get control of the thrift, make Shenker's friend chief executive officer, and approve loans to Shenker.

A former Bloomfield official told Detroit *Free Press* reporter Bernie Shellum, who dug up much of the Bloomfield story, that Bazarian's approach at the meeting was that he was a partner in the thrift, he wanted to help it make money, and one important step it should take was to loan to his company in Oklahoma City. The former thrift official said Bazarian was "loud and aggressive—a pound-the-table type guy" whose message was, "Here's what you should do, you dummies." The thrift's chairman evidently agreed, saying in a memo to thrift directors that Bazarian would bring "the huge loan demand and deep pocket which we have been trying to find."

Bank records show that on April 22 the thrift approved a $15 million loan for Bazarian (the loans-to-one-borrower limit at Bloomfield at that time was $3.5 million) backed primarily by real estate that regulators later said turned out to be overappraised or already pledged as collateral for another loan someplace else. Court records showed Shenker was to share in a finder's fee for taking Bazarian to Bloomfield.

The new president at Bloomfield (promoted to the position in February), unfortunately for Shenker, was a career banker who vehemently opposed the Bazarian loan, and within two weeks the thrift was trying, without success, to get its money back.[36] By late 1988 Bloomfield was hopelessly insolvent and regulators seized control.

Shenker's assault on the thrift industry was massive. No one will ever know its true extent. As this book was going to press, we learned that Shenker had tried to borrow from Freedom Savings in Tampa, and a highly placed law-enforcement official told us he had just discovered that Shenker had borrowed from Liberty Federal Savings in Leesburg, Louisiana (Liberty later collapsed), a thrift with connections to an incestuous Texas banking network we discuss later in this book.

In 1988 Shenker, 82, suffered two heart attacks, and when we tried to contact him at his St. Louis office, a spokeswoman told us he was in poor health in a St. Louis hospital. In February 1989 he was indicted in Nevada on two counts: conspiracy to commit bankruptcy fraud (by concealing money from creditors) and conspiracy to defraud the IRS. A Nevada Gaming Control Board investigator told us that when he had investigated Shenker years ago he found him to be "a financial Svengali with over 105 corporations between which he was shuttling money."

In 1982 Congress passed the Garn-St Germain Act, which allowed thrifts to begin to invest in areas other than home mortgages so they could diversify their portfolios of investments and protect themselves against swings in interest rates and other market fluctuations. No one suggested that casinos were a great hedge against inflation, deflation, or stagnation, but within months after thrifts were deregulated, millions of dollars in loans were flowing into casino operations. Casinos also used junk bonds, many arranged through Drexel Burnham Lambert, to finance their acquisitions and expansion, and some of those junk bonds, we discovered, ended up in the portfolios of troubled thrifts who bought them hoping that their potentially high returns would pull their thrifts out of trouble.[37]

"These guys are going to have a rude awakening when the day comes that junk bonds live up to their name," one thrift analyst told us.

Of all the thrift/casino deals we discovered, not a single one resulted in anything but substantial losses for the thrifts. Like the union pension funds that came before them, thrifts were always the losers in the casino game, while the high rollers—some with long-standing mob ties—emerged unscathed. The casino connection was a financial black hole that sucked millions in insured deposits off to who knows where.

CHAPTER FIFTEEN

Gray, Stockman, and the Red Baron

In the summer of 1984 swindlers like Mike Rapp were looting thrifts like Flushing Federal with wild abandon, unobserved and unobstructed. But some isolated cases of abuse had begun to surface, enough to convince FHLBB Chairman Ed Gray that deregulation had been carried too far. No sooner had Empire Savings in Dallas collapsed in March 1984 than the problems at San Marino Savings in Southern California came to his attention[1] (the failure of the two thrifts cost the FSLIC an estimated total of $600 million), and on their heels came word from the San Francisco FHLB to brace for more of the same. At least a dozen more San Marinos were in various stages of insolvency, they told Gray, and Gray's people in Texas were sending back the same message. In the first half of 1984, Gray faced one crisis after another.

In April the industry got unwanted publicity when the San Francisco *Examiner* reported on what it said was a land flip orchestrated by San Francisco loan broker J. William Oldenburg at State Savings of Salt Lake City. Reportedly Oldenburg bought 363 acres of land in Richmond, California, in 1977 for $874,000 (he actually paid only $80,000 in down payment, the paper reported). In 1979 he hired an appraiser who appraised the land at $32.5 million. Just a little over two years later, in 1982, the same appraiser decided the land was worth $83.5 million. In 1983 Oldenburg bought State Savings for $10.5 million. In 1984 he sold the Richmond property to State Savings for $55 million, the *Examiner* reported.[2] Oldenburg resigned as chairman of State soon after a searing article appeared in *The Wall Street Journal* in June 1984.[3]

On July 31 a congressional committee released a report that made public for the first time the causes for the collapse in March of Empire Savings near Dallas. Pressure on Gray to do something about the emerging problem was building. But do what? The growing number of insolvencies presented Gray with a heads-I-win, tails-you-lose dilemma. If he ordered all the insolvent institutions closed, as the law required, the FSLIC would be liable for billions of dollars in losses. If the dying thrifts were allowed to continue operating, they would only sink deeper into the red. Gray began to gear up for an extended battle to get the thrift industry back under control and to try to develop a plan for responding to the emerging crisis.

The last thing he needed then was a run-in with Charlie Knapp. Knapp was dashingly handsome, a young, self-styled financial visionary whose gold-plated faucets, in the lavatory of his company's $14 million Lear jet, have become part of the lore of those go-go S&L years. He ran Financial Corporation of America (FCA) in Irvine, California, south of Los Angeles. FCA in turn owned American Savings and Loan of Stockton, California, which was at the time the largest thrift association in the country. FCA was one of Gray's rapidly emerging headaches. The company was on a growth curve that pointed straight up. In just one year, 1983 to 1984, FCA had grown from an already staggering $22 billion in assets to an unbelievable $32 billion. Regulators said Knapp used brokered deposits and jumbo CDs sold through his own money desk[4] to invest in fixed-rate mortgages and sophisticated hedging instruments that regulators and the Securities and Exchange Commission had a very difficult time understanding or evaluating. They couldn't see how FCA was coming up with the profits it was reporting while at the same time it was drowning in repossessed real estate.

FCA had invested billions in old, fixed-rate loans at the very time the rest of the industry was rushing to safe adjustable-rate loans. And court documents later revealed that FCA had its share of risky commercial development projects in California and Texas as well. Delinquencies piled up and regulators said FCA was making outrageous deals in order to sell the properties it had already had to repossess. At one time, Knapp told us, he had 300 people working in FCA's repossessed properties department.[5]

Among Knapp's borrowers was the ubiquitous Morris Shenker. FCA had loaned millions to the Las Vegas-based Dunes Hotels and Casinos when Shenker was chairman. (When Shenker ran into financial woes, FCA was partly bailed out by Jack Bona, who purchased the Atlantic City Dunes project in 1983.[6] However, as of October 1985 FCA was reportedly the Dunes' largest creditor with a $51 million mortgage on the Las Vegas Dunes' building.)

Another borrower was Leonard Pelullo. Pelullo and American Savings and Loan eventually became entangled in litigation over a $13 million mortgage. (The Atlantic City *Press* reported that circumstances surrounding Pelullo's business relationship with American prompted a grand jury investigation in 1986 but no indictments resulted.[7] In 1988 Pelullo's Royale Group Ltd. bought the Atlantic City Dunes.)

Gray didn't like Charlie Knapp's way of doing business and wanted him out of the thrift industry. If FCA failed, the weight of its $32 billion portfolio would pull the FSLIC fund down in one swoop.

From Washington, Gray called Knapp at his offices in Irvine, California, and said he wanted to see him in Washington as soon as possible. Knapp flew straight to Washington to confront the chairman on his own ground.

"Mr. Gray will see you now," the receptionist told Knapp, a dapper dresser nicknamed "the Red Baron" by his friends because he flew a vintage P-38 World War II fighter. But this was one dogfight Knapp wasn't going to win. The meeting between Gray and Knapp began at 2:15 p.m. and Gray had another meeting scheduled for 2:30 that he could not miss. Gray told us he read Knapp the riot act, quoting chapter and verse on everything he disliked about FCA's operations. He accused Knapp of running FCA in an "unsafe and unsound manner." The phrase was a provocative one and Knapp could not miss its significance—it was the very phrase the FSLIC used when it closed thrifts and sued former owners for the losses.

"Because of your irresponsible actions," Gray said he continued, "you've placed in jeopardy the entire savings and loan industry, Mr. Knapp, and I'll do everything in my power to make sure you are removed from this industry. I'm putting you on notice." Gray looked down at his watch. It was 2:30, and he was a busy man.

Knapp remembered the meeting a little differently. He told us Gray greeted him with, "I understand that your loan portfolio is not sound."

Knapp said he asked Gray, "What do you base that on?"

Gray pulled out of his shirt pocket an article from the business section of *The New York Times* and started reading. As Knapp later recalled it to us, "I just threw up my hands and said, 'The hell with this, I've gotta get out of here.' I couldn't get out of there fast enough."

Regardless of the version you believe, it was clear that the normally flamboyant, self-assured Knapp was caught by surprise by the vigor of Gray's attack. This was not the dopey "Mr. Ed" his friends in the industry had told him to expect. The Red Baron had been shot down in flames.

"I fly all the way from California and the guy gives me 15 minutes and shows me the goddamn door," Knapp told us later.

Shocked, Knapp returned to California, formulated a plan, and called Gray to make a proposal. This time Gray had to listen because FCA was too big to shut down, no matter how rotten it may have been. Somehow Gray had to keep the company going, like a ward of the FHLBB, until its problem assets could be disposed of in an orderly manner over a long period of time. Knapp knew the bind that Gray was in and offered him a deal. Knapp agreed to leave voluntarily on two conditions: first, that he be allowed to select his successor, pending Bank Board approval, and, second, that Gray agree to a $2 million golden parachute for Knapp. Gray agreed.

Knapp hung up the phone and called Washington again. This time he phoned the Office of Management and Budget.

"David Stockman, please. Tell him Charlie Knapp's on the line."

Knapp told us he called Stockman[8] and said that Gray had forced him out of FCA. Knapp asked Stockman if he would be interested in the job. Stockman had been President Ronald Reagan's spokesman on budget matters since Reagan took office in 1981, and he had made it known he was getting tired of taking the heat—outspoken and opinionated, he had attracted a lot of press coverage. He also may have been getting tired of taking trips to the Oval Office woodshed whenever he "misspoke." The prospect of running a $32 billion company must have seemed an easy matter after what he'd been through. He agreed to Knapp's proposal. Knapp told Stockman to get Ed Gray's approval. Stockman called Gray.

"Come on over, David," Gray said.

Within 30 minutes Stockman had arrived at Gray's office. Gray told us Stockman said he had talked to Knapp about the FCA job and was interested. He said he was tired of Washington and wanted to return to the private sector, and the FCA job was an attractive challenge. Gray listened patiently, thinking to himself that Knapp must have offered Stockman a lot of money to take the job and to act as Knapp's mouthpiece. But Gray let Stockman present his case. Gray's friend and the FHLBB's general counsel, Norm Raiden, sat quietly in a corner chair. Finally Gray spoke up. Out of curiosity he asked, "How soon could you leave your job at OMB, David?"

"Five days," Stockman shot back. But Gray had already made up his mind.

"I understand you're a nice man and a quick study, David, but you've never operated a thrift before. I'm sorry, but I've already lined up Bill Popejoy for the job."[9] A half hour after Stockman left Gray's office, James Baker, the president's chief of staff, phoned and Gray told us he asked angrily:

"Why are you trying to hire Stockman away from us? There's an election coming up. We need him."

"I didn't," Gray answered. "He wanted the job and I suggested he forget all about it." Baker hung up the phone. Later that day Stockman called Gray and said he didn't want the job anyway. He was going to stay at OMB. (As of early 1989 Knapp had not been charged criminally or civilly in connection with FCA's huge insolvency. However, FCA's troubles cost the FSLIC over $2 billion and spawned nearly 1,200 separate lawsuits, many naming Knapp, and he had sued FCA. By press time about half the suits had been settled, ruled on, or dismissed.)

As Gray mapped his strategy for stopping the abuses at thrifts and dealing with the damage already done, he realized he could not do the job with regulations alone. He would need help from Congress. He knew he was pushing a stick into a beehive, but he felt the situation was deteriorating so fast that he had little choice. To get Congress to act he would have to have public support, so he took his battle public. In speech after speech Gray attacked some of the elements he identified as being at the root of the industry's problems. Among them were: brokered deposits, risky lending, direct investments,[10] and inaccurate appraisals. He proposed restrictions, and he even introduced the idea of a risk-based premium program that would require individual thrifts to pay special assessments to the FSLIC if they engaged in risky behavior.

His candor produced a vigorous counterattack in Washington. Gray claimed Don Regan had the Treasury Department[11] back a bill in Congress that would actually *further* deregulate the thrift industry. Gray was appalled and vigorously opposed the bill. It was defeated. Score one for Gray.

A short time later, Gray believes, Don Regan exacted his revenge. On September 13, 1984, Regan spoke on the state of the economy to a convention of mortgage executives in Washington. At the news conference that followed, Stan Strachan, editor of the *National Thrift News*, asked Regan if the Treasury would guarantee losses at FCA in the event of a run on the company by depositors. After all, Strachan reminded Regan, Treasury had done just that a few years earlier during a run on Continental Illinois bank in Chicago.

"No," Regan shot back. Pressed by Strachan, Regan categorically ruled out any kind of Treasury backing for FCA. That public statement created exactly the kind of turmoil Gray had been trying to avoid by moving slowly on the FCA matter. He had eased Knapp out and Popejoy in with as little fanfare as possible. So far his strategy had worked—until Don Regan's remarks. The next day there was a run on FCA and $400 million in deposits walked (or ran) out the door as customers and deposit brokers rushed to remove their money. It was the largest one-day run in thrift history, and Ed Gray was furious at Regan. Regan's careless remarks had been devastating to Gray's FCA rehabilitation program. Gray shot off an angry letter to Regan, asking him to check with the FHLBB the next time he planned to speak out like that.

Regan replied with an angry letter of his own in which he said, "I was surprised and frankly displeased by your letter. . . . Candidly, I do not have to be reminded of my responsibilities in areas of concern to you or, for that matter, any of the other areas of government in which economics and finance play a role."

Soon Regan had another opportunity to throw stumbling blocks in Ed Gray's path. To repair the damage done at FCA by the massive outflow of deposits in the wake of Regan's remarks, Gray turned to brokered deposits as a quick fix. Ironically, Gray, the very man who was death on brokered deposits, was now turning to them to buy time. For help he approached his predecessor at the Bank Board, Richard Pratt, now an executive with Merrill Lynch, and Pratt agreed to have Merrill Lynch place $1 billion in deposits with FCA within days. But he soon called Gray back with the news that he'd been overruled by his superiors at Merrill Lynch and the deal was off. Gray was forced to raise the money from other brokerage houses. Later Pratt told Gray privately that Don Regan had personally intervened at Merrill Lynch to kill the deal. It was almost as if Regan were taunting Gray for his opposition to brokered deposits. Gray thought Regan was trying to get back at him for Gray's suggestion that Regan check with him before commenting publicly about S&L matters.[12] Regan, who had promised he would not involve himself with matters relating to his former employer Merrill Lynch after he joined the Reagan cabinet, denied intervening with Merrill Lynch about the $1 billion in brokered deposits for FCA. Pratt declined to comment.

After Gray's brokered-deposit regulation was rejected by a federal court, which ruled that only Congress could make such a prohibition, Gray decided that if he couldn't limit brokered deposits, he'd better limit what thrifts did with those federally insured deposits. At every insolvent S&L, Gray found both excessive brokered deposits and risky direct investments. In Gray's view thrifts chartered in states with liberal thrift regulations were using federally insured deposits to take far too many risks.[13] The thrift industry was turning into a crap shoot, with the bets insured by the FSLIC. Gray thought that was wrong, and he made it known that his next move would be to draft new regulations that would curb direct investments by FSLIC-insured state thrifts[14] and limit thrifts' growth.[15]

"It had to stop," he was telling everyone who would listen. S&Ls were padding their financial statements with too many direct investments that seemed on the books to be worth millions but whose quality couldn't really be determined until the project was completed. If the project was a ripoff, no one would know until it was too late.

Gray had first proposed a new direct investment regulation in May 1984. In early December 1984, shortly before he actually issued the new regulation, Gray said Bill O'Connell of the U.S. League of Savings Institutions phoned and pleaded with him not to go through with it.

"If he had been at Gray's office, you can guarantee that O'Connell would've been down on his hands and knees," an aide said later.

O'Connell denies he asked Gray to kill the whole regulation, but only to modify it. Whatever the case, Gray was unmoved.

In January the regulation was finally enacted, to go into effect in March. In general it would limit direct investments to just 10 percent of a thrift's total assets,[16] and it would also limit a thrift's rate of growth to 25 percent a year.[17] Some thrifts had been growing at rates of 100 to 500 percent a year.[18]

Gray says that the U.S. League again tried to kill the regulation. O'Connell remembers events differently, repeating that, rather than wanting to kill Gray's growth restrictions, the League had simply wanted them modified and calling

Gray's version "overkill." Gray says "nonsense." He believes O'Connell is trying to rewrite history.

"During the late afternoon of the day before both of these regs [the growth regulation and the direct investment regulation] were proposed in open hearing of the Bank Board, Mr. O'Connell called me," Gray recalled. "My recollection is that the calls came in at around 5 to 6 p.m. Mr. O'Connell begged me to not go through with the growth regulation, not to propose it the next day, and he said if I did so my career would be ruined if I ever decided to go back to the thrift industry. The call was a long one, as I recall, probably 30 to 40 minutes. I told him that if I had to be the son-of-a-bitch to do it so be it. It would be done."

Regarding the direct investment regulation, Gray said it was only after the regulation was adopted by the Board that the U.S. League "grudgingly" supported it.

As 1985 dawned it was beginning to appear to Ed Gray in Washington that Texas was especially out of control. Gray's shorthanded and underpaid examiners were coming in from the field with stories about Texas thrift owners and managers that made J. R. Ewing look like a minister. They told Gray about thrift board meetings attended by hookers whose services were paid for by the thrift, chartered jet-set parties to Las Vegas, gala excursions to Europe, luxurious yachts, ocean-front mansions, and Rolls-Royces—princely life-styles built on mountains of bad loans and bad investments. The state's long-standing liberal thrift and banking practices, the oil and real estate booms of the late 1970s, and the state's entrepreneurial, wild-cat business traditions had all combined to make Texas a hothouse for deregulated thrifts, and the signs of abuse were starting to show. In the newly deregulated environment new thrifts had sprouted throughout Texas like rye grass after a spring rain. Old, long-established thrifts were snatched up by young speculators eager for the opportunity to wheel and deal with insured deposits. Even out-of-state thrifts, many from California, opened loan offices in Texas hoping to catch a ride on the Texas wave.

Within a year of Garn-St Germain's passage Texas was embroiled in a construction-loan feeding frenzy. Acquisition and Development Loans (ADLs) and Acquisition, Development, and Construction Loans (ADCs), for commercial projects, were the main-line products. Home loans went begging. The money, in large part, flowed into construction. Yet thrifts were not doing sufficient market surveys to see if the marketplace could absorb the new office buildings and condos, and they were not coordinating with other thrifts to make sure they weren't all going to flood the market at the same time with the same kinds of projects. In Texas in the early 1980s the emphasis was on building, and the future would take care of itself because the boom would never end.

Building permits in Texas increased from $4.3 billion in 1976 to about $17 billion in 1983.

Texas thrifts lived only for today: today's deals, today's profits, today's kick-backs. By 1985 the Dallas and Houston skylines were filled with what locals began to refer to as "see-through office buildings." So much commercial con-struction had been financed by thrifts that it far outstripped the local market demand, and glass skyscrapers stood empty. There were so many unsold condos littering Houston and Dallas and their suburbs that a favorite joke among lenders went: "What's the difference between V.D. and condominiums?" The answer: "You can get rid of V.D."

With supply vastly exceeding demand in 1985, many Texas thrifts kept from going under only by turning more deals and inflating their financial statements with more fees and up-front interest. Their portfolios became little more than huge pyramid schemes, Ponzis, that required constant trades, refinancings, swaps, participations, and loans on yet more new projects. They had to take in more brokered deposits to fund more loans so it would appear that they were making more profit, even though the loans were risky (risky loans carried the potential for the highest profits—and losses). As a result Texas thrifts grew at an astronomical rate. In 1984 and 1985 they grew three times faster than the national average.[19] As long as the S&Ls could keep pedaling, they wouldn't fall. But every day that passed they had to pedal faster and faster to maintain the illusion that they were moving forward. Gray's proposed limits on direct investments and growth were going to be *very* unpopular with thrift owners in Texas—men like Don Dixon, who owned Vernon Savings and Loan, headquartered in Dallas. By 1985 Don Dixon was living like a king, and Gray's new rules threatened his kingdom.

Don Dixon, his petite blond wife, Dana, clinging tightly to his arm, strode proudly toward the front of the crowd of 40,000 assembled in the piazza in front of St. Peter's Basilica in the Vatican. Pope John Paul II, dressed entirely in white, had just made his weekly Wednesday address in six languages and was now descending the white throne to mingle with the special guests seated around the platform.

The Bishop of San Diego, the Reverend Leo T. Maher, was hosting the Dixons for their personal meeting with the Pope. Dixon was in his late forties. Expensively dressed, and with collar-length gray curls around a tanned face, he stood out as a businessman in the crowd of worshipers. He had a drooping mustache and beady eyes that could look warm and trustworthy or calculating and condescending. He had the air of a let's-shake-on-it kind of guy.

Dixon noted the grandeur of the 300-year-old piazza surrounded by Gian Lorenzo Bernini's grand colonnade. It is one of the most awesome places on earth, and Dixon noticed that the normally loquacious Dana was uncharacteristically silent. As the Pope neared, Dixon, too, felt the uniqueness of the moment. He was not a Catholic, and he had an arrogant self-confidence, but even he could not resist this Pope's stature and personal power.

"I was very well aware of everything I said and that I was in the presence of someone very special," he would later recall.

Pope John Paul II greeted the Dixons with a handshake and his characteristic off-to-one-side nod. Dixon thanked the Pope for the opportunity to meet with him and presented him with a gift he had brought for the occasion, a $40,000 Olaf Wieghorst original oil painting of an Indian on horseback, "Night Sentry." The Pope admired the painting and said it would hang in the Vatican Museum. Dixon told the Pope how much that meant to him. What Don failed to tell His Holiness was that the painting was not his to give. He had "borrowed" it from Vernon Savings and Loan back home.[20]

After their stop at the Vatican the Dixons continued their European fling with visits to Bulgari and Guzzi spas. They stayed at the finest European hotels, such as the Grosvenor House in London, the Hotel Ritz in Madrid, and the Bristol Hotel in Paris, and while in the neighborhood they stopped by the Palais de Margaux in Bordeaux, a château Dixon and some partners were converting into a restaurant and hotel. Then it was time to head for home. The Dixons made their May 1985 European jaunt in Vernon Savings' tri-jet Falcon 50 and, regulators later discovered, charged the trip's expenses on Vernon's tab.

Flying into Dallas on the last leg of their trip, the Dixon entourage looked out of the windows of their private jet at the city where the Dixons had made their fortune. Dallas, the eighth largest city in the United States, was an exciting town of soaring glass buildings, wild night spots, and businessmen in gray suits and cowboy boots. Business had traditionally been done differently in Dallas than in the rest of the country—on gambling instincts, eternal optimism, and the myth of the reliability of a Texas man's word. In the early 1980s the brash city vibrated with the pulse of money being pumped into the local economy from a booming oil business and mushrooming real estate speculation.

Don and Dana must have enjoyed the view as their private jet swooped down over North Dallas, a cluster of about 20 high-rise office buildings that had sprung up 15 miles due north of downtown Dallas. North Dallas straddled the Dallas Tollway just north of its intersection with the LBJ Freeway. It was the hub of a new Dallas financial center, and Dixon's Vernon Savings and Loan owned the 15-story high rise right in the middle.

There, too, was State Savings and Loan of Lubbock, under the control of Dixon's friend Tyrell Barker. And Sunbelt Savings and Loan, playfully known around town as Gunbelt Savings for its quick-draw deals. Sunbelt was run by Ed McBirney, nicknamed "Fast Eddie"—a man people said was "so smart it was frightening." McBirney became famous in Dallas for lavish parties filled with wine, women, and debauchery at places like the Dunes Hotel and Casino in Las Vegas. Near Sunbelt were a host of other entrepreneurial thrifts. North Dallas was Texas-thrift mecca.

Also in North Dallas was Jason's, the famous restaurant that became a favorite watering hole for deal makers who flocked to Dallas from around the world. At Jason's the manager, in desperation, had to cover some tables with butcher paper to prevent speculators from scribbling deals on the linen tablecloths. And, finally, in North Dallas were the swanky homes and condos where many of the S&L deal-makers (including Dixon, Barker, and McBirney) lived. The setting was right out of the script for the popular TV nighttime soap opera *Dallas*, which was shot on location at the South Fork Ranch about five miles away. North Dallas buzzed 24 hours a day with the frenetic seven-days-a-week pace of millionaires chasing their next million. For entrepreneurs in the early 1980s, North Dallas was where it was at.

The Dixons gathered their belongings as the Vernon Savings jet dropped down into Addison Municipal Airport (also in North Dallas) where Vernon Savings kept its fleet of planes. The clerical staff that had accompanied the Dixons to Europe settled back in their seats for the landing. It had been a tiring but rewarding trip, and it was good to be home. Europe was terrific, but no place in the world could quite compare at that time to the brave new world of Dallas.

Don Dixon was a man in a big hurry and he had made it to the top fast. Even as a child Dixon had been in a hurry, always looking for ways to cut corners, always trying to get from here to there in the quickest and easiest way. He grew up in Vernon, Texas, a small town 150 miles northwest of Dallas and 10 miles from the Oklahoma border, and his Type A tendencies had first shown themselves in high school, where, eager to get on to college, Dixon combined his junior and senior years so he could graduate a year early. His mother reinforced this "go get 'em" behavior by presenting young Don with a brand-new, money-green, 1956 T-Bird two-seater convertible for graduation. Dixon reportedly once told a high school friend that his goal was to make so much money he'd "never be able to put a dent in it."

From high school Dixon went to Rice Institute in Houston, where he studied architecture for two years. Then he transferred to the University of California at Los Angeles and began a lifelong love affair with the Pacific beaches of Southern California. In June 1960 Dixon graduated from UCLA with his degree in business administration. That same year, over a thousand miles away in Dixon's hometown, R. B. Tanner cut the ribbon to open his little Vernon Savings and Loan. No one could have imagined how intertwined the two disparate launchings would become.

Dixon went from college straight to where the money was in those days —residential development. The year 1960 marked the height of the migration to the suburbs. Like honeysuckle vines, freeways sprouted from crowded cities and turned once-flat farm and grazing lands into sprawling residential developments. The tide was rushing out and Dixon was there to catch the crest of the wave.

He formed Raldon Homes with an associate, Raleigh Blakely, and the company did well until the 1973–74 recession hit. Like most development companies, Raldon depended upon a steady stream of loans to provide the capital the company needed to buy land and build homes. With the recession the bottom dropped out of the housing market, and, according to published reports, Raldon found itself stuck with millions in development loans it could not pay off. Bankers complained about business cycles but didn't accept them as excuses for nonpayment, so, in a deal worked out between Raldon and its creditors, "Ral and Don" were forced to resign.

With Raldon's liabilities off his back, Dixon waited the recession out, and when the real estate market picked up again, he formed Dondi Construction (DON DIxon). In short order he was back on the top of the heap. Hundreds of homes bearing Dondi's unique signature trademark—Spanish styling topped with red tile roofs—began to pop up in the suburbs of Dallas. By 1981, at 45 years of age, Dixon was the head of a large, successful construction company that employed hundreds of people. He took to wearing gold chains, leather vests, and open-collared shirts around the office. People often said he reminded them of entertainer Kenny Rogers. *Texas Monthly* reported that his office staff handed out phony $3 bills with Dixon's picture on the front, under which was inscribed "Chairman of the Bored" and "In Don We Trust." The reverse side featured a picture of one of Dondi Construction's homes with the caption, in mock Latin, "Red Tilebus Roofum."

Dixon was riding high in the saddle when he teamed up with soul mate Tyrell Barker. Barker was a Northern California builder who had come to Texas recently when someone reportedly told him, "Hey, come on down to Dallas. We're making lots of money down here." Barker had already done very well in California real estate, and even after he moved to Dallas, government investigators said, he continued to maintain his $1.5 million home in Hillsborough, an exclusive community 20 miles south of San Francisco. He had purchased the home from the millionaire Hearst family. Barker was in his early forties, about three years younger than Dixon. He was noticeably hyperactive, an energetic workaholic with no family. Friends said he lived to "do deals." He was stocky, wore glasses and a mustache, and he talked a lot—except when he was with Dixon, to whom he deferred. He was smart and articulate, a man who had learned to compensate for a potentially crippling dyslexia that had kept him from graduating from high school or, he later told a judge, being able to read beyond a third-grade level.

Both Dixon and Barker were "deal junkies," as one FBI agent later described them, but their motivations were slightly different. Dixon had an appetite for the good life. He liked money and the pleasures it could buy. Barker, on the other hand, thrilled to the deal-making game and money was just the way he kept score. Dixon was a showman who enjoyed the parties and social amenities of his power. Barker was a loner who lived for his job. But neither of them was ever satisfied. Dixon and Barker measured themselves by the Texas oil yardstick of the day, which rated one's personal fortune in "units," with one unit equaling $100 million. At chic Dallas cocktail parties each new arrival was sized up in whispered rankings, such as "I hear he's a four-unit man." Dixon and Barker were "no-unit men," and they wanted to change that. A partnership Barker formed soon after he came to Texas in 1980 left no doubt where his priorities lay. He called it "MLMQ#1"—Make Lots of Money Quick #1.

Though Texans traditionally made their money in oil, neither Dixon nor Barker knew one end of an oil rig from the other so they could not hitch their wagons to that star. What they did know was development and, through that, the banking and thrift business. They had also heard about thrift deregulation, which had begun in 1980. And while as developers they had always had to go begging to lenders for money, they knew that if they could own their own S&L they would have ready access to all the cash (deposits) they wanted. So if they couldn't pump oil, maybe they could pump something better—money.

They each decided to buy a savings and loan.

Buying a savings and loan would cost more money than they had on hand, but Dixon had a close friend who was only too willing to help with the financing. He had become friends with a wealthy Shreveport, Louisiana, businessman, Herman K. Beebe. Beebe must have been everything Dixon wanted to become. He traveled in a chauffeured limo and lived on a gracious southern-style plantation estate near Shreveport. He also had homes and businesses in Dallas and Southern California. Dixon and Beebe had met about five years earlier, and Dixon had become an unofficial member of the Beebe family. He often visited Beebe on his Louisiana plantation and the two men frequently traveled together, playing gin rummy and drinking bourbon on Beebe's plane.

Beebe's flagship company, AMI, Inc., was an enormous conglomerate whose primary interests were insurance and nursing homes. One of the products AMI specialized in was credit life insurance. (Banks making large loans often required a borrower to take out a life insurance policy in the amount of the loan. If the borrower died, the insurance would pay off the loan.) Selling credit life insurance policies was a lucrative business, and Beebe had built close ties with many Texas and Louisiana banks. Dixon was so taken with Beebe that he introduced Tyrell Barker to him and soon they were a threesome.

"Terry and Beebe were on the phone to each other all the time," a friend said later. When Dixon and Barker decided they wanted to make their move into the soon-to-be-deregulated thrift industry, Beebe said he'd get them started by helping to finance their acquisitions.

CHAPTER SIXTEEN

Going Home

Don Dixon and his friend Tyrell Barker each began a search for an established thrift they could acquire with the minimum of fuss. Herman Beebe had solved their financing problems—all they had to do was find willing sellers. Barker hit pay dirt first when he landed State Savings and Loan of Lubbock, Texas. Lubbock (population 178,500) was a cattle town in West Texas at the center of prime Texas ranching country, about 300 miles west of Dallas. There 22 local citizens owned State Savings and Loan, a small, conservative thrift with $65 million in assets, primarily mortgages on single-family homes. But State/Lubbock was struggling because the interest it had to pay to attract deposits was higher than the interest it was earning on its 30-year home mortgages. State/Lubbock's owners were in the throes of a classic 1980–81 thrift squeeze.

With financial backing from Beebe, Barker gained formal control of State/Lubbock on December 3, 1981. Two weeks after buying State, Barker removed much of the thrift's management, and regulators later said that from then on Barker and his attorney, Lawrence B. Vineyard, were in control. (Later Barker would tell the FBI that Vineyard was the guy who read his paperwork for him, since Barker, because of his dyslexia, had only a third-grade reading ability.) Barker wasted no time opening a headquarters office in Dallas, where the action was, and he bought two corporate planes for State so he could fly back and forth, even though it cost only $34 to fly from Dallas to Lubbock on a commercial airline.

Barker later said he felt like a kid in a candy store. His oak-paneled office was on the first floor of a North Dallas high rise, and outside the sliding glass doors he had a miniature swimming pool built for his two dogs, an English bulldog and a Labrador retriever, who traveled with him wherever he went. Inside, he had a bar, a kitchen, and a fireplace, all the comforts of home. He even had a pull-down bed, just in case. He often entertained customers dressed in his jogging suit or jeans and suspenders. He worked from 7 a.m. until 11 p.m. *Newsweek* quoted him as saying his motto was "If I rest, I rust."

Word quickly spread among Dallas speculators, and Barker's waiting room was soon jammed with developers waiting their turn to pitch projects. Barker's message to them, some said later, was simple: "You bring the dirt, I bring the money. We split 50-50." The easy money produced a rush of customers eager to take advantage of Barker's lenient loan policies.

"How do you know what property to buy?" someone reportedly asked a developer scurrying to get one of Barker's loans.

"Wherever my dog lifts his leg I buy that rock and all the acreage around it," came the reply.

With his friend Tyrell Barker up and running, Don Dixon was searching in earnest for his place in the sun. That search took him back to his roots in little Vernon, Texas, where, the same spring Dixon had graduated from college in California, R. B. Tanner had opened Vernon Savings and Loan. Dixon decided to ask Tanner if he'd like to sell out to a local boy.

Vernon Savings and Loan, with $82 million in assets and only $90,000 in delinquent loans, was one of the soundest thrifts in the state. Tanner had run Vernon since he opened it in 1960 as though every paper clip and rubber band were hard cash. Friends said he even worked an entire year without a salary just to improve Vernon's balance sheet. Vernon Savings was his baby and he nurtured it lovingly. His small, modest office was dominated by a large oil painting of the First State Bank of Dumas, Texas, the very first bank he had audited as a young bank examiner in 1937.

Dixon arrived at Tanner's home that spring day wearing humility on his sleeve. R.B., dressed in shirt, tie, and suspenders, sat across from the stylishly dressed Dixon and listened to Don talk lovingly about his roots in Vernon. (Later Mrs. Tanner would recall sadly that Dixon displayed "perfect manners.") Dixon said he had benefited greatly from his wholesome upbringing there and he wanted to give something back to the community. He showed Tanner some of the plaques he had been awarded for his real estate developments. Though R.B. had not known the Dixon family well, young Don had grown up with the reputation of someone who would amount to something, so Tanner wasn't surprised that the successful young developer had the will and means to buy his savings and loan. But he was surprised at the generosity of Dixon's offer. The deal: Dixon would pay $5.8 million for Vernon's outstanding shares, $1.2 million in cash. The balance, Dixon told him, would be secured not only by Vernon stock but also by a rich business friend of his from Louisiana, Herman K. Beebe. How could Tanner lose?

Tanner took Dixon's offer to the other Vernon shareholders, who agreed it was generous, and on January 10, 1982, the deal was done. Don Dixon now owned Vernon Savings and Loan. Dixon told Tanner and the other board members that he was busy with his construction company and really had no interest in running Vernon. He asked if they would stay on board. They agreed. But Tanner was in for a rude awakening.

A month later the Vernon Savings board of directors held their first meeting since the change of ownership. Dixon did not attend, but he sent word to an astonished board that he had purchased, with the thrift's money, a $125,000 three-foot-tall bronze sculpture of a squatting Indian. Art was a great investment, he said, especially Western art, and he wanted the board to rubber-stamp the purchase. The slack-jawed directors looked around in stunned silence and then glumly approved the purchase. For the prudent, conservative Tanner, the shock of this extravagance was too much. He resigned his position on Vernon's board and went home to reflect, he told us later, upon the man to whom he had sold his pampered thrift.

Dixon soon forgot any gratitude for his wholesome small-town roots and promptly moved Vernon's administrative offices to a 15-story building in North Dallas. His business plan for Vernon was to attract brokered deposits and use them to finance commercial real estate projects (an abrupt departure from Vernon's traditional role as a local home lender). Our investigation of Mario Renda had already tipped us that First United Fund had brokered huge deposits into Vernon. Some of Renda's former employees (Manning's Seven Dwarfs) said Vernon Savings was one of First United Fund's "special deal" institutions (which meant that in exchange for getting the deposits, Vernon agreed to make loans to designated borrowers).

Dixon, who was above all a developer, not a banker, could have used some of that financing too. But he was faced with thrift regulations that prohibited large loans to "affiliated persons," and by owning all of Vernon's stock Dixon was about as affiliated as a person could be. Later, regulators said that to get around that thorny problem he created a complex web of some 30 subsidiary companies, layered in three tiers, at the apex of which was Dondi Financial Corporation. Dixon was a controlling owner of Dondi Financial and Dondi Financial was made controlling owner of Vernon Savings. But Dondi's other subsidiaries did not own Vernon Savings stock so they could promptly take their place in line to receive loans from the thrift. Dixon had pulled off a brilliant Trojan horse maneuver. And once Vernon Savings' money entered Dixon's maze of subsidiaries, regulators complained, it was rarely seen or heard from again.[1]

To run this empire Dixon built a loyal entourage of managers. He refused to give us his side of the story, but according to court records and federal regulators, he purchased his employees' loyalty with extravagant perks. Each head of a subsidiary received a new Mercedes sedan, for example. Offices and bonus plans were lavish. The result was a go-along, get-along, get-rich-too crew, many of whom asked few questions and did what they were told. Their loyalty and cooperation allowed Dixon to enjoy the fruits of this enterprise while appearing to maintain distance from the day-to-day activities that eventually led to Vernon's demise. One exception to the go-along was Jack Brenner, who, for example, was asked to check out some property Vernon Savings had bought in California. When Brenner called home he told Vernon president Woody Lemons that the property was worthless. It was a "boulder farm," he said.

"Now, Jack, you go look at it again," Brenner said Lemons told him. "You go look and tell me if you don't see a Gulf Stream 50 [a top-of-the-line corporate jet] in that land." Brenner said he realized in a flash that the whole project was just a way to siphon money out of Vernon and into something quite different, in this case a very expensive toy.

"I just said, 'Aw the hell with ya,' " Brenner recalled.

In just a few months Dixon converted little country-bumpkin Vernon Savings into a high-rolling, multitiered corporate conglomerate and for the next four years he took the S&L for the ride of its life. Vernon Savings had reported assets of $82.6 million in early 1982. In 1986 it would report assets of $1.3 billion. Regulators, who had begged entrepreneurs to step in and save the ailing thrift industry, were delighted. They soon added Vernon Savings to their published list of "High Performance Associations." Vernon was just one more shining example of what American business could do when government got out of its way, they said.

Regulators later charged that Dixon and some senior officers at Vernon wasted no time turning on Vernon's spigots and directing the money flow in their direction. Between July 6, 1982, and January 3, 1986, Vernon declared $22.95 million in dividends, of which Dondi Financial Corporation received $22 million. Thus millions of dollars were transferred from Dixon's regulated thrift, which had to account to federal and state regulators for every dollar, to his holding company, Dondi Financial Corporation, where he could use the money however he chose. But even with his Dondi Financial coffers bulging with Vernon's money, Dixon seems to have dipped directly from the Vernon Savings till whenever possible. It appeared that his every need, his every scratched itch, became a legitimate business expense for Vernon. Regulators later charged in court that Dixon and his senior officers "wrongly extracted" at least $40 million from Vernon.

In early 1983, for example, one of Vernon's subsidiaries paid $1.9 million for a Swiss-style chalet, built of stone, in the exclusive Colorado ski community of Beaver Creek. The 85 homes at Beaver Creek, nestled in the Rocky Mountains in prime skiing territory, were strictly for the rich and powerful. Homeowners were transported to and from the ski lifts by Beaver Creek's chauffeured limos, which served hot coffee and doughnuts on the way to the lifts and sparkling wine on the way back home.

Many of the houses at Beaver Creek, records showed, were built with money provided by a half dozen go-go Texas thrifts, Vernon among them, and each S&L made sure it had its own posh retreat there. Western Savings and Loan owner Jarrett Woods had a $2 million cabin, as did Morton Hopkins, owner of Commodore Savings of Dallas, and Chuck Wilson, owner of Sandia Savings of Albuquerque, New Mexico. According to news accounts, Wilson particularly liked to watch the skiers from his hot tub in his rooftop cupola with its heated slate floor. Sandia Savings purchased its stone castle retreat, complete with ponds and towers and waterfall, with a $5 million loan from Vernon.[2] All four thrifts, and their management, were inside players in the Texas thrift game, making loans back and forth to each other, and by 1988 they would all be insolvent or struggling to survive.

Beaver Creek was fine when Don and Dana were in the mood for snow, but their first love was Southern California and a $1 million Solano Beach house just north of San Diego. Dixon's role model, Herman Beebe, had located the house when, in early 1981, his vacation home at La Costa Resort in Southern California was being redecorated and he needed a place to stay in the interim. When Beebe found the Solano Beach house he had Dixon and Barker fly out west for a look. They liked it and Dixon entered into a lease option on the six-bedroom, 5,000-square-foot home. Beebe moved in and stayed there until the renovation of his La Costa house was complete. After Don and Dana Dixon were married in 1982 (regulators later charged Vernon Savings paid for the wedding), the Solano Beach home became their favorite hideaway. They commuted on Vernon's jet between Dallas and California, spending three and four days a week at Solano Beach. Barker visited on weekends. Dixon had the Solano Beach house remodeled, and when the work was complete he named two of the master bedrooms—one the Dixon Suite, the other the Beebe Suite.

Dixon must have realized that deregulation was a gift from Washington, and what Washington giveth, Washington could taketh away. Vernon needed a way to show its appreciation and just the item was tied up at a yacht harbor in Florida. Even the name, *High Spirits*, was apropos. She was docked in Boca Raton, Florida, and what a dream boat she was. Built in the late 1920s, she was 112 feet long and she reeked of Gatsby-era charm. Her sleek white hull was topped by two levels of cabins made of lacquered natural wood. Shining brass handrails enclosed her promenade and poop decks. Her main parlor was as spacious and luxurious as the living room of a country manor. Her staterooms rivaled those of fine old hotel suites. And to cap it all off she was the sister ship to the presidential yacht, *Sequoia*. How was that for a political attention getter? She was a beauty. She was perfect. She was $2.6 million.

Federal regulators might have found it a bit hard to justify the purchase of a yacht for a landlocked Dallas thrift, so Vernon executives and customers formed the High Spirits Limited Partnership. According to the FSLIC, Vernon routed over $2 million to the "partners" (by overfunding on a $10 million loan to a San Antonio shopping center, according to the FSLIC),[3] so they could "buy" their shares of the partnership. FSLIC claimed that the partners were never required to make any payments whatsoever and that Dixon in turn used the *High Spirits* as though it were his and Vernon Savings' personal flagship.

High Spirits, with its permanent crew of three, became a migratory bird. In the cold winter months Dixon docked her in Boca Raton. But as soon as the cherry blossoms were out up north, he had her moved to Washington, D.C., where he used her as a floating party platform to wine and dine some of this country's best-known and most powerful politicians. The bill for flowers alone was reportedly $800 a day. By far the most frequent sailor on Vernon's yacht was Representative Tony Coelho, who, according to the captain's log, used *High Spirits* almost as often as Dixon. (A four-term congressman from California's San Joaquin Valley, Coelho had been a fund-raiser par excellence since becoming chairman of the House Democratic Campaign Committee in 1981. After federal bank examiners discovered that Coelho and the campaign committee had used the *High Spirits* for 11 political fund-raising events in 1985 and 1986, Coelho and the committee repaid Vernon $48,450. In 1987 Coelho would become House majority whip, a position he held until he resigned from Congress in 1989 rather than face an ethics probe.) Others sailors included Texas Congressmen Jake Pickle (D-Austin) and Jim Chapman (D-Sulphur Springs), Texas lobbyist Durward Curlee (who reportedly lived on the *High Spirits* when he was in Washington),[4] and House Majority Leader Jim Wright (D-Texas).

Yachting was all well and good, as far as it went, but rich people, *really rich people*, jetted regularly to the Continent. In 1983 off the Dixons flew on a private chartered jet to Europe. Dixon justified the tour as a business trip because, he told associates, he and Dana were researching three-star restaurants on the possibility that Vernon might open a French eatery of its own, maybe in Dallas. Dixon said he might even hire a famous French chef to run the place. (*The Wall Street Journal* reported that in Lyons Paul Bocuse, a well-known French chef, actually assembled his 12 sous chefs in the restaurant courtyard for Dixon's review.) Don and Dana hopscotched across Europe from one three-star Michelin diner to another, eating their way through France. All in all, they sampled seven different world-class restaurants, in what Dana described in her diary as a "flying house party . . . a gastronomique-fantastique!"

Dana wrote that as they traveled on their comfortable chartered jet, or in Rolls-Royces, in the company of a group of European socialites, their way was prepared for them by Philippe Junot, the former playboy-husband of Princess Caroline of Monaco. He had found his way onto Vernon's payroll as a "consultant" for all things European. When the trip was over the Dixons had run up a $22,000 tab—paid for, said an FHLB examiner, by Vernon Savings, even though Dixon was neither an officer nor a director of the thrift. Later, responding to criticism of the trip, Dixon told James O'Shea of the Chicago *Tribune*, "You think it's easy eating in three-star restaurants twice a day six days a week? By the end of a week, you want to spit it [the food] out."

Aside from the stress of eating in three-star restaurants twice a day, Dixon had no real complaints about the trip itself, but using a "rent-a-jet" dulled the gloss a bit, so when he returned he went jet shopping. He wound up with what regulators would later call "a small air force." In another apparent effort to keep frivolous items out of regulatory view, Dixon made a deal with a small company, Coronado Air, Inc., whereby Vernon Savings loaned Coronado Air the money to buy the aircraft and Vernon then leased the planes from them. An FHLB examiner said the first purchase was a Falcon 50, considered the Rolls-Royce of corporate aircraft. The lease cost Vernon Savings $39,500 a month and eventually rose to $65,000 a month. Dixon liked the Falcon and quickly made it his personal aircraft, but that left other Vernon executives facing the disgrace of commercial air travel. So Vernon loaned another $1.7 million to Coronado Air, this time for the purchase of a 1978 Lear Jet 35A. Vernon then leased the aircraft back for $23,125 a month. By 1985 the lease had jumped to $35,000 a month. Those two jets alone were costing Vernon nearly $100,000 a month by 1985.

But Vernon's many subsidiaries employed many executives. To make certain none of the loyal troops felt slighted, Vernon bought three airplanes, a Cessna Citation, a Cessna 414A, and a King Air E-90 long-range twin turbo prop. And for those short hops to the store, a helicopter. Planes needed pilots, and Vernon kept six full-time pilots on the payroll in its corporate "ready room" at Addison Municipal Airport in North Dallas.

Vernon's jets, three of which were baby blue, were rarely idle. The logs of the Falcon, now in possession of the FSLIC, listed only Don and Dana as passengers on at least six flights. Also, like the Dixon navy, the Dixon air force played host to a gaggle of politicians. Among them, according to the logs, were former President Gerald Ford and his wife, Betty, Vernon's neighbors at Beaver Creek, who hitched several rides at costs ranging from $6,000 to $13,000, *Texas Monthly* reported. Other high-flying political guests included Representative Jack Kemp of New York; Senator Pete Wilson and Congressman-cum-boatswain's mate Tony Coelho, both from California; Senator Paul Laxalt of Nevada; and Representative Jim Wright of Texas (later to become speaker of the House). Dixon's air force was proving a handy alternative to commercial travel for Dixon's politician friends. (In just three years this fleet of aircraft cost Vernon Savings $5,574,942.40 to lease and operate, an FHLB examiner later testified.)

A review of the people listed on the flight logs of Vernon's jets turned up many other names familiar to us: Larry Taggart, former California S&L commissioner; Ed Mittlestet, the president of Charles Bazarian's company, CB Financial; and Eric Bronk, attorney for Consolidated Savings and Loan's owner Robert Ferrante.[5] We were starting to feel right at home at Vernon. It was becoming clear that whatever the network was that we were piecing together, Don Dixon had definitely plugged himself and Vernon into it.

One of the Good Ole Boys' favorite Texas pastimes was hunting, and as a boy Dixon had particularly enjoyed quail hunting with his dad in West Texas, so a partnership chipped in $2.4 million for a posh hunting club. The huge Sugarloaf Lodge sat atop a loaf-shaped mountain about 30 miles southwest of Vernon. Suites had magnificent views overlooking a canyon, and hot tubs with Jacuzzis soothed the woodsmen's aching muscles.

To the hunting club's armory were added $40,000 worth of handmade Italian shotguns embellished with gold and silver inlay. But hunting, even with fancy guns, could be a hit-or-miss proposition, as one guest later recalled, so live quail were flown in from Illinois the day before the hunt. Their wings were clipped and tail feathers plucked so they couldn't possibly fly. "Hunters" then stood on Sugarloaf's sweeping deck, overlooking the canyon, while hired hands crouched on a ledge below and threw the quail into the air as the guests blasted away. If a bird survived one volley, it was recycled until someone finally nailed it. A lot of Illinois quail met an ignoble end at Sugarloaf.

Although diverting, skiing at Beaver Creek and shooting plucked quail at Sugarloaf did not alter Dixon's preference for California and its sunny beaches. He and Dana threw lavish parties at their Sola no Beach home, mixing with Southern California's Who's Who, and it wasn't long before Dixon came to the conclusion that he should become a pillar of the community like other socialites. He had an office there and some real estate projects in the works. Now he should contribute to a worthy cause.

After looking for such a cause he finally settled on the University of San Diego. He wasn't ready to part with money, mind you. Instead he donated Dondi Financial Corporation stock to the university, and he threw in a written commitment that, if asked, he would buy the stock back for $3 million cash. The donation was a stroke of genius. It cost Dixon nothing (and would ultimately be worth nothing, after Dixon filed for bankruptcy in 1987), but it brought instant pillardom and covered nearly every conceivable social, political, and karmic (an important consideration in California) base. Suddenly Dixon was the darling of USD's influential alumni, who in turn plugged him directly into a powerful circle of local, state, and federal politicians. Among them was Congressman Bill Lowery (R-San Diego), for whom Dixon promptly threw a $7,000 campaign fund-raiser. He also took Lowery for rides on Vernon's jet and threw parties for him on the *High Spirits*. Lowery later told reporters he thought Dixon himself owned the jet and the yacht, but Dixon charged it all to Vernon Savings.

The congressman reimbursed Dixon, but somehow, according to the FSLIC, those reimbursements never made their way back to Vernon.

To enhance their enjoyment of the Southern California scene, the Dixons joined the private Moonlight Beach Club in Encinitas, just north of Solano Beach. A membership cost them $2,500. The club wanted to expand and buy a condo project nearby that the Dixons (and Vernon Savings CEO Woody Lemons) owned. The Moonlight Beach Club didn't have enough money to buy the condos from Dixon so regulators said he helped the club raise the cash this way: When businessmen wanted to borrow money from Vernon, some were told they first had to join the Moonlight Beach Club. Memberships, for them, cost $77,500 to $155,000 depending on how large a loan they wanted from Vernon.

To reward high-performance employees Dixon and Vernon's executive committee decided to distribute Vernon's booty through a Bean Program, regulators later alleged in court. Under the Bean Program, "beans" were awarded instead of bonuses to Vernon executives and employees based on their performance. Between June 1983 and June 1986, a FSLIC lawsuit revealed, Vernon paid out $15 million in beans. $10 million of the beans were subsequently redeemed for cash and Vernon kept $5 million, calling it deferred compensation.

There was a hitch—one that regulators said benefited Dixon at Vernon Savings' expense. Employees participating in the Bean Program were also required to buy stock in Dondi Financial Corporation. Dixon would arrange loans from Vernon for them to buy the stock. (Vernon made over $678,000 in such loans.) Employees were then required to use part of their bean bonuses to make the payments on the loans. Buying stock in Dixon's Dondi Financial was what qualified them to participate in the Bean Program. Eighty employees took part in the plan, which appeared, in fact, to be simply another scheme to funnel money from Vernon to Dondi Financial. The plan seems to have helped turn some of Vernon's top executives into an army of little Jacks ready to climb the magic beanstalk whenever Dixon snapped his fingers.

By the dawn of 1984 the Vernon Savings of 1982, with its $82 million in assets, was a distant memory. The thrift now boasted assets of $450 million, made up of what would later turn out to be a murky stew composed of brokered deposits, bad loans carried as sound ones on the books, and properties Vernon carried on its balance sheet at grossly inflated values. Vernon was wildly making loans without regard to their intrinsic value because the thrift made its money up front, in large origination fees. The S&L charged up to 5 points for originating a loan, so on a $100 million loan Vernon immediately "made" up to $5 million. The thrift also charged 1 percent to 2 percent to renew the loan every six months (once a year was standard practice in the industry). So what if the borrower later defaulted on the loan? Vernon had already made its profit. And who else was to know? The Federal Home Loan Bank Board's $14,000-a-year examiners? Vernon's sophisticated maze of business dealings left those shavetail accountants scratching their heads. Besides, the Federal Home Loan Bank for District 9 (Arkansas, Louisiana, Mississippi, New Mexico, Texas), where there were about 300 S&Ls, had just reduced its agents and supervisors from 34 to 12, in the spirit of deregulation. It now took up to two years just to schedule an examination of a thrift, and some had not been examined in over three years.

Eventually, though, Dixon's ostentatious life-style began to raise questions. When federal auditors got around to examining Vernon's 1983 books, they became alarmed by the institution's headlong dive into brokered deposits, helter-skelter development, and loans to the maze of subsidiaries bearing the mark of "Dondi." Bank records show that in August of 1984 regulators forced Vernon's board to sign a supervisory agreement binding Vernon to strict guidelines. The feds had no idea what was going on at Vernon because it was all moving too fast. They wanted to slow things down until they could figure out whether what they were seeing was the promise of deregulation incarnate or a thrift regulator's darkest nightmare.

The supervisory agreement was a sobering event to Vernon's board of directors, who still conducted their board meetings in Vernon, 150 miles from the Dallas action. All in their sixties and seventies, holdovers from R. B. Tanner's day, they never really understood Dixon's fast-moving deals so they had to trust him and his officers to make the right decisions for the thrift. Their confusion allowed Dixon (who served on the thrift's powerful loan committee, where the decision was made to approve or disapprove a loan or investment, even though he was never an officer at Vernon) and his associates to blunt the effect of the supervisory agreement, as Vernon employees later testified. Deals the board had never approved were added to the minutes of the board meetings *after* the meetings were held. Boilerplate language, designed solely to comply with the supervisory agreement, was added to the minutes so the directors thought they were complying. After the board meetings the real minutes and tape recordings of the board meetings were destroyed in the Dallas office. The board was also given inaccurate data on the condition of Vernon's loan portfolio, and the list of delinquent loans submitted to the board of directors was woefully incomplete. In short, the supervisory agreement apparently was little more than an annoying roadblock that Dixon and his associates quickly found a detour around. It would take more than regulatory saber rattling to stop the Don Dixons of Dallas.

Dixon's sidekick, Tyrell Barker, hadn't been idle either. His State Savings of Lubbock had also mushroomed into a megathrift using brokered deposits, high-risk lending, direct investments, and—as was later proven in court—fraudulent deals. While federal regulators were focusing on Dixon, Texas state regulators were wringing their hands over Barker, who was not only looting State Savings but was branching out and acquiring other thrifts as well. Barker had bought Brownsfield Savings in Brownsfield, Texas, and Key Savings, located just outside Denver.[6]

Barker had also struck up a friendship with Tom Nevis, 39, the president of Nevis Industries in Yuba City, California. Nevis Industries described itself in a corporate profile as "a highly diversified real estate development and agribusiness concern with major holdings throughout California as well as in Arizona, Colorado, Kentucky, Mississippi, Oregon and Nevada." The company reported that its holdings were worth $100 million in 1981. Tom Nevis sat astride this megabusiness in an elaborate office with a macho Western motif of stuffed trophy animals, pictures of Nevis on hunting trips, pictures of Nevis in a bar riding a mechanical bull.

Nevis Industries had borrowed heavily to acquire this far-flung empire, bellying up, for example, to the troughs of State Federal Savings and Loan of Corvallis, Oregon. Federal investigators said Nevis walked off with about $81 million in loans in a gross violation of loan limits to a single borrower after Beverly Hills loan broker Al Yarbrow introduced him to the thrift. (Federal investigators said State/Corvallis paid Yarbrow $900,000 in commissions for loans he placed there. Yarbrow was later indicted for one deal in which he took his commission in the form of an $88,000 white Rolls Royce.) An FSLIC lawsuit revealed that regulators believed Nevis had participated in defrauding State Savings of Corvallis by using straw borrowers and cash-for-trash schemes.[7]

U.S. Attorney Lance Caldwell and lone FBI agent Joe Boyer spent nearly three years piecing together the dozens of mind-numbing deals at State/Corvallis, which they said could cost the FSLIC over $150 million. As a result of their work, a grand jury indicted Nevis, Yarbrow, Mitchell Brown, and others on numerous counts of conspiracy, bank fraud, and mail fraud. Nevis was found guilty on 28 counts in May 1989. The Yarbrow and Brown trials were pending as of this writing.

Published reports and regulatory documents indicated that Nevis Industries had run up an impressive loan tab of at least $8 million at Eureka Federal Savings and Loan of San Carlos, California, before showing up at State[8] and had borrowed heavily from Fidelity Savings and Loan of New York, Coast Savings and Loan of San Diego, and American Savings and Loan of Stockton, California. Nevis's S&L take totaled more than $100 million, law enforcement officials told us.

In 1983 a friend had introduced Nevis to Tyrell Barker, to the mutual benefit of both men.[9] For example, regulators said, $8 million of the money Nevis got from State/Corvallis went to purchase a Texas resort from Barker. And Barker helped Nevis with a complex transaction that involved the Sioux City Hilton (in Sioux City, Iowa), which Nevis had acquired.

The hotel was losing $50,000 a month, but Nevis wanted to sell it at a profit. To accomplish such a magical maneuver, Barker, records showed, agreed that State/Lubbock would loan a Georgia company the money to buy the Hilton from Nevis. Nevis immediately channeled $2 million of the proceeds to a company called Doe Valley, Inc., that regulators said he controlled. After State/Lubbock failed and investigators tried to unravel that deal, they couldn't figure out who owned what. The Georgia company said State/Lubbock (Barker) owned the Hilton. Barker said, "Hotel? What hotel?" Nevis said Barker owned Doe Valley. Barker said, "Huh?" Federal investigators dug into Doe Valley's books, only to discover that they were unauditable. (In 1988 a Texas court ruled in favor of State Savings/Lubbock and ordered Nevis to repay $11.3 million in connection with the Sioux City Hilton/Doe Valley case.)

Regulators warned Barker that he had to stop making risky loans and needed to get the thrift's records in shape. Barker reacted by hiring four auditors to straighten out the mess at State/Lubbock, but after a look at the books they just threw their hands up in despair, finding the situation beyond comprehension. Through it all there was one thing that didn't concern Barker in the least, and that was the loss that the FSLIC would sustain if it had to close State/Lubbock and pay off the depositors.

"I bought the institution, and that's what I buy insurance for," he said, referring to the premiums State/Lubbock paid to the FSLIC. With Barker displaying that kind of cavalier attitude, the next step was probably inevitable. In May 1984 the regulators kicked him out (though they say they believe he continued to exercise influence over State/Lubbock until they finally closed the institution in December 1985). Barker's unceremonious ouster as the president of State/Lubbock came only two months after Ed Gray in Washington saw the video of Empire Savings' I–30 condos (the "Martian landing pads" on the outskirts of Dallas) and closed Empire Savings.[10] The assault on the two major thrift institutions shocked Texans, and an uneasiness crept into the back rooms of North Dallas's financial district.

CHAPTER SEVENTEEN

Dark in the Heart of Texas

Slowly, throughout 1984, the regulatory noose tightened in Texas. Ed Gray sought support for his regulation that would go into effect March 1985, limiting direct investments and placing a 25 percent annual growth limit on S&Ls. Regulators also began to demand that thrifts acquire more accurate appraisals. But during the heat of the debate that surrounded these moves, even as it became increasingly evident that Ed Gray wasn't going to back down, no one would have guessed a thing was wrong at Vernon Savings and Loan. Vernon looked great—on paper. Trade journals routinely listed Vernon among the country's soundest and most profitable institutions, and Vernon itself crowed that it was the most profitable thrift in America. Vernon looked so hot, in fact, that a month after California Savings and Loan Commissioner Larry Taggart left that post in January 1985 he went to work for Dixon as a consultant. Taggart had no regrets for having presided over the deregulation of the California thrift industry, and he believed Texas thrifts' recent problems were simply caused by the downturn in the oil economy. He viewed with alarm the frantic attempts by his former friend Ed Gray to tighten S&L regulations. He felt that, as someone who had been a regulator, he could help the industry by lobbying politicians in Washington to remain steadfast in their commitment to thrift deregulation. And he set off to do just that.

With Taggart in Washington singing the company song, the *High Spirits* docked in Washington keeping politicians happy, and a fleet of planes giving politicians rides home, Dixon must have felt he had his bases covered and had little to fear from the lackluster and politically impotent Ed Gray. Dixon continued to improve his bottom line at Vernon's expense. He decided to abandon the Solano Beach house in favor of more elaborate quarters down the road in Del Mar, where he had one of Vernon's subsidiaries buy a luxurious $2 million home. The house fronted a long expanse of beach. It was two stories, with rounded corner windows and verandas overlooking the Pacific. Tall palms surrounded the porch, and wide steps led to the fine white-sand beach below.

Although the money for the purchase came from Vernon Savings, regulators said Vernon's board of directors was never consulted. Dixon then set up two bank accounts at Vernon Savings and filled them with Vernon money, which he used to pay the $561,874 in living expenses he incurred during his 18 months in the Del Mar house. Some of the items paid out of the accounts, according to regulators, included:

Flowers—$36,780

Pool service—$4,420

Car service—$23,845

Catering—$13,446

Pet services—$386

Graduation Party—$2,408

Telephone—$37,339

Utilities—$29,689

Cable TV—$1,794

Plants—$5,901

Political fund raiser for San Diego Congressman Bill Lowery—$7,238

Miscellaneous—$101,075

Petty cash—$44,095

A bottle of perfume—$110

Life was sweet in California and the Dixons spent about 40 percent of their time at the Del Mar house, where they became known for their gracious dinner parties and where they kept an extra Rolls-Royce parked in the garage just for weekend guests. Their West Coast homes also served as a political lobbying platform for Dixon, who reportedly hosted political figures such as former Texas Governor John Connally, former Texas Lieutenant Governor Ben Barnes,[1] and Edwin Edwards, the colorful governor of Louisiana, among many others.

"It was a real circus," said one who was around at the time. "They had something going at that house every weekend."

A succession of friends stayed at the Solano Beach house after the Dixons moved to Del Mar. One of those friends was Charles Bazarian of Oklahoma

City. Fuzzy, we learned, met Dixon in 1985, thanks to loan brokers Al Yarbrow and Jack Franks, who made the introductions. Once again it was driven home to us the key role played by loan brokers in this drama, as they scurried around the country connecting round-heeled bankers with horny borrowers.[2]

Bazarian became a prominent figure in the Dixon entourage in both Dallas and Southern California.[3] Later Bazarian would tell us that for a time Dixon was a good friend who, he was sure, had never set out purposefully to loot a savings and loan.

Bazarian did agree, though, that Dixon definitely was a high liver.

"Didn't we have wonderful parties?" he sighed.

Jack Brenner, the contractor employed to manage some of Vernon's California assets, confirmed the party rumors. "They were always having parties at that house in California. I went to only one, and we just turned around and walked out. The house was a maze of hookers," Brenner told a reporter.[4]

Later an East Coast banker recalled for us the time Dixon paid his expenses to fly to San Diego and had a limousine pick him up at the airport.

"We went to that famous Del Mar beach house of his. Dixon was there with his wife, and there were these women there. I said to Dixon, 'Who are these women? They are gorgeous honeys.' Dixon told me, 'These are your dates for the night, a little female companionship. You might get a little lonely at the beach house. You might want a little company for the night.'

"I wasn't expecting that. My face turned bright red. I told Dixon, 'Gee, I was thinking of going back to my room to work on this loan deal.' And the subject quickly changed to hunting."

Prostitutes became just another perk for Vernon's employees and customers—sort of human "beans," if you will. Later Vernon's senior vice president, John V. Hill, would be indicted on a federal felony charge of bank bribery (he ultimately pleaded guilty to a conspiracy charge and agreed to cooperate with prosecutors). He was indicted for what the government quaintly termed giving "a thing of value in excess of $100," making "sexual favors . . . available to Vernon officers and directors in connection with their service to Vernon and to Vernon's owner, Don R. Dixon." Hill admitted he had arranged for Vernon Savings to hire two Dallas women and up to ten San Diego women to attend the first and third nights of a three-day celebration during a Vernon Savings board meeting in Southern California in 1985.[5]

When Dixon wasn't hosting such affairs he used the Del Mar house to maintain his status with the Southern California upper crust. But not everyone invited to the Del Mar mansion liked what he saw. Old Rolls-Royce money could smell new stretch-limo money a mile away. A wealthy California publisher recalled later, "My wife and I felt very strange about them [the Dixons]. Everything was too lavish, too big. It seemed to us if they were *real* they wouldn't be so socially and politically aggressive."

The Dixons decided to make another trek to the Continent. This time Dixon and the little lady hit the high spots of France, England, and Denmark and justified this trip by forming a new subsidiary, VernonVest, based in Munich. Dixon claimed that VernonVest would attract foreign deposits to Vernon, but records showed all it ever attracted were expense vouchers for the Dixons' trips abroad.

And still Vernon Savings continued to grow. By 1985 Vernon's assets stood at a staggering $1 billion. (Brokered deposits made Vernon look better than the truth would have it.)

Just months after their second European tour the Dixons decided the time was right for another. This trip took form one day when Dixon was chatting with his new friend, Roman Catholic Bishop of San Diego Leo T. Maher, and discovered that the bishop and Monsignor I. Brent Eagen, pastor of Mission San Diego de Alaca, were planning a trip to Europe soon. The Dixons were ready to go again, so they invited the two holy men to ride along with them on Vernon's Falcon. Thus in May 1985 Maher and Eagen were entertained at Vernon's expense in Paris, London, and Rome—where they in turn arranged the Dixons' introduction to the Pope. The trip was charged to Vernon Savings, and Dixon justified the expense as entertainment for Vernon customers. But what customers? The bishop and the monsignor? Perhaps the notation was simply a rare moment of candor by Don and Dana, who most certainly *were* Vernon's best customers.[6]

Vernon's records showed that Don and Dana went to Europe again in 1985. This time they visited Ireland, Great Britain, Switzerland, Italy, Spain, France, and Denmark. The stated purpose for the trip was to conduct business,[7] of course, but the visible spoils were $489,000 worth of furniture and antiques, paid for by a Vernon subsidiary but delivered to the Dixons. There was also a 1951 Rolls-Royce Don picked up in London. (Vernon Savings reimbursed the Dixons over $68,000 for the European trips they made between 1983 and 1985.)[8]

Don had loved cars since he was a kid, and in May of 1985 he had Vernon buy Symbolic Motors, a Rolls-Royce and Ferrari dealership in affluent La Jolla, just south of Del Mar. Rare and expensive autos stood reflected in the polished tile floors, each car exhibited like a rare gem in its own section of the display room. Dixon justified the purchase of the dealership by saying that it would offer Vernon an opportunity to "break into the consumer lending market."

The Dixons had moved from the $1 million Solano Beach house to the $2 million Del Mar house in late 1984, but within months they were ready for another move up. In 1985 Dixon decided to build a Spanish-style manor house in the ultraexclusive Rancho Santa Fe subdivision, a few miles inland from Del Mar in the coastal hills. The land alone, 16 hillside acres, cost Vernon $5 million, regulators complained. The mansion, as he and Dana envisioned it, would sprawl across five acres like a white stucco Spanish castle. It would have a six-car garage and a two-story stable. Several man-made waterfalls would grace the grounds. Dana would do the decorating, starting—an FHLB examiner later charged—with the $489,000 worth of furniture the Dixons had just brought home from Europe and 514 yards of carpet they ordered for $26,000.

Dixon wasn't alone in his fearless pursuit of the good life. It seemed all of Dallas was on a roll by 1985 and no one was having more fun than young Edwin T. McBirney III at Sunbelt Savings and Loan. McBirney was chairman, CEO, majority shareholder, and ruler of the Sunbelt fiefdom, and Sunbelt was a star sapphire in the Texas crown of thrift debauchery. While careering his institution toward staggering losses that culminated with a shortfall of $1.2 billion, the darkly handsome McBirney threw some wild and crazy parties. Regulators said that in 1984 and 1985 Sunbelt spent over $1.3 million on Halloween and Christmas parties. One Halloween McBirney entertained at his palatial North Dallas home dressed as a king. He served broiled lion, antelope, and pheasant and had a fog machine going for atmosphere. The following Halloween he expanded to a warehouse that he decorated like a jungle, and he wore a pith helmet, khakis, and binoculars. And, yes, the elephant was real—until a magician he had hired made it disappear. That Christmas he decorated a warehouse like a Russian winter, with strolling Russian peasants and a bear.

Gifted with a retentive mind and a sharp intelligence, McBirney often had groups of borrowers in several rooms at one time at Sunbelt Savings' office in North Dallas. Cigar in hand, he could circulate between rooms and never miss a nuance or forget a concession. When a deal couldn't be structured traditionally, "figure a way to paper it" was often his response, observers said. If a borrower didn't qualify for a loan, find someone to "kiss the paper" for him.[9] More than one man who had tried to negotiate a deal with McBirney called him a shark.

Sunbelt had seven aircraft, one of which he bought with financing provided by Don Dixon's Louisiana friend, Herman K. Beebe. McBirney flew business associates on trips to Las Vegas, Kona, and Capo San Lucas. He liked to gamble, and associates told the story of the trip to the Dunes in Las Vegas when he bet $15,000 on one hand of 21 and won. Then he went over to the craps table and won again. And again.

"It was amazing," said a fellow junketeer. "I couldn't figure out how he always won."

Sunbelt later sued McBirney, claiming that in three years Sunbelt spent $61,800 for him on Christmas gifts (including $54,000 at Neiman Marcus), $15,100 for lodging on trips, $100,000 for meals (including $57,000 at Jason's—no wonder they didn't mind taking the time to cover his table with paper so he wouldn't scribble his deals on their tablecloths), $22,000 at the

Texas Stadium, and $70,000 for limousine service. According to several firsthand accounts, McBirney produced whores for his customers the same way an ordinary businessman might spring for lunch. A visiting developer told us he checked into his Dallas hotel room and found a hooker sitting on his bed.

"Hello," she said.

"What are you doing here?" he asked.

"I'm for you," she purred.

Just then the phone rang. It was McBirney. "Get my little gift?" he asked.

McBirney prowled one of Dallas's hottest night spots, the Rio Room—along with such jet setters as Sammy Davis, Jr., and Adnan Khashoggi—where $1,000 bar tabs were common and the big sellers were $150 bottles of champagne. Real estate night was Thursday, and many a deal was celebrated or even consummated then. *Wheeler Dealers*, a 1963 spoof of Texas millionaires that starred James Garner and Lee Remick, showed up on late-night TV and some thought it was a perfect parody of the times, 20 years later. Dallas reporter Byron Harris wrote that a fellow who had been celebrating an especially lucrative deal stumbled out of the Rio Room into the parking lot and kicked in the door of a Rolls-Royce just for fun.

Vernon Savings, State/Lubbock, and Sunbelt were only three of dozens of Texas thrifts running amok at the end of 1985. Deregulation was barely three years old but the level of greed and corruption at Texas thrifts had reached biblical proportions. Questions were being raised about Commodore Savings, Western Savings, Independent American Savings, Sandia Savings, Lamar Savings, Paris Savings, Midland Savings, Mainland Savings, Stockton Savings, Summit Savings, Continental Savings, Mercury Savings, Ben Milam Savings— the list went on and on. Texas was rocking and rolling to the deregulation rag.

"I remember one closing we had," said a real estate salesperson, describing how they flipped land to raise its value. "It was in the hall of an office building. The tables were lined all the way down the hall. The investors were lined up in front of the tables. The loan officers would close one sale and pass the papers to the next guy. It looked like kids registering for college. If any investor raised a question, someone would come over and tell them to leave, they were out of the deal." At the end of the day's flipping, huge loans, based on the inflated values created by the flip sales, would be taken out on the properties.

Texas was careening out of control, but Ed Gray returned from his Christmas break in January 1986 refreshed and optimistic that his direct investment regulation and the limit on growth were bringing excesses like those in Texas to a halt. He couldn't have been more wrong. In 1986 the lid would blow off the Texas pressure cooker.

Gray's illusions were shattered when reports from the field in Texas indicated that the wildcat thrifts had found ways around most of Gray's roadblock regulations and were falling deeper into the morass.

Gray told us later he was surprised to find that the people in charge of supervising Texas thrifts, Joe Settle at the Dallas Federal Home Loan Bank and L. Linton Bowman III, the Texas savings and loan commissioner, were more sympathetic to the Texas thrift owners than to the Federal Home Loan Bank Board.[10] Gray claimed Settle was "too chummy" with the Texas thrift establishment, and he told a congressional subcommittee that under Settle's administration, supervision of Texas thrifts had been virtually nonexistent. Gray brought in veteran thrift regulator Roy Green to baby-sit the Dallas district bank, and he needed someone with top-notch credentials to run Green's supervisory staff. Gray's first order of business in 1986 was to get someone with a strong stomach in that job. Green recommended Washington veteran Joe Selby.

About that time Selby was seriously thinking about quietly slipping into semiretirement. A Texan by birth, he was thinking about returning to his home state to look for some light work, or maybe to do some part-time jobs for the International Monetary Fund. He was 54 years old and had already served 31 of those years as a regulator in the office of the comptroller of the currency. His forte was the supervision of large national commercial banks.

Gray had met Selby at a luncheon in Boston before Christmas. Gray liked what he saw and told Selby he'd be delighted to have him in the FHLBB camp if he ever decided to leave the comptroller's office. From Gray's vantage point Selby had all the right qualifications for the Texas job. He was a native of Ganado, Texas, 90 miles west of Houston, so the Texas cowboys couldn't accuse him of being a Yankee troublemaker. As a teenager he'd worked as a teller in his father's bank. Then he went on to earn a banking and finance degree from the University of Texas. His co-workers in the comptroller's office had affectionately nicknamed him "The Great White Father"—a reference to his snowy white hair. In January, Green visited Selby in his Washington office and asked him to be executive vice president and head of supervision at the Dallas FHLB. Selby accepted.

Selby moved to Dallas to assume his FHLB position in May 1986. By that time the worsening financial condition of the state's oil and real estate economy was on the front pages almost daily. But the ups and downs of local economies didn't concern Selby. Such cycles were as perennial as the grass. Anyway, he soon discovered that the problems facing Texas thrifts were rooted in a much more troubling soil.

It was only about a month after Selby got on the job that he met Don Dixon. Dixon strolled arrogantly into Selby's office one Monday morning wearing his permanent California tan, beige suit, and alligator shoes. Roy Green and Selby greeted Dixon and asked him what he had on his mind. Green had briefed Selby about the deep concerns he had about Vernon, so both men were shocked when Dixon confronted them with his plan. Dixon had heard all about "the troubles" the Bank Board was having with insolvent thrifts, and he was there to help them out. He wanted them to allow Vernon to absorb about ten ailing thrifts and, in so doing, create one giant $9 billion superthrift.

Selby later said that he and Green fought to keep a straight face while Dixon smoothly explained his plan. They thanked him for his concern over the FSLIC's well-being and told him they'd get back to him. When Dixon left the two men burst out laughing. Was this guy for real? Ironically, two years later, in 1988, the Bank Board's own plan for dealing with failed thrifts in Texas would closely resemble Dixon's plan. Regulators called Dixon's idea crazy. They called theirs "The Southwest Plan."

Dixon was among the most visible of the ostentatious S&L rogues, and he justified his good life by pointing to Vernon's profits. But those profits were built on shifting sand. For example, Vernon had loaned millions to Dondi Residential Properties, Inc. (DRPI) to build condos all over Dallas and the suburbs. By 1985 DRPI (or "Drippy," as it was called) was stuck with over 700 unsold units (nicknamed "the Drippies") on which, examiners warned, Vernon faced a potential $11 million loss. But Vernon kept right on loaning and DRPI kept right on building.

Vernon also made huge loans to favorite developer friends of Dixon's like Jack Atkinson, who borrowed tens of millions of dollars from Vernon ($56 million of which went into default, bank records showed). Atkinson owned his own Gulfstream 50 jet, which Dana Dixon was rumored to prefer because she liked its gray leather interior.

To keep those loans from going into default, Vernon Savings—and sister thrifts like State/Lubbock and Sunbelt—made the loans large enough to allow for an interest reserve that could cover the payments for a year or so. When that money ran out Vernon renewed the loan. And each time Vernon renewed a loan it was able to book new loan fees. If examiners were due for a visit, Vernon officers farmed out ("participated") really bad loans to other, like-minded thrifts where the loans would be out of sight until the examiners left.

In June 1985 representatives from 19 Texas savings and loans met secretly in Houston to discuss what mutual actions they could take to keep regulators off their backs. According to a report in the Houston *Post*, the S&L executives discussed:

Selling loans ("participations") to other S&Ls to get rid of dead wood and to avoid Ed Gray's growth limits.

Using straw borrowers to avoid loans-to-one-borrower limits and to avoid Ed Gray's growth limits.

Selling loans to each other, with agreements to buy them back later.

Sources told the *Post* the effect of these actions would have been to "move bad loans around to hide them from regulators and make the S&Ls appear to be in better financial shape than they actually were." (Among those attending the meeting held in Houston were Terry Barker as well as representatives from Vernon, Western, Lamar, Mainland, and Continental Savings. Of the approximately 19 thrifts represented at the meeting, about 15 would later fail.)[11]

Even after the loans went into default, thrift officials had ways of postponing the day of reckoning. When Vernon officials compiled the thrift's delinquent loan list for regulators at the end of 1985, for example, they reported $36 million in delinquent loans. The accurate figure, regulators later learned, was $212 million.

"It was just a big Ponzi scheme that probably only had four good years in it to begin with," a Dallas contractor later explained, referring to Texas savings and loan operations in the early 1980s. Someday, when the loans finally went into default, a chain reaction would spread the damage from one Texas thrift to the next and into other states as interlocking loans and participations, buyback agreements, and letters of credit all began coming home to roost at once.

Since even the best juggler reaches the limit of how many balls he can keep in the air at one time, by 1986 no one around Vernon or its subsidiary operations had a clue as to how many balls they were juggling or where those balls were. When the balls started hitting the ground like hailstones in a Texas hailstorm, startled regulators slapped Vernon with a cease-and-desist order that instructed Vernon Savings to clean up its act. Dixon knew that a cease-and-desist order was a serious step in a process that led to almost inevitable seizure by the regulators.

A few days after he got the order in June 1986, Dixon called his employees together for a party in a hangar at the company's facility at the Addison Municipal Airport. Employees of Vernon were accustomed to parties at company expense so they probably didn't find Dixon's sudden party announcement particularly unusual. They were greeted at the hangar with a full bar and hors d'oeuvres. After healthy rounds of drinks and small talk among Vernon's baby-blue air force, Dixon called for everyone's attention.

Employees gathered around their leader, expecting the usual Dixon pep talk. Instead he shocked them with the news that he would be withdrawing from active involvement at Vernon. He would still hold control over Vernon's stock but would not be around the office anymore. Some employees who attended the party said they greeted Dixon's announcement with a secret sigh of relief.

They hoped that once the colorful Dixon was gone so, too, would be the regulators.

In the same month McBirney got the same idea, and he resigned as president of Sunbelt Savings. And the U.S. attorney indicted Terry Barker and his seeing-eye attorney, Larry Vineyard, for fraud and conspiracy in connection with an exchange of loans they had made with a banker friend.[12] June 1986 marked the climax of the most dramatic five years in the history of the Texas thrift industry.

Even these better-late-than-never actions were no match for the harvest of woe regulators would now face. Events were tumbling out of control in Texas, and every agency with an interest in what was happening was scrambling to catch up. In July, Ed Gray rounded up examiners from around the country and sent a "hit squad" of 250 specially trained examiners into Texas to help the Dallas FHLB investigate thrifts suspected of being insolvent. But as pressure was put on the Texas thrift industry by the small army of FHLBB examiners, Gray and Joe Selby became increasingly unpopular with both crooked thrift owners and honest ones. The crooks feared exposure and indictment while the straight thrift owners feared that the write-downs (reductions in the inflated values crooked thrifts were assigning to their Texas real estate holdings and loan portfolios) would depreciate the value of everyone's real estate holdings and hurt the innocent as well as the guilty.

In August, Nancy Reagan received an anonymous letter saying that Ed Gray was a "Nazi" and that the Bank Board was using "gestapo tactics" in its supervision of Texas thrifts. The president's wife, who was still friendly with Gray, forwarded the letter to him for his growing collection.

Larry Taggart (Gray's former friend and California savings and loan commissioner), working as a lobbyist and consultant for Don Dixon and other thrift owners,[13] sent an angry six-page letter to White House Chief of Staff Don Regan with copies to Senator Jake Garn and Representative Doug Barnard. In the letter Taggart complained bitterly about Gray and his policies. Taggart had broken with Gray long ago, as he had sided with California's go-go thrifts against Gray's re-regulation of the industry. They openly feuded in the press. Their relationship had hit rock bottom when Gray forced Charlie Knapp, a close friend of Taggart's, out of FCA in August 1984.[14] But nothing Taggart had said before compared with the vitriol of this letter.

Taggart's letter all but demanded that Don Regan kick Gray out of office. Taggart wrote that "the attitude of the FHLBB and Chairman Gray has been contrary to that of the Reagan administration." He noted that Gray's regulation of the industry was "likely to have a very adverse impact on the ability of our party to raise much needed campaign funds in the upcoming elections. Many who have been very supportive of the Administration are involved with S&Ls which are either being closed by the Bank Board or threatened with closure . . ." Taggart also stated that Gray's contention that there was widespread fraud occurring at thrifts was not true and that fraud was a factor "at very few of the thrifts" being closed by the Bank Board. Taggart parroted the Texas thrift industry party line . . . any problems the thrift industry was having were due to the temporary downturn in the state's oil-based economy and Ed Gray's regulations, not fraud.[15]

Around the time that Taggart's letter reached Washington, Selby testified before the Bank Board, seeking approval to close Dallas-based Western Savings and Loan, owned by Jarrett Woods. Board member Don Hovde asked Selby whether the mess in Texas was the fault of the economy or the fault of the people who had run the thrifts down there. Selby didn't have to search for an answer.

"I think a majority are a result of poor underwriting and basically it might be said that even if the economy were good, these loans would never be good."

Selby's straight talk and tough enforcement policies were not winning him any friends in Texas. Between May 1986, when he went to work at the Dallas FHLB, and December 1986, the Dallas FHLB placed at least 100 supervisory actions on thrifts. By September constituents' cries of anguish were ringing in Texas congressmen's ears, and then House Majority Leader Jim Wright (D-Texas) called Gray over to his office.[16] When Gray and his party arrived he was surprised to find Congressmen Steve Bartlett (R-Texas), John Bryant (D-Texas), and Martin Frost (D-Texas) lounging about. Gray felt like he was being ambushed. He was right.

The meeting, on September 15, lasted almost two hours, though Wright had to leave unexpectedly after half an hour. The congressmen minced no words. "Gestapo tactics—bullying examiners—hit squads—Joe Selby's a financial Rambo—what the hell are you trying to do to Texas?" They all took their turn beating on Gray, parroting complaints they'd heard from such financial wizards as Don Dixon, Tyrell Barker, and Ed McBirney. Like a beaten boxer in the tenth round, Gray absorbed each punch without complaint and tried to reassure them that the FHLBB was being circumspect and cautious and fair. Gray said he left the meeting deeply depressed. He was amazed that the congressmen had so little understanding of what the Bank Board was up against in trying to protect the FSLIC fund.

A few days later Wright[17] called Gray to say that he'd been contacted by fellow Texan Craig Hall, who was having problems renegotiating loans with a thrift that the Bank Board had taken over, Westwood Savings and Loan in California.[18] Wright asked Gray if he would check into the matter, and he particularly complained that Scott Schultz, the regulator responsible for Westwood, was not as "flexible or understanding" as he should be. Gray told Wright he'd check out the Hall loans and see what all the flap was about.

Hall was a slick young Dallas real estate syndicator who owned one of the nation's largest private real estate limited partnership firms and was one of the biggest owners of real estate in Texas. He also controlled at least one thrift and had interests in others. He had been hit hard by the downturn in the Texas economy and was now stuck with nearly $500 *million* in syndication loans he couldn't repay. He claimed that so many of the loans were from S&Ls that if he went bankrupt, 29 thrifts would immediately be insolvent. Gray asked Bank Board negotiators to do what they could for Hall, but Gray later noted, "If a piece of real estate was only worth $1 million and an S&L had it on its books as having a value of $2 million, then what were we supposed to do? Look the other way?"

On September 26 Wright tightened the screws. Gray's bill to replenish the FSLIC fund, seriously depleted after covering so many costly thrift failures, was scheduled to be considered by the House soon, but Wright removed it from the calendar. Through scuttlebutt and media reports Gray and his people got what they later said they considered to be the clear message that Wright would take care of the FSLIC recapitalization bill (the "recap") when Gray took care of Hall.

Gray had begun to feel desperate about the recap bill. Almost a year earlier he had realized that the FSLIC would not have enough money to close and liquidate all the insolvent thrifts that regulators were now identifying. When a thrift was liquidated all its deposits up to $100,000 each had to be repaid to depositors, and that money came out of the FSLIC fund. A single medium-sized thrift liquidation could cost the FSLIC $500 million. There had already been several, and the fund would soon be running on empty. It was down to a reserve of only $2.5 billion to cover deposits of $800 billion in 3,249 S&Ls. At the time 252 thrifts, with assets of almost $95 billion, were in serious trouble. If the FSLIC fund did not have enough money to close insolvent thrifts, they would be left open and continue to lose millions of dollars a month. The specter of insolvent S&Ls continuing to operate around the country had driven Gray to propose the recap bill in the spring of 1986. Now the year was almost over and Gray's apprehension had increased daily.[19]

For the sake of the recap bill, Gray decided to replace Schultz at Westwood with someone he hoped would be more acceptable to Wright. He selected a highly respected official from the FHLB in New York ("I felt that I would not be caving in by asking a person of very high stature in the Federal Home Loan Bank system to come out and do this," Gray later explained to a congressional investigator) and instructed him to see if there was any way to justify restructuring Hall's loans. Schultz's replacement ultimately did agree not to foreclose on the $200 million in Hall syndication loans at Westwood Savings, thereby giving him some breathing room. Wright told the Associated Press that Gray's action "saved [Hall's] business, saved several S&Ls, and saved the market from panic."

The move was very unpopular at the FHLBB, however. Replacing an official in Schultz's position (conservator of an insolvent thrift) just wasn't done. It was a slap in the face to the FHLBB's enforcement staff, and the Bank Board chief of staff later said, "We didn't like what we did. . . . [W]e felt terrible about the choices posed for us and I personally took a great deal of time to torment over the fact that from our perspective . . . we [felt] we crossed a line between what we felt was permissible or not. On the other hand . . . there was a very difficult problem [getting Wright to release the recap bill] that we were trying to address."

Gray called Wright to report that the Hall matter had been tended to and asked for a private meeting with the majority leader. Gray had decided that Wright's problem was that he just didn't understand how the thrift regulatory business ran, so on October 3 he went to Wright's office to give him what Gray called a "civics lesson on FSLIC." The meeting lasted about 20 minutes. Gray told Wright the FSLIC was almost broke.

"We need your support on the recap," he said.

Wright once again mentioned that people he trusted in Texas were saying Gray and Selby were acting like the gestapo in dealing with insolvent S&Ls down there. Once again Wright likened the FHLBB to the Nazis and added that Texas examiners were operating like hit squads in his home state. He said he was afraid the FHLBB would use the extra money from the recap bill to crack down unfairly on Texas S&Ls and cause needless bankruptcies. Sitting on a couch in Wright's office, Gray told Wright point-blank, "Whether you like it or not, there are too many crooks in this business."

In parting, and with an eye toward prying the recap bill loose, Gray told Wright to let him know if he ever needed anything further. Three days later Wright released his hold on the recap bill.

On October 10 Wright wrote to Gray saying that he had received a letter from Scott Mann, chairman of CreditBanc Savings in Austin,[20] that detailed some "very inappropriate actions by regulators." Wright said he'd been hearing many such complaints since his discussions with Gray had "come to the public's attention." Wright was especially concerned, he wrote, about Mann's detailed charges that Selby and other regulators in the FHLB of Dallas had unreasonably harassed CreditBanc and were threatening to declare the thrift insolvent without good reason and in spite of an agreement reached between CreditBanc and Texas Savings and Loan Commissioner Bowman. Mann had complained in his letter to Wright, "The FHLB of Dallas had become a high-handed adversary of Texas savings and loan associations and has effectively usurped the authority of the

Texas Savings and Loan Commissioner to regulate state-chartered institutions in Texas."

Wright wrote to Gray, "This kind of high-handed and arbitrary attitude can only create fear, mistrust and a climate of great instability." He said the regulators' actions, as described by Mann, "would seem clearly outside the realm of acceptable regulatory behavior. . . . Some in the regulatory force seem not to understand the fundamental principle that it is government's aim and objective to save legitimate businesses, not to destroy them." Wright later said the letter was intended as an expression of concern about the Texas S&L industry as a whole, not a particular S&L, and was "a very common thing" for a congressman to send to "a bureaucrat."

This time Gray could not deliver. CreditBanc was too far gone. By the time Gray wrote back to Wright four months later, after what he called a lengthy investigation, he reported that CreditBanc was nearly insolvent because of "deep-seated financial problems, most of which have surfaced since Mr. Mann acquired control of CreditBanc in July 1985" and as "a direct result of the failure of [CreditBanc's] management to invest in safe and sound assets." Regulators later forced Mann to resign and reported CreditBanc had a net worth of minus $216 million.

The political pressure from Texas thrift owners intensified daily. On October 21 Wright hosted a catered luncheon at the Ridglea Country Club in Fort Worth, arranged by Wright's good friend and business partner Fort Worth developer George Mallick. The purpose of the get-together was to give about 20 of Wright's S&L constituents a chance to recount directly to the majority leader the unspeakable things the Bank Board, Joe Selby, and Ed Gray were doing to their lives. Advance word of the luncheon meeting spread quickly throughout the Texas thrift community and soon Mallick was besieged with phone calls from people who wanted to attend. By the time Wright got to the country club he faced a veritable lynch mob of 110 angry Texas S&L executives and developers.

As lunch got under way each stood and told his or her own horror stories. They said that Ed Gray and Joe Selby were kicking their teeth in and forcing them to list their real estate at its true current value rather than at its projected inflated value. They complained that they were being vilified and accused of being corrupt. Local sheriffs were being used to escort deposed S&L chiefs out of their institutions right in front of the whole world. A minister who was building a nursing home complained that he was almost finished with the project but couldn't complete the building because S&L regulators had told thrifts to stop lending to him. After the meeting a Wright aide reported that Wright's office was besieged with calls from other people in the industry who had heard that Wright had expressed an interest in their problems.

A week or two after the Ridglea meeting, Wright called Gray again.

"Congressman Jim Wright's on the phone for you, Mr. Gray."

Lighting a cigarette, Gray wondered what it would be this time. He took a deep drag and punched the lighted button on the phone.

This time Wright asked Gray to meet with his friend Tom Gaubert, who owned Independent American Savings Association in Irving, between Dallas and Fort Worth, and who was also under the regulators' gun—in January 1986 the Bank Board had banned him from ever operating an FSLIC-insured thrift.

Scrappy Tom Gaubert reminded many of George C. Scott with a beard. He had a gruff voice and he smoked cigars, a Texas-type man's man, a real roll-up-the-sleeves kind of guy. Gaubert was a tough negotiator. He had been waging a war against S&L regulators since they had criticized his management of Independent American and his involvement with what appeared to be a land flip in connection with a loan from Capitol Savings and Loan in Mount Pleasant, Iowa. He had agreed to resign in December 1984. Independent American had then continued under the leadership of Gaubert's brother and others until May 1986, when the FHLBB installed a team of its own. But Gaubert went on fighting for reinstatement.[21]

Gaubert told us that he believed most of the troubles he and his friends were having were because regulators had first encouraged developers to own savings and loans in the early 1980s to revitalize the industry, and then they suddenly panicked and switched gears four years later, throwing the industry into a tailspin by "re-regulating" it. Everything he had done, he said, had been approved by regulators who had encouraged him every step of the way. It was a familiar theme. Without exception, virtually every deposed thrift officer we spoke to, beginning with Erv Hansen at Centennial, claimed that deregulation was a trap, a trick, that there never had been any real deregulation of the thrift industry, and that thrifts were in trouble because they believed what regulators had first told them, only to have the rules changed later and the ground pulled out from under them. (No doubt much of that was true. In the early 1980s regulators did encourage many of the behaviors that they later forbade.) Tom Gaubert made no secret of his hatred for thrift regulators. In his mahogany-paneled office, adorned with stuffed birds, he kept a toy shooting gallery where he had tacked pictures of regulators Ed Gray, Rosemary Stewart (who headed the Bank Board's enforcement division in Washington), and Roy Green (president of the FHLB in Dallas).

The Wall Street Journal reported that in 1985 Gaubert had organized a political action committee for Democratic candidates that raised $101,000 from 66 Texas thrift owners, officers, borrowers, and wives. Donations came from Gaubert, Dixon, McBirney, other Vernon Savings and Sunbelt Savings officers, and Dallas developers who had borrowed hundreds of millions of dollars from the clique of Texas S&Ls. *The Wall Street Journal* said Sunbelt Savings may have paid fees to its directors to subsidize their contributions to the fund.

Besides raising funds for his little thrift owners' defense fund, Gaubert had other fund-raising positions that gave him even more political pull. In 1986 Gaubert was treasurer of the Democratic Congressional Campaign Committee, when Representative Tony Coelho was chairman, and in his 12 months as treasurer he raised $9 million for House candidates, according to *Newsweek* magazine. [22] In 1987 he was chairman of an event that grossed $1 million for his good friend Representative James Wright, who became speaker of the House in January 1987.

Gaubert told us, in fact, that it was he who arranged Wright's 1984 flight from Los Angeles through Dallas to Shreveport and back on the Vernon Savings jet, a flight that would make headlines a few years later and cause Wright considerable political embarrassment. Gaubert said he arranged Wright's flight on the Vernon plane because other transportation was not available on short notice. He said he had always expected Vernon Savings to bill Wright for the flight. Wright did not know at the time that he was on a Vernon plane, Gaubert added.

"Bullshit," said an FBI agent when we told him Gaubert's story.

When it came to being the queen bee of Texas thrift activists, no one could hold a candle to Tom Gaubert. And he had a real friend in Jim Wright. When Wright spoke to Ed Gray on Gaubert's behalf, Wright told Gray he had known Gaubert for a long time and had total confidence in him. Selby wanted to boot Gaubert out of Independent American Savings permanently, and Wright complained that Gaubert was being treated unfairly. Gaubert had assured Wright he had done nothing wrong. Instead, the Bank Board had violated its rules and abused its authority, Gaubert said. He ridiculed the regulators who removed the Dixons and McBirneys and then caused even more losses when they themselves tried to run the S&Ls. [23]

It was highly unusual for a congressman to intervene directly in FHLBB regulatory matters, as Wright was doing, and it was against Bank Board rules for Gray to meet with anyone involved in action before the Board, but since Congress had not yet acted on the recap bill and the bill was therefore still vulnerable to Wright's displeasure, Gray agreed to meet with Gaubert and listen to his complaints. For over two hours Gaubert bent Gray's ear. According to Gray, Gaubert alternately buttered Gray up and evoked Wright's name to remind Gray who his patron was. Gaubert asked Gray to review Gaubert's removal as CEO of Independent American. Gray bit his tongue and agreed—for the recap, he told himself. Gaubert left Gray's office a happy man. [24]

Later Gaubert told us that he advised Wright not to pass the recap while Gray was in office. "I told the Speaker it would be stupid to give Ed Gray $15 billion. He'd just piss it away."[25]

Not long after Wright called Gray on behalf of Tom Gaubert, he called Gray yet again to repeat his concern for the way thrifts in Texas were being treated. He especially complained to Gray about what he considered to be Joe Selby's heavy-handed methods. He asked if Gray could get rid of the man. Gray refused. When reasoning failed him Wright turned to hardball again. He said he had heard from his people in Texas that Selby was a homosexual and that he was hiring homosexual lawyers to work for the Federal Home Loan Bank in Dallas. Again Wright wondered pointedly if Gray couldn't find someone more suitable for the job.

Gray replied, "I feel he is doing a fine job in Texas and I see no justification for firing him."

Wright had to call his friends in Texas and tell them he had been unable to dislodge Selby from his job at the FHLB of Dallas.

Later, when we asked Wright in writing about the above incident, he replied by having his attorney write to McGraw-Hill, the publisher of this book, and deny that any such conversation took place. Wright's attorney wrote, "Mr. Wright does not and would not presume to tell the head of any agency who should be hired or fired." He wrote that Wright had no specific knowledge concerning Selby's personal life "and never would express any judgments about him without such knowledge."

The 1989 report of a congressional ethics probe of Speaker Wright, however, concluded that the conversation did indeed take place. The report noted that Selby's sexual orientation, whatever it might have been, was "completely irrelevant to his qualification for employment in the Federal Home Loan Bank System." Every credible witness who knew Selby "had only the highest praise for the man's character and ability" and none believed "the incredible rumor embraced by Wright" that Selby "had established a ring of homosexual lawyers" to do the FHLB's supervisory work in Dallas. The report concluded that Wright's request that Gray get rid of Selby "greatly exceeded the bounds of proper congressional conduct. . . . An attempt to destroy the distinguished career of a dedicated public servant because of his rumored sexual orientation or because of a wild accusation hardly reflects creditably on the House. Such an attempt is a direct violation of House Rule XLIII."

Selby continued to be a particular target of Texas thrift owners, who viewed him as a colonial governor representing the imperialist power in Washington, Ed Gray.[26] If Wright had made life hot for Ed Gray in Washington, Wright's friends in Texas turned Joe Selby's life into a living hell. Soon after Selby returned from a Washington meeting with the Bank Board, in which he had obtained approval for the closure of Jarrett Woods's Western Savings and Loan in Dallas, one of the Dallas FHLB examiners noticed his home phone was not functioning properly. He unscrewed the mouthpiece and discovered the problem—an electronic listening device—a bug. Selby knew he had annoyed some powerful people, but not until now had he imagined how deep those waters were. Selby wasn't taking any chances. He had his office and the entire supervisory floor swept for bugs. None were found.

A few weeks later Selby received a call from a Dallas savings and loan executive whom he respected.[27]

"Joe, can we get together for lunch? I have something I think you should know, but I don't want to talk about it on the phone."

Over lunch the bank president recounted a strange occurrence.

"I was attending a thrift conference last week and walked in on a meeting full of Texas savings and loan guys from around town here. I only picked up the end of the conversation, but I can tell you they were talking about hiring somebody to kidnap you, Joe."

Selby thought for a moment. If someone had told him that story a few weeks earlier, he would have considered them nuts, but now, after the phone bug, he wasn't so sure. "Don't tell me any more. I don't want to hear about it," Selby told his friend. "I don't even want to know who was at the meeting." Selby said later he felt like he was in the cross hairs of a rifle scope.

"God, it was an electric atmosphere during those days," Selby told us. "I feared for my mental and physical health. I was afraid for my own life. There were bad guys robbing millions from S&Ls. . . . I had no idea I'd run into the crooks I ran into when I got down to Dallas."

CHAPTER EIGHTEEN

The Last Squeezing of the Grapes

Don Dixon had stepped down at Vernon after the FHLB issued its cease-and-desist order. He no longer participated in the thrift's day-to-day activities, but he still controlled Vernon's subsidiary Dondi Financial. Though gone from the office, his presence continued to be felt in the vault. After clearing out at Vernon, Don Dixon began to cash in his Southern California empire. Since Vernon Savings would no longer be paying the bills, something certainly had to be done with all his homes there: the Solano Beach house, the Del Mar house, and the Rancho Santa Fe home that he was building. He tried to find someone to buy the Solano Beach house (the only one of the three that Vernon Savings was not on the hook for). Jack Atkinson, who regulators said borrowed (with his affiliates) over $56.2 million from Vernon, told an FHLB examiner he paid the Solano Beach rent for a while. So did John Riddle, a developer who bank records showed had borrowed about $10 million from Vernon.

Our old friend Charles Bazarian showed up next, renting the home for several months during 1986. Bazarian actually made two offers to buy the home from its owners after Dixon stopped making the monthly payments. In March, Bazarian offered $1.75 million, and he said Paris Savings and Loan (in North Dallas around the corner from Vernon Savings) had agreed to finance the purchase. However, Dixon's man Friday in California said Dixon told him the Bazarian offer was bogus, intended simply to buy time for Dixon.[1]

Bazarian's heart attack that year sent Dixon scrambling for another "buyer," but Bazarian came back in September with another offer, $1.45 million. Paris Savings backed out of the deal, however, when they read in the *National Thrift News* that Bazarian had been indicted in September for the Florida Center Bank scam with Renda and Rapp. Eventually Dixon lost the home.

As for the Del Mar house, in June 1986 Dixon negotiated its sale to a company owned by Bruce West, another major Vernon borrower. An FSLIC lawsuit revealed that Dixon arranged to have Vernon loan West $2.8 million to buy the house, but first Dixon removed the expensive artwork, for which Vernon had paid $900,000.[2] After the sale of the Del Mar house the Dixons continued to occupy it for about six months, paying West's company, Lawton Industries, $7,100 a month rent. During that time the Dixons abandoned hope of moving into the Rancho Santa Fe mansion, under construction a few miles away, and in December 1986 the Dixons moved into a home in nearby Laguna Beach that was owned by Jack Franks, a California loan broker who would later be indicted with Tom Nevis at State/Corvallis.[3]

In July Dixon held an auction at Symbolic Motors in La Jolla and sold 19 vintage cars. Eight of them belonged to him, he said, including a classic Hispano-Suiza, a stunning 1930 Duesenberg, and a 1936 Mercedes. Regulators said the auction grossed $2.3 million, of which Dixon pocketed $1.8 million. Symbolic Motors paid all the auction fees, and it (and, therefore, Vernon Savings) lost $204,000 on the auction.

After Dixon withdrew from Vernon Savings, some of his loyal cadre must have known their days were numbered. In August 1986 they made some strategic moves for what they apparently hoped would be a clean getaway. Their bonus and "bean" commissions, over a million dollars of which was being held in bonus accounts at Vernon Savings, would be forfeited if they quit (or if the thrift were seized). So, the FSLIC charged, they took out personal loans in the exact amounts contained in their bonus accounts and never made a single payment on the loans. In effect, they withdrew the money from their bonus accounts by defaulting on the loans. Attorneys for the FSLIC would later tell a federal judge of their amazement at the boldness displayed by the Vernon executives:

> But even as it became increasingly difficult to continue the cover-up and as the investigator's net began to tighten, the Senior Officers schemed one last desperate maneuver to divert another $1,211,792 into their own pockets. . . .
>
> The persistence and boldness of the Senior Officers in putting this last scheme into effect, after the commencement of a special investigation by the FHLB, is truly breath-taking.

Appearing later for depositions, in response to the attorney's charges, all of the senior officers refused to answer questions. (By press time, three had been indicted on bank fraud charges, two of whom had pleaded guilty.)

By December 1986, the dozens of examiners sniffing around in Vernon's books began to piece together a frightening picture. What emerged was a $1.7 billion financial institution in worse shape than the Alamo after the smoke cleared. Dead and dying properties and loans littered Vernon's portfolio. Vernon assets—office buildings, shopping centers, condo projects—hemorrhaged before their eyes. At the same time new casualties staggered in the door every time the examiners glanced up. Losses mounted by the hour. Regulators started calling the thrift "Vermin Savings." Roy Green, president of the Dallas FHLB, told congressional investigators that Vernon was the worst-run, worst-managed debacle he'd ever seen in the thrift industry.

Vernon Savings had reported a $17 million negative net worth in November 1986. A month later, as examiners got a better handle on the situation, that figure rose to $350 million. Then regulators discovered that Vernon had sold more than $449 million in loans to other thrifts, to get the loans off of Vernon's books, and had promised to buy many of the loans back if the borrowers ever defaulted. That meant Vernon was still on the hook for those loans, but if Vernon were ever liquidated by the FSLIC and unable to uphold its end of the participation agreements, thrifts around the country would take direct losses every time one of the loans they had bought from Vernon turned sour. The health of a number of S&Ls around the country depended upon Vernon's survival.

In December 1986 regulators decided to seek a consent-to-merger agreement from Vernon.[4] The agreement would impose certain restrictions on management and authorize the FSLIC to arrange a merger or sale of the thrift. It also would give regulators the right to replace Vernon's directors and officers.

Dixon saw control of Vernon Savings slipping away from him, and he didn't intend to give up his thrift without a fight. He tried to contact Representative Jim Wright.[5] When Wright didn't return his call, he got in touch with Representative Tony Coelho and Coelho called Wright's right-hand man John Paul Mack,[6] who got Wright to call Dixon.[7] Wright later told congressional investigators that Dixon said, "Look, they are getting ready to put me . . . and all the stockholders completely out of business. . . . If I can be given a week, I have located a source of income, a source of loans, financing in Louisiana . . . a person who will take over all the nonperforming notes and provide capital to continue and redo our operation here, if they will just give me that time." Dixon asked Wright to intercede for him with Gray, and near Christmas 1986 Wright called Gray at home in California.

According to Wright, he said, "Ed, I don't know anything about Vernon Savings and Loan. I don't know if it's valid or not. I don't know if it's meritorious. But the man claims he's being kicked out of business. He's got a week or three or four days that he can save it and avoid foreclosure. Why don't you look into it?"

Gray told Wright he thought there must be a misunderstanding. Only the

Bank Board could authorize closing an institution and no such authorization had been given. He agreed to find out what was going on.

Later Gray would lament over the Christmas call: "I have done things as a results of his [Wright's] calls that I would not have done and never did before."

But Gray kept his promise and called Roy Green at the FHLB in Dallas. Green said regulators planned to seek a consent-to-merger agreement, not a closing, and Gray and Green called Mack to explain the difference. They told Mack a consent-to-merger agreement wouldn't affect the Louisiana business-man's ability to invest in Vernon, and Gray said if there was an investor foolish enough to commit $300 million to a massively insolvent institution, the Bank Board would certainly be interested.

On January 2 the Dallas FHLB received four proposals to invest in Vernon and rejected them all. In the case of the Louisiana group, it proposed to put up no cash whatsoever.

Jim Wright was elevated to the post of speaker of the House of Represent-atives, the third most powerful post in government, in January 1987. Gray's recap bill then was truly in the hands of a powerful hostile force. Roy Green and Joe Selby decided to take a crack at Wright next. They knew better than anyone else what was yet to come in Texas, and they felt Wright had to be made to understand that their examiners were only doing what needed to be done. The examiners were not victimizing innocent constituents. Until Wright un-derstood the situation they felt he would continue to punish the Bank Board by failing to support the critically needed recap bill. "I wanted the speaker to understand exactly what was going on in Texas," Green said. Selby wasn't so sure the meeting would do any good. Some thought Wright's actions grew more out of self-interest than out of ignorance of the facts. But Selby reluctantly agreed to accompany Green.

Ed Gray said he was not invited to attend the February 10 meeting because Wright didn't want him there. The six who did go included Green, Selby, and William Black, who was the FSLIC's aggressive young deputy director. Wright invited his Texas developer friend and partner George Mallick, George's son Michael, and others to observe the meeting. Wright had asked Mallick to write a report on the cost of cleaning up all the insolvent S&Ls and the reasons for the problems, and Mallick was presenting his completed report today.[8] Black later told us he and the other regulators were astounded to see the Mallicks and the others in the room. He said their presence made it vir-tually impossible to discuss highly confidential regulatory matters openly with Wright.

Wright trusted Mallick's views. He and Mallick had been partners since the 1970s, according to published accounts, and Wright's wife, Betty, received $18,000 a year as an employee of a firm they jointly owned. A Justice Department official told the Washington *Times* the relationship between Wright and the Mallicks appeared to be "a classic gratuities case . . . official acts prompted by financial favors," and it later became one focus of an ethics probe of the speaker.

The February 1987 meeting in the speaker's office began with Roy Green and Joe Selby explaining the serious problems they faced in Texas. Green told Wright that the innuendos about gestapo tactics in Texas were nonsense. Regulators were just doing their jobs.

Wright was unmoved. If they were so smart, Wright wanted to know, why couldn't the FSLIC handle these problems more creatively? He felt the FSLIC was forcing thrifts into insolvency by requiring them to take huge write-downs on property they owned.

"Why can't you guys work out some kind of deals with these people?" Wright wanted to know.

There's disagreement on just who brought up Vernon at the meeting. Wright claimed he didn't, Black said he most certainly did, others said Green did. One thing was clear—Wright was furious with Gray, whom he felt had lied to him about Vernon.

"When I talk to the head of a federal agency and he tells me something, you know, I believe him," Black quoted Wright as saying. "And I asked Gray when they were going to shut down Vernon Savings and Loan and he personally assured me that they were not going to do that, and then I discover that you did just exactly that, and the very [same] day."

Black realized that the speaker just didn't understand the difference between a consent-to-merger agreement and a seizure.

Black was an articulate, liberal Democrat in his late thirties. A striking man, with a full head of red hair and a red beard, he was well versed on the FSLIC's growing crisis. Unlike Gray, there was nothing folksy about Black. He was professional and blunt.

"You don't seem to understand what's going on down there," Black said to the speaker.

"I don't understand what's going on down there?" Wright boomed, his face turning bright red. "I'm the speaker of the House, goddamn it. Goddamn it, I listened to you people and now you're going to listen to me. You're talking semantics to me, jargon, and I don't like it."[9]

Wright complained bitterly that it was Ed Gray who didn't know what he was doing, especially in Texas. Black, choosing his words more carefully this time, tried to explain to Wright that Vernon was hopelessly insolvent, that it would cost hundreds of millions of the FSLIC's dollars—maybe as much as a billion—just to clean up after Don Dixon.

Wright turned to Joe Selby.

"You're the guy who's carrying the big hammer down there. They're scared of you," Wright said, cocking an angry eye at Selby. Selby wasn't about to get into a shouting match with Wright, so he just didn't reply. (Friends later said Selby told them he was afraid of the speaker.) The meeting lasted about an hour, but Wright remained unmoved and nothing was accomplished. Two weeks after the meeting, Roy Green threw in the towel and resigned from the Dallas Bank Board. He later denied that his resignation had anything to do with his meeting with Wright.

The meeting with Green and Selby was good background for Wright for what happened six weeks later. On March 27, 1987, the inevitable could be delayed no longer and the FHLBB ordered that Vernon Savings be closed. When the extent of the damage at Vernon began to leak out in the press, the seizure became a major embarrassment to the speaker. His press secretary quickly issued a statement:

"The Speaker has no personal knowledge one way or other of this or any other individual savings and loan. . . . The Speaker's aim from the beginning has been to make sure that depositors are protected and that sound and salvageable private businesses are not forced into bankruptcy or foreclosure whenever that can be avoided."

A full-fledged damage-control operation swung into action to protect the new speaker from himself. Representative Frank Annunzio (D-Ill)[10] rushed to Wright's side and told the Washington *Post*, "If this [the closing of Vernon] is an attempt to embarrass Jim Wright then Mr. Gray is lucky that the Speaker is an advocate for the homeless because after June, when Mr. Gray is out of a job (Gray's term as FHLBB chairman was due to expire in June 1987) he may be sleeping on a grate."

Regulators went on the offensive. They seized thrift after thrift in Texas in the months that followed the closure of Vernon. But it wasn't the end, not by a long shot. They began the task of dismantling the rogue thrifts one piece at a time, dissecting them, like a mortician would dissect a cadaver to determine the cause of death, reading out the list of maladies and malignancies as they were found. In Vernon's case the list was a long one, just part of which was a long list of loans FSLIC compiled that were in default at the time of the takeover. For us some of the names were familiar ones: John Atkinson and related companies, $56.2 million; Dixon-related companies, $44.9 million; Larry Vineyard, $16.3 million; John B. Anderson, $11.7 million; John Riddle, $9.7 million; Tom Gaubert, $6.76 million; Bruce West, $4.85 million; Charles Bazarian and related companies, $4.6 million; Frank Domingues, $995,000; Durward Curlee, $502,600; Jack Franks and related entities, $300,000; Tom Nevis, amount unspecified.

In a case where staggering figures and tall tales were the order of the day, it was hard to pick one figure that summed up Vernon, but if we had to choose one it would be this: By the time Vernon failed on March 20, 1987, an unbelievable 96 *percent* of all its outstanding loans were in default. 96 percent! Virtually every loan Vernon had made was a bad loan.[11]

On April 27, 1987, the FSLIC filed a civil racketeering lawsuit against Dixon, Dondi Financial, and a baker's dozen of Vernon former officers, charging that they had looted Vernon of more than $540 million. The suit alleged, among other things, that they had made loans of up to $90 million each to friends and business associates without, the suit said, any "reasonable basis for concluding the loans were collectible." At the time the civil suit was the largest in the FSLIC's history. Then regulators faced the long and messy job of trying to clean up the books, repay depositors, and dispose of Vernon's overencumbered real estate in a Texas market that had gone bust. Cleaning up Vernon would ultimately cost $1.3 *billion*. Later Vernon CEO Woody F. Lemons was indicted for bank fraud and two of the six senior officers named in the FSLIC suit pleaded guilty to bank fraud. Spokesmen said the investigation was continuing.

The day after the FSLIC sued Dixon, et al, Speaker Wright and the House Banking Committee Chairman St Germain did a public about-face and, in what *The New York Times* characterized as "a startling reversal," agreed to support the $15 billion recap bill. Wright later said his sudden decision had nothing to do with Vernon Savings. He said Secretary of the Treasury James Baker had met him in Fort Worth on April 24 and personally asked him to support the $15 billion bill.

While the FSLIC was filing its half-billion-dollar lawsuit, Dixon was going into his lame-bird routine and declaring bankruptcy. He claimed to have lost $100 million and to be flat broke, and he warned creditors that they "couldn't get blood out of a turnip." He estimated his income in 1987 would be a modest $104,500, compared to $1.9 million in 1986 and $2.9 million in 1985. Dixon appeared at a bankruptcy court hearing in June 1987 in Southern California with Dana clinging nervously to his arm. When the judge questioned him about the extravagant life-style he had led while he controlled Vernon Savings, Dixon tried to paint a picture of prudence. He left spectators shaking their heads when he insisted that his Ferrari was not an extravagance.

"It was a family Ferrari," he told the court. How so? Well, he explained, because it had an automatic transmission. Laughter spread throughout the courtroom. As Dixon answered the bankruptcy court judge's questions, he glanced out into the audience, where he spotted a familiar face, Dallas reporter Byron

Harris, who had closely covered Dixon's rise and fall. Dixon smirked, as if to say "What a pain in the ass, huh?" Dana, on the other hand, looked terrified by the whole public spectacle. She held tightly to Don's arm as they sat at the witness table and afterward in the hall as they passed the phalanx of reporters and television cameras.

The "family" Ferrari was not the only asset Dixon's 85 creditors wanted to get their hands on. There were the custom-made shotguns, now valued at $25,000 apiece, and Dana's $75,000 diamond solitaire ring. And the $31,000 worth of French wines Dixon had picked up on his European tours. All were listed in the bankruptcy filings.

In an attempt to gauge the depth and breadth of Dixon's five-year spending binge, his own attorney compiled a list of about 400 people and 150 banks and S&Ls Dixon had done business with ("every one he'd ever driven by," quipped an associate) who might need to be notified about any action taken in his bankruptcy case. On the list were many names familiar to us: Larry Vineyard, Tyrell Barker, Jack Atkinson, former U.S. Secretary of the Treasury John Connally, Ben Barnes (former lieutenant governor of Texas), Robert Ferrante, Jack Franks, John Riddle, Bruce West, Charles Bazarian and his company, CB Financial. There were also several familiar savings and loans: Sunbelt, Key, Paris, and Vernon.

And there on the list was R. B. Tanner, 71, founder of Vernon Savings. Dixon continued to promise Tanner he would pay him the more than $2 million that Dixon still owed him for Vernon Savings and that the Tanners had counted on for their retirement, but it was hard to see where the money would come from.

"We are hurting terrifically," Mrs. Tanner told us, and R.B.'s health hadn't been the same since Vernon's collapse. But they found strength through doing mission work for their church. "R.B. lived a life of integrity," Mrs. Tanner said proudly, and that was something, at least, that Don Dixon could not take from them. Months later the Tanners were on television, praying for Don Dixon's soul.

Bad as things were, Vernon wasn't an exception in Dallas, it was the rule. FBI officials scoffed at Federal Home Loan Bank Board statements that the losses were attributable to the oil recession. Vernon, for example, was already in trouble in 1983, over two years before oil prices collapsed. Government auditors and Justice Department investigators estimated that there were $15 billion in losses in institutions in the Dallas area that were under criminal investigation. In Houston half the failed institutions there were under investigation as well. Every time investigators looked at a failed thrift, they found fraud.

"My god," an overwhelmed FBI agent said to us, "the only thing that is ever going to get me out of here is the statute of limitations." (The statute of limitations for bank fraud is five years.)

"This is the biggest Keystone Cops debacle to happen to U.S. financial institutions since the Great Depression," one veteran thrift executive, hired by the FSLIC to help untangle the mess, told *The Wall Street Journal*. "The failure on the regulatory side is every bit equal to the failures committed by the other side."

"If you know the Vernon story," a FSLIC attorney told us, "you know three percent of what happened in Texas."

HUGE FRAUD PROBE OF DALLAS THRIFTS

Thus read newspaper headlines across the United States in mid-August 1987. The U.S. Department of Justice had convened a special task force of 20 FBI agents, two assistant U.S. attorneys, four IRS agents, 14 Justice Department lawyers and special prosecutors, and at least one federal grand jury. They seized the records of about 400 players in the Dallas S&L game, involved in 25 to 35 thrifts, and they announced that the largest white-collar crime probe of its type in U.S. history was under way. Their investigation, they said, could take from two to five years to complete.

The Dallas *Times Herald* obtained a copy of the list of 400 people whose records had been seized while investigators repeatedly stressed that seizure of a person's records did not indicate that person himself was under investigation. On the list were many names familiar to us: Jack Atkinson, Tyrell Barker, Herman Beebe, Mitchell Brown, Durward Curlee, Don and Dana Dixon, Jack Franks, Tom Gaubert, Craig Hall, Morton Hopkins, Ed McBirney, Tom Nevis, John Riddle, Larry Vineyard, Jarrett Woods. The list also included some heavyweight Texans, including Richard Strauss, the son of Robert Strauss, the former national Democratic Party chairman; Ben Barnes; John Connally; former Texas Savings and Loan Commissioner L. Linton Bowman, III; and Gene Philips, president of Southmark, a $10 billion Dallas-based investment company. An eerie silence fell over what had been a mecca for wild, free-wheeling S&L action.

Many suspected the task force investigation was no more than a temporary inconvenience for Texans. As Molly Ivins, columnist for the Dallas *Times Herald*, once said, "When they crap out, Texans are very good-natured about it and just start over with something else. It's the game they like . . ."

Texas differed only in scale from what we had discovered virtually everywhere else in the country, even in places where the only oil being pumped was at the corner gas station. Texas had attracted almost every swindler in the country who was traveling the thrift circuit because Texas thrifts wheeled and dealed like no others in the nation. Texas, we had discovered, was the most glaring example of how ultraliberal state thrift regulations, coupled with new federal powers and FSLIC deposit insurance, produced a machine that sucked in deposits from across the nation and channeled them into a network of excess, fraud, and corruption the likes of which had no equal in the history of this nation.

CHAPTER NINETEEN

The Godfather

We had spent several months investigating the Texas savings and loan industry when a source slipped us a startling document. It was a copy of a series of secret reports prepared in 1985 for the comptroller of the currency.[1] The report had been ordered by the comptroller in order to "determine the breadth of [Herman] Beebe's influence or control over financial institutions." We knew of Beebe's involvement in banking through his credit life insurance business. We also knew he had bankrolled Dixon and Barker when they bought Vernon and State/Lubbock and he had loaned money to McBirney to buy an airplane for Sunbelt Savings. But Beebe's interest in financial institutions apparently went far deeper than that.

The 22-page report listed *over 100* banks and savings and loans that the comptroller's investigators suspected were either directly or indirectly controlled by Beebe or over whom he had some kind of influence. Listed among the thrifts they suspected Beebe of controlling were, of course, Vernon and State/Lubbock. The report also outlined a complex structure of personal relationships, corporate shells, and stock partnerships that secretly underlaid ownership of dozens more institutions throughout Texas, Louisiana, Colorado, California, Mississippi, Ohio, and Oklahoma. And beneath it all, the report alleged, was the guiding hand of Herman K. Beebe. When we scanned the list of thrifts and banks, we saw many that we knew had failed or were on the verge of insolvency. Suddenly Herman Beebe appeared to be in the class of Mario Renda and Charles Bazarian. If the report was correct, Herman Beebe was a veritable godfather of thrifts and banks.[2]

Herman Beebe in 1987 was 60 years old. For over 20 years he had been quietly manipulating financial institutions for his own benefit and the benefit of a close-knit circle of influential friends. We learned that Beebe was a business associate of the most powerful men in Louisiana and Texas, and we heard the rumors that he was also associated with one of the Mafia's most powerful god-fathers, Carlos Marcello.

His influence in banking circles was so pervasive by the mid-1980s that he could be connected in some way to almost every dying bank or savings and loan in Texas and Louisiana, yet few people had ever heard his name—that is until U.S. Attorney Joe Cage set out to change all that. The confrontation between Joe Cage and Herman Beebe was a clash played out in Louisiana courtrooms between 1985 and 1988. It would match in significance Mike Manning's pursuit of Mario Renda.

Herman Beebe grew up in Rapides Parish in central Louisiana. Beebe was a common name in the Arkansas, Louisiana, and Texas area, and Herman came from solid rural stock. In 1943 he entered Northwestern State University in Natchitoches, just a few miles from home, and swept the floors of Caldwell Hall for his room and board. But World War II intervened, and he had to give up school for Navy shipboard duty in the Pacific. After the war he finished college at Louisiana State University in Baton Rouge, and the same year, 1949, he married Mary. They would have four children: Easter Bunny, Pamela, Ruth Anastasia, and Herman, Jr. Beebe had majored in agricultural education, and he worked as an assistant county agent in northern Louisiana until called into the Navy reserves during the Korean War. While in the Navy he decided to sell insurance when he got out.

In 1956 he moved back to Rapides Parish and within two years he was vice president of Savings Life Insurance Company in Alexandria (eventually one of the largest mortgage life insurance companies in Louisiana). In 1961 he started his own company, investing in motels, mostly Holiday Inns. He originally called his company American Motel Industries, but gradually his investments spread from motels to insurance to nursing homes and finally banking. American Motel Industries became simply AMI, Inc. Over the next 25 years he would build AMI into a multimillion-dollar conglomerate only to see it crumble as U.S. Attorney Joe Cage probed Beebe's business dealings and bombarded him with indictments and back-to-back investigations.

Whatever Horatio Alger elements there may have been in Beebe's success story, investigators said he joined the dark side early. In January 1965 the Securities and Exchange Commission accused Beebe and a partner of withholding important information when they tried to sell AMI stock.[3]

Beebe shrugged off the SEC judgment and went right back to building his empire. Nearly two years later, in October 1966, he made a decision that would change his life. It would also change the fortunes of more than 100 banks and thrifts over the next 20 years. In 1966 Herman Beebe bought his first bank, Bossier Bank & Trust, in Bossier City, Louisiana. As AMI had become the cornerstone of his business empire, so Bossier Bank & Trust would become the cornerstone of his banking empire. On a roll, he parlayed that purchase into eight more banks in Louisiana, Oklahoma, and Texas. Beebe had come up with a way to create his own captive customer base for his insurance company. By owning his own banks Beebe could require the banks' prospective borrowers to buy AMI's credit life insurance. No insurance, no loan, though it might not be so crudely put.

Beebe quickly became one of Louisiana's major employers and a one-man conglomerate. Soon he was in demand. The mayor of Shreveport, Louisiana, 120 miles northwest of Alexandria, tirelessly wooed him, even attending AMI board meetings. He urged Beebe to consider the benefits of basing his company in Shreveport. Beebe agreed—after all, his bank, Bossier Bank & Trust, was in Bossier City, a suburb just across the Red River from Shreveport. In 1971 he made the move. For the next 14 years he would work and live in Shreveport, 200 miles due east of Dallas.

Even as Beebe's star was rising in Louisiana, he was getting some unasked-for attention outside the state. Two thousand miles away, on the West Coast, the San Diego police were looking into Beebe's growing contacts there and notified the Metropolitan Crime Commission in New Orleans. The San Diego authorities reported that they had discovered that Beebe was negotiating to purchase a casino. His partners in the deal were familiar to the San Diego police, who considered them undesirables.

About the same time the rumors began to circulate that Beebe was "connected" in some way to Carlos Marcello, the powerful New Orleans Mafia boss. Among Beebe's growing businesses were his nursing homes. Carlos Marcello liked nursing homes too. In fact, in 1966 he had been arrested in a New York restaurant with East Coast Mafia boss Carlo Gambino and Florida boss Santo Trafficante, and he had told authorities he was in New York to arrange financing for a nursing home. Aaron Kohn, who was on the Metropolitan Crime Commission at that time, said one of Marcello's "messenger-boy attorneys" was seen serving as a courier between Marcello and Beebe in the mid-1970s.[4] Later Beebe's attorney would tell us vehemently that Beebe absolutely did not have any association with Carlos Marcello or any organized crime figure.[5]

Whatever relationships might have been developed underground, Beebe was forging powerful political connections above ground. In the early 1970s he and former Texas Lieutenant Governor Ben Barnes developed a complex business association, the tentacles of which would be found 15 years later entwined in the Texas thrift crisis.

When Ben Barnes was only 22 he was elected to the Texas House of Representatives. For 11 years he was one of Texas's most up-and-coming young politicians. In 1968 he was nominated for lieutenant governor and became the first candidate in Texas history to receive two million votes. He was lieutenant governor from 1968 to 1972, but his political career ended after his name was involved in a bank and stock fraud scandal.

In 1971 a group of Texas banks were looted by a network of businessmen who borrowed money from the banks and used it to buy and sell stock from firms that belonged to Texas businessman Frank Sharp.[6] Ben Barnes had owned stock in one of the companies under investigation by the SEC, according to the Texas *Observer*, and he had had loans at Dallas Bank & Trust, owned by Sharp (Barnes and Beebe later bought the bank). Though Barnes was never indicted, the Texas media speculated that his involvement may have raised questions in the voters' minds. He placed third in the 1972 race for the Democratic gubernatorial nomination.

In July 1973 Beebe and Barnes began to form banking and insurance associations,[7] and by mid-1976 they controlled or had major influence over 19 banks and savings and loans in Texas and Louisiana.

Dallas, where Beebe's Savings Life had an office, was the center of the pair's business activity together. They often held their meetings in a North Dallas apartment, and it was sometime during 1976, Beebe later said, that Ben Barnes introduced Beebe to aggressive young Dallas developer Don Dixon.

Financially, Beebe and Barnes did very well together. The Dallas *Morning News* reported that by 1976 Beebe claimed a net worth of $8.2 million, and Barnes' prospects had certainly improved—from a net worth of $100,000 when he left the political arena in 1972 to $5.4 million in 1976. Unnoticed, they quietly went about the business of amassing a banking and insurance empire. Unnoticed, that was, until August 29, 1976, when Dallas *Morning News* reporters Earl Golz and Dave McNeely shattered the silence:

PYRAMID SCHEME, UNSECURED LOANS
POSE THREAT TO SEVERAL
STATE BANKS

So read the main headline on the Golz/McNeely series. The lead paragraph of their story could have run almost unchanged in any Dallas newspaper during the savings and loan crisis ten years later:

"A multimillion dollar looting of state banks, with links to political figures and possibly to organized crime, could cause several state banks in Texas to fail unless severe corrective measures are taken, according to informed sources."

The gist of the stories was that a network of 14 businessmen had borrowed money to buy Texas banks and thrifts, used those banks and thrifts to get loans to buy others, and so on, in pyramid fashion. Then, once they had acquired the institutions, they had used depositors' money to make loans to themselves and their friends.[8] Among the men named in the story were Herman Beebe and Ben Barnes.

Aside from the financial wheeling and dealing outlined in their Dallas *Morning News* series, Golz and McNeely revealed disturbing information about some of the men in the network they said officials believed were looting state banks.[9] Beebe, they said, had "drawn the interest of several federal investigative agencies, which have reported that he has had associations with individuals who have organized crime connections."

Again the allegation: "One agency has reported that Beebe has had frequent contact with one of the personal attorneys of reputed New Orleans Mafia boss Carlos Marcello." And:

"Usually reliable federal sources report that Bossier Bank & Trust is suspected of being a conduit for funds skimmed by organized crime from Las Vegas gambling receipts and placed in foreign bank numbered accounts."

Two of the men named in the *Morning News* series, Carroll Kelly and David Wylie, would later get financing from Beebe to take over Continental Savings and Loan in Houston, according to court documents. A Houston dentist (who was a former investor in two thrifts merged to form Continental) said in an affidavit that one of the men's former partners told him New Orleans Mafia boss Carlos Marcello controlled Continental Savings through Beebe.[10] Officials with Continental Savings denied the institution had anything to do with anybody in organized crime. (Continental Savings failed in October 1988.)

Ben Barnes was in Reno, Nevada, negotiating to build a Holiday Inn at Lake Tahoe, when the 1976 Dallas *Morning News* series began. He was livid, and with great fanfare and bluster ("I am sick and tired of having my personal business affairs subjected to continuous harassment. My family and I have endured enough persecution from the awesome power of a giant newspaper") he sued the *Morning News* for $20 million.

Within a few days Beebe followed with a $12 million suit. But for all their threats, the cases never came to court. After a lot of jawboning attorneys for the defense said Barnes and Beebe abandoned their monetary demands in return for the newspaper's promise that it would not release any of the information it had collected on them and would seal the files. Barnes told us he did not pursue his suit because he could not show he had been damaged financially by the story.

But that was by no means the end of the story. A House subcommittee,[11] chaired by Representative Fernand St Germain (D-R.I.), held hearings in San Antonio later that year (1976) to investigate the closing of Citizens State Bank in Carrizo Springs and what became known as the rent-a-bank scandal. The hearings dragged up all the dirt again and added more.[12] A former executive vice president of Citizens State Bank testified at the hearing that an associate had attended a meeting with Beebe and Harper and later told him "that Beebe was supposedly connected with the Mafia." Beebe denied the rumor.

In the documents filed as part of the 1976 congressional hearings was a letter from loan broker Donald E. Luna to Barnes and Beebe about a loan Luna was arranging for an associate of theirs. We remembered Don Luna: Ten years after he wrote this letter to Barnes and Beebe, he would be indicted with Cardascia at Flushing Federal for allegedly extorting $1.75 million from a Swiss developer. (Sometime during those ten years, federal authorities said, Luna had been convicted of running a confidence scam.) Cardascia was cleared of the charge and Luna was awaiting trial as this book went to press.

As with the congressional hearings on brokered deposits involving Mario Renda, the Citizens State Bank hearings in 1976 had virtually no impact. Beebe continued to build up AMI, Inc., from his corporate headquarters in Shreveport. But the people of Shreveport began to notice that Herman Beebe had changed. In 1979, saying he needed to devote more time to his business, he stepped down as chairman of the board of Bossier Bank & Trust (though he maintained his ownership) and seemed to withdraw from the mainstream of daily commerce. He stopped going to civic and social functions in Shreveport, and he sank into the anonymity of corporate AMI, Inc. He spent his days doing million-dollar deals concluded in a matter of minutes and sealed with a handshake. His habit was to rise before dawn and work late.

An associate later described to us Beebe's way of doing business: "He just kind of walked on the edge of fire, just defying people. He lived by the sword and he died by the sword. But I don't think he was a crook. I do think he violated federal banking laws and savings and loan laws, as most people do who do a lot of creative things, so he was guilty of that, sure."

Beebe adopted a jet-setting life-style, flying out of nearby Shreveport Municipal Airport for business meetings around the country or taking an entourage by limousine to Dallas, which was a straight three-hour shot west on Interstate 20 from Shreveport. When he wasn't engrossed in business he was at home with his family at their private compound near AMI headquarters, a woodsy secluded colony of stately Southern mansions, pine trees, and vast gracious lawns. Beebe's home in the family compound was described in the Shreveport *Times* as an 11,000-square-foot, $1 million Colonial mansion complete with swimming pool, tennis courts, and private pond. There were seven bedrooms, 24-karat-gold-leaf chandeliers from Spain, separate barbecue and smokehouse, bronze-trimmed winding staircase in the foyer, murals on the dining-room walls, and a six-car garage. There were also separate, more modest houses for the Beebe children —in the half-million-dollar range.

Beebe maintained a second home at La Costa Country Club in Southern California. La Costa was built by Rapp's buddy Moe Dalitz and others in the mid-1960s with $97 million from the Teamsters Central States Pension Fund. Beebe had owned property there for 17 years and was an established member of an important social and business circle.[13] Most notably, Pete Brewton reported in the Houston *Post*, he was a business partner with Scott Susalla, whose father, Edward D. "Fast Eddie" Susalla, was a general partner in La Costa.[14] Beebe and Susalla owned a loan brokerage and real estate firm called TLC (Texas, Louisiana, California). Susalla also worked with Don Dixon on condo deals in the La Costa area. (In 1985 Scott Susalla would plead guilty to possession of cocaine in one of the biggest drug busts in Southern California history. Federal authorities had accused him and about 100 others of importing a large percentage of Peru's cocaine into the United States.)

But Beebe's primary interests were still in Louisiana and Texas, where he continued to expand. When Congress announced that it intended to deregulate thrifts—taking the first step with the Depository Institutions Deregulation and Monetary Control Act of 1980—Beebe immediately saw the possibilities. Real estate in Texas was red-hot, and deregulated thrifts could make more commercial real estate loans than ever before, with fewer restrictions than ever before. Beebe began to "diversify," investing in more S&Ls, and he helped his friends do the same. Word got around that anyone who needed money to get control of a thrift should see Beebe.

"He was the man," said an FBI agent later. "Herman was the man to see," a thrift regulator agreed. Thus, Beebe became known to a handful of the observant as "the Godfather of Texas Savings and Loans."

Among the authorized visitors to AMI headquarters and the Beebe family compound during this time was Don Dixon, who had become a close family friend and with whom Beebe had made several investments, including a Holiday Inn in Shreveport. Dixon, about ten years younger than Beebe, had adopted the older man as a paternal role model, even calling Beebe "Papaw." (Some people would later speculate that Dixon's high-living life-style at Vernon was just an attempt to outperk his mentor, Papaw.) Dixon brought his friend Tyrell Barker into the Beebe clan.

Later U.S. Attorney Joe Cage said, "Beebe created Barker and Dixon for his benefit, their benefit, everybody's benefit but the American taxpayers." Both Dixon's and Barker's thrifts sold Beebe's credit life insurance policies to their borrowers. Beebe's right-hand man at AMI, Dale Anderson, later said that AMI netted $2.5 million in two years through Vernon's sales alone. For a time Beebe even kept a two-room suite in the Vernon Savings building. Anderson explained how it worked:

"We were very careful about how we worded it. If a borrower said he'd talk to his own insurance man, we'd say, 'Fine. That's probably where you need to get your loan.' "

Beebe, Dixon, and Barker also networked with the burgeoning S&L community in Texas, arranging millions of dollars in loans for themselves, loans that regulators would later claim weren't always repaid.

"Basically it all boiled down to back scratching," said the U.S. attorney who later prosecuted Barker. Tom Nevis's testimony, about a time when Barker approached him for a loan, showed how the back scratching worked:

"He (Barker) said, 'You owe me a loan. Try to get me a loan.' . . . I never crossed Barker. . . . Barker was always saying, 'You do this and I'll help you out.' . . . He done a lot of that."[15]

A deal negotiated with a Beebe-controlled bank or savings and loan, according to former Beebe associates, might work something like this: Someone who wanted a real estate development loan would be required to borrow more than he needed and to use the excess as Beebe directed (to pay off a loan that Beebe owed or that was owed to him, or to buy stock in a Beebe bank). And once the development was completed, a Beebe associate might buy it with another (overfunded) loan from a Beebe-controlled institution. The whole process resembled a Ponzi scheme (that could only last as long as real estate values were climbing).

"What happened was that people who came to us for money had to buy something," a Beebe associate told the Dallas *Morning News*.

Beebe built a number of important relationships, each serving a particular need, each giving Beebe access to an important arena. With Barnes, Beebe was plugged into old-Texas banking, insurance, and political circles. With Dixon and Barker, he was part of the wild-'n'-crazy thrift owners of Dallas.[16] With Louisiana Governor Edwin Edwards and Judge Edmund Reggie, Beebe would gain entry into the highest circles of political power in Louisiana.

Edwin Edwards was an ambitious politician, and beginning in 1954 he would hold political office in Louisiana for almost 30 years. He started as a city councilman in Crowley and subsequently served in the Louisiana Senate and the U.S. House of Representatives. He was governor of the state of Louisiana from 1972 to 1980, took a break for one term, and served again from 1984 to 1988. Until he lost his bid in 1988 for an unprecedented fourth term as governor, he had a campaign record of 16–0.

Edwards was a flamboyant gambling man, a self-admitted "proud and egotistical person" who reportedly used to boast that the only way he could lose an election was "to be caught in bed with either a dead girl or a live boy." He gambled in Las Vegas under aliases like T. Wong, and U.S. Attorney Joe Cage said Edwards and Beebe traveled together to Las Vegas and Southern California. For two years during Edwards's four-year sabbatical from the governorship (1980 to 1984) he was on Beebe's payroll, earning $100,000 a year working for AMI. (Later Cage would say the accommodation seemed to exhibit "the hallmark of influence peddling.")

When Edwards was governor of Louisiana his administration became embroiled in the federal government's pursuit of Carlos Marcello, boss of the New Orleans Mafia. In 1981 Charles Roemer, then Edwards's commissioner of administration, and Marcello were convicted of federal charges of racketeering. The prosecution played in court some tapes they had made in 1979 of Marcello's conversations with associates. On the tapes Marcello said, "Man, I know better than you, man, 'bout them politicians. . . . Edmund [referring to Edwin Edwards] and me all right, but I can't see him every day. . . . He's the strongest sonofabitchin' governor we ever had. He fuck with women and play dice, but won't drink. How do you like dat?" Edwards's lieutenant governor in 1979 was James Fitzmorris. Marcello was recorded as saying, "Fitzmorris? All he can do is ask a favor. He ain't worth a shit."[17]

Dallas *Morning News* reporters Bill Lodge and Allen Pusey reported that at this same time Marcello was a borrower at Beebe-controlled Pontchartrain State Bank near New Orleans. James McKigney, Pontchartrain's president, testified[18] that Pontchartrain had lent money to Marcello, Marcello's son Joseph, and several corporations connected with Marcello. McKigney replaced Beebe as president of Beebe's Bossier Bank & Trust when Beebe resigned in 1979.[19] Marcello attorney Anthony J. Graffagnino[20] was a director in 1983 of Sunbelt Life Insurance Co., which had its headquarters in Beebe's Shreveport office (another Sunbelt director was Governor Edwards's commissioner of financial institutions, who supervised state-chartered banks and savings and loans).

Edwards' close associate Judge Edmund Reggie was a former Crowley city judge in the town where Edwards had once practiced law. Some observers felt Reggie may have been the real power behind Edwards, that it was Reggie who pulled the governor's strings. He was Edwards's personal attorney, served as his executive counsel while he was governor, and headed up Edwards's transition team when he resumed the governorship in 1984. Reggie also was a close personal friend of Senator Ted Kennedy and had been Louisiana campaign manager of John Kennedy's 1960 campaign.[21]

Judge Reggie was a Louisiana power broker. And he was both a banker and a thrift owner. He owned the National Bank of Bossier City, in the same Shreveport suburb as Beebe's Bossier Bank & Trust.[22] He started Acadia Savings and Loan in Crowley in 1957 and had been a director ever since. And he and Beebe owned stock together in several financial institutions. Reggie told us they had been friends for about 30 years, and they were associates in nursing homes, insurance companies, and real estate ventures. Investigators for the comptroller of the currency said several of Judge Reggie's real estate projects were financed by Beebe banks, and Reggie's banks made loans to Beebe-related entities.

Herman Beebe had positioned himself at the vortex of each of these separate but interlocking circles of influence—the Ben Barnes, Dixon/Barker, and Edwards/Reggie axes. By the end of 1981 Beebe was a man to be reckoned with. Beebe was prepared to use everything he had learned over the years about banking and newly deregulated thrifts to build potentially the most powerful and corrupt banking network ever seen in the U.S.

CHAPTER TWENTY

Beebe Gets Caged

On January 8, 1982—just two days before Dixon took control at Vernon Savings in Texas—Joe Cage was sworn in as a U.S. attorney and assigned to the Shreveport office. Cage grew up in Monroe, about 100 miles due east of Shreveport in northern Louisiana, and throughout his high school career he was an outstanding athlete. When he was a sophomore—in spite of the fact that the school had no track team—he threw the javelin 203 feet, a U.S. record at the time. He served a tour of duty in the Marine Corps, returned to college, and at one time aspired to become an FBI agent. Instead he became a practicing attorney and spent the next ten years as a prosecutor in U.S. attorneys' offices and in private practice. In January 1982 President Ronald Reagan appointed him U.S. attorney, and he and his family moved to Shreveport.

Through the years Cage had worked on several cases of financial fraud and, unfortunately for Herman Beebe, he had developed a keen interest in white-collar crime. He liked to quote a line from an old Woody Guthrie song ("Pretty Boy Floyd") that went:

As through this world I've rambled, I've seen lots of funny men. Some will rob you with a six-gun, some with a fountain pen.

Joe Cage was to white-collar swindlers what Elliot Ness was to bootleggers. It was (and remains) rare to find a U.S. attorney familiar with the ways and methods of the professional white-collar criminal, their intricate paper trails and byzantine multimillion-dollar frauds. Untangling the deals is in itself an art, and explaining them to a jury of twelve honest men and women borders on the miraculous. But Cage found the cases both challenging and fascinating, and when he moved to Shreveport in 1982 he ran up against the Dr. Moriarity of his career—Herman K. Beebe.

When Cage arrived in Shreveport a white-collar fraud case was already in the early stages. It involved a smooth and wealthy French businessman who lived in Texas, Albert Prevot, who was accused of defrauding the Small Business Administration by getting SBA loans and then diverting the money to his own uses. Assigned to work with Cage on the case was FBI Special Agent G. Ellis Blount.

Blount became Cage's indispensable right-hand man. He had a background in business law and shared Cage's interest in white-collar crime. They actually liked the challenge of wading through thousands of documents to piece together complex business transactions designed specifically to leave a cold trail. They developed a close working relationship, and eventually the two of them together would bring down the Beebe empire.

Cage and Blount worked through the months on the Prevot case, and as they tightened the screws Prevot decided to try to make a deal. He offered to tell Cage what he knew about Shreveport businessman Herman Beebe, who was, he said, involved in all kinds of illegal activities. Cage said he was interested, and by September 1982 he had two plea agreements in the Prevot case and enough information about Beebe's affairs to justify empaneling a federal grand jury. What Cage had stumbled onto was Beebe's maze of business relationships with banks and corporations. In November, Cage convened the grand jury and he and Blount went to work unraveling Beebe's tangled affairs for the jurors.

"We'd have, say, 10 issues, trying to get them resolved with the grand jury, and in solving those 10, 15 more would come up," Cage told us later. It was like trying to nail jelly to the wall. Beebe's business deals were five dimensional. They went in every direction, and in every direction Cage said he saw transactions that worried him. He discovered that many banks and thrifts in Louisiana and surrounding states had participations and take-out agreements (interlocking financial arrangements) with Beebe's Bossier Bank & Trust, and Cage began to fear for the integrity—and safety—of the area's banking system. Cage and Blount alone handled all the grand jury documents, all the witnesses. They worked long hours, determined to get to the bottom of the complicated case. As Cage called witnesses to testify before the grand jury, word of the investigation trickled back to Beebe. Gradually, tension grew in the Beebe camp.

At first Beebe just tried to shrug it off. 1983 should have been one of the best years of his life. He was flush with what seemed like an endless supply of money from numerous financial institutions, institutions whose owners or officers were in place because Herman Beebe had put them there. He embarked upon an expansion program. In April he broke ground on a $12 million seven-story glass office building in his AMI complex that became known around town as the AMI Tower. Shreveport people called it an ivory tower because it was "out in the middle of nowhere." On the top floor were four palatial offices, one at each corner, where Beebe and his top echelon of officers directed a fast-paced operation that employed almost 6,000 people, over 1,000 of whom lived and worked in the Shreveport area. AMI had 17 subsidiaries and connections with 14 other companies, with after-tax income of over $4 million and assets of $155 million.

In March 1984 a mutual friend arranged for Beebe's now ex-wife, Mary, to visit the Reagans at their Santa Barbara ranch, near her own second home in Santa Barbara, and the public relations blitz was on. The Shreveport *Times* ran a full-page article in March 1984, most of it a fawning account of her visit written by Mary, along with pictures of her standing with President Ronald Reagan and Mrs. Reagan at their ranch. It made its point—Beebe had friends who had friends in very high places.

Across town from the AMI Tower, in a plain corner office on the third floor of the Federal Building,[1] Cage and Blount were spending hundreds of hours combing through evidence and laying their trap. Cage became so convinced that Beebe was a danger to the banking and thrift community that he personally conducted the Beebe investigation. The grand jury was meeting once a week in Alexandria, over 100 miles south of Shreveport, so Cage was absent from his Shreveport office for days at a time. Under his personal direction the grand jury heard 150 witnesses and stayed in session for two years. Cage and Blount methodically formed a cordon around Beebe and AMI, and then they closed in step by step. On Halloween 1984, Beebe was indicted, along with three AMI officers and the CEO of Bossier Bank & Trust. They were charged with 21 counts of fraud.

Beebe was accused of having an AMI subsidiary illegally borrow $1 million from the Small Business Administration in a series of complex transactions that had taken place on New Year's Eve 1980. He was also accused of having Bossier Bank & Trust loan $1.85 million to Albert Prevot (the French businessman whose plea agreement spawned the empaneling of the Beebe grand jury), who then passed it through four corporations and on to AMI, thus allowing Beebe to avoid regulations against banks making loans to their owners. In response to a defense motion the judge separated the charges into two trials—the SBA case and the Bossier Bank case.

Beebe maintained an ominous silence in the wake of the indictments, but AMI, Inc., came out swinging, releasing a strong statement in defense of the five accused men.

"They [the accusations] are the product of an investigation by a U.S. attorney and an FBI agent who for more than two years have demonstrated the desire to obtain an indictment at any cost." The accuseds' high-powered defense team of 15 attorneys included flamboyant attorney Richard "Racehorse" Haynes of Houston and Camille Gravel, who was one of Louisiana's leading criminal defense lawyers, an advisor to Governor Edwin Edwards and Judge Reggie's best friend.

The Beebe children, who had heretofore stayed out of the public eye, fell in behind their father. Though the children were grown and Mary and Herman were divorced, the Beebes remained a close family. Beebe's son, Herman, Jr., and Beebe's two sons-in-law worked for him. Throughout the two-year grand jury investigation, they had all believed it would come to nothing.

"I am a human being and I make a lot of mistakes," daughter Pam told reporters, "and my daddy does, too, but I know he would never set out to harm or deceive somebody or take anything that didn't belong to him."

Daughter Easter Bunny's husband, David, was one of the accused (though charges against him were later dropped).

"It was almost comical," said Bunny in her Louisiana drawl, "to think David could be indicted. Anybody who knows David would think, 'not sweet little David.' We are just thankful Camille [Gravel, defense attorney] was available. He is the kindest, most caring person. We must have looked to him like two little lost lambs."

Many of the 1,000-plus AMI employees in Shreveport took personal offense at the attack on their employer. They held prayer meetings in the AMI Tower and turned out at important times to show support for their boss. The grumbling against Cage had begun.

"The ones [AMI employees] I've talked to," said an employee, "wondered what Mr. Cage has against our boss. It seems so personal, like a vendetta. We wondered why the government is spending so much money to go after one man."

When the first trial began in January 1985, Beebe's family and friends, including ex-wife Mary, faithfully took their places on wooden benches in the courtroom at the Federal Building in Shreveport. During breaks they huddled in small groups, speaking in quiet tones, exchanging subdued smiles, obviously under tremendous strain. Outside the courtroom the whole town of Shreveport waited to see what would happen to one of Shreveport's best-known citizens.

Within a few days the prosecution and the defense rested their cases and the judge sent the jury out to deliberate. On January 17, 1985, the jurors came back in with a verdict. All eyes in the standing-room-only courtroom were on Judge Tom Stagg when at 1:10 p.m. he read the jury's decision: *Guilty*. The jury had found Beebe guilty of the overall charge of defrauding the SBA. They did not find him guilty, however, of several specific charges of lying or benefiting from the loans. Beebe was sentenced to 200 hours community service and ordered to pay a $21,000 fine and $1 million in restitution.

With hardly time to catch their breaths, the attorneys, defendants, family, friends, and reporters gathered on February 4 in a courtroom in Lafayette, Louisiana, 200 miles south of Shreveport. There the second half of the trial, dealing with the Bossier Bank charges, was to be held. Cage charged that Beebe had defrauded his Bossier Bank & Trust by having the bank make a loan to Albert Prevot that was secretly routed to AMI. Cage said the purpose of the transaction, which took place on New Year's Eve 1980, was to improve the looks of AMI's balance sheet at the end of the year. Then Beebe returned the money, via Prevot, to Bossier Bank. Beebe was again represented by Camille Gravel, a distinguished white-haired Southern gentleman who sounded like a Baptist preacher in the courtroom.

"Herman Beebe is a builder," thundered Gravel, "the kind of man that has helped to build this country. He has risen from the red clay hills of north Louisiana to the position he now occupies as a leader of the business community. . . . Any conviction of any of the defendants in this case carries with it a life sentence. Mr. Beebe's career as a prominent and successful businessman would be over. The blight of a conviction would stain him for the rest of his life."

Gravel told the jury that whatever loans Mr. Beebe received were in the course of legitimate business. The loans had all been repaid. Besides, what was illegal about trying to make your financial statement look better at the end of the year? Where was the harm?

Cage was unmoved. "It wasn't a legitimate loan, merely a true and classic sham loan to a person who agreed to do a favor."

But this time Cage did not prevail. It took the jury 50 minutes to acquit Beebe of all charges. They just could not believe Beebe had intended to defraud his own bank. When Judge Tom Stagg read the verdict the courtroom erupted in shouts of joy. Beebe seemed stunned and declined comment, but Mary Beebe said emotionally, "I'm so grateful. I don't know what to say. I really am so thankful. So grateful to God, so grateful to the lawyers and the judge and so grateful to the jury." Someone in the background yelled about a phone call to the governor. Smiling supporters hugged each other and pumped every friendly hand. A disappointed Joe Cage led his team from the courtroom without a word. The score stood even at one-to-one. Cage went back to his office, and he and Blount started all over again, spreading out the deals, looking at the connections, following the money. Three months later, on June 4, Cage convened a second grand jury to investigate Herman Beebe.

Cage's onslaught took its toll on Beebe. He began to have difficulty finding people willing to do business with him. He was a convicted felon—convicted of loan fraud. He found it increasingly difficult to borrow money. His name, and the names of his companies, became like red flags when a bank examiner found them on a list of loans. Many of the officials of the 200 to 300 banks and savings and loans that he typically did business with were called to testify before the grand jury, and many of them decided Beebe was just too hot to handle. They stopped associating with him.

Beebe, a man who had lived a very private life in recent years, suddenly found himself and his business affairs laid open to public view. "My company was leveraged, like so many companies are," he explained to Shreveport *Times* reporter Linda Farrar. "And the turn the investigation took just cut my credit off totally. I had no choice but to start liquidating. I just had so much bad publicity . . . it had just pretty well done away with my opportunity to make a living. . . . It just went downhill in a hell of a hurry."

Loss of insurance business was especially difficult for Beebe to sustain because it had been an important source for the cash flow his other businesses required. He began what appeared to be a liquidation of the Beebe empire. Eventually financial institutions, even those with ties to Beebe, were forced to foreclose on most of his holdings (including the AMI Tower), and he sold whatever was not mortgaged to the hilt. But federal investigators said he had put many of his assets into his children's names, and they believed he continued to control still more investments through third parties.

Cage and Blount proceeded to prepare the new case against Beebe. Their investigation drew the attention of other federal agencies. Two conferences were held, in Baton Rouge, Louisiana, and Memphis, Tennessee, between federal prosecutors and state and federal regulators, and between April and June 1985 the comptroller of the currency prepared the series of secret reports on Beebe's banking activities that first clued us in to the scope of Beebe's influence. After we obtained a copy of the reports, federal officials told us that while the documents might contain minor errors, they stood behind them as a fair and accurate assessment of Beebe's influence in banking and savings and loan circles in 1985. Compiled independently of Cage's investigation, the reports revealed 12 national banks that could "in some way be controlled or influenced by Beebe." Key Beebe figures at those banks included Edmund Reggie and Don Dixon, the reports said. Listed, too, was Harvey McLean, who owned Palmer National Bank in Washington, D.C., and who had a multimillion-dollar line of credit at Bossier Bank & Trust. McLean was also a director of Paris Savings and Loan, which Dixon associates had said was Dixon's "junk S&L."

The comptroller of the currency report then listed 13 national banks that Beebe might "exert some influence over." Listed as being the link between Beebe and some of these banks were Ed McBirney (owner of Sunbelt Savings), Jarrett Woods (owner of Western Savings),[2] Carroll Kelly (part of the network exposed by the failure of Citizens State Bank in 1976 and now an owner of Continental Savings in Houston), and Tyrell Barker.

The OCC study listed 55 state banks (in Arkansas, Florida, Louisiana, Mississippi, and Texas) and 29 savings and loans (in Colorado, California, Louisiana, Mississippi, Ohio, Oklahoma, and Texas) "controlled by Beebe and his associates. . . ." Among the S&Ls listed were Key, Continental, Mercury, Paris, State/Lubbock, Sunbelt, Vernon, and Western. Among the people mentioned as a Beebe-bank associate was Rex Cauble, described in the report as "a convicted drug dealer [who] has had massive debt at Bossier Bank & Trust." Cauble owed two other Beebe-related banks $1.5 million and owned stock in two others. (See Appendix A for full, unedited OCC report.)

One hundred and nine banks and thrifts had been pinpointed by the comptroller of the currency's investigators as having a tight enough relationship with Beebe to be worthy of serious concern. The report so worried the comptroller that it was brought to the attention of Attorney General Ed Meese, the FSLIC, and the FDIC at a joint meeting of the Justice Department's new Bank Fraud Working Group. They realized that with Beebe's extended network of influence, he could shift fraudulent deals not only from institution to institution but from regulatory system to regulatory system—which would make him almost impossible to stop. A loan he wanted to hide could be structured through federally regulated or state-regulated thrifts, banks, and insurance companies all over the country.

The information in the OCC report would not have startled U.S. Attorney Joe Cage and FBI Special Agent Ellis Blount had they known of it, but it was not shared with them. On their own they forged steadily ahead, presenting documents, evidence, and witnesses to the second Beebe grand jury.

Joe Cage's hot breath got to be too much for Beebe and suddenly in late 1985 he packed up and moved from Shreveport to Dallas to start a new life.

"I left town," Beebe said later, "because the atmosphere was such that I just felt like it would be very difficult to—" He interrupted himself and then continued, "It's not difficult for me to make a living. I could make a living on the Sahara Desert. But I had to get to an atmosphere that was at least better than where I was."

Beebe started life in Dallas on a high note by marrying his girlfriend from Shreveport. Ostensibly, they were building a new life together from scratch, and 1986 was a hard year to get started. S&Ls were dropping like flies—that summer Dixon resigned from Vernon, McBirney resigned from Sunbelt, and Barker was indicted—and the atmosphere in North Dallas, where Beebe had an office, was one of deepening gloom. The runaway real estate development craze had resulted in such a glut that shopping centers and condos stood vacant all over town. Dallas had about 38 million square feet of unused office space (equivalent to 17 Empire State Buildings). Dallas reporter Byron Harris said of 1986, "The silence of deals not being made was deafening." Still Beebe somehow always seemed to have money. With his empire in shambles, where was he getting it?

"If you're interested in Beebe, you should be interested in Southmark," a source told us one day. "Have you seen the transcripts of Southmark's casino licensing hearings in Las Vegas? I think you'd find them interesting."

We had found this Dallas-based company in some of our other thrift investigations. Now we were to learn that Southmark had made nearly $30 million in loans to Beebe (and Beebe related companies) *after* his conviction. Altogether, Southmark conducted nearly $90 million in business deals with Beebe. Some of the business was paid for in Southmark stock. The company's 1985 10-K showed that Herman Beebe held nearly 62 percent of Southmark's Series E Preferred stock. (FSLIC later charged that Beebe used some of that stock to pay off a loan he had at Edmund Reggie's Acadia Savings and Loan.)

Southmark was a "Forbes 500" company based in Dallas and run by Gene Phillips, a calculating, tough negotiator, described by competitors as one of the most astute real estate men in the country. He was of medium height and build, sandy-colored hair, not particularly imposing. But he took a hard-nosed, structured approach to deals that awed people on the other side of the negotiating table. Phillips was a chemical engineer who had been bitten by the real estate bug. *BusinessWeek* reported that in 1973, when Phillips was 35, he had dealt his way right into bankruptcy in South Carolina. To pay off his debts he went to work for one of his larger creditors and later bought the company. In 1978 he tried to buy a bank in Georgia, but the comptroller of the currency blocked the purchase because Phillips, he said, had not told the truth on his application. But, true to form, Phillips still made $2 million on a $4 million investment when he sold the bank shares he had bought before his application was denied.

Then in 1979 he and his partner, New York city attorney William Friedman, began to buy up the stock of a defunct Dallas real estate investment trust. By 1981 they had acquired control, and five years and about 35 acquisitions later, they had built Southmark into a publicly traded financial services company with 27,000 employees (including subsidiaries) and nearly $10 billion in assets. Southmark's extraordinary increase in assets attracted a lot of attention, and Phillips's eagerness to take unorthodox risks raised eyebrows. *Forbes* magazine said he and Friedman ran Southmark more like their own private investment company than a big public corporation. For example, when one of Phillips's own companies was called upon to repay a construction loan, Phillips sold the company to Southmark and let Southmark repay the loan. The deal cost Southmark $9.5 million. Pressed to explain Southmark's willingness to take on the debt, a Southmark officer told reporters the venture "looked like an attractive project."

After thrifts were deregulated, Phillips hurriedly searched for one to finance his acquisitions. In 1983 Southmark acquired San Jacinto Savings, and for three years the S&L was under Phillips's control. But in 1986 worried regulators ordered the S&L to stop funding Southmark's purchases, and Phillips had to rely on another favored way to raise cash. That year he raised $950 million through Drexel Burnham Lambert. In fact, much of Southmark's explosion in assets, according to SEC filings, was financed by junk bonds marketed for Phillips by his close friend Michael Milken, Drexel Burnham Lambert's junk bond king. (*Forbes* reported Drexel Burnham made well over $50 million in fees by financing Southmark and its subsidiaries.) When Phillips borrowed money,[3] he took more than he needed and used the extra to invest in other companies' junk bonds being marketed by Milken—a common practice of many of Drexel Burnham's favorite customers. (The practice bore a disturbing resemblance to the cash-for-trash deals, where a thrift borrower was required to take more money than he wanted and to use the excess to buy a piece of junk property from the thrift. One year, *The Wall Street Journal* reported, Drexel raised $450 million for Southmark, and Phillips used *all* of it to buy other junk bonds Drexel was promoting.)[4] Southmark became the largest real estate-based conglomerate financed by Milken.[5] It may also have been one of the most complex. Even seasoned Wall Street analysts admitted to reporters they couldn't figure out the company's maze and layers of debt. What they did know, however, was that Southmark had a lot of debt coming due all at once in the early 1990s.

That outstanding debt didn't seem to phase Phillips. Records showed that Southmark paid him over $1 million in 1988. He and his wife owned a $1 million condominium on Wilshire Boulevard in Los Angeles and a $10 million estate in Dallas (previously owned by Lamar Hunt and, then, James Ling). He traveled in a $3.5 million DC-9 that used to belong to singer Kenny Rogers.

Perhaps it was his hunger for cash that sent Southmark to the gaming tables, a move that unwittingly exposed the company's close ties to Herman Beebe. Whatever the reason, the afternoon of November 5, 1986, found Phillips, Friedman, and their attorney sitting at attention before the Nevada Gaming Control Board. The commission's job was to make sure no one with criminal associations or backgrounds got a casino license. Southmark owned the land where the Silver City Casino in Las Vegas was located and had worked out an agreement with the owners of the casino that Southmark could collect a percentage of the casino's gambling revenues if the gaming control board approved.

But from the opening of the session it became clear that what the gaming control board wanted to talk about was Herman Beebe. As soon as the board had dispensed with preliminaries, one member got to the point:

"Mr. Phillips, could you please describe first of all how the relationship, business relationship or otherwise, with Mr. Beebe came about occurring? Secondly, how it's evolved and, if you would, what the current relationship with Mr. Beebe is?"

Phillips said that in 1984, shortly before Beebe was indicted, he and Beebe had reached an agreement for Southmark to purchase Beebe's nursing homes for almost $100 million. Beebe owned 62 nursing homes in five states with over 6,500 beds.

Then, Phillips said, before they could close the deal Beebe "ran into severe financial difficulties" (a euphemism for Beebe's indictment and the resulting fallout) and Southmark, Phillips contended, had to loan him money to keep him afloat. Otherwise, Phillips said, Beebe might have gone into receivership and the contract between Phillips and Beebe would have been voided. Phillips assured the gaming control board that Southmark would have had nothing to do with Beebe after his indictment had it not been for Phillips's desire to consummate the purchase of the nursing homes.

"Obviously," said Phillips, "Mr. Beebe would not be the appropriate or suitable type of individual to have an ongoing relationship with."

But, the commission member persisted, ". . . you loaned Mr. Beebe an additional $29.6 million in a total of five other loans and made three other purchases from Mr. Beebe, all *after* the date of his conviction." He enumerated the transactions: February, $500,000 loan; April, $14.2 million nursing-home purchase; May, $1 million purchase and $2.3 million loan; June, $1 million loan; August, $25.5 million loan; and December ("almost a year after his conviction on fraud and wire fraud and other charges"), a $7 million purchase of Beebe's Savings Life Insurance Company.

"Now, that adds up to $29.6 million[6] in loans after the man was convicted," the commission member concluded. Then he got to the crux of the commission's concern. "Mr. Beebe . . . had a $700,000[7] restitution levied [as a result of his 1985 conviction]. Would you know whether Mr. Beebe paid his fine with proceeds of loans from your companies?" and again: "It appears that [Southmark's loans to Beebe] were for the benefit of Mr. Beebe, to keep his head above water, in a business sense, so that he could continue operating even after he had been convicted of federal charges."

Phillips and Friedman stood their ground.[8] They readily admitted that for a time they were propping Beebe up. They said they even tried to get control of Bossier Bank & Trust. But all of those transactions were part of the original nursing-home purchase agreement, made before Beebe was indicted, or were attempts to keep him in business until they could conclude the deal. And all the loans they made to Beebe, they said, had been repaid with the exception of $1 million.

Phillips's explanations evidently satisfied the gaming control board, and after a lengthy discussion of other topics, such as Phillips's 1973 bankruptcy, the board approved Southmark's request. And there our interest in Southmark might have ended, except for the fact that the company had shown up in some of our earlier investigations. We went back to our files and began compiling a list of Southmark's appearances. Time and time again the company had turned up at the *end* of our investigation of a failed thrift. Southmark would appear, most often, in the role of scavenger, acquiring the troubled assets of those who had contributed to the failure of the institution. We had found, for example, Southmark or a Southmark subsidiary acquiring assets formerly owned by Mario Renda, Robert Ferrante, Morris Shenker, John B Anderson, and Tom Nevis. Now many of these deals were further confirmed by Phillips's testimony before the gaming control board:

Southmark's Pratt Hotel division acquired the Palace Hotel and Casino project in Puerto Rico, which investigators told us was being developed by Mario Renda and Robert Ferrante until their empires crumbled; Southmark bought the Double Diamond A. Ranch near Reno that had belonged to Tom Nevis;[9] Southmark bought some of Morris Shenker's stock in the Dunes Hotel and Casino when Shenker and John Anderson fell on hard times and tried to buy control of the casino but lost out to a Japanese group; Southmark tried to buy Eureka Federal Savings' liens against Anderson secured by his Maxim Hotel and Casino; Southmark tried to fund the purchase of the Aladdin Hotel and Casino by Harry Wood, a Shreveport native who ran the Dunes's junket operations;[10] Southmark's S&L subsidiary, San Jacinto Savings, got media attention when it tried to buy troubled Continental Savings in Houston (Beebe had bankrolled Carroll Kelly and David Wylie in their purchase of Continental).[11] And, finally, we discovered on a 1988 trip to Shreveport that Southmark now owned the AMI Tower.

Then there were the "coincidences." For example, Southmark's 10-K showed Southmark owned 37 percent of Pratt Hotel Corporation,[12] and in 1986 Pratt was trying to buy Resorts International (which had opened Atlantic City's first casino and which was building the $525 million Taj Mahal casino hotel there). Funny, we thought. We'd just learned from Cage that Judge Edmund Reggie had been a $10,000-a-month consultant for Resorts International for about a year. When we checked with Reggie, he said the two events were unrelated.

Then we found Southmark's fingerprints at Silverado Savings and Loan in Denver.[13] Neil Bush, son of then Vice President George Bush, became director on Silverado's board in 1985 but resigned just days after his father was nominated in 1988 as the Republican candidate for president and just three months before Silverado was forced by regulators to establish nearly $200 million in loan loss reserves to cushion the thrift from expected losses on shaky deals. Neil Bush said he resigned for personal reasons. Others said his resignation was to spare his father the embarrassment of Silverado Savings' condition. (Silverado collapsed in late 1988.) After all, one of George Bush's jobs as vice president during Ronald Reagan's first term had been to chair the Bush Task Group on Regulation of Financial Services. (The group was part of Ronald Reagan's deregulation apparatus. It died a quiet death in August 1983 after accomplishing very little.)[14]

After we had collected all of this information about Southmark, we asked ourselves what it meant, that Southmark, a giant corporation, had turned up in investigations that we had thought at the outset were entirely unrelated. A disturbingly large number of our trails led to Southmark in one way or another. The company appeared to be a major player in the network of people we had been tracking—often there to pick up the pieces whenever one of our thrift pirates hit rough water. Apparently someone else was wondering as well. When the Dallas *Times Herald* printed the list of the 400 individuals whose records were subpoenaed by the Justice Department's fraud task force in 1987, Gene

Phillips was among them. Southmark itself began to show up on the business pages of daily newspapers, as Phillips and Friedman were increasingly forced to deny that Southmark was in deep trouble. Its Houston thrift, San Jacinto, was put under a supervisory order in 1988 and forced to take almost $140 million in write-downs. Regulators forced Southmark to remove two of its three directors from San Jacinto's board, and in early 1989, under pressure from Southmark investors and directors, Phillips and Friedman resigned from their positions at Southmark.

The Southmark puzzle was one of those black holes into which a reporter could disappear and never be heard from again. One normally reliable source even told us he had phone records showing that a real estate broker who had close dealings with both Southmark and Carlos Marcello had also made phone calls to Major General John Singlaub, of Contra-gate fame. We were intrigued, but we had a deadline to meet and we had to leave the further unraveling of Southmark for later. But we had discovered a powerful player in the thrift game and we had learned who it was that had kept Beebe afloat after Cage convicted him. Thanks to associates like Southmark, Beebe was not ever likely to be down and out.

CHAPTER TWENTY-ONE

Round Three

After Herman Beebe's 1985 conviction he was assigned five years probation and ordered to perform 200 hours of community service in Dallas. In early 1987 he was performing that community service at the Dallas Life Foundation, a shelter for the homeless. He was also selling employee benefit packages out of his office in a new North Dallas complex near the Addison Municipal Airport, and he claimed he was making $5,000-a-month payments toward the $1 million restitution the court had ordered. He divided his week between Dallas and his California retreat at La Costa, hardly the life-style of a so-called ruined man.

Joe Cage's long arm soon served Beebe with a subpoena, and in February 1987 Beebe was grilled for six hours in front of the Louisiana grand jury that was still investigating his affairs. Shortly thereafter he agreed to an interview with Shreveport reporter Linda Farrar, who had covered his 1984 indictment and trial. She traveled to Dallas for the interview.

This second grand jury, he said, was also going to indict him. "I asked them [the jury], 'Just what do you want from me? I need to pay the people I owe . . . just what are you seeking? I'm not a liar. If I did something, if you'll ask me, I'll tell you.' "

He said to Farrar, "If you give me the money that's been spent on [investigating] me, I can put you, your mother, President Reagan, and everybody else in jail."

With a rueful smile he denied again the old allegations of Mafia ties and casino skimming: ". . . try to find where I've ever been in the Mafia, where I've been in drugs, where I've done anything unethical in business. If I really had, after ten years, somebody would find something really highly criminal.

"Given a little time to be left alone, I can pay off my debt because I'm smart enough to do that. . . . I need the government to leave me alone so I can put my life back together. I'm a good businessman, I work hard, and I'm smart enough. If they'll leave me alone, I'll be right back on top after two or three years."

That was exactly what worried Joe Cage, exactly what drove him in his dogged pursuit. The second Beebe grand jury had been in session almost two years, meeting week after week, examining mountains of tedious evidence. And then Cage got a real break. Late one winter evening, a Friday night after work, Cage was sitting on the floor in his office studying documents and he came upon a smoking gun that would become known as the Bussell notes. Beebe had been claiming that he was just another victim of the scam Cage was investigating, but these notes, written by his associate David Bussell,[1] appeared to prove otherwise. The notes consisted of a list of figures with dates and notations like "we owe half of this because we own one-half of the farm," and Cage believed they proved Beebe had been a full partner in the deal. "They were handwritten notes of a defendant, an admission of what we were trying to prove," Cage told us later. He could hardly believe his eyes.

In the spring of 1987 Cage's grand jury indicted Beebe and charged him with fraud involving $30 million in loans from over 16 financial institutions spread from Colorado to New Orleans.[2] The loans had been made in 1983 and 1984—during the *very time* the grand jury had been investigating Beebe the first time—to Richard Wolfe, who was also indicted. (Charges against Wolfe were later dismissed.) The indictment charged that Beebe arranged for Wolfe to get loans from institutions where Beebe had "influence" (including Continental, Ponchartrain, Vernon, Key, and State/Lubbock savings and loans) without the loan papers reflecting that Beebe got a lot of the money. And this time Cage didn't mince words. The charge, he said, was *bank robbery*.

Beebe later explained that Ben Barnes had introduced him to Richard Wolfe 10 or 12 years earlier, and a few years later he had run into Wolfe again at Vernon Savings. They decided to do some business together.[3] Richard Wolfe and his Dallas attorney, David Wise, were hip-deep in Beebe's bank network. Wise himself chartered at least five banks that the comptroller's report identified as Beebe banks.

One of the companies named in the 1987 indictment against Beebe and Wolfe was League, Inc. We thought there was something familiar about that name. We checked with Cage and, sure enough, at one time a Southern California developer, G. Wayne Reeder, had discussed becoming a partner in League, Inc. We looked in our files and found a League, Inc., document with Reeder's signature on it, right next to Beebe's. In fact, said Beebe's former right-hand man Dale Anderson, Beebe and Reeder had tried to do several deals together. "Herman must have run into Reeder while staying down at La Costa," Anderson said. (Both men had homes at La Costa.) We had run into Reeder often ourselves, beginning months earlier during our investigation of San Marino Savings in San Marino, California. (San Marino, one of the first thrifts where we ran into Mario Renda, failed in late 1984.) Reeder was a multimillionaire said to have holdings in 16 states, and the Justice Department confirmed that by mid-1989 he was under FBI investigation in Tennessee, Rhode Island, Arizona, Texas, California, and Florida in connection with a number of his business deals in those states (no charges had been filed as of this writing). Once again a trail we had been following had unexpectedly wound up at Beebe's door.[4]

The walls were closing in on Beebe and his small legion of surrogates. The FSLIC filed a civil suit in June (Beebe was mentioned but not sued) and claimed that in 1982 and 1983 State/Lubbock had loaned $4.5 million to Fred Bayles and others who were straw men for Beebe. Beebe, they said, had actually gotten the money. The comptroller of the currency report listed Fred Bayles as a key member of Beebe's banking consortium. He had bought stock in several banks with Beebe's help, including stock in a bank where Judge Reggie was a director. When Beebe needed it Bayles would have his own institution place deposits at Beebe-controlled banks at a very low interest rate. And then when Bayles got into financial trouble, records showed, AMI absorbed his banks. When asked about his business Bayles replied, "What we are is, we're in the borrowing business." In 1985 Bayles pleaded guilty to bank fraud in Mississippi, and in 1988 he was convicted of bank fraud in New Jersey.

"That old boy," said one acquaintance about Bayles, "could sell the Brooklyn Bridge. He was going to court to get sentenced to five years (for the Mississippi bank fraud), and he spent 20 minutes with the judge and the judge gave him five years probation." He got one year for the New Jersey conviction.

Bayles interested us because we had run across him earlier at North Mississippi Savings and Loan in Oxford, Mississippi, where he was a big borrower. Some law-enforcement officials wondered out loud to us if he had fronted for Beebe there too. The man who owned the S&L, a Dr. Joseph Villard, claimed he had been Beebe's physician when Beebe lived in Alexandria, Louisiana, before he moved to Shreveport. When we talked to Villard he mentioned that San Antonio loan broker John Lapaglia was his friend. In fact, he said, "John might be a second or third cousin to me, just by accident."[5] (In January 1984 North Mississippi's president and owner were indicted for several counts of wire and bank fraud. They pleaded guilty to some of the counts.)

We had originally taken a look at North Mississippi not because Beebe had ties there (in fact, when we first looked at North Mississippi, we had never heard of Herman Beebe) but because Mario Renda's First United Fund was involved in "special deals" there. Now we learned that both Renda and Beebe, or their associates, were working deals out of North Mississippi Savings. Apparently when word traveled the thrift grapevine that an S&L was willing to deal, both Renda and Beebe quickly got the news.

An FBI agent investigating thrift failures in the Sunbelt area said it reminded him of the Depression days when hobos would paint a large "X" on the sides of a barn to tip other hobos that the barn was a friendly spot to curl up for the night. Hundreds of S&Ls must have had big X's scrawled on their backsides.

Beebe continued to try to do business out of his office in North Dallas, but the grand jury indictment in the spring of 1987 and the FSLIC lawsuit filed soon thereafter made it more and more difficult for him to maneuver. And behind it all, in Beebe's mind, was Joe Cage. Cage was ruining him. He was dragging him down. Cage was like a mad dog who wouldn't let go of Beebe's leg. Something had to be done. Beebe decided to hire Gerry Spence.

Spence was a famous millionaire cowboy attorney from Jackson Hole, Wyoming. He had gotten national recognition in 1979 by winning a $10.5 million settlement against the Kerr-McGee Corporation in the Karen Silkwood plutonium-contamination suit. In 1981 he got a huge judgment against *Penthouse* magazine for allegedly libeling Miss Wyoming in a cartoon. He was credited with having mastered a courtroom style that went from the easy manner of a front-porch philosopher to what *Esquire* magazine described as the "fevered pitch of the country preacher in the grip of divine inspiration." Spence said he viewed the courtroom as a place of "blood and death," and in 30 years as a lawyer, he claimed to have seldom lost a case. Beebe decided to hire Spence to represent him in his third round with Cage.

Spence agreed to take Cage on and came out swinging. He filed an 80-page motion with the Louisiana court in the summer of 1987 requesting that Cage be disqualified from prosecuting Beebe's case. In his motion he charged Cage with "prejudicial and vindictive misconduct." He accused Cage of having conducted a personal vendetta against Beebe. He said the whole witch-hunt was politically motivated, that Cage was trying to make a name for himself at Beebe's expense, that Cage showed no sense of justice, fair play, or decency. He told the judge that Cage had harassed Beebe's business associates and had offered Beebe freedom if Beebe would "give [to Cage] the governor and Judge Reggie." Judge Stagg, who had presided over the first two Beebe trials, agreed to hear the motion and for six and a half days Spence raked Cage over the coals before the judge.

Spence was in rare form. A massive man, six feet two and more than 200 pounds, he wore a brown suit and cowboy boots and carried a Stetson into the courtroom on the opening day of the hearing. He had long gray hair that was swept back on the sides in ducktails and hung down over his collar. He stalked the courtroom, hands in his pockets, at times leaning back on his heels, clutching his glasses in his teeth, his demeanor rich with histrionics. Spence called Cage to the witness stand and kept him there over two days.

"Isn't it true that one of the overriding compulsions of your life has been the prosecution of Mr. Beebe?" Spence demanded.

"No, sir," Cage replied.

"Would you grant me that it has been the most important case of your career?" Spence asked.

"Yes, sir, that's true," Cage answered.

"In all the Beebe cases, wouldn't you take all the witnesses that Beebe could use to defend himself and threaten them with prosecution?"

"No, that hasn't been my tactic."

Cage kept his cool. Sometimes he appeared amused, sometimes irritated. But he was polite to the bitter end, answering questions with "Yes, sir," and "No, sir" while steadfastly maintaining that his investigation and prosecution of Beebe had been completely fair.

Spence, on the other hand, couldn't seem to think of an analogy too venal for Cage. He accused him of criminal acts, of conspiring with another attorney to set Beebe up. In one two-hour diatribe Spence began by referring to the "blessed liberty" of constitutional rights and the dangers in abuse of prosecutorial power.

"A prosecutor has the power to destroy human beings," he said. "Like mold on an otherwise scrumptious pie, it has to be removed."

He referred to Cage's behavior as "repulsive" and "patently silly." Cage's occasional "I don't remember" he characterized as "a lie that can't be proven."

He equated Cage and a former Beebe defense attorney who was a friend of Cage's as "twin black holes in space. These people should be called the Euripides twins." As with black holes, "information was sucked in and nobody heard or saw anything after." They were, he said, a "double-headed monster." Beebe, he said, "was hog-dressed. The last hair was scraped off his naked hide" by Cage and his team.

Spence's attack sounded so vile that shocked courtroom spectators turned to whisper to each other. Several times Judge Tom Stagg admonished Spence, sometimes calling him to the podium for consultation. At one point during a particularly thunderous oration by Spence, Stagg pointedly commented that poor hearing wasn't one of his problems.

Spence's charges were more than empty rhetoric or courtroom drama. If the judge had ruled in his favor, there could have been serious career repercussions for Cage. When Spence finally ran out of steam, Cage was livid and began work on a written response to Spence's allegations, which he filed with the court.

"The charge that my professional life has focused on the goal of toppling the Beebe empire is completely ridiculous. I am accused of questioning almost every person who has ever conducted business or been associated with Mr. Beebe. Then I'm accused of failure to seek out material evidence favorable to Mr. Beebe that was readily available to me. If the questioning of almost every person Mr. Beebe has dealt with would not reveal anything favorable to Mr. Beebe, what would? . . . If the investigation and resulting 19-count indictment is considered 'Beebe-hunting,' then so be it."

After taking under consideration Spence's motion to remove Cage from the case, Judge Stagg ruled that Cage's investigations had been fairly done and the case could proceed.

"We have excellent lawyers here," he said. "Both sides are intractable in their belief they are right."

The adversaries met again in the courtroom in the fall of 1987—Spence for the defense, Cage for the prosecution. The trial was again being held in Lafayette, 200 miles south of Shreveport, so Cage and his team were staying in a motel near the Lafayette courthouse. This time Cage knew he had Beebe nailed. Along with all the other documentation and evidence he had amassed, he had the Bussell notes, which were an admission of guilt in the handwriting of one of Beebe's close associates.

The trial proceeded as Cage had expected until the day before the case was to go to the jury. In a surprise move Judge Stagg decided in favor of a defense motion that Cage not be allowed to refer to the Bussell notes in his closing arguments. Cage was devastated. The Bussell notes were the key to his case. He had intended to hammer them home to the jury the next day in his closing arguments. In a moment of frustration he told a Texas reporter that "the judge has sabotaged my case."

The next morning Cage did not show up in the courtroom. His assistant appeared to handle the case. Word spread quickly that Cage had disappeared. Rumors ran wild. Where was he? What had happened? After all these years, the thousands of hours, where was he?

The jury deliberated two days and on the third day sent word that they were unable to reach a verdict. Judge Stagg declared a mistrial. Cage, who had been monitoring the progress of the trial from the motel, saw years of work slip away into nothingness. He couldn't understand why Judge Stagg had made the ruling about the Bussell notes. But he knew why he had refused to go back into the courtroom. It was a matter of principle with him. Even though he knew Judge Stagg would hold him in contempt of court and could even put him in jail, even though he knew he could very well be fired, the Beebe case was too important not to register his protest in the strongest possible manner. He and Blount believed they knew the extent to which Beebe's scams threatened the financial fabric of Louisiana and surrounding states. They also believed they knew how deep within the political power structure Beebe's influence ran. They had successfully prosecuted Beebe once, and they wanted a second felony conviction to make sure he wouldn't be able to worm his way back into action. They had put everything they had into a thorough prosecution of the case.

A sober prosecution team headed back to Shreveport. Judge Stagg found Cage in contempt of court and a panel of judges reprimanded Cage for abandoning the Beebe case to his assistant. But they could have done much worse, and Cage believed their comparatively gentle treatment of him also sent a message to Stagg, who removed himself from further involvement in the case. The ball was once again in Cage's court. Should he go for a retrial? Plenty of people told him he should drop the case, but he decided to go for it. One more time. You could have almost heard Beebe's sigh of despair. Stagg was gone and Cage was back.

Beebe's fourth trial was set for May 31, 1988. But this time Cage had company. The U.S. attorney in Texas had indicted Beebe on charges stemming from Cage's investigation, including a $4.4 million loan Beebe had gotten from State Savings/Lubbock. The one-two punch was too much for Beebe. And with Judge Stagg out of the case, who knew what the new judge would be like?

In March, Beebe told the Shreveport *Times* he'd done nothing wrong and "this is a bunch of bull." But on April 29 he threw in the towel and cut a deal. . . . He agreed to plead guilty to two counts of bank fraud and he agreed to cooperate with the ongoing criminal investigations into fraud at banks and S&Ls in Texas and Louisiana. In return the government agreed not to prosecute him for any other fraud then under investigation in northern Texas (which excluded large parts of Texas) or western Louisiana. Beebe's lawyer said Beebe pleaded guilty because he was out of money and wanted to put six years of litigation and harassment behind him.

At his sentencing, before a Louisiana judge, Beebe sat in silence while the three lawyers representing him—former Louisiana Governor David Treen, former Shreveport U.S. Attorney J. Ransdell Keene, and Jim Adams—argued vigorously that Beebe should not have to serve any time in prison. Cage was also mysteriously silent, not challenging Beebe's attorney and not demanding that Beebe do some time. As a result U.S. District Judge John M. Shaw, who could have sentenced Beebe to ten years in prison, gave him instead only a year and a day. Later Shaw said Cage had not asked for any jail time for Beebe, but "I just felt he had to see the inside of a jail."

When word got out that Beebe would spend, at the most, a year in prison, Cage was widely criticized for devoting so much time to the Beebe pursuit and then not fighting for a stiffer sentence. In response Cage said Beebe had agreed in the plea bargain to give "complete, truthful, and accurate information and testimony," and Cage expected him to cooperate in the prosecution of other bank frauds that he hoped would land bigger fish. If he didn't, Cage said he and the Texas prosecutor could drop the plea bargain and prosecute Beebe.

Besides, Beebe now had three felony convictions (the 1985 conviction and the two included in the 1987 plea bargain) and that ought to be sufficient to keep him out of the banking business.

Bigger fish? What bigger fish? Bigger than Beebe? Carlos Marcello was already in prison. Who was left that was bigger than Beebe?

Cage had turned his sights on Judge Edmund Reggie. He had begun to dig into financial transactions at Judge Reggie's Acadia Savings and Loan in Crowley, Louisiana. Though Cage would not discuss his investigation, which was still in progress when we went to press, the FSLIC filed a civil suit in August 1988 against Reggie and other officers and directors of the thrift (citing 20 loan transactions, involving over $40 million, that regulators alleged caused the collapse of Acadia in August 1987) and in that suit we could see the direction Cage's case might be taking.[6]

Between 1982 and 1986 Acadia Savings had, according to regulators, made several loans that benefited Beebe and Judge Reggie. (Our favorite was the loan that went to bail Reggie family members out of the Daddy's Money Condominiums.) But even more interesting, regulators said that in June 1985 the Acadia Savings board had loaned Gilbert Beall (of Texas and Florida) and Frederick Mascolo (of Connecticut) each $2.95 million. The collateral for the loans was 106 acres in an area in the Pennsylvania Poconos where gambling was under consideration.

The Poconos property rang a bell with us, and we located it in our Aurora Bank file. Documents in our file showed that Beall and Mascolo had acquired the property from Anthony Delvecchio and Jilly Rizzo, whom we had met at Flushing Federal working with mob stockbroker Mike Rapp. Aurora Bank in Denver had been busted out in 1984 and 1985 by John Napoli, Jr.'s racketeering scheme. The FDIC sued Rizzo and Delvecchio (and others) in the case,[7] alleging that Rizzo and Delvecchio tried to hide their Aurora Bank take from the FDIC by laundering it through the Poconos property. When Rizzo and Delvecchio sold the property to Beall and Mascolo, regulators in Colorado and Pennsylvania filed lawsuits claiming that the sale was a sham attempt to keep the FDIC from confiscating the 106 acres.[8]

Even more troubling to Cage, however, was what Beall and Mascolo allegedly did with the $2.95 million they each borrowed—and never repaid—from Acadia Savings. Regulators alleged they spent only about $700,000 on the Poconos property. The rest, they said, was divided up:

Beall and Mascolo allegedly bought $2 million worth of stock in Louisiana Bank & Trust of Crowley, where Reggie was also a stockholder and was chairman of the board. The bank was about to collapse, regulators said, and they saw this move as a way for Reggie to recapitalize his troubled bank.

They loaned another $490,000 of the money to a Reggie partnership, which secured the loan with an IOU from Beebe's AMI, the FSLIC alleged.

And they bought $1 million worth of stock in a company controlled by themselves in partnership with Mike Rapp's associate Lionel J. Reifler,[9] who was also said to be involved in the plans to develop gambling on the Poconos property. Reportedly they also paid Reifler another $500,000 that Mascolo owed him.

Regulators alleged that Acadia Savings had made another such loan. In May 1985 Acadia loaned $1.8 million to a company to buy 154 St. Tropez tanning beds, but they said much of the money really went to Reifler, Mascolo, and Beall. When regulators tried to file a claim with the company that bonded the loan, it turned out to be an offshore company in the Grand Cayman Islands and it didn't have enough money to pay the claim.

Cage had been untangling these relationships at the very time that Beebe's high-powered attorney, Gerry Spence, had attacked him personally in open court and asked the judge to remove Cage from the Beebe case. At that time Cage had retired from the field of battle and prepared a blistering written rebuttal that not only attacked Beebe but laid out Beebe's relationship with Reggie in damning detail. We obtained a copy of the extraordinary affidavit, which Cage had filed with the court.

In the affidavit Cage tore into Beebe, Governor Edwards, Judge Reggie and their relationship to each other. He was worried, he said, about their plans to bring casino gambling to Louisiana[10] and he was worried about what he called "the Reggie connection with organized crime, Mafia, or La Cosa Nostra figures."[11]

Cage told in his affidavit about the Acadia Savings loans that he said indirectly benefited Reifler. He said that Reggie's Louisiana Bank & Trust of Crowley in 1985 had made $1.5 million in loans (secured by worthless annuities) that "benefited Reifler and Reggie." He quoted the Woodie Guthrie line—which was the source for the title of Jonathan Kwitny's book, *The Fountain Pen Conspiracy*—to point out that Reifler appeared in Kwitny's book[12] as an associate of Edward Wuensche, one of the nation's leading dealers in stolen securities who worked with Reifler at the same time that he (Wuensche) was deeply involved with the New Jersey mob.[13]

In his affidavit Cage pleaded with the court to understand that he was not some obsessed prosecutor:

"[My] motivation was and is not political but one of grave concern for the stability of the financial institutions in the Western District of Louisiana. The appearance of organized crime in the Western District of Louisiana, likewise, causes [me] a great deal of concern. The indicia of organized crime is truly frightening and worthy of the most relentless pursuits by those in law enforcement."

The Cage affidavit infuriated Judge Reggie. He told coauthor Mary Fricker that he believed Cage was pursuing him for political reasons (Cage was a Republican appointee). "The Cage affidavit is absolutely a lie. That affidavit did more to damage me than anything in my lifetime. . . . He [Cage] has made me a target of his investigation for nearly seven years. . . . If he thought I had connections with the Mafia, where was his evidence?" Reggie said he met Reifler through Beall, who had been an attorney with Fulbright and Jaworski in Houston. All of the Beall loans were approved in advance by state regulators, he said, and, anyway, by that time he was no longer active in the thrift's affairs.

In regard to the FSLIC civil suit, Reggie told us he had never benefited improperly from any of the S&L's transactions. "I never drew a single expense account. I never charged them a nickle. Never charged them a legal fee.[14] Because we loved the savings and loan. I bet not another law firm in America can say that. That's why my feelings are just crushed. . . . I loved Acadia Savings and Loan."

"Yeah, he loved it to death," one Reggie critic quipped.

Cage agreed. In May 1989 the grand jury indicted Reggie for bank fraud. A week earlier Beall and Reifler had pleaded guilty to violating banking laws and were said to be cooperating with Cage's investigation. Just five months earlier the SEC had charged the two men with fraud in connection with a Boca Raton, Florida, penny stock scam. Both the Acadia Savings and the SEC cases were pending as of this writing. Whatever the outcome, Acadia Savings had clearly been victimized by the hit-and-run gang of swindlers we knew very well.

In July 1988 Herman Beebe finally went to prison, courtesy of Cage and Blount. But his sentence was only one year and a day. We well remembered his words to reporter Linda Farrar, "I'll be right back on top after two or three years," and we didn't doubt it for a minute. Beebe had opened a window for us into the world of banking as it was done "down home" in Texas and Louisiana. The mob was active there, but in addition there was a good-ole-boy "mob" that had been fleecing financial institutions as a matter of birthright for generations. A group of Arkansas-Louisiana-Texas businessmen with the most powerful political connections had been using financial institutions for their own purposes for years. Fiduciary duty meant little to them. They ran their banks the same way they would have run their cattle ranches. They walked the thinnest possible line between legal and illegal, and some of them regularly crossed that line.

The occasional attempts to blow the whistle on the ring went nowhere. Regulators, prosecutors, and reporters came and went, but the Southern power structure remained.

The wholesale looting that occurred in the thrift industry in Texas and Louisiana (and later spread to surrounding states) in the 1980s would not have been possible in an environment that unambiguously condemned such behavior. Texas and Louisiana, in particular, lacked such an ethic. In fact, when it came to changing management at a bank or thrift, the attitude was perhaps best characterized by what a voter said when Edwin Edwards was finally defeated as governor. Asked if he felt the new governor and his people might be more honest, he replied, "No, it's just turning the fat hogs out and letting the lean hogs in." So it was with Texas and Louisiana banks and thrifts. The U.S. taxpayer will pay a high price for that erosion of ethical business standards—an erosion facilitated and exacerbated by deregulation of the thrift industry, which sent the wrong message to the wrong people.

CHAPTER TWENTY-TWO

A Thumb in the Dike

The last three years had been very difficult for Ed Gray. When he took the job of Federal Home Loan Bank Board chairman on May 1, 1983, he was the darling of the thrift industry's chief lobbying group, the U.S. League of Savings Institutions, and a Reagan administration insider. Eighteen months later it would have been hard to find anyone to say a nice word about him. The U.S. League worked overtime to lobby against his proposed regulations, and forces high in the administration worked for his ouster—all because of Gray's attempt to stem the avalanche of thrift failures by putting a lock on brokered deposits and by limiting a thrift's direct investments and rapid growth. In an administration where any form of deregulation was applauded, Gray had become an outcast, "the great re-regulator."

Ed Gray could not have been prepared for this fire storm. No FHLBB chairman in the entire 50-year history of the post had been faced with the kind of crisis Gray faced. The job had always been an easy one, with clearly defined responsibilities, chief among them being to do the thrift industry's bidding. The chairman was expected to serve out his relatively low-paying post ($79,000 a year), after which he would be rewarded with a well-paying thrift industry position. But these were not ordinary times. The seeds of the thrift crisis had been planted nearly three years before Gray arrived, but it was Ed Gray who faced the bitter harvest.

Texas thrifts had reacted most violently to Gray's restrictive regulations. A "get Gray" movement began to take form in Texas, spearheaded by Texas thrift lobbyist Durward Curlee and loan broker and Republican activist John Lapaglia. Lapaglia, whom we had originally encountered brokering loans for Norman B. Jenson and Philip Schwab, owned Falcon Financial in San Antonio. He fired the opening salvo with a full-page ad attacking Gray's new regulations.[1] The ad was entitled "An Open Letter to the Congress of the United States." It ran in the Dallas *Morning News* during the Republican National Convention in August 1984. Lapaglia followed up by stalking the halls of the convention handing out copies of his weekly newsletter, *Falcon Newsletter*, to attendees. The newsletter became a weekly denunciation of Ed Gray and his policies. Lapaglia told us he mailed the letter to 380 Southwestern thrift executives.

In September Lapaglia shot off a letter to President Reagan. He complained bitterly that Ed Gray's policies were strangling the Texas thrift industry, which had been doing just fine before Gray began to interfere. He begged the president to do something about Gray. But he also knew an election approached, and he let the president know that if Reagan didn't fire Gray right away, he would understand:

> We are very mindful of our obligations to not raise sensitive issues until November; accordingly, I shall personally take no action that would not be beneficial to the Administration. After that time I expect to lead an industry-wide effort, which at this moment consists of fifty-five savings institutions, in bringing a class-action suit against Chairman Edwin J. Grey [sic] and the FHLBB.

Lapaglia kept his word and waited until after the November elections before acting. Then in December, he told us, he organized a trip to Washington, D.C. He was accompanied by thrift attorney Robert Posen,[2] John Mmahat, who was CEO of Gulf Federal Savings of Louisiana, and singer Wayne Newton, whom Lapaglia said was "having some problems with millions in loans he had on a resort in the Poconos."[3] Also attending the Washington meeting were Texas thrift lobbyist Durward Curlee[4] and Frank Fahrenkopf, Jr., chairman of the Republican National Committee. They met with Danny Wall in the offices of the Senate Banking Committee, which was chaired by Senator Jake Garn. Wall was Garn's chief administrative aide. (In 1987 Wall would succeed Ed Gray as chairman of the FHLBB.) Posen, who led the meeting, protested to Wall that Gray's new policies were too extreme and they would strangle the industry. Wall listened but did not respond.

Suddenly the secretary stuck her head in the room. "Mr. Newton, the First Lady is on the phone for you." (Newton was a close friend of the Reagans.)

Newton left the room to take Nancy Reagan's call. When he returned the meeting resumed. A few minutes later the secretary knocked. "Mr. Newton, the phone again. It's the president."

Newton left the room again, returning a few minutes later to summon Fahrenkopf. "The president wants to talk to you now, Frank," he told Fahrenkopf.

When Fahrenkopf returned from talking to the president, he called the meeting to a close, telling the others that he would look into the matter. According to Lapaglia, President Reagan had asked Fahrenkopf to rein in FHLBB chairman Ed Gray. Mmahat later described the meeting in a manuscript he commissioned entitled "To Kill An Eagle." He summed up the outcome of the meeting: "It later became clear that Gray's friend, supporter and sponsor, Attorney General Edwin Meese, prevailed over any influence that Wayne Newton and the Chairman of the Republican National Committee had with the President of the United States. As a result of that support, Edward Gray continued on his course of conduct which, it is now clear, aggravated the present crisis."

Like so many who villified Gray, Mmahat exaggerated Gray's involvement in day-to-day details. As extraordinary as this meeting and conversations with the president were, Gray later told us he was unaware the meeting even occurred and denied Fahrenkopf ever put any pressure on him about FHLBB policies in Texas. He did tell us, though, that at about that time he began giving Fahrenkopf regular briefings on his actions in Texas because he felt that Fahrenkopf had the president's ear.

"I'd been told by a high White House staffer to stay away from the White House," Gray told us. "He told me that if I made an appointment with the president, Don Regan would bad-mouth me before I got there, sit in on the meeting, and bad-mouth me after I left." So, Gray said, he hoped he could get his messages to Reagan through Fahrenkopf.

The appearance of Frank Fahrenkopf at that meeting was puzzling. What stake could the Republican National Committee have in all this? Maybe Fahrenkopf was responding to Lapaglia's warning that Gray's actions could cost the party the support of the thrift industry. But we learned that he also may have had a business relationship to protect. According to the Colorado Springs *Gazette Telegraph*, Fahrenkopf and Newton—for whom Fahrenkopf sometimes performed legal services[5]—were at that time involved in a complex transaction with the holding company of United Savings Bank (a thrift) in Wyoming. Fahrenkopf was borrowing $100,000 and Newton $200,000 to invest in an RV park in Bullhead City, Arizona, not far from Las Vegas.[6] The RV investment was being orchestrated by a Las Vegas loan broker, John Keilly, who had shown up in our Centennial investigation—he had introduced Norman Jenson to Sid Shah. (In the 1970s Keilly did 27 months in prison for bribery in connection with a $1.25 million loan from a Teamsters Union pension fund, according to published reports.) Another investor in the Bullhead City RV park was John Pilkington, described to us by a Nevada Gaming Control Board investigator as a longtime associate of Morris Shenker.

So Newton had at least two reasons to support thrift deregulation: one in the Poconos and one with partner Fahrenkopf in Bullhead City, and Fahrenkopf may also have had his own investments in mind at the Washington meeting with Wall.

· · ·

Gray was still struggling at that time to get a sense of just how big a problem he had on his hands. His examiners in the field were giving him one story—that the situation was bad and getting worse—while industry "experts" were saying that the problems were temporary, caused by the recession, and were nothing to worry about. Gray received a letter from respected economist Alan Greenspan (later to be appointed Chairman of the Federal Reserve Board) telling him he should stop worrying so much. Greenspan wrote that deregulation was working just as planned, and he named 17 thrifts that had reported record profits and were prospering under the new rules. Greenspan wrote the letter while he was a paid consultant for Lincoln Savings and Loan of Irvine, California, owned by a Charles Keating, Jr., company.[7] Four years after Greenspan wrote the letter to Gray, 15 of the 17 thrifts he'd cited would be out of business and would cost the FSLIC $3 billion in losses.

Gray's regulation limiting direct investments and growth had finally taken effect in mid-March 1985 and a lot of thrifts did not measure up. Centennial Savings, Vernon Savings, Flushing Federal—the list ran into the hundreds. The U.S. League had opposed the new regulation fiercely before it was adopted by the Bank Board, but they suddenly changed sides when they saw Gray had Senator William Proxmire, the powerful Senate Banking Committee chairman, on his side. Also, the growing number of thrift failures had begun to scare the League. It was becoming clear that accommodating the bad-boy S&Ls was eventually going to cost the other thrifts billions. In fact, they realized, if the carnage were really severe, it could lead to public pressure to re-regulate the entire industry.

But in Congress the old adage that money was the mother's milk of politics held true. Following deregulation the thrifts became the cows, and there were certain congressmen who never missed a milking. Go-go thrift operators had plenty of money, and they were sharing it with their friends in Washington. We'd already seen that Congressman Tony Coelho (D-Calif.) had nuzzled right up to Don Dixon at Vernon; Congressman Doug Bosco (D-Calif.) had Erv Hansen at Centennial; and Speaker Jim Wright (D-Tx.) had Tom Gaubert at Independent American in Dallas. Now we learned that Charles Keating, Jr., his employees, business associates, friends, and family had donated $220,000 to Arizona politicians, $85,000 to California worthies, $34,000 to Ohioans, and more—$440,000 in all.

While Keating and his associates were giving politicians money, Ed Gray was giving them only headaches. No sooner had Gray's direct investment regulation gone into effect than 220 members of the House of Representatives had signed a resolution asking the Bank Board to delay the implementation of the new rule. Congressional hearings were scheduled for late March 1985:

Representative Frank Annunzio (D-Ill.) looked down the long table at Gray,

U.S. League President Bill O'Connell, and others who had come to testify in favor of the direct investment regulation.

"We ask that the agency postpone the effective date of this rule," Annunzio boomed.

"That's impossible, Congressman," Gray said he replied. "It's been in effect since March 18."

Annunzio countered, "The Bank Board is acting too hurriedly in putting the regulation into existence. It could well be the beginning of the end to the dual banking system in this country."[8]

Gray reminded the congressman, "It's the FSLIC, not the states, that has to pick up the tab for thrift failures, Congressman."

Annunzio was unswayed and again demanded that Gray delay applying the new regulation.

"Mr. Annunzio"—Gray bristled—"if it is rescinded or postponed, losses . . . will fall squarely on the shoulders of the Congress itself. We cannot delay implementation."

Gray said Annunzio flushed with anger, took a deep breath, glared down the table, and then stormed out of the hearing room in protest. With Annunzio gone, Representative St Germain, chairman of the House Banking Committee, finally came to Gray's aid. He said he agreed with the Bank Board's new regulation, adding, at long last, that he had little sympathy for thrifts that asked for concessions.

"They can just go jump in a lake," St Germain said as he gaveled the hearing to a close.

Everyone knew the fight couldn't be over. There were too many shaky thrifts across the country that would not be able to survive under Gray's new rules. If they had to dispose of some of their direct investments, which they were carrying on their books at inflated prices, their houses of cards would tumble because they would have to take large losses. Still, the regulation went into effect and FHLBB examiners across the country began measuring thrifts by the new yardstick. Then Gray had to turn his attention to another old problem. There weren't enough examiners. Gray needed more eyes and ears in the field if he was to enforce his new regulation. He had 3,200 thrifts (handling a trillion dollars in deposits)[9] but his examination staff numbered only 679. That was about one examiner for every four and a half thrifts. Some institutions had gone over two years without an examination. Gray figured he needed to double his examination staff, at least, if he was to effectively enforce his new regulation—or any of the old ones for that matter.

Gray picked up the phone and called Dave Stockman at the Office of Management and Budget. Stockman held the purse strings and would have to approve any increase in staff at the Bank Board.[10] But Stockman had no interest in helping Gray, who a year earlier had humiliated him by shooting the FCA job out from under him, and Gray had to meet with his assistant, Connie Horner. Horner said she was a busy person, but she said she could squeeze him in over lunch at the White House.

As Gray walked through the iron gates of the White House on the way to the executive lunchroom, he reflected that the root of the thrift problem was the "high fliers," as he liked to call them—the wild and crazy guys like Dixon, McBirney, and Hansen. Gray had made his high-fliers speech many times, and that day he planned to tell Horner again that high fliers were using brokered money to engage in risky and complicated investments, many of them fraudulent. To stop the abuses he needed more examiners to ferret the con men out of the system. Gray had butted heads with Horner over staffing before, but he was sure this time she'd see the wisdom of his case.

As they settled in for lunch at the White House senior mess, an oak-paneled dining room where only the cabinet and senior aides to the president were allowed to dine, Gray laid his cards on the table. He wanted to double the examination staff to 1,400. What's more, with a turnover rate exceeding 30 percent, he needed to raise examiners' base pay from an average of $14,000 a year to a level more competitive with private industry examiners. Gray said Horner ate and let Gray talk. She had been through all this with him before. Like the Dickens character in *Oliver Twist*, Horner always responded the same way to Gray's requests for additional staff: "You want *more* examiners??"

She told him it wasn't a matter of money but of philosophy. The administration's philosophy was one of *deregulation*. That meant *fewer* regulators, not more. As Gray listened to her recite the administration mantra, he reflected on her own bloated staff. Each time Horner trooped over to his office for a meeting she dragged with her a staff of eight. They filed in behind her like baby quail behind their mother. He could never understand why she brought them along, since they never seemed to do or say anything.

Gray looked around the lunchroom while Horner lectured, noticing how much the senior mess resembled the interior of a ship. Horner speculated out loud that maybe, just maybe, she could swing 30 more examiners for him if Gray would be more cooperative and get back into step with the administration. Gray said Horner also issued a thinly veiled warning, reminding Gray of his expense-account troubles. She even suggested he could go to jail if his overages proved to be a violation of something called the "Anti-Deficiency Act," which mandated how much the Bank Board could spend. Gray was already over that amount, she claimed, way over it. Gray said there must be some mistake and he'd clear it up. (A few months later it was discovered that an OMB accountant had "misplaced" a decimal point and Gray was, in fact, within his budget.) But the message Horner sent was clear: The administration could play hardball with one of its own if that person strayed too far off the reservation.

Gray, however, had a card up his own sleeve. His months of being knocked around by Washington pros had taught him that he wasn't going to make any friends in this job anyway and hardball was the only way to play the game if you wanted to win.

"Okay, Connie," Gray said when she finished her speech. "Then I'm transferring the examiners to the district banks."

Horner was stunned. What Gray was proposing to do was to transfer responsibility for all future thrift examinations and supervision from Washington to the 12 district banks across the country. The district banks, although answerable to the Bank Board in Washington, were independent entities, owned and operated by the thrifts within their district.[11] The FHLBB had oversight over the 12 district banks, but the OMB did not. In making such a transfer Gray would remove any authority OMB had over the number of examiners the FHLBB had or how much they were paid.[12]

"You mean you're going to have *nongovernment* employees regulating?" Horner gasped.

"They're already doing it," Gray said. "I don't see a problem with it."

Horner, Gray recalled, just glared at him across the remnants of lunch. Although decentralization of federal government was one of the goals of Reaganomics, transferring 700 federal examiners away from the interfering hands of the White House and Congress was something else.

"Well, I've got to get back to the office, Connie. Thanks for the lunch." Score another one for Gray.

A week later Horner trooped into Gray's office at the Bank Board, her eight assistants in tow. "I'll offer you a deal, Ed," she snapped, sitting herself down at a large dining-room table Gray had had brought to the office for such meetings. The table sat only six comfortably, so Horner's staff had to squeeze in around the edges. "If you agree not to transfer the examiners to the district banks, I'll give you 39 new ones," Horner said, as though she were making a major arms-control proposal.

Gray was flabbergasted. He looked around the table at the blank expressions on the faces of Horner's staff. Finally, running his hand through his thin gray hair, Gray told her it was a deal he simply could not make.

"Really, Connie, I need 1,100 examiners," he insisted.

As soon as Horner and her minions trooped off, Gray, his general counsel, Norm Raiden, and his chief of staff, Ann Fairbanks, finalized the transfer of the examiners to the district banks. The move, effective July 1985, greatly strengthened the district banks and got Washington bureaucracy out of their lives—two things the industry liked. Gray told the district banks to begin making arrangements to bring on board at least 700 new examiners immediately and to raise starting salaries from the current $14,000 to a more competitive $21,000.[13] The transfer of examiners was accomplished just at the time that Centennial Savings and Consolidated Savings were teetering on the brink.

If Gray's end run around OMB made him some new friends outside Washington, it did nothing for his standing on Capitol Hill or for the congressmen's vocal thrift constituency. The last thing in the world Don Dixon and his kind wanted was more examiners. To their mind there were too many regulators poking their noses into thrifts' books already. Those S&L owners, heavy contributors to congressional and senatorial candidates, renewed their call for Gray's ouster. First he had attacked brokered deposits, the lifeblood of the industry, then he had limited direct investments and growth, and now he was sending 700 more examiners into the field. He also was insisting that supervisors on the district level issue supervisory agreements and cease-and-desist orders more firmly and promptly. He was very unhappy with what seemed to him to be a lax enforcement of his new regulations.[14]

In the midst of the intramural skirmishing Gray was making regular trips to Capitol Hill to answer questions from angry congressmen on various committees. He and his general counsel, Norm Raiden, took a particularly tough grilling in July before a House subcommittee[15] investigating the failure of Beverly Hills Savings in April. Before Raiden had become general counsel for the FHLBB he had been an attorney with the Los Angeles firm of McKenna, Connor and Cuneo (one of the top S&L law firms in the country), and he had represented Beverly Hills Savings during the time that Beverly Hills management was making insider loans and speculative investments.[16] Congressmen accused Raiden of "severe and extreme conflict of interest" in his handling of the Beverly Hills case after he became counsel for the FHLBB. Gray defended Raiden (and kept him in his post), and Raiden denied any conflict of interest.[17]

Representative Thomas A. Luken then called Gray on the carpet for not acting sooner against Beverly Hills, saying "Mr. Gray is following an Alice-in-Wonderland approach" to thrift problems. He said the FHLBB "lacks the incentive to take aggressive action."

Gray replied that "a very important contributory factor" to the lack of timeliness in dealing with Beverly Hills was a shortage of examiners, which had now been corrected by transferring them to the FHLBs.

Luken then demanded that Gray "do the decent thing and resign" because he had implied that he couldn't do the job with the personnel he had.

Representative John D. Dingell (D-Mich.), chairman of the subcommittee, came to Gray's defense, saying that it was "a national disgrace" that the Bank Board lacked the funds to have a sufficient and properly trained examination force. Dingell, on several occasions during the hearings, characterized Gray as "an honorable man," but he denounced Raiden for his failure to stop the abuses at Beverly Hills when he was the thrift's attorney.[18]

In other appearances on Capitol Hill, Gray testified on the worsening condition of the industry insurance fund, the FSLIC. The insurance fund, Gray said, did not have enough money left to close all the insolvent thrifts. He projected that the cost would run into the billions of dollars. In July he testified the FSLIC would need $15 billion to clean up the industry. His numbers were based on a report by Bank Board economist Dan Brumbaugh. Congress was stunned. Where would the industry get that kind of money?

Gray was at such a hearing when his driver tiptoed into the hearing room and whispered in his ear, "Sir, there's an urgent call for you on the car phone." It was Bank Board member Mary Grigsby. She asked Gray to call her back on a regular phone. She didn't want to discuss this matter on the car phone where it could easily be monitored by any ham radio operator.

When he returned to the office he called Grigsby.

"Ed, I just got a phone call from someone representing a substantial California savings and loan," she said. "They want to offer you a job."

"Who?" Gray asked, wondering who thought he might be available. Speculation was always floating around Washington that he was leaving office, but he had denied all the rumors.

Grigsby didn't want to be more specific over the phone. Gray said he'd be available to chat later that afternoon, and he set a time for Grigsby to meet him at his office. When she arrived she told him just who the suitor was. It was Charles Keating, Jr., of American Continental Corporation (which owned Lincoln Savings and Loan in Irvine, California), a leader of the chorus that was singing for Gray's removal.

The offer stunned Gray. He knew regulators were crawling all over Lincoln's books and complaining that Lincoln was in gross violation of his new direct investment regulation. Lincoln was one of Gray's nightmare thrifts. (Lincoln grew from $2.2 billion in deposits in 1984, when Keating's company acquired the thrift, to $4.2 billion by 1987, and some of that money was invested in high-risk junk bonds.) In 1985 regulators said Lincoln had only $54 million in passbook accounts and $2.1 billion in large CDs.

Gray told us he consulted Bank Board general counsel Norm Raiden on the Keating offer. "He wants to get you out of the way," Raiden told Gray. The offer had been a vague one, so Gray sent Ann Fairbanks to a breakfast meeting with Keating to verify that this was a real offer. She came back and said that it was, though later Keating denied ever making such a proposal. Just what Keating might have been prepared to pay Gray was never disclosed. Executives at American Continental Corporation were very well paid. Keating, who earned $1.9 million in bonuses and compensation in 1987 as head of American Continental, was reportedly the second highest-paid executive in the thrift industry. Three other American Continental executives, including Keating's son Charles Keating III, were among the ten highest-paid industry executives. Keating the III made $863,494 in 1987. Another son employed by Keating's American Continental Corporation was Mark Connally, son of the powerful former Texas Governor John Connally.

Keating, with palatial estates in Arizona and the Bahamas, private jets and helicopters, was rich beyond Ed Gray's dreams. He had a reputation as an anti-pornographer and a philanthropist, and one of his favorite charities was politicians. He also encouraged his friends, employees, and business associates to contribute. Keating knew no political party. His largesse flowed equally to Democrats and Republicans alike.

Though now head of a multibillion-dollar thrift empire (Lincoln Savings made up about 85 percent of American Continental Corporation's assets), SEC documents revealed that in 1979 Keating had been accused by the Securities and Exchange Commission of misusing bank funds in Ohio by lending $14 million to friends and associates between 1972 and 1976. The SEC alleged that Keating, Carl Lindner, and Donald Klekamp, all officers of American Financial Corporation of Cincinnati, used Provident Bank, which American Financial controlled, for their own benefit. They accused the three men of a long list of SEC violations, including permitting Provident Bank to make loans to them without collateral, extend them new loans to cover the interest they owed on the old loans, roll over loans as they matured without demanding payment, and guarantee loans that other banks had made to Keating and others.

Keating and two associates consented to the SEC judgment without admitting or denying the allegations in the SEC complaint. After reading the charges, and even knowing that the SEC never had to prove them in court, we still wondered how Keating later got control of a thrift. In late 1988 published reports revealed that Keating, through American Continental, had gotten caught up in another SEC investigation, this one centering around MDC Holdings Inc. (a major borrower at Silverado Savings in Denver and an associate of a Southmark subsidiary), and that the SEC was investigating American Continental's accounting methods.

Gray said he turned down Keating's job offer without ever talking to him. When a reporter from the *National Thrift News* called Keating and asked if he had tried to hire Gray away from the Bank Board, Keating simply said, "No. That's all I have to say at this time. Good-bye." Click.

Though Gray turned Keating down, he was thinking that it was time for him to keep his promise to his wife and bow out of the Washington scene. After all, he'd already stayed on several months longer than he had meant to. But he had no intention of being forced out. He was determined to orchestrate his own departure from public life. But his enemies were impatient, particularly Don Regan, who now decided it was time to put the pressure on Gray again. He knew Gray was on the outs with a lot of people in the industry, most recently because Gray had told them the insurance fund was down to $3 billion in reserves to cover $1 trillion in deposits and member thrifts were going to have to set aside 1 percent of their assets to make up the shortfall.

That news was a sour pill that thrift officers did not want to take, and Regan seized the moment to leak to *The Wall Street Journal* the "news" that Gray was resigning. It was Regan's way of saying to Gray, "Here's your hat. What's your hurry?" It was also no secret that Regan wanted his old friend, former stock exchange president James Needham, in Gray's place.

When reporter Monica Langley of *The Wall Street Journal* called Gray for comment on the rumor that he was resigning, Gray was stunned.

"I am?" he said. "I think I'd know if I was resigning."

Langley told Gray she had gotten the news "from the highest possible authority."

"You mean the president?" Gray asked, half fearing the answer.

"No," Langley responded, but a very high source.

Ah, Gray thought . . . Don Regan. Gray was tired and mad.

"No, I'm not resigning," he told Langley, and he hung up the phone. At that moment Gray knew he was going to have to break that promise he kept renewing to his wife that he would retire soon. He was staying on.

The decision brought with it more than personal hardship. It meant financial hardship as well. Gray's $79,000-a-year salary was quickly eaten up by the cost of living in Washington and maintaining a home base in San Diego. He also had two daughters in college. Gray said he took out small personal loans from Washington banks to support himself. He even borrowed from his mother. (By the time he left the Bank Board his personal loans exceeded $80,000, Gray said.) He chaffed at the thought of having to scrape and beg while people like Don Dixon and Ed McBirney and Charles Bazarian lived the life of Reilly.

But once again Ed Gray had outfoxed the Washington pros. One could almost hear the sighs of frustration when they read Gray's remarks in *The Wall Street Journal*: "Resigning? Why no. I'm staying on."

A week later White House spokesman Larry Speakes reaffirmed the administration's support for Gray. "Ed Gray can stay as long as he wants," Speakes said.

By the time 1985 rolled to a close it looked to Gray as though he might finally have turned the corner. They'd passed the regulations to curb direct investments and growth, and they'd gotten more examiners in the field—major accomplishments that should at least hold the high fliers in check while regulators and law-enforcement officials mopped up the damage that had already been done. As Gray flew out of Washington to spend the holidays with his family in San Diego, he felt the first optimism he had enjoyed in months. He sat back in his seat and watched from the window as his plane left Washington—and the thrift crisis—behind. He thought maybe the worst was over.

CHAPTER TWENTY-THREE

The Touchables

While officials at the Federal Home Loan Bank Board in Washington caught their breath, enjoying what they did not yet realize was simply a lull before another storm, pressure was building down the street at the Department of Justice to pay more attention to the thrift industry. But they were no more prepared to handle the thrift crisis than the FHLBB had been—and for many of the same reasons.

The Department of Justice was understaffed. FBI special agents and U.S. attorneys in field offices around the country were battling a war on drugs that had already stretched them far beyond their resources. It took awhile for them to realize how many swindlers had infiltrated the thrift industry, and once they did they found they were woefully short of FBI agents and U.S. attorneys with accounting backgrounds who could unravel the paper trails of sophisticated bank fraud. Regulators who contacted the FBI for assistance were often put on hold —literally.

"I had to phone the Los Angeles FBI office 17 times trying to get them to open a case when North American Savings and Loan failed," California Savings and Loan Commissioner Bill Crawford complained later. "After 17 calls an agent finally returned my call and told me, 'Look, if you're telling me that North American is more important to you than Consolidated Savings and Loan, I'll drop my Consolidated investigation and come right over.' " If not, he said, he could get around to North American in about two years.[1]

Particularly in hot spots like Texas and California, the FBI simply did not have enough agents to investigate all the thrift fraud cases. In 1983 the FBI had only 258 agents assigned to bank fraud investigations, and within a year they would have over 7,000 cases to investigate. Three years later there would be only 337 special agents to investigate what by 1987 would increase to over 11,000 cases. To make matters worse, bank fraud was an incredibly complex white-collar crime. Each major case took from two to four years to investigate and prosecute. The FBI just didn't have the manpower. In San Francisco, for example, the FBI's white-collar crime unit had only 34 FBI agents to handle not only bank fraud but also drug-money laundering, corruption of public figures, and espionage. Part of their district (15 California counties from south of Monterey to the Oregon border) included Silicon Valley, which was waist-deep in spies trying to get information on nearly $7 billion a year in Defense Department projects. The head of the San Francisco FBI office told us he needed nearly twice as many FBI agents (60) for his white-collar crime unit.

Even if the FBI had the manpower, the United States attorneys' offices did not have enough assistant U.S. attorneys to take the cases to court. When an assistant U.S. attorney took on a major thrift fraud case that attorney was lost to the department for up to two years. The cases were backbreakers and budget busters. To make matters worse, there was a lot of turnover in U.S. attorneys' offices. Assistant U.S. attorneys could earn about $70,000 a year prosecuting federal cases for a few years and then retire to the private sector, where they could earn twice (or three times) as much representing the crooks.

But something far more damaging than lack of manpower was undermining the Department of Justice's response to criminality within the thrift industry. The biggest threat to the proper prosecution of these cases—and the hope of deterring further such abuses—was the thrift and bank regulators' penchant for secrecy. Ironically, the best accomplice that thrift crooks had after they were discovered was the federal regulators, who secreted away the evidence of the crime and sat on it.

On an increasingly regular basis, starting in 1985, FBI agents around the country saw thrifts in their jurisdiction being seized by federal regulators. Insiders or informants would tell them of massive fraud at the failed thrift, but regulators were referring only a handful of the cases to the FBI. The agents wondered why their phones weren't ringing off the hook. The Bureau contacted Federal Home Loan Bank officials and asked why they had not reported these alleged crimes to the FBI. The answer they got could have come right out of a Kafka novel.

"We can't discuss these cases with you," they were told. "That would be against the law."

The law the regulators were referring to was the Right to Financial Privacy Act, which Congress passed in 1978. It mandated that a person's business with a financial institution was privileged, like his business with his doctor, attorney, or priest. Regulators told FBI agents that, yes, many of the thrift failures had been caused by insider and customer fraud, but the law forbade regulators to discuss any thrift's relationship with any customer (which regulators interpreted as meaning even fraudulent relationships). And, no, they wouldn't be in a position to supply the agents with any evidence to help them in their investigations. That meant there could be no investigation because when the FSLIC seized an institution it sucked up every atom of information on the spot, and immediately it all became as secret as plans for the stealth bomber. Without the evidence that was in the regulators' possession, no United States attorney could hope for a conviction of a bank swindler. He needed those phony appraisals, postdated documents, fraudulent financial statements, endorsed checks.[2]

The problem wasn't a new one. The Bureau had had earlier problems with banking regulators over the same issue. After the collapse of the Butcher brothers' banks in Tennessee in 1983, the FBI actually had to complain to a Senate subcommittee to get FDIC regulators to release the phony loan documents they needed to convict the brothers. The regulators fought the Justice Department every inch of the way, leading *The Wall Street Journal* to wonder in an editorial if regulators might be worried less about bank secrecy than they were about what the documents said about their own ineptitude.

"Since the FDIC was the main agency keeping watch over the Butchers' banks, its documents afford the best picture of what went on. But every time its files have been subpoenaed it has asked the court for a sweeping protective order. . . . Similar cover-ups blanket a multitude of other cases, including one in which the defendants contend the plaintiff FDIC sought the protective order to 'hide its own culpability.' "

Concerned that serious white-collar criminal investigations involving the theft of hundreds of millions of dollars were going nowhere while FBI agents fought with federal regulators in public over scraps of information, the Justice Department in December 1984 had called for a sit-down with regulators. Together they formed a joint working group to which they gave a $50 name: "The Attorney General's Interagency Bank Fraud Enforcement Working Group." The group's mission was to mesh the needs of prosecutors, FBI agents, and bank supervisory personnel and to "identify, address, and resolve issues of major significance relating to the detection, reporting and prosecution of bank-related crimes, focusing especially on crimes by insiders of financial institutions."[3]

The Justice Department began to teach bank examiners how to spot bank fraud, and the FBI began work on a computerized tracking system that would contain the names of known bank swindlers. When crooks moved from one FBI jurisdiction to another, agents could just type in their names and get a complete history on them. Unfortunately that system was not scheduled to go on line for several years.

Regulators were told in no uncertain terms that the Right to Financial Privacy Act in no way prohibited them from releasing information to the FBI on suspected criminal activity at a financial institution. They were provided with criminal referral forms and told to file one anytime they had suspicion of a crime. But old habits died hard. To a regulator financial information was as sacred as the Holy Sacrament was to a priest. One just didn't hand something that precious to the uninitiated, the great unwashed—and particularly not to ham-handed

FBI agents with lumps under their coats. Agents were still required to get a federal court subpoena for anything they wanted from regulators.

An example of passive-aggressive behavior by Bank Board examiners was their "redacted" criminal referral, which satisfied the letter of the law while totally avoiding the spirit. One veteran FBI agent recalled his first run-in with a redacted criminal referral.

"You would not believe it. It read kind of like this:

> Loan officer A made a loan to borrower B. Borrower B supplied fraudulent financial information on the loan application. Loan officer A knew the information to be false. Appraiser C supplied an inflated appraisal on the property. He and Borrower B and Loan Officer A knew the appraisal was false. When the loan was funded Borrower B paid Loan Officer A and Appraiser C $25,000 kickbacks out of the loan proceeds.

"I called that character [the examiner] back and asked him just what he expected me to do with this piece of shit. I told him I couldn't investigate people with code names, that he had to put their real names in the referral. What the hell did those clowns call us for? They wanted us to investigate someone but they wouldn't tell us *who*?" (The FHLBB is the only agency in government that employs redacted criminal referrals.)

Secrecy at the 12 district banks became an obsession and got even worse after Danny Wall succeeded Ed Gray at the FHLBB. If we called to speak with Bill Black or Mike Patriarca at the San Francisco Bank, at least one "listener" would stay on the line to make sure Bill or Mike didn't spill any unauthorized beans. Black, before Danny Wall took over as FHLBB chairman, was well known to Washington reporters for his good rapport with the press. However, once Wall became chairman that changed. Black reportedly wrote a memo to Wall criticizing the FHLBB's new Southwest Plan (Wall's much-ballyhooed answer to the S&L crisis in Texas that called for selling bankrupt thrifts), which was costing the FHLBB billions of dollars.[4] Wall, according to former regulators, put Black on an informal muzzle, threatening to fire him if he criticized FHLBB policy again. Wall brought in the FBI as a consultant to help the agency keep a lid on information. He hired a security officer to track leaks. This Nixonian paranoia reached its peak when Wall's chief of staff recommended that the FHLBB offer a $20,000 reward for anyone who could turn in a leaker. (Wall decided against the plan.) Washington columnist Jack Anderson reported that the year after Wall took office he convened the FHLBB for only three public meetings but held at least 70 meetings behind closed doors.

Such secrecy inevitably raised suspicions that the regulators had something to hide. We began to wonder why we never found a single instance where federal regulators had filed a criminal referral against one of their own examiners. Were we to believe that, while crooked thrift officials were busily bribing appraisers, accountants, and contractors, and receiving kickbacks and bribes themselves, not a single $14,000-a-year FHLB examiner ever took a bribe to cover up? Regulators said no, but we began to hear differently. One California examiner was quietly fired by the San Francisco FHLB after it was discovered he had received a $6,000 check from a crooked thrift officer. In Texas an officer of a failed thrift actually let a grand jury charge him with perjury rather than repeat to the jury what he had already told two different FBI agents three times in different interviews: Two days before he was subpoenaed to appear before the grand jury, an employee of the FSLIC whom he had known for years had called and told him to "get dumb" if it came to testifying before a federal grand jury. Still, not until 1989 did we find a single FHLB examiner or supervisor charged with wrongdoing.

Then the facade began to crack. We learned that the FSLIC had hired Stuart Jones in Washington to help dispose of Texas S&L assets while he was reportedly being investigated by the FBI in Dallas for alleged criminal wrongdoing at Richardson Savings in Dallas, which had collapsed. Jones was a commercial loan officer at Richardson until he was fired in March 1986. The *National Thrift News* reported that the FHLB in Dallas had filed not one but two criminal referrals on Jones, both of which the FSLIC was blissfully unaware.

A couple of weeks later the FBI arrested twin brothers Philip and Thomas Noons and charged them with defrauding the FSLIC while employed by the agency to help liquidate insolvent Mainland Savings in Houston. The men were charged with setting up a complex web of offshore banks to acquire assets of Mainland at below-market value. They pleaded not guilty and their trial was pending at press time.

Then the FHLBB announced it had asked the Justice Department to investigate charges that the former head of the FSLIC, Stuart Root, had given Silverado Savings in Denver (where Neil Bush had been a director) advance warning that regulators were going to seize the thrift in December 1988. Root denied the charges.

These were all just allegations. No one had pleaded guilty or been convicted by a jury at this writing. But this cascade of allegations in early 1989 reinforced our own suspicions that all the confusion and sense of urgency surrounding the faltering thrift industry might become fertile ground for a second wave of thrift fraud, this time perpetrated by the very people sent to save the industry.

Apparently we weren't alone in our concerns. In mid-1989 we learned the FBI had spent over $11,000 flying two suspected Texas thrift swindlers around the country. According to court testimony, the pair met with important elected and appointed officials in Washington under the guise that the two men wanted to acquire troubled Texas thrifts. The FBI wired them and recorded the conversations. In all, 38 hours worth of body tapes were collected by the pair. While in Washington meeting with congressional aides, the pair met in June 1988 with none other than FHLBB Chairman M. Danny Wall, a meeting they said had been arranged for them by Texas Senator Phil Gramm. Wall later confirmed the meeting. When the San Antonio *Light* ran a story that Wall was a subject of an FBI probe, the FHLB and the Justice Department vehemently denied Wall was a target. The tapes were put under court seal when the U.S. attorney argued that their release could jeopardize the probe. At press time precisely what that probe involved remained under wraps.

Secrecy at the FHLBB succeeded for a long time in keeping the public from finding out that fraud was rampant at S&Ls. Occasionally someone on the inside would speak out, but that was rare. In January 1987 William Weld, assistant attorney general and head of the Justice Department's criminal division,[5] said in a speech to the American Bar Association: " . . . both FBI and [FDIC] figures confirm that a large percentage of bank failures involve allegations of criminal misconduct on the part of the bank's senior management. . . . We have even got organized crime types taking a look at thinly capitalized financial institutions which are candidates for takeover, and then using [various specified fraudulent schemes] to create a paper financial asset which they can then pull the plug on after a year and a half or two, and leave the FDIC or FSLIC, i.e., the taxpayers, holding the bag. . . . Insider fraud thus obviously plays a major role in bank failures, and we now have evidence to suggest a nationwide scheme linking numerous failures of banks and savings and loan institutions throughout the country."

Unfortunately Weld's words didn't get much attention (we didn't hear about them until 18 months later), and regulators continued to play the secrecy game. In late 1988 we called the San Francisco FHLB to ask about complaints we were still getting from FBI agents that they weren't receiving criminal referrals. A public relations person took our message and said she'd have an official call us back. Half an hour later she told us the official was "not comfortable talking to you about this."

We did talk later, but only after we told the PR person that we already had the FBI side of the story and if the FHLB didn't want their side presented, we were "comfortable" with that. Then we were invited to a meeting with the Bank's criminal referral staff. At that meeting we were told that, indeed, the regulators had "fouled things up in the past" when it came to timely criminal referrals and providing information to the FBI. But since April 1988, they said, a new system was in place and the machinery was functioning much better. They, in turn, now criticized the Justice Department, saying that many cases referred to the FBI were not being prosecuted. Congress released the results of a confidential internal FBI audit that painted a bleak picture of the FBI's ability to investigate sophisticated financial crimes. Some federal prosecutors, the report said, were giving their bank fraud cases to IRS agents or Secret Service agents to investigate, and some were going so far as to hire outside accountants to do the sleuthing.

Criminal referrals remained the chafing point between the Justice Department and thrift regulators. But civil suits that the FSLIC filed against thrift abusers, to try to recover some of the FSLIC's dwindling fund, were another important stumbling block in the complicated task of bringing criminal charges against thrift looters, though regulators would never admit it. When a thrift failed the FSLIC hired a high-powered private law firm to represent its interests against the thrift's former management and customers. Those attorneys were called "fee counsel" because the FSLIC paid them a fee for their services—a fat fee. In a short 18-month period between January 1986 and September 1987, the FSLIC reported it paid out a staggering $108 million in legal fees to independent fee counsel working on thrift failures nationwide (prompting one attorney to suggest they rename the Garn-St Germain Act the Lawyer's Relief Act of 1982).

Fee counsels' job was to figure out how the thrift's assets had disappeared and to go after them. They sued thrift officials who were guilty of self-dealing and borrowers who had defaulted on their loans. And they had no interest in seeing those people arrested because the accused might start squirreling their money away to pay for criminal attorneys and say they didn't have enough money to pay the civil judgment. Fee counsel complained further that when they filed a criminal referral, FBI agents flashed badges in the faces of their civil defendants, scaring them, and everyone immediately clammed up. Defendants being deposed in a civil case would suddenly start taking the fifth amendment on the grounds that a criminal investigation was under way and anything they said in the civil action might be used against them in the criminal case. For these reasons many fee counsels just counted to ten whenever they were tempted to file a criminal referral and kept counting until the temptation went away. The issue became one of priorities: Was it more important to collect the missing money or punish the offenders?[6]

At the FHLB in Topeka we ran across a prime example of regulators' reluctance to make criminal referrals to the FBI. After discovering what appeared to be fraud at SISCorp, an Oklahoma thrift servicing company heavily influenced by Charles Bazarian, attorneys met with Kermit Mowbray, president of the Topeka Federal Home Loan Bank, to advise him of their findings. A transcript of the meeting included the following exchange:

"I can't minimize what I feel to be suspicions of criminality . . ." an attorney told Mowbray. But, apparently concerned about the conduct of possible civil proceedings, he quickly added, "I think if there was a stampede now by certain investigating agencies, I wonder if it wouldn't set off somewhat of a situation where people would become immobilized.

"For example, if we called up the FBI . . . they're hot on white-collar crimes anyway. And that if the FBI was to hit the streets and investigating who knows . . . I wonder if it would help or harm in the short term . . . everybody retreating into a very defensive posture and not saying anything to anybody without four lawyers and a monsignor present."

Mowbray replied, "I'm not sure that we need that. We usually do not call the FBI in until we have done our own investigation."

"Well, that's fine," the lawyer replied, apparently satisfied that no ham-handed FBI agents would be muddying his civil waters.

The end result of the strained relations between regulators and the Department of Justice was clearly visible in the numbers. Even as late as 1987 (three years after the working group's formation) the San Diego division of the FBI would be working on only nine bank fraud investigations in the $100,000 to $250,000 category (a category large enough to exclude garden-variety embezzlements). *None* of those investigations was referred by the FSLIC or the FDIC. Two were referred by the district attorney, two by an FBI informant, and two were started after agents learned of alleged bank fraud while reading the morning paper over coffee. The other three referrals also did not come from regulators.

In Los Angeles in 1987 the federal prosecutor would receive 78 criminal referrals in cases involving losses between $100,000 and $250,000. *None* of those cases was referred by the FSLIC. Informants referred seven of the cases and seven more were initiated by the FBI on its own after it stumbled over information while investigating unrelated crimes.

In cases where the loss exceeded $250,000 nine investigations were initiated in the San Diego division, and none of those was referred by the FSLIC. In Los Angeles 143 criminal referrals were filed in the $250,000-plus category, of which the FSLIC was responsible for only five.

When regulators did make criminal referrals and forked over supporting documentation, the Justice Department often refused to keep them informed of the progress of the case (or to give them the information the FBI gathered that might help the FSLIC locate some of its missing money) and prosecutions were uneven, depending entirely upon the individuals called upon to handle the case: the FBI agent, the U.S. attorney, the judge, and the jury. If an FBI agent pursued his suspects with vigor and collected all the necessary information to support an indictment, he then had to "sell" the case to an assistant U.S. attorney who would decide whether or not to prosecute the case. The system worked best when there was a team of an FBI agent and a U.S. attorney who were both dedicated to the prosecution of the case, like U.S. Attorney Joe Cage and FBI Agent Ellis Blount in Louisiana (Herman Beebe) or U.S. Attorney Lance Caldwell and FBI Agent Joe Boyer (State Savings/Corvallis) in Oregon. But those were the rarest of exceptions. (In late 1988 a congressional report stated that 60 cases in which the FBI in the Northern District of California had completed its investigation had gone unprosecuted.)

If the U.S. attorney gave the go-ahead to prepare evidence for a grand jury, and if the grand jury handed down indictments, the U.S. attorney had another chance to decide how much he believed in his case. Could he spare the long months it took to prepare for trial? And then the weeks in court? If the answer was no, the U.S. attorney would dispose of the defendants one by one by offering them relatively light sentences or even probation in exchange for a plea to one count of bank fraud. For the U.S. attorney's career scorecard a plea bargain counted as a conviction, just as if he had sent the crook up the river for 20 years.

But suppose the U.S. attorney decided to bite the bullet and take the case to court. Then he and the FBI agent faced the tedious work of building a case, and they nearly always did so by reinventing the wheel. The fraternity of high fliers and professional white-collar criminals who looted thrifts seldom confined their efforts to one financial institution. Yet FBI investigators rarely looked beyond the thrift in their jurisdiction. Time and again when we asked an FBI agent about a suspect we were investigating we discovered the agent had had no knowledge that the same person was under FBI investigation for bank fraud 1,000 miles away. Crooks networked—FBI agents did not. In fact, we found that reporters like Byron Harris at WFAA-TV in Dallas and Pete Brewton at the Houston *Post* were far better informed about the network of major players in the thrift bust-out game than many FSLIC attorneys, U.S. attorneys, and FBI agents actually working the cases.

Once FBI agents and the U.S. attorney had gathered their information and made a case, they had to endure the uncertainty of the outcome. Would a jury understand the complicated financial deals? Would they understand what a cash-for-trash deal was, what a land flip was, and how they were used to bilk a thrift? And if they got a jury to convict, would the judge hand down a sentence tougher than the prosecutor could have gotten if he'd just plea-bargained at the start? Every inch of the path, from discovery of the crime through prosecution, was littered with uncertainty.

Judges and juries had a hard time dealing with white-collar criminals. White-collar criminals didn't look like crooks—they looked like businessmen. In more than one instance we saw them con FBI agents, U.S. attorneys, judges, and juries. Swindlers are by definition likable folks. They'd be damned poor con men if they weren't. A few hours with a Charles Bazarian or a Mario Renda had most folks wondering why everyone was picking on them. All too often we saw people like Beverly Haines and Herman Beebe come before judges who could not bring themselves to view the defendants as serious criminals. Instead, they were treated like characters out of some Greek tragedy . . . victims of fate . . . in the wrong place at the wrong time . . . choosing the wrong fork in the road but otherwise fine fellows . . . when in fact they were criminals, plain and simple. They were swindlers who, when given the chance to make a decision between right and wrong, *freely chose wrong.*

"These guys are con men," complained California Savings and Loan Commissioner William Crawford during congressional testimony in 1987. "First they con the banker, then they con investigators, then they con prosecutors, and lastly they con the judge and the jury."

The odds against the successful prosecution of a bank fraud case were enormous. The vast majority of looters would never see a day in jail or ever have to pay any restitution. Admitting the obvious, Attorney General Richard Thornburgh told Congress in early 1989, "We'd be fooling ourselves to think that any substantial portion of these assets is going to be recovered."

Sometimes the obstacles came from within the Justice Department itself, as when then-Attorney General Ed Meese decided to transfer a million dollars to the department's obscenity unit from the travel budget of the Fraud Section just when it was beginning to make headway in its investigation of failed thrifts in Texas. (Meese was on his way out of office, having resigned after questions were raised about his ethical standards.) Suddenly prosecutors around the country were told there was no money to have witnesses flown in to testify before the grand jury and FBI agents were told they could not go to other states to conduct interviews because there wasn't enough money to pay the air fare. Then in October 1988 it was announced that, because of budget restraints, the Criminal Division at the Department of Justice had a hiring freeze in effect and U.S. attorneys would be cut back by 10 percent in 1989. By the end of 1988 there were still 128 vacant U.S. attorney positions that would apparently go unfilled. As regulators began referring more cases the understaffed Justice Department fell further behind in its investigations and prosecutions. In Chicago the U.S. attorney between 1985 and 1988 charged 300 people with embezzlement (250 were convicted or pleaded guilty) and 120 cases involving losses of perhaps $100 million were under investigation in December 1988. "Despite that," the U.S. attorney said, "the bank frauds continue to grow." In 1989 Thornburg announced that one-third of the major bank fraud cases were not being pursued because the Justice Department lacked the resources.

The only solution to this crunch was to filter the flood of fraud cases. U.S. attorneys' offices in areas like Los Angeles, San Diego, San Francisco, and Dallas simply established an arbitrary $100,000 cutoff point. If a case under $100,000 was reported to them, it generally went unprosecuted. In some jurisdictions a fraud had to exceed $250,000 before the U.S. attorney would even look at it. One U.S. attorney on the Organized Crime Strike Force told us, "I think sometimes that I could quit this job and go out and do bank scams. As long as I kept my take under $100,000 per scam I know I'd never get prosecuted." In Southern California and Texas, the cutoff became $1 million.

The simple fact remained that whether the mob or just your generic swindler busted out a savings and loan (or bank), the risk he incurred was very low but the potential for gain was staggeringly high. If a person was stupid enough to walk into a thrift and stick a gun in a teller's face, he would get out the door with a couple of thousand dollars at the most, have his picture taken in the process, get caught, and spend years in prison, where, for a handful of cigarettes, he'd become the personal property of the cellblock guerilla. But if he (or she) pulled a well-oiled loan scam, he would walk out the door arm in arm with the thrift president, with a check for a couple of million dollars in hand. If caught, and chances were excellent he would not be, and if convicted, and the odds were against it, he faced a very small chance of ever spending a day behind bars. The problem challenges us as a nation. For some reason our system has seen nothing unjust in slapping an 18-year-old inner-city kid with a 20-year prison sentence for robbing a bank of a couple of thousand dollars while putting a white-collar criminal away for just two years in a "prison camp" for stealing $200 million through fraud.

The average sentence for an executive who defrauds an S&L and gets sentenced to prison is three years, compared to 13 years for someone who sticks up the same institution. Of the 960 people convicted in federal courts of fraud against lending institutions in one year, only 494 were sentenced to prison terms; of 795 people convicted of embezzling, only 227 were sentenced to prison terms. *But* of 996 people convicted of *robbing* banks and S&Ls, 932 went to prison.

Even the Justice Department's much-ballyhooed task force of 50 federal law-enforcement officers who moved into Dallas in 1987 to investigate S&L fraud had failed to produce much results almost two years later. They had 25 convictions, but most were for minor violations or were the result of plea agreements. About 25 percent of those sentenced got probation. Hampered by a lack of funds, most of the attorneys on the task force commuted from Washington to Dallas a couple of times a month while many defendants seemed to have huge financial resources and hired teams of high-powered attorneys to represent them.

If Ed Gray hoped that furious prosecution of thrift crooks was going to help him chase the bandits out of the industry, he was destined for disappointment.

CHAPTER TWENTY-FOUR

Friends in High Places

By 1986 the biggest issue facing Ed Gray in Washington became the growing insolvency of the FSLIC insurance fund itself. All the new regulations and beefed-up regulatory staff would be for naught if the FSLIC lacked the money necessary to close and liquidate insolvent thrifts once they were identified. When a thrift was liquidated all its deposits up to $100,000 had to be repaid to depositors. That money came out of the FSLIC fund. A single medium-sized thrift liquidation could cost the FSLIC half a billion dollars,[1] and the fund was down to $2.5 billion from $6 billion just two years earlier. Gray told Congress, as he had been doing for a year, that he needed the authority to raise at least another $15 billion, through bond sales, to cover the anticipated cost of closing all the rotten thrifts.

In May, Gray sent to Congress a bill that he said would provide up to $25 billion to deal with the FSLIC's problems. But the bill, dubbed the "recap" (short for FSLIC recapitalization), soon became the hottest political potato in town. At times it seemed to Gray that everyone was lining up against the bill. Legitimate thrift owners bristled at the notion that they should pick up the tab[2] for poorly run thrifts. They wanted the recap to be as small as possible, $5 billion at the most.

One day, after a particularly grueling session before Congress, Gray ran into one of the U.S. League's chief lobbyists in the hall outside the hearing room.

"Why are you guys fighting me on the recap?" Gray asked him.

"Listen, Ed," the lobbyist answered, pulling Gray off to one side. "In 1989 we'll have a new administration running things. By that time everyone will know this problem is so big that the industry can't pay for it. The taxpayer will have to pay for it then, not the industry." (The U.S. League did not speak for the entire industry. The smaller, and much less politically powerful, National Council of Savings Institutions supported immediate passage of Gray's recap bill.)

The crooked thrift owners, on the other hand, wanted no recap at all. As far as they were concerned the best FSLIC was a broke FSLIC because it couldn't shut them down. That meant more time at the till and more time to gamble on hitting it big.

The lobbying against the recap was furious, and the bill was going nowhere fast. Then once again, just when Gray's credibility was his most potent weapon, *The Wall Street Journal* ran a story that examined Gray's cozy relationship with the U.S. League—which was curious since Gray had been fighting with them now for two years. The story examined the question of the League's "influence on Gray" and noted that the group had paid some of his travel expenses over the years. The Office of Government Ethics launched a probe to investigate whether the League regularly paid Gray's expenses when he traveled to speak at League functions.[3] A Washington *Post* reporter wrote that some of these stories originated with law firms Charles Keating, Jr., hired to leak reports that would embarrass and undermine Gray.

It had all gotten to be too much. Soon after the story broke Gray's two board counterparts, Mary Grigsby and Don Hovde, announced they would be leaving. Gray knew he would not be allowed much of a hand in picking their successors, and he also believed Don Regan would seize the opportunity to insert two of the biggest thorns he could find. Those being named as possible candidates did little to reduce Gray's concerns. There was conservative Democrat George Benston, who had written a report just 15 months earlier for Charles Keating, Jr. Benston blamed high interest rates (that thrifts had to pay to attract deposits), not brokered deposits or direct investments, for the industry problems. Another possible choice was Durward Curlee, Texas League lobbyist who had led the opposition to Gray in Texas. Then there was another Keating loyalist, Lee Henkel, a lawyer who resembled silent movie actor Fatty Arbuckle. Just a week earlier the *National Thrift News* had reported that Henkel-related businesses had received a number of large loans from Lincoln Savings, the thrift that Keating controlled.

In November 1986 the White House announced its choices for the two vacant seats. The Democratic seat on the Board went to Larry White, 43, an economist from New York University. White was young and bright and didn't seem to have ties to anyone in particular. Gray was surprised. He had been certain Don Regan would put someone in that seat to keep an eye on him.[4]

The second seat went to Lee H. Henkel. Gray learned that Lincoln Savings had given Henkel a $250,000 personal loan and had loaned him more than $55 million on real estate projects in Georgia. Henkel's law firm was also employed by Lincoln Savings. Keating and Henkel, it turned out, went way back together. They had reportedly met during John Connally's campaign for the presidency in 1980, when Henkel was Connally's East Coast finance chairman and Keating was the West Coast chairman. The evidence tying Henkel to Keating was so overwhelming even the U.S. League was embarrassed by the mounting disclosures and the League came out against his appointment to the Board.

Gray suspected that since Keating had failed to hire him away from the FHLBB, he was now trying to put his own man on the Board to neuter him. Henkel's first move did little to change Gray's theory. Henkel no sooner took his seat than he introduced a new regulation that would grant a sweeping clemency to thrifts that had violated Gray's tough direct investment regulation and would allow them to keep the investments they had made before the regulation went into effect. Among the thrifts that would have benefited from Henkel's regulation was Lincoln.

A federal ethics investigator had reviewed Henkel's background, and Henkel told the investigator he had repaid the personal loan from Lincoln Savings and had put all his Lincoln-financed real estate projects into a blind trust. The reviewer had ruled that Henkel's relationship with Keating posed no ethics problems. However, Senator William Proxmire, the 66-year-old Democrat from Wisconsin and chairman of the Senate Banking Committee, made it known that he had major reservations about the Henkel appointment. It had been made by the president during the winter recess and until now the Senate had not had time to study or comment on it.[5] Proxmire reportedly felt Henkel might be unfit to serve as a FHLBB member because of the potential conflict of interest caused by the loans he'd received from Lincoln Savings. The senator had also supported Gray's direct investment regulation and strongly opposed Henkel's new proposal to amend it. Proxmire announced he'd hold hearings on the Henkel matter. With Proxmire on Henkel's trail, it didn't appear to Gray that Henkel would be a board member very long.

Gray's priority at that juncture was to get the recap bill away from Jim Wright, who was holding it hostage as a favor to his Texas thrift constituents. The FSLIC insurance fund didn't have enough money to bail out a few small thrifts with the flu, much less the estimated 400 thrifts that were now functionally insolvent and just hadn't been so declared. (Regulators coined the phrase "brain dead" to describe thrifts that regulators were allowing to operate after they became insolvent simply because there wasn't enough money in the FSLIC fund to close them and pay off depositors.) The recap had to be passed and fast. Gray's best estimate was that brain-dead thrifts were experiencing operating losses totaling $10 million a day.

For months Gray fenced with Jim Wright over the recap.[6] Time after time Wright took Gray to the woodshed for his Texas thrift and developer constituents.

In January 1987 Wright was elevated to speaker of the House. In February Gray had an aide call Wright to see if the bill would soon be sent to the floor for debate. Gray's aide also told the speaker's office that if they needed any information that would be helpful in moving the recap bill along, please call and Mr. Gray would go right over. Gray's aide made several such offers in the days that followed, but Wright's office didn't return any of the calls. At one point, Gray told us later, his office called Wright every 15 minutes for a solid week. At the end of that week (late February) a spokesman for Wright finally returned the call. Gray was out, so he left a message: "Don't call us. We'll call you."

Later Gray would recall those hectic days with bitterness. "I have worked with all kinds of guys in government since 1966. I've seen people who were honest and straightforward and those who were something else, but I never saw anything like this. The speaker used his power and influence to bring about behavioral changes in a regulator. It was an abuse of power and improper. I felt he was putting us through hoops to do his bidding. I wish I had told him off, but when you have no money left in your fund you do things you would normally never do. I certainly would not have done what I did, unless I felt it was the only way to get the recap bill passed."

Wright's chief of staff would later (1988) send the following mind-boggling rationalization to *Banker's Monthly*:[7]

One of the first hints of serious troubles in America's S&Ls came to then-Majority Leader Wright in 1986. Into his office one day came a young woman whose husband had lost his job six months earlier. Even though the family had been making timely payments for eight years and was, in fact, only two months in arrears, their home was being repossessd.

Looking into the matter, Wright found that this case, like many he would see later, was the result of a federal regulator's arbitrarily dictating policy to a savings institution under federal supervision. The regulator had ordered the lender to foreclose on all due mortgages—no delays, no forbearances, no ifs, no ands, no buts. In this case and several others Wright was able to help the young couple save their home. They were allowed to work out an arrangement to get their house payments current once more.

That, after all, is the job of a Congressman. There is nothing unusual or sinister about a citizen coming to a member of Congress for help. In each mail Speaker Wright receives a stack of letters from people caught in the web of an impersonal bureaucracy and appealing for help. In every congressional office it is the same.

This is what makes America the great country that it is. If government should ever become so remote and so aloof that the plain, everyday citizen has no influence, no access and no intercessor, then we will have lost our precious Constitutional right "to petition the government for a redress of grievances."

The fact remained, however, that Wright intervened, not on behalf of some poor woman whose husband had lost his job, but on behalf of big campaign contributors who had lost (or were about to lose) their savings and loans, men like Tom Gaubert, Don Dixon, and Craig Hall. Hall had had half a billion dollars in troubled debt at thrifts when Wright exerted pressure on Gray to get Hall some forbearance.

By the end of February the burgeoning savings and loan crisis was making news. Washington reporters began asking Speaker Wright daily about the recap bill and why it wasn't moving. The break in the impasse came on April 27, 1987, when the FSLIC filed a civil lawsuit seeking $540 million in damages from Dixon and six other former Vernon officers, the largest such claim the agency had ever filed. The next day Wright announced he would support the $15 billion version (Gray's current version) of the FSLIC recap bill. But he continued to peddle influence for his Texas thrift constituents and was eventually successful in getting a forbearance provision added to the recap bill, a provision that instructed regulators to grant forbearance to thrifts whose problems were determined to have been caused by temporary economic conditions. Gray blasted the forbearance provision, saying it would hamstring regulators.[8]

In May, after intense lobbying by the U.S. League for a smaller $5 billion recap bill, the House passed a $5 billion recapitalization plan[9] and the Senate passed a $7.5 billion version. A conference committee began the process of reconciling the two versions of the bill.

Two months before the end of Gray's term, which was scheduled to expire in June 1987, things finally started to break his way. His old nemesis at the White House, Don Regan, ran into a buzz saw named Nancy Reagan and was sent packing.[10] Though no one could have imagined it earlier, Gray had actually outlasted Regan. To sweeten Gray's victory Regan had learned that he was "retiring" while watching a morning news program, after which he submitted his resignation in a huff. Those who lived by the news leak sometimes died by the news leak. It was a sweet moment for Ed Gray, whose friends broke out a bottle of champagne for a small impromptu office party.

Just a week later pressure from Senator Proxmire and rumors that the Justice Department might probe his relationship with Charles Keating forced Lee Henkel to resign his seat on the FHLBB, saying he was "fed up with the whole process" of defending himself against conflict-of-interest charges concerning Lincoln Savings. Gray thought he just might be able to leave Washington with some scalps of his own under his belt.

And there was more good news: No action would be taken against Gray for using expense money from the district banks for his travel expenses. The GAO and the Department of Justice had conducted an investigation of charges that he had traveled on FHLBB business and billed his expenses to district banks and that he had used expense money for golf and yacht outings. Gray had written a letter to Congress apologizing for his "flawed judgment" and had repaid the district banks $28,000. Investigators reported that using district bank money for FHLBB expenses would not be tolerated in the future and henceforth could result in criminal charges, but Gray would not be indicted.

Early in April, a couple of days after Henkel resigned, Senator Dennis DeConcini (D-Ariz.) called. "Ed, can you drop by my office?" he asked.

When Gray arrived at DeConcini's office the senator met him at the door. Gray had walked into another ambush. Waiting in DeConcini's office were three more senators: John McCain (R-Ariz.), John Glenn (D-Ohio), and Alan Cranston (D-Calif.). The four men had something in common besides being United States senators—campaign disclosure forms showed they each had received healthy political donations from Charlie Keating and his associates. Of the contributions Keating and his associates had made since 1984, these four men or their associates had received: DeConcini, $55,000; McCain, $112,000; Glenn, $200,000; Cranston, $889,000. Each man claimed Keating as his personal constituent because Lincoln Savings was based in Irvine, California, and American Continental Corporation, Lincoln's parent company, had been incorporated in Ohio and had its headquarters in Phoenix, Arizona.

Suddenly Gray felt tired. With only weeks to go as chairman, he was in no mood for this. In the four years since he'd taken office his hair had thinned noticeably. His middle-age spread hung over the belt of his trousers. In the early days as chairman, Gray, with his silver hair and boyish smile, had looked distinguished, though often tired. Now he looked haggard, like a boxer who'd taken too many punches.

The four senators wanted to know why the examiners from the Eleventh District FHLB in San Francisco were being so tough on Charlie Keating. The FHLB wanted Lincoln in line with Gray's new direct investment regulation, but Keating claimed that the new regulations were the equivalent of changing the rules in the middle of the game and should not be retroactively applied to thrifts that had operated under the old rules. (Keating had filed suit in federal court challenging Gray's regulation. The case was later dismissed.)

DeConcini took the lead: "Look, this is what we'll do. We agree with the idea that Lincoln not making more home loans is bad. That's what they're supposed to do." (Prior to Keating's acquisition of Lincoln in 1984, the thrift had been a heavy single-family mortgage lender. But in 1985 Lincoln originated only 11 mortgages and four were for employees. For a $3.6 billion S&L with 24 branches that was unusual behavior.)

"What do you want?" Gray asked.

DeConcini offered a deal: "We'll assure you that they'll make more home loans and get into the basic business of home lending if you do something— you have to withdraw the equity-risk regulations." (Equity-risk regulations required thrifts that were heavily involved in direct investments to set aside additional cash reserves to compensate for the risk inherent in those investments.)

Gray was puzzled. He had four U.S. senators trying to negotiate business with him on behalf of a savings and loan. Gray reminded them that Lincoln was suing the FHLBB over the direct investment regulation. He also offered his opinion that it was highly irregular for him, as FHLBB chairman, to be asked to discuss a savings and loan that was presently being examined by a FHLB.[11] Gray told them it would be impossible for him to withdraw the direct investment rule.

DeConcini made one last try. He suggested that the regulation be withdrawn until a court could determine if the rule were legal or not.

"If I withdraw it," Gray told him, "then they'll just withdraw their suit." He reiterated, "The rule is very important."

Gray told the senators if they had any more questions about Lincoln to direct them to Jim Cirona, president of the Eleventh District FHLB in San Francisco. Supervision had been transferred to the district banks, and the Eleventh District was responsible for whatever examinations were in progress at Lincoln.

A few days later DeConcini called Cirona and asked if he and his staff could come to Washington to discuss "the Lincoln problem." A meeting was scheduled at DeConcini's office for April 9 at 6 p.m.

Cirona flew to Washington along with his second-in-command at the San Francisco FHLB, Michael Patriarca, and Richard Sanchez, the supervisor in charge of Lincoln's examination. In Washington they picked up Bill Black over at the FSLIC. He was transferring out to San Francisco soon to be the general counsel at the San Francisco FHLB.

When the four arrived at DeConcini's office they found senators DeConcini and McCain in attendance. Senator Glenn arrived a few minutes late and Senator Cranston dropped by briefly. Also present was Senator Don Riegle (D-Mich.), next in line to replace Proxmire as chairman of the Senate Banking Committee. Riegle, like the other senators there that day, had received large donations from Charles Keating and his associates ($76,100 in Riegle's case). Keating had raised the money for Riegle in March at a fund-raiser attended by over 100 Keating employees.

The meeting lasted just over two hours. All four regulators and four of the five senators stayed the entire time. Cranston, who had appointments to keep on the Senate floor, stopped by to tell Cirona, "I just want to say that I share the concerns of the other senators on this subject." The meeting was confidential. Bill Black was the only person taking detailed notes, which became an unofficial transcript of the meeting prepared at Ed Gray's request, and the basis for the following. (The entire, uncut transcript is reproduced in Appendix B.)

Jim Cirona began the meeting by introducing his colleagues from the district bank. After the introductions DeConcini got right to the point. He told the regulators, "We wanted to meet with you because we have determined that potential actions of yours could injure a constituent." The constituent, of course, was Lincoln Savings.

DeConcini said that Keating was afraid the FHLB was going to seize Lincoln because Keating disagreed with the Bank Board's rules on direct investments. He said Lincoln also strongly disagreed with the Bank Board over appraisals it had made on Lincoln properties. They were low, way too low, and "grossly unfair."

Senator McCain, from Tempe, Arizona, spoke up to try to put the meeting into a more benign light. "ACC [American Continental Corporation, headquartered in Arizona, was Lincoln Savings' parent company] is a big employer and important to the local economy. I wouldn't want any special favors for them. . . . I don't want any part of our conversation to be improper. We asked Chairman Gray about that and he said it wasn't improper to discuss Lincoln."

Senator John Glenn jumped in to complain that the district bank had taken an "unusually adversary view toward Lincoln." He complained that normal examinations took up to six months, but the Lincoln exam had dragged on and on. "To be blunt, you should charge them or get off their backs," Glenn said.

Riegle said the way it looked to him was that the standoff between Lincoln Savings and the FHLBB had become a "struggle between Keating and Gray. . . . The appearance is that it's a fight to the death." Riegle added that he just wanted to make sure the San Francisco regulators were acting in a fair and professional manner.

Cirona finally spoke up. Contrary to rumor, he told the senators, Ed Gray was not out to get Charles Keating. "We [at the San Francisco FHLB] determine how examinations are conducted," he told them. "Gray never gave me instructions on how to conduct this exam or any other exam. At this meeting you'll hear things that Gray doesn't know."

Cirona then put the senators on notice. "This meeting is very unusual, to discuss a particular company."

"It's very unusual for us to have a company that could be put out of business by its regulators," DeConcini shot back. "Richard [Sanchez], you're on, you have 10 to 12 minutes." (The senators had a vote coming up on the floor.)

Sanchez began presenting the Bank Board's case. "An appraisal is an important part of underwriting [a loan]. It is very important. If you don't do it right you expose yourself to loss. Our 1984 examination [of Lincoln] showed significant appraisal deficiencies. Mr. Keating promised to correct the problem. Our 1986 exam showed the problems had not been corrected, that there were huge appraisal problems. There was no meaningful underwriting on most loans." Sanchez cited as an example an appraisal redone for the FHLB by Merrill Lynch that corroborated a "significant loss."

DeConcini countered Sanchez. "Why not get an independent appraiser?"

"We did," Sanchez answered. (The FHLB had hired Merrill Lynch to do the appraisals.)

"No, you hired them," DeConcini replied. "Why not get a truly independent one or use arbitration if you're trying to bend over backwards to be fair?" (DeConcini didn't specify how the FHLB might go about getting a "truly independent appraiser" without hiring one.) The senators broke for a vote on the floor.

When the meeting resumed Sanchez told the senators, "Lincoln had underwriting problems with all their investments, equity securities, debt securities, land loans, and direct real estate investments." He said that out of 52 real estate loans Lincoln made between 1984 and 1986 there were no credit reports in the file on the borrowers in all 52 cases. Examiners found $47 million in loans made to borrowers who didn't have adequate credit to assure repayment.

"They're flying blind on all their different loans and investments," Patriarca told them.

Glenn asked, "Some people don't do the kind of underwriting you want. [But] is their judgment good?"

Patriarca replied, "That approach might be okay if they were doing it with their own money. They aren't. They're using federally insured deposits."

Riegle piped up. "Where's the smoking gun? Where are the losses?"

"What's wrong with this if they're willing to clean up their act?" added DeConcini.

Cirona couldn't believe the resistance. "This is a ticking time bomb," he told them.

Patriarca's patience had worn thin. "I've never seen any bank or S&L that's anything like this," he told the senators. ". . . They [Lincoln's practices] violate the law and regulations and common sense."

Then he dropped his bombshell. "We're sending a criminal referral to the Department of Justice. Not maybe, we're sending one.[12] This is an extraordinarily serious matter. It involves a whole range of imprudent actions. I can't tell you strongly enough how serious this is. This is not a profitable institution. . . . Let me give you one example. Lincoln sold a loan with recourse [the buyer had the right to back out] and booked a $12 million profit. The purchaser rescinded the sale, but Lincoln left the $12 million profit on its books. Now, I don't care how many accountants they get to say that's right, it's wrong."

Still fighting, DeConcini countered, "Why would [the accountants] say these things [that the regulators' exam was inordinately long and bordered on harassment]? They have to guard their credibility too."

"They have a client," answered Patriarca, referring to the fact that thrifts pay the accounting firms to perform the required annual audits.

"You believe they [private accounting firms] would prostitute themselves for a client?" DeConcini asked.

"Absolutely," said Patriarca. "It happens all the time."

The senators left for another vote, then returned.

After some discussion Sanchez said, ". . . [Lincoln has] $103 million in goodwill[13] on their books. If this were backed out, they would be $78 million insolvent."

"They would be taken over by the regulators if they were a bank," added Patriarca.

Cirona told DeConcini that the regulators had tried to compromise with Keating. "I've never seen such cantankerous behavior," Cirona said. "At one point they said our examiners couldn't get any association documents unless they made the request through Lincoln's New York litigation counsel."

Patriarca's comment that he was filing a criminal referral on Keating must have been still ringing in the senators' ears. They began to soften their opposition. DeConcini, although still unhappy with the way the FHLB was appraising Lincoln's properties, nevertheless commented, "Frankly the criminality surprises me."

"What can we say to Lincoln?" a stone-faced Glenn asked.

"Nothing with regard to the criminal referral," Black said. ". . . Justice would skin us alive if [they knew we had discussed it]."

Patriarca ended the meeting by telling the senators, "I think my colleague Mr. Black put it right when he said that it's like these guys put it all on 16 black in roulette. Maybe they'll win, but I can guarantee you that if an institution continues such behavior it will eventually go bankrupt." Nine months after this meeting the *National Thrift News* acquired a copy of Black's secret transcript and broke the story. Shortly thereafter Don Riegle returned the $76,100 in donations to Charles Keating and his friends, stating that he wanted to avoid any appearance of misconduct.

Lincoln Savings' attorney commented on the allegations of impropriety raised at the meeting: "From what you've told me these are malicious statements based on false information."

In January 1989 Senator Riegle, now in Proxmire's old post as chairman of the Senate Banking Committee, appeared on *Meet the Press* and flatly denied he'd ever interceded on behalf of Lincoln.

"I did not intervene on behalf of a company [Lincoln]. I did attend a meeting at the request of other senators who represented the state in which that institution was. I came as a member of the banking committee to help try to understand the maze of regulation that is obviously very complex. But I took no action on behalf of that savings and loan or any other at any time."

A year after the meeting between the five senators and San Francisco FHLB representatives, Keating and the San Francisco district bank were still fighting. The president of the district bank, Jim Cirona, later told a congressional committee that Lincoln Savings had given regulators in Washington a secret file about him.

"He [Roger Martin, an FHLBB member] told me that he had in his possession information that was furnished to him by Lincoln that would be very damaging to me."

When asked by reporters about the file, Martin at first denied its existence. Then he recanted and said he had indeed had such a file given to him by Lincoln

Savings but he had not looked inside it. He said, though, that it was his impression that the file contained nothing of a personal nature, only more complaints about the manner in which the San Francisco regulators were conducting their long examination of Lincoln.

San Francisco regulators completed that examination in May 1987. They reported what they considered to be substantial irregularities at Lincoln and they recommended seizure of the institution. But Danny Wall became chairman of the FHLBB in June, and Keating complained to him that the regulators at the San Francisco FHLB were out to get him. He said they had leaked confidential material to the press to undermine him and his company. Wall prohibited the San Francisco regulators from moving against Lincoln. Instead, he moved the responsibility for Lincoln's examination and supervision from the San Francisco FHLB to the FHLBB in Washington—something that had never occurred in the 50 years of Bank Board history. San Francisco regulators complained that Wall's action had "crippled" the independence of his examination staff and "undercut every regulator in the country."

When Keating was asked if his financial support influenced politicians to support his cause, the Orange County *Register* reported that he told reporters, "I want to say in the most forceful way I can: I certainly hope so."

In November 1987 the FHLBB in Washington initiated its own examination of Lincoln Savings, which would last for over a year. In 1988 a meeting was held at the White House with select members of the White House staff and a handful of Republican congressmen. One of those attending that meeting said he was astounded to hear a close advisor to the president conclude that the best cure for the thrift industry was to "keep moving in the direction of the Charles Keatings. They're the only hope." Keating, however, had different ideas. He decided he didn't want to be in the thrift business anymore and put Lincoln up for sale.

Finally even the folks in Washington could not ignore conditions at Lincoln. The FHLBB completed its examination at the end of 1988 and soon demanded that Keating relinquish control of Lincoln. He responded by throwing Lincoln's parent company, American Continental, into bankruptcy on April 13, 1989, and regulators moved in to seize Lincoln the following day. Keating promptly called a dramatic televised news conference in Phoenix and, visibly upset, hands shaking, he told the citizens of Arizona that their economy would be destroyed if regulators—whom he described as malicious, politically motivated bureaucrats—brought Lincoln down (American Continental claimed to employ 2,300 Arizonans).

The same day Danny Wall was forced to admit that San Francisco regulators had been right about Lincoln, and he confirmed that the Bank Board had made several referrals to the Justice Department involving Lincoln Savings. He said the Bank Board audit had uncovered evidence of assets being shifted from Lincoln Savings to American Continental and documents being destroyed.

Two weeks later the Orange County *Register* reported that it obtained a copy of an FHLBB memo that reportedly accused American Continental of "cooking the books" to make both it and Lincoln Savings appear healthy and of making deals with insiders and affiliated companies that cost Lincoln Savings more than $100 million.

Company spokesman Mark Connally responded, "I don't put a whole lot of stock in anything the Bank Board says. All it is is a lot of hot air and unfortunate innuendo." As of this writing, Keating was threatening "to challenge in court those who would destroy us, and [to] call for a full federal investigation of the abusive power by one or more regulator offices."

Regulators said the collapse of Lincoln Savings would cost $2.5 billion.

In June 1987 Ed Gray cleaned out his desk at 1700 G Street to make room for the new chairman, M. Danny Wall—the same Danny Wall who in 1982 had helped shape much of what became known as the Garn-St Germain Act when he was staff director of the Senate Banking Committee, and the same Danny Wall who had opposed Gray's brokered deposit regulation. Treasury Secretary James Baker called Jim Wright in Fort Worth to give him the good news.[14] Wall had come to Washington with Senator Jake Garn (R-Utah), chairman of the Senate Banking Committee, from a savings and loan in Salt Lake City and had served as Garn's chief administrative aide. Bald, bearded, energetic, and always impeccably dressed in three-piece suits, Wall was more in tune than Gray with the U.S. League: *The New Republic* reported that a journalist examining the disclosure statements of top congressional staffers a few years earlier had discovered that Wall led the pack in lobbyist-subsidized junkets—30 in one year. Wall was obsessed with making certain no unauthorized documents leaked to the press. And he stressed the positive side of the S&L industry. Over and over he repeated how pleased he was to head an industry in which "80 to 90 percent of the thrifts were healthy and thriving." He said it was only a small minority of thrifts that were in trouble and he'd have a handle on them just as soon as the recap bill passed the Senate (which it finally did in August).

Wall vehemently denied charges that he was systematically misinforming Congress and the American public about the depth of the FSLIC problem when he projected a $20 billion FSLIC deficit at the same time the General Accounting Office was estimating the debt to be more like $70 billion and private forecasts were coming in at over $100 billion. But after George Bush's nomination speech at the Republican National Convention, Americans might have wondered how Bush's "read my lips, no new taxes" and FSLIC's huge debt could coexist,[15] so mum was the word. By 1989, however, Wall's sleight of hand with the S&L numbers had become so outrageous that House Banking Committee Chairman Henry Gonzalez called loudly for Wall to be fired. It was hard to argue with

Gonzalez's reasoning: Anybody who couldn't figure out how bad the problem was shouldn't be in charge of fixing it.

As for Ed Gray, he was glad his term was over. He knew only too well that 80 to 90 percent of the industry was nowhere near "healthy and thriving." Gray knew he was still being vilified by almost everyone touched by the scandal. Federal Reserve Board Chairman Paul Volcker and Treasury Under Secretary George Gould were two of his few supporters. To the high fliers in Texas and California, Gray was still the Darth Vader of the Bank Board. To the U.S. League he was an unpredictable public relations nightmare and a loose cannon on their deck. To congressmen and senators he was the guy who had caused them to be reminded that money had strings and their mouths moved when someone pulled those strings. Almost everyone was glad to hear that Ed Gray was cleaning out his desk.

Perhaps it was a tragedy that someone of greater national stature had not been chairman at this critical time, someone like Gray's friend Volcker, who could have gone to Congress and thrown down the gauntlet. It's difficult to imagine Jim Wright treating Volcker the way he routinely mistreated Ed Gray. But whatever Gray lacked in stature, he more than made up for in personal commitment. When he left Washington he left with bitter memories of a president and administration that had turned their backs on him when he most needed support. He also left in debt, while the crooks he had tried to chase out of the industry had stuffed offshore bank accounts with hundreds of millions of ill-gotten dollars.

The movie *The Untouchables* opened in Washington the last week before Gray's departure, and Gray rushed to see it. It was about FBI Agent Elliot Ness's battles against mobster Al Capone and his bootleggers, and it struck a chord with Gray. Being under attack from every side for over four years left him feeling like Ness—one man, alone against the corruption of an entire system. The next day Gray had scheduled exit interviews with the major newspapers, and he invoked the name of Elliot Ness, comparing himself to the crime-fighting loner. Only one newspaper, *The American Banker*, mentioned Gray's embellishment.

Gray never got to see Congress pass the recap. Two months after he left office reconciliation between the House and Senate versions was completed and the bill—which gave the FSLIC $10.8 billion in borrowing authority—was signed into law in August 1987. Two precious years had been wasted in political wrangling since Gray had first begun his campaign to get more money for the FSLIC so that insolvent thrifts could be closed and a permanent stop put to their hemorrhage of red ink—two years at $10 million dollars a day in additional losses. (By August 1987 some analysts felt this figure was too low. At the end of 1988 analysts said the insolvent thrifts were costing the FSLIC $35 million a day.) But Ed Gray's ordeal was over. Danny Wall had the wheel now, and his job would be to keep a lid on the problem until the Reagans got out of town in 1989. Once again political expediency would win out over statesmanship.

CHAPTER TWENTY-FIVE

What Happened?

We set out in 1986 with a simple question: How had thrift deregulation gone so terribly wrong? To find the answer we decided to take a look at a few dozen failed savings and loans that we selected virtually at random, attempting only to obtain a fair geographic sampling. Three years later we had our answer: A financial mafia of swindlers, mobsters, greedy S&L executives, and con men capitalized on regulatory weaknesses created by deregulation and thoroughly fleeced the thrift industry. While it was certainly true that economic factors (like plummeting oil prices in Texas and surrounding states) contributed to the crisis, savings and loans would not be in the mess they are today but for rampant fraud.

Yet to this day diehard apologists for thrift deregulation flatly refuse to admit that purposeful fraud was, in fact, chiefly to blame for the FSLIC's $200 to $300 billion debt. A few stubbornly adhere to their denials because they still don't realize what was going on around the country, but most—especially members of lobbying groups like the U.S. League—are simply trying to cover up their own culpability. They pushed hard for deregulation and they share responsibility for the results.

Even the part of the industry that did not participate in the orgy of avarice and fraud must share some degree of blame. They knew what was going on but they kept their silence, fearing that Congress would re-regulate the industry if legislators found out what rogue thrifts were up to.

As Edmund Burke said, "The only thing necessary for the triumph of evil is for good men to do nothing." Fraud became the thrift industry's dirty little family secret.

When Ed Gray tried to clamp down on renegade thrifts, the industry and Congress fought his every move. Like rebellious teenagers bristling over parental intrusion, thrift lobbyists and many thrift executives complained bitterly that Gray was cramping their style, that he didn't understand them, that he was old-fashioned. Congress, always sensitive to the complaints of large contributors, listened well. In the end too many politicians became net beneficiaries of the fraud that swept the thrift industry. WFAA-TV in Dallas reported, for example, that in 1987–88 the three largest S&L political action committees gave more than $883,000 to candidates for Congress. As a result, just when the country needed the best regulators money could buy, those regulators were stopped cold in their tracks by some of the best politicians money had bought.

These powerful forces easily outmaneuvered Ed Gray and systematically undercut his effectiveness. From the very beginning of our investigation we were told that Gray had bungled the job, that he was "an idiot, a buffoon." People like John Lapaglia, Charles Bazarian, Charlie Knapp, and Tom Gaubert railed about Gray and his misguided policies, blaming him for virtually the entire thrift crisis.

"If your book comes off sympathetic to Gray," Lapaglia warned us, "you'll be the laughingstock of the industry."

But we spent many hours interviewing Ed Gray and people who worked with him during those critical years, and we came away with a different opinion. It was true that nothing Gray had done in his life had in any way prepared him for handling a crisis of this magnitude and complexity. He was a public relations man by trade. Still, even with some of the most powerful forces in government breathing fire down his back, he didn't fold and he didn't run away. Instead he took highly unpopular positions that he believed were right and necessary and he stuck with them. He was one of the first to correctly assess the magnitude of the problem and react accordingly.

Ed Gray's biggest fault was that he didn't go public when it became clear that a cabal of political and industry forces were conspiring against his remedial efforts. He should have blown the whistle on them and blown it loud. He should have named names. He should have turned the spotlight on what seems to us to have been sleazy legislative extortion by Jim Wright and others.[1] He should have held a press conference and exposed the OMB's refusal to give him more examiners. But Gray believed that common sense would eventually overcome partisan self-interest. He was wrong.

If those who authored thrift deregulation didn't see the potential for fraud, others certainly did. The likes of Mario Renda and Mike Rapp and Charles Bazarian were swinging into action even before the Garn–St Germain bill was signed. Renda actually followed the progress of the bill through Congress, making notes in his daily desk diary. And when Garn–St Germain passed, Renda and the others moved in like German tank divisions in the early days of World War II, grabbing territory virtually unopposed. Instead of acting to stop the looting, Congress and regulators debated over *whether* they should do anything. They couldn't even seem to decide if the people looting thrifts were crooks or just misunderstood "entrepreneurs."

Such a chaotic state of affairs was fertile ground for the mob. And for them thrift deregulation could not have come at a better time, because the Justice and Labor departments had just cracked down on the mob's pipeline to the Teamsters' Central States Pension Fund, which had for so long been a ready reservoir of capital for wise guys who didn't mind paying kickbacks. The 1986 President's Commission on Organized Crime reported that Jimmy Hoffa, who became Teamster president in 1957, was indisputably a direct instrument of organized crime, and his control over the Central States Pension Fund was convenient for wise guys who couldn't get loans elsewhere. In the mid-1970s, for example, 89 percent of the fund's investments were in real estate loans, mostly to small, speculative businesses (such a portfolio was highly unusual for such a large fund, analysts said). "In short," wrote author Steven Brill (*The Teamsters*), "the mob had control of one of the nation's major financial institutions and one of the very largest private sources of real-estate investment capital in the world."

The president's commission revealed that Hoffa shared his pension-fund kickbacks with Allen Dorfman, asset manager and consultant to the Central States Pension Fund, and one of their favorite investments for pension-fund money was Las Vegas real estate.[2] After Hoffa was convicted of jury tampering in 1964 and went to prison in 1967, Dorfman and members of the mob continued to control the fund. But at the end of 1982 Dorfman was indicted along with Mafia and Teamster officials for trying to bribe Nevada Senator Howard Cannon with favors from the Central States Pension Fund, and a month later, January 20, 1983, Dorfman was gunned down in a parking lot.

That same year the U.S. Department of Labor finally forced the fund to operate according to guidelines enforceable by the courts. That decree resulted in a dramatic shift in the way the Central States Pension Fund invested its money.[3] The message was clear. Wise guys had to find a new "friendly" lender, one that offered the same easy, no-questions-asked access to money and the same liberal nonrepayment terms. Like a gift out of nowhere, deregulated thrifts became the answer to their prayers. President Reagan had just signed the Garn-St Germain Act, in October 1982, and the covey of swindlers who had fluttered around the Teamsters flocked to savings and loans. Simply put, deregulation was the best thing to happen to the mob since Congress passed Prohibition. It also provided organized crime with the best money-laundering environment since the invention of bearer bonds. No one will ever know how many hundreds of millions, or billions, of dollars the mob and drug organizations pumped through thrifts during this "anything goes" period.

But we were told repeatedly by regulators, and even Justice Department officials, that the Mafia, the mob, organized crime, the Syndicate, whatever label you choose, had not and could not infiltrate the thrift industry in any serious way. Well, we asked, then why had these people shown up in our investigations?

Martin Schwimmer, Mario Renda's "associate," was, according to Organized Crime Strike Force investigators, an investment advisor for Frank "the Wop" Manzo, a reputed member of New York's Lucchese crime family. (The five New York crime families were Lucchese, Gambino, Genovese, Bonanno, and Colombo.)

Mario Renda, who was credited with helping destroy dozens of thrifts and banks (possibly a hundred or more), was a friend of Sal Piga, whose rap sheet listed him as an associate of the Tramunti crime family (Carmine Tramunti was the boss of the Lucchese crime family) and enumerated a criminal record of grand larceny, assault and robbery, burglary, first-degree assault, carrying dangerous weapons, and criminal possession of stolen property.

Michael Rapp, a.k.a. Hellerman, who looted Flushing Federal Savings and Loan, among others, said in his autobiography that he had worked his swindles on Wall Street in the 1970s on behalf of the Lucchese and Gambino families, and a law-enforcement official said the dividing of the loot from his S&L swindles in the 1980s was the subject of a sit-down between the Lucchese and Genovese families.

John Napoli, Jr., a Rapp associate who was convicted with Heinrich Rupp in the Aurora Bank case, was identified in an FDIC lawsuit as having been associated with "a well-known, Eastern organized crime family" (identified by a law-enforcement official as the Lucchese family).

Lawrence Iorizzo told investigators he was a Colombo family lieutenant and that Renda invited him to join him in his scheme to bust out banks and thrifts.

Iorizzo said in federal depositions that Mario Renda told him that he (Renda) was handling business for Paul Castellano, a Gambino crime family boss who was assassinated in 1985.

Murray Kessler, indicted with Richmond Harper (identified by the Dallas Morning News as a member of the Beebe banking network in the 1970s) for smuggling arms to Mexico in exchange for heroin (the case ended in a mistrial), was identified by federal officials as an associate of the Gambino family.

Beebe's friend and associate, former Louisiana Governor Edwin Edwards, was implicated through federal wiretaps in dealings with New

Orleans Mafia boss Carlos Marcello. Marcello in 1979 bragged to an FBI undercover agent that he and two or three other mob bosses "owned the Teamsters."

A Beebe-controlled bank made loans to Marcello, his son, and several corporations connected to Marcello, according to the bank's president.

The *American Banker* revealed that Anthony Russo, a former attorney and a director at Indian Springs State Bank, had represented Kansas City's Civilla mob family, and bank records showed the Civillas had several loans at Indian Springs. For years Nick Civella was the man to see about getting favors from the Teamsters, according to the President's Commission on Organized Crime.

David Gorwitz, who was with Dick Binder in Santa Rosa (Binder listed $1.5 million in loans from Centennial on his bankruptcy papers), worked with Binder in Boston. The Boston *Globe* reported that the pair were suspected by law-enforcement officials in Boston of laundering money for fugitive mobster Salvatore Caruana, a capo in the New England Patriarca crime family. Gorwitz was also described in court testimony in the 1970s as a muscleman for the mob.

Lionel Reifler, who indirectly received money from loans made by Judge Reggie's Acadia Savings, was a career white-collar criminal associated with Mike Rapp and organized crime figures.

Morris Shenker, who surfaced time and again in our investigation, was identified in congressional hearings on organized crime as a close associate of the Civella crime family. He was Jimmy Hoffa's attorney and also a close associate of Allen Dorfman, the insurance executive and sophisticated money manager who had extensive connections to the Chicago mob (which is reportedly called "the Outfit") and to the Teamsters Central States Pension Fund. The President's Commission on Organized Crime reported that Shenker borrowed millions of dollars from the fund. Individuals or companies in this book whom we found had done business with Morris Shenker included Norman B. Jenson, Philip Schwab, Charlie Bazarian, Kenneth Kidwell, Southmark, John B. Anderson, Jack Bona, Mario Renda, the Indian Springs State Bank bunch, Al Yarbrow, FCA, Sun Savings and its president, Dan Dierdorff.

Jimmy "the Weasel" Fratianno in *The Last Mafioso* told of Jilly Rizzo, Frank Sinatra's sidekick, associating with him and other mob figures. Rapp, in his biography, said Rizzo was his close friend. Rizzo was a borrower with Rapp at Flushing and regulators said he was involved with Delvecchio at Aurora Bank. Rizzo and Delvecchio sold property in the

Poconos that became collateral for a loan at Edmund Reggie's Acadia Savings and Loan.

Guy Olano of Alliance Savings and Loan was said by the FBI to be connected to people with ties to major Colombian drug families. He had arranged casino financing through John Lapaglia for Las Vegas attorney Norm Jenson, who himself was later identified in evidence collected by Organized Crime Strike Force investigators as a key figure in a $300 million drug-money-laundering operation that the Justice Department said also involved Centennial Savings vice president Sid Shah.

Philip Schwab failed to get a Nevada gaming license because officials had more questions for him than he apparently wanted to answer on the subject of his associations with certain Italian surnamed individuals, one of whom they described as a convicted heroin trafficker. Consultants he hired to help him get the license said in their report, "We can only presume at this point that the Gaming Control Board has information from law-enforcement authorities associating these individuals with organized crime activities."

At nearly every thrift we researched for this book we found clear evidence of either mob, Teamster, or organized crime involvement. Only one conclusion was possible: The mob had played an important role in the nationwide fraternity that looted the savings and loan industry following deregulation.

Of course the mob and swindlers didn't suck all the billions out of the thrift industry, although they certainly got their share. People who had never committed a crime in their lives fell prey to deregulation's promise of easy money. Thrift officers watched as the professional swindlers worked their scams and never got caught and decided, why not? Buttoned-down appraisers, plugging along in boring jobs making $200 to $600 per appraisal, learned that by simply raising their opinion of a property's value to match a borrower's needs or desires, they could raise their own standard of living as well—and the higher their opinion, the bigger their paycheck. Contractors, attorneys, title company executives, and auditors each found their own ways to get a seat on the gravy train by perverting their particular business functions for the cause. As Erv Hansen so correctly observed in 1983, "The beauty of this is that there's going to be enough money in it for everyone." And there was.

Something else was going on at thrifts too. We avoided dealing with it in detail because we never seemed to be able to get our arms around it, but it disturbed us and bears mention. Time and time again during our research we ran into people at failed thrifts who claimed to have connections with the CIA. We ran into individuals whom we discovered were dealing secretly with the

Contras, moving large sums of money here, there, and off to nowhere for what they claimed were covert purposes.

At San Marino Savings in Southern California we heard about a major borrower, G. Wayne Reeder (who also attempted a couple of failed ventures with Herman Beebe), meeting in late 1981 at an arms demonstration with Raul Arana and Eden Pastora, Contra leaders who were considering buying military equipment from Reeder's Indian bingo-parlor partner, Dr. John Nichols. Among the equipment were night-vision goggles manufactured by Litton Industries and a light machine gun.[4] Nichols, according to former Reeder employees and published accounts, had a plan in the early 1980s to build a munitions plant on the Cabezon Indian reservation near Palm Springs in partnership with Wackenhut, a Florida security firm. The plan fell through. Nichols was a self-described CIA veteran of assassination attempts against Castro in Cuba and Allende in Chile. Authorities said he was a business associate of members of the Los Angeles Mafia. He was later convicted in an abortive murder-for-hire scheme and sentenced to prison.

At Indian Springs State Bank we found Farhad Azima, who financed part of his Global International Airways operations with loans from Indian Springs bank. Mario Renda had relationships with Adnan Khashoggi and another deposit broker who, federal investigators confirmed, was a former CIA operative who laundered millions of dollars through financial institutions for Baby Doc Duvalier, the former ruler of Haiti. Investigating Mike Rapp we met Heinrich Rupp, a self-described CIA contract pilot, and his associate, who claimed the CIA was using banks to launder drug money and get loans that went to finance the Contras.

And there was more, much more. Experts had wondered how so many billions of dollars could just vanish from the thrift industry without a trace. If some of that money were channeled into the Contra pipeline or used to serve other legal or illegal covert purposes, that could certainly be one answer. One respected law-enforcement official told us that a man in prison for bank fraud had agreed to cooperate with him in an investigation of another bank fraud case, in exchange for a good word to the judge, until he was suddenly granted a White House pardon. The official said he was told the pardon was obtained through CIA chief Bill Casey. And as we were going to press we were working with a fellow reporter digging up information that Southmark may have had a relationship with some members of the covert Iran-Contra crowd.

We don't *know* what all that means. We didn't have time to investigate both that story and this one, but we want to be on the record as saying that we finally came to believe *something* involving the CIA and Contras was going on at thrifts during the 1980s. After all, deregulation created enough chaos to accommodate just about anyone's purposes. And taking out loans from federally insured institutions, giving the money to the Contras, and letting federal insurance pick up the losses does have the flavor of what Ollie North might think was a "neat idea."

The S&L industry-inspired "see no evil" approach to the looting at thrifts helped keep the mounting crisis out of the public consciousness until 1988. It surfaced then only because nonindustry analysts began to insist loudly that the FSLIC's losses were approaching $100 billion. Suddenly the American public started paying attention. For two years the three of us had worked in near isolation. With the exception of a handful of other reporters around the country, we couldn't find anyone who understood what was happening or seemed to care. But suddenly everyone wanted to talk to us about the problem. We were just winding up our investigation when the General Accounting Office in Washington sent two investigators out to Guerneville. The two buttoned-down bureaucrats wanted to know if any "La Cosa Nostra types," as they so quaintly put it, had infiltrated the thrift industry after deregulation. A producer for CBS's *60 Minutes* contacted the House Committee on Government Operations to get background for a *60 Minutes* segment on the thrift crisis, and an attorney for the committee referred him to us. He, too, made the trek to Guerneville to spend a few days going through our files.

The FBI announced that fraud and embezzlement cases settled at financial institutions were up 42 percent in 1987 and more than doubled (to $2.1 billion) in 1988. In October 1988, Congress finally caught up and announced their findings that the country's financial institutions were targets for bust-outs by organized crime syndicates and generic swindlers. A House committee reported, "At least one-third (and probably more) of commercial bank failures and over three-quarters of all S&L insolvencies appear to be linked in varying degrees to [serious misconduct by senior insiders or outsiders]."[5]

In 1988 the comptroller of the currency surveyed recent bank failures and found that less than 10 percent were caused solely by economic factors. The FSLIC began issuing profiles of the failed thrifts it was trying to dispose of (sell, merge, give away), and the profiles almost always included tales of looting and insider abuse.[6]

Finally even FHLBB Chairman Danny Wall, who had made a profession out of denying that there was a problem, admitted to the House Banking Committee's Subcommittee on Financial Institutions in March 1989 that the FHLBB was finding more and more instances of fraud and mismanagement: "In virtually all cases, the boards of directors of resolved [handled by the FHLBB in 1988] institutions were found to not have acted prudently."

But after all was said and done, what would come of it? Had anything been learned? Probably not. As far back as 1976 key members of Congress knew what might happen if they deregulated thrifts. That year Congressman Fernand St

Germain (D-R.I.) had chaired the House banking subcommittee investigating the failure of Citizens State Bank in Carrizo Springs, Texas, and the network of businessmen (including Herman Beebe) whom authorities believed were abusing dozens of financial institutions in the area. As we read the hearing transcripts 11 years later, it was clear that Congress and federal regulators knew in 1976 what kind of people were out there just waiting for an opportunity to victimize financial institutions if given the slightest opening.

During those 1976 hearings St Germain said about bank failures:

> We have been repeatedly told that most major bank failures have been caused by criminal conduct. . . . Insider loans have been the principal cause of bank failures over the past 15 years. . . .

Yet, he noted:

> Of the 56 banks that failed in the United States between 1959 and 1971, 34 had passed their most recent examination in a "no-problem" category, and 17 of the 34 had been given an "excellent" rating. Undeniably, this fact alone points to an increasingly apparent deficiency in the existing examination process.
>
> . . . All too frequently examiners do not "look behind the loan" as to the adequacy of collateral and do not inquire into relationships between institutions due to agency coordination difficulties. . . .
>
> There has been a growing feeling in recent years of the need for greater uniformity in statutes and regulations relating to self-dealing loans, conflict of interest, duties and responsibilities of boards of directors, and loan limitations for directors and stockholders.

With those words St Germain had summed up not only the situation in the banking industry in 1976 but also predicted with stunning accuracy the fate of hundreds of S&Ls less than ten years later.

Federal regulators who testified at the Citizens State Bank hearings (among those testifying, by the way, was Rosemary Stewart, the regulator whose picture would be a target in Tom Gaubert's mini-shooting gallery ten years later) warned that their ability to keep swindlers out of the banking industry was severely hampered by privacy laws that made it illegal to keep lists of undesirables who had a history of abusing financial institutions. Furthermore, anyone who wanted to buy a bank could. Only officers and directors, not owners, were required to meet certain minimum standards.

Committee member Representative Henry B. Gonzalez (D-Tx.) also sat on the subcommittee investigating Citizens State Bank and he made the most ironic comment of the hearings:

Here, however, we have found the one bright spot: namely, that the Federal Home Loan Bank Board is aware of the situation and is plainly working hard to turn it around. Even here we probably must consider strengthening enforcement powers of the Federal Home Bank Board. . . .

Remember, this was 1976.

But then Representative Gonzalez gave this wise and eloquent summation:

Charters issued to financial institutions are given for public reasons. Banks are supposed to serve the public. They have a public character. It is the public that suffers when bank owners and officers buy and sell banks like used cars, when they engage in self-dealing, when they plunder and steal. We have seen the pattern of flagrant and squalid misconduct in these institutions. There is no reason to doubt that other institutions are being stripped and raided this very day.

We have found regulation that is forgetful, benign, and on some levels pitiful. Inadequate regulation is what has made possible the kind of outlandish sordid conduct we have discovered. We have lifted only a corner of the rock. What we have seen is enough to disgust anyone.

Corrective action is needed both at the state and federal level. Administrative regulation can be—and must be—strengthened. State statutes need to be strengthened. Federal statutes probably need updating, and yet at the bottom this is the ultimate truth: no law is going to replace efficient, honest and aggressive regulation.

Six years later Congress, led by St Germain, voted to *deregulate* the savings and loan industry with the Garn-St Germain Act in 1982. (Gonzalez voted against both the 1980 and 1982 deregulation legislation.) Had St Germain forgotten everything he saw and learned at Citizens State Bank?[7] It would appear so. During the time his deregulation bill was pending in 1981 and 1982, St Germain was dining around Washington on the U.S. League of Savings Institutions' charge accounts.[8] That little indiscretion earned him a special Justice Department probe into his cozy relationship with the U.S. League and the $10,000 to $20,000 a year in entertainment they reportedly spent on him but he never reported. Though the Justice Department decided not to prosecute St Germain, it found "substantial evidence of serious and sustained misconduct." A House ethics committee investigation in 1986 alleged that he understated his assets by more than $1 million for several years and took at least seven trips on Florida Federal Savings' jet (St Germain reportedly had a close relationship with the CEO of Florida Federal Savings in St. Petersburg), but they recommended no punishment. St Germain's home-district voters voted him out of office in the 1988 election, and he thus became the first major Washington politician to succumb to the thriftgate scandal. Because any legislation to clean up the savings and loan industry would have to go through the House Banking, Finance and Urban Affairs Committee, which St Germain had chaired, we hoped his ouster was a good omen. He was replaced by Representative Henry B. Gonzalez, who had spoken so eloquently during the Citizens State Bank hearings in Texas 12 years earlier and later voted against deregulation.

St Germain wasn't the only person who demonstrated a flat learning curve when it came to the thrift industry.

In 1988 Wall remembered his benefactor, Senator Jake Garn, by committing the bankrupt FSLIC to donating $6,000 to the Jake Garn Institute at the University of Utah. When a reporter asked Wall about the donation, she reported that he replied, "So?"

In the fall of 1988 members of the U.S. League—who as late as the summer of 1987 argued, against all reason, that the FSLIC needed only $5 billion to get back on its feet—held their annual convention in sunny Honolulu. Network television ran colorful footage on the evening news of thrift executives partying on the sandy beaches, showing no apparent concern for the billions in losses their industry had incurred, losses they had every intention of asking the taxpayer to cover.

Only a few weeks earlier three officials of the Federal Home Loan Bank of San Francisco flew at bank expense to Italy and Spain to choose granite samples for the bank's new 20-story headquarters building. (After a public outcry they decided to use American sandstone from a quarry in Pennsylvania.)

In 1987 an annual survey of executive salaries and benefits showed that for the second time in three years thrift chief executive officers got much larger increases than CEOs in other industries. In 1987 total compensation for thrift CEOs increased 13 percent, 5 percent more than for CEOs in other industries and nearly triple the 4.4 percent rise in the consumer price index.[9]

Taken altogether, it was enough to make a taxpayer scream, since by the end of 1988 it was being widely reported that taxpayers would probably have to fund most of a *$200 to $300 billion* FSLIC bill, an amount equal to the entire NASA budget for the next 20 to 30 years. The potential cost to the average American taxpayer was estimated to be at least $2,000 each (or $200 a year on every person's 1040 for ten years) *assuming* the hole wasn't deeper than estimated, and that was not a very safe assumption. By the end of 1988 insolvent thrifts yet to be closed were costing the FSLIC $35 to $40 million a day in additional red ink, or at least $12.7 billion a year.

In March 1989 President Bush's point man on the thrift crisis, Richard Breeden, warned thrift industry leaders meeting behind closed doors in Los Angeles that the new administration's broom was about to sweep the industry clean and not to get underfoot.

"This is a very delicate and very dangerous situation," Breeden said. He warned that the administration was in no mood for trouble from either thrifts or their lobby groups. "I'm here today to tell you that it would not be in the long-term best interests of this industry to oppose our plan. We don't have ten months this time to sit around and debate this thing. This is a very dangerous situation."

CHAPTER TWENTY-SIX

Taking the Cure

The American savings and loan industry has been damaged beyond repair. Little can be done now to mitigate the damage done by careless and thoughtless deregulation. Over the next five or ten years the savings and loan industry as we know it today will quietly disappear into history, one of the last relics of post-Depression New Dealism. The FHLBB, FSLIC, etc., may gradually be merged with the bank regulatory agencies, and the few remaining distinctions between thrifts and banks will vanish, or the thrift regulatory apparatus will remain to supervise financial institutions still called S&Ls but very unlike today's thrifts. Perhaps we will be left with community banks—to handle mortgages, consumer loans, and small business loans—and commercial banks. In any case, the country will have institutions offering home mortgages and a safe haven for deposits, but they will bear little resemblance to traditional savings and loans. As deregulation progresses, more and more Americans may have to turn to unregulated mortgage bankers[1] for home loans because banks and thrifts lulled by the siren song of developers will have little interest in mortgages.

While the thrift industry plays out its last hand, the American taxpayers must concern themselves with how the industry's little $200 to $300 billion problem can be solved. There has been and will continue to be a great deal of effort expended in Washington to disguise the politically dangerous fact that American taxpayers are the only people with deep enough pockets to pay the bill. The remaining members of the thrift industry can't pay it.[2] Already, thrifts are paying premiums two times higher than banks are paying and that extra expense makes it very difficult for them to compete in the financial marketplace. Forcing them to pay even more would only create more casualties. We believe it would be inherently unfair to expect the prudently managed thrifts to pay the entire cost of this debacle (even though their silent acquiescence allowed the situation to get so far out of hand) because the primary responsibility for the

310

huge losses belongs to those who plundered and to politicians who were seduced by the thrift lobby and campaign contributions.

But as with any such sticky issue, officials in Washington were looking for a way to fix the problem without personally taking any heat. A wide-open debate over the thrift crisis was the last thing Congress, the Federal Home Loan Bank Board, or the thrift industry lobby wanted. Too much dirty laundry would get aired in the process. To avoid just that the same people who brought us this $200 to $300 billion problem began cooking up schemes for quietly dealing with it.

To get a jump on any new Bush administration (nonindustry) initiative, and because Congress wouldn't give them the money to close the institutions down, the FHLBB initiated a crash program to "sell" 220 of the sickest institutions before changes in the tax laws at the end of 1988 made such acquisitions less attractive. But to attract buyers the Bank Board had to offer huge financial and regulatory incentives.[3] Analysts[4] said that selling the institutions in this manner actually cost up to 40 percent more than simply closing them immediately, paying off insured depositors, and selling the institutions' assets. When the FHLBB sold American Savings and Loan (a subsidiary of Charlie Knapp's FCA) in 1988 to the Robert Bass Group, the buyer put $350 million cash into the deal, with a promise of $150 million more within three years. The FSLIC subsidized the balance of the transaction with nearly $2 billion of its own money. In another "take my wife, please" deal, the FSLIC sold failed Eureka Savings to former Bank of America executive Steve McLin's group, America First. As part of the deal the FSLIC agreed to pay for all future losses from bad loans on Eureka's books and contributed $291 million in cash to make Eureka solvent for the new owners. The FSLIC agreed to share the tax-loss benefits with America First on a 50-50 basis, just to sweeten the deal, and guaranteed America First a built-in profit on troubled assets that came along with the thrift. One source close to the FSLIC/McLin negotiations described dealing with the FSLIC negotiators as "taking candy from a baby," and in the first seven months of ownership America First reported a $10 million profit from its Eureka Federal operations.[5]

For the first time, *The Wall Street Journal* reported, thrifts are being run by corporate raiders, with assets guaranteed by the government.

These arrangements were attractive to the FHLBB and some politicians because many of the costs were in the form of tax breaks[6] and interest payments[7] that can be spread out over many years and may go quietly unnoticed. But the losers will be the U.S. taxpayers, who several years from now may have to pay an even larger thrift bill than is due today if these same (but even sicker) S&Ls wind up back in the taxpayers' laps. It is especially troubling that some of the buyers of these insolvent thrifts are other thrifts who are themselves almost insolvent or developers with no banking experience but a lot of uses for money—those ubiquitous "entrepreneurs." These deals are simply a new batch of ticking time bombs.

Representative Jim Leach (R-Iowa) said the deals were too good for the buyers but not good enough for the government. What has developed, he said, is a giveaway system where the potential profit has been privatized while the potential loss has been socialized—exactly the problem that brought us the thrift crisis in the first place.

In 1988 regulators put together what they called the "Southwest Plan," in which they created 15 large thrifts out of 87 smaller, insolvent ones and threw in some federal "assistance." The very first Southwest Plan deal in Texas merged four sick thrifts into one large thrift, Southwest Savings Association of Dallas, owned by Caroline Hunt, the daughter of one of the Texas Hunt brothers.[8] The FSLIC forgave Hunt a debt estimated at $15 billion and contributed $2 billion to the new megathrift. Within ten months Southwest Savings was reportedly seeking an additional $200 million in federal assistance. In March 1989 the comptroller general of the General Accounting Office was saying that the Southwest Plan had little chance of succeeding. He told the House Banking Committee that the FHLBB didn't even audit the 87 Texas thrifts involved in the Southwest Plan before arranging their mergers.

Other mergers and purchases the FHLBB had arranged were already falling apart. Ramona Savings in Fillmore, California (its president, remember, was arrested at the San Francisco passport office as he tried to flee the country for the Grand Cayman Islands), was sold to Midwest Federal in February 1988. Within a year Midwest Federal had also failed and news reports alleged fraud and misconduct by the Midwest chairman, who was reportedly under FBI investigation.

In March 1989 the GAO told the Senate Banking Committee that the FSLIC was so disorganized and its record-keeping so sloppy that it was impossible to tell how much the deals would eventually cost the federal government and whether or not some White Knights got preferential treatment.

In February 1989 the new Bush administration moved swiftly to take the initiative away from the FHLBB and presented a complex plan that was still being revised as this book went to press. The most immediate aspects of the Bush plan called for the FHLBB to be placed under the direct supervision of the Treasury Department and the watchful eye of the comptroller of the currency. The FSLIC's job of seizing and liquidating the nation's junkyard of insolvent thrifts would be handed over to the FDIC. The complex plan also called for $50 million for the Department of Justice's white-collar crime and fraud divisions.

The Bush plan was a clear improvement over the status quo, but the idea of the FDIC shouldering the additional burdens of the thrift industry gave little comfort. The same people who decided it was a good idea to lend billions of dollars to Argentina, Mexico, and Brazil would be deciding what was best for thrifts.

The FDIC said its assets at the end of 1988 stood at around $18 billion— not a lot of money for an agency with plenty of problems of its own. In 1987 a record 184 banks failed, costing the FDIC more than $3 billion, and 221 were closed in 1988 at a cost of $3 billion to $9 billion. FDIC examiners said there were an unprecedented (since the Depression) 1,500 problem banks around the country at the end of 1988—three times the number of problem thrifts that remained to be dealt with. In late 1988 a banking industry watch group, the Shadow Financial Regulatory Committee, reported that the FDIC was itself nearly insolvent but wouldn't admit it. The shadow group said the FDIC had only $400 million left.

The FDIC record in dealing with those troubled banks was not much better than the FSLIC's in many cases and, like thrift regulators, the FDIC was politicized. Jake Butcher, who with his brother was close to the Carter administration and looted 23 banks in Tennessee and Kentucky until they collapsed in 1983 (even though the insider dealing was identified as early as 1977), bragged to a journalist that he had helped name a member of the FDIC board. (The Butcher brothers are serving 20-year prison sentences for bank fraud.)

But the Bush administration proceeded with its plan to put the FDIC in charge of closing more than 200 insolvent thrifts, and even before Congress began to debate the Bush plan the FDIC moved in. Closing those brain-dead institutions resolved two immediate problems: first, it stopped the losses that such a thrift racked up each day it remained open—an open, insolvent thrift is like an open artery; and second, each closure removed another piece of the excess capacity created in the thrift industry when everyone rushed to open his own money machine after deregulation. But it mired the FDIC in a problem the FSLIC had been wrestling with for some time—how to operate and then dispose of the assets of the seized thrifts. Regulators did not make good real estate managers or brokers, and the stories of their inefficiency and wasted millions of dollars came to us by the dozens.

Acknowledging the magnitude of the problem, FDIC Chairman Bill Seidman said, "The amount of real estate that will be up for sale is likely to exceed $100 billion, so it is a huge task, the biggest liquidation in the history of the world."

Immediately reports began to surface that with the FDIC turning its attention to thrifts, banks were going dangerously unsupervised. The House Committee on Government Operations had reported in October 1988 that the FDIC examination staff was understaffed then and "failed badly" at meeting its examination schedule. In 1986 and 1987, 79 out of 189 state banks that failed had not been examined within a year of their failure, 39 had not been examined within 18 months, and 29 had not been examined within three years prior to their failure. The *American Banker* reported in March 1989 that hundreds of state-chartered banks in Texas were operating essentially unsupervised, just as bank failures in the state had soared from 22 in 1987 to 44 in 1988 to a projected 50 in 1989.

Clearly, the only way to successfully tackle the thrift crisis was with a co-ordinated, overall attack approved by the Bush administration and Congress. Piecemeal efforts had proved inadequate time and time again, and siccing the FDIC on thrifts without adequately increasing its staff was just one more example. President Bush entreatied Congress to act on his proposal in 45 days, but there was no chance whatsoever that they would. And the $35 to $40 million-a-day losses continued.

While Congress tried to deal with the Bush plan, the savings and loan industry continued to operate under regulations (especially on the state level) that hadn't changed much since the heady days of deregulation. It was true that some important improvements had been made. For example, when California Savings and Loan Commissioner William Crawford succeeded Larry Taggart in early 1985, he stopped the expansion of the state thrift industry dead in its tracks until he could get the out-of-control situation in hand. From 1981 through 1984, California regulators had approved 172 thrift charters. From 1985 through 1988, Crawford approved one.

Federal and state regulatory agencies were in general beefing up their staffs with more regulators and examiners. And some important re-regulation had occurred on the federal level, including: standards were raised for thrifts seeking FSLIC insurance; in 1985 Gray placed limits on growth, raised minimum net-worth requirements, and limited direct investments; in 1986 he increased reserve requirements; and the FHLBB began demanding more accurate appraisals. In addition, savings and loans had to start carrying assets on their books at values that more closely reflected actual market values. While the new standards came with qualifications that blunted some of their effectiveness, and the philosophy of forbearance continued, these were important steps in the right direction. But regulators and Congress still needed to develop a comprehensive program to ensure that savings and loans (and banks) would stop acting like drunken sailors.

Banks and thrifts should be held to the same standards when they are serving the same market, and the following points must be addressed in any future legislation:

Politics:

The issue of politics as played in the halls of Congress hardly needs further mention here except to report the ironic results of the ethics probe of Speaker Jim Wright. The outside counsel to the House Ethics Committee, Richard Phelan, submitted his report February 21, 1989, and concluded that in savings and loan matters Wright broke House rules four times:

> When he removed the recap bill from House consideration in order to pressure the Bank Board to change its resolution of the Craig Hall matter.

> When he sought a change in the Bank Board's decision to oust Tom Gaubert from Independent American Savings.

> When he attempted to "destroy [Joe] Selby's career" based upon the accusation that he was a homosexual.

> When he tried in early 1988 to get Danny Wall to fire William Black (by then Black was working for the FHLB in San Francisco and was not within Wall's jurisdiction).

But the House Ethics Committee ignored Phelan on the S&L matters. Members concluded that Wright violated House rules 69 times, but not when he tried to get a little service for his thrift constituents.

Still, the savings and loan issue wouldn't die. In May 1989 during the Dallas trial of some Commodore Savings Association officials (for allegedly illegally funneling corporate money into a political action committee headed, coincidentally, by Wright's friend Tom Gaubert), defendant John Harwell, a former Commodore vice president, said Wright solicited campaign contributions for Democrat Jim Chapman during a meeting of S&L executives in Dallas and also said Wright understood the problems that pending direct-investment legislation could create for thrifts. Subsequently, the PAC received large donations, some of which went to Chapman, according to press reports, and the legislation never made it to the House floor. Wright denied any connection, saying, "You can look until you're blind, ask until you're hoarse, listen until you're deaf and you will never find anybody of whom I've asked anything in return."

If the FHLBB remains in operation, several changes need to be made to help keep political pressure from playing such a strong role in the regulation process. The Bush plan called for the elimination of the three-member Bank Board, but if it is retained, the three members should be appointed for six-year terms rather than the current four-year terms. The requirement that no more than two members can belong to the same party should be eliminated—the White House should select the best-qualified people regardless of their political affiliation. The FHLBB should not oversee the FSLIC—the FSLIC should be a separate entity, free from any political pressure the FHLBB might exert.

Though transferring examiners to the district banks served an important purpose when Gray couldn't get Stockman's approval for more examiners, it created a possible conflict of interest when a president of a troubled S&L was sitting on the board of the supervising district bank (FHLB directors are elected by the member S&Ls). Charles Keating raised the further objection that his company's thrift, Lincoln Savings, was being regulated by officials (the San Francisco FHLB board, which was made up of savings and loan executives in his district) who were in competition with him. But even under the old system the potential for conflict of interest existed. For example, when examiners from the FHLBB were examining Empire Savings' books in 1982, Empire Chairman Spencer Blain was an official of the FHLB of Little Rock, which was responsible for any disciplinary measures that might grow out of the examination.

The Topkea Federal Home Loan Bank, under its president, Kermit Mowbray, became embroiled in several political controversies, and an official said Mowbray was sharply criticized by Ed Gray for not being tough enough in his supervision. For example, regulators said, the Topeka bank had been receiving warnings since 1985 that Silverado Savings of Denver was on a collision course with disaster, and Silverado borrowed heavily from the Topeka FHLB, but no significant supervisory action was taken against the $1 billion thrift until it was finally declared insolvent in December 1988. (The thrift fell within the jurisdiction of the Topeka FHLB.) A former analyst for the Topeka FHLB, James Moroney, went public with his conviction that politics was the reason. Moroney declined to elaborate, but published reports said Larry Mizel, a Republican activist who had raised over $1 million for the Republican party, was a borrower at Silverado; Neil Bush, son of then-Vice President Bush, sat on Silverado's board of directors;[9] and Silverado's chairman, Michael Wise, was reported by the Denver *Post* to be a favorite of the thrift lobbying organization, the U.S. League.

"The problem in my assessment," said Moroney, "was the lack of separation between the examination and supervision function at the Topeka bank."[10]

Deposit insurance:

There is a place for the entrepreneurial bank or thrift in today's marketplace, but the risks such a nontraditional institution takes should not be underwritten by federally backed deposit insurance. Until the politically powerful in the thrift industry are willing to let go of the FSLIC security blanket in return for the right to wheel and deal, all their talk about free enterprise is simply hypocrisy. Deposit insurance was established so the common person could be assured that his relatively meager life savings could be invested safely. It's time to get back to that concept.

Deposit brokers:

Deposit brokers' access to thrifts was limited in the 1960s precisely for the reasons Gray wished to limit them again in 1984: Their ability to scour the countryside for the highest rate in the nation creates an atmosphere that pushes rates up, as institutions compete for the easy-to-get institutional deposits, and encourages thrifts to use the expensive deposits in high-risk ventures. Insured brokered deposits also are too easy a source of fuel for fraudulent deals.

We believe, however, that the problem is not necessarily the brokers themselves but, again, the insurance coverage. Deposit brokers can perform a legitimate and important function by efficiently moving money around the country, but we should limit FSLIC insurance coverage to $100,000 per deposit broker, per institution. Even Mario Renda would have had difficulty getting normally honest thrift officials to sell their integrity for a $100,000 deposit.

Capital requirements:

Before deregulation, thrifts were supposed to have 5 percent of their total assets in tangible reserves to cover unexpected losses. But regulators dropped the requirement to 3 percent in 1981 as fewer and fewer institutions were able to meet the 5 percent standard. The 3 percent rule, coupled with a regulation adopted in 1972 that allowed thrifts to meet the reserve requirement by averaging reserves over a five-year period, allowed thrifts to grow much too fast, if they were so inclined, and the crooked ones were. This high leveraging capability was one of the chief elements that attracted "entrepreneurial" owners into the industry. The brake on lending that the reserve requirement achieved disappeared.

A high capital requirement is a key element to a healthy banking or thrift industry, and we applaud a movement within the industry to support an 8 percent reserve requirement that would increase as a thrift's investment risks increase. The FHLBB attempted a decade ago to develop a risk-based reserve requirement but abandoned the plan in 1980 when the thrift industry objected. If the FHLBB had stuck to its guns, much of the artificial growth that followed would not have been possible.

Regulatory agencies:

Deregulation of the financial services sector has blurred the distinctions between financial institutions. Mortgage brokers and commercial banks, as well as thrifts, now provide traditional home-loan mortgage services. As a result many people feel a separate thrift industry is no longer needed.[11] But if thrifts do continue to exist as a separate entity, they must be prepared to fund an adequate regulatory staff and be able to offer auditors and examiners salaries equal to what they could earn at private auditing firms—only then can they expect to attract quality staff. If thrifts are at all reluctant to pay the bill for such a regulatory structure, Congress could take this opportunity, this crisis atmosphere, to swiftly put the industry out of its misery. They could liquidate the twelve district banks and apply to the FSLIC's deficit the estimated $13 billion in equity that the district banks hold, fill the rest of the FSLIC hole with a federal bailout, and liquidate the FSLIC. Close all the sick thrifts immediately and send the healthy ones out for applications to become banks.

Accounting principles:

Accounting practices used by thrifts (Generally Accepted Accounting Principles and Regulatory Accounting Principles) were practically impenetrable except by specially trained accountants. They looked like something authored by Lewis Carroll. In dozens of ways thrifts could legally doctor their balance sheets, and they used those smoke-and-mirror accounting methods—usually with the regulators' blessing—to hide the sorry truth of their deteriorating condition from the public and, to some extent, from themselves. Thrifts should be required to adhere to accounting methods that reflect reality, no matter how distasteful that reality may be. They should be required to regularly revalue their assets to current market conditions ("mark to market").

Screen the thrifts' officers, directors, and owners:

Set up a process modeled after the New Jersey and Nevada Gaming Control Boards, which screen and thoroughly investigate applicants for gambling licenses. Look into applicants' pasts, their records in other jurisdictions, and their associates. Determine the source of the funds that applicants are using to capitalize their new institution. (Herman Beebe grubstaked more than one unethical banker.) And after they are approved for a charter, recall thrift owners for a thorough reevaluation at the slightest breath of scandal. If it's determined that they hang around with crooks, show them the door. Don't let con men be bankers. Don't let borrowers be lenders. Remember the words of California's tough Savings and Loan Commissioner Bill Crawford: "The best way to rob a bank is to own one." And the words of Willie Sutton when he was asked why he robbed banks: "Because that's where the money is."

Rewrite bank secrecy laws:

It's high time to bury the Depression-era fear of runs on banks. That phobia is one of the underlying justifications for the secrecy that surrounds Bank Board actions, but, in fact, the best thing that could have happened to the thrifts in this book would have been an early run on deposits to force more timely action by regulators. Secrecy was the single most important factor in allowing losses at thrifts to get so large. It played directly into the hands of anyone who had something to hide. It even prevented ethical S&L managers from monitoring their own industry, because when they reported their concern about a high flier to regulators, they never heard another word about the case.

The secrecy was inevitably carried to ridiculous extremes, as when regulators sent us several short biographies ("bios") of themselves, prepared for the media . . . and each one was stamped "confidential."

We recommend opening thrifts and banks to the light of day, and if depositors don't like what they see and decide to take their money elsewhere, so be it. Examination reports, for example, should immediately be made public. If Vernon Savings' depositors had discovered the kinds of screwball deals that thrift was involved in when its assets were only, say, $300 million, and there'd been an ugly little run on deposits, forcing regulators to pay attention, think how much the FSLIC would have saved. Instead, secrecy let Vernon swell to over $1 billion in assets before it finally collapsed—all in the name of "privacy."

Law enforcement:

The nation's legal systems weren't prepared for the upheaval that followed deregulation. Prosecuting financial fraud cases became a nightmare, partly because it was a fairly simple matter to bust out a thrift or bank without *clearly* breaking a single law: Borrow (or have your associate borrow) lots of money, never pay it back, blame a bad local real estate market or (if the scam was in the Southwest) the falling price of a barrel of oil, and enjoy the proceeds tax-free since debt is not taxed. Prosecutors had a tough time proving intent to defraud.

"Let me wave a pair of bloody underwear in front of a jury in a murder trial and I can have their undivided attention," complained one U.S. attorney. "But let me wave a handful of phony deeds and loan applications in front of that same jury and their eyes just glaze over."

Congress should pass legislation that expands and redefines bank fraud and establishes new and more severe penalties, particularly for those who have a history of abuses at institutions. There are too many cracks in the law through which highly sophisticated criminals can slip.

White-collar crime is a growth industry and the Justice Department's small fraud task forces are not an adequate weapon against it. Nor are individual FBI agents chasing swindlers around their own blocks. Just as the Justice Department created permanent regional organized crime strike forces around the country, they now need to establish similar white-collar crime strike forces. Such strike forces could keep track of these highly mobile swindlers as they move from jurisdiction to jurisdiction, state to state. And, as the strike forces did with the mob, they could penetrate the network of associations that white-collar criminals use to facilitate their schemes. They could establish long-term sting operations and place in the field undercover agents who would act as an early warning system when a scam was about to go down. Only then would prosecutors have an effective weapon against the growing number of economic terrorists bleeding today's financial services industry.

Not only is no such white-collar crime strike force being considered but, remarkably, one of the first suggestions made by Attorney General Richard Thornburgh upon taking office in 1989 was that the 24 regional organized crime strike forces be eliminated. We found incontrovertible evidence of organized crime involvement in the thrift crisis, but Thornburgh wanted the strike forces disbanded and merged with the U.S. attorneys, who have so often proven themselves ineffective in battling bank and thrift fraud. The battle was a bureaucratic one, with Thornburgh supporting the U.S. attorneys, who didn't like having independent strike forces operating in their jurisdiction. But we remembered the trouble Mike Manning had finding a U.S. attorney who would take the Mario Renda case, and we strongly agreed with assistant U.S. Attorney Bruce Maffeo, who prosecuted Renda in Brooklyn, when he said, "The First United Fund case provides a vivid example of why the organized crime program is necessary to effectively investigate and prosecute complicated financial crimes. Without the institutional dedication of resources and time that the organized crime section uniquely affords, this case and others like it would never have been solved." The strike forces should not only be retained, but they should be expanded to include non-mob white-collar crime. Another change in the works, moving white-collar crime out of the jurisdiction of civil racketeering laws (RICO), is another bad idea. Securities, accounting, commodities, and other industries are lobbying against the Racketeer Influenced and Corrupt Organization Law, but it is a powerful tool against economic, white-collar crime. As Thornburgh said, it is one of the few federal laws designed "to attack the business of crime."

The Bush plan did call for a token increase of $50 million in the Justice Department's white-collar crime budget, but it would be a mere drop in the bucket. When we considered that just one of our alleged thrift abusers, Tom Nevis, got over $80 million in loans from a single failed thrift, according to the FBI, $50 million seemed insignificant—and so would be its effect.

Federal judges need to be schooled on the damage that white-collar criminals do. Too many major white-collar swindlers, like Herman Beebe, get meaningless short sentences. Judges need to get away from the notion that a person who robs a bank with a gun and one who defrauds it with a pen are somehow different. They are not. Only their techniques differ. Either way, the money has been *stolen*. In fact, bank robbers usually run out the door with only several thousand dollars, while the average swindle nets hundreds of thousands, or millions, of dollars. White-collar criminals should be sentenced to hard time at regular mainline federal prisons, not minimum-security "country clubs." Anything less fails to establish a creditable deterrent to bank fraud. A new sentencing law should include a clause for bank fraud that reads: "Use a Pen, Go to Jail."

Fortunately, new federal sentencing guidelines that went into effect November 1987 prescribe minimum prison terms based partly on the amount of money stolen, regardless of whether the theft was robbery or fraud. Unfortunately, the law went into effect too late to apply to many of the S&L looters. Meanwhile, the five-year statute of limitations is running out on many of their crimes, and they are laughing up their silk sleeves.

FSLIC legal action:

The FSLIC typically files civil lawsuits against officers and directors of institutions they believe have been "mismanaged." If the officers and directors of a failed thrift have assets, the FSLIC should take them. If they don't, the FSLIC should go after the officers' and directors' insurance coverage. Too often we saw the FSLIC spend millions of dollars to get a civil judgment against a crooked former thrift officer, only to agree later to a settlement that was a farce.

In 1988 regulators settled secretly with Frank Domingues and Jack Bona, whom they had sued in connection with $200 million in loans that contributed to the failure of San Marino Savings and Loan, San Marino, California.[12] When we contacted regulators in Washington to find out the terms of the settlement, we were told the terms were secret, put under court seal at the request of both the plaintiffs and defendants. If the FSLIC is going to spend a small fortune in legal fees to sue these people, then they must be prepared to demand settlements that are not just one more travesty, and those settlements should be made public.

The FSLIC hired a law firm to sue David Butler, former CEO of Bell Savings and Loan, San Mateo, California,[13] and in the settlement that followed Butler agreed he was responsible for $165 million in losses incurred by Bell while he was in charge. Butler had been an extravagant spender, even having a $6,000 leather toilet seat installed on his corporate jet and reportedly buying his secretary a new Maserati. The final judgment the FSLIC agreed to, however, limited Butler's actual liability to $290,000 in cash and to what the judge described as some nearly worthless stock. Butler was allowed to keep his $190,000 home and his $40,000 vintage biplane, and the FSLIC agreed to pay him $110 a day for his time and trouble while he cooperated with its investigation. A federal judge vacated the settlement in 1988, calling it a disgrace and saying,

"The court feels FSLIC owes more of a responsibility to the American taxpayers." The legal fees collected by the firm representing the FSLIC in the Bell case would have dwarfed the quarter million in cash they "recovered" from Butler. Anyone who admits to causing $165 million in losses should be stripped naked of assets. But apparently the FSLIC felt that a man and his biplane should not be parted.

Ethics in government:

The relationships that developed between politicians and thrift abusers constituted a breach of ethics at best and in some cases smacked of corruption. It's outrageous that politicians who helped protect and perpetuate much of the thrift scandal were allowed to wrap their actions in the disguise of "constituent service." Their real constituents should give them the boot (as Rhode Island voters did St Germain in 1988), because those congressmen and senators weren't helping constituents, they were protecting their financial supporters. When they should have been guarding the public's interest, they were instead repaying old debts. And to prove that nothing had changed, the Federal Elections Commission revealed that in 1988 333 congressmen and 61 senators received donations from thrift lobbyists. Voters should vote out of office legislators who do not demand from themselves and others the highest possible ethical standards. When powerful leaders like Jim Wright can hold up a piece of emergency legislation like the recap bill, in order to extort concessions for constituents from federal regulators, they have violated the public's trust (to the tune of more than $100 billion, said some analysts who believed losses could have been held at $15 billion if regulators could have closed institutions as soon as they became insolvent). If Congress and the Justice Department haven't the stomach to do what is necessary, then the voters should.

Appraisers:

Appraisers played a critical role in much of the looting that occurred at thrifts. Behind nearly every fraudulent loan was a phony appraisal. Time and time again properties were grossly overappraised to justify large loans that were never paid back. At one Southern California thrift, regulators found a half dozen appraisals on a single piece of property that began at $2 million and went up to $175 million. "The last appraisal even had a big red seal on it," recalled California Commissioner Bill Crawford. "I'd never seen one with a seal on it. It looked real official." The FSLIC later sold the property for $2.5 million. States should license appraisers. Most states now license real estate salespersons and brokers, and the slightest accusation of illegality, misrepresentation, or fraud can result in suspension or revocation of that license. All states license barbers. Why should appraisers be any different? Currently, appraisers can belong to private professional organizations that allow them to put official-sounding letters after their names, but nowhere are they licensed.

Auditors:

Many thrifts failed not long after receiving perfectly clean bills of health from their auditing firms. By March 1989 the FSLIC had sued ten accounting firms that had audited the books of failed S&Ls and more suits were on the way.[14] The auditors deflected criticism by saying that their audits could only be as good as the information provided to them by the thrift's management, and if that information was fraudulent, they weren't responsible.

When auditors examined a thrift's books, they were not required to look for fraud, but if they should *happen* to see any, they were required to report it to thrift management, which might not be the best move if the thrift management itself was involved in the scam. Auditors should be required to look for fraud and to report to federal regulators, who can then confirm the suspicions and contact the FBI. Auditors also do not now have to include in their annual audit any suspicion they may have that the company might be about to collapse. Clearly, they should be required by law or by industry standards[15] to include such information. If thrift officials pressured auditors (or promised them rewards) to overlook fraudulent deals or other discrepancies, auditors should be required to report the pressure to federal regulators. Auditing firms that were found to routinely certify thrifts that fail should be barred from auditing thrifts.

Adjustable rate mortgages:

Ironically, the deregulation thrifts most needed in the 1970s was one of the simplest: allowing thrifts to offer adjustable rate mortgages. The industry lobbied heavily for the ARMs in the 1970s, but Congress—trying to please consumers—refused.[16] Deregulating interest rates on both the deposit and loan sides would have allowed thrifts to make all the adjustments they really needed during both inflationary and deflationary periods. Rates on deposits were finally freed up by the Depository Institutions Deregulation and Monetary Control Act of 1980, and rates on loans were freed up in April 1981 when then-chairman of the FHLBB Richard Pratt authorized thrifts to use ARMs. But by then it was too late. Forces for thorough deregulation had already been set in motion by the interest rate crisis of the late 1970s. The savings and loans that did survive the 1980s steered a conservative course, ignored deregulation as much as possible, and simply took advantage of unregulated deposit and loan rates.[17]

• • •

What we hope will come from the thrift industry carnage is a careful reassessment of what can and cannot be deregulated in this country and a recognition that deregulation is one thing while *unregulation* is something else entirely. Deregulating segments of the financial services industry is, conditionally, a good idea. Federal meddling in private financial services, like placing tariffs and import quotas, can smother the most efficient business and turn it into a lumbering U.S. Postal Service-type beast. But Congress must learn to treat financial service deregulation like brain surgery, realizing that if too much is cut away, the patient will begin acting in bizarre, unpredictable, and, often, self-destructive ways.

Congress now is besieged with banking industry pleas to deregulate commercial banks.[18] Banking lobbyists are clamoring for bank deregulation today the same way thrift lobbyists clamored for thrift deregulation a decade ago. Even their arguments are the same, as bankers complain that they need more "freedom to compete." They, too, want freedom from what they see as a "regulatory straitjacket."

In the late 1970s, when thrifts found themselves caught in the interest rate squeeze caused by inflation, thrifts begged for the right to diversify their investments. Today banks, being squeezed by ill-advised loan decisions they have made over the past two decades (loans to Third World countries, in particular), also want to diversify into fields where they hope they can make up the losses, particularly into underwriting securities and insurance. They want the restrictive features of the Glass-Steagall Act removed, and they certainly never mention that one of the reasons Congress passed the Glass-Steagall Act after the Depression was that risky transactions conducted between banks and their securities affiliates[19] led to many bank failures when the market crashed in 1929.[20] Robert Glauber, Treasury undersecretary for finance, said in May 1989, "Once we get the thrift industry legislation passed, we are going to go back to our agenda of structural reform" (a euphemism for bank deregulation).

Banks are crying for deregulation, but they are not offering to give up federal deposit insurance or accept a risk-based insurance system. That would be more "deregulation" than they have in mind.[21] And bankers are not offering to pay for more examiners, examiners trained in the ways of the complicated and risk-ridden securities industry. What they say they will do is erect so-called fire walls that would theoretically keep their federally insured banks separate from their Wall Street stock-trading operations. But when the stock market crashed in October 1987, Continental Illinois National Bank and Trust in Chicago[22] promptly lent its option-trading subsidiary over $90 million to cover margin calls, in *direct violation* of an existing fire wall.[23] For another example of fire walls that didn't work, we have to look no further than the thrift industry: Thrifts were limited in the amount of money they could loan to themselves or to their own projects, so they found other thrifts who wanted to play and they made quid pro quo loans back and forth to each other. Banks, too, will work out back-scratching arrangements with their friends. So much for fire walls.

It's hard to believe Congress would contemplate significant deregulation of banks before they have come to grips with the monumental mess they created by deregulating thrifts. And look who's giving Congress advice on the subject —Alan Greenspan, chairman of the Federal Reserve Board. He assured Congress in 1988 that deregulating banks and abolishing the 55-year-old Glass-Steagall Act was a great idea and held nothing but benefits for the nation and for banking. Just four years earlier the very same Alan Greenspan had advised Ed Gray to stop worrying so much about deregulated thrifts because things were just fine and would only get better.

Swindlers have always targeted banks, but with mixed success prior to de-regulation. An FBI agent in Texas told us, "The only difference [between banks and thrifts in Texas] is that the FDIC still has its head in the sand. When I looked at the banks that closed between 1984 and 1987, in many of them I found people I knew, the same S&L crowd I'm investigating from the failed thrifts here." Attorneys at private law firms who worked for both the FDIC and the FSLIC told us the same story.

About bank deregulation, U.S. Attorney Joe Cage said, "Some of the same people who took down savings and loans, they're out in the securities business and banking, already in place, just waiting for Congress to abolish the Glass-Steagall Act. When it happens I'm afraid they'll take the banks just like they did the savings and loans."

Our conclusion that S&Ls were in large part looted by a hit-and-run network that would pose the same threat to deregulated banks was reinforced by the Housing and Urban Development (HUD) scandal breaking as this book went to press. While the national press focused on powerful Republicans who got huge consulting fees for pedaling their influence with insiders at HUD (for HUD approval of their clients' projects and the low-interest loans and tax credits such approval carried), we saw other patterns emerging:

The ethics report on Speaker Wright said that in 1983 he personally appealed to HUD Secretary Samuel Pierce for approval of a HUD grant to help a company owned by Wayne Newton, Billy Bob Barnett, William Beuck, Steve Murrin, Don Jury, and others restore the Fort Worth stockyards. When the application was denied, Wright got Senator Paul Laxalt to write to Pierce in support of the grant and the project was eventually approved. (It later went into bankruptcy in spite of efforts by Wright's friend George Mallick to bail it out.)

An FBI affidavit filed in a Washington, D.C., court (in support of a request for a warrant to search the offices of DeFranceaux Realty Group [DRG] and its affiliates) revealed that the Justice Department believed DRG (approved by HUD to act on its behalf) in 1988 sold repossessed property to Southmark at below-market value (for example, Southmark paid $2.3 million for Dallas property DRG had loaned $6.4 million on just two years earlier). At the time DRG was trying to get a $15 million loan and a $25 million line of credit from San Jacinto Savings and Loan, a Southmark subsidiary. HUD was liable for 85 percent of the "loss" on such sales.

The affidavit also claimed that in September 1984 DRG loaned Colonial House Apartments in Houston $47 million based on DRG's appraisal that the property was worth $60 million. In 1988 DRG had to foreclose. A few months later HUD appraisers said the apartments had been only 6 percent rented when the loan was made and were worth at that time only $13 million, not $60 million. In 1989 HUD estimated it would lose over $35 million on the deal. The Houston *Post* reported that Colonial House Apartments apparently was owned at least part of this time by a limited partnership (in a tax-shelter investment) headed by a group of syndicators that included Howard Pulver. Pulver's group in 1984 and 1985 sold $333 million in mortgages (appraised at the time by the county for only $192 million, according to the *Post*) to Mainland Savings in Houston, where Martin Schwimmer and Mario Renda placed some of their pension deposits and where Adnan Khashoggi also did business (in 1985, for example, Mainland reportedly paid Khashoggi $80 million for 21 acres the county was appraising at only $41.5 million). Reporter Pete Brewton discovered that Pulver lived practically across the street from Schwimmer in an exclusive Long Island neighborhood, yet the two men did not admit to knowing each other. Mainland collapsed in 1986.

In 1988 Charles Bazarian was actively involved in locating property that qualified for HUD tax credits. It was then packaged and sold as tax shelters. The FBI was said to be investigating Bazarian's relationship with HUD.

So the S&L and HUD scandals were not two separate stories. They were the same story. The fund that insured HUD's Federal Housing Administration (FHA) mortgages was reported to be at record lows and whispers of another taxpayer bailout had begun.

Would banks be next?

Those considering bank deregulation should go slow. Very slow. Keeping in mind that two simple, well-thought-out adjustments—flexible deposit rates and adjustable rate mortgages—were all that was needed in the 1970s to save the thrift industry, while sweeping deregulation and expanded powers destroyed it. Deregulation is powerful medicine. A little goes a long way.

And the money lost in the savings and loan crisis, as horrendous as it is, would pale beside a similar fleecing of the banking industry: There were only 3,200 savings and loans in the United States, but there are over 14,000 banks.

▪ ▪ ▪

We leave this project knowing this will probably be the most important story the three of us, as journalists, will ever work on.

We have tried to give the reader a sense of the vast scope and depth of this scandal, but there was no way we could cover everything in the space allowed. We investigated many more failed thrifts than we could mention in this book. For every scam we chronicled, we left a hundred out. For every connection we made between key players, organized crime figures and thrifts, we had to leave dozens out. It would have literally taken several volumes to chronicle this story in its totality. There was so much more that we would have liked to have told you.

We began this project as seasoned reporters, but we were not prepared for the depth of corruption and the pervasiveness of white-collar crime that we found. "Sometimes I think the only thing keeping this economy going anymore are bust-out scams," a business reporter quipped to us one day. The words of one exhausted FBI agent seemed to sum it up: "Trouble today is that too many people in business are just no damn good."

But besides the criminality we discovered a pervasive feeling that anything not actually illegal or specifically prohibited by thrift regulation was fair game. Traditional standards of right and wrong were ignored. Too many people in the thrift industry simply sold their fiduciary responsibilities to the highest briber. Whatever had infected Wall Street in the 1980s found its way into S&Ls as well—a burning greed that consumed long-standing American ethical standards.

"An ethical person is someone who does more than is required and less than is allowed," said Michael Josephson, former law professor turned ethics teacher. The thrift rogues turned that maxim on its head. If this book has a message, it is that the fabric of American society is being systematically weakened by the growing number of people willing to sell their values and principles for a fast buck.

But perhaps most dangerous of all was the willingness of honest people to tolerate, rationalize, and even do business with the crooks. Erv Hansen could never have flown as high as he did for three years without the cooperation of many people in Sonoma County, California. As a respected Nevada judge said:

"It won't be the bad people who destroy this country. It'll be the good people who rationalize the bad people's conduct."

Epilogue

As we finished our investigation we looked back at what had become of the key players in our drama. The answer was—not much.

Erv Hansen died in his sleep, uncharged of any crime, after nearly two years of FBI investigations. His victim, Centennial, on the other hand, lay dead with a $165 million hole in her broadside.

Hansen's accomplice, **Beverly Haines**, spent just 67 days (of a five-year sentence) in prison before a soft-hearted federal judge (Robert Peckham) released her to a halfway house in San Francisco, where she was allowed to dine out at local restaurants. At press time she was spending her weekdays in the halfway house and going home on weekends.

Sid Shah was indicted for drug-money laundering, but he was not indicted in connection with the Centennial case. The FSLIC sued him to try to recoup some of its losses at Centennial, and both the drug trial and the FSLIC civil case were pending at press time. (In April 1989 the government's key witness in the drug case, Michael Stevenson, was reported missing.) The FBI said their investigation of Shah's activities at Centennial remained open and active, but at press time, over four years after Centennial closed, Shah remained uncharged with any wrongdoing involving Centennial's downfall. He was living and working in Santa Rosa.

Norman Jenson cut a deal with federal Organized Crime Strike Force prosecutors for some level of immunity in the drug-money-laundering case. Since it wasn't a crime at the time, Jenson wasn't prosecuted for paying thrift president Guy Olano a $50,000 kickback—Jenson called it a legal fee—in return for his $4 million casino loan. At press time Jenson continued to live and work in Las Vegas.

The Soderling brothers pleaded guilty to bank fraud and were sentenced to seven years in prison with all but one year suspended. They were released in late 1988 after serving about six months.

Robert Ferrante of Consolidated Savings and Loan, which failed in 1985, was the subject of a disorganized, on-again off-again FBI investigation and remained uncharged at press time. He hired a public relations person to take his calls and aggressively maintained his complete innocence.

Jack Bona and Frank Domingues, who, regulators said, pulled $200 million out of San Marino Savings in loans secured by only about $100 million in property, settled with the FSLIC before their civil trial began. That settlement was sealed upon the request of both the defendants and the FSLIC and neither would disclose how much, if anything, the pair agreed to repay. Neither man was charged criminally. The U.S. attorney declined the San Marino case reportedly because FHLB examiners had failed to supply the FBI with the necessary evidence. Bona disappeared after his fling at the Atlantic City Dunes. At press time Domingues, authorities told us, was still the subject of an ongoing FBI investigation for loans he got from South Bay Savings and from Vernon Savings, but he remained uncharged.

Ed McBirney, former CEO of Sunbelt Savings and Loan (a $2 billion failure), started a new investment firm in Dallas. By press time he had not been charged with any wrongdoing. The FSLIC sued him for $500 million, and the case was pending at this writing.

Tom Gaubert, Representative Jim Wright's friend and fund-raiser, was charged with bank fraud at an Iowa thrift but he was found innocent. At press time Gaubert was working in Dallas.

Charlie Knapp, former head of $30 billion FCA, the failure of which cost the FSLIC nearly $2 billion, formed Trafalgar Mortgage in Los Angeles in partnership with Larry Taggart, the former California savings and loan commissioner. At press time they were packaging mortgages and selling them on Wall Street as mortgage-backed securities.

Don Dixon, the former head of Vernon Savings and Loan, had not been charged at press time but was the focus of an ongoing FBI investigation. *The Wall Street Journal* reported that he was "dabbling in offshore insurance companies and playing golf at the La Costa Hotel and Spa."

Herman Beebe pleaded guilty and was sentenced to one year and a day in prison. He also got immunity from additional prosecution for whatever he may or may not have done at dozens of failed thrifts and banks in northern Texas and western Louisiana.

Mario Renda faced a potential 25-year prison term as part of his plea bargain in the pension-fund bribery and embezzlement case in Brooklyn. After testifying against his former associate, Martin Schwimmer, Renda was given a five-year sentence and ordered to repay over $10 million in restitution to the FSLIC and the FDIC. In Kansas City, where he had pleaded guilty in the Indian Springs State Bank and Coronado Savings cases, he got two years, to run concurrent with the Brooklyn five, and five years probation. Ditto for his five-year Florida Center Bank sentence. At worst, Renda probably faced no more than 42 months in a country-club federal facility.

Charles Bazarian received a five-year sentence for his involvement with Rapp at Florida Center Bank. At press time his appeal had just been denied and he was living and doing business out of his Oklahoma City mansion. Bazarian, according to federal sources, cut a deal early with the Justice Department. Though the terms of the deal remained confidential, sources told us Bazarian wanted total immunity from prosecution for anything he did at thrifts in return for his testimony against others. He also agreed to plead guilty to some nonthrift-related frauds involving HUD deals. Bazarian confirmed to us that he had been given immunity but would not elaborate. "I can't tell you any more. My life might be in danger," he said. Meanwhile, when CBS's *60 Minutes* tracked him down in February 1989, they found him in a New York City hotel suite equipped with four ringing telephones. Assistants buzzed in and out with stock buy-and-sell slips.

Michael Rapp took the hardest fall. His abuse of the federal witness protection program was a major embarrassment to federal prosecutors. He was sentenced to 32 years for his involvement at Flushing Federal Savings and Florida Center Bank and was expected to serve about eight years.

Sam Daily (Renda and Franklin Winkler's associate in the Indian Springs State Bank deal) was sentenced to five years in a federal facility.

At press time **Franklin Winkler** was still fighting extradition from Australia. His father, Leslie, died of natural causes in Israel while awaiting extradition to the United States.

Tyrell Barker pleaded guilty to misapplication of bank funds and was sentenced to five years in prison with all but six months suspended.

Loan broker **Jack Franks** was charged with bank fraud, pleaded guilty, and agreed to cooperate with the government. Franks was sentenced to five years in prison.

Tom Nevis, Tyrell Barker's associate, convicted on 28 counts related to bank fraud at State Savings and Loan of Corvallis, Oregon. Nevis received a two year sentence, no fine.

Jilly Rizzo was indicted in May 1989 for using overvalued security as collateral for loans. His trial was pending at press time.

Judge Edmund Reggie was indicted for bank fraud in May 1989 and his trial was pending at press time.

Endnotes

Original Sin

1. Ivan Boesky pleaded guilty in 1986 to insider trading and securities fraud in one of the most celebrated white-collar crime cases in the nation's history, and he implicated Drexel Burnham Lambert and their junk bond king Michael Milken. Dan Walker pleaded guilty to bank fraud in 1987. Neil Bush's and Andrew Cuomo's forays into the bright new world of deregulated savings and loans ran into troubles of a different sort: Bush resigned as a Silverado Savings director just days after his father was nominated as the Republican candidate for president and three months before Silverado had to set aside $275 million to cover expected losses (regulators finally seized Silverado in December 1988), and Cuomo's investment group became entangled in a bitter lawsuit with the chairman of a related thrift. (They reached a settlement in 1988.)

2. The Federal Home Loan Bank Board, a quasi-independent agency in the executive branch of the federal government, is responsible for all federal regulation of savings and loans. Gray became chairman in May 1983.

3. By April 1989 the Justice Department had convicted over 100 people in relation to the I-30 scandal and more convictions were expected.

4. The Federal Savings and Loan Insurance Corporation insured deposits at member thrifts.

5. The FHLBB's definition of insider abuse and fraud included breach of fiduciary duty, self-dealing, engaging in high-risk speculative ventures, excessive expenditures and compensation and conflicts of interest, among others.

6. The General Accounting Office is the auditing arm of Congress.

7. Among them was the Federal Deposit Insurance Corporation which insures banks and some savings banks.

8. Centennial's net worth at the time was $1.87 million.

9. The *National Thrift News* was awarded the 1989 George Polk Award in Journalism for Financial Reporting for its coverage of the savings and loan industry.

Chapter 1. A Short History Lesson

1. The Federal Reserve System also loaned money to banks when deposits were in short supply, but thrifts had no such source for funds and had to borrow from banks, their prime competitors, when they needed extra money.

2. Mortgage foreclosures increased from 75,000 in 1928 to over 275,000 in 1932, as Americans were increasingly unable to meet their house payments and thrifts were left holding mortgages on property that was worth less and less as the Depression deepened.

3. The thrifts were members of their regional FHLB.

4. Congress created the Federal Deposit Insurance Corporation (FDIC) to perform the same function for banks and the National Credit Union Share Insurance Fund for credit unions.

5. Membership was mandatory for federally chartered thrifts, optional for state-chartered thrifts. In ensuing years S&Ls consolidated and gradually joined the FSLIC until in 1987 there were 4,600 savings and loans—2,000 federally chartered, 2,600 state-chartered, and only 600 not insured by the FSLIC.

6. Inflation in the U.S. had traditionally fluctuated in a range below 5 percent. The rate from 1959 through 1969, for example, averaged 2.3 percent. But when OPEC flexed its muscle in the early 1970s, oil prices rose and so did inflation. In 1972 inflation was at 3.4 percent, in 1974, 12.2 percent, in 1979, 13.3 percent.

7. The interest rate ceiling established in the 1960s limited thrifts to paying only 5.25 percent interest on passbook savings accounts, raised to 5.5 percent in July 1979. Rate ceilings on time deposits of $100,000 and over had been phased out in the early 1970s.

8. Investors could place any amount of money in money market funds anytime they wanted, earn rates that were even with or greater than the inflation rate, and withdraw their money anytime they wanted.

9. Even when inflation began to abate in the early 1980s, the public believed it would return and they continued their flight from thrifts. The public was also withdrawing their savings from banks.

10. The first major legislative effort by Congress to deregulate federally chartered S&Ls came in 1973, but the movement failed. Instead, throughout the 1970s the FHLBB and Congress continued to tighten regulations. But the support of deregulation grew as those new regulations failed to stem thrift losses.

11. In 1974 the ceiling had been increased from $20,000 to $40,000.

12. Lyndon Johnson's protégé, Bobby Baker, convicted of stealing $100,000 and evading taxes in one of the most publicized political scandals of the 1960s, wrote in his book *Wheeling and Dealing* that Troop gathered money from S&L executives and funneled the money through Baker to pay off a senator for killing some legislation the executives opposed. Troop died in 1982.

13. Thrift lobbyists were said to have more influence over their regulators than any other regulated industry, and the U.S League had traditionally participated in regulatory and legislative decisions, even going so far as to write some of the regulations. Bankers complained that they did not get treated as generously by Congress as did savings and loans because their lobbyists were not as powerful.

14. And a wide variety of other kinds of accounts.

15. Up from 20 percent.

16. In opening up nonresidential real estate lending to thrifts, Congress was blurring one of the key differences between banks and savings and loans: banks traditionally made commercial real estate and construction loans and thrifts were supposed to stick to home mortgages.

17. Technically, from that moment forward the American taxpayer was on the hook for thrift industry debts, but as a practical matter Congress could not have allowed the savings and loan industry to collapse, with or without the Joint Current Resolution, because such a massive default would have posed too much of a threat to the country's financial stability.

18. In 1978 Congress passed the Change in Control law, which gave regulators the right to deny an application for a thrift charter, but in actual practice regulators exercised control over directors and officers but not owners. The FHLBB maintained they couldn't disapprove applications unless there was hard evidence of incompetence or wrongdoing, and they believed they should not limit the freedom of stockholders to sell their institutions.

19. This change was authorized by the Garn-St Germain legislation but did not take effect until August 1983.

20. This FSLIC regulation took effect in 1980.

21. Entrepreneurs could start a savings and loan for $2 million (raised to $3 million in 1983) or buy an old one; attract, say, $300 million in brokered "hot money" deposits; loan that $300 million on trendy condominium units; pocket $18 million in points and fees; package the loans and sell them to other thrifts; and start all over.

22. Starting salaries in 1984 were $14,000.

23. Regulation and examination were two separate functions. Examiners were fact finders; regulators made the decisions.

Chapter 2. Shades of Gray

1. Pratt, chairman of the FHLBB from 1981 to 1983, was called by many in the thrift industry "The Savior of the Industry" because he presided over much of the deregulation of savings and loans.

2. The Federal Reserve Board, which is the Federal Home Loan Bank Board's counterpart in the world of banking, has no such partisan staffing requirements. Many believe some of the thrift industry's problems stemmed from the politicizing of the FHLBB.

3. Paul Volcker was the highly respected chairman of the Federal Reserve Board from 1979 to 1987.

4. And they still do.

5. CDs had terms that ranged from as long as 15 years to as short as 30 days. The long-term brokered CDs were not considered a problem. The short-term CDs were.

6. This was especially true of thrifts chartered in states where regulations were even more lenient than on the federal level.

7. The FDIC insured deposits placed with banks.

8. Isaac was chairman of the FDIC from 1981 to 1985. He was succeeded in that post by L. William Seidman.

9. Federally chartered S&Ls were required to join the FSLIC.

10. Oil prices collapsed in late 1985 and early 1986 and the Texas economy sank into a devastating depression.

11. Curlee, by the way, once attended an S&L party dressed as Elvis Presley, wearing a gold and rhinestone-studded jump suit.

12. Democratic Governor Edmund Brown, Jr., 1975–1983.

13. In 1978 California had 172 state-chartered institutions. That dropped to 55 by 1983.

14. In 1988 Nolan, an assemblyman from Glendale who became Assembly minority leader, resigned his position as minority leader on reports that he, among other state legislators, had been targeted by an FBI sting operation investigating influence peddling and political corruption. Nolan denied all wrongdoing, saying he was resigning because his party lost two Assembly seats in the November election. Assemblyman Bill Filante told the Santa Rosa *Press Democrat*, "He's under a lot of stresses."

15. According to their seminar outline.

16. Larry Taggart had been a vice president of Great American First Savings Bank in San Diego.

17. The weapon used to murder Masegian was a 32-inch nylon cord with wooden knobs. The FBI said the commando-styled method for death had not been used in the United States for 16 years. "I can't remember another case like this one," said the Dade County medical examiner.

18. A tiny island cluster in the Caribbean south of Cuba.

19. Texas and California were by no means the only states with problems. Wyoming, which had relatively few total cases, had the most bank fraud per capita in the nation.

20. The FSLIC insurance fund got its money from member thrifts who made payments to the fund, but it was also backed by the full faith and credit of the U.S. government, which meant that when the fund ran out of money, taxpayers would have to cover the losses.

Chapter 3. Centennial Gears Up for Deregulation

1. Norman Raiden, general counsel to the FHLBB during the Gray years, told us that of the failed savings and loans he was familiar with, the one he had the hardest time under-standing was Centennial Savings, because Hansen had been so well known in the thrift industry and had had such a good, and conservative, reputation.

2. Piombo Corporation was owned by Piombo Construction Company.

3. This was a common practice among lenders and only became a problem for thrifts when faulty appraisals were used to justify loans much larger than the value of the collateral.

4. This bookkeeping anomaly resulted in the most desperate thrifts making the most, the largest, and the riskiest loans in an attempt to make the S&Ls' financial statements look better—or to give the borrowers a couple of years getaway time.

5. Prior to deregulation, boards of directors of thrifts were mainly figureheads who typically

rubber-stamped management's requests. Primarily for that reason, they were unprepared to assume the tougher role that deregulation thrust upon them, and they continued rubber-stamping for far too long.

6. An attorney working on a related case told us he had discovered that the BIA violated regulations and failed to exercise prudent fiduciary care in investing the trust-fund money. Federal officials knew about his discoveries, he said. The BIA admitted their record keeping was inadequate and they computerized their system. But as far as we could tell, no one had investigated the charges of bribery. We notified the Office of the Inspector General of the U.S. Department of the Interior ourselves and an investigator spent a day with us, promising to conduct a thorough review. Later he said the case was "very big" and had high priority with his department. But it was all hush-hush, he said, so he couldn't tell us the details. Still, we'd be the first to know when arrests were made. Up to press time, a year later, there were no further developments.

7. The limit that a thrift could loan to one borrower varied from thrift to thrift, based on a formula established by regulators. Golden Pacific's limit at that time, according to a former loan officer, was $500,000.

8. The FSLIC later sold the building for an undisclosed sum under $1 million.

Chapter 4. $10,000 in a Boot

1. In response to our questions about his loans from Centennial, Bosco wrote to McGraw-Hill, the publishers of this book, and admitted to receiving two loans that totaled less than $200,000 in 1979 and 1980 ("before any scandal attended the operation of Centennial," he wrote) but he failed to mention the two loans totaling $124,000 that he got in 1982 and 1983, while Hansen was riding high.

2. In an advance-fee scheme a middleman promised to get a borrower a loan if the borrower would pay the middleman an up-front fee. Of course the middleman took the fee and disappeared and the borrower never saw the loan. A U.S. attorney told us he had decided that S&L deregulation had permitted an updated version of the advance-fee scheme: Now middlemen could actually produce the loan by setting the borrower up with a cooperative thrift.

3. Senator Dolwig, Kaplan, and Gorwitz formed a company on Grand Cayman Island that offered to obtain large loans for prospective commercial borrowers who were having trouble finding a willing lender. In return for a loan guarantee borrowers would pay the company $25,000 for every $1 million of financing requested. But when borrowers paid the fees Gorwitz flew the money to Freeport, in the Bahamas, where it disappeared, presumably into the coffers of fugitive mobster Salvatore Caruana. The borrower, of course, would never get the promised loan. Admitted hitman Jimmy "the Weasel" Fratianno said in his biography that Gorwitz and his partners had tried to interest him in joining them in the scam, but Jimmy, a veteran of scams, predicted that Kaplan was out of his league and would end up taking a fall on the scam, which was precisely what happened.

4. In 1986 Binder declared bankruptcy and Centennial (by that time having been taken over by the FSLIC) sued for relief, stating that Binder had pledged to them security he had already pledged for other loans, listed real estate he did not own, and counted his home twice on his financial statement, once as his personal residence and again as "real estate." In his bankruptcy Binder listed his total unpaid debt at $5,851,755.45. He claimed cash on hand at the time of filing at just $239.

5. This figure does not include the hundreds of thousands of dollars the FBI would later discover Hansen was embezzling from Centennial and borrowing from Columbus-Marin as well.

6. The FHLB's Eleventh District encompassed California, Arizona and Nevada.

7. Alexander Grant later changed its name to Grant Thornton after it became enmeshed in a scandal in which a managing partner in Florida pleaded guilty to accepting $225,000 in bribes to falsify financial statements for ESM Government Securities Inc. and hide ESM's shaky financial situation.

8. After the deal between Atlas Savings and Columbus-Marin Savings that let Hansen and Shah take $1.6 million in bonuses in 1984, auditors gave Centennial a clear audit even though a Centennial executive told Pizzo the contracts clearly indicated that Centennial had agreed to buy the properties right back in early 1984.

Chapter 5. The Downhill Slide

1. They also had to agree to submit a detailed business plan to regulators and tighten up their investment procedures and policies. Regulators didn't issue many supervisory agreements until 1984 when Ed Gray, upset with lax enforcement, insisted that regulators crack down on wayward thrifts. That year they issued 116, including Centennial's.

2. The $35 notes had the effect of creating an artificially high price for Centennial stock. Since Hansen had Centennial stock pledged as security for loans, he had to keep the price of the stock as high as possible.

3. The FHLBB is the regulatory agency that closes insolvent thrifts, whether state or federal, when they are insured by the FSLIC.

4. Regulators consider it normal for up to 20 percent of a thrift's deposits to be brokered deposits.

5. The interim management team from Great Western Savings and Loan, baby-sitting Centennial for the FSLIC after the takeover, discovered Bev's check-kiting scheme.

6. Federal sources later told us that Bank of America was less than cooperative in their investigation into the Haines matter.

7. She also granted us several interviews.

8. Joseph P. Russoniello, U.S. attorney for the northern district of California, said that of the 400 persons prosecuted federally for bank embezzlement in his district since 1983, half reported drug use or alcohol abuse.

9. One month earlier two Golden Pacific loan officers had become part of a small group who, according to a federal indictment, first bought and then defrauded Bank of Northern California in San Jose out of nearly $2 million in just 16 days before regulators threw them out. The group allegedly made their last payment for the purchase of the San Jose bank with $700,000 cash which, authorities said, the group's leader, Rodney Wagner, delivered in a satchel. Later Wagner was indicted by Organized Crime Strike Force attorneys who accused him of being a major international drug-money launderer. John L. Molinaro, owner of Ramona Savings in Ramona, California, who was arrested trying to flee the country using a dead man's passport, was also a shareholder of Bank of Northern California.

10. Attorneys working the criminal side of the investigation forged ahead as well, and a

year later Hansen's friend at the head of Columbus-Marin Savings, Ted Musacchio, was formally indicted by a federal grand jury on two counts of misapplying bank funds and two counts of receiving benefits from bank transactions, a euphemism for allegedly taking $40,000 in kickbacks for arranging loans to Erv Hansen. A few months after that indictment he was indicted a second time on charges that he conspired with a couple of developers to defraud Columbus Savings. Musacchio's attorney said the charges were "outrageous."

11. One of those indicted along with Shah was a James Schlichtman, who, the indictment alleged, had distributed drugs for the ring. An IRS affidavit said Schlichtman had also worked for San Francisco investment advisor W. Franklyn Chinn from 1985 through 1987. Chinn, Attorney General Ed Meese's former financial advisor, would later become the focus of an intense federal investigation into Meese and the defense contracting firm of Wedtech Corporation. The IRS affidavit said Schlichtman was cooperating with the Wedtech investigation under an immunity agreement.

12. This loss of experienced prosecutors to private practice was a major problem facing the overworked and understaffed Justice Department.

13. Regulators could put insolvent thrifts into conservatorships or receiverships. The purpose of a conservatorship was to keep the institution open and operating while a new management team tried to "conserve" the thrift's assets. A receivership was instituted when the institution was beyond repair. When the FHLBB took over Centennial Savings in 1985 and removed Erv Hansen and his team, they placed the S&L in a conservatorship. They brought in a team from Great Western Savings and Loan to operate Centennial from the time of the takeover in August 1985 until its purchase by Citizens Federal in April 1987. When Citizens Federal purchased Centennial, Centennial's assets were transferred to a receivership, a FHLB team that would slowly liquidate those assets, while Citizens Federal opened shop in the old Centennial offices.

14. The Citizens Federal purchase of Centennial greatly slowed the forward march of the FSLIC's civil suit against the Centennial defendants. The Great Western team managing Centennial had employed a law firm to help them conduct an investigation. When Citizens Federal bought Centennial, the Great Western team went back to Great Western and a federal receivership team picked up where they left off. The receivership hired a different law firm, which then took months to get up to speed on the complicated case. We found that this kind of duplication of effort was common.

15. According to reporter Allen Pusey of the Dallas *Morning News*.

Chapter 6. *Lazarus*

1. Federal regulations allowed only 40 percent.

2. Ferrante told us later, when we talked to him by telephone, that he had at one time looked into the possibility of purchasing Golden Pacific Savings from the Soderlings, but it had not been strong enough financially to suit him. .

3. The Israeli Mafia is said to be headquartered in Los Angeles.

4. The bribes were allegedly funneled through a complex web of subcontractors who then passed the money back to Mitchell, according to the indictment.

5. Patrick Connolly was acting state savings and loan commissioner when Ferrante applied

for a charter. A year later he retired to become an officer for Centennial Savings while its CEO, Erwin Hansen, looted it into insolvency.

6. Ferrante's associate in the Carson deal, and others, was W. Patrick Moriarity, the manufacturer of Red Devil fireworks, who founded the Bank of Irvine. The bank failed in 1984, the victim of fraud and mismanagement, according to regulators. In 1985 Moriarity pleaded guilty to mail fraud in a case that became the biggest political scandal in California in 30 years. Over 10 prominent politicians, including one state senator, were indicted for taking bribes from Moriarity.

7. Although the FSLIC claimed Consolidated loaned just over $15 million on the Carson property, the thrift had actually committed to loaning the project $20 million. Appraisers later told regulators the property was worth only $6.2 million. Angotti told us the FSLIC had hired appraisers who purposely underappraised the Carson property.

8. "Participations," loans sold to other institutions, were an accepted (and perfectly legal) way for an institution to manage its loan portfolio. An institution that needed to get rid of a loan (because it exceeded the loans-to-one-borrower rule, for example, or just to raise additional capital) could sell all or part of the loan to a thrift that was looking for an investment. The selling thrift improved its cash flow and the buying thrift improved its portfolio of loans.

9. These two institutions would make headlines nationwide and come to ignominious ends two years later when United Federal was declared insolvent and closed and SISCorp was forced into involuntary bankruptcy, both in 1987.

10. The commission paid to loan brokers was negotiable. Sometimes it was paid by the lender in return for bringing the thrift a valuable borrower or deal. In other cases the borrower paid the loan broker out of his loan proceeds as thanks for finding him a lender. In other cases the lender and borrower shared the cost of the commission. Or the loan broker was sometimes given a percentage of the project or future profits as his commission.

11. Phoenix Federal Savings and Loan of Muskogee, Oklahoma, sued him for a scheme it claimed defrauded several S&Ls out of millions of dollars, according to published reports.

12. Among them were the following S&Ls: Homestead in Oklahoma City, Freedom in Tampa, Sunbelt in Dallas, Vernon in Dallas, Phoenix Federal in Muskogee, Oklahoma.

13. A FHLBB attorney described Charlie's alleged transgressions this way: "A prime example of borrower misconduct was discovered at Consolidated, where the former management [Ferrante] made a loan and participated in advances in the amount of $9 million to a corporation owned by a convicted felon by the name of Charles Bazarian. These advances were made without any loan application and financial information, and they were made with only cursory, one-page letter opinions from the appraisers as to the value of the secured property. Not one payment was made on these loans and they appear to be substantial—if not total—losses."

14. When we interviewed Bazarian we had to consciously struggle against the temptation to like him, to care about his mounting troubles, even his health. He, like other white-collar con men we met during our investigation, has about him a kind of magic, a psychic novocaine that dulls the senses and relaxes the listener. We recalled Assistant U.S. Attorney Peter Robinson, who told us that whenever he was with Beverly Haines he "always felt he should be doing something for her." Bazarian was a master of that old black magic. But we got an interesting insight into his thinking when coauthor Mary Fricker asked him if the deal he was working on at the time was honest. "Sure," he replied. "It's just a scam."

15. Angotti said he believed the FHLBB had a vendetta against him because he fought vigorously for the rights of small thrifts and ran (unsuccessfully) for election as a director of the Eleventh District FHLB in San Francisco in 1985. He also was a supporter of deregulation.

16. If regulators determined, in an examination of a thrift, that problems were developing at the institution, they would send the institution a supervisory letter that asked for corrections. If improvements weren't forthcoming, regulators would enter into a supervisory agreement with the thrift's officers in which the officers had to agree to follow the regulators' instructions. If that didn't work, regulators could issue a cease-and-desist order. If the cease-and-desist order was ignored, officers could then be removed from their jobs. At each step in this process there were innumerable opportunities for challenge and delay.

17. FSLIC vs. Ferrante et al.

18. After Pizzo interviewed Angotti, Angotti sent him an invitation to join the Italian-American Foundation, which he co-chaired with U.S. Congressman Dante Fascell. "Would be great to have you among the Italian-American leadership," Angotti wrote on the invitation. "By honoring others we honor ourselves."

19. Virtually every "entrepreneur" at the helm of a savings and loan that ran into trouble with regulators sang the same tune.

20. In a memo written by a California state examiner after the takeover, the examiner explained, "I spoke to the examiner in charge of the first exam who indicated that the Newport police called the Department of Savings and Loan to schedule a meeting concerning how officers of Consolidated were intertwined with various individuals suspected of being affiliated with the 'Mob.' . . . Apparently, the police were following Ferrante and Angotti."

21. The reporter sent the 1987 Christmas card to us, and we tacked it up on our bulletin board beside Angotti's invitation to Pizzo to join the Italian-American Foundation.

22. Then director of the FBI.

23. When the FSLIC estimated its loss on a thrift failure, the figure included the cost of repaying all the money on deposit at the time of closure, losses on direct investments made by the thrift, legal fees, and receivership expenses, all of which the FSLIC had to pay. The loss figure was typically much larger than the amount of any suit they might bring against the people they believed were responsible for the thrift's insolvency.

24. Fifteen percent of the thrift industry's loss in 1987 was in Orange County in Southern California, where Consolidated was located. The county was in the midst of an economic boom, so the failures could not be blamed on a recession.

Chapter 7. Back in Washington

1. Penn Square Bank, a small shopping-center bank in Oklahoma City, failed in 1982 after financing much of its risky lending with brokered deposits. Its demise threatened Continental Illinois National Bank and Trust Company in Chicago, which had to be bailed out by the federal government to the tune of $4.5 billion, the largest federal bailout in bank history.

2. Limits on brokers' commissions were not removed until 1982, however, so it wasn't until 1982 that the use of brokered deposits really skyrocketed. The Depository Institutions Deregulation Committee chaired by Don Regan removed the limits.

3. Richard Pratt, Gray's predecessor as chairman of the FHLBB, became head of the mortgage-backed securities department for Merrill Lynch after he resigned from the FHLBB.

4. Blain was an FHLB director for four years (1979 to 1982), vice chairman of the FHLB of Dallas, and a prominent member of the Texas Savings and Loan League before his two-year stint as chairman (1982 to 1984) at Empire Savings netted him and six others an 88-count indictment on charges of racketeering and fraud. Regulators reported the I-30 condo loans had been supported by doctored appraisals and land flips. Prosecutors charged that Texas developer D. L. (Danny) Faulkner—a sixth-grade dropout who professed not to be able to read or write, according to reporter Allen Pusey—and associates bought land along I-30, flipped it among themselves to artificially inflate its value (in one case the value of 117 acres reportedly increased from $5 million to $47 million in a few weeks), and then sold it to investors who got the money for the purchase (and sometimes additional bonuses for themselves) by borrowing from Empire Savings. Regulators banned Blain from the thrift industry, and in April 1987 he settled a civil racketeering suit with the FSLIC for $100 million. The criminal trial of Blain, Faulkner, and five others began in early 1989 and was in progress as of this writing. Reportedly the government had to hire a moving van to carry 4,000 documents to court. Whether the jury would understand a case of such complexity remained to be seen. Defendants faced a possible 1,696 years in prison if convicted.

Chapter 8. Tap-Dancing to Riches

1. Money that had been flowing out to money market funds began to go instead to federally insured institutions. Thrifts with brokered deposits that exceeded 5 percent of their total deposits went from 32 to 258 that year.

2. Organization of Petroleum Exporting Countries.

3. Ten years later Khashoggi would be ridiculed for his role as a middleman in the Iran-Contra affair, and OPEC's reduced circumstances would make it increasingly difficult for him to come up with the $250,000 a day it reportedly cost him to live.

4. Khashoggi was not often in Riyadh. He spent most of his time jetting around the world in his Boeing 727 to close deals or visit one of his other seven estates (in London, Rome, Paris, Cannes, New York, Beirut, and Jidda) where servants and lovely, expensive women catered to his needs.

5. Air America was a charter airline that flew CIA flights in the Far East during the Vietnam War.

6. The Kansas City *Star* confirmed with Azima and the U.S. State Department the airline's business association with Egyptian American Transport and Services Corporation (EATSCO). EATSCO was formed in 1979 by Thomas Clines, former CIA director of training (and in 1986 a prominent figure in the Iran-Contra scandal), and Hussein Salem, a former Egyptian government official and a friend of Azima. Other partners included Edwin Wilson, former CIA operative found guilty of selling arms to Muammar Quaddafi in the late 1970s. EATSCO had an exclusive contract with Egypt to ship billions of dollars of military equipment to Egypt as part of the 1979 Camp David accords. For five years, half of Global International's cargo business would be with EATSCO. (In 1983 Clines and Salem would plead guilty to overcharging the U.S. government $8 million. Global International was not linked to any wrongdoing.)

7. When we were investigating Mario Renda and Indian Springs State Bank in early

1987, the Iran-Contra scandal was in full flower. Americans had just learned that Adnan Khashoggi had played his familiar middleman role in raising $15 million for the complicated arms transaction. The Iran-Contra affair exposed a shadowy covert crowd of which Global certainly had been a part. But Global International attracted very little attention during the scandal because the airline had filed for bankruptcy in 1983 and slid from public view. After bankrupting Global, Azima took the helm of another airline, RACE Airways headquartered in Madrid. In July 1986 a RACE jet reportedly carried 23 tons of arms to Iran, via Spain and Yugoslavia, as part of the Iran-Contra deals, according to *The Chronology* by the National Security Archives. When we tried to telephone Azima in 1988 we learned that he was then chairman of Aviation Leasing Group, which had offices in Kansas City and London.

8. Shenker was licensed in 1975 to operate the Dunes.

9. The President's Commission on Organized Crime reported in 1986 that the leaders of the International Brotherhood of Teamsters, the nation's largest union, had been "firmly under the influence of organized crime since the 1950s." The report said Hoffa and Teamster President Roy Williams (president from 1981 to 1983) were "indisputably direct instruments of organized crime."

10. When Shenker filed bankruptcy in 1984 he listed debts of $197 million and he left banks, savings and loans, and pension funds holding the bag for tens of millions in unpaid loans. The IRS said he owed $66 million in taxes.

11. In 1987 former Teamster President Roy L. Williams testified during a federal racketeering trial in Manhattan that he was controlled by Nick Civella, who was identified in the trial as the boss of the Mafia family in Kansas City.

12. Linked financing has been practiced for years by mob-dominated unions who could offer union deposits (and kickbacks if necessary) to bankers in exchange for loans. Jonathan Kwitny describes the practice in *Vicious Circles*, W.W. Norton & Co., 1979, as does Steven Brill in *The Teamsters*, Simon and Schuster, 1978.

13. Individuals who posed as borrowers but who then turned the loan money over to someone else.

14. Renda didn't bother to share with the banks and thrifts the little matter of the higher interest rate he was quoting to his customers. He simply told the bank or thrift a block of money was heading their way (via the Federal Reserve Bank Telecommunications System, the Fed Wire), and he accepted whatever rate they were paying at the time. They, of course, were delighted to receive these CD funds, and as an added incentive Renda waived the traditional 1 to 2 percent brokerage commission normally paid by the institution. If the CD owners noticed (and they often did not) that the banks were not paying them the rate Renda had quoted them, Renda coughed up a check for the difference (from money generated by the loan end of the scheme). Later, after First United Fund collapsed, regulators compiled a partial list of 160 institutions that accepted deposits from Renda under these terms. By October 1988, 104 of them had failed.

15. The straw borrowers were also called "mortgage pullers."

16. Often the loans the bank agreed to make totalled half the amount placed on deposit there by First United Fund.

17. Applications and references that the bank or thrift required from the straw borrowers would be provided by Winkler or Daily. Often the references were Winkler or Daily.

18. La Costa resort, in northern San Diego County, was the resort built with up to $100 million in Teamster financing and rumored to be a hangout for organized crime since 1975 when *Penthouse* magazine did a major exposé of the resort. La Costa general partner Edward "Fast Eddie" Susalla appears in the chapter on Herman Beebe.

19. Indian Springs State Bank.

Chapter 9. Buying Deposits

1. Thanks to OPEC solidarity, oil prices went from $7.64 per barrel in 1975 to $34.50 in 1981.

2. Its failure almost toppled Continental Illinois National Bank and Trust Company in Chicago, which held millions of dollars' worth of participations from Penn Square. Only a $4.5 billion federal bailout (of Continental's holding company, Continental Illinois Corporation) in 1984, the largest rescue in banking history, would prevent Continental's collapse.

3. Morris Shenker's bankruptcy in 1984 revealed that he had defaulted on a Penn Square loan.

4. One FSLIC attorney told us Winkler introduced Ferrante to Renda. Winkler had an office in Southern California.

5. Ultimately, however, most of the loans were made good when the borrowers realized the heat was on the bank and the FBI would probably be the next to talk to them about their tardy payments.

6. On December 8, 1983, Renda scribbled in his desk diary, "Winkler Sr. going to Kansas City to talk to FBI re: conspiracy to kill Winkler and Lemaster." We could not tell if this was a smoke screen they hoped would get the FBI off their scent or if Leslie Winkler had actual knowledge of a conspiracy that resulted in the death of Lemaster and the shooting of Franklin. Perhaps Franklin's father was simply trying to feed the FBI information that would isolate and discredit Daily. The FBI wouldn't say, and no one was ever charged in either case.

7. Keep in mind, these amounts were in addition to his salary at First United and the money flowing to him from straw borrowers he had in place around the country. He and Schwimmer also were stuffing their secret bank accounts with $16 million garnered from their business deal with the two union funds, a business deal they weren't telling the IRS about, court records showed.

8. In 1989 the case was still pending.

9. Indian Springs State Bank had an asset value of $8 million when Lemaster took over. Using brokered deposits, he increased the value of its assets to $43 million. When regulators closed the institution, asset value had dropped to $28 million.

Chapter 10. Renda Meets the Lawyer from Kansas

1. The FDIC reported that of the 90 commercial banks that failed from 1982 through March 23, 1984, 46 had brokered deposits.

2. By the end of 1983 brokered deposits at FSLIC-insured institutions in the San Francisco district were 11.7 percent of deposits; in the Dallas district, 7.5 percent.

3. The regulation said that as of March 26, 1984, brokered deposits would be limited to

5 percent of assets by associations with less than 3 percent net worth. Then, beginning October 1, the FSLIC would insure only $100,000 per institution per broker.

4. Barnard was chairman of the Commerce, Consumer and Monetary Affairs subcommittee of the House Government Operations Committee.

5. Published March 26, 1984, by the *American Banker*.

6. The report cited First United Fund's dealings with an unnamed thrift and an unnamed savings bank.

7. When the Barnard committee later issued its report, in October 1984, it concluded that there was no correlation between bank failures and brokered deposits and that there was "neither concrete evidence nor a coherent logical argument that insured deposit brokerage is inherently harmful to the banking system." The report did admit, however, that there were instances where brokered deposits had been misused. Isaac later commented, "I think we were maybe ahead of Congress in seeing this problem and trying to deal with it."

8. Gray's supporters alleged the leakers operated at Treasury Secretary Don Regan's behest.

9. Rumor had it that Renda leased the jet to a movie studio for actor Michael Douglas to use in *Wall Street*, a movie about greed and corruption on Wall Street.

10. Renda used his brokered deposits for a variety of scams. He cheated the IRS, as in the union deals with Schwimmer. Or he did linked financing deals à la Indian Springs. Or he exaggerated the interest rate to his depositors to attract their deposits and keep his commissions coming. Or he skimmed from the proceeds in a variety of ways, as Beverly Haines told us he did at Centennial. Investigators say they will never know all the scams Renda was pulling.

11. Manning was hired by both the FDIC and FSLIC in a joint suit involving Indian Springs State Bank and Coronado Savings and Loan.

12. What Manning did not yet know was that on the last day of his interrogation of the Seven Dwarfs, Rexford State Bank in Rexford, Kansas, had failed, brought down entirely by Renda and his special deals. It was the beginning of a cascade of failures regulators would later lay at Renda's door.

13. Frank Manzo, identified by the Justice Department in court documents as an alleged member of the Lucchese crime family (Manzo is a character in Nicholas Pileggi's book *Wise Guy*), was talking to associate William Barone.

14. Bearer bonds bore no one's name and whoever held them could cash them in. Once money was invested in the bonds it became virtually untraceable. Bearer bonds were so abused by organized crime the government discontinued their use.

15. The Butcher brothers were convicted of bank fraud following the 1983 collapse of their Tennessee and Kentucky banking empire. The Seven Dwarfs told Manning and Byrne that Steve Black was Renda's connection to State Savings in Clovis, New Mexico, among other S&Ls, and his deals were referred to around First United Fund as "Black Magic Deals." Black was never charged with any wrongdoing.

16. The Houston *Post* revealed that Adnan Khashoggi and Howard Pulver, who had been Martin Schwimmer's neighbor in an exclusive Long Island community for 11 years (Houston *Post* reporters discovered the neighborly arrangement quite by accident when they went to Pulver's Long Island home to try to interview him and then later went to Schwimmer's home

for the same purpose. When asked, Schwimmer and Pulver did not admit that they knew each other), had done millions of dollars worth of business with Mainland. When the S&L collapsed in April 1986, with assets of $800 million, it was at that time the largest S&L failure in U.S. banking history.

17. In 1983 First United Fund had described itself in a brochure as "the single largest purchaser of certificates of deposit in the United States."

19. In 1988 the FDIC compiled a partial list of 104 thrifts and banks that received brokered deposits from First United Fund and later failed.

18. The suit asked $20 million in actual damages but charged the defendants under the Racketeering Influence and Corrupt Organizations Act, RICO, which tripled the damage award.

20. It was scheduled to go to trial in 1989. Ironically, the first attorney Renda called, in his search for a lawyer to represent him, was Manning. Renda did not know then that Manning had already been hired by the FDIC to work on the Indian Springs State Bank case.

Chapter 11. *The End of the Line*

1. In September 1987 Franklin Winkler would be found living quietly in Australia and Leslie would be located in Israel. The government started extradition procedures. They dragged on and on. Leslie died in Israel in November 1988. As of this writing, Franklin was still in Australia.

2. FSLIC attorneys said he moved the money to Brazil and Switzerland.

3. Renda promised the Kansas City prosecutor that he would cooperate in bank fraud investigations in Louisiana and Texas, but a Louisiana attorney who questioned him later told us Renda was evasive, at best.

4. The U.S. attorney obtained pleas of guilty from many of the little straw borrowers who had made up Daily's and Winkler's army of "investors." Most received suspended sentences and were ordered to repay the loans.

5. Renda testified in Schwimmer's trial, and Schwimmer was convicted in 1988. During the trial Schwimmer's attorney asked Renda, "But in the past you've never hesitated to lie when you could make money off of it, have you?" and Renda replied, "That's correct, Mr. Fink." (From a transcript of the trial.)

Chapter 12. *"Miguel"*

1. The $50 billion figure, compiled for the President's Commission on Organized Crime in the mid-1980s, included income from traditional mob enterprises such as narcotics, loan-sharking, prostitution, and gambling. It did not include billions in income from the mob's "legitimate" businesses.

2. Wharton Econometric Forecasting Associates estimated that average Mafia members made $222,000 a year between 1979 and 1981.

3. "Wise guy" was a term used by the mob to describe those at the lowest echelons of the mob organization who carried out the day-to-day chores, assignments, and scams. It was an entry-level position in the family and the manpower pool from which the mob selected its future soldiers, lieutenants, and capos. In the old days a wise guy might strong-arm someone

who was late on his payments to the mob. Today's wise guy might just as well be a teller, an accountant, or a real estate broker, organizing financial scams for himself and the family.

4. A sit-down is a meeting held by mob hierarchy, sometimes made up of various mob families for extraordinarily important discussions. They can be held to resolve territorial disputes between mob families or to plan major mob operations.

5. Federal investigators claimed that Sid Shah and Norman B. Jenson used some of these techniques to launder money through real estate projects that were ultimately cashed out by Centennial Savings. (Centennial bought them. Thus, Shah and Jenson received clean Centennial money in place of the allegedly dirty money they spent on the projects.)

6. For example, consider a quit claim deed: that instrument's legitimate purpose was to allow someone to deed to someone else whatever interest he might have in a property. It was used most often to clear a title. By signing a quit claim deed a person pronounced that whatever interest he had in the property was thereby renounced or transferred, even if it were no interest at all. In a money-laundering operation a quit claim deed was a diversion. An investigator seeing that Joe quit-claimed his interest in a given property to Dick could spend weeks backtracking to find out where Joe got his interest in the property in the first place. Using several dozen such quit claim deeds in a money-laundering operation could tie up investigators for months as they checked out each and every deed. It only took five minutes to file a quit claim deed, and filing a phony one was not illegal.

7. Proceeds from drug trafficking, prostitution, and illegal gambling, primarily.

8. Also brokerage houses, currency exchange businesses, and, added in 1985, casinos.

9. Nevertheless, the federal government successfully prosecuted several well-publicized cases of money laundering through financial institutions. One of the most notable was Operation Greenback in Florida, which led to 211 indictments, 63 convictions, $38.5 million in dirty money seized, and $117 million in fines to financial institutions.

10. Russian for reorganization.

11. Sit-downs, at which such operations might have been discussed in the past, had become a target of Justice Department electronic surveillance probes and landed more than one godfather in jail.

12. Joseph Pistone, testifying before the Senate subcommittee on investigations in 1988.

13. The details of Hellerman's early life, up to 1977, come from his authorized biography, *Wall Street Swindler*, Thomas C. Renner, Doubleday & Co., 1977.

14. His father was a certified public accountant who worked for Chemical Bank of New York and eventually became a bank vice president.

15. Roselli was also the CIA's contact with the Mafia in the intelligence agency's ineffectual schemes to kill Castro.

16. From *The Last Mafioso*, by Ovid DeMaris, Bantam Books, 1981.

17. Hellerman would later dedicate *Wall Street Swindler* to Morvillo, among others.

18. Rapp and Rizzo's relationships with others in this chapter were as described in sworn depositions given by Anthony Delvecchio and Ronald Martorelli.

19. A U.S. attorney said that Jilly's Enterprises was a private company organized by Jilly Rizzo, Anthony Delvecchio, and another for the purpose of developing the Poconos property.

At the time there was talk of bringing legalized gambling into the Poconos, but it never materialized. In 1983 World Wide Ventures acquired 50 percent of Jilly's Enterprises and the right to develop the Poconos property. The property would later surface in at least two other troubled institutions, Aurora Bank in Denver and Acadia Savings and Loan in Crowley, Louisiana. See chapters on Herman Beebe.

20. Hiring appraisers to provide inflated appraisals was a common way that borrowers and thrift officials justified large loans.

21. Delvecchio said in a 1985 deposition that World Wide had at one time been called World Wide Ventures/Jilly's Enterprises Inc. Lorenzo Formato, who served as World Wide's president, was a former stockbroker. Regulators later revealed that in 1982 the Securities and Exchange Commission had banned Formato from any association with any broker or dealer for two years for violating various provisions of federal securities law.

22. According to a November 1986 civil lawsuit filed by the FDIC against John Antonio, Angelo Carnemolla, Fuad C. Jezzeny, William J. Vanden Eynden, Jilly Rizzo, Anthony Delvecchio, and others, Rizzo and Delvecchio secured the loans from Aurora in July 1984 using 500,000 restricted shares of World Wide Ventures Corporation as collateral, "which stock in fact had little or no actual value as collateral for the loans." Aurora Bank failed in November 1985. Two other Colorado banks lost hundreds of thousands of dollars after becoming involved in the scheme and both later failed. Napoli, a former president of Aurora Bank, Heinrich Rupp, and two others were convicted of bank fraud in connection with the Aurora Bank failure. Court documents in the case read like a dime novel, with tales of money laundering, gold bars, and a robbery of $475,000 cash. Napoli was also charged in an unrelated case with dealing in narcotics. In the Aurora case Napoli copped a plea and was sentenced to nine years in prison, but his sentence was suspended and he was put on five years' probation. Rupp, who could have gotten 42 years, got two. After the judge handed down the sentence on February 24, 1989, a government attorney remarked, "He'll be out this summer, you watch."

23. He testified, "In many cases, I think the people involved—of the ones I knew of—they were a very specialized group of people. They—they played on two, I think, very significant factors: One was a certain amount of patriotism that the banker would demonstrate by going along with whatever the current scheme was—and there were a number of schemes used. . . . And secondly, that the banker himself—the banker would enrich himself by doing so; and he would do so at the expense of the insurance company, not at the expense of the depositors. In some cases that, of course, didn't work; but in many cases it did."

24. We were unable to verify this story, and the witness was later indicted for perjury (case pending) for other statements he made about this case. But Rupp's attorney told us he believed the reason the judge in early 1989 reduced Rupp's sentence from 42 years to two years was because he believed the CIA story.

Chapter 13. Flushing Gets a Bum Rapp

1. According to a September 16, 1985, deposition given by Ronald J. Martorelli.

2. According to an August 1, 1986, deposition given by Anthony Delvecchio. Also, according to testimony given by Anthony Delvecchio in 1986, Rapp was filtering loan money he'd obtained from Flushing to his wife through a company he'd set up called Any Name, Inc.

3. The interest rates charged on the Rapp group loans were not exactly tough. Rapp and his cohorts were paying only the prime rate plus one percentage point on the lines of credit Rapp had obtained from Flushing. Most commercial bank customers paid at least prime plus 2 (for valued customers) or prime plus 3. Brazil or Argentina would kill for such a deal.

4. Later the Federal Reserve Board denied the application.

5. According to depositions given by Ronald J. Martorelli, September 14 through September 17, 1985.

6. The Federal Reserve Board ultimately turned down the application.

7. September 1985 deposition given by Anthony Delvecchio.

8. Rapp was quite familiar with the Regency. In *Wall Street Swindler* he wrote that back in the late 1960s he'd attended a number of mob sit-downs there and in 1971 it was at the Regency that Rapp wore a concealed microphone in the investigation that led to the indictment (and conviction) of Robert Carson, the administrative aide to Hawaiian Senator Fong.

9. *American Banker*, March 31, 1986.

10. Investigators later speculated that Renda's sloppy handling of this scam illustrated just how desperate he was for money at the time.

11. Florida Center Bank collapsed in April 1986, less than seven months after Rapp's deal began to unfold.

12. When Bazarian put his company, CB Financial, into bankruptcy, among those listed who owed him money was The Muhammad Ali Fan Club, which owed him $62,000.

13. But was it their plan? In his book *The Last Mafioso*, Jimmy Fratianno told of a conversation he had with Teamster executive Allen Dorfman in the 1970s when Dorfman faced trial for a pension-fund scam he had pulled in New Mexico. Dorfman reminded Jimmy of another case where a boxer helped out. Fratianno described his conversation with Dorfman: "So Allen brings up the time Joe Louis walked into the courtroom in Washington when Hoffa was on trial for bribery and shakes hands with Hoffa. All the blacks on the jury, and there must have been eight or nine of them, see this and they acquit the sonovabitch in about two hours flat. So Allen's thinking how great it would be if Muhammad Ali walked into the courtroom and shook his hand." That never happened. Dorfman was convicted and then assassinated while his case was on appeal.

14. William Smith, the alleged former CIA agent, was also convicted of conspiracy and bank fraud in the Florida Center caper.

15. In August 1986 Rapp pleaded guilty for running a check-kiting scheme that defrauded Flagship National Bank of Miami. The institution's name was later changed to Sun Bank.

16. Farrell and Wolk were former business partners of John A. Zaccaro, the husband of 1984 Democratic vice presidential candidate Geraldine A. Ferraro, in an unrelated business deal. Zaccaro was not implicated in the indictment.

Chapter 14. Casino Federal

1. The Teamsters Central States Pension Fund, for example.

2. Junk bonds marketed by the securities firm Drexel Burnham Lambert were a favorite.

3. A series of articles in the Las Vegas *Review-Journal* revealed that entertainer Wayne Newton was an original investor in the Shenandoah when it opened in 1980 but tough state gaming officials would not approve a casino license for the owners. Newton had an abiding interest in owning a hotel-casino. After he backed out of the Shenandoah deal, he tried unsuccessfully to purchase the Aladdin, Stardust, and Fremont in Las Vegas, according to published reports. He also invested in the Poconos in Pennsylvania when he believed voters would approve gambling in the state.

4. The DeVille was in Las Vegas, the Crystal Palace in Laughlin.

5. A Reno businessman told us an associate of Lapaglia's boasted that Lapaglia had brokered loans in connection with at least four casinos. Lapaglia told us he had brokered only one.

6. Lapaglia claimed he never personally earned more than $2 million in his entire life.

7. And Eureka Federal Savings and Loan, San Carlos, California.

8. Alliance was one of the thrifts that Renda and Schwimmer used for their pension fund scam.

9. Irving Savings near Dallas had first agreed to make the loan, but regulators forced them to back out. An associated thrift, Home Savings in Seattle, then agreed to assume the loan in one year (Home was run by John Shepard, who had taught a seminar at Lapaglia's company for a short time before going on to run Home Savings), so Lapaglia went to Olano for interim financing.

10. Alliance was under a strict court order not to make such loans without FHLBB approval, regulators later charged.

11. Officials from three federal agencies also gave details to a New Orleans judge of at least six other investigations involving Olano, including allegations of ties with organized crime and cocaine trafficking, according to published reports.

12. Later officials would allege in bankruptcy court that some of the collateral (machinery and scrap steel from his demolition jobs, for example) may not have existed.

13. Until he was removed by regulators later in 1984.

14. Players Casino, the Dunes, Maxims, and the Treasury. A renovation loan for the Treasury came from Ed Forde's San Marino Savings in Southern California.

15. The gaming investigators even looked to the source of funds being used by the applicant to buy the casino. If they didn't like where the money had been, they turned down the applicant. One year after making Schwab his Players loan, Eureka Federal was declared an unfit source of funds for casino purchases. The gaming control board never publicly explained why.

16. Schwab also bought controlling interest in the Rushville National Bank in Rushville, Indiana. The bank's attorney was former U.S. Senator Vance Hartke. When Paul called him in May 1987 to ask him about Schwab, Hartke replied, "I've met him. But I've never been in business or represented him."

17. The FHLBB approved a regulation that established a formula for raising the minimum net-worth requirements for a thrift. The purpose of the regulation was to eliminate the excessive leveraging that was contributing to fast growth and careless lending.

18. Letter to the chairman of Freedom Savings from Schwab.

19. The Philadelphia project was an old distillery that the EPA in 1987 placed in their Superfund cleanup program, estimating the cleanup might cost $10 million. Schwab would not be on the hook for the cleanup costs, however, because Freedom Savings had foreclosed on his loan, and the FSLIC had closed Freedom Savings, so the FSLIC was the proud new owner of, and therefore responsible for, the toxic site.

20. The *Daily Oklahoman* reported that Bazarian brought Kohnen into CB Financial after having dealt with him when Kohnen was in the Washington, D.C., office of the Robert Strauss law firm. (Strauss was chairman of the Democratic National Committee 1972–76.) Strauss told us an associate in the law firm confirmed that Kohnen did work there, but Strauss said he had never met him.

21. Court documents revealed that in late 1985, after Bazarian had bought into Freedom Savings, attorney Eric Bronk's firm represented Consolidated Savings and Loan on several trips to Tampa to convince Freedom Savings to purchase some of Consolidated's troubled loan portfolio. In 1988 First Federal Savings and Loan of Shawnee, Oklahoma—one of four failed Oklahoma thrifts to whom Bazarian owed millions—would sue Bazarian and Freedom Savings and others, charging they participated in a racketeering scheme headed by Bazarian to defraud the thrift. Freedom Savings denied the charge. The case was pending at press time.

22. Schwab had conducted a 20-year battle with the IRS. He freely admitted to Gaming Control Board agents that he formed companies to hide his homes from the IRS. And he admitted that every year he filed incomplete tax returns, on purpose. He claimed $200,000 in commissions every year, saying that he owed no taxes but would file an amended return soon.

23. In the Abscam sting in 1980, FBI agents posed as bribe-offering sheiks to obtain criminal evidence against members of Congress and others.

24. Donald P. Crivellone was president of First American Bank and Trust. We had run into Crivellone at Consolidated Savings, where he was a director from May 1984 to March 1985. He was not charged with wrongdoing at either institution.

25. When Anderson took over the Dunes Hotel one of his first moves was to hire the former chairman of the Gaming Control Commission to work for him at the Dunes. A regulation was later established to prevent such moves.

26. His partner at First National Bank of Marin was E. Morton Hopkins, a Texan who later owned Commodore Savings and Loan in Dallas, which failed. Hopkins was indicted in January 1989 for election fraud, for allegedly hiding from regulators the use of Commodore funds for political purposes.

27. Mario Renda brokered $550.4 million in deposits into San Marino. A key loan officer at San Marino during the time Bona and Domingues received some of their loans later became CEO at South Bay (owned by Bona and Domingues) and a consultant to Robert Ferrante's Consolidated Savings.

28. FHLBB memo of 9-28-83 and documents on file with the California savings and loan commissioner.

29. At that time the largest liquidation of a thrift in FSLIC history.

30. The Dallas *Morning News* reported that Robert Ferrante of Consolidated Savings borrowed $3.1 million from South Bay. Regulators removed Domingues from the helm at

South Bay in November 1984, 18 months after the thrift opened. South Bay was seized by regulators in March 1987.

31. Who listed his name on an Atlantic City gaming license application as Jack Bonacorte, according to the Dallas *Morning News*.

32. Bank records show Domingues arranged $2 million in loans from Vernon Savings in Dallas to buy out Bona. Domingues also borrowed between $10 million and $14 million from Eureka Federal Savings for Texas real estate projects, according to an FSLIC attorney.

33. Cost of completing the project was estimated at $287 million in a 1986 prospectus.

34. The FBI didn't know how much money the pair put into the project. They questioned us on the subject when we tried to pry information from them about the Palace Casino.

35. Another buddy of Michael Rapp, John Dioguardi (Johnny Dio), was reportedly a close friend of Paul "Red" Dorfman, father of Allen Dorfman, who became the power behind the fund after Hoffa went to prison. Allen Dorfman was a "special consultant" to the fund and was later convicted of racketeering and then shot to death in a Chicago parking lot in 1983.

36. Later, in a court settlement, it did get $8.5 million from the FHLB in Topeka, which supervises thrifts in Oklahoma.

37. One of the thrifts that bought the Drexel Burnham junk bonds was Southmark's San Jacinto Savings and Loan. See chapter 20.

Chapter 15. Gray, Stockman, and the Red Baron

1. San Marino was put in the hands of a conservatorship in February 1984 and closed permanently in December 1984.

2. Seven times more than State Savings was allowed to invest in a single project.

3. State/Salt Lake City failed in April 1985—at the time the largest failure in the history of the FSLIC in terms of deposits ($416 million). We ran into Oldenburg when he was brokering loans into Eureka Federal Savings in San Mateo, California. He once owned the defunct Los Angeles Express football team. The FSLIC sued Oldenburg and others for $50 million, alleging fraud and self-dealing. Then, in February 1989, with less than three days left to run on the statute of limitations, Oldenburg was indicted by the San Francisco United States attorney. He was accused of grossly inflating the value of land so he and others could sell it to State Savings at an enormous profit. Oldenburg angrily denied the charge and hired former San Francisco Mayor Joseph Alioto to defend him. Alioto claimed the government had waited until the last minute to indict Oldenburg in order to take full advantage of the growing public "lynch mob mentality" over bank fraud cases. Both civil and criminal cases against Oldenburg were pending when this book went to press.

4. Not all go-go S&Ls relied on brokered deposits. Some, like American of Stockton, established their own deposit solicitation department, often called a money desk.

5. In the industry such properties were called REOs, short for "real estate owned." REO was a benign-sounding pseudonym for real estate that the thrift had to repossess because the borrower defaulted on his loan.

6. Was it coincidence, then, that American—owned by FCA—agreed to purchase a package of loans from San Marino Savings that included $100 million of Bona and Domingues

loans (on which regulators later claimed American lost $17 million)? Or was it all part of one large quid pro quo, as one investigator told us he suspected? Odds are, we will never know.

7. *BusinessWeek* reported that in 1989 Pelullo again went to Knapp (then doing business as Trafalgar Holdings Ltd. with former California Savings and Loan Commissioner Larry Taggart) to finance an unsuccessful takeover bid for DWG Corporation controlled by corporate raider Victor Posner. (For eight months in 1987 and 1988, according to *BusinessWeek*, Pelullo had earned $1.2 million as a consultant for Posner.) A profile of Victor Posner in *The Wall Street Journal* said the SEC had charged Posner and others with a series of securities-law violations in 1977 (Posner agreed to an injunction related to the charges without denying or admitting guilt) and in 1987 he was convicted in Miami of tax evasion (the verdict was later thrown out and a new trial was pending). *The Wall Street Journal* said Posner was obsessed with security and was almost always accompanied by bodyguards. *BusinessWeek* reported that in 1987 Posner earned $8.4 million in salary and bonuses from DWG. In 1988 he was sued by the SEC, on charges of illegal stock trading in 1984, as part of the SEC's massive case against Drexel Burnham Lambert, built largely from information provided by Wall Street trader Ivan Boesky.

8. David Stockman was director of the Office of Management and Budget from 1981 to 1985.

9. Popejoy had operated thrifts in California and he had headed up the Federal Home Loan Mortgage Corporation, a quasi-governmental agency that bought mortgages from thrifts.

10. Garn-St Germain allowed thrifts to invest more of their deposits in direct investments, as opposed to simply making loans on projects. Centennial Savings, for example, invested in Sid Shah's mushroom farm project. Gray did not believe such investments were a prudent way for thrifts to use federally insured deposit money, and he was proposing strict new limits on what percent of a thrift's assets could be in direct investments. The difference between a direct investment and a loan was primarily that in a direct investment the thrift provided 100 percent of the financing, participated in the losses, and had no recourse to the borrower's other assets if the borrower defaulted on the loan. Thrifts confused the two, often on purpose, because they wanted to collect the points, fees, and interest that characterized a loan and they also wanted to participate in any profit from the appreciation of equity. Regulators didn't establish clear distinctions between the two until 1985.

11. Regan was Secretary of the Treasury from 1981 to 1985.

12. The Bank Board resolved the FCA problem by selling American Savings to the Bass Group in 1988. The resolution cost the FSLIC over $2 billion.

13. By the end of 1984 more than one-third of the states had given their thrifts investment powers beyond those of federally chartered institutions. California, for example, had no limit whatsoever on direct investments in real estate, and Texas limited real estate investments only to 100 percent of the S&L's net worth (unless the state commissioner approved the investment).

14. Failure rates for S&Ls relying heavily on direct investments were high. For example, the FHLBB staff identified 37 institutions with direct investments exceeding 10 percent of their assets in late 1983. Three years later 21 of those institutions had failed or were in serious trouble.

15. Growth was measured by the size of an institution's assets (loans and investments), not by the size of its liabilities (deposits).

16. Or twice its net worth, whichever was greater.

17. Or twice its net worth, whichever was greater.

18. The regulation required additional net worth for institutions growing more than 15 percent per year.

19. Texas thrift assets: 1980, $35.3 billion; 1981, $38.2 billion; 1982, $43.5 billion; 1983, $57.3 billion; 1984, $78.4 billion; 1985, $94.5 billion; 1986, $97.3 billion; 1987, $100.1 billion. Source: "Where Deregulation Went Wrong" by Norman Strunk and Fred Case, published in 1988 by the U.S. League of Savings Institutions.

20. Art collections became a favorite investment for deregulated savings and loans. CenTrust Savings of Miami, for example, had a $28 million art collection in 1988 when regulators announced they had ordered CenTrust to sell the collection, much of which they discovered was kept at the thrift chairman's home.

Chapter 16. Going Home

1. Later Dixon reorganized, making Dondi a subsidiary of Vernon.

2. Vernon also loaned over $15 million to borrowers who wanted to purchase Sandia stock (one of the buyers was Tom Gaubert, who was the power behind Independent American Savings Association in Dallas), and Sandia Savings bought over $80 million in participations from Vernon.

3. The shopping center loan later went into default.

4. The *High Spirits* was non-partisan. Democrat Tom Gaubert of Independent American Savings told *BusinessWeek* he remembered being asked to leave the yacht because Republican Ed Meese was coming aboard.

5. The Dallas *Morning News* reported that Ferrante and a partner borrowed $8 million from Vernon to buy real estate from Dixon's Dondi Group, Inc.

6. Barker and Vineyard bought the thrifts in a deal that involved Texas banker Sam Spikes. Barker, Vineyard and Spikes would later be convicted for the loans they made to one another to facilitate their mutual bank acquisitions.

7. In a cash-for-trash transaction, a thrift officer said, in effect, "We'll make you the loan you want, on the condition that you use the extra money we loan you to buy a piece of repossessed real estate we have on our books." Cash-for-trash schemes were popular among poorly run and crooked savings and loans because as long as the thrift could keep reselling repossessed properties to phony buyers (thereby hiding their past mistakes), and collect phony fees and make a phony profit, it could hold off suspicious federal auditors. Of course the trash property usually went back into default within a year or two, since the borrower really had no interest in it. But that wasn't necessarily bad news for the thrift, which could then recycle the property to another cash-for-trash customer.

8. Eureka Federal, under chairman Kenneth Kidwell, made the loan (brokered by John Lapaglia) to Philip Schwab to renovate the Players Casino and gave John Anderson the $25 million letter of credit to fund his purchase of the Dunes Hotel and Casino in Las Vegas. Nevis was a business associate of California farmer John Anderson, who, federal investigators said, also borrowed heavily from State/Corvallis after being introduced to the thrift by loan broker Al Yarbrow. Among other things, Nevis and Anderson were both tomato farmers in the Sacramento Valley.

9. When a mysterious fire destroyed Nevis Industries' corporate jet, Barker loaned Nevis one of State/Lubbock's, ostensibly because Nevis had become such a valuable customer. When federal regulators seized State/Lubbock, they would have to go to court to get Nevis to give the plane back. Nevis claimed Barker had given it to him.

10. Empire was located in Mesquite, near Dallas.

Chapter 17. Dark in the Heart of Texas

1. Published accounts showed that a Connally/Barnes partnership borrowed $40 million from Vernon. Connally was Secretary of the Navy 1961–62, wounded in the Kennedy assassination in 1963, governor of Texas 1963–68, Secretary of the Treasury 1971–72, and candidate for the Republican presidential nomination in 1980.

2. Yarbrow and Franks were the two Southern California loan brokers who the Justice Department alleged were involved in deals with Tom Nevis at State/Corvallis. Yarbrow introduced Charles Bazarian to Consolidated Savings (who then connected Bazarian to Mario Renda), according to Consolidated's chairman, Ottavio Angotti, and Yarbrow reportedly took Anderson to both Bazarian and Vernon Savings.

3. When we checked Bazarian's bankruptcy papers we found that he and/or his company, CB Financial, had listed Vernon as a creditor, delineating over $11 million in unpaid loans, including $118,000 on a 1985 Rolls-Royce and $13,000 on a Mazda.

4. WFAA-TV, Dallas, news reporter Byron Harris, in an on-camera interview.

5. Hill also pleaded guilty to making an illegal $2,000 campaign contribution, with Vernon's money, to Representative Jack Kemp and others. In 1988 Kemp was appointed Secretary of Housing and Urban Development for the Bush administration.

6. Two years later, after Dixon filed for bankruptcy, the trip made the newspapers and caused the Catholic Church some embarrassment. Maher and Eagen denied knowing the trip was at Vernon's expense. They pointed out that the Dixons had other guests and that they, Maher and Eagen, returned to San Diego on a commercial jet, leaving the Dixons behind to continue their European holiday. Maher told the San Diego *Union* he accepted the trip as a matter of convenience because he had business in Rome and Dublin. Then he stopped discussing the trip with the press at all.

7. To drum up foreign investment in Vernon.

8. Regulators later claimed the thrift received no benefit from the trips whatsoever.

9. When a borrower couldn't qualify for a loan he could pay someone with a strong financial statement to join him as a partner in the project. Once the loan was made the borrower would buy out his partner with a portion of the loan proceeds. The buyout was actually the partner's fee for "kissing the paper."

10. *Texas Business* magazine reported that Bowman had owned thrift stock that he sold at a considerable profit to Ed McBirney. *The Wall Street Journal* revealed he also was a partner in a real estate venture with Patrick G. King, a friend who was chairman of Vernon Savings and has been accused by the feds of having looted the institution. Both activities occurred after Bowman became the commissioner, but state officials have said Bowman's actions did not constitute a conflict of interest. Bowman resigned as Texas S&L commissioner in 1987. He did try to get authority for state regulators to seize an S&L without having to go to court first. He drafted a bill that passed only after he reached a private agreement with an S&L

owner who thought the bill was aimed at him. Bowman later told *BusinessWeek*, "I had to negotiate with people I didn't want to be in the same room with."

11. The meeting was called by Continental Savings President David Wylie and Chairman Carroll Kelly, the *Post* reported. Regulators told the *Post* that information about the meeting had been turned over to the Justice Department "as part of an ongoing criminal investigation."

12. Sam Spikes helped them buy Key Savings and Loan near Denver in return for loans from Key. Barker and Vineyard were later found guilty and sentenced to five years in prison. Barker cooperated with federal investigators in their investigation of Tom Nevis and Jack Franks.

13. Including Charles Keating, Jr., of Lincoln Savings.

14. The day Gray removed Knapp from FCA, Gray had tried to coordinate the move with Taggart in California, only to discover Taggart had gone hiking in the Sierras and could not be reached.

15. In January 1989 the House Banking Committee grilled Taggart about his letter. Taggart replied that none of his actions as a regulator were ever politically motivated and his reference to campaign contributions in the letter was only an effort to "get Don Regan's attention." Congressman Jim Leach (R-Iowa) denounced Taggart during the hearing: "You are part and parcel of a group who turned thrifts in this state [California] into private piggy banks for speculators and developers. . . . Your testimony proves my contention that the thrift crisis was caused by cooked books with regulators acting as chefs and legislators stirring the pot."

16. *BusinessWeek* reported October 31, 1988, that Wright got $240,000 (20 percent of his total) for his 1986 campaign from savings and loan and real estate interests.

17. Everyone knew that House Speaker Tip O'Neill planned to retire in the near future and Jim Wright would be tapped to become speaker of the House, the third most powerful position in the government. Wright became speaker in January 1987.

18. Regulators had declared Westwood Savings insolvent in March 1986, claiming the thrift's problems stemmed mainly from its participation in land flips. They said Westwood bought property from real estate syndicators (one of whom, they alleged, was Hall, who made a healthy commission on each sale) and then simultaneously, or nearly simultaneously, resold the property to affiliates of the syndicators at a substantial profit (with Westwood providing the loans for that final transfer). When the borrowers defaulted on the loans Westwood was left with the properties, which were not worth the amount of the loans, regulators said.

19. It would be August 1987 before a compromise recap bill would finally pass both houses of Congress and be signed into law.

20. *The Wall Street Journal* reported that Mann donated $2,000 to Wright's 1985 re-election campaign.

21. Using brokered deposits to invest in commercial real estate development, Independent American grew from $40 million in assets in 1983 to $1.8 billion by the summer of 1986. Gaubert got control of Independent American in October 1982.

22. Over a 15-month period ending in September 1986, Dixon and people with ties to Vernon donated about $60,000 to the Democratic Congressional Campaign Committee. Hall and others with ties to his company donated $4,700, according to the Chicago *Tribune*.

23. Regulators' management of assets that they acquired from insolvent thrifts would make an interesting topic for another book. Their record was dismal.

24. Gray decided that the only way Wright would be satisfied that the FHLBB's handling of Gaubert had been fair would be if Gray appointed an independent counsel acceptable to Gaubert to conduct an investigation. Regulators later characterized the appointment as "extremely unusual, even extraordinary." The independent counsel ultimately upheld the Bank Board's decision, discovering that, though there had been some procedural errors committed by the Bank Board at Independent American, the outcome of the examination would have been the same even if the errors had not occurred.

25. Ironically, the last thrift closed by the FSLIC prior to the passage of the recap was Capitol Savings in Mount Pleasant, Iowa. When regulators got control of Capitol and dug into its books, they found a deal they didn't like and made a criminal referral to the Justice Department on Tom Gaubert. Later a grand jury indicted him for loan fraud. He told us he had simply been doing the thrift a favor, and he believed the indictment was an attempt by the Reagan administration to embarrass Representative Wright. The Justice Department said Gaubert made at least $5.6 million off of a 1983 land flip. A Bank Board official told a congressional investigator, ". . . our own enforcement people had . . . documented a pattern of land flips and fraud. . . . None of this had been proved in a court of law, but it is as solid a finding as you were going to find." Gaubert was acquitted in October 1988.

26. Selby was asked to leave the Dallas FHLB after Wall took over the FHLBB chairmanship from Gray in 1987. In an interview Selby hinted that some of the thrift owners he forced out had friends in Congress and he had become "a political liability" for the FHLBB in Washington.

27. Selby refused to name the man, saying he had assured him confidentiality.

Chapter 18. The Last Squeezing of the Grapes

1. Dixon associates said in depositions later that Dixon's California attorney told them Paris Savings was Dixon's "junk S&L," meaning presumably that Dixon could place his bad loans with them. A director of Paris Savings was Harvey McLean, whom regulators believed was an associate of Herman Beebe, according to a report by the comptroller of the currency.

2. A later appraisal commissioned by regulators put the artworks' real value at only $443,000.

3. Franks pleaded guilty to a charge that he helped defraud Vernon Savings, and he cooperated with authorities.

4. Vernon's directors had to agree to the consent-to-merger agreement, which they did December 31, 1986.

5. The following account of the Wright telephone call on behalf of Don Dixon and Vernon Savings is as recounted by the report of the special counsel investigating Jim Wright, Richard J. Phelan, for the House Committee on Standards of Official Conduct, February 21, 1989. When Dixon appeared before the committee, he asserted his fifth amendment right against self-incrimination and refused to testify.

6. In May 1989 the Washington *Post* revealed that in 1973, when he was 19, Mack brutally attacked a young woman, a stranger. He pounded her skull with a hammer, stabbed her five times near the heart, slashed her repeatedly across the throat, drove around for a while

with her unconscious body in the car, then parked the car and went to the movies. Incredibly, the woman lived. Mack pleaded guilty to malicious wounding and was sentenced to 15 years in the Virginia State Penitentiary, but in what the *Post* said a state attorney called "highly unusual" treatment, he never served time in the penitentiary. Instead he did 27 months in the county jail and was paroled to a job as staff assistant to Wright, who even before sentencing had had the judge notified several times that Mack had a good job waiting for him. Mack's brother was married to Wright's daughter. By 1989 Mack was earning $90,000 as perhaps the most powerful staff member on Capitol Hill, and the *Post* reported that his history was known to many on Capitol Hill. Responding to comments that the victim never received restitution or even an apology from Mack, Tony Coelho, who described himself as "very close" to Mack, said, "Rightly or wrongly, under our system of law John Mack owed his debt to society, not to this young woman." If Wright were to let Mack go, Coelho told the *Post*, "members would be lined up to hire him." Mack was a model of rehabilitation, his supporters said. Journalist Brooks Jackson reported that in 1981 Coelho wrote to a judge on behalf of another convicted murderer (who bludgeoned, stabbed, choked, and buried alive his victim) whose father had contributed to Coelho's campaign. The judge was unmoved by Coelho's plea. The Phelan report said that Wright in 1975 wrote a letter requesting leniency for another convicted felon, William Carlos Moore. The Justice Department accused Moore, a Teamster lobbyist for eight years, of misappropriating Teamster funds for his own use. Moore said Frank Fitzsimmons, Teamster president, and Jimmy Hoffa, former Teamster president, were aware of the diversion and the money was used to make cash contributions to politicians. Moore eventually pleaded guilty to one count of income tax evasion, and Wright wrote the judge on Moore's behalf, saying he'd been a personal friend of Moore's for more than 20 years. Moore was sentenced to two years in the penitentiary (he served 4½ months). In 1984 Moore published Wright's *Reflections of a Public Man* which became one focus of the 1989 Phelan report on Wright to the House ethics committee.

7. Wright has said he did not know Dixon personally. Dixon has said he met Wright in Washington twice.

8. According to the Phelan report, Mallick placed the blame for the thrift crisis in Texas on regulators. Green later said Mallick "did not have an intimate knowledge of the bank system nor the savings and loan industry." He said Mallick's lack of knowledge "was somewhat of a surprise," given his responsibility for the investigation. Green said he had thought Mallick and Wright wanted a balanced perspective but "the balanced perspective . . . that they wanted is completely absent. . . . [T]his is not even close to a fair exposition of the problem as I would view it."

9. Black said he heard that Wright later referred to him as "that red-bearded son-of-a-bitch" in private. The Phelan report referred to Black as "one of the most impressive witnesses to appear before the Committee." Wright tried to get Black fired in early 1988, the Phelan report said.

10. Frank Annunzio of Illinois was close to the U.S. League for years and represented the Chicago congressional district of U.S. League President (until he retired in 1988) William O'Connell. Journalist Kathleen Day reported in *The New Republic* that Annunzio's chief banking aide, Curt Prins, told Gray he wouldn't be able to get a job in the industry after he stepped down as FHLBB chairman if he didn't stop speaking out about the industry's problems.

11. S&L analysts generally believed a failure rate of 4 percent was something to worry about and 10 percent was leading almost certainly to insolvency.

Chapter 19. The Godfather

1. The comptroller has principal supervisory responsibility for the nation's national banks.

2. In the back of this book is a copy of the comptroller of the currency's report on Herman Beebe's influence over banks and savings and loans. A careful reading of that report explains how the Beebe network interrelated during the 1980s.

3. The SEC said Beebe hadn't told investors that he sold to AMI the stock of companies he controlled, including one company that hadn't made a profit for nine years; he sold stock to AMI without disclosing what he had paid for it or what AMI paid him; he arranged for AMI to loan money to companies he owned; he told investors of a $28,000 AMI asset that was really worthless; and he included in the AMI prospectus $281,288 in "other assets" that were in large part just hot air.

4. Beebe reportedly owned a Holiday Inn that Marcello was interested in buying at the time.

5. Marcello was convicted in 1981 of mail and wire fraud (the result of the FBI's BRILAB investigation, which has been called the most massive undercover operation against a single individual in the FBI's history), and in 1983 of attempting to bribe a California federal judge. After a widely publicized trial, he was sentenced to a total of 17 years in prison.

6. One of Sharp's attorneys, according to reports published in the Dallas *Morning News*, was Jake Jacobsen, White House legislative aide to President Lyndon Johnson from 1965 to 1967, who also controlled three savings and loans involved in the scandal. Jacobsen was indicted for misapplication of funds. (Before Jacobsen's indictment, John Connally, while he was the nation's top bank regulator as secretary of the Treasury, 1971–1972, telephoned the Justice Department several times to express fear that Jacobsen was being treated unfairly, the *Morning News* reported. Later Connally was accused of accepting a $10,000 bribe in 1971 from Jacobsen acting on behalf of the dairy industry, but Connally was completely cleared of all charges. Jacobsen pleaded guilty.)

7. Barnes told us they originally met through a mutual friend or at a Holiday Inn convention. Like Beebe, one of Barnes' businesses was developing Holiday Inns.

8. The information had begun to come to light after Citizens State Bank in Carrizo Springs, Texas (about 30 miles as the crow flies from Mexico and the Rio Grande), was closed by state banking officials June 28.

9. One member of the Texas banking network was Richmond Chase Harper, Sr., who also owned banks. According to documents and testimony entered into the congressional record, Harper was sued by the Labor Department for feeding horse meat to *braceros* and was arrested in 1972 in connection with a plot to smuggle guns to Mexico to be used to overthrow Castro. Indicted along with Harper was Murray Kessler, who had a record of six convictions in federal and state courts and who was well known to law-enforcement authorities in New York as an associate of the Carlo Gambino organized crime family. The case ended in a mistrial. Barnes helped Harper get loans of $1.9 million and $180,000 from savings and loans with whom Barnes and Beebe had a close association. Barnes told us he was introduced to Harper by the chairman of the Board of Regents of the University of Texas. He said he did not know Kessler.

10. As reported in the Houston *Post*.

11. Committee on Banking Currency and Housing, Subcommittee on Financial Institutions Supervision, Regulation and Insurance.

12. Regulators testified that George John Aubin and J. B. Haralson had had control or influence over more than a dozen banks that were part of the network. Still there was no reason to worry about the pair, regulators claimed in 1976, because ". . . neither is active in Texas banking now, having been removed from control well over 18 months ago." That optimism would prove to be nothing more than wishful thinking because in the 1980s Aubin and Haralson got control of two Texas S&Ls, Mercury Savings Association in Wichita Falls and Ben Milan Savings in Cameron. The Dallas *Morning News* reported that in 1984 Aubin was a $15,000-a-month consultant to the two thrifts. In 1985 the Texas savings and loan commissioner warned that the thrifts were engaged in "extremely dangerous and questionable practices" such as "major loans to insiders," including Aubin, according to *Fortune* magazine, and in 1986 regulators took over the two thrifts, even as E.F. Hutton was wailing that Aubin had defrauded them of millions of dollars with an elaborate stock and commodity trading scam. In granting E.F. Hutton a $48 million judgment against a Haralson company in a related matter, the judge nevertheless admonished E.F. Hutton for not being more careful in who they dealt with, saying, "That Aubin was an obfuscating liar is no excuse not to examine corporate records before assuming an obligation."

13. Interestingly, reporter Pete Brewton discovered that Renda and Beebe both had bank accounts at San Dieguito National Bank in Vista, near La Costa.

14. Another source of funds for La Costa, according to *Penthouse* magazine, was C. Arnholt Smith's United States National Bank of San Diego, which collapsed in 1973. Smith, at one time a member of President Richard Nixon's inner circle, pleaded no contest to bank fraud in 1975. Smith and related entities owed United States National Bank more than $400 million when it collapsed, but Tom Nevis eased the pain in 1977 by paying the FDIC $7.4 million for a 12,400 acre ranch once controlled by Smith.

15. Testimony of Tom Nevis in State Savings of Lubbock vs. Doe Valley. Nevis also testified that he met Beebe in Barker's office.

16. Beebe's old partner Ben Barnes also benefited from Beebe's relationships with the 1980s S&L owners. In the 1980s Barnes was in partnership with John Connally. WFAA-TV, Dallas, reported that the Barnes/Connally partnership borrowed from 17 S&Ls in three states, including $40 million from Vernon and an unspecified amount from CreditBanc, where Barnes's son worked. So well known were Barnes and Connally on the thrift circuit that even officers at Centennial Savings traveled to Texas to try to interest Connally in a project they were promoting. John Connally went bankrupt when the Texas S&L industry collapsed. Connally was later hired by a Houston advertising firm to make commercials for University Savings Association, Texas's fourth largest S&L. In the ads he urged people to set aside savings. In February 1989 the FHLBB threw University Savings into a conservatorship and in the first quarter of 1989 it posted losses of $1.14 billion.

17. From material gathered by author John H. Davis for *Mafia Kingfish*, McGraw-Hill, 1988.

18. In a sworn deposition relating to a 1979 lawsuit filed in Louisiana.

19. He had also been president of Colonial Bank in New Orleans, which the *Morning News* reported was owned by Beebe and Reggie.

20. Graffagnino was convicted in 1983 for obstruction of justice, according to the *Morning News*.

21. When Reggie retired, he bought a house next door to Ted Kennedy's home in Nantucket and lived there about four months a year.

22. In 1982 Reggie purchased the bank's stock in his name as trustee, with no indication of whom he was a trustee for, and he gave as his address the headquarters of AMI, Inc., according to the comptroller of the currency report on Beebe.

Chapter 20. Beebe Gets Caged

1. The Federal Building was named, ironically, the Joseph D. Waggonner Federal Building after Shreveport's longtime congressman, who was also a director of Beebe's Bossier Bank & Trust and an investor in at least one other Beebe-dominated bank, according to the comptroller of the currency report. In 1989 the FDIC sued Beebe, Waggonner, and others for their involvement in the 1986 collapse of Bossier Bank & Trust.

2. George Aubin and Jarrett Woods, both of Houston, grew up together. Both were involved financially with the banking network that was exposed during the congressional hearings in Texas in the mid-1970s and surfaced again in the S&L scandal of the 1980s, according to congressional testimony and numerous published reports. Aubin said he introduced Woods to Beebe. Western Savings grew more than 6,000 percent in the four years Woods was at the helm, 1982 to 1986. The Dallas *Morning News* reported that another close associate of Woods was James D. Hague, vice chairman and owner of Liberty Federal Savings and Loan of Leesburg, Louisiana, which was closed by regulators who said they had uncovered self-dealing, poor underwriting, risky lending, and the usual litany. Just as this book was going to press a law-enforcement official informed us she had just discovered that Morris Shenker had borrowed heavily from Liberty.

3. By marketing junk bonds through Milken.

4. Drexel Burnham capitalized on the Reagan administration's lax view of federal antitrust laws and pioneered the use of junk bonds to finance corporate raids and takeovers. Congress debated cracking down on the controversial operation, and Drexel contributed hundreds of thousands of dollars to congressional campaigns. Among the top recipients of their largess was Rep. Tony Coelho, who was a friend of Drexel's junk bond king Michael Milken. In 1989 it was revealed that the chairman and CEO of Columbia Savings (Beverly Hills, California), Thomas Spiegel, bought and held $100,000 in Drexel junk bonds for Coelho until Coelho could come up with his own financing. Eventually half the money, according to Spiegel, came in the form of a low-interest loan from Columbia Savings (which was itself a heavy investor in Drexel's junk bonds) which Coelho admitted he failed to report on his financial disclosure statement the next year. *The New York Times* reported Coelho made nearly $13,000 on the junk bond investment. The Justice Department opened a preliminary investigation, the House ethics committee proposed an investigation, and Coelho resigned his House seat in May 1989.

5. When Milken was indicted for his alleged role in the Wall Street insider trading scandal that began with the arrest of Ivan Boesky, the government revealed that in 1987 Milken earned a staggering $550 million from his junk bond operation. His earlier compensation was: 1986, $294.8 million; 1985, $135.3 million; 1984, $123.8 million; 1983, $45.7 million.

6. Actually it adds up to $29.3 million, but who's quibbling?

7. It was $1 million.

8. Phillips said $27.8 million went to a company affiliated with Beebe but not to Beebe himself.

9. Published accounts said Nevis sold an option on the property to George Benny, who

was convicted for kiting nearly $40 million in checks through banks and thrifts and who sold the option to Southmark.

10. Wood arranged junkets to the Dunes for some of the Texas S&Ls, including Sunbelt. Phillips said Wood's contact in the Texas S&L family was Joe Grosz, who was an executive with San Jacinto Savings and Loan in Houston. San Jacinto Savings was owned by Southmark and held millions in Drexel Burnham's junk bonds. Grosz borrowed from Sunbelt Savings to the tune of over $5 million, in transactions that Sunbelt officials later charged were fraudulent. Grosz, in turn, had San Jacinto loan $75 million to an Ed McBirney partnership, the Sunbelt officers charged in a civil lawsuit.

11. Continental Savings failed in October 1988.

12. Among Pratt's properties was the Sands Hotel and Casino in Atlantic City.

13. Southmark's involvement at Silverado was through its subsidary construction company, J.M. Peters, and another Colorado company, MDC Holdings Inc. The two had been involved in an acquisition deal which, had it been completed, would have allowed Southmark to book a much-needed $25 million profit. Instead, the deal fell apart. MDC Holdings Inc. was another junk bond junkie, having sold $700 million worth through Drexel Burnham Lambert. The Denver *Post* reported that its chairman, Larry Mizel, lobbied in Washington on behalf of Drexel's junk bond operation. The *Post* described Mizel as one of Colorado's most powerful businessmen. By the end of 1988, MDC Holdings, whose affairs were intricately involved with those of Silverado Savings, was suffering severe losses and trying to regroup.

14. "They took a lesson from the Vietnam War: Declare victory and pull out," quipped Lester Lave, a regulatory expert at Carnegie-Mellon University, to a *Fortune* magazine reporter.

Chapter 21. Round Three

1. See the comptroller of the currency report in the appendix for some of the details of his involvement with Beebe.

2. Indicted with Beebe was an associate of Spencer Blain, chairman of Empire Savings, the first big Dallas S&L to fail.

3. Both Beebe and Wolfe had been indicted in Shreveport in 1984 and convicted in separate and apparently unrelated cases. Wolfe was convicted of defrauding the government of $139,000 by fraudulently obtaining milk subsidy payments. He was placed on five years probation.

4. Reeder ran Carlsberg Management, a former subsidiary of Carlsberg Corporation, which 10-Ks and Reeder said was a subsidiary of Southmark; federal investigators told us Reeder was associated with John Boreta, a business partner of casino owner John B. Anderson; when the Tennessee banking empire of C. H. and Jake Butcher collapsed in 1983 due to fraud (in the nation's third largest banking collapse since the Great Depression, costing the FDIC $1 billion) and the pair were indicted, the Knoxville *Journal* reported that Reeder guaranteed their $1 million bail and formed a company, Reeder Equities, to acquire their properties out of bankruptcy; Reeder tried to play White Knight for San Marino Savings, offering to buy the thrift when it was on the verge of collapse, according to the thrift's chief operating officer; in August 1988 Reeder and a partner bought Litton Industries' microwave division and within three months threw it into bankruptcy (critics said the company had been looted in a bustout operation; Reeder said Litton defrauded him by selling him a bankrupt company); in 1989 the FBI was investigating allegations that he purchased insurance companies and had them

invest in questionable business ventures that benefited him (Reeder said an employee he later fired was responsible for these moves).

5. Lapaglia spent a lot of time in New Orleans with his friend Guy Olano at Alliance Federal Savings, and a U.S. attorney told us Beebe also knew Olano.

6. Regulators claimed in the suit that they had been warning Acadia since early 1984 to stop unsafe loan practices and avoid conflicts of interest.

7. Interestingly, as Judge Reggie pointed out to us, the FDIC was complaining on behalf of Aurora Bank that Rizzo and Delvecchio had undervalued the property and the FSLIC was complaining on behalf of Acadia Savings that Beall and Mascolo had overvalued it.

8. John Lapaglia told us Wayne Newton had millions in shaky loans on property in the Poconos, too, and investigators said Newton's property was not far from the Rizzo-Delvecchio property. There had been much talk that legalized gambling might be introduced into the northeast Pennsylvania resort area, and federal investigators told us developers were using the well-known names of Wayne Newton and Frank Sinatra to attract investors. According to Cage, World Wide Ventures, run by Rapp's buddy Lorenzo Formato, was one of the intended developers of the Poconos project. World Wide Ventures borrowed heavily from Flushing Federal.

9. Reifler, then a resident of Fort Lauderdale, Florida, was no stranger to law-enforcement authorities. He had at least four criminal convictions—in Florida and elsewhere, going back to 1970—for stock fraud and extortion.

10. One of Governor Edwards's pet projects during his last term in office was to bring big-time casino gambling to Louisiana, and Reggie had been hired by Resorts International as a $10,000-a-month consultant. Resorts International, the number one gambling presence in Atlantic City, made no secret of the fact that they wanted to open a casino in New Orleans.

11. From Cage's affidavit.

12. Kwitny's *The Fountain Pen Conspiracy*, 1973, is the story of a band of international swindlers who in the 1960s and early 1970s were "fleecing hundreds of millions of dollars from banks, businesses, and private investors . . . and getting away with it." Besides Reifler, two other Kwitny characters showed up in our investigation. One borrowed millions from Oklahoma thrifts through SISCorp (tied to Charles Bazarian) on grossly overvalued Las Vegas properties. The other was suspected by FSLIC attorneys of being behind a Texas group that took over at least one Kansas thrift that later failed. The group borrowed $5 million from Ed McBirney's Sunbelt Savings to purchase the Kansas thrift. No indictments have been handed down in these cases.

13. Cage quoted Kwitny: "The associates [Wuensche] identified for the McClellan Committee might constitute a quorum at a high-level meeting of the New Jersey Mafia: Frankie 'The Bear' Basto, named by a previous witness as the foremost member of the New Jersey mob's murder squad. Anthony 'Little Pussy' Russo, who ran the rackets over a large area and employed the politically powerful Wilentz family to provide his legal help in netting hundreds of thousands of dollars from land speculation financed by banks with which the Wilentzes are associated. Angel 'The Gyp' DeCarlo, subject of some of the FBI eavesdropping transcripts made public in 1969. Joseph 'Bayonne Joe' Zicarelli. And bloodstained enforcers like Charlie 'The Blade' Tourine and Harold 'Kayo' Konigsberg. Wuensche also said he worked with Satiris Galahad 'Sonny' Fassoulis and Lionel Reifler, who participated in the Community National Life Insurance Co. swindle."

14. Reggie's law firm did accept fees from Acadia customers.

Chapter 22. A Thumb in the Dike

1. Lapaglia believed Gray's insistence on tighter appraisal standards were the cause of the industry's collapse.

2. Posen worked for Caplin and Drysdale, a law firm heavily involved in representing S&L interests, and he had been the keynote speaker at the Acapulco conference sponsored by Lapaglia and Eureka Federal Savings in 1983. Government attorneys told us Caplin and Drysdale represented Herman Beebe and Vernon Savings and employees confirmed Judge Edmund Reggie's daughter, who was also an attorney, worked there.

3. Newton was also a friend of Charles Bazarian, an associate of loan broker Bill Oldenburg, and an associate of Eureka Federal Savings President Kenneth Kidwell, and a casino investor. His investment in the Poconos was just down the road from the property owned by Jilly Rizzo and Anthony Delvecchio.

4. Curlee represented the Texas League and 20 of Texas's most aggressive thrifts, including Vernon and Sunbelt. S&L records show he also had several loans from Vernon.

5. For example, the Associated Press reported that Fahrenkopf represented Newton in his bid to get control of the Aladdin Hotel in Las Vegas in 1980.

6. Involved in the complicated transaction were the Buena Vista Bank & Trust in Buena Vista, Colorado (population 2,000), which collapsed in August 1986, United Savings Bank and its holding company, Uniwest Financial Corporation in Denver. The Colorado Springs *Gazette Telegraph* reported that Newton filed a lawsuit in 1987 in which he charged that he and other investors had to purchase $1.75 million in stock from Uniwest Financial Corporation in order to qualify for a loan from one of its subsidiaries. A spokeswoman for the FHLB of Seattle told the *Gazette Telegraph* that if Newton's description were correct, the deal could have been a "kickback, which means it's bribery and a crime." The FDIC, SEC, and FSLIC were investigating the transactions surrounding the collapse of Buena Vista Bank. A key figure in the collapse was a wheeler-dealer from Dallas who was said to have worked for a special CIA team in Southeast Asia in the 1960s. Newton declined to discuss the case with *Gazette Telegraph* reporter Julie Bird, but Fahrenkopf told her he repaid his loan on time and he was disillusioned with his partners in the project and with the project itself. He said he was trying to get his $100,000 out of the RV park but, "My lawyers have been unable to get documentation . . . I could have gone anywhere to get a loan. This raises some real questions. I didn't have to go to Buena Vista. It was presented to me that the financing was all lined up." Neither Newton nor Fahrenkopf replied to our calls and registered letters.

7. Keating owned American Continental Corporation, which owned Lincoln S&L.

8. A reference to state and federally chartered thrift institutions. The direct investment regulation was aimed at state-chartered thrifts that were FSLIC-insured.

9. The FSLIC fund that insured those deposits had only $4.6 billion on hand at a time when thrift failures were piling up like wrecks in a demolition derby, some costing the FSLIC as much as a billion dollars each.

10. Although the FHLBB was funded through assessments on its member thrifts, its budget was by law included in the appropriations' process and had to be approved by OMB before submission to Congress. Staffing levels at the FHLBB, therefore, were subject to OMB control.

11. Each member thrift owned a number of shares in their district bank and voted as the bank's shareholders.

12. There was precedent for Gray's move. FDIC examiners did not fall under OMB control.

13. The average savings and loan examiner's salary was 25 percent less than the lowest-paid federal bank examiner in 1984.

14. Supervisory agreements and cease-and-desist orders were binding instructions to thrifts, attempts to force them to adhere to regulations and to manage their assets responsibly. Gray issued lengthy memoranda in April 1985, December 1985, and February 1986 pressing for stronger and faster regulatory enforcement.

15. House Subcommittee on Oversight and Investigations of the Committee on Energy and Commerce.

16. Beverly Hills Savings was the subject of several congressional hearings after it was revealed its failure would cost the FSLIC between $700 million and $900 million. Regulators said one of the thrift's customers, a mysterious Swiss financier named Werner K. Rey, had tried to gain control of the thrift and there was speculation among the congressional staff that he may have been acting on behalf of fugitive financier (and suspected drug smuggler) Robert Vesco, for whom Rey had at one time operated a bank.

17. When the committee issued its report months later they concluded that the FHLBB was not adequately supervising thrifts. They also complained bitterly that the FHLBB had failed to supply the documents the committee requested, and they finally had to subpoena them.

18. In the ensuing years the FHLBB would be criticized for not suing law firms when those firms failed to give S&Ls the legal advice they needed to stay out of trouble, and eventually regulators did begin to file such suits. In 1987 the FSLIC sued Larry Vineyard's law firm, the third largest law firm in Dallas, for its role in the collapse of State Savings/Lubbock. In August 1988 the Philadelphia firm of Blank, Rome, Comisky & McCauley agreed to a $50 million settlement with the FSLIC concerning their alleged failure to properly advise Sunrise Savings of Boynton Beach, Florida, which collapsed in 1985 amid a swirl of intrigue. Also in August the FSLIC sued the law firm of Reggie, Harrington and Boswell for its alleged role in the collapse of Acadia Savings and Loan in August 1987. In December 1988 the FSLIC won a $35 million judgment against the firm of Mmahat and Duffy, which was paid $5 million for advising Gulf Federal Savings Bank of Metairie, Louisiana, while the thrift repeatedly granted loans in excess of Bank Board limits. Gulf Federal failed in November 1986. In some cases the attorneys also owned stock in the thrift.

Chapter 23. The Touchables

1. North American Savings and Loan failed in 1986 and cost the FSLIC $209 million.

2. Such problems existed, for example, at Vernon Savings and also at San Marino Savings, where, according to a U.S. Attorney, ". . . the [FSLIC] had notice of possible criminal fraud almost two years before the institution failed . . . [but] did not make a referral until the institution closed. The delay created severe document control problems" that destroyed any possibility of connecting certain documents to the chief executive officer suspected of fraud.

3. It was to this group, about eight months later, that regulators presented the 1985 comptroller of the currency report on Herman Beebe.

4. The FHLBB had to offer prospective buyers billions of dollars in assistance (notes, IOUs) as an incentive to take the thrifts.

5. Weld later submitted his resignation in protest over Attorney General Ed Meese's refusal to resign from office amid questions about his business dealings.

6. Many observers faulted the fee attorneys for suing directors of a thrift instead of filing immediately to collect on the insurance coverage the directors carried. Often the directors were bankrupt and had no assets to satisfy a civil judgment anyway, critics reasoned, and the only result of pursuing them in court was higher fees for the fee counsel.

Chapter 24. Friends in High Places

1. Vernon and Sunbelt Savings each cost the FSLIC over $1 billion.

2. The FSLIC bond issue would be repaid through increased assessments on thrifts. The amount they paid each year to belong to the FSLIC would be increased until the bond issue was retired.

3. It had been a long-standing tradition that the U.S. League subsidize the chairman's accommodations when he spoke at U.S. League functions. The chairman would be booked into a more expensive room than the government payroll allowed for and the League would pick up the difference.

4. Don Regan was now chief of staff at the White House. He and James Baker had switched jobs in 1985.

5. FHLBB members were selected by the president and approved by the Senate.

6. Both House and Senate had passed versions of the recap bill in 1986 but too late to hammer out a compromise. Wright had voted for the bill at that time, after he said he got assurances from the FHLBB that it would cooperate with Texas S&Ls. The recap was reintroduced when Congress reconvened in January 1987. In February the U.S. League announced an alternative plan for borrowing only $5 billion.

7. In 1988 attorney Robert Strauss represented Wright in a dispute with *Bankers Monthly* over a two-part series that detailed Wright's alleged unethical conduct in intervening with Ed Gray on behalf of Don Dixon. The compromise they reached allowed Wright to submit a rebuttal to the series. Strauss was a powerful Texan with deep roots. When John Connally was governor, Strauss was his appointee to the Texas Banking Commission. Strauss was a Texas banking commissioner from 1963 to 1976. He became known as "Mr. Democrat" while serving as a Democratic National Committeeman from 1968 to 1972 and chairman of the Democrat National Committee from 1972 to 1976. In the 1980s he was a law partner in the prestigious Akin, Gump, Strauss, Hauer and Feld law firm, which had offices in Dallas, Austin, San Antonio, Fort Worth, Washington, New York, and London. Charles Bazarian brought Sig Kohnen into CB Financial from the Strauss law firm (Strauss told us Kohnen had worked for the firm but they never met), and Strauss' son Richard was a Dallas real estate developer whose records were subpoenaed by the fraud task force. He was not accused of any wrongdoing. When Roy Green, head of the Dallas FHLB, decided in early 1987 that he and Joe Selby should meet with Wright (the meeting attended by the Mallicks), he contacted Strauss to set up the meeting.

8. The issue of forbearance was first raised by the U.S. League during House Banking Committee hearings in January 1987. Wildcat Texas thrift owners immediately began to lobby their friends in Washington for forbearance because all they needed to get back on their feet, they insisted, was time. Forbearance became a popular buzzword of the thrift crisis.

9. Largely because the House Banking Committee, under the leadership of Representative Fernand St Germain (D-R.I.) capitulated once again to the S&L lobbyists.

10. Regan had been chief of staff at the White House since 1985.

11. The San Francisco FHLB examined Lincoln's books from May 1986 to December 20, 1988—the longest examination into an S&L in the history of the industry.

12. The Phoenix *Gazette* obtained a copy of the Eleventh District criminal referral list, which showed Lincoln had been on it since December 1984.

13. Goodwill is what a business says its customer's support is worth. The use of goodwill in valuing thrifts has come under attack. As late as 1987 nearly 45 percent of total net assets claimed by thrifts was goodwill.

14. Columnist Anthony Lewis revealed.

15. By October 1988 Wall had started to change his tune and went so far as to say that the FSLIC cleanup could cost anywhere from $30 billion to $50 billion.

Chapter 25. What Happened?

1. Writer James Ring Adams reported that when the FSLIC closed down FirstSouth Savings in Arkansas in 1986, members of the Arkansas congressional delegation wrote letters of protest to the FSLIC. Then, when they saw the magnitude of FirstSouth's problems, they wrote the FSLIC again, asking for the first set of letters back.

2. In 1977, $261 million of the $1.6 billion Central States Pension Fund was in Nevada (mostly casino-related) investments.

3. By 1985 the fund would have $5.3 billion, but only 6.3 percent—$336 million— would be invested in real estate and only $34.7 million in Nevada real estate.

4. In an unrelated deal described in published accounts, Reeder in 1988 purchased the microwave division of Litton Industries, paid no bills after acquiring it, and placed it in bankruptcy three months later. The FBI was reportedly investigating Reeder's Litton acquisition.

5. Seventy-second report by the House Committee on Government Operations, "Combating fraud, abuse, and misconduct in the nation's financial institutions: current federal efforts are inadequate," October 13, 1988.

6. The GAO studied the documentation from 184 banks that failed in 1987 and 26 S&Ls that represented 57 percent of the FSLIC's losses through September 1987. It compared those failed institutions to a group of similar but solvent banks and thrifts and concluded in January 1989: "Some within the financial institutions industry have expressed the view that the unprecedented problems and resultant failures are largely due to economic downturns in certain regions. However, both of our reviews lead to a different conclusion. Well-managed institutions with strong internal controls appeared able to remain viable despite downturns in local economies. . . . Under the Bank Board's definitions, fraud or insider abuse existed at each and every one of the failed thrifts; allegations of criminal misconduct involved 19 of the 26. . . .

Either insider abuse or fraud was present in 64 percent of the 184 [bank] failures." The Bank Board's definitions of insider abuse and fraud included breaches of fiduciary duty, self-dealing, engaging in high-risk speculative ventures, excessive expenditures and compensation, and conflicts of interest, among others.

7. St Germain did not return our phone calls.

8. The thrift charge accounts and free golfing trips were reportedly provided by thrift lobbyist James Freeman.

9. According to the third annual survey of executive compensation at publicly held thrifts published by MCS Associates in Newport Beach, California.

Chapter 26. Taking the Cure

1. Reliance on unregulated mortgage bankers carries risks of its own. A thrift director who worked with the real estate investment trusts, which failed in huge numbers in the 1970s, said he saw there the same appraisal scams, phony sales, double books, and theft that characterized the S&L failures of the 1980s, and he believed the parasites that moved from REITs to S&Ls have now moved into the unregulated mortgage banking industry, where they will steal from middle-income Americans trying to buy homes.

2. $100 billion borrowed at the 1988 10-year Treasury bond rate would cost $15.5 billion a year for 10 years or $10.8 billion a year for 20 years. Meanwhile, thrift losses continue to mount at least $12 billion a year—between 1986 and 1988 the loss increased an average of $16.3 billion a year.

3. Some deals even promised the buyers they would not be on the hook if any of the real estate they acquired in these deals turned out to be sitting on top of toxic waste. We wondered if regulators had Consolidated Saving's Carson property or Philip Schwab's Philadelphia distillery in mind.

4. McKinsey & Co., a consulting firm.

5. To solve the Vernon Savings problem the FSLIC promised $5 billion in government aid to MacAndrews & Forbes Holding, Inc.[4] which took control of five thrifts, including Vernon. When industry analyst Bert Ely heard about the MacAndrews & Forbes deal, he said, "I am amazed by the [$5 billion] number. . . . It's just further confirmation that the losses are of a far greater magnitude in Texas than the Bank Board has ever been willing to admit." Ely worried that these deals were a quick fix that will come back to haunt us. "It appears that we're looking at deals that the country will regret in the not-too-distant future," he said. "Someday all this is going to come unglued." Another analyst, Robert Litan of the Brookings Institute, agreed. "Many of those institutions were far too far gone and should have been shut down. But the regulators didn't have the cash to just shut them down, so they arranged these mergers instead. A few of them may actually work. But a lot of them won't. The whole thing is like Las Vegas."

6. The new owners could write off the thrift's losses, they could deduct their interest expense, and, to add insult to injury, the substantial cash assistance extended by the FSLIC (like the $2 billion pumped into American Savings to facilitate the Bass acquisition) is exempt from federal income tax.

7. Congress has authorized the FSLIC to issue promissory notes to cover debts at failed

thrifts. The notes will come due at staggered intervals and as each note comes due the Treasury will be quietly tapped.

8. In the early 1980s the U.S. government had to bail the two brothers out of trouble when they overinvested in silver before the price fell.

9. The *National Thrift News* reported that Bush's oil and gas company had a $1 million line of credit at a bank owned by a developer who owned large amounts of Silverado's preferred stock and received more than $40 million in loans from Silverado. (Bush also sat on the board of directors of a Florida company that borrowed over $80 million from failed Western Savings of Dallas.)

10. Moroney said he was astounded at the incompetence he saw at the Topeka FHLB. "I've often analogized it to hospital orderlies doing brain surgery," he told us. After he went public with his complaints, he said he had to close his S&L consultancy because the FHLB Topeka wouldn't do business with him.

11. Competition in the marketplace is also phasing out thrifts. Ten years ago thrifts wrote nearly 50 percent of Americans' home mortgages; in 1987 that share was down to 39 percent.

12. Regulators took over San Marino in 1984.

13. Regulators took over Bell Savings in 1985 and said the institution's failure would cost the FSLIC fund $565 million.

14. Sued were Anderson, Alford & Ritter (State Savings in Salt Lake City), Cole & Armbrister (Mountain Security Savings Bank, Wytheville, Virginia), Coopers & Lybrand (First Federal Savings of Shawnee, Oklahoma), Deloitte Haskins & Sells (Sunrise Savings of Boynton Beach, Florida), Grant Thornton (Sunbelt Savings, Dallas), Jeffrey & Pallazolla (North American Savings, Santa Ana, California), Mike Sage (Ramona Savings, Fillmore, California), Regier Carr (Territory Savings of Seminole, Oklahoma, and Oklahoma Federal of Oklahoma City), Touche Ross (Beverly Hills Savings of Beverly Hills), and Vanasco & Resnick (Intercapital Savings of Jacksonville Beach, Florida).

15. The American Institute of Certified Public Accountants has been working on this issue.

16. Congressional Banking Committee Chairman Senator William Proxmire and Representative Fernand St Germain, and powerful building and consumer groups, opposed ARMs. The Bank Board could at any time have approved ARMs by regulation, as FHLBB Chairman Richard Pratt did in 1981, but the Bank Board in the 1970s deferred to Congress' judgment in the matter.

17. By 1988 solid institutions like giant Great Western Savings (now Great Western Bank) held loan portfolios that were 90 percent, or more, ARM.

18. A number of versions of bank deregulation are under consideration by Congress, some far more restrictive than others.

19. Martin Mayer wrote about these 1920s securities affiliates in *The Bankers*: "These organizations were without exception a disaster, as the Comptroller of the Currency had warned in 1920 that they would be: he saw them borrowing from their parents and other national banks 'in an endless chain . . . for the accommodation of speculative cliques.' "

20. The Glass-Steagall Act in 1933 forbade commercial banks to own common stock or to underwrite and sell stock or corporate bonds to their customers or depositors.

21. Banks' premiums pay for the FDIC insurance, but like the FSLIC, the FDIC insurance is backed by the full faith and credit of the United States government, which means that if the FDIC went broke, as the FSLIC has, the American taxpayer would have to pay its debts.

22. Bailed out by the federal government in 1984 to the tune of $4.5 billion.

23. According to David Silver, president of Investment Company Institute, in remarks before the National Center on Financial Services in New York, April 22, 1988.

Glossary

ADL (Acquisition and Development Loan): Loans that include enough money to both acquire and develop a property. These loans were very popular at rogue thrifts for several reasons: They were very large loans, allowing thrifts to book big points and fees; they allowed crooks to borrow huge amounts of money, never buy the land or develop it, and walk off with the money.

Alligator: A piece of property that produces no income and is a financial burden because of its large carrying costs, such as real estate taxes and other ongoing expenses. The FSLIC was left to wrestle a lot of alligators.

Appraiser: Defined by bankers as a person qualified by education, training, and experience to estimate the value of real estate (and personal property). Anyone can call himself an appraiser. Although there are fraternal organizations of appraisers, there are not universally established or enforced standards. One fraternal organization designates its members as "MAI" appraisers (Members Appraiser's Institute). Many high fliers used to contend the letters actually stood for "Made As Instructed," a reference to appraisals done to suit the needs of the borrower.

ARM (Adjust Rate Mortgage): Loans that allow the lender to adjust the interest rate charged up or down within a certain range as market interest rates rise or fall.

Broker: A person who, for a fee or commission, brings parties together and assists in negotiating contracts between them.

Bust-out: A mob term used to describe a scam designed to extract large sums of money from an unsuspecting company or financial institution. The mob has used bust-outs for decades to gut small firms of their assets. After deregulation they began busting out thrifts as well.

Capital: The net worth of a business represented by the amount that its assets exceed liabilities.

Cash for Trash: Rogue thrifts with lots of repossessed properties on their books would lend new borrowers more money than they requested and require them to buy one of the thrift's repossessed properties with the difference as a condition of the loan. Such deals were dubbed "cash for trash" because the repossessed property was usually of questionable value.

Caveat Emptor: Latin for "let the buyer beware."

Certificate of Deposit: A written document issued by a financial institution formalizing an arrangement between a depositor and institution that outlines the term (length of time) of the deposit and the rate of interest the institution promises to pay on those deposits during the agreed-upon term.

Closing Costs: Money paid by borrowers (and sellers) to effect the closing (issuance) of a loan. Such costs normally include the thrift or bank's loan origination fees, points, and attorney's fees. Such fees are booked by the loaning financial institution as income. Fees and points are often "built in" to the loan so the borrower does not have to take money out of pocket.

Collateral: Property pledged as security for a loan. Collateral can be the property being loaned on or another property owned by the borrower. It can also be stock, a promissory note, or other personal property. Whatever is put up as collateral is supposed to be worth at least as much as the loan it secures.

Commission: A broker's fee for negotiating a transaction, often expressed as a percentage of total transaction. Loan brokers were paid a percentage of the total loan. Deposit brokers were paid a commission ranging from 1 percent to as high as 5 percent of the deposit placed at an institution.

Commitment: An agreement in writing between a lender and borrower to loan money at an agreed-upon rate and terms at some future date.

Cosigner: One who agrees to assume the debt of the principal borrower if that borrower defaults on the loan. See also "Kissing the Paper."

Daisy Chain: Rogue thrifts often banded together into what regulators later called "daisy chains." By helping one another they discovered they could thwart regulators' efforts to ferret out regulatory violations. These rogue thrifts would make loans to one another's officers, for example, to circumvent the $100,000 regulatory limit on how much a thrift could loan one of its own officers. They also shuffled troubled loans and properties among themselves to hide them from examiners.

Dead Horses for Dead Cows: Rogue thrifts quickly ended up with their portfolios full of bad loans and repossessed (REO) properties that were real alligators. To keep thrift examiners from discovering such bad assets, these thrifts worked together with other rogue thrifts, swapping loans and properties. They would agree that "if you buy my dead horse, I'll buy your dead cow." When they'd buy a delinquent loan from another thrift, they would then "roll it over," or refinance the loan, thereby extending the due date into the future. To examiners it would simply appear as a new loan on the thrift's books.

Deed of Trust: A document used to both convey title to a property while also evidencing that the property is security for a loan and that ownership is conditioned upon repayment of that loan. Defaulting on a deed of trust results in foreclosure.

Default: Nonpayment of a loan or other breach of the terms and conditions under which the loan was granted.

Delinquency: When payments on a loan go into arrears the loan is considered delinquent until payments are brought current. If a loan continues being delinquent, the lender can, and often will, foreclose.

Directors & Officers Liability Insurance (D&O): Insurance protecting both a corporation and its top managers from legal damages. Thrift officers and directors began to find it difficult to get D&O coverage beginning in 1985 when many of the companies providing the coverage became alarmed at what they saw going on at thrifts.

Disintermediation: When deposit money chases the highest rate of return. When rates in money market funds were higher than thrifts could pay before 1980, money left the thrift industry by the billions of dollars and flowed to money market funds. That was disintermediation.

Encumbrance: Anything that affects or limits title to a property such as loans, leases, or restrictions.

Equity: The difference between a property's fair market value and what the owner owes on the property. If the property is 100 percent financed, meaning the borrower has borrowed the exact amount the property is worth, then the borrower is said to have no equity left in the property.

FADA (Federal Asset Disposition Agency): An agency created by the FSLIC in 1986 to dispose of billions of dollars in repossessed thrift properties.

Federal Home Loan Bank Board (FHLBB): The regulatory agency that oversees federally chartered savings and loans. It is also the parent agency of the FSLIC (Federal Savings and Loan Insurance Corporation), which insures deposits at nearly all thrifts, both federal and state-chartered. Therefore the FHLBB also sets standards for state-chartered thrifts with FSLIC insurance coverage.

Finders Fee: A commission or fee paid to the person who brings a client or deal to another person, company, or institution.

Fixed-Rate Mortgage: A loan on which the interest rate and repayment schedule are set for the duration of the loan and do not change.

Foreclosure: A legal process by which a lender can repossess property from a borrower when the borrower fails to fulfill the conditions of the loan for which the property is security. The most common reason property is foreclosed on is nonpayment of the loan.

Forbearance: The act of refraining from legal or supervisory action. Forbearance, when applied to the thrift industry, means that, even though a thrift may not be in compliance with federal regulations, regulators do not take disciplinary action against the thrift. Instead they give the noncomplying institution time to resolve its compliance problems.

FSLIC (Federal Savings and Loan Insurance Corporation): An agency of the Federal Home Loan Bank Board that insures deposits at savings and loans up to $100,000 each.

GAAP (Generally Accepted Accounting Principles): GAAP accounting is considered slightly preferable to the system employed by thrifts. (See RAP.)

Liquidation: When a seized thrift cannot be repaired by the FSLIC, the institution is liquidated. Its assets are sold off and the proceeds distributed to the former thrift's creditors, primarily the FSLIC.

Kickback: Payment in return for favor. Kickbacks differ from commissions in that kickbacks are generally not an open part of a transaction and are often illegal. Thrift officials were often paid kickbacks for making shaky or fraudulent loans. Appraisers received kickbacks for overappraising properties, etc.

Kissing the Paper: When a borrower was too financially weak to qualify for a large loan, he would pay someone with a strong financial statement to join him as a partner in the project. Using that person's financial statement, the borrower could then get his loan. Once the loan was made the borrower would "buy out" his partner with a portion of the loan proceeds, thereby relieving that person of any future liability. The buyout was actually the partner's fee for allowing the weak borrower to use his financial strength to get the loan. This was called "kissing the paper" because, in essence, that's all the partner did.

Land Flip: In order to inflate a property's value well above its actual worth in order to justify the largest possible loan, swindlers would engage in a number of sham sales of the property, each time raising the sales price. No real cash ever changed hands during these sham sales. The only purpose of the sales was to record a new deed, each time reflecting a new, higher price. A property could be "sold" and resold several times in a single day. Once the desired value was reached the borrower would get a loan for that amount and later default on it, leaving the lender stuck with a grossly overencumbered property. Such sham sales were called "flips."

Lender Participation: A loan arrangement in which the lender receives a portion of the project or its profits as part of the deal. Lender participations were very popular with rogue thrifts, which would make their loans conditional upon "getting a piece of the action."

Loan Fee: A charge made by a loan broker for negotiating a loan. Also a fee charged directly by the lender either for a commitment or at the time the loan funds are actually advanced. An additional income device used by lenders.

Loans to an Affiliated Person: There are limits on the amount of money an FSLIC-insured institution can loan to a person affiliated with the institution. The thrift can make loans that are secured by the person's principal residence or his savings accounts and loans for home improvements, consumer purchases or education. These loans are limited to the value of the collateral. The thrift can also make unsecured commercial loans to affiliated persons up to a maximum of $100,000.

Loans to a Single Borrower: There are limits on the amount of money an FSLIC-insured thrift can loan to each borrower. For unsecured commercial loans, the limit is 15 percent of the thrift's capital. For real estate loans the limit is the greater of (1) 10 percent of total deposits or 10 percent of capital, whichever is less or (2) $500,000.

Loan-to-Value Ratio: The ratio of mortgage to property value. Conservative lenders like to keep their loans at no more than 80 percent of the property's real value in case they must repossess the property. Rogue thrifts routinely made 100 percent loans on properties and they also often made loans far exceeding the value of the land securing the loan. In some cases loans exceeded the value of the property by several hundred percent. The term used for the money in excess of that required for the project was "walking money."

Mortgage Broker: An individual who brings a borrower and lender together and receives a commission if a loan is made. The commission is generally a percentage of the loan. Occasionally loan brokers take their fees in other ways, including a participation in the property or project. Loan brokers who represented unqualified borrowers found that they could demand higher fees for putting together shaky deals. The shakier the deal, or borrower, the higher the fee.

Net Worth: The value of total assets less total liabilities.

Nonrecourse Loan: A kind of loan in which the lender's remedies in the event of default are limited to foreclosing on the property only. The borrower is not personally liable for any losses suffered by the lender if the property's value does not cover the outstanding balance on the loan.

Origination Fee: A fee charged by a lender for preparing the loan documents, credit checks, and property inspections. Origination fees are generally computed as a percentage of the loan amount.

Participation Loan: Thrifts often do not keep the loans they make but sell all or part of them to other lenders who are looking for the interest income. When a thrift sells a loan that is called a "participation." Also thrifts can join together and make a loan together. That, too, is a participation loan. Rogue thrifts liked participations because they allowed them to sell off to unsuspecting thrifts loans they knew would eventually go into default.

Points: Lenders traditionally charge "points" along with loan and origination fees. Points are a percentage of the loan and can run from 1 percent to 8 percent of the loan amount. Lenders use points to increase their yield on a loan without raising the interest rate.

RAP (Regulatory Accounting Principles): An accounting system designed especially for thrifts that allowed them to book as assets such intangible items as "goodwill." RAP accounting is credited with obscuring the worsening conditions within the thrift industry until they were beyond repair. Traditional accountants used to using GAAP (Generally Accepted Accounting Principles) characterize RAP accounting as "smoke-and-mirrors accounting."

Receiver: A court appointee whose responsibility it is to preserve and manage the assets of a defunct company or institution for the benefit of all its creditors. When a thrift fails the FSLIC is appointed receiver and the old thrift is referred to as a receivership.

REO (Real Estate Owned): The term stands for property acquired by a thrift through foreclosure. Troubled thrifts ended up with a lot of REOs.

Scraping: When swindlers take out a large loan to develop a property, they often steal some of the loan proceeds by using such methods as double invoicing. They call this "scraping off some of the loan." If they scrape off too much, the project will go bankrupt, and they often did.

Second Mortgage: A loan that is placed on a property behind an existing first mortgage. A second mortgage's rights are subordinate to the first mortgage. If the property goes into default, the first mortgage holder gets paid first. If any equity remains after paying the first, the second mortgage holder gets what's left.

Straw Borrower: A person who poses as the borrower on a property but in fact is fronting for another. Thrifts were limited by regulation from loaning too much to a single borrower. Straw borrowers were used to get around this limitation. The straw borrower was generally paid a fee by the borrower for his or her services.

Walking Money: That amount of a loan that exceeds the value of the property securing it, so named because walk is what the borrower usually does, leaving the lender with an overencumbered piece of property.

White Knight: White Knights were employed by thrift crooks and high fliers to forestall unpleasant actions like foreclosure or seizure of their thrift by federal regulators. The White Knight would suddenly appear, offering to pay top dollar for a troubled asset. Sometimes the deal would never close, but negotiations bought the owners additional time. When a deal did close on a White Knight purchase, it would usually be discovered that the White Knight got his money for the purchase from another friendly thrift and that loan would later go into default.

Appendix A:
The Comptroller Report on
Herman K. Beebe

MEMORANDUM

Comptroller of the Currency
Administration of National Banks
Washington, D.C.

To: Robert Ahrens, Director, Special Projects
Robert E. Sharpe, Director, Enforcement & Compliance Div.
Rovert M. Krasne, Attorney, Legal Services Div.

June 3, 1985

Re: Final Status Report on the Analysis of Herman K. Beebe's Partici-
    pation in the Affairs of National Banks.

As you know, last December I was asked by the Chief Counsel to spend up
to six months analyzing the banking interest of Herman K. Beebe, Sr. ("Beebe")
of Shreveport, Louisiana. The primary objective of the analysis was to determine
the breadth of Beebe's influence or control over financial institutions.

Beebe is neither an officer nor director of any national bank. To the best of
my knowledge, he does not *personally* own the stock of any national bank. His
influence and control flows through an extensive web of corporate enterprises
and nominees. Two of the more popular vehicles for Beebe's activities involving
financial institutions are AMI, Inc., his Shreveport holding company, and Bossier Bank and Trust Company, the $265 million state chartered bank he dom-
inates. Because Beebe owns two residences in Southern California and spends
the majority of his time there, speculation abounds that he is involved with

376

financial institutions on the West Coast. To date, none of his California activities
or operations have been identified.

I have reviewed dozens of examination reports generated by the OCC, FDIC,
FHLBB and the Louisiana and Mississippi state financial institutions regulatory
agencies. I have talked with examining personnel from Louisiana and Texas, as
well as many of the Southwestern District's bank analysts. I have also talked with
representatives of the Federal Reserve, FDIC, SEC, IRS, and two United States's
Attorney's offices. Counsel for several business partners of Beebe have also contacted me.

Beebe's Involvement in National Banks:

Beebe's influence or control over national banks does not appear as extensive as
his influence or control over state banks, savings and loans, and insurance
companies. Based on information presently available, the following banks may
in some way be controlled or influenced by Beebe:

1. National Bank of Bossier City, Bossier City, Louisiana.

Ownership: Control Group led by Patterson Affiliates.

Most Recent Examination: 2/28/85

Rating: 3

Asset Size: $113 million

Administrative Action: Cease and Desist Order dated 12/01/81

Jimmy Patterson, principal behind Patterson Affiliates, purchased National Bank of Bossier City from Judge Edmund Reggie ("Reggie") (See
attached memorandum for details). In addition, Reggie obtained a
standby letter of credit from the First National Bank of Lafayette, Lafayette, La., to secure debts of Patterson Affiliates at Bossier Bank and
Trust Co. incurred during their purchase of National Bank of Bossier
City.

2. The First National Bank of Ruston, Ruston, La.

Ownership: Control Group led by Texas State Senator Peyton McKnight.

Most Recent Examination: 11/30/84

Rating: 4

Asset Size: $42 million

Administrative Action: Formal Agreement dated 7/20/82. A Notice of Charges was served 3/26/85.

Peyton McKnight of Tyler, Texas, purchased his interest from Don Dixon (Dondi Group and Vernon Savings and Loan).

Eleven other entities combine with McKnight to control the bank. Change in Bank Control Act information on the McKnight and Dixon acquisitions is not available. In 1982, Dixon contested the OCC's presumption of control and the OCC agreed that CBCA (Change in Bank Control Act) filings were unnecessary. McKnight did not submit CBCA filings either.

Since the last examination, a large kite was discovered which may result in loss to the bank. The bank's former president was implicated. The matter was referred to Joe Cage (United States Attorney, Western District of Louisiana) and should be reviewed at the next examination so that a removal action can be considered.

3. Bowie National Bank, Bowie, Texas

Ownership: AMI, Inc.

Most Recent Examination: 1/31/85

Asset Size: $17 million

Administrative Action: Cease and Desist Order dated 2/23/83. Enforcement of the Order is in process. The FDIC has initiated a section 8(a) action.

Richard Wolfe acquired controlling interest with funds borrowed from AMI, Inc. (Wolfe's Change in Bank Control Act application could not be found in Central Records). In November 1984 AMI foreclosed on Wolfe's loan and assumed control of the bank. AMI contested requests for CBCA information. On December 7, 1984, Wolfe was convicted of making false statements and conspiring to make fraudulent claims against the U.S. Department of Agriculture. On February 5, 1985, Wolfe was suspended by the OCC from further participation in the conduct of the affairs of any bank. On May 5, 1985, I discussed Wolfe's activities with Bill Alexander, Assistant U.S. Attorney, Northern District of Texas, and Joe Cage, who indicated that they will investigate Wolfe's potentially illegal activities (e.g. fictitious loans, misapplication of bank funds).

4. First National Bank in Terral, Terral, Oklahoma

Ownership: Kenneth O. Arnold

Most Recent Examination: 2/28/85

Rating: 5*

Asset Size: $4 million

Administrative Action: Formal Agreement dated 11/21/83. A Cease and Desist Order proposal is to be presented to ERC in early June.

Arnold is currently subject to a removal action for Regulation O violations he purportedly committed at Republic Bank, Blanchard, La., another institution he controls. (In addition to Republic Bank, Arnold also has controlling interest in the Bank of Benton, Benton, La., American Bank and Trust, Coushatta, La., and Lake Area State Bank, Hawthorne, Florida.) Arnold has various other business interests, including insurance and mortgage companies, that are experiencing financial difficulties.

5. Energy Bank, N.A., Dallas, Texas

Ownership: Voting Trust, David Wise, Trustee

Date of Opening: 6/15/82

Declared Insolvent: 5/16/85

6. Park West Bank, N.A. Farmers Branch, Texas

Ownership: Voting Trust, David Wise, Trustee

Date of Opening: 10/03/83

Most Recent Examination: 11/30/84

Rating: 4

Asset Size: $21 million

Administrative Action: Notice of Charges served 5/15/85

7. Executive Center Bank, N.A., Dallas, Texas

Ownership: Voting Trust, David Wise, Trustee

Date of Opening: 5/16/84

---

* A rating of 1 is best, a rating of 6 the worst.

Most Recent Examination: 7/31/84

Rating: 1

Asset Size: $11 million

Administrative Action: None

8. Financial Center Bank, N.A., Dallas, Texas

Ownership: Voting Trust, David Wise, Trustee

Date of Opening: Preliminary Charter revoked.

9. First National Bank in Carrollton, Carrollton, Texas

Ownership: Voting Trust, David Wise, Trustee

Date of Opening: Preliminary Charter granted. Final approval under review in BOS.

David Wise, former ANBE and attorney for Richard Wolfe, assembled investor groups interested in owning national bank stock and submitted charter applications for the five banks listed above. His banking consultant was Charles Gray, former CEO at Citizens State Bank, Princeton, Texas (owned by AMI, Inc.), and AMI's representative in Texas. Gray served as advisory director of several Wise banks and received generous compensation. Questionable insider transactions, brokered funds, and an insurance fraud helped promote the demise of Energy Bank. These activities were referred to Alexander and Cage on May 15, 1985, for possible criminal investigation.

Wise is resigning from the other two banks presently operating and CBCA applications are pending for William C. Kennedy, Jr. According to NBE Rod Burgett, Kennedy claims that Gray introduced him to Wise. In 1975, Kennedy was barred from the securities business by the SEC because of his participation in a stock manipulation scheme. Kennedy has also been associated with individuals from the Andover Fund, which was involved with Peoples National Bank of Rockland County, Ramapo, New York.

10. The First National Bank of Jefferson Parish, Gretna, La.

Ownership: Elton Arceneaux, Preston Wailes, David K. Smith, Gerald H. Smith

Most Recent Examination: 2/28/85

Rating: 2

Asset Size: $471 million

Administrative Action: None

Beebe, Dale Anderson (Vice Chairman of the Board, AMI), James McKigney (Chairman of the Board, Bossier Bank and Trust Co.), and Edmund Reggie together own $1.6 million par value debentures in First Continental Bancshares, the parent corporation of The First National Bank of Jefferson Parish.

11. The First National Bank of Lafayette, Lafayette, La.

Ownership: Braxton Moody and William Trotter (First Commerce Corporation, New Orleans, has agreed to purchase the bank)

Most Recent Examination: 1/31/85

Rating: 4

Asset Size: $411 million

Administrative Action: Formal Agreement dated 11/08/84

Reggie has a $625 million unsecured standby letter of credit (OAEM) which purportedly secures debts of Patterson Affiliates at Bossier Bank and Trust Company. The debts were incurred when Patterson Affiliates purchased the National Bank of Bossier from Reggie. The credit exceeds the lending officer's limit for unsecured lending, the Discount Committee approved the credit in favor of FNB Shreveport and not Bossier Bank and the officer apparently based the credit decision on the strength of the guarantor, Reggie's brother-in-law. Jimmy Ardoin, the lending officer, is Vice Chairman of the Board and brother of Clarence Ardoin, the CEO of Louisiana Bank and Trust, Crowley, La., which is controlled by Reggie.

12. Palmer National Bank, Washington, D.C.

Ownership: Harvey McLean

Date of Opening: 6/83

Most Recent Examination: 9/23/83

Rating: 2

Asset Size: $11 million

Administrative Action: None

The charter application for the bank could not be located in Central Records. McLean, a real estate developer and investor, has a multimillion dollar line of credit at Bossier Bank and Trust Company, a portion of which is classified. McLean is involved with Beebe and Don Dixon in University Springs Joint Venture. McLean is CEO of Paris Savings and Loan, Paris, Texas.

In addition to the aforementioned banks, Beebe may exert some influence over the following banks:

City National Bank, Plainview, Texas and

Pan American National Bank, Dallas, Texas:

These banks have been controlled by Robert Holmes. Beebe purportedly had borrowings at the Plainview bank and Jack Pilon, the Dallas bank's CEO, has been linked to Beebe.

First National Bank, Killeen, Texas

Fort Hood National Bank, Fort Hood, Texas

United National Bank, Houston, Texas: Jerold B. Katz, the controlling owner of these banks and Killeen Savings and Loan, has been linked to Beebe through Ed McBirney (Sunbelt Savings), and Jarrett Woods (Western Savings), and Carroll Kelly.

Center Bank, N.A., Dallas, Texas: William C. Kennedy, Jr., is director of this bank.

First National Bank & Trust Co., Frederick, Ok: Harold M. McBee, a director at Vernon Savings and Loan, is a director of this bank.

Groos National Bank, San Antonio, Texas: Tom Benson, the controlling owner of this bank, has purchased Pontchartrain State Bank, Metairie, La., from Beebe's interests and has other business relationships with Beebe's associates.

Banks related to Sam Spikes and Reed Chittin: These individuals and their institutions had business dealing with State Savings and Loan (Lubbock), and Brownfield Savings and Loan, owned by Tyrell Barker. Barker, who also has ownership interests in Key Savings and Loan, Englewood, Colorado, and Woodland Savings Bank, Cincinnati, Ohio, is a Beebe business associate.

American National Bank, Mt. Pleasant, Texas, and

City National Bank, Kilgore, Texas, and

Huntsville National Bank, Huntsville, Texas: Each of these banks has or has had a significant correspondent banking relationship with Bossier Bank and Trust Co. Each relationship includes the purchase of participations from Bossier Bank & Trust Co.

The following is a list of state banks controlled by Beebe and his associates or which conduct significant correspondent banking with banks controlled by Beebe and his associates:

Arkansas:

Bank of Bradley, Bradley

Florida:

Lake Area State Bank, Hawthorne

Louisiana:

American Bank & Trust, Coushatta

American Bank, New Orleans

Bank of Benton, Benton

Bank of Commerce, Shreveport

Bank of Coushatta, Coushatta

Bank of Logansport, Logansport

Bank of Louisiana, New Orleans

Bank of Marigouin, Marigouin

Bank of Ringgold, Ringgold

Bank of Southwest Louisiana, Oakdale

Bossier Bank & Trust Co., Bossier City

Capital Bank & Trust Co., Baton Rouge

Citizens Bank, Springhill

City Savings Bank & Trust, DeRidder

Claiborne Bank, Homer

Colonial Bank, New Orleans

Farmerville Bank, Farmerville

First Bank of Natchitoches, Natchitoches

First Republic Bank, Rayville

First State Bank, Plain Dealing

First United Bank, Farmerville

Jonesville Bank, Jonesville

Mansura State Bank, Olla

Pelican State Bank, Pelican

Peoples Bank, Minden

Planters Bank, Haynesville

Pontchartrain State Bank, Metairie

Republic Bank, Blanchard

United Mercantile Bank, Shreveport

Webster Bank, Minden

Mississippi:

American Bank, Moss Point

Central Bank of Mississippi, Brandon

Commonwealth Bank, Bay Springs

First Bank, McComb

First United Bank, Meridian

Southwest Mississippi Bank, Quitman

Valley Bank, Cleveland

Texas:

Allied Lakewood Bank, Dallas

Azle State Bank, Azle

BancTexas, McKinney

Chandler State Bank, Chandler

Citizens State Bank, Princeton

Commercial State Bank, San Augustine

First State Bank, Frisco

Dallas International Bank, Dallas

Guaranty Bank, Dallas

Liberty City State Bank, Kilgore

Medical Place Bank (in organization)

South Main Bank, Houston

Western State Bank, Denton

The following is a list of savings and loans controlled by Beebe and his associates or which conduct significant correspondent business with institutions controlled by Beebe and his associates:

Colorado:

Key Savings & Loan, Englewood

California:

Beverly Hills Savings and Loan, Beverly Hills

Far West Savings and Loan, Newport Beach

Southern California Savings and Loan, Beverly Hills

Louisiana:

Acadia Savings and Loan, Acadia

Audubon Federal Savings and Loan, New Orleans

First Federal Savings and Loan, Oakdale

Mississippi:

American Savings and Loan, Biloxi

North Mississippi Saving and Loan, Clarksdale

Ohio:

Woodland Savings and Loan, Cincinnati

Oklahoma:

American Federal Savings and Loan, Anadarko

Texas:

Bonham Savings and Loan, Bonham

Brownfield Savings and Loan, Brownfield

Commerce Savings Association, Angleton

Continental Savings, Angleton

First Savings and Loan, Fort Stockton

First Savings Association, San Augustine

Killeen Savings and Loan, Killeen

Mainland Savings and Loan, Houston

Mercury Savings Association, Wichita Falls

Paris Savings and Loan, Paris

Parkway Savings Association, Dallas

San Jacinto Savings and Loan, Houston

State Savings and Loan, Lubbock

Sunbelt Savings and Loan, Dallas

Texana Savings and Loan, Texarkana

Texoma Savings Association, Sherman

Vernon Savings and Loan, Vernon

Western Savings and Loan, Gatesville

MEMORANDUM

The Enforcement Review Committee
From: Robert Krasne, Attorney
March 4, 1985
Re: The First National Bank of Ruston, Ruston, Louisiana, and Herman
    K. Beebe Related Banking Interests.

(This memorandum preceded Krasne's more comprehensive one dated June 3. This memorandum began by outlining a cease-and-desist order just issued to the above Beebe-related bank which we do not reproduce here in the interest of space. The order required FNB-R to accept no further broker deposits, strengthen its loan collection procedures, and to obtain satisfactory credit information before making loans, among other things. The balance of the March 4 memorandum deals with Beebe's alleged influence over banks and thrifts.)

First National Bank of Ruston (FNBR) Control Group:

Peyton McKnight, 9.7%.

Principal Relationships: McKnight is a Tyler, Texas, resident; purchased stock from Dondi Group, which involved Don Dixon and Vernon Savings and Loan.

FNB-R Corp, 6.86%

Principal Relationship: Dale Hooper, David Bussell, Dale Anderson, J. Pat Shows, and H. K. Beebe, Sr., all present or former AMI officers, each own 20% of FNB-R.

Other Institutions Influenced by H.K. Beebe, Sr.

Based upon information I have gathered to this point, H. K. Beebe, Sr., apparently directly owns one bank. However, his corporation, family members, friends, business associates, and their corporations own banks which are frequently used by Beebe as sources of credit and conduits for his financial dealings.

1. Beebe:

Beebe owns 39.5% of Pontchartain State Bank, Metairie, La., a $47 million, "4" rated institution. Beebe's children indirectly own another

39.5% of the bank. As of the most recent (1-6-84) examination. David Bussell was the CEO.

2. AMI, Inc.:

AMI, Inc., Beebe's primary business entity, owns Bowie National Bank, Bowie Texas, and Citizens State Bank in Princeton, Texas. AMI owns 81% of Citizens State Bank, a $18 million, "4" rated institution. H. K. (Ken) Beebe, Jr., is a director and strong influence in the bank. At the most recent (10-1-84) examination, Ken Beebe and President James Wood attributed all of Citizens Bank problems to former Chairman Charles Gray. Wood came to Citizens from Metro Bank, Dallas, in 1978 and became COB in July 1984.

Bowie National Bank was acquired by AMI, Inc., when they foreclosed on the stock carry loan of the majority owner, Richard Wolfe. The bank is in precarious condition. David Bussell is the AMI representative most active in Bowie's communications with the Southwestern District Office.

3. Beebe's Children:

H.K. Beebe, Sr., has four children: H. K. (Ken) Beebe, Jr., Easter Bunny Beebe Dixon, Pamela Beebe Gray, and Ruth Anastasia Beebe Chreene. Each child owns a corporation which holds bank stock. Their corporations, respectively are WMA, Inc., Easter Bunny, Inc., P. B. Gray, Inc., and ARIC, Inc.

In addition, the four children own KEPA Investments, Inc., which owns Louisiana Nursing Homes, Inc. (a First National Bank shareholder).

Beebe's children's corporations, Dale Anderson (AMI's Vice Chairman of the Board and a defendant in the recent criminal action involving Beebe), 6001 Financial Corporation (owned by Beebe and Anderson), Saving Life Insurance Company (an AMI, Inc. subsidiary), and Beebe own approximately 55% of Bossier Bank and Trust Co. . . . . During the past few years, BB&T has been a participation mill, selling tens of millions of dollars in loan participations to dozens of other institutional lenders.

Beebe's four children own 50.28% and Dale Anderson owns 33.8% of Bank of Southwest Louisiana, Oakdale, La. (BSWL). As of the most recent examination of this $36 million, rated "4" institution David Bussell was Chairman and Henry Dickens was President.

Beebe's daughters Easter Bunny and Pamela own just under 50% of the stock of City Savings Bankshares, Inc., the parent of City Savings Bank and Trust Company of DeRidder, La. Edmund Reggie's six children and Frem Boustany's three children together also own just under 50% of CSB&T's holding company. Reggie is the former owner of National Bank of Bossier City and was a frequent business partner of Beebe. Boustany is Reggie's brother-in-law. When the bank holding company was created, Beebe, Reggie and Boustany transferred the bank stock to their children for $160/share; $2 cash and $158 debt. The children then exchanged the stock for BHC stock and the BHC assumed the $158/share debt. CSB&T is a $5 million "5" rated bank . . . David Bussell was COB and Thomas Glass, previously of Bossier Bank & Trust, was president. . . .

4. Beebe's Friends, Business Associates, and their Corporations:

Richard O'Dom or Odom, former owner of First National Bank in Butler, Alabama, is or was a senior vice president of AMI and director of BB&T. He has massive debt (nearly $4 million originated at BB&T), most of which is classified II. Odom owns various banks in Mississippi, most of which are held under the umbrella of First United Financial Corp. . . . . Odom owns a small portion of Southwest Mississippi Bank in Quitman.

David Wise, et al. Wise, a Dallas attorney (he represented Richard Wolfe) and former ANBE, is a promoter responsible for the chartering of several national banks in Texas. Wise has several partners in his banking ventures: William C. Kennedy, Jr., a director of Center Bank, N.A.; Kenneth Hathaway, an investor who has debt at CSB; Glenn Loch, CEO of Loch Exploration and shareholder in Gainesville National Bank, Gainesville, Texas, and Michael R. Lewis. Lewis is CEO and president of Shannon Oil Company. Lewis, Loch, and Wise own Shannon Oil stock. WMA, Inc., Easter Bunny, Inc., P. B. Gray, Inc., and ARIC, Inc., also own significant quantities of Shannon Oil stock. Lewis has $184 million debt at Consolidated Bankers Life Insurance Co. of Shreveport, a wholly owned subsidiary of Savings Life Insurance Co., and $68 million at CSB classified II. Consolidated Bankers Life Insurance Co. owns 28 million of the 950 million shares of common issued by Energy Bank, N.A. (Dallas).

The Banks Wise, et al, are involved in are Energy Bank, N.A., Executive Center Bank, N.A., Park West Bank, N.A., National Bank of Carrollton (in organization), Financial Center Bank, (in organization). All of these banks are in the Dallas area.

Energy Bank, the oldest bank in the group, was opened in 1982. Wise is Chairman of the Board. At the most recent examination total assets had ballooned to $51 million. . . . The preliminary approvals for the two banks in organization are being reconsidered.

Shannon Oil has a line (of credit) both in violation of 12 U.S.C. section 84 and classified II at Energy Bank. AMI guarantees a portion of the credit.

K. O. Arnold has been involved in various businesses which have been funded by Beebe or Beebe's related entities. Arnold owns interests in the First National Bank of Terral, Ok., Republic Bank, Blanchard, La., American Bank and Trust, Coushatta, La., and Lake Area State Bank, Hawthorne, Florida. Arnold once held stock in Bossier Bank & Trust. The FDIC is contemplating section 8 action against Arnold for his actions in his Louisiana state banks.

Harvey McLean had $3.5 million in debt at Bossier Bank & Trust of which $1.4 million was classified (overdue). Collateral for the debt is 202 thousand shares of Palmer National Bank in Washington, D.C. (PNB). According to the most recent examination, McLean owned 173,400 shares (57.8%) of PNB's bank holding company. McLean is a director of PNB, a $11 million bank. McLean also apparently owns a significant share of Paris Savings and Loan, Paris, Texas.

Edmund Reggie is believed to own Louisiana Bank and Trust Co., Crowley, La. ($41 million in assets) and Acadia Savings and Loan of Crowley ($138 million in assets). Reggie has been indebted to Bossier Bank and Trust in amounts exceeding $3 million at various times and has classified credits at various banks. The CEO at Louisiana Bank & Trust is the brother of the Vice Chairman at First National Bank of Lafayette, La. ($436 million in assets).

Roland Dobson, a member of the control group of First National Bank of Ruston, is Chairman of the Board at First Bank of Natchitoches, La., and owns interest in Moreauville State Bank and Bank of Coushatta, La.

John Bennet Waters, President of AMI, Inc., and Senior Vice President and Director of Savings Life Insurance Co., an AMI subsidiary, is believed to own a significant portion of Moreauville State Bank, Moreauville, La. ($20 million in assets). Waters has had debt classified II at FNBR and NBBC, as well as debt classified II, III, and IV at Bossier Bank and Trust and debt classified IV at CSBB&T and BSWL. His business, Fireside Commercial Life Insurance Co., presently has $1.3 million in II debt at NBBC.

Rex Cauble, a convicted drug dealer, has had massive debt at Bossier Bank and Trust, much of which has been participated out. (FNBR has $188,000 at II and NBBC has $563,000 at II) BSWL has over $1 million of Cauble's paper. PSB has $500,000 of Cauble's paper and shows stock in Dallas International Bank and Western State Bank as collateral for Cauble's loans.

Gus Mijalis had $4.8 million in debt at Bossier Bank & Trust, of which $3.5 million was participated out. The balance was classified II and III. His debt at FNBR, $142,000, is classified II at the most recent examination. He is Chairman of the Board of the Bank of Commerce in Shreveport. He was indicted by a federal grand jury on February 28, 1985, for his involvement in the nursing home certificate scheme that also yielded the indictment of Gov. Edwin Edwards. (Later acquitted.)

Dr. Arnold Kilpatrick, a Bossier Bank & Trust director, has $2 million in debt which originated at Bossier Bank. His $200,000 debt at BSWL and $97,000 debt at PSB is classified III. Kilpatrick is Chairman of the Board of Pelican State Bank, Pelican, La. David Bussell is a director of Pelican Bank.

Fred Bayles was involved in the motel business with and received financial support from Beebe. At one time he owned stock in FNBR and Colonial Bank, New Orleans, La. AMI apparently guaranteed Bayles' purchase of the Colonial Bank stock. Bayles also apparently bought American Bank of Jackson Count, Moss Point, Miss., using money borrowed at Colonial. When he had financial difficulties, Colonial Bank acquired American Bank and AMI acquired Colonial Bank. David Bussell is Chairman of the Board of Colonial Bank and a director of American Bank. Edmund Reggie is also a Colonial Bank director.

Don Dixon, a former FNBR shareholder and Bossier Bank & Trust borrower, apparently has close ties to Vernon Savings and Loan, Vernon, Texas. Dondi Group, of which Dixon is a principal, is involved in a joint venture with Beebe, University Springs Joint Venture. This enterprise has $300,000 debt at Bossier Bank & Trust classified II and $100,000 at Bank of Benton.

Appendix B:
"The Five Senators Meeting"

The following memorandum was prepared by Federal Savings and Loan Insurance Corporation official William "Bill" Black. Black accompanied three San Francisco regulators who had been summoned to Washington, D.C., by five U.S. senators, each of whom had received sizable campaign contributions from Charles Keating, his company, American Continental Corporation, its subsidiary, Lincoln Savings and Loan, or Keating's employees or associates. The subject of the meeting was to be the San Francisco FHLB's extended examination of Lincoln Savings. Regulators contended Lincoln was exaggerating the value of properties in which it had invested or on which it had made loans.

Black's boss, Federal Home Loan Bank Board Chairman Ed Gray, had asked Black to report back to him on the meeting, and he took the notes that formed the basis for this memorandum.

MEMORANDUM

DATE: April 10, 1987

TO: Edwin J. Gray, Chairman, FHLBB

FROM: William K. Black, Deputy Director, FSLIC

RE: April 9, 1987, Meeting of FHLB-SF Personnel with Senators Cranston, DeConcini, Glenn, McCain and Riegle

At your request I am providing you this memorandum, which reflects the substance of yesterday's meeting with Senators Cranston, DeConcini, Glenn, McCain and Riegle. The Federal Home Loan Bank of San Francisco (FHLB-SF) personnel who attended the meeting were James Cirona, (President and Principal Supervisory Agent), Michael Patriarca (Director of Agency Functions), myself (general counsel) and Richard Sanchez (the Supervisory Agent for Lincoln S&LA of Irvine, Calif.). The meeting commenced at 6:00 p.m. and ended at approximately 8:15 p.m., with two breaks of approximately 15 and 10 minutes during which time the Senators voted. Senator Cranston was present only very briefly, because of his responsibilities on the Senate floor. The other Senators were present for substantially the entire meeting.

This meeting was the product of an earlier meeting among yourself and Senators Cranston, DeConcini, Glenn and McCain. At that meeting, as related by you (and by these same Senators in yesterday's meeting) each of the Senators raised their concerns regarding the examination of Lincoln by the FHLB-SF and you noted your unfamiliarity with any specifics of the examination, your confidence in the FHLB-SF and your suggestion that the Senators hear from the FHLB-SF our supervisory concerns regarding Lincoln.

I was the only one at the April 9 meeting who took notes. While not verbatim, my notes are very extensive. At your request, I called you last night and read these notes to you. I have attached a copy of those notes to this memorandum. I have used these notes and my independent recall of the meeting to prepare this memorandum and provide the fullest possible record of the discussions at yesterday's meeting. I have circulated this memorandum to Messrs. Cirona, Patriarca and Sanchez for their review to ensure the accuracy of this memorandum. I believe that this memorandum is an accurate and complete record of the substance of yesterday's meeting.

CIRONA: I am Jim Cirona. I am president of the Federal Home Loan Bank of San Francisco. I have held that position for four years. I am here in my capacity as principal supervisory agent. We have jurisdiction over California, Arizona and Nevada savings and loans. Before becoming president I was in the industry for 20 years.

DECONCINI: Where?

CIRONA: In New York.

DECONCINI: Did you know Bud Bavasi?

CIRONA: Yes. Bud is a good guy.

DECONCINI: Yes. He's great.

CIRONA: With me is Mike Patriarca, head of our agency function. Mike has joined us recently from the Comptroller of the Currency, where he was in charge of multi-national banks. Before that he was a lawyer for seven years.

McCAIN: We won't hold that against you.

CIRONA: You were a litigator.

PATRIARCA: No, I was in enforcement for seven years.

CIRONA: Also with me is Bill Black, our general counsel. Bill was formerly director of litigation for the Bank Board for three years. Next to Bill is Richard Sanchez. He's been with the San Francisco bank for __ years. Before that he was an auditor for a commercial bank and before that he was in school.

DECONCINI: Thank you for coming. We wanted to meet with you because we have determined that potential actions of yours could injure a constituent. This is a particular concern to us because Lincoln is willing to take substantial actions to deal with what we understand to be your concerns. Lincoln is prepared to go into a major home loan program—up to 55% of assets. We understand that that's what the Bank Board wants S&Ls to do. It's prepared to limit its high-risk bond holdings and real estate investments. It's even willing to phase out of the insurance process if you wish. They need to deal with, one, the effect of your reg . . . Lincoln is a viable organization. It made $49 million last year, even more the year before. They fear falling below 3 percent (net worth) and becoming subject to your regulatory control of the operations of their association. They have two major disagreements with you. First, with regard to direct investments. Second, on your reappraisal. They're suing against your direct investment regulation. I can't make a judgement on the grandfathering issue. We suggest that the lawsuit be accelerated and that you grant them forbearance while the suit is pending. I know something about the appraisal values [*Senator Glenn joins the meeting at this point.*] of the Federal Home Loan Bank Board. They appear to be grossly unfair. I know the particular property here. My family is in real estate. Lincoln is prepared to reach a compromise value with you.

CRANSTON: [*He arrives at this point.*] I'm sorry I can't join you but I have to be on the floor to deal with the bill. I just want to say that I share the concerns of the other Senators on this subject. [*Cranston leaves.*]

DECONCINI: I'm not on the Banking Committee and I'm not familiar with how all this works. I asked Don Riegle to explain to me how the Federal Home Loan system works because he's on Senate Banking. He explained it to me and that's why he's here.

McCAIN: Thank you for coming. One of our jobs as elected officials is to help constituents in a proper fashion. ACC is a big employer and important to the local economy. I wouldn't want any special favors for them. It's like the Apache helicopter program that Dennis and I are active on. The Army wants to cut back the program. Arizona contractors make major components of the Apache helicopter. We believe that the Apache is important to our national defense. That's why we met with General Dynamics and tried to keep the program alive.

I don't want any part of our conversation to be improper. We asked chairman Gray about that and he said it wasn't improper to discuss Lincoln. I'd like to mention the appraisal issue. It seems to me, from talking to many folks in Arizona, that there's a problem. Arizona is the second fastest growing state. Land values are skyrocketing. That has to be taken account of in appraisals.

GLENN: I apologize for being late. Lincoln is an Ohio chartered corporation, and . . .

CIRONA: Excuse me. Lincoln is a California chartered S&L.

GLENN: Well, Lincoln is wholly owned by ACC.

DECONCINI: You said Lincoln was Ohio chartered. It's California.

GLENN: Well, in any event, ACC is an Ohio chartered corporation. I've known them for a long time but it wouldn't matter if I didn't. Ordinary exams take maybe up to 6 months. Even the accounting firms says you've taken an unusually adversary view toward Lincoln. To be blunt, you should charge them or get off their backs. If things are bad there, get to them. Their view is that they took a failing business and put it back on its feet. It's now viable and profitable. They took it off the endangered species list. Why has the exam dragged on and on? I asked Gray about his. Lincoln has been told numerous times that the exam is being directed to continue by Washington. Gray said this wasn't true.

RIEGLE: I wasn't present at the earlier meeting. There are things happening that may indicate a pattern that do raise questions. There is broad concern on the Banking Committee about the *American*

Banker article on the FADA and FSLIC feud. Gray has great confidence in you as a team. He says you are some of the finest people in the system. The appearance from a distance is that this thing is out of control and has become a struggle between Keating and Gray, two people I gather who have never even met. The appearance is that it's a fight to a death. This discredits everyone if it becomes the perception. If there are fundamental problems at Lincoln, OK.

I've had a lot of people come through the door feeling that they've been put through a meat grinder. I want professionalism, and your backgrounds attest to that professionalism. But I want not just professionalism, but fairness and the appearance of fairness. So I'm very glad to have this opportunity to hear your side of the story.

GLENN: I'm not trying to get anyone off. If there is wrongdoing I'm on your side, But I don't want any unfairness against a viable entity.

CIRONA: How long do we have to speak to you? A half-hour, an hour?

DECONCINI: As quickly as possible. We have a vote coming up soon.

CIRONA: First, if there's any fault to be had concerning the length of the examination, it's on my shoulders. We determine how examinations are conducted. Gray never gave me instructions on how to conduct this exam or any other exam. At this meeting you'll hear things that Gray doesn't know.

DECONCINI: Did Gray ever talk to you about the examination of Lincoln?

CIRONA: Gray talked to me when that article ran in the Washington *Post*.

PATRIARCA: Gray asked for a written response from us to the Washington *Post* article about the length of the exam at Lincoln. Jim is correct. We received no instructions from Gray about the exam of Lincoln. We decide how to do the exam.

CIRONA: This meeting is very unusual. To discuss a particular company.

DECONCINI: It's very unusual for us to have a company that could be put out of business by its regulators. Richard you're on; you have 10–12 minutes.

SANCHEZ: An appraisal is an important part of underwriting. It is very important. If you don't do it right you expose yourself to loss. Our 1984 exam showed significant appraisal deficiencies. Mr. Keating promised to correct the problem. Our 1986 exam showed that the problems had not been corrected—that there were huge appraisal problems. There was no meaningful underwriting on most loans. We have independent appraisals. Merrill Lynch appraised the Phoenician [Hotel]. It shows a significant loss. Other loans had similar losses.

DECONCINI: Why not get an independent appraisal?

SANCHEZ: We did.

DECONCINI: No, you hired them. Why not get a truly independent one or use arbitration—if you're trying to bend over backwards to be fair. There's no appeal from your reappraisal. Whatever it is you take it.

SANCHEZ: If it meets our appraisal standards.

CIRONA: The Phoenician reappraisal process is not complete. We have received Lincoln's rebuttal and forwarded it to our independent appraisers.

[*At this point the Senators left to vote. We resumed when Senators DeConcini and Riegle returned.*]

SANCHEZ: Lincoln had underwriting problems with all of their investments, equity securities, debt securities, land loans and direct real estate investments. It had no loan underwriting policy manual in effect when we began our 1986 exam. When the examiners requested such a manual they were informed that it was being printed. The examiners looked at 52 real estate loans that Lincoln had made since the 1984 exam. There were no credit reports on the borrowers in all 52 of the loan files.

DECONCINI: I have trouble with this discussion. Are you saying that their underwriting practices were illegal or just not the best practice?

CIRONA: These underwriting practices violate our regulatory guidelines.

BLACK: They are also an unsafe and unsound practice.

DECONCINI: Those are two very different things.

SANCHEZ: You need credit reports for proper underwriting.

[*Senator Glenn returns at this point.*]

RIEGLE: To recap what's been said for Senator Glenn: 52 of the 52 loans they looked at had no credit information. Do we have a history of loans to folks with inadequate credit?

SANCHEZ: $47 million in loans were classified by examiners due to lack of adequate credit to assure repayment of the loans.

PATRIARCA: They're flying blind on all of their different loans and investments. That's what you do when you don't underwrite.

GLENN: How long had these loans been on the books?

SANCHEZ: A fairly long time.

GLENN: How many loans have gone belly-up?

SANCHEZ: We don't know at this point how many of the 52 have defaulted. These loans generally have interest reserves.

GLENN: Well, the interest reserves should run out on many of these.

CIRONA: These are longer term investments.

BLACK: I know that Lincoln has refinanced some of these loans.

GLENN: Some people don't do the kind of underwriting you want. Is their judgement good?

PATRIARCA: That approach might be okay if they were doing it with their own money. They aren't; they're using federally insured deposits.

RIEGLE: Where's the smoking gun? Where are the losses?

DECONCINI: What's wrong with this if they're willing to clean up their act?

CIRONA: This is a ticking time bomb.

SANCHEZ: I had another case which reported strong earnings in 1984. It was insolvent in 1985.

RIEGLE: These people saved a failing thrift. ACC is reputed to be highly competent.

BLACK: Lincoln was not a failing thrift when ACC acquired it. It met its net worth requirement. It had returned to profitability before it was acquired. It had one of the lowest ratios of scheduled assets in the 11th District, the area under our jurisdiction. Its losses were caused by an interest spread problem from high interest rates. It, as with most other California thrifts, would have become profitable as interest rates fall.

DECONCINI: I don't know how you can't consider it a success story. It lost $24 million in 1982 and 1983. After it was acquired by ACC it made $49 million in one year.

McCAIN: I haven't gotten an answer to my question about why the exam took so long.

SANCHEZ: It was an extremely complex exam because of their various investments. The examiners were actually in the institution from March to October—8 months. The asset classification procedure is very time consuming.

McCAIN: What's the longest exam you ever had before?

CIRONA: Some have technically never ended, where we had severe problems with a shop.

McCAIN: Why would Arthur Young say these things about the exam—that it was inordinately long and bordered on harassment?

GLENN: And Arthur Anderson said they withdrew as Lincoln's prior auditor because of your harassment.

RIEGLE: Have you seen the Arthur Young letter?

CIRONA: No.

RIEGLE: I'd like to see the letter. It's been sent all over the Senate.

[*Hands Cirona the letter.*]

PATRIARCA: I'm relatively new to the savings and loan industry but I've never seen any bank or S&L that's anything like this. This isn't even close. You can ask any banker you know about these practices. They violate the law and regulations and common sense.

GLENN: What violates the law?

PATRIARCA: Their direct investments violate the regulation. Then there's the file stuffing. They took undated documents purporting to show underwriting efforts and put them into the files sometimes more than a year after they made the investment.

GLENN: Have you done anything about these violations of law?

PATRIARCA: We're sending a criminal referral to the Department of Justice. Not maybe; we're sending one. This is an extraordinarily serious matter. It involves a whole range of imprudent actions. I can't tell you strongly enough how serious this is. This is not a profitable institution. Prior year adjustments will reduce that reported $49 million profit. They didn't earn $49 million. Let me give you one example. Lincoln sold a loan with recourse and booked a $12 million profit. The purchaser rescinded the sale, but Lincoln left the $12 million profit on its books. Now, I don't care how many accountants they get to say that's right. It's wrong. The only thing we have as regulators is our credibility. We have to preserve it.

DECONCINI: Why would Arthur Young say these things? They have to guard their credibility too. They put the firm's neck out with this letter.

PATRIARCA: They have a client. The $12 million in earnings was not unwound.

DECONCINI: You believe they'd prostitute themselves for a client?

PATRIARCA: Absolutely. It happens all the time.

[*The Senators left at this point for another vote.*]

[*We resumed when Senators DeConcini, McCain, and Riegle returned.*]

CIRONA: I also wanted to note that the Bank Board has had a lot of problems with Arthur Young, and is thinking of taking disciplinary action against it.

BLACK: Not for its actions here. Primarily because of its Texas office, which has never met a direct investment. They think everything is a loan. This has quite an effect on the income you can claim.

Empire of Texas is a perfect example. It did acquisition, development and construction loans that were really direct investments because the borrowers had no equity in the projects. It booked all the points and fees up front as income. It created interest reserves so the loans couldn't go into default. It provided take-out financing and then end loans so that the loans couldn't go into default for many years. All this led it to report record profits. Even when the losses started, as long as it grew fast enough and could book new income up front it could remain "profitable." It gets to be kind of a pyramid scheme with rapid growth. Lincoln has grown very fast.

Many congressional hearings have been very critical of the Bank Board for not acting more quickly against unsafe and unsound practices. Representative Dingell our . . . our . . . I grew up in the 16th District. His hearings were very critical about Beverly Hills [Savings], which had a clean accounting opinion, and then, at last count, is over $900 million insolvent.

Then there was Sunrise [Savings], also with a clean opinion and it is expected to cost FSLIC over $500 million. And Congressman Barnard's hearing was very critical there.

CIRONA: Also San Marino.

BLACK: Yes. I can tell you from my experience as former litigation director, where I sued for many of these failed shops, that it is routine for the accounting firm to serve as management's expert witnesses and adopt an extremely adversarial tone.

            What it all comes down to is that Congress has been on our ass, and many of us think rightly, to act before an institution fails. That's what we're doing here, and I think it is laudable.

DECONCINI: What?

BLACK: Laudable.

SANCHEZ: Our exam has found that millions has to be written off Lincoln's books. That will leave them with a regulatory net worth of $25 million. They will fail to meet their net worth requirement. They have $103 million in goodwill on their books. If this were backed out they would be $78 million insolvent.

PATRIARCA: They would be taken over by the regulators if they were a bank.

DECONCINI: You're saying they're insolvent.

BLACK: They'd be insolvent on a tangible capital basis, which is basically the capital standard for banks.

DECONCINI: They'd be insolvent if they were a bank, but by law you have to use a regulatory capital standard, and under that standard they have $25 million in capital. Is that what you're saying?

PATRIARCA: By regulation we have adopted a regulatory capital standard.

DECONCINI: And you'll take control of them if they fail your net worth standard—you'll take operational control of them.

CIRONA: That's speculative. We'd take steps to reduce their risk exposure.

RIEGLE: What would require them to sell?

CIRONA: We'd probably have them decrease their growth. Time and again we've found rapid growth associated with loss. Lincoln has grown rapidly.

BLACK: Are you sure you want to talk about this? We haven't made any recommendation to the Bank Board yet. The Bank Board decides what action to take. These are very confidential matters.

DECONCINI: No, then we don't want to go into it. We were just asking very hypothetically and that's how you [indicating Mr. Cirona] were responding.

CIRONA: That's right.

DECONCINI: Can we do something other than liquidate them?

CIRONA: I hesitate to tell an association what to do. We're not in control of Lincoln, and won't be. We want to work the problem out.

McCAIN: Have they tried to work it out?

CIRONA: We've met with them numerous times. I've never seen such cantankerous behavior. At one point they said our examiners couldn't get any association documents unless they made the request through Lincoln's New York litigation counsel.

RIEGLE: Well, that does disturb me—when you have to go through New York litigation counsel. What could they do? Is it too late?

CIRONA: It's never too late.

McCAIN: What's the best approach? Voluntary guidelines instead of a compulsory order?

DECONCINI: How long will it take you to finish the exam?

PATRIARCA: Ten days.

GLENN: Have they been told what you've told us.

PATRIARCA: We provided them with our views and gave them every opportunity to have us hear what they had to say. We gave them our classification of asset materials and went through them loan by loan. This is one of the reasons the exam has taken so long.

SANCHEZ: We gave them our classification materials on January—. On March 9 we received 52 exhibits, amounting to a stack of paper this high [indicating approximately two feet of material] responding to that. We went through every page of that response.

PATRIARCA: We didn't use in-house appraisers. We sent the appraisals out to independent appraisers. We sent the reappraisals to Lincoln. We got rebuttals from Lincoln and sent them to the independent appraisers. I don't think there was any case that Lincoln agreed with the reappraisal.

SANCHEZ: None where the reappraisal indicated insufficient collateral.

PATRIARCA: In every case, after reviewing the rebuttal, the independent appraiser has stood by his conclusion.

DECONCINI: Of course. They had to.

PATRIARCA: No. The rebuttals claim specific problems with the independent appraisers reappraisals: "You didn't consider this feature or you used the wrong rental rate or approach to value." The independent appraiser has come back to us and answered those specific claims by saying: "Yes, I did consider that, and here's why I used the right rate and approach."

DECONCINI: I'd question those reappraisals. If you want to bend over backwards to be fair I'd arbitrate the differences.

      The criminality surprises me. We're not interested in discussing those issues. Our premise was that we had a viable institution concerned that it was being over regulated.

GLENN: What can we say to Lincoln?

BLACK: Nothing with regard to the criminal referral. They haven't, and won't be told by us that we're making one.

GLENN: You haven't told them?

BLACK: No. Justice would skin us alive if we did. Those referrals are very confidential. We can't prosecute anyone ourselves. All we can do is refer it to Justice.

DECONCINI: They make their own decision whether to prosecute?

BLACK: Yes. I also want to mention that we are already investigating Arthur Anderson because of their role in the file stuffing. We don't know whether they knew the purpose for which they were preparing the materials. I don't want to get harassed . . . no, that's not the right word; I don't want to get criticized if we find out that Arthur Anderson was involved criminally and we have to make a referral on them. We don't want them to claim retaliation. We're in a tough spot.

      With regard to what you can say to Lincoln, you might want to simply have them call us. If you really want to talk to them you can say that it will take us 7 to 10 days to finish the exam.

RIEGLE: Is this institution so far gone that it can't be salvaged?

PATRIARCA: I don't know. They've got enough risky assets on their books that a little bad luck could nail them. You can't remove the risk of what they already have. You can reduce what new risks they would otherwise add on.

BLACK: They have huge holdings in Tucson and Phoenix. The market there can't absorb them for many years. You said earlier that ACC was extremely good but ACC has gotten out of its former primary activity, home building. I'm not saying they're bad businessmen but they had to get out of one home-building market after another. They had to get out of Colorado when they had bad models and soil problems. They also had to get out of their second leading activity, mortgage banking. They're now down to Arizona.

That's not a bad market but no one knows how well it will do over the many years that it would take to absorb such huge holdings in Tucson and Phoenix.

DECONCINI: So you don't know what you'd do with the property even if you took them over?

BLACK: Bill Black doesn't. Bill Black is a lawyer. We hire experts to do this work. Our study of their Arizona holdings was done by top experts. Our study of below investment grade corporate debt securities—what folks usually call junk bonds, but I avoid it because I don't know where you stand on such bonds—was done by top outside experts. I see in this Arthur Young letter that they criticize us for having an accountant with "only" eight years of experience. Well, I think . . . I don't see how you can claim eight years as inexperienced. But we didn't simply rely on him. We had . . . wasn't it Kenneth . . .

SANCHEZ: Yes. Kenneth, Laventhol.

BLACK: We had Kenneth, Laventhol, outside accountants, work on this. These are also some of the reasons the exam took time.

PATRIARCA: I think my colleague Mr. Black put it right when he said that it's like these guys put it all on 16 black in roulette. Maybe, they'll win, but I can guarantee you that if an institution continues such behavior it will eventually go bankrupt.

RIEGLE: Well, I guess that's pretty definitive.

DECONCINI: I'm sorry, but I really do have to leave now.

[*The meeting broke up at this point, approximately at 8:20 p.m.*]

Source Notes

Our goal as we researched this book was to listen carefully to all sides and to try to understand how so much money could have been drained out of the S&L industry. We found unmistakable evidence of widespread fraud and unethical behavior in the savings and loan industry and we wrote this book to expose it. Some of the people in *Inside Job* will feel we have treated them unfairly because we listened to their stories and drew our own conclusions.

Inside Job presents what we believe, after years of research, to be the accurate version of events. Those who disagree, many of whom we interviewed, have told us they intend to write their own books and we hope they do. At least now readers will have this book by which to measure theirs, and vice versa.

We have made every effort to avoid errors. We have been over the material time and again looking for mistakes. But because we and our sources are human, we recognize that, somewhere in this mass of 150,000 words, there may still reside errors. If that be the case, we apologize and would like to take a page from Jonathan Kwitny who wrote at the end of his book on organized crime, *Vicious Circles*:

> For any errors in this book, I sincerely apologize, and if informed of them, I will be glad to apologize publicly and do my best to see that they are corrected in any future editions. I am confident that if any errors exist, they will not be such as to stain the essence of this book; that nobody else could have done it a whole lot better; and that some of the ones I got right were real beauts, and more than make up for any slips.

We attempted to interview all of the people who played significant roles in this book. If we couldn't reach them, we contacted their attorneys. To those who failed to return our telephone calls we mailed by certified mail, return receipt requested, a list of our questions. Any responses we received, by telephone or mail, we incorporated into *Inside Job* where appropriate.

The Federal Savings and Loan Insurance Corporation and the Federal Home Loan Bank Board are the sources for all estimates of the net worth of an institution and the losses incurred by an institution or by the FSLIC.

The descriptions of the loans and transactions discussed in this book are based primarily on allegations made in civil suits filed by the FSLIC and further details provided by participants (borrowers, brokers, S&L officers and directors), regulators, and investigators (FBI agents, FSLIC attorneys, U.S. attorneys).

Where we had no firsthand knowledge, we obtained descriptions of people and settings through interviews with people familiar with the characters and the scene.

Some of the dialogue is reconstructed as described to us by participants, and therefore it is only an approximation of the real discussion. The potential for inaccuracy concerned us, so we kept dialogue to a minimum, even though we wished we could have enlivened *Inside Job* with more conversation.

We interviewed S&L borrowers, officers and directors, loan and deposit brokers, developers, bankers, journalists, FBI agents, defense and prosecution attorneys, private investigators, associates of the principals, regulators and others. We synthesized what they told us, and then told the story in our own words. We will not attempt in these notes to attribute each bit of information. However, we do want to note the important documents and published material that we used or that would be useful to others researching this subject.

For those readers who wish to expand their knowledge of the thrift industry, good overviews of the Federal Home Loan Bank system are *A Guide to the Federal Home Loan Bank System*, published by the FHLB System Publication Corp., 655 Fifteenth Street, N.W., Suite 510, Washington, D.C. 20005, March 1987; and *Fifty Years of Service: Federal Home Loan Bank Board*, June 1982, Volume 15, Number 6 issue of the *Federal Home Loan Bank Board Journal* published monthly by the FHLBB.

Excellent technical discussions of thrift problems are:

Where Deregulation Went Wrong, by Norman Strunk and Fred Case, United States League of Savings Institutions, 1988; and *Thrifts Under Siege*, by R. Dan Brumbaugh, Jr., Ballinger Publishing Company, 1988.

Testimony before the U.S. House of Representatives Subcommittee on Commerce, Consumer and Monetary Affairs, June 13, 1987; testimony before the Subcommittee on Financial Institutions Supervision, Regulation and Insurance of the House Committee on Banking, Finance and Urban Affairs, June 9, 1987.

FHLBB Rules and Regulations for FSLIC-insured Institutions, and FHLBB and

FSLIC Outline of Information to be submitted in support of an Application for Insurance of Accounts or a Request for a Commitment to Insure Accounts.

Background on the California thrift industry: Commerce, Consumer and Monetary Affairs Subcommittee of the Committee on Government Operations, U.S. House of Representatives, June 13, 1987, in Los Angeles, California; also, extensive interviews with California Savings and Loan Commissioner William Crawford.

MEDIA OVERVIEWS:

The *National Thrift News* and the *American Banker* have continually provided the best coverage of thrift deregulation, beginning with the deregulation debate in the late 1970s. Both publications continue to distinguish themselves in this area.

Nonindustry print media has also done its part in chronicling this crisis and many reporters around the country have written superb regional stories worthy of notice. They include:

"Inside Jobs," by Cris Oppenheimer and Scott Herhold, San Jose *Mercury News*, Nov. 1–3, 1987.

"This Is an Epidemic," by Jonathan Lansner and Ann Imse, *The Orange County Register*, Nov. 8–11, 1987.

"S&Ls: How They Self-Destructed," by Allen Pusey, The Dallas *Morning News*, Nov. 8, 1987.

"Inside Jobs: New War on Bank Fraud," by Tom Furlong and Douglas Frantz, Los Angeles *Times*, Jan. 3, 1988.

"Federal Fiasco," by Jeff Bailey and G. Christian Hill, *The Wall Street Journal*, March 25, 1988.

"Who to Thank for the Thrift Crisis," by Nathaniel C. Nash, *The New York Times*, June 12, 1988.

Series by James O'Shea that began in the Chicago *Tribune* Sept. 25, 1988.

BusinessWeek cover story, Oct. 31, 1988, by Catherine Yang, Howard Gleckman, Frederic A. Miller, Mark Ivey, Teresa Carson, Tod Mason, Todd Vogel, Paula Dwyer, Joseph Weber, Antonio Fins, and Gail DeGeorge.

Series by Allen Pusey and Lee Hancock in the Dallas *Morning News* that began Dec. 4, 1988.

Chapters 1–3

The Rose Garden scene: Several newspaper articles, the White House press office, Ed Gray, and the National Weather Service.

Ed McBirney party at the Dunes: *Texas Monthly* article of June 1987, by Byron Harris and a confidential source who attended the party.

FHLBB viewing of the Empire Savings and Loan video: FHLBB Chairman Ed Gray.

Depository Institutions Deregulation and Monetary Control Act of 1980, Public Law 96-221, March 31, 1980.

Garn-St. Germain Depository Institutions Act of 1982, Public Law 97-320, Oct. 15, 1982.

Ex-Governor Dan Walker's bank fraud case, covered in the Chicago *Tribune,* especially Aug. 6, 1987, by William B. Crawford, Jr., and Mitchell Locin.

Example of seminars offered by law firms: Course offered by Jeffer, Mangels & Butler, Los Angeles law firm, copyright 1984 by James R. Butler, Jr.

For sources of information about Ed Gray and developments in Washington, see notes listed under Chapters 23–25.

North American Savings: Several articles in *The Orange County Register*, by Ann Imse, Jonathan Lansner, Cathy Taylor in 1987 (especially Jan. 21, Feb. 1, and Oct. 4); article by Richard W. Stevenson in *The New York Times*, June 30, 1988; article in Los Angeles *Times* by James S. Granelli, Oct. 4, 1987; the FSLIC vs. Janet F. McKinzie, et al, 87-00861 HLH(Tx), U.S. District Court, Central District of California; bankruptcy filing of James R. Hodges LR88-163M, U.S. Bankruptcy Court, Eastern District of Arkansas, Western Division; article by Edna Buchanan in the Miami *Herald*, Aug. 30, 1987 (Masegian's death).

Ramona Savings: The FSLIC vs. John L. Molinaro, et al, 86-6016 AHS(Gx); passport personnel in San Francisco passport office; articles in *The Orange County Register*, by Adam Dawson and Jonathan Lansner in 1987; articles in Los Angeles *Times*, by Jane Applegate, John Spano, and Maria L. LaGanga in 1987 and 1988; USA vs. John Lee Molinaro and Donald P. Mangano, Sr., CR 87-952-Kn(A), U.S. District Court for the Central District of California.

Chapters 4–6

Centennial Savings was in our hometown, and we covered the Centennial story for six years. We interviewed the principals numerous times for newspaper stories. Much of the information for this chapter comes from six years of interviewing the people involved and those who knew them. We also conducted extensive interviews with Beverly Haines in 1987 and 1988. Confidential sources close to the inner working of Centennial, the FSLIC workout of Centennial, and the FBI investigation provided important leads. Other important sources for anyone researching Centennial:

The FSLIC vs. Siddharth S. Shah, et al, C871197 RHS, U.S. District Court for the Northern District of California.

Bureau of Indian Affairs trust funds: USA vs. Mark Twain Bank, et al, 84-0380-CV-W-9, in the U.S. District Court of the Western District of Missouri, Western Division, especially depositions of Terrence Miller and John W. Vale.

Participations with Atlas Savings: San Francisco *Examiner*, Aug. 25, 1985.

The FSLIC vs. Leif D. Soderling, et al, C88-0401 JPV, U.S. District Court for the Northern District of California.

Siddarth Shah: The Santa Rosa *Press Democrat* article by Joyce Terhaar, Jan. 11, 1987.

Erv Hansen's 1971 Mercedes: William B. Grover, trustee, vs. Centennial Savings, 1-86-0228, U.S. Bankruptcy Court for the Northern District of California, regarding bankruptcy of Erwin Hansen, 1-86-01529.

Congressman Doug Bosco's relationship with Centennial: Article by Steve Hart in the Santa Rosa *Press Democrat*, April 19, 1986; article by Seth Rosenfeld in the San Francisco *Examiner*, Sept. 15, 1986.

Sheriff Roger McDermott's relationship with Erv Hansen and Centennial: Article by Bony Saludes in the Santa Rosa *Press Democrat*, Oct. 17, 1986.

Drug indictment: United States of America vs. Ronald Richard Stevenson, et al, CR87-737-EFL, U.S. District Court for the Northern District of California.

Information about David Gorwitz, Paul Axelrod, and Morris Shenker: *The Last Mafioso*, by Ovid Demaris, Bantam Books, 1981, and story by Stephen A. Kurkjian, Daniel Golden, and Jan Wong about Richard Binder and David Gorwitz in the Boston *Globe*, Oct. 21, 1984.

Stories about David Gorwitz and Richard Dolwig, by Drew McKillips in the San Francisco *Chronicle*, June 1975.

Richard Neil Binder bankruptcy, Chapter 7, I-86-01236, U.S. Bankruptcy Court for the Northern District of California.

Centennial Savings and Loan Association vs. Richard N. Binder and Debra L. Binder, I-86-01236, filed in the U.S. Bankruptcy Court for the Northern District of California.

$6 million land deal: Series of stories in the Santa Rosa *Press Democrat*, April and May 1986.

Congressman Doug Bosco's response to the seizure of Centennial Savings: Article by Dick Phillips in the Santa Rosa *Press Democrat*, Aug. 25, 1985.

FBI questioning Congressman Doug Bosco: Article by Bony Saludes in the Santa Rosa *Press Democrat*, Sept. 16, 1986.

Financial condition of Centennial Savings at takeover: Articles by Bob Klose and Dick Phillips in the Santa Rosa *Press Democrat*, Aug. 21, 1985, and by Joyce Terhaar and Bob Klose, Oct. 17, 1986.

United States of America vs. Beverly Haines and Raleigh Yasinitsky, criminal complaint filed in U.S. District Court, Northern District of California, Sept. 2, 1986.

Details of FBI's investigation of Erv Hansen: FBI memorandum of 10-5-87 concerning Operation Buckpass (investigation of Erwin A. Hansen), which we obtained through the Freedom of Information Act.

Erwin Hansen bankruptcy, Chapter 7, U.S. Bankruptcy Court, Northern District of California, 1-86-01529.

Soderling sentencing (on same page with sentencing of man convicted of ransoming a parrot): The Santa Rosa *Press Democrat* article by Bob Klose, June 2, 1987.

Transcript of Soderling sentencing hearing, United States of America vs. Leif Soderling and Jay Soderling, CR-87-0143 RFP; hearing held June 1, 1987, before Judge Robert F. Peckham.

The FSLIC vs. Leif D. Soderling, et al, U.S. District Court for the Northern District of California, C88-0401 JPV.

The FSLIC vs. Siddharth S. Shah, et al, U.S. District Court for the Northern District of California, C87-1197 RHS.

United States of America vs. Ted Musacchio, U.S. District Court for the Northern District of California, filed in Oct. 1987.

United States of America vs. Ted Musacchio and Peter Frumenti, U.S. District Court for the Northern District of California, filed in June 1988.

Bank of Northern California: Bank of Northern California vs. Orange Bancorp et al, 612275, Superior Court of California, County of Santa Clara; Belmont F. Kelly, et al, vs. Orange Bancorp, et al, C86-20645 RPA, U.S. District Court, Northern District of California; U.S.A. vs. Rodney Vernon Wagner, et al, CR 88-20003WAI, U.S. District Court, Northern District of California; article by Dick Phillips in the Santa Rosa *Press Democrat*, Dec. 11, 1986; article in the *Press Democrat*, Aug. 9, 1987; article by Cris Oppenheimer in the San Jose *Mercury News*, Nov. 21, 1986.

Secret recording by federal investigators: Transcript of a conversation between Norman B. Jenson, Siddharth Shah, and Michael Stevenson, July 1, 1985, Miyako Hotel, San Francisco.

Details of the drug investigation came from stacks of documents we received from a member of the defense team; articles in the Santa Rosa *Press Democrat*, Oct. 6 and 7, 1987, by Bob Klose and Bony Saludes.

James Schlichtman: Article by Mary Thornton in the *Washington Post*, Jan. 21, 1988.

Jan. 24, 1986, search warrant affidavit, and Jan. 25, 1986, receipt for property received from Norman B. Jenson law offices in Las Vegas, Nevada.

Peter Robinson statements concerning his resignation: *The Recorder*, June 30, 1988.

Chapter 7

The FSLIC vs. Robert A. Ferrante, et al, U.S. District Court, Central District of California, CV-86-3332 MRP.

Robert Ferrante: FHLB Biographical and Financial Report; stories by Jeff Weir in *The Orange County Register*, especially May 24, 1986.

Redondo Beach Police Department incident report of April 12, 1982.

Chester W. Anderson, et al, vs. Condor Development, etc., et al, Superior Court of California for the County of Los Angeles, NWC 73316.

Quote from Mrs. Ferrante: "Maverick Bankers," Los Angeles *Times*, Jan. 22, 1987.

Robert Ferrante declaration of May 10 and 12, 1982.

Robin Bohannon declaration of May 12, 1982.

Walter Mitchell stories: April 13, 1982, May 23, 1983, July 9, 1983, July 14, 1983, all by Dirk Broersma, Redondo Beach *Daily Breeze*. May 12, 1983, story by Dan Morain and Rich Connell, Los Angeles *Times*.

United States of America vs. Walter L. Mitchell, Jr., U.S. District Court for the Central District of California, indictment CR 83-385 and trial memorandum.

Ferrante loans to Mitchell and Hawaii employment: The SLIC vs. Robert A. Ferrante, et al, CV-86-3332 MRP. Notice of motion and motion by plaintiff . . . to compel production of documents by defendant . . . , Feb. 1, 1988.

Martha Gravlee information: May 24, 1986, story in *The Orange County Register*, by Ann Imse.

Department of Savings and Loan Organizing Permit of May 12, 1983, signed by Deputy Savings and Loan Commissioner William J. Clayton.

W. Patrick Moriarty and the Carson City Council: Los Angeles *Times* of March 27, 1986.

Charles Bazarian: Numerous articles in *The Oklahoman* by Kevin Laval and Glen Bayless, 1985–88; and a three-part series in the Tulsa *Tribune*, beginning Feb. 11, 1987, by Edward M. Eveld and Mark Davis; numerous articles in the *National Thrift News*.

Charles Bazarian bankruptcy, U.S. Bankruptcy Court for the Western District of Oklahoma, 87-03927-A.

CB Financial Corp. bankruptcy, U.S. Bankruptcy Court for the Western District of Oklahoma, 87-03928-A.

Sig Kohnen on Bazarian: Tulsa *Tribune* series.

Process server story: The FSLIC vs. Robert A. Ferrante, et al., CV-86-3332 RG, transcript of proceedings May 28, 1986.

Ferrante's statements: The FSLIC vs. Robert A. Ferrante, et al, counter-claim/ third party complaint of Robert A. Ferrante for damages, declaratory relief, injunctive relief, and recoupment; Ferrante's contentions of fact re motion for temporary and limited stay of discovery and for protective order.

Ottavio Angotti: FHLB Biographical and Financial Report; articles by James S. Granelli, Los Angeles *Times*, 1985 and 1986; Angotti's answer to the FSLIC vs. Robert Ferrante, et al suit; "Open Letter to My Friends of the Press from Ottavio A. Angotti: The Quackery within FSLIC System Calls for Your Immediate Attention," by Ottavio A. Angotti on July 8, 1986; letter to FHLBB chairman Ed Gray, Oct. 14, 1986; letter to FHLB/San Francisco President James M. Cirona, July 7, 1986.

Ongoing criminal investigation: The FSLIC vs. Robert A. Ferrante, et al, transcript of proceedings May 27, 1986; Eric Bronk vs. FSLIC, et al, declaration of Bartly A. Dzivi; Sept. 18, 1987, letter from Frederick D. Friedman to Don A. Proudfoot, Jr.

Trust Fund Federal Savings Bank: The FSLIC vs. Robert A. Ferrante, et al, CV-86-3332 MRP, first amended counter-claim/third party complaint of Robert A. Ferrante for damages, declaratory relief, injunctive relief, and recoupment.

Angotti threat: Declaration of Darrell S. De Castro and the FSLIC vs. Robert Ferrante, et al, suit.

Raid on Eric Bronk's office, picture taking, smuggling documents, shredding documents: Eric C. Bronk vs. the FSLIC, et al, CV-86-5977-MRP, declaration of Bartly A. Dzivi, declaration of John T. McCullough, memorandum of points and authorities in support of motion for summary judgment and for an order specifying facts and issues without substantial controversy—declarations in support of motion; declaration of Janice H. Burrill; declaration of Stephen T. Owens; the FSLIC vs. Robert A. Ferrante, et al, CV-86-3332 RG, transcript of proceedings May 28, 1986, notice of motion and motion by plaintiff FSLIC to compel production of documents by defendant Robert A. Ferrante—joint contentions of law and fact—joint stipulation of counsel re individual requests, stipulation of counsel re motion by plaintiff FSLIC to compel deposition testimony of defendant Robert A. Ferrante and for sanctions.

Cheap suit quotes: The FSLIC vs. Robert A. Ferrante, et al, CV-86-3332 RG, transcript of proceedings May 27, 1986.

Chapters 8–12

Information on broker deposit ban: *National Thrift News*, Feb. 20, 1984 (including Grell quote and Tower information).

Ed Meese: Articles in the San Diego *Tribune* in February and March 1984 by Marcus Stern and Denise Carabet.

For other sources on Ed Gray's activities, see notes in section for Chapters 23–25.

Mario Renda and First United Fund: "Linked Financing" series by Richard Ringer and Bart Fraust in the *American Banker*, Nov. 15, 16, and 19,

1984; "The Rise and Fall of a Money Broker," by Bart Fraust in *Newsday*, Sept. 14, 1987, telephone interview with Sy Miller; transcripts of the trial of U.S.A. vs. Martin Schwimmer, CR-87-423, U.S. District Court for the Eastern District of New York; official "Profile" of First United Fund with Feb. 29, 1984, message from Mario Renda, First United Investment Company, Ltd.; First United Management Company, Ltd.; First United Contractors, Ltd.; rough draft of Annual Report, Jan. 26, 1984; Profile of First United Investment Co.; First United Fund financial statement as of Dec. 31, 1982; Renda's desk diaries and appointment calendars, 1981–84; summary of Mario and Nina Renda's American Express records.

Adnan Khashoggi: *Fortune* article by Louis Kraar, June 1977, and telephone interview with Kraar in Hong Kong; *Time* stories by George J. Church and Richard Stengel, Jan. 19, 1987.

"It was almost an afterthought . . ." quote: Dallas *Morning News* story of Nov. 8, 1987, by Allen Pusey.

Renda and Schwimmer: Transcripts of the trial of USA vs. Martin Schwimmer and Mario Renda, CR-87-423, U.S. District Court for the Eastern District of New York; U.S.A. vs. Martin Schwimmer and Mario Renda, CR-87-0123(S) in U.S. District Court for the Eastern District of New York; U.S.A. vs. Martin Schwimmer, CR-86-00528, U.S. District Court of the Eastern District of New York; transcript of wiretapped telephone conversation between Frank Manzo and Bill Barone on Aug. 15, 1983; numerous articles in *National Thrift News* (Nov. 10, 1986, for Schwimmer's income at First United Fund).

Indian Springs State Bank: Stories in the Kansas City *Star* by Lori Shein (especially Oct. 11, 1987); "Linked Financing" series by Richard Ringer and Bart Fraust in the *American Banker*; FDIC examinations of Aug. 23, 1982, Dec. 10, 1982, Dec. 5, 1983; FDIC meeting with directors, Feb. 15, 1983.

Fahad Azima: "The CIA, Arms & Global," by James Kindall in the Kansas City *Star*, June 10, 1984.

RACE Airways: *The Chronology*, by the National Security Archive, Scott Armstrong, executive director, Warner Books, 1987.

Civellas and Tropicana case: Numerous stories in the Kansas City *Star*, including story by Elizabeth Drake about convictions; story ran July 1, 1983.

Henry Tager: Stories in Kansas City *Star*, including Nov. 18, 1984, story by Brant Houston (conviction) and Mar. 6, 1985, no byline (sentencing).

The Winklers: The FDIC vs. Mario Renda, et al, 85-2216-0, in the U.S. District

Court for the District of Kansas; U.S.A. vs. Franklin Winkler and V. Leslie Winkler, 87-20049-02 and 03, in the U.S. District Court for the District of Kansas, including affidavits of Stanley Tobias, Joseph J. DeCarlo, and Michael A. Brenesell in support of request for extradition; FDIC vs. F&I Real Estate Holding Company, et al, 83-2477, in the U.S. District Court for the District of Kansas.

Renda, Winkler, and Daily's "Linked Financing" scheme: FDIC vs. Mario Renda, et al, 85-2216-0, in the U.S. District Court for the District of Kansas, including especially Stanley Tobias's testimony in that case; affidavit of Michael C. Manning in the matter of the application of the U.S.A. for a search warrant for the offices of First United Financial Corp. filed in U.S. District Court for the Eastern District of New York; transcripts of tapes produced by Frederik A. Figge of meetings of Indian Springs State Bank borrowers for Haiku Partners and Haiku Holdings; FDIC vs. (numerous straw borrowers including) Peter Michael Chessen, 83-2476, and Edward Michael Berr, 83-2461, all in the U.S. District Court for the District of Kansas; correspondence between Renda, Winkler, Daily, Russo, and the straw borrowers from 1982 to 1987.

Information and copies of correspondence about Seaside Ventures came from FSLIC and FDIC attorneys; U.S.A. vs. Mario Renda, 87-CR-423 (S)(JMM), in the U.S. District Court of the Eastern District of New York, temporary restraining order and transcript of the trial.

Palace Hotel: Eric C. Bronk vs. the FSLIC, et al, CV-86-5977 MRP, U.S. District Court, Central District of California.

Indictment of East Indian: *American Banker* article of Aug. 1, 1983, by Richard Ringer.

American Banker, March 26, 1984, story by Jay Rosenstein and Robert Trigaux and FHLBB report on brokered deposits.

The New York Times, "Money Broker's Books Subpoenaed," by Kenneth B. Noble, May 17, 1984.

Coronado Savings and Rexford State Bank: FDIC vs. Mario Renda, et al, 85-2216-0, in the U.S. District Court for the District of Kansas.

Renda plea agreement: May 26, 1988, in case of U.S.A. vs. Mario Renda, 87-CR-423(SS)(JMM), U.S. District Court for the Eastern District of New York.

Lawrence S. Iorizzo: Affidavit in support of request for extradition of V. Leslie Winkler and Franklin A. Winkler in U.S.A. vs. V. Leslie Winkler and

Franklin A. Winkler, 87-20049-02 and 03, in the U.S. District Court for the District of Kansas.

Chapters 13–14

Mafia, Teamsters, money laundering: President's Commission on Organized Crime established by Executive Order 12435 on July 28, 1983, several volumes between Oct. 1984 and April 1986; "Vicious Circles," by Jonathan Kwitny, W. W. Norton, 1979; "The Crime Business," by Roy Rowan, *Fortune*, Nov. 10, 1986; numerous 1988 newspaper articles about trials of Mafia and Teamster figures; article by Anne B. Fisher in *Fortune*, April 1, 1985; transcripts of the hearing held by the Permanent Subcommittee on Investigations, Senate Committee on Government Affairs, concerning money laundering in Puerto Rico, July 25, 1985; testimony before Senate subcommittee on investigations of Joseph D. Pistone, 1988, and his book *Donnie Brasco: My Undercover Life in the Mafia*, New American Library, 1988; *The Teamsters*, Steven Brill, Simon & Schuster, 1978.

Michael Rapp: *Wall Street Swindler: An Insider's Story of Mob Operations in the Stock Market*, by Michael Hellerman and Thomas C. Renner, Doubleday & Co., Garden City, N.Y., 1977; "A Swindler, a U.S.-issued ID, and a Web of Fraud," by Bart Fraust, the *American Banker*, Mar. 31, 1986; further Fraust stories in the *American Banker* on April 22, 1986, May 16, 1986, June 2, 1986, June 18, 1986, March 17, 1987.

Jilly Rizzo: *The Last Mafioso*, by Ovid DeMaris, Bantam Books, 1981.

Flushing Federal Savings vs. Michael Rapp, et al, 85 Civ. 2356 (JBW), U.S. District Court, Eastern District of New York.

Depositions of Ronald Martorelli (Sept. 13–17, 1985) and Anthony Del Vecchio (Sept.–Oct. 1985, June 1986, August 1986).

The FSLIC vs. Carl Cardascia, et al, Civ. 87-0002, U.S. District Court, Eastern District of New York.

The Fountain Pen Conspiracy, by Jonathan Kwitny, Knopf, 1973.

July 1985 affidavit filed by Andrew B. Donnellan, Jr.

Aurora Bank: U.S.A. vs. Heinreich Rupp, 88-CR-112, U.S. District Court for the District of Colorado; numerous stories in the *Rocky Mountain News* and the Denver *Post* 1985–87; story in the *American Banker*, by Bart Fraust, Nov. 17, 1986, Aurora Bank vs. Juad S. Jezzeny, John A. Napoli, Sr., John A. Napoli, Jr., Michele A. Propato, filed in May 1985; FDIC vs.

John Antonio et al, 85-C-1298, U.S. District Court for the District of Colorado.

Rapp threatened Nigrelle: The *American Banker*, March 31, 1986.

John Lapaglia: Several stories in the *San Antonio Light* in 1985. Testimony in the trial of USA vs. Joseph S. Ascani, et al, CR-86-202R, U.S. District Court, Western District of Washington at Seattle.

Wayne Newton: Las Vegas *Review-Journal* article by Richard Cornett, May 17, 1984.

Philip Schwab: Buffalo *Evening News*, several stories, Jan. through April 1966; St. Petersburgh *Times* story by Bradley Stertz, Sept. 27, 1987; "The Rushville Connection," a series in the Indianapolis *Star* beginning Oct. 18, 1987.

Philip Schwab sang to Mary: Buffalo *Evening News*, May 7, 1970.

Players Casino: 73-page description/proposal subsequent to Eureka Federal Savings' foreclosing on Schwab; a Reno *Gazette Journal* story by Susan Voyles, Nov. 8, 1986.

Kenneth Kidwell and Eureka Federal Savings: San Francisco *Examiner* story by Paul Shinoff, April 12, 1985; San Francisco *Chronicle* story by Gail E. Schares, July 15, 1985; several stories in the Santa Rosa *Press Democrat*, 1984–86; Eureka Federal Savings and Loan Association, et al, vs. Kenneth L. Kidwell, et al, C86-1245, U.S. District Court for the Northern District of California; the Santa Rosa *Press Democrat*, July 28, 1984, and Sept. 11, 1984.

Freedom Savings: The *National Thrift News*, in March and July 1985.

Sig Kohnen on why Bazarian bought stock in banks and S&Ls: The Tulsa *Tribune* series by Edward M. Eveld and Mark Davis, Feb. 11–13, 1987.

Florida Center Bank: U.S.A. vs. John A. Bodziak, Jr., et al, GJ 86-1-26, U.S. District Court, Middle District of Florida, Orlando Division; the Tulsa *Tribune* series, which began Feb. 11, 1987.

Wolk, Farrell, Zaccaro business relationship: *National Thrift News* article on July 27, 1987.

Chapter 15

Home Savings, Irving Savings, and Alliance Savings actitivies: U.S.A. vs. Joseph S. Ascani, et al, CR-86-202R, in the U.S. District Court, Western

District of Washington at Seattle, especially superseding indictment and trial brief; FSLIC vs. Guy W. Olano, Jr., et al, 86-0472, U.S. District Court in the Eastern District of Louisiana, including depositions of Convention Center Investments Co., Inc., and Michael Speaks vs. Norman B. Jenson, et al, A243197, Judicial District Court of the State of Nevada in and for the County of Clark; Minor Leasing, Convention Center Investments Co., Inc., Norman B. Jenson, Michael Speaks vs. FSLIC, et al, CV-S-86-494 HDM, U.S. District Court for the District of Nevada, especially depositions of Norman B. Jenson, May 5–7, 1987, and file of supporting documents; numerous stories in the *National Thrift News*, 1986–88 (Oct. 27, 1986, article by Bill Voelker gives information about other investigations of Olano).

Norman B. Jenson: Las Vegas *Sun*, March 25, 1980; financial statements of Nov. 15, 1980; UPI article of April 28, 1981; Las Vegas *Review-Journal* article by Richard Cornett, May 17, 1984.

Philip Schwab's quid pro quo: June 26, 1986, letter from Schwab to chairman of the board and CEO of Freedom Savings, F. Philip Handy.

Eric Bronk's trips to Tampa: Exhibits for the FSLIC vs. Robert A. Ferrante, et al, 86-3332, U.S. District Court, Central District of California.

First Federal Savings of Shawnee sued Bazarian: *National Thrift News* story, by Kevin Laval, May 16, 1988.

Report prepared by Casino Control Corp. for Philip Schwab regarding his application for a casino license for the Players Casino in Reno, Nevada.

Schwab bankruptcy: *The New York Times* story, by Albert Scardino, Jan. 11, 1988; list of Cuyahoga Group and/or Mr. & Mrs. Schwab banks and creditors. Also Brad Stertz of the St. Petersburg *Times*.

John Anderson: Numerous stories between 1981–86 in *The Valley Times*, Las Vegas *Sun*, Las Vegas *Review-Journal*, Reno *Gazette Journal* (especially Sept. 18, 1985), *The Wall Street Journal*, May 24, 1984; St Louis *Post-Dispatch* story as described by the Las Vegas *Sun*, Nov. 16, 1982.

Mitchell Brown: Marin *Independent Journal* article, March 28, 1987, by Renee Koury; 1987 Dun and Bradstreet report on Wells International, Inc.

State Savings/Corvallis: U.S.A. vs. Brian John Olsvik, et al, filed May 1988, U.S. District Court for the District of Oregon; FSLIC vs. numerous related parties, 86-676, 86-1436, 86-1205, 86-1436, 86-1390, 86-1648, 87-1025; numerous stories in the *National Thrift News* and the *Portland Oregonian*, 1986–88; interviews with two defense attorneys.

San Marino Savings: The FSLIC vs. Edward A. Forde, et al, U.S. District Court for the Central District of California, 85-774-WDK; San Marino Savings joint proxy statement and offering circular of Dec. 28, 1982; April 15, 1983, Report of Examination by FHLBB Office of Examinations and Supervision; San Marino Savings Annual Report to the FHLBB/FSLIC for fiscal year ended Dec. 31, 1982; McGladrey Hendrickson & Co. report of Jan. 12, 1983, and letter of Jan. 20, 1983; memo to files by G. N. Lubushkin on Oct. 29, 1983; FHLBB letter to San Marino Savings board of directors March 14, 1983; FHLBB recommendation for appointment of conservator, Feb. 3, 1984; San Marino Savings vs. FHLBB, et al, 84-0776 RJK, in U.S. District Court for Central District of California, including declaration of Edward A. Forde and defendants' opposition to application for temporary restraining order.

First United Fund deposits at San Marino Savings: *American Banker* series by Richard Ringer and Bart Fraust, Nov. 15, 16, and 19, 1984.

Bona and Domingues: *The Orange County Register* four-part series by Jonathan Lansner and Ann Imse, Nov. 8–11, 1987; the *Atlantic City Press* three-part series by Daniel Heneghan, Oct. 7–9, 1985; FHLBB memo of Sept. 28, 1983, from Glen Sanders to Donald McCormick; April 8, 1984, story by Jon Standefer in the San Diego *Union*; marketing agreement of July 21, 1982, between San Marino Savings (Forde and Casanova), Bona and Domingues; various correspondence between San Marino Savings and Bona-Domingues; Feb. 8 and Feb. 24, 1983, analysis of Bona-Domingues projects; D&B Development Company, Inc., vs. Frank J. Domingues, CV-85-774-WMB, in U.S. District Court, Central District of California; article by Michael Kinsman in San Diego *Tribune*, Oct. 5, 1987; Dunes Casino Development, Ltd., prospectus of April 11, 1986; Domingues' ouster, Los Angeles *Times* story of March 4, 1985.

Zulu projects: Edward V. Casanova deposition, June 25 and 26 and July 1, 1987, for the FSLIC vs. McGladrey, Hendrickson & Co., et al, CV-85-2975-WMB, and the FSLIC vs. Edward A. Forde, et al, CV-85-774-WMB, both in U.S. District Court for the Central District of California.

Steve Goodman: The FSLIC vs. Robert A. Ferrante, et al, CV-86-3332 MRP, notice of motion and motion by plaintiff FSLIC to compel production of documents by defendant Robert A. Ferrante; joint contentions of law and fact; joint stipulation of counsel re individual requests.

Report on condos: San Marino Savings in-house memo of Feb. 7, 1983; Edward V. Casanova deposition, June 25 and 26 and July 1, 1987, for the FSLIC vs. McGladrey, Hendrickson & Co., et al, CV-85-2975-WMB, and the FSLIC vs. Edward A. Forde, et al, CV-85-774-WMB, both in U.S. District Court for the Central District of California.

American Savings and Loan vs. Leonard Pellulo, et al, 86-2261 RMT(Tx), U.S. District Court, Central District of California.

Morris Shenker, Teamsters, Mafia: President's Commission on Organized Crime, report to the President and the Attorney General on organized crime, business, and labor unions, Dec. 31, 1985; several bankruptcy articles in St. Louis *Post-Dispatch* in 1984; bankruptcy 84-00001, U.S. Bankruptcy Court, Eastern District of Missouri, Eastern Division; see listings under Chapters 13–14.

Sun Savings: U.S.A. vs. Daniel W. Dierdorff, CR 88-0542-R, U.S. District Court, Southern District of California; Sun Savings and Loan Association Form 10-K for fiscal year ended Dec. 31, 1985, and Form 10-Q for quarter ended March 31, 1986.

Chapters 16–19

William J. Oldenburg: San Francisco *Examiner*, April 29, 1984; *The Wall Street Journal*, June 8, 1984.

Charles Knapp: "Lender's Lament," by David B. Hilder in *The Wall Street Journal*, June 23, 1987; several articles in *The Wall Street Journal*, Aug. 16, 23, 29, 1984; article by Thomas C. Hayes in *The New York Times*, July 11, 1984; article in *Fortune* by Gary Hector, July 12, 1982.

For further source material on Ed Gray's activities, see listings for Chapters 23–25.

Texas: Article in *Texas Business*, by Geoffrey Leavenworth, Feb. 1988; article in Dallas *Times Herald*, by Ross Ramsey, Aug. 16, 1987; "The Party Is Over," by Byron Harris in *Texas Monthly*, June 1987; several news reports by Byron Harris on WFAA-TV in Dallas 1986–88; "S&Ls: How They Self-Destructed," by Allen Pusey in the Dallas *Morning News*, Nov. 8, 1987; "Loan Stars Fall in Texas," by Bill Powell and Daniel Pedersen in *Newsweek*, June 20, 1988; "Texas S&L Disasters Are Blamed, in Part, on Freewheeling Style," by Leonard M. Apcar in *The Wall Street Journal*, July 13, 1987; "S&L Trouble Felt Beyond Texas Border" (about participations) by Robert Dodge, the Dallas *Morning News*, Sept. 28, 1987; series by Allen Pusey and Lee Hancock that began in the Dallas *Morning News*, Dec. 4, 1988.

Don Dixon and Vernon Savings: "Beware of Texan Bearing Gifts," by Susan Burkhardt in the San Diego *Union*, Aug. 9, 1987; "Break the Bank," by Byron Harris in *Texas Monthly*, Jan. 1988; supervisory agreement between the FSLIC and Vernon Savings, Aug. 16, 1984; cease-and-desist order issued by the FHLBB to Vernon Savings, June 19, 1986; FHLBB approval of Dondi Financial Corp.'s acquisition of Vernon Savings, June 29, 1982; Vernon Savings list of allowances for loan losses, Sept. 30, 1986, and Nov. 30, 1986; Vernon Savings workout list of projects, Feb. 8, 1987; the FSLIC vs. Don R. Dixon, et al, CA 3-87-1102-G, in the U.S. District Court for the Northern District of Texas, Dallas Division, including affidavits of Norman G. Oldham, Daryl Ray Tucker, Gordon J. Reid, Gralee P. Parr, William H. Degan, James E. Poole, James R. Alberts, Jim Wright, Charles Galindo, James S. Hinman, Robert Torres (and exhibits), Gene Webb, and Alfred Beltran-Romero, statements of Linda Shivers, Chris Barker, and Nancy Horne, the FSLIC's supplemental memorandum of law in support of its motion for preliminary injunction; Jack R. Brenner and Construction Financial, Inc., vs. Vernon Asset Management Corp., et al, 581981, Superior Court of the State of California, County of San Diego; U.S.A. vs. John G. Smith, CR 3-88-016-T, in the U.S. District Court for the Northern District of Texas, Dallas Division; U.S.A. vs. John V. Hill, CR 3-88-0059-H, in the U.S. District Court for the Northern District of Texas, Dallas Division, and subsequent guilty plea on March 24, 1988; U.S.A. vs. Roy F. Dickey, Jr., CR 3-88-160-T, in the U.S. District Court for the Northern District of Texas, Dallas Division; flight logs; U.S.A. vs. Woody F. Lemons, CR 3-88-234-T, U.S. District Court, Northern District of Texas, Dallas Division.

Dixon's Solano beach house: Walter J. Van Boxtel and Roseann S. Van Boxtel vs. Harvey McLain, et al, 581506, Superior Court of the State of California, County of San Diego, especially depositions of Glenn Edward Billingsley, Walter J. Van Boxtel, and Roseann Van Boxtel.

Terry Barker and State/Lubbock: U.S.A. vs. Donald W. Nahrwold, CR 3-88-019-T, U.S. District Court for the Northern District of Texas, Dallas Division; U.S.A. vs. Larry K. Thompson, CR-5-88-002 and 024, U.S. District Court, Northern District of Texas; U.S.A. vs. Tyrell Barker, CR-3-88-017-D, U.S. District Court, Northern District of Texas; guilty pleas of Larry K. Thompson and Tyrell G. Barker, Feb. 8, 1988; story by Pete Brewton in the Houston *Post*, July 10, 1988; U.S.A. vs. Sammy Wayne Spikes, et al, CR 5-86-041, in the U.S. District Court for the Northern District of Texas, Lubbock Division; story by Pat Graves in the Lubbock *Avalanche-Journal*, Jan. 31, 1987; the FSLIC vs. Laurence B. Vineyard, Jr., et al, CA 5-87-

124, in the U.S. District Court for the Northern District of Texas, Lubbock Division; U.S.A. vs. Donald D. Campbell, CR-3-88-144-T, U.S. District Court for the Northern District of Texas.

Tom Nevis and Nevis Industries: Numerous stories in the Yuba-Sutter *Appeal Democrat* 1977–88; Eureka Federal Savings vs. Nevis Industries, Inc., et al, 298371, Superior Court of California, County of San Mateo; Cargill, Inc., and Universal Rice and Grain Establishment vs. Pacific International Ag-Products, Inc., et al, 35098, in the Superior Court of the State of California in and for the County of Sutter; 1981 corporate profile of Nevis Industries, Inc.; State Savings of Lubbock vs. Doe Valley of California, Inc., et al, 92253, in the Superior Court of the State of California in and for the County of Butte, especially depositions of Thomas E. Nevis; Dun and Bradstreet report on Nevis Industries, Inc., and Doe Valley, Inc., June 15, 1987; Nevis Industries, Inc., Adams Esquon Ranch, Inc., Thomas E. Nevis, Samuel A. Nevis, Doe Valley of California, Inc. vs. Eureka Federal Savings, et al, 298371, cross-complaint; Rick L. and Gay Lee Willard, Roland K. Martin vs. Sioux Corp., et al, 13-221, in the U.S. Bankruptcy Court in and for the District of Nevada, especially 2004 examination of Thomas E. Nevis on Feb. 25, 1985; promissory note June 25, 1981, for $2 million payable to Joseph F. Arroyo, signed by Thomas E. Nevis.

Jack Franks: JDF Financial Corp. corporate profile and Jack D. Franks personal profile; U.S.A. vs. Jack D. Franks, CR 3-88-196-R, U.S. District Court, Northern District of Texas, Dallas Division.

Nevis ordered to pay $11.3 million: Yuba-Sutter *Appeal Democrat* story, Oct. 3, 1988, by Eric Vodden.

Flipping land like registering for college classes: Series by James O'Shea for the Chicago *Tribune* that began Sept. 25, 1988.

Joe Selby: Article by Jim McTague in the *American Banker*, June 6, 1988.

Westwood Savings: FSLIC vs. Edward Israel, et al, CV-87-04124 WDK (Tx), U.S. District Court, Central District of California.

Scott Mann: Article by Brooks Jackson in *The Wall Street Journal*, June 30, 1988; report to California S&L Commissioner William Crawford from Lynn Gray, Oct. 20, 1988.

Tom Gaubert: U.S.A. vs. Thomas A. Gaubert, CR88-44, in the U.S. District Court for the Southern District of Iowa.

George Mallick: Article by Brooks Jackson in *The Wall Street Journal*, Aug. 5, 1987.

Political pressure: Article by Andrew Mangan of the Associated Press in the *Arkansas Gazette*, July 19, 1987; articles by George Archibald in the Washington *Times*, June 24 and Aug. 24, 1988; *Honest Graft*, by Brooks Jackson, Knopf, 1988; "The Wright Man to See," by Rich Thomas and David Pauly in *Newsweek*, June 29, 1987; "Loose Lending," by Leonard M. Apcar in *The Wall Street Journal*, July 13, 1987 (Sunbelt paid fees illegally); "The Speaker and the Sleazy Banker," by William M. Adler with Michael Binstein, *Banker's Monthly*, March and May 1988 (includes Wright's reply); numerous stories in the *National Thrift News*; *BusinessWeek*, Oct. 31, 1988.

Dixon bankruptcy: 387-33941-M-11, U.S. Bankruptcy Court, Dallas.

Dallas task force probe and subpoena list: Dallas *Times Herald*, Aug. 16 and 27, 1987, stories by Steve Klinkerman.

Conditions in Houston: Numerous articles in the Houston *Post*, by Pete Brewton, specifically the article that appeared Aug. 18, 1987, by Gregory Seay and Brewton.

Chapters 20–22

Herman K. Beebe: Numerous stories in the Shreveport *Times*, by Larry Burton, Jane M. Allison, Charles Cornett, and especially Linda Farrar, 1984–88; numerous stories in the Houston *Post* by Pete Brewton, especially Feb. 11, March 13, and May 3–4, 1988; "Lone Stars Fall in Texas," by Bill Powell and Daniel Pedersen, *Newsweek*, June 20, 1988; the FSLIC vs. Laurence B. Vineyard, Jr., CA5-87-124, in the U.S. District Court for the Northern District of Texas, Lubbock Division; U.S.A. vs. Herman K. Beebe, Sr., CR 3-88-124-D, in the U.S. District Court for the Northern District of Texas, Dallas Division; U.S.A. vs. Herman K. Beebe, Sr., CR 87-50015, U.S. District Court, Western District of Louisiana, Lafayette-Opelousas Division.

Edwin Edwards: *Newsweek* article by Daniel Pedersen, Oct. 26, 1987; *The Almanac of American Politics*, published by *The National Journal*, 1986 and 1988; *Mafia Kingfish*, by John H. Davis, McGraw-Hill Publishing Co., 1989.

Continental Savings and Carlos Marcello: Affidavit filed in state district court in Houston by Dr. James Fairleigh as reported by Pete Brewton in the Houston *Post*, March 13, 1988.

Carlos Marcello: *Mafia Kingfish*, by John H. Davis, McGraw-Hill Publishing Co., 1989.

Hearings held in San Antonio, Texas, Nov. 20 and Dec. 1, 1976, before the Subcommittee on Financial Institutions Supervision, Regulation and Insurance to investigate the closing of Citizens State Bank in Carrizo Springs, Texas, H241-10, and appendices, H241-11.

George Aubin: "How Hutton Took a Texas-sized Bath," by Brian O'Reilly in *Fortune* magazine, Oct. 13, 1986.

Memorandum prepared for the Comptroller of the Currency, June 3, 1985, by Robert V. Ahrens, Ralph E. Sharpe, and Robert M. Krasne; memorandum prepared for the Enforcement Review Committee of the Comptroller of the Currency by Robert Krasne, March 4, 1985; memorandum prepared for Deborah S. Hechinger, director of the Securities and Corporate Practices Division of the Comptroller of the Currency, by Robert Krasne, April 16, 1985.

Southmark Corporation: Phil Hevener column in the Las Vegas *Sun*, Jan. 16, 1986, and story by Phil Hevener and Jeffrey M. German, Feb. 7, 1986; articles in the Las Vegas *Review-Journal*, April 2, May 7, May 8, Sept. 29, Nov. 6, all 1986, and Oct. 2, 1987; articles in *The Wall Street Journal*, July 8, 1986, Sept. 19, 1986, Sept. 11, 1987, Feb. 11, 1988, Nov. 14, 1988; Houston *Post* story by Pete Brewton and Gregory Seay, April 10, 1988, and by Seay, April 19, 1988; *Barron's*, April 18, 1988; San Francisco *Chronicle*, Sept. 8, 1988; *The New York Times* News Service story by Nina Andrews, Sept. 7, 1988; Reno *Gazette-Journal*, Aug. 8, 1986, Oct. 6, 1988; *Real Estate Securities Review*, Oct. 7, 1988; Thomas C. Hayes story for *The New York Times*, Oct. 17, 1988; San Jacinto Savings Association and Subsidiaries Consolidated Statements of Financial Condition, June 30, 1984, and June 30, 1985; story for *Forbes* magazine by Howard Rudnitsky and Matthew Schifrin, March 7, 1988; *BusinessWeek* story by Todd Mason, May 19, 1986; transcript of hearings before the Nevada State Gaming Control Board, Nov. 5, 1986; Southmark Corp. Form 10-Ks for fiscal years ended June 30, 1985, and June 20, 1987.

Drexel Burnham Lambert, Inc., and Michael Milken: *Wall Street Journal* stories by James B. Stewart and Daniel Hertzberg, Sept. 8, 1988.

George I. Benny: San Francisco *Chronicle* stories on April 16, 1986, and July 14, 1987.

North Mississippi Savings: Mario Renda's desk diaries; U.S.A. vs. John R. Swaim 84-4583, U.S. District Court for the Northern District of Mississippi.

George Wayne Reeder: Knoxville *Journal* series by Joe Krakoviak, Aug. 19–21, 1985; numerous articles by Sanford Nax in the *Desert Sun*, 1985–88;

depositions of G. Wayne Reeder and John Patrick McGuire in case of John Patrick McGuire vs. Wayne George Reeder, et al, 86-0663-CV-W-3, in the U.S. District Court for the Western District of Missouri; Hill Top Developers, Inc., consolidated financial statements of May 31, 1983; Aug. 7, 1987, story in the Los Angeles *Times*; May 2, 1986, story in the Los Angeles *Times* by Bill Ritter.

Acadia Savings: The FSLIC vs. Edmund M. Reggie, et al, CV88-2013, U.S. District Court, Western District of Louisiana, Lafayette-Opelousas Division; the *Times-Picayune* stories by Mark Schleifstein, Oct. 16 and 19, 1988; the Baton Rouge *Advocate* story by Bruce Schultz, Aug. 28, 1988; the FDIC vs. John Antonio, et al, 85-C-1298, U.S. District Court for the District of Colorado; FDIC vs. Anthony Del Vecchio and Jilly Rizzo, 87-0626, U.S. District Court, Pennsylvania.

John Connally, Jake Jacobsen, Mike Myers, Robert S. Strauss: San Diego *Union* publication of a Reuters story on Aug. 9, 1987; *Mother Jones* cover story by Kaye Northcott, Jan. 1980; several stories by Earl Golz in the Dallas *Morning News* in 1971, 1973, 1974, 1979.

Ben Barnes: Several stories in the Dallas *Morning News* in 1971, 1975 by Earl Golz.

Robert Strauss representing Jim Wright: New York *Post*, June 16, 1988.

Sig Kohnen worked for Strauss law firm: *The Sunday Oklahoman* "Mystery Man" article by Glen Bayless of April 21, 1985; independently confirmed.

Chapters 23–25

Most of the material for these chapters comes from extensive interviews with regulators and law-enforcement officials.

Lapaglia trip to Washington: *To Kill an Eagle: The Dismantling of Gulf Federal Savings Bank*, by Thomas A. Kehoe, Sr., Harahan, Louisiana, 1988.

Frank Fahrenkopf, Wayne Newton, United Savings Bank, Buena Vista Bank & Trust: Series by Julie Bird, beginning June 5, 1988, in the Colorado Springs *Gazette Telegraph*.

The Federal Home Loan Bank Board, by Thomas Marvell, Praeger Publishers, 1969.

The U.S. League: Article by Monica Langley in *The Wall Street Journal*, July 16, 1986.

Ed Gray: Article by Michael Binstein in *Regardie's*, Oct. 1988.

John M. Keilly: "Shenandoah Probe Widens," by Clyde Weiss in the Las Vegas *Review-Journal*, Aug. 20, 1980.

Alan Greenspan letter: "Federal Fiasco," by Jeff Bailey and G. Christian Hill in *The Wall Street Journal*, March 25, 1988.

"Consolidating the Administration and Enforcement of the Federal Securities Laws within the Securities and Exchange Commission," report by the Subcommittee on Oversight and Investigations of the House Committee on Energy and Commerce, April 1987 (hearing on Beverly Hills Savings, ESM Government Securities, Inc., Marvin Warner, American Savings and Loan of Miami).

Charles Keating: Articles by Michael Binstein in *Regardie's*, July 1987, *Arizona Trend*, Sept. 1987, and the *Washington Post*, May 1988; article by Andrew Mollison in the Mesa *Tribune*, Dec. 28, 1986; articles by Bill Roberts, Terry Smith, and Ben Winton in the Mesa *Tribune*, Dec. 29, 1986, and Stephen Kleege of the *National Thrift News*.

Regulatory and law enforcement: "Report of the National Commission on Fraudulent Financial Reporting (Treadway Commission)," Oct. 1987, presented to House Committee on Energy and Commerce's Subcommittee on Oversight and Investigations; "Combatting fraud, abuse and misconduct in the nation's financial institutions: current federal efforts are inadequate," seventy-second report by the Committee on Government Operations, U.S. House of Representatives, Oct. 13, 1988, House report 100-1088; *The Wall Street Journal*, "Review & Outlook," Sept. 21, 1988; "What's So Secret About the Bank Secrecy Act?" by Margery Waxman and Linda Madrid in *Outlook* of the Federal Home Loan Bank System, July/August 1986; San Diego *Tribune* article by Michael Kinsman, Oct. 5, 1987; testimony of Jeffrey J. Jamar and others before the U.S. House of Representatives Subcommittee on Commerce, Consumer and Monetary Affairs, June 13, 1987; several articles in the *Washington Post* by Kathleen Day in 1988; remarks by William F. Weld, assistant attorney general, criminal division, to the Fidelity and Surety Committee of the American Bar Association, Jan. 23, 1987; article by Seth Kantor for the Cox News Service as it appeared in the San Francisco *Banner Daily Journal*, March 14, 1988; "Bank office and director liability—regulatory actions," by Thomas P. Vartanian and Michael D. Schley in *The Business Lawyer*, May 1984.

Testimony that an FSLIC employee told defendant to "get dumb": U.S.A. vs. Wayne Barnhart, CR 3-88-206-G, U.S. District Court for the Northern District of Texas, Dallas Division.

Danny Wall: Several Jack Anderson columns in 1988.

Fees to independent fee counsel: FHLBB Office of General Counsel Outside Counsel Questionnaire Summary Compilation, April 22, 1988.

Banker's Monthly, May 1988.

Chapters 26 and 27

Teamster investments: President's Commission on Organized Crime.

Dr. John Nichols: The following stories in the *Desert Sun*: March 24, 1981, by P. G. Torrez and John Hussar; Sept. 28, 1984, by Gale Holland; Oct. 3, 1984, by Gale Holland; March 21, 1985, by John Hussar; March 26, 1985, by John Hussar; May 27, 1987, no byline; May 28, 1987, no byline; 1985 Annual Report to the California Legislature on Organized Crime in California by the State Department of Justice; March 30, 1988, story in the Los Angeles *Times* by Kim Murphy.

McKinsey & Co. study that concluded the FHLBB search for merger partners may cost the government as much as 40 percent more: As reported by Nathaniel C. Nash for *The New York Times* News Service, Nov. 14, 1988.

Federal Reserve Bank solution: Article by William Greider in *Rolling Stone*, Aug. 11, 1988; William Isaac in the *Washington Post*, Oct. 9, 1988.

FSLIC vs. David L. Butler, et al, 85-3845, U.S. District Court, Northern District of California.

The Bankers, by Martin Mayer, Ballantine Books, 1974.

Conditions of banks and the FDIC: Two articles in the *National Thrift News*, Dec. 12, 1988.

Index

429

434 · Index